Diagnosis and Correction in Reading Instruction

Second Edition

Dorothy Rubin
Trenton State College

Allyn and Bacon

Boston   London   Toronto   Sydney   Tokyo   Singapore

With love to my understanding and supportive husband, Artie,
my precious daughters, Carol and Sharon,
my delightful grandchildren, Jennifer, Andrew, and Melissa,
my charming sons-in-law, John and Seth,
and my dear brothers and sister.

Acquisitions editor: Carol Wada
Editorial/production supervision: Tara Powers-Hausmann
Interior design: Karen Buck
Cover design: 20/20 Services, Inc.
Prepress buyer: Debra Kesar
Manufacturing buyer: Mary Ann Gloriande

Copyright © 1991, 1982 by Allyn and Bacon
A Division of Simon & Schuster, Inc.
160 Gould Street
Needham Heights, Massachusetts 02194

Library of Congress Cataloging-in-Publication Data
Rubin, Dorothy.
    Diagnosis and correction in reading instruction / Dorothy Rubin. —
— 2nd ed.
      p.   cm.
    Includes bibliographical references and index.
    ISBN 0–13–208760–X
    1. Reading.   2. Reading—Ability testing.   3. Reading—Remedial
teaching.   I. Title.
LB1050.42.R83   1991
428.4′2—dc20   90–20030
                                                                CIP

Printed in the United States of America
10 9 8 7 6 5 4 3 2 1   95 94 93 92 91 90

Contents

Preface

Diagnosis and Correction in Reading Instruction, Second Edition, as in the first edition, is based on the premise that diagnosis and correction are essential parts of reading instruction. If diagnosis and correction are practiced as an integral part of reading instruction on a daily basis, there should be less need for remediation. I have designed this book to help preservice and in-service teachers acquire the skills necessary to make diagnosis and correction integral parts of their reading program. To achieve this goal, *Diagnosis and Correction in Reading Instruction* combines theory, basic knowledge and skills, practical application, and hands-on materials.

This book starts with the role of the teacher in the diagnostic-reading and correction program because the teacher is the key person in the program, and teachers today are becoming more autonomous; this is good. However, with autonomy comes a great deal of responsibility. Teachers need as much information as possible so they can develop a program best suited to their students, whether they use a literature-based program or a combined basal reader and literature-based program.

In a viable diagnostic-reading and correction program, teachers must be able to envision the totality of the reading program. They must have basic developmental reading skills at their fingertips, as well as strategies to help their students become proficient readers. They must recognize that reading is a thinking act, and that the emphasis in the 1990s is on higher-order thinking skills. They must have knowledge of educational and noneducational factors that affect the reading act and be knowledgeable of diagnostic techniques and instruments, as well as be able to administer and interpret them; they must have a working knowledge of corrective techniques. To help teachers accomplish this kind of program, nothing should be taken for granted. In this book, nothing is taken for granted.

Part I sets the stage for a diagnostic-reading and correction program. I explain what a diagnostic-reading and correction program is and define special terms so that there is no confusion when these terms are met later; then I present the teacher as the key person in the reading program, and his or her role in the program is explored. This part also presents an overview of those things a classroom teacher must know about tests, measurement, and evaluation. I introduce teachers to testing terminology and explain the differences between standardized tests and teacher-made tests, and norm-referenced and criterion-referenced instruments. In Part II, I am concerned with the nature and interrelatedness of factors that affect reading performance. Teachers must know about the individual differences of children, including multicultural differences, and about the educational and noneducational factors that can affect a child's ability to read if they are to provide proper instruction for their students. I explore the relationship of reading to language development, concept development, and listening; I also present a chapter on determining which students are underachieving in reading so that teachers can identify those students who need further help.

Part III presents instruments and techniques for the assessment and diagnosis of students' reading performance. In this part I explain and give examples of many kinds of diagnostic tests and techniques. I give special attention to the informal reading inventory and observation as diagnostic tools because, if used properly, these can be two of the classroom teacher's indispensable tools.

Part IV, the last part of the book, presents the diagnostic-reading and correction program in action. In this part I present scenarios of children with reading problems and show how step by step the teacher helps each child. In Chapters 12, 13, and 14 I give an analytical review of the basic skills teachers should have at their fingertips, including study skills, and provide numerous diagnostic and corrective strategies teachers can use. There is also a chapter on helping special children and one on parents as partners in a diagnostic-reading and correction program.

To help the teacher further, a complete informal reading inventory is included in Appendix A. Instructions on how to administer it, as well as how to mark and score errors, are presented in Chapter 8. The Fry Readability Formula is included in Appendix B as an additional aid to the teacher.

In *Diagnosis and Correction in Reading Instruction* I have tried to give principles in practical, comprehensible language as often as possible, for a book overburdened with esoteric terminology tends to obscure rather than to clarify concepts. Often, some explanations cannot be given without names, but whenever I use a technical term, I define the term and then use it. I hope that readers will find that I have succeeded in cutting down on the number of new terms, and that they will benefit from a concentration on practical principles rather than one on terminology and theories.

Throughout this book the emphasis is on helping the classroom teacher incorporate diagnosis and correction as part of the ongoing developmental program on a daily basis. It is hoped that this book will help to raise the teacher's level of consciousness so that diagnosis and correction are interwoven with instruction.

D.R.
Princeton, N.J.

Acknowledgments

I would like to thank my editor, Carol Wada, for her continuous support, valuable suggestions, intelligent insights, and cheerfulness. It is a pleasure to work with her. I would also like to thank Tara Powers-Hausmann for being such a patient, kind, considerate, and very helpful production editor. In addition, I would like to thank my proofreader, Carol Smith, for reading the manuscript so carefully, and for all her excellent suggestions and insights. I would also like to express my appreciation to Dr. Phillip Ollio, Dean of the School of Education, Trenton State College, and Dr. Eileen Burke, Chairperson, for their continued support. Finally, I would like to give special thanks to the following for taking such excellent photographs in a timely manner: Carol Smith, Monticello School System, Arkansas; Sharon Johnson, Dublin, Ohio; Russell Stanley, Lawrence Township School System, New Jersey; Marcie Feinberg, Happy Acres School, Hauppauge, New York; and Laura Nathanson, Half Hollow Hills School District # 5, New York.

1

Introduction to a Diagnostic-Reading and Correction Program

Scenario: A Diagnostic-Reading and Correction Program in Action

Whenever you walk into Ms. Johnson's third-grade classroom, you sense that something special is taking place; you sense the excitement of learning. Often no one notices your arrival because everyone is so engrossed in what he or she is doing.

Ms. Johnson's classroom is not a quiet one. It's a room in which children and teacher are involved in a dynamic, interactive teaching-learning program, which includes a diagnostic-reading and correction program.

During any one day, you can usually see Ms. Johnson working with an individual child, a group of children, or a whole class. In Ms. Johnson's room grouping is tailored to the needs of children and is very flexible. Children flow from one group to another depending on need. It's not unusual to find one child in more than one reading group, working individually, or working in a one-to-one relationship with Ms. Johnson. Ms. Johnson tries to correlate reading with all the language arts and sees to it that she meets individually with each child in a special conference at least once during the week. She believes in "nipping problems in the bud," so she keeps very close tabs on her students. Whether children are reading from trade books or from their basal readers (in her class, they do both), she keeps records of their progress in word recognition and comprehension skills.

Ms. Johnson is always probing, questioning, and keeping a sharp eye out for potential problems; she interweaves diagnosis with instruction. When she notices a problem, she talks to the child to try to determine whether the child recognizes that he or she has a problem. She then sets up a conference to meet and discuss it further.

At the conference, Ms. Johnson helps the child recognize that it's important to ask for help when you need it. She also tries to elicit from the child what he or she thinks the problem is. Ms. Johnson has at her fingertips various informal diagnostic strategies, which she employs to learn more about the child's problem. If she feels it is necessary, she will use more formal techniques or contact the special reading teacher for suggestions.

Ms. Johnson also contacts the parents to discuss with them what is taking place and to

1

solicit their help. She believes strongly that parents should be partners in their children's learning and that their help and support are important and needed.

Ms. Johnson is a good teacher, and she gets better with experience. Her students are fortunate to have her.

This chapter will introduce you to a diagnostic-reading and correction program and discuss the relationship of diagnosis to the ongoing reading program. Also, in the field of reading, there is often confusion because similar terms are used to convey different meanings. Because communication cannot take place unless there is a consensus of meaning, this chapter will define a number of terms that are used in the reading field.

KEY QUESTIONS

After you finish reading this chapter, you should be able to answer the following questions:

1. What is a diagnostic-reading and correction program?
2. What is remedial reading?
3. What is a developmental reading program?
4. How is reading defined in this book?
5. What is a total integrative reading program?
6. How does a definition of reading influence the diagnostic-reading program?
7. What are some principles of a good diagnostic-reading and correction program?
8. What are some reading theories?

KEY TERMS IN CHAPTER

You should pay special attention to the following new terms:

affective domain
bottom-up reading models
cognitive domain
corrective reading program
developmental reading
diagnosis
diagnostic-reading and
   correction program
functional reading
interactive reading models
metacognition
perception
perceptual domain
reading
reading process
reading recovery program

recreational reading
remedial reading program
top-down reading models

WHAT IS A DIAGNOSTIC-READING AND CORRECTION PROGRAM?

Diagnostic-reading and correction program
Reading instruction interwoven with diagnosis and correction.

A diagnostic-reading and correction program (DRCP) consists of reading instruction interwoven with diagnosis and correction. This program is based on the premise that diagnosis and correction are an integral part of the daily developmental reading program and that teachers can and should be able to implement such a program if they have the necessary skills (see Chapter 11).

Figure 1.1 This teacher has a diagnostic-reading and correction program that focuses on "nipping problems in the bud."

WHAT IS REMEDIAL READING?

Corrective reading program
Takes place within the regular classroom.

Remedial reading program
Takes place outside the regular classroom and is handled by special personnel.

Corrective reading programs take place in the regular classroom. Remedial reading programs usually take place outside the regular classroom and are handled by special personnel such as a special reading teacher, a therapist, or a clinician. The special reading teacher usually works with students who have severe reading problems that cannot be handled in the regular classroom. The students are usually referred for help by the regular classroom teacher.

WHAT ARE THE ADVANTAGES OF A DIAGNOSTIC-READING AND CORRECTION PROGRAM?

A diagnostic-reading and correction program is superior to remedial reading programs because it focuses on potential reading problems or those related to reading and tries to head them off. It is part of the ongoing reading program, and it takes place in the regular classroom under the leadership of the classroom teacher. The sooner an astute teacher recognizes a problem, the sooner the problem is diagnosed; and the sooner steps are taken to correct the problem, the less need there will be for later remediation.

A diagnostic-reading and correction program can help to stop the "failure cycle." For example, if children continually have reading difficulties, they begin to see themselves as failures; their self-concept is destroyed. The more they perceive themselves as failures, the more they fail. And so the cycle continues.

A diagnostic-reading and correction program will not make the jobs of special reading personnel obsolete, but it will make their load lighter and easier. It would be foolhardy to presume that the initiation of a diagnostic-reading and correction program would eliminate all reading problems. It will not. However, its implementation would free special reading personnel so that they could spend more time with those students who have severe reading problems, and it would give reading therapists more time to act as consultants to the regular classroom teachers.

WHAT IS A DEVELOPMENTAL READING PROGRAM?

Ask three different reading authorities to give you a definition of *developmental reading*, and the chances are high that you will receive three different definitions. (This is, of course, not limited to merely *developmental reading* or a few terms but seems to be the general rule in the field of reading.) The difficulty with such terms is that they are so commonly used that many persons assume that they are using them in the same manner. This can be an erroneous assumption and lead to confusion. For example, some reading authorities differentiate among developmental reading, functional reading, and recreational reading. For these people, *developmental reading* refers to those activities "in which the main purpose of the teacher is to bring about an improvement in reading skills—activities in which learning to read is the main goal. *Functional reading* includes all reading in which the primary aim is to obtain information. . . . *Recreational reading* consists of reading activities that have enjoyment, entertainment, and appreciation as major purposes."[1] Some reading authorities differ-

Functional reading Includes all reading in which the primary aim is to obtain information.

---

[1] Albert J. Harris and Edward R. Sipay, *How to Increase Reading Ability*, 7th ed. (New York: Longman, 1990), p. 95.

Figure 1.2 Andrew is involved in recreational reading; he is reading for enjoyment.

Recreational reading
Reading primarily for enjoyment, entertainment, and appreciation.

Developmental reading
All those reading skills that are systematically and sequentially developed to help students become effective readers throughout their schooling.

entiate among the developmental reading program, the corrective reading program, and the remedial reading program; whereas some others look upon the developmental reading program as encompassing the corrective and remedial program.

Developmental reading, in this book, refers to all those reading skills that are systematically and sequentially developed to help students become effective readers throughout their schooling. "All those reading skills" refers to learning-to-read skills as well as reading-to-learn skills and reading for appreciation. Developmental reading is the major reading program, and the diagnostic-corrective program that takes place in the regular classroom is part of the developmental reading program; all other programs are adjuncts to the developmental program, but they are also developmental in nature. For example, the remedial reading program that takes place outside the regular classroom has as its prime purpose the task of helping students attain those developmental skills that they lack. This program, which usually employs different strategies and techniques, is not a replacement for the student's classroom developmental instruction in reading; it is reading instruction that is given in *addition* to the reading instruction in the regular classroom, and therefore it must be related to or considered part of the developmental program. This is imperative because studies show that there is a consistent negative relationship between the time students spend in "pull-out" classes and reading.[2] Many times the "pull-out" program becomes the complete reading program for severely retarded readers, and

[2] G. V. Glass and M. L. Smith, *Pull-Out in Compensatory Education*, paper prepared for Office of the Commissioner, U.S. Office of Education, 1977.

rather than spending more time, the students spend less time in reading. Also, if the remedial program is looked on as separate from the developmental reading program, there is usually a lack of coordination between the teaching of the regular classroom teacher and that of the remedial reading teacher. (See: "Scenario: Integrating the Remedial Reading Program With the Regular Classroom Reading Program" Chapter 11.)

WHAT IS READING RECOVERY?

Reading recovery program
An early individualized, one-on-one intervention program for first-graders who are experiencing difficulty in learning to read.

The best kinds of programs are those that intervene as early as possible to help children overcome their difficulties in reading. Reading Recovery is an early-intervention program that was designed to help young readers who are experiencing difficulty in their first year of reading instruction.[3] In this program, which is not supposed to be a long-term or permanent one, a child who is one of the lowest achieving readers in a first-grade class receives daily individual 30-minute lessons by a specially trained teacher that are in addition to the regular classroom instruction. The program is tailored to the individual child, and the emphasis is on engaging the child in reading and writing activities that will help the child catch up with peers.

This collaborative one-on-one early intervention program is very promising; however, as the designers of the program aptly note, there are many variables that determine how well someone will do in school, not least of which is socioeconomic circumstances (see Chapter 4). "There is no one answer to problems in education."[4]

DEFINING READING

The relationship of reading to diagnosis is important in a diagnostic-reading and correction program. To fully understand this relationship it is first essential to define reading. The definition that we choose will influence not only the instructional component of the program but also the diagnostic component. (See "Diagnosis and the Definition of Reading" in this chapter.)

John is able to decode correctly all the words in a passage; however, he cannot answer any questions about it. Is John reading? Susie makes a number of errors in decoding words, but the errors she makes do not seem to prevent her from answering any of the questions on the passage. Is Susie reading? Maria reads a passage on something about which she has very strong feelings; she has difficulty answering the questions based on the passage because of

---

[3] Gay Su Pinnell, Mary D. Fried, and Rose Mary Estice, "Reading Recovery: Learning How to Make a Difference," *The Reading Teacher* 43 (January 1990): 283.

[4] Ibid., p. 293.

her attitude. Is she reading? José can decode the words in the passage, and he thinks that he knows the meaning of all the words; however, José cannot answer the questions. Is José reading?

To answer these questions, we would have to state: They depend on our definition of reading. A definition of reading is necessary because it will influence the choice of goals that will be set in the development of the reading program. A teacher who sees reading as a one-way process, consisting simply of the decoding of symbols or the relating of sounds to symbols, will develop a different type of program from that of a teacher who looks on reading as getting meaning from the printed page.

Reading
The getting of meaning from and the bringing of meaning to the written page.

There is no single, set definition of reading. As a result, it is difficult to define it simply. A broad definition, which has been greatly used, is that reading is the bringing to and the getting of meaning from the printed page. This implies that readers bring their backgrounds, their experiences, as well as their emotions, into play. Students who are upset or physically ill will bring these feelings into the act of reading, and the feelings will influence their interpretative processes. A person well versed in reading matter will gain more from the material than someone less knowledgeable. A student who is a good critical thinker will gain more from a critical passage than one who is not. A student who has strong dislikes will come away with different feelings and understandings from those of a pupil with strong likings.

By defining reading as the bringing to and the getting of meaning from the printed page, Susie is actually the only child who is reading, because she is the only one who *understands* what she is reading. She is the only one who is able to integrate information from the text with what she already knows. Although John can verbalize the words, he has no comprehension of them. Maria can also decode the words, but her strong feelings about the topic have prevented her from getting the message that the writer is conveying. "Reading is a process in which information from the text and the knowledge possessed by the reader act together to produce meaning."[5] In Maria's case this has not happened. José can decode the words and knows the meanings of the individual words, but either he is not able to get the sense of the whole passage or he does not know the meaning of the words in another context.

It could be that José is having difficulty with the presentation of the material. The way that the writer presents the information will influence how well the reader will gain the presented concepts. The more clear and logical the presentation and organization of the writing, the easier it is to gain meaning from the text. It is possible, too, that José does not have the motivation, skill, or background

[5] Richard C. Anderson, Elfrieda H. Hiebert, Judith A. Scott, and Ian A. G. Wilkinson, *Becoming a Nation of Readers* (Washington, D.C.: National Institute of Education, 1985), p. 8.

Figure 1.3 Without understanding, there is no reading.

experience to interpret the text material. Good readers are good problem solvers who must construct "meaning through the dynamic interaction among the reader, the text, and the context of the reading situation."[6]

Reading as a Total Integrative Process

Reading process
Concerned with the affective, perceptual, and cognitive domains.

By using a broad or global definition of reading, we see reading as a total integrative process that starts with the reader and includes the following domains: (1) the affective, (2) the perceptual, and (3) the cognitive.

The Affective Domain

Affective domain
Includes the feelings and emotional learnings that individuals acquire.

The affective domain includes our feelings and emotions. The way we feel influences greatly the way we look at stimuli on a field. It may distort our perception. For example, if we are hungry and we see the word *fool*, we would very likely read it as *food*. If we have adverse feelings about certain things, these feelings will probably influence how we interpret what we read. Our feelings will also influence what we decide to read. Obviously, attitudes exert a directive and dynamic influence on our readiness to respond.

The Perceptual Domain

Perceptual domain
Part of the reading process that depends on an individual's background of experiences and sensory receptors.

In the perceptual domain, perception can be defined as giving meaning to sensations or the ability to organize stimuli on a field. How we organize stimuli depends largely on our background of experiences and on our sensory receptors. If, for example, our eyes are organically defective, those perceptions involving sight would be distorted. In the act of reading, visual perception is a most important factor. Children need to control their eyes so they move from left to right across the page. Eye movements influence what the reader perceives.

[6] Karen K. Wixson, Charles W. Peters, Elaine M. Weber, and Edward D. Roeber, "New Directions in Statewide Reading Assessment," *The Reading Teacher* 40 (April 1987): 750.

Although what we observe is never in exact accord with the physical situation,[7] readers must be able to accurately decode the graphemic (written) representation. If, however, readers have learned incorrect associations, it will affect their ability to read. For example, if a child reads the word *gip* for *pig* and is not corrected, this may become part of his or her perceptions. Whether children perceive the word as a whole, in parts, or as individual letters will also determine whether they will be good or poor readers. The more mature readers are able to perceive more complex and extensive graphemic patterns as units. They are also able to give meaning to mutilated words such as

Town

Perception
A cumulative process based on an individual's background of experiences. It is defined as giving meaning to sensations or the ability to organize stimuli on a field.

Perception is a cumulative process which is based on an individual's background of experiences. The perceptual process is influenced by physiological factors as well as affective ones. As already stated, a person who is hungry may read the word *fool* as *food*. Similarly, a person with a biased view toward a topic may delete, add, or distort what is being read.

Betts presents a number of factors on which the perceptual process of decoding writing into speech is dependent. Here are most of them:[8]

1. Motivation, for example, the attitudinal factor *need* to identify the unknown part or parts of a particular word.
2. Attention as a powerful selector of stimulus information to be processed and as a constant feature of perceptual activity.
3. Set, a determiner of perception, which, among other things, causes the pupil to regard reading as a poverty-stricken word-calling process or as a thinking process.
4. Grouping of stimuli into recognizable syllables, phonograms, and other patterns for making optimum use of a limited span of attention.
5. Meaning, both structural and referential, needed for the closure of perception.
6. Contrast, such as the contrastive letter patterns which represent contrastive sound patterns.
7. Feedback, a circular process, from the examination of letter groupings of the written word to the sounds of the spoken word;

[7] Julian E. Hochberg, *Perception* (Englewood Cliffs, N.J.: Prentice-Hall, 1964), p. 3.

[8] Emmett A. Betts, "Linguistics and Reading," *Education* 86 (April 1966): 457–58.

for example, the *application* of word perception skills to the written word during silent reading.

8. Closure, as in the identification of the word *noise* after the usual sound represented by *oi* is recalled.

The Cognitive Domain

Cognitive domain
Hierarchy of objectives ranging from simplistic thinking skills to the more complex ones.

The cognitive domain includes the areas involving thinking. Under this umbrella we would place all the comprehension skills (see Chapter 13). Persons who have difficulty in thinking (the manipulation of symbolic representations) would obviously have difficulty in reading. Although the cognitive domain goes beyond the perceptual domain, it builds and depends on a firm perceptual base. That is, if readers have faulty perceptions, they will also have faulty concepts. (See Chapter 4 for a discussion of concept development.)

Research about the human brain and cognition is providing interesting information that may affect our teaching practices. The human brain is actively involved in selecting, transforming, organizing, and remembering information;[9] in many ways, it is analogous to a computer's information-processing system. However, the human brain, unlike the computer, is constantly reprograming itself, generating new strategies, and learning new knowledge. The better strategies a learner has for processing information, the better able the learner is to retain and retrieve the information. Studies on the brain are looking at the kinds of strategies that people use to organize, encode, and store information. The researchers are also interested in how individuals differ in their information-processing strategies; that is, researchers are interested in the cognitive styles that the individuals use.

Research on the brain and cognitive processes have implications for teaching and instruction. By looking at the brain as an active consumer of information, able to interpret information and draw inferences from it as well as ignore some information and selectively attend to other information, the learner is "given a new, more important active role and responsibility in learning from instruction and teaching."[10]

METACOGNITION

The term *metacognition* is used "to refer to both students' knowledge about their own cognitive processes and their ability to control these processes."[11] It literally means thinking critically about thinking.

[9] Merlin C. Wittrock, "Education and the Cognitive Processes of the Brain," *The National Society for the Study of Education Seventy-seventh Yearbook*, Part II (1978): 64.

[10] Ibid., p. 101.

[11] Claire E. Weinstein and Richard E. Mayer, "The Teaching of Learning Strategies," *The Handbook of Research on Teaching*, 3rd ed. (1986): p. 323.

Metacognition
Thinking critically about thinking; refers to students' knowledge about their thinking processes and ability to control them.

Good readers are engaged in active learning strategies. They use good monitoring strategies whereby they establish learning goals for an instructional activity, determine the degree to which these are being met, and, if necessary, change the strategies being used to attain the goal.[12] Good readers know what to do, as well as how and when to do it; they have the metacognitive abilities that make them active consumers of information.

The "what to do" includes such strategies as "identifying the main idea, rehearsing (repeating) information, forming associations and images, using mnemonics, organizing new material to make it easier to remember, applying test-taking techniques, outlining, and note-taking."[13]

The "how and when" includes such strategies as "checking to see if you understand, predicting outcomes, evaluating the effectiveness of an attempt at a task, planning the next move, testing strategies, deciding how to apportion time and effort, and revising or switching to other strategies to overcome any difficulties encountered."[14]

Good readers are good thinkers.

READING THEORY AND TERMINOLOGY: A SPECIAL NOTE

The field of reading is replete with numerous theories, and different catch phrases are sometimes assigned to the same general theories, further confusing the field. An area that has caused much heat and debate among reading theorists is that of beginning reading. Controversy has centered on whether the reading process is a holistic one (emphasis on meaning), that is, a top-down model of reading, or a subskill process (code emphasis), that is, a bottom-up model, and more recently whether it is an interactive model, which is somewhat but not entirely a combination of both top-down and bottom-up in that both processes take place simultaneously depending on the difficulty of the material for the individual reader.

Top-down reading models
Depend on the reader's background of experiences and language ability in constructing meaning from the text.

Although various types of each reading model have been proposed, and within each group there have been extremists as well as middle-of-the-road advocates, each model has certain elements.

The top-down reading models depend greatly on the reader's background of experiences and language ability in constructing meaning from the text. In the top-down models readers continuously make predictions about the text based on their prior knowledge, the specific material being read, and the context of the material. For the

---

[12] Ibid.

[13] Anita Woolfolk, *Educational Psychology*, 4th ed. (Englewood Cliffs, N.J.: Prentice-Hall, 1990), p. 252.

[14] Ibid.

top-down theorist, "the skilled readers go directly from print to meaning without first recoding print to speech."[15]

Bottom-up reading models
Models which consider the reading process as one of grapheme-phoneme correspondences; code emphasis or subskill models.

The bottom-up reading models, on the other hand, consider the reading process as one of grapheme (letter)–phoneme (sound) correspondences—that is, a decoding process. After the written code has been broken, the reader associates meaning to the written symbols if the words are in the reader's listening experience. For the bottom-up models, the printed material is supposed to supply more information than the reader, which is the converse of the top-down models. Some theorists claim that the bottom-up models describe what readers do when first learning to read and that a top-down model is for more skilled readers.[16]

Interactive reading models
The top-down processing of information is dependent on the bottom-up processing, and vice versa.

The interactive models of reading, which are currently the most widely held, seem to be somewhat but not completely a cross between the top-down and bottom-up models. In these models, the top-down processing of information is dependent on the bottom-up processing, and vice versa. In others words, if the material is difficult to decode, this difficulty will obviously influence comprehension; similarly, if the material is difficult to understand, the impediment will slow down the decoding process. However, there is not "complete agreement among the interactive theorists as to which kind of processing initiates the reading process, or if the processes occur almost simultaneously."[17] There is agreement, however, that "reading involves the skillful combination of linguistic and semantic knowledge with visual information in order to reconstruct the meaning intended by the author."[18]

Practices in classrooms are based on the theories that teachers embrace. Those who believe in a bottom-up model would emphasize decoding to the exclusion of meaning; and the converse would be true of those who believe primarily in a top-down model. Those who believe in an interactive model would probably use a combination of both.

Theories often tend to be exclusive; they emphasize their own approach and generally neglect others. The classroom teacher, however, should not accept an either-or dichotomy, but rather should seek a synthesis of all the elements that have proved to be workable; that is, the classroom teacher usually takes elements from each theory based on the individual needs of students. It is not a contradiction of any one of the theories to use elements of each. Good teachers realize that the reading process is a very complex one and that there is no simple answer.

---

[15] Albert J. Harris and Edward R. Sipay, *How to Increase Reading Ability*, 9th ed. (New York: Longman, 1990), p. 13.

[16] Ibid., p. 12.

[17] Ibid., p. 14.

[18] Ibid.

WHAT IS DIAGNOSIS?

Some educators are disturbed by the term *diagnosis* because it seems to connote illness or disease, and they do not like the analogies that are often made between medicine and education. *Diagnosis* is a term that has been borrowed from medicine. For example, the first definition in *Webster's Third New International Dictionary* is as follows: "the act or art of identifying a disease from its signs and symptoms. . . ." The third definition given for *diagnosis* is, however, a more general one: "investigation or analysis of the cause or nature of a condition, situation, or problem. . . ." Reread the first definition, and replace the term *disease* with the phrase *reading difficulties and strengths*. Now reread the first and third definitions. You should have the following: Diagnosis is the act or art of identifying reading difficulties and strengths from their signs and symptoms, and diagnosis involves the investigation or analysis of the cause(s) or nature of a condition, situation, or problem. This definition does describe diagnosis as it is used in reading. It seems obvious that we should not be concerned with where the term comes from, that is, from which field it has been borrowed, but rather whether the definition that we use is valid for our purposes.

Diagnosis
The act of identifying difficulties and strengths from their signs and symptoms, as well as the investigation or analysis of the cause or causes of a condition, situation, or problem.

Let us analyze the definition further.

1. The first step in diagnosis is the identification of strengths and weaknesses by observing certain signs or symptoms. Some examples of these signs or symptoms would be a child's inability or ability to read fluently, a child's inability or ability to decode words; or a child's ability or inability to answer questions on comprehension.
2. The second step is to determine the cause or causes of the difficulty by analyzing the kinds of difficulties the child is having. This is done through a careful investigation of the strategies and techniques the child uses in reading. It may include looking for some of the underlying factors, noneducative or educative, that could be causing the reading problem.

Note that in the first step, we look for both reading difficulties and strengths; knowledge of what a child can do is helpful many times in giving us an insight into a child's reading problem. In the second step, we generally find that a reading problem is due to a number of factors rather than to just one. (See Chapter 6 for information on a diagnostic pattern.)

DIAGNOSIS AND DEFINITION OF READING

As has already been stated, the definition that is chosen for reading also influences the diagnostic program. If we see reading as a total integrative process, diagnosis should also be seen as a total integrative process. If a global definition is chosen, then the diagnostic program will be a broad one. Under a global definition, when one makes a diagnosis, it is recognized that a reading problem is usually caused by many different factors. Therefore, a diagnosis of a reading problem would include considerations of ecological (environmental), personal, and intellectual factors. Educative factors, as well as noneducative ones, are scrutinized. It is recognized that learning takes place in some kind of relationship; that is, not all children respond in the same way, and not all children respond to the same person. An atmosphere conducive to growth is recognized as important, as well as the maxim that success breeds success. Diagnosis is looked on as continuous, as underlying prevention as well as remediation, and as interwoven with instruction. The emphasis in diagnosis is on determining the child's reading problems and the conditions causing them. Here is a list of some principles of diagnosis:

The Principles of Diagnosis

1. Diagnosis underlies prevention.
2. Early diagnosis is essential.
3. Diagnosis is continuous.
4. Diagnosis and instruction are interwoven.
5. Diagnosis is a *means* to correction.
6. Diagnosis is not an end in itself.
7. Teacher-made as well as published instruments are used in diagnosis.
8. Noneducative as well as educative factors are diagnosed.
9. Diagnosis identifies strengths as well as deficiencies.
10. Diagnosis is an individual process; that is, in diagnosis the teacher focuses on the individual child. (Diagnostic information can be obtained from working in a one-to-one relationship with a child, from observing a child in a group, or from observing a child doing seatwork.)
11. The diagnostician looks for a number of causes of reading difficulty rather than just one.
12. The diagnostician is able to establish rapport with the student.
13. The diagnostician avoids labeling students.
14. The diagnostician treats each student as an individual worthy of respect.

SUMMARY

Chapter 1 is an introduction to a diagnostic-reading and correction program. Such a program consists of reading instruction interwoven with diagnosis and correction. Since the definition that is chosen for reading will influence the diagnostic program, reading is defined in a global manner: Reading is the bringing to and the getting of meaning from the printed page. By using a broad defintion, we look on reading as a total integrative process. Under a global definition when one makes a diagnosis, it is recognized that a reading problem is usually caused by many different factors.

SUGGESTIONS FOR THOUGHT QUESTIONS AND ACTIVITIES

1. You have been assigned to a special committee to develop a reading program in your school that would help stem the number of reading problems that now exist. You have decided to advocate the implementation of a diagnostic-reading and correction program. Give your rationale for doing so. How would you go about implementing such a program?
2. Make a study of the ways that persons in a school district are defining *developmental reading*.
3. Make a study in your school district to see whether remedial reading is a "pull-out program" that is or is not integrated with the developmental reading program.
4. Ask a number of teachers how they define reading. Observe their classes and try to discern whether their reading program reflects their definition of reading.

SELECTED BIBLIOGRAPHY

Anderson, Richard C., Elfrieda H. Hiebert, Judith A. Scott, and Ian A. G. Wilkinson. *Becoming a Nation of Readers*. Washington, D.C.: National Institute of Education, 1985.

Clymer, Theodore. "Research in Corrective Reading: Findings, Problems, and Observations." In *Corrective Reading in the Elementary Classroom*, ed. Marjorie S. Johnson and Roy A. Kress. Newark, Del.: International Reading Association, 1967.

Harris, Albert J., and Edward R. Sipay. *How to Increase Reading Ability*, 9th ed. New York: Longman, 1990.

Mullis, Ina V. S., and Lynn B. Jenkins. *The Reading Report Card, 1971–1988*, National Assessment of Educational Progress. Princeton, N.J.: Educational Testing, 1990.

Pinnell, Gay Su, Mary D. Fried, and Rose Mary Estice. "Reading Recovery: Learning How to Make a Difference." *The Reading Teacher* 43 (January 1990): 282–95.

Rayner, Keith, and Alexander Pollatsek. *The Psychology of Reading*. Englewood Cliffs, N.J.: Prentice-Hall, 1989.

Rickelman, Robert J., and William A. Henk. "Reading Technology and the Brain." *The Reading Teacher* 43 (January 1990): 334–36.

Strange, Michael, and Richard L. Allington. "Use the Diagnostic Prescriptive Model Knowledgeably." *The Reading Teacher* 31 (December 1977): 290–93.

Wittrock, Merlin C., "Learning and the Brain." In *The Brain and Psychology*, ed. Merlin C. Wittrock. New York: Academic Press, 1980.

2

The Teacher's Role
in the Diagnostic-Reading
and Correction Program

Scenario: Rachael S.—The Making of a Dropout

Rachael started the third grade in the top reading group. By March she was in the lowest one. She was confused because she didn't understand why her teacher, Ms. Graves, kept putting her in lower reading groups. The only thing Ms. Graves told her was that she couldn't do the work.

When Rachael's mother tried to elicit from the teacher what Rachael's problems were, she was told that her daughter "just didn't seem to have it together." When Rachael's mother asked Ms. Graves what she could do to help, Ms. Graves was unable to give her any suggestions.

Toward the end of March, Rachael came home hysterical. Ms. Graves was sending her and her whole group to the "resource room" with a special reading teacher while the other groups stayed in the regular classroom and had reading with Ms. Graves. Rachael's mother phoned the teacher to find out what was happening.

Ms. Graves said that the children would be taking the standardized achievement tests soon and she feared that Rachael would not do well in reading, so she wanted her to go to the resource room for reading. Rachael's mother explained that her daughter was very upset about going out of the classroom and asked why Ms. Graves couldn't give her the help she needed in the regular classroom. Ms. Graves said that Rachael's whole group was going to the resource room and if Rachael didn't go, she'd be the only one left from her group. Obviously, she did not have the time to work with Rachael. Rachael's mother said that she would be happy to come in and work with her daughter if Ms. Graves would tell her what to do. She explained that her daughter was very, very upset and did not want to go out of the classroom to the "dummy" room. Ms. Graves said that under no circumstances could she come to class and work with Rachael.

Meanwhile, Rachael was becoming more and more upset. In the mornings she would have dreadful stomachaches. At times she would cry and beg her mother to let her stay home. She said that she felt like a dummy and she couldn't do the work. Rachael's mother wondered how a cheery, happy little girl who loved school and reading could change so radically.

Do you agree with the way Ms. Graves is handling Rachael and her mother? If you were Ms. Graves, would you have sent Rachael to the "resource room"? For that matter would you have sent a whole group to the "resource room"? What insights can you draw from this scenario about Ms. Graves's ability as a reading teacher? How is Ms. Graves's attitude toward Rachael affecting Rachael?

This chapter discusses the teacher's role in the diagnostic-reading and correction program and focuses on the characteristics of a good reading teacher in the regular classroom. It focuses on you, the classroom teacher, as a teacher of reading in a dynamic diagnostic-reading and correction program.

KEY QUESTIONS

After you finish reading this chapter, you should be able to answer the questions presented at the end of the scenario, as well as the following:

1. What is the role of the teacher in a diagnostic-reading and correction program?
2. What skills are needed to implement a diagnostic-reading and correction program?
3. Why is the teacher considered the key person in a diagnostic-reading and correction program?
4. What are some important characteristics of a good reading teacher?
5. What is "self-fulfilling prophecy"?
6. What should a teacher know about planning and instructional time?
7. What should the teacher know about classroom management and organization?
8. What is direct instruction?
9. What is interactive instruction?
10. How does a teacher "model" thinking strategies for students?

KEY TERMS IN CHAPTER

You should pay special attention to the following new terms:

direct instruction
interactive instruction
modeling strategy
self-fulfilling prophecy

THE TEACHER IN A DIAGNOSTIC-READING AND CORRECTION PROGRAM

The role of a teacher in a diagnostic-reading and correction program is broad. The teacher must observe individual children, understand individual differences and the factors that influence them, build readiness for reading at various reading levels, identify children who are having reading difficulties, combine diagnosis and correction with everyday reading, and help children gain an appreciation of reading. Teachers must have knowledge of the various word recognition and comprehension skills at their fingertips and be able to teach these effectively. They must know the techniques of observation and be aware of the factors that influence children's reading behavior. Teachers must be able to administer and interpret such diagnostic techniques as the informal reading inventory and word analysis tests. If teachers cannot construct their own informal diagnostic tests, they should be aware of those that are commercially available. Obviously, teachers in a diagnostic-reading and correction program must be well prepared and well informed.

THE TEACHER AS THE KEY TO A GOOD READING PROGRAM

Although a school may have the best equipment, the most advanced school plant, a superior curriculum, and children who want to learn, it must have "good teachers" so that the desired kind of learning can take place. With today's emphasis on accountability, the spotlight is even more sharply focused on the teacher. Although there is no definitive agreement on how to evaluate teachers, researchers and educators agree that teachers influence students' behavior and learning.

Studies show that it is difficult to compare different methods or sets of materials in researches and that students seem to learn to read from a variety of materials and methods.[1] More importantly, researchers of these and other studies point to the teacher as the key to improving reading instruction. For example, the authors of *Becoming a Nation of Readers* state that "studies indicate that about 15 percent of the variation among children in reading achievement at the end of the school year is attributable to factors that relate to the skill and effectiveness of the teacher."[2] In contrast, "The largest study ever done comparing approaches to beginning reading found that about 3 percent of the variation in reading achievement at the end of the first grade was attributable to the overall approach of the program."[3] The teacher is obviously the key to improving reading instruction:

[1] Guy L. Bond and Robert Dykstra, "The Cooperative Research Program in First-Grade Reading Instruction," *Reading Research Quarterly* 2 (Summer 1967): 1–142. Albert J. Harris and Coleman Morrison, "The CRAFT Project: A Final Report," *The Reading Teacher* 22 (January 1969): 335–40.

[2] Richard C. Anderson, Elfrieda H. Hiebert, Judith A. Scott, and Ian A. G. Wilkinson, *Becoming a Nation of Readers* (Washington, D.C.: National Institute of Education, 1985), p. 85.

[3] Ibid.

The main lesson, it seems to me, is that the teacher is of tremendous importance in preventing and treating children's reading and learning disabilities . . . good teaching is probably the best way to help children.[4]

Although most persons agree that the teacher is the key to improved instruction, there is no unanimity on what factors affect teaching performance and student learning or on the objective criteria for evaluating teacher performance.

TEACHER EVALUATION

Effective teaching is usually determined by a teacher's ability to produce desirable changes in students' learning behavior, in students' achievement. If evaluation were only based on such changes, the task of teacher evaluation would be somewhat simplified. Students would be given pretests at the beginning of the term and posttests at the end of the term. The students' achievement, based on desired outcomes, could then be determined. But there are recognizable difficulties with this method. One is the assumption that students' achievements or nonachievements are directly due to their teachers. This is not so. Yes, as stated earlier, teachers have a profound affect on students' learning, but there are many variables that affect student achievement, such as home environment, ability level, motivation, peers, television, illness, and so on. (Many of these factors will be discussed in subsequent chapters.)

What on the surface may appear to be simple is really not. In one class, children may produce better results on standardized tests than in another, but they may have grown to dislike the subject so intensely that they will avoid it in the future. These learned attitudes are not desirable, and they will remain with the children longer than the subject matter they have learned. How should such teachers be evaluated?

It is beyond the scope of this book to try to answer or resolve the teacher-evaluation controversy. We will concern ourselves with possible descriptions and means for evaluating the characteristics, traits, and competencies that teachers in a diagnostic-reading and correction program should possess.

SOME IMPORTANT CHARACTERISTICS AND PRACTICES OF GOOD READING TEACHERS

Although unanimity does not exist among educators as to which characteristics are the most salient in producing good teachers, most would agree that verbal ability; good educational background includ-

[4] Jeanne Chall, "A Decade of Research on Reading and Learning Disabilities," *What Research Has to Say About Reading Instruction* (Newark, Del.: International Reading Association, 1978), pp. 39, 40.

Figure 2.1 This teacher is setting a good example for her students.

ing such knowledge as the content of reading, ability to read with skill oneself, and ability to do higher-order thinking; good planning and organizing ability; instructional strategies; and positive teacher expectations and attitudes would be ones that reading teachers should possess.

Studies have shown that teachers who have a good educational background and verbal ability are usually better teachers than those who do not.[5] This information makes good sense and should come as no surprise. What is surprising is that there are some teachers who themselves lack necessary reading skills. A four-and-one-half-year study measuring the reading skills of almost 350 teachers found "many of the teachers tested demonstrated a wide range of deficiencies or discrepancies in their reading abilities."[6] Although researchers stated that care should be taken not to generalize from these results, it is clear that teacher deficiencies in reading ability should warrant concern. Another study found that teachers scored low on tests of study skills intended for children completing elementary or junior high school.[7] Obviously, if a teacher feels insecure about a subject,

[5] Charles E. Bidwell and John D. Kasarda, "School District Organization and Student Achievement," *American Sociological Review* 40 (February 1975): 55–70. Eric Hanushek, "The Production of Education, Teacher Quality and Efficiency," paper presented at the Bureau of Educational Personnel Development Conference: "How Do Teachers Make a Difference?" Washington, D.C.

[6] Lance M. Gentile and Merna McMillan, "Some of Our Students' Teachers Can't Read Either," *Journal of Reading* 21 (November 1977): 146.

[7] Eunice N. Askov, et al., "Study Skill Mastery Among Elementary School Teachers," *The Reading Teacher* 30 (February 1977): 485–88.

that teacher will tend to avoid teaching it, and when it is taught, concepts and skills may be taught erroneously. If teachers lack a broad vocabulary, are unable to read critically, and have not mastered study skills, their students will suffer. How can teachers construct questions that challenge students' higher levels of thinking if the teachers lack the ability to read at high levels of comprehension? They can't. How can teachers diagnose students' problems if they do not know what skills the students are supposed to have? They can't. How can teachers instill a love for books in students if they themselves are not reading? They can't. Obviously, if teachers are seen by students as not placing a high value on reading, students may begin to feel likewise. The section in Chapter 13 on "Attitudes and Reading" discusses how important the role of the teacher is in helping to instill a love of books in children. (Chapters 12 to 14 present reading skills that teachers should have at their fingertips and help teachers learn how to interest their students in books.)

TEACHER PLANNING

Teachers in a diagnostic-reading and correction program must also be good planners. Planning helps guide teachers in making choices about instruction; it helps them to clarify their thinking about objectives, students' needs, interests, and readiness levels, as well as to determine what motivating techniques to use.

The teacher in a diagnostic-reading and correction program bases instruction on continuous analysis of students' strengths and weaknesses. The teacher is flexible and is always alert to student feedback to determine whether to proceed with instruction, to slow down instruction, or to stop and correct or clarify some misconception.

The teacher in a diagnostic-reading and correction program must wisely plan time allotments for reading.

TIME SPENT IN READING

Reading helps reading! Hardly any person would disagree with that statement, nor with the statement that children need to be helped to acquire comprehension skills; without the ability to comprehend, reading would not take place. The question is: How much time is spent on comprehension instruction in the schools? Durkin, a noted reading researcher, undertook a study to determine the answer to this question. She found that teachers spend very little time on comprehension instruction; they attend to written assignments; and none of the teachers in the study views social studies as a time to help with reading instruction.[8] In that part of the study dealing with

---

[8] Dolores Durkin, "What Classroom Observations Reveal About Reading Comprehension," *Reading Research Quarterly* 14, No. 4 (1978–1979): 533.

Figure 2.2 Reading helps reading.

fourth grade, the researcher reports that "less than 1 percent (28 minutes [out of 4,469 minutes]) went to comprehension instruction."[9] The results are startling; however, another researcher reexamined Durkin's data and found that by broadening the definition of comprehension instruction, she could state that "some teachers are attempting to teach reading comprehension approximately one-fourth of the time they are involved in teaching reading and social studies."[10] These findings seem more realistic.

What is devastating is that reading authorities in the late 1970s did not expect to find comprehension instruction in the primary grades. For example, Durkin did not initiate her study in the primary grades because she felt that there is less comprehension instruction "in the primary grades because of the concern there for decoding skills."[11] Durkin also states that she chose fourth grade as one part of her three-prong study "because it is commonly believed that at that level a switch is made from *learning to read* to *reading to learn*. It is also at that level that content subjects begin to be taken seriously."[12]

Learning to read and *reading to learn* are not two mutually exclusive processes; they can and should take place together. Children in the lower grades as well as in the higher grades should be involved in both. And fortunately in the 1990s the trend is in that direction. (See "Helping Children Acquire Comprehension Skills" in Chapter 13.)

---

[9] Ibid., p. 497.

[10] Carol A. Hodges, "Toward a Broader Definition of Comprehension Instruction," *Reading Research Quarterly* 15, No. 2 (1980): 305.

[11] Durkin, p. 493.

[12] Ibid., p. 494.

Not only is the amount of time spent in reading essential for success in reading, but the amount of actual reading accomplished is also vital to reading achievement. Researchers have found that differences do exist between poor and good readers. One researcher found that "poor readers do not complete equivalent amounts of reading in context generally, and have few opportunities to practice silent reading behaviors particularly."[13] Even though the teacher spends equal amounts of time with the two groups of students, the quality of the time is different. Teachers appear to have poorer readers spend more time on oral reading, and more time is spent correcting oral reading errors.[14]

The Nation's Report Card has consistently found a positive correlation between achievement and exposure to intensive reading experiences: "Students at all ages who read books, newspapers, and magazines most often also displayed the highest reading achievement."[15] In addition, positive relationships were found between students' proficiency and the time spent in homework.[16] (Certainly homework involves various aspects of reading, so it is being reported here.) What is sad is that approximately one-tenth of the students who were interviewed in the study said that they never read for pleasure.[17]

Direct Instruction Time

Direct instruction Instruction guided by a teacher, who uses various strategies to help students understand what they are reading.

There is no question that the more time one spends in reading, the better reader that person should be, but must the time spent in reading be direct instruction time with a teacher or reading independently? Both are probably important.

Some studies suggest that direct instruction time is related to reading achievement at the lower grades; however, at the upper grades direct instructional time seems to be more necessary for low-socioeconomic-status children. The researchers hypothesize a reason for this difference:

> Middle-class children tend to spend substantial amounts of time reading outside school, increasing their total reading practice and reducing the significance of differences in amount of instructional reading time in school, while lower socioeconomic children are less likely to do so.[18]

[13] Richard L. Allington, "Poor Readers Don't Get to Read Much in Reading Groups," *Language Arts* 57 (November/December 1980): 874.

[14] Ibid., pp. 872–76.

[15] Ina V. S. Mullis and Lynn B. Jenkins, *The Reading Report Card, 1971–1988*, National Assessment of Educational Progress (Princeton, N.J.: Educational Testing, 1990). p. 43.

[16] Ibid.

[17] Ibid., p. 42.

[18] Albert J. Harris, "The Effective Teacher of Reading, Revisited," *The Reading Teacher* 33 (November 1979): 136.

Other studies claim that direct instruction in reading is effective for children in basic skills programs.[19] The direct approach is characterized by a structured classroom environment under the control of the teacher; it includes goals, activities to accomplish the goals, direct explanation, and immediate feedback.[20] Still others claim that "direct instruction may be the most effective way to teach most subjects including reading."[21] Teachers are cautioned that they must decide what is best for their students and classrooms.[22] What is good for one group of students may not be effective for another (see Chapter 15).

TEACHER INSTRUCTION

It makes sense, too, that the kind of instruction teachers use to directly teach reading will affect how well their students acquire reading skills, especially higher-order thinking skills. Good teachers know a number of strategies and attempt to help students become active consumers of information. Good teachers recognize that good readers interact with the text and bring their background of experiences to the reading act. Good teachers also attempt to become part of the interactive process by using interactive instruction.

Interactive Instruction

Interactive instruction
The teacher intervenes at optimal times to enhance the learning process.

In interactive instruction, what the teacher does is all-important:

> The teacher has a powerful role in classroom reading and learning from text. The teacher can modify the text, increase or decrease the demands on reader resources, add to reader resources, set goals that are difficult or easy in relationship to reader resources. Indeed, depending on what the teacher does, the students in one class may be successful in reading while in another class they might fail.[23]

In other words, the teacher plays a crucial role in determining the instructional outcomes. The teacher intervenes at optimal times with optimal strategies to achieve desired learning.

[19] Barak Rosenshine, "Content, Time, and Direct Instruction," in *Research on Teaching: Concepts, Findings, and Implications*, ed. Penelope L. Peterson and Herbert J. Walberg (Berkeley, Calif.: McCutchon, 1979), pp. 28–56.

[20] Timothy R. Blair, "Teacher Effectiveness: The Know-how to Improve Student Learning," *The Reading Teacher* 38 (November 1984): 139–40.

[21] Fran Lehr, "Direct Instruction in Reading," *The Reading Teacher* 39 (March 1986): 706.

[22] Ibid., p. 708.

[23] Mariam J. Dreher and Harry Singer, "The Teacher's Role in Students' Success," *The Reading Teacher* 42 (April 1989): 614–15.

Modeling Strategy

Modeling strategy
Thinking out loud; verbalizing one's thoughts to help students gain understanding.

A technique that is especially helpful in getting students to attain important reading skills is that of modeling or "thinking aloud." A teacher using this technique says aloud all of his or her thoughts while trying to figure out a solution to a problem. This strategy helps students gain an insight to the kind of thinking involved in reading comprehension and helps them recognize that reading comprehension is analogous to problem solving. Here is a scenario illustrating how one teacher uses this modeling technique:

Scenario: A Sample Modeling Lesson

A teacher and five students in a fourth-grade class are engaged in a reading comprehension lesson. They are reading a trade book about the Civil War. They have been studying the Civil War, and this is a short novel depicting the lives of two different families during that period. Mr. Rojas, the teacher, prepares his students for the book by showing them a picture of President Lincoln reading the Gettysburg Address and uses this as a stimulus to discuss what they have learned about the Civil War. He then presents some key vocabulary words that he feels students may need to read the chapter. Next he tells them that they will be acting as investigative reporters. Even though they had previously discussed what investigative reporters do, he wants to go over it again with them because he wants them to read as if they are investigative reporters.

Today he will help them become better investigative reporters. He tells them that before they return to their seats to read the first chapter silently, he wants to make sure they know how to collect information, especially if the information is not directly stated. Mr. Rojas hands out a short selection to each of the students. He asks them to read the short selection to try to determine how many soldiers had started out on the mission and in what direction they were headed. (None of the information is directly stated in the selection.) After the students finish reading the short selection, Mr. Rojas says that he will tell them how he figures out the answers. He tells them that he will "talk aloud" to give them his thoughts.

Mr. Rojas says that as he reads the selection to answer the first question, he notices some key information, namely, that the remaining one-third of the soldiers were exhausted. It also says that the nine remaining ones could not last much longer. From this information, he can determine that two-thirds have died or are missing. If 9 equals $\frac{1}{3}$ of the original number, then there were 27 soldiers at the beginning of the special mission. The selection also states that the soldiers were walking toward the mountain range, and in another sentence it states that the sun was setting behind the mountain range. He says that he knows the sun rises in the East and sets in the West. Since the soldiers are walking toward the mountain range and the sun is setting behind the mountain range, they are heading west.

Mr. Rojas has them read another selection and has them answer questions based on information that is not directly stated. He asks them to explain how they went about answering the questions.

He then tells them that he wants them to go back to their seats and read silently the first chapter in their book. While they are reading he wants them to collect evidence from this chapter to make some predictions about the two main characters who are introduced in the chapter. They should record the predictions. Tomorrow, they will discuss them, and as they read the book, they will check to see how accurate their predictions were.

THE TEACHER AS A GOOD ORGANIZER AND CLASSROOM MANAGER

Teachers in a diagnostic-reading and correction program must be good organizers and classroom managers. It is simply not practical, and it probably is not possible, to provide a completely individualized reading program for each student. Teachers must be able to work with large groups, small groups, the whole class, and individual students. Usually the basis for selection in reading groups is the achievement level of students. During the first few weeks of the term, teachers collect data concerning the achievement levels of each of the students in their classes through observation, teacher-made tests, and standardized tests. After evaluating the collected data, tentative groups are organized. The number of groups in a skill area depends on the amount of variability within the class. For some areas, there may be three or four groups; for some, there may only be two groups; for some, the teacher may decide to work with the whole class as a unit; and for some areas, the teacher may have a number of children working individually. The grouping pattern is a flexible one, and the groups themselves are recognized as flexible units; children can easily flow from one group to another.

The teacher as a good classroom manager is able to deal with more than one situation at a time. A teacher working with a group should be aware of what is going on not only in that group but also with the other children in the class. A teacher cannot "dismiss" the rest of the class because he or she is working with a particular group. Even though the children have been given challenging work based on their individual needs, the teacher must be alert to what is happening. A teacher who ignores the rest of the class while working with one group will probably have a number of discipline problems. The following scenario presents an example of a good classroom manager. Notice especially how Ms. Mills is able to manage a number of ongoing activities at the same time. Notice how she is always aware of what is going on in her class, and notice how she prevents problems from arising.

Scenario: Ms. Mills—A Good Classroom Manager

One teacher and six children are seated at a round table engaged in reading. The rest of the class is involved in a variety of activities: A number of children are working individually at their seats or at learning centers; one child, sitting in a rocking chair, is reading; two children are working together; and a group of children are working together in the rear of the room.

The teacher says to her group at the round table, "We've talked about what inference means, and we've given examples of it. Who can tell us what we mean by inference?" A few children raise their hands. Ms. Mills calls on one, and he gives an explanation of inference. "Good," says Ms. Mills. "Now, I'd like you to read the paragraph about Mr. Brown and then tell us what inferences you can make about Mr. Brown. Be prepared to support your inferences with evidence from the paragraph."

Ms. Mills looks at each of the children as

they are reading. She then glances around the room. She says, "Judy, may I see you for a moment?" Judy comes to Ms. Mills. The teacher asks Judy in a very quiet tone if she can help her. She says, "Judy, you look confused. What's wrong?" Judy says that she is having trouble figuring out a question. Ms. Mills tells Judy to work on something else for about ten minutes, and that then she will help her. As Judy goes back to her seat, Ms. Mills again quickly glances around the room. As her eyes catch some of the children's, she smiles at them. Ms. Mills then looks at the children in her group. She sees that they are ready and asks them what inferences they can make about Mr. Brown. All the children raise their hands. Ms. Mills calls on one of the children, who makes an inference about Mr. Brown. Ms. Mills asks the rest of the group if they agree with the inference. Two students say that they do not agree. Ms. Mills asks all the students to skim the paragraph to find clues that would support their position. Ms. Mills again looks around the room. A child approaches and asks her a question. She answers the question and then goes back to the group. After a while Ms. Mills and the group discuss whether they have accomplished what they were supposed to. They then discuss, for a moment, what they will be doing next time. They all go back to their seats. Before Ms. Mills calls another group, she checks off in her plan book the objectives that have been accomplished by the group. She also makes some remarks in her record book about the individual children in the group. Ms. Mills puts down her book and walks around the room to check on what the students are doing. She smiles to a number of the students, says "good" to some others, helps Judy with her problem, and listens in on the group that has been working together on a special project. Ms. Mills asks the group how they are doing and how much more time they will need before they will be ready to report their progress to her and the class. Ms. Mills then goes back to the reading table and calls the next group.

TEACHERS' EXPECTATIONS

Self-fulfilling prophecy
Teacher assumptions about children become true, at least in part, because of the attitude of the teachers, which in turn becomes part of the children's self-concept.

The more teachers know about their students, the better able they are to plan for them. However, teachers must be cautioned about the self-fulfilling prophecy—where teachers' assumptions about children become true, at least in part, because of the attitude of the teachers, which in turn becomes part of the children's self-concept. Studies have shown that teachers' expectations about students' abilities to learn will influence students' learning.[24] For example, if a child comes from an environment not conducive to learning, the teacher may assume that this child cannot learn beyond a certain level and thus treat this child accordingly. If this happens, the teacher's assumptions could become part of the child's own self-concept, further reinforcing the teacher's original expectations.

Teachers who are aware of the effect that their expectations have on the learning behavior of students can use this to help their students. For example, teachers should assume that *all* their students are capable of learning to read; they should avoid labeling their students; and they should use positive reinforcement whenever feasible to help students become motivated.

[24] Robert Rosenthal and Lenore Jacobson, *Pygmalion in the Classroom* (New York: Holt, Rinehart and Winston, 1968). Douglas A. Pidgeon, *Expectation and Pupil Performance* (London: National Foundation for Educational Research, in England and Wales, 1970).

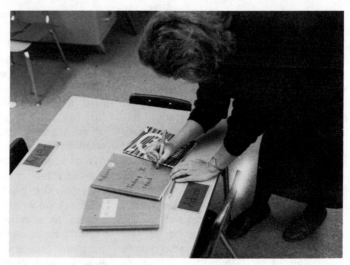

Figure 2.3 This teacher has strong, positive feelings toward each of her young students. She plans carefully to help students experience success.

ANOTHER LOOK AT RACHAEL S.—THE MAKING OF A DROPOUT

By now you should be able to answer the questions posed at the end of the introductory scenario. Here are some comments about the introductory scenario. See if you agree with them.

Ms. Graves is a very poor teacher. She is insensitive to Rachael's needs and appears to be incapable of helping her. If she had had a diagnostic-reading and correction program in her classroom, she would have been able to "nip in the bud" Rachael's reading problems. She would not have sent Rachael nor her whole group to the "resource center," but would have worked with them in the regular classroom; she would not have segregated them from the rest of the class. These children needed additional help and encouragement. She would have sought help from the special reading teacher and worked closely with Rachael's mother, as well as with the other parents. She would have created a nonthreatening atmosphere in which children feel they can learn and succeed—an atmosphere where the children are the center of the curriculum and tests are not used as ends in themselves.

SUMMARY

Chapter 2 focuses on the teacher as the key person in a diagnostic-reading and correction program. The teacher is seen as that person who should help children when they come to school regardless of their backgrounds. The role of a teacher in a diagnostic-reading and correction program is viewed as broad, so a teacher must be well prepared and well informed. A discussion of a number of studies shows that teachers influence students' behavior and learning and that the teacher is more important than the method of instruction or the materials used. Chapter 2 also discusses what characteristics a good teacher of reading should have: verbal ability, a good educational background including such knowledge as the content of reading, an ability to read, and positive expectations and attitudes. Teacher planning, instructional time, and instruction are also discussed, as well as the importance of teachers being good organizers and classroom managers. In addition, teachers are cautioned about invoking the self-fulfilling prophecy.

SUGGESTIONS FOR THOUGHT QUESTIONS AND ACTIVITIES

1. Make a list of all the characteristics you think a good teacher of reading should have in a diagnostic-reading and correction program.
2. Think of one of the best teachers you have ever had. Write down the characteristics of the teacher you remember best.
3. Think of the worst teacher you have ever had. Write down the characteristics that you feel made him or her your worst teacher.
4. Observe a teacher during a reading lesson. Check off all the characteristics he or she exhibits that you listed in question 2.
5. Make a videotape recording of yourself teaching a reading lesson. Check off all the characteristics you exhibited that were in your list in question 2.
6. You have been assigned to a special committee that is concerned with teacher accountability. What are your views concerning teacher accountability? What suggestions would you have for the committee?
7. Videotape a lesson in which you use a modeling approach.

SELECTED BIBLIOGRAPHY

Ashton-Warner, Sylvia. *Teacher*. New York: Simon & Schuster, 1963.
Bagford, Jack. "Evaluating Teachers on Reading Instruction." *The Reading Teacher* 34 (January 1981): 400–404.
Brown, Linda A., and Rita J. Sherbenou. "A Comparison of Teacher Perceptions of Student Reading Ability, Reading Performance, and Classroom Behavior." *The Reading Teacher* 34 (February 1981): 557–60.
Buike, Sandra, and Gerald G. Duffy. "Do Teacher Conceptions of Reading Influence Instructional Practice?" Paper presented at the American Educational Research Association Convention, San Francisco, April 1979.
Do Teachers Make a Difference? Department of Health, Education and Welfare Report No. OE 58042. Washington, D.C.: U.S. Government Printing Office, 1970.

Dreher, Jean Mariam, and Harry Singer. "The Teacher's Role in Students' Success." *The Reading Teacher* 42 (April 1989): 612–17.

Guthrie, John T. "Time in Reading Programs." *The Reading Teacher* 33 (January 1980): 500–502.

Harris, Albert J. "The Effective Teacher of Reading, Revisited." *The Reading Teacher* 33 (November 1979): 135–40.

Jackson, Phillip W. *Life in Classrooms*. New York: Teachers College Press, 1990.

Kidder, Tracy. *Among School Children*. Boston: Houghton Mifflin, 1989.

Pidgeon, Douglas A. *Expectation and Pupil Performance*. London: National Foundation for Educational Research, in England and Wales, 1970.

Rosenthal, Robert, and Lenore Jacobson. *Pygmalion in the Classroom*. New York: Holt, Rinehart and Winston, 1968.

Steiglitz, Erza L., and William J. Oehlkers. "Improving Teacher Discourse in a Reading Lesson." *The Reading Teacher* 42 (February 1989): 374–79.

Taylor, Gail Cohen. "Findings from Research on Teacher Effectiveness." *The Reading Teacher* 34 (March 1981): 726–30.

Woolfolk, Anita E. "Teachers, Teaching, and Educational Psychology," in *Educational Psychology*, 4th ed. Englewood Cliffs, N.J.: Prentice-Hall, 1990.

3

What a Teacher Should Know About Tests, Measurement, and Evaluation

Scenario: Ms. Smith Learns about Assessment

Ms. Smith is a new teacher. She's excited about having a position and wants to be the best teacher possible; however, she's a little overawed and confused. At the orientation meeting at the beginning of the school term, the principal talked about the school district's testing program, and then the reading specialist talked about the various kinds of reading tests that the teachers were expected to give. They talked about norm-referenced tests, informal tests, and criterion-referenced tests. They also talked about group and individual tests. Ms. Smith regretted that she had never had a course in tests and measurements, but rather than lamenting this fact, she decided to gain as much background information as possible in this area.

She agrees with the principal and reading specialist that a good teacher must be able to administer and interpret various types of tests, not only for evaluation but also for diagnostic purposes. At the meeting, knowledge of different types of diagnostic techniques was especially emphasized since the school is committed to a diagnostic-reading and correction program.

Toward the end of the meeting two teachers who are strong proponents of the whole language movement raised their hands and said that they felt all standardized reading tests should be outlawed. The silence that followed was deafening. Then, as if on cue, everyone started talking at once.

Ms. Smith listened carefully to the heated debate among those who felt there should be no standardized testing and those who disagreed. The teachers who believed in the whole language movement were vitriolic against the use of standardized reading achievement tests. Others claimed that these tests may not measure the kinds of behaviors they are supposed to.

The principal said that he was aware of the testing controversy, but rather than less testing, it appears that there will probably be more because of the increased emphasis on accountability. Actually, national standardized testing is just about here. Even though the legislation governing National Assessment has decreed that the state-by-state comparison portion of the National Assessment will be voluntary, 37 states, two territories, and the District of Columbia have chosen to participate. Therefore, regardless of what an individual's position is, it's important that teachers know what is taking place and be knowledgeable about the various types of tests that they may have to administer or evaluate. He emphasized also that in a diagnostic-reading and correction program, teachers must know how to use various types of teacher-made and commercial tests to assess their students' reading difficulties.

This chapter should help Ms. Smith and others like her to gain background information on the various types of tests.

KEY QUESTIONS

After you finish reading this chapter, you should be able to answer the following questions:

1. What are the differences among test, measurement, and evaluation?
2. What are the values of measurement?
3. What are some of the criteria of good tests?
4. What are standardized tests?
5. What are some differences between group and individual tests?
6. What are criterion-referenced tests?
7. What are some of the different kinds of reading tests that are available?
8. How is the whole language movement influencing test makers?

KEY TERMS IN CHAPTER

You should pay special attention to the following new terms:

classroom tests
content domain
criterion-referenced tests
diagnostic reading tests
evaluation
grade equivalents
group tests
individual tests
informal tests
measurement
norm-referenced tests
norms
objective
objectivity
percentile

raw score
reliability
scale score
standardized tests
stanine
suitability
survey batteries
teacher-made tests
test
validity
whole language

EVALUATION, TESTS, AND MEASUREMENT

> Examinations are formidable, even to the best prepared, for the greatest fool may ask more than the wisest man can answer.
>
> *C. C. Colton*

The word *evaluation* seems to bring shudders to most people. Although some individuals may look on evaluation as necessary, it is often considered an intrusion on privacy and is avoided for as long as possible. The following remarks were overheard in one school. Do they sound familiar to you?

Person A: "Shh, everyone be alert! Keep the kids quiet! We're being evaluated!"
Person B: "Oh no! Don't tell me we're being evaluated again. We just finished testing our students."

Test
A standard set of questions to be answered.

Measurement
Part of the evaluative process; broader than test; involves quantitative descriptions.

To some the terms *evaluation, test*, and *measurement* are synonymous. But they are not. *Test*, which is the narrowest of the terms, is confined to "a standard set of questions to be answered. From a person's responses to a series of questions, we obtain a measure (that is, a numerical value) of a characteristic of that person."[1] Measurement, which is broader, "can measure characteristics in ways other than by giving tests. Measurement involves using observation, rating scales, or any other nontest device that allows us to obtain information in a quantitative form."[2]

Evaluation is the broadest of the terms and goes beyond test and measurement. Evaluation has to do with the passing of personal judgment on the accuracy, truthfulness, and validity of something. Evaluation can be done with either qualitative or quantitative data. Obviously, the more data available, the better the evaluation. Since evaluation is carried on by humans, good evaluators should avoid emotional bias in making their value judgments. This objectivity is

---

[1] William A. Mehrens and Irvin J. Lehmann, *Using Standardized Tests in Education*, 4th ed. (New York: Longman, 1987), p. 7.
[2] Ibid., p. 8.

Evaluation
A process of appraisal involving specific values and the use of a variety of instruments in order to form a value judgment; goes beyond test and measurement.

often hard to achieve. For this reason it is essential that evaluation should occur at the beginning of, during, and at the end of the educative process; be based on an adequate collection of data; and be made in terms of desired objectives and standards.

In addition, it is important to note that "we never measure or evaluate people. We measure or evaluate characteristics or properties of people: their scholastic potential, knowledge of algebra, honesty."[3]

The positive values of measurement outweigh the negative connotations often associated with it. Measurement is useful for diagnostic, review, and predictive purposes. It can be used as a motivating technique for students, as well as a basis for grades and promotion. Through ongoing measurement, teachers are also able to reevaluate their own teaching methods.

In order for measurement to be an effective part of the evaluative process, teachers must master varied techniques and be able to administer and interpret them. Such measurements include standardized tests and teacher-made tests. Direct observation of student behavior is also necessary in order to collect data for valid evaluations.

CRITERIA FOR A GOOD TEST

Before looking at specific criteria of tests, it's important to note that in the past decade tests and testing have come under a great deal of criticism. This criticism is focused not only on test purposes but also on test users. For example, Anastasi, a noted psychologist and psychometrician, has made the following statements:

> A conspicuous recent trend in mental measurements is the increasing recognition of the part played by test users. Common criticism of testing and popular antitest reactions are often directed not to the characteristics of the tests but to the misuses of the tests in the hands of inadequately qualified users in education. . . .[4]
>
> For practical purposes, the most effective tests are likely to be those developed for clearly defined purposes and for use within specified contexts.[5]

Certainly test users must know their purposes and be qualified to administer and interpret test results. They must know, too, that regardless of the tests they choose, there are certain criteria that all good tests should meet:

Objectivity
The same score must result regardless of who marks the test.

1. *Objectivity:* The same score must result regardless of who marks the test. Since essay questions do not lend themselves to a high degree of objectivity, the users of such tests should give specific

[3] Ibid.

[4] Anne Anastasi, "Mental Measurements: Some Emerging Trends," *The Ninth Mental Measurements Yearbook* (Lincoln, N.B.: Buros Institute of Mental Measurements, University of Nebraska, 1985), p. xxiii.

[5] Ibid., p. xxix.

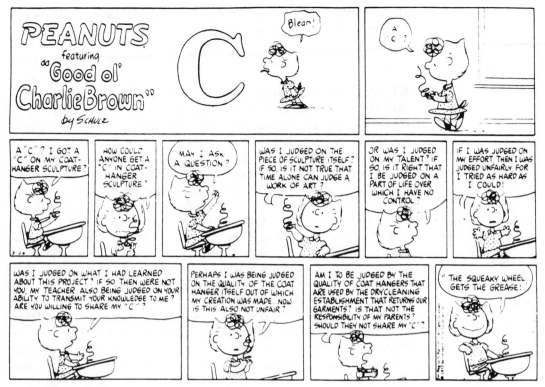

© 1972 United Feature Syndicate, Inc.

Figure 3.1 Sally recognizes the subjectivity involved in grading. She should receive an A in question asking.

directions for scoring and should make the essay question as explicit as possible.

2. *Validity:* "Validity can best be defined as the degree to which certain inferences can be made from test scores or other measurements."[6] A nontechnical definition of validity would be that the test measures what it purports to measure. Reading teachers are concerned primarily with the content of a test. In order to determine the content aspect of validity, the test should be compared with instructional content.

3. *Reliability:* The test is reliable if it consistently produces similar results when repeated measurements are taken of the same students under the same conditions. (Conditions include no changes in students' knowledge from one measurement to the next.)

4. *Suitablity:* In selecting or preparing a test, the teacher must determine not only whether it will yield the type of data desired but

Suitability
The appropriateness of a test for a specific population of students.

---

[6] Mehrens and Lehmann, p. 74.

also whether the test is suitable for the age and type of students and for the locality in which they reside.

Validity

Validity
The degree to which certain inferences can be made from test scores or other measurements; the degree to which a test instrument measures what it claims to measure (nontechnical definition).

Educators often talk about the validity of a test and generally define validity as the degree to which a test measures what it purports to measure. However, technically we do not measure the test's validity but rather the validity of the inferences made from the test.

According to the *Standards for Educational and Psychological Testing*, "Validity is the most important consideration in test evaluation. The concept refers to the approriateness, meaningfulness, and usefulness of the specific inferences made from test scores. Test validation is the process of accumulating evidence to support such inferences."[7]

The three categories of validity evidence are content-related, criterion-related, and construct-related evidence of validity. However, "the use of the category labels does not imply that there are distinct types of validity or that a specific validity strategy is best for each specific inference or test use."[8]

For reading teachers, as stated earlier, the content aspect of validity of achievement tests is probably the most important. The content aspect of validity is concerned with how adequately the test items represent what is being tested so that inferences can be made concerning a student's degree of attainment of the subject matter.

Reliability

Reliability
The extent to which a test instrument consistently produces similar results.

Reliability is concerned with consistency. A test's reliability depends on how consistent it is in measuring whatever it is measuring. Therefore, reliability can be defined "as the degree of consistency between two measures of the same thing."[9] Any test that is valid must be reliable, but reliability is not a sufficient condition for validity. It is possible to get a consistent measure of something, but consistency does not always mean that the measure is correct or truthful.

It is to be hoped that when a student takes a test, the score will remain consistent, even if conditions under which the test are taken change slightly, even if different scorers are used, or even if similar but not identical test items are used. There are a number of reasons why a student's test score could vary: The test may not be testing

---

[7] *Standards for Educational and Psychological Testing*, prepared by the Committee to Develop Standards for Educational and Psychological Testing of the American Educational Research Association, the American Psychological Association, and the National Council on Measurement in Education (Washington, D.C.: American Psychological Association, 1985), p. 9.

[8] Ibid.

[9] Mehrens and Lehmann, p. 54.

what it is supposed to; the student may not have good rapport with the tester; the student may not be motivated; the student may be ill; or the student may be tired. Another reason may be that the student has good or bad luck in guessing. Still another may be that the student has acquired new knowledge between testings.

Special Note

It is beyond the scope of this book to go into an in-depth discussion of validity and reliability. There are many excellent test and measurement books that supply this information.

STANDARDIZED TESTS

Standardized tests
Tests that have been published by experts in the field and have precise instructions for administration and scoring.

Standardized tests are published tests which generally have been constructed by experts in the field and are available from publishers. They are usually developed in a very precise fashion, and they should be precisely administered. Standardized tests contain exact instructions on how to administer them, and these instructions are supposed to be followed by all testers.

Confusion may exist concerning the definition of standardized tests because of changes in the way the term is currently being used in comparison with how it has been used in the past and is still being used by many, especially in the reading field. *Good's Dictionary of Education*, the *Penguin Dictionary of Psychology*, the *Dictionary of Behavioral Sciences*, and the *International Dictionary of Education* all include *norm-referenced* as one of the criteria for a standardized test; however, today the definition does not necessarily include that criterion. Today, a standardized test may or may not be a norm-referenced test. A test is considered to be a standardized test if it is a published test with specific instructions for administration and scoring.[10] Michael Zieky, director of technical assistance and training at Educational Testing Service, defines a standardized test "as any published test in which rules exist such that the test is administered to all examinees under the same conditions.[11] In this text, a test that has been published by experts in the field and has precise instructions for administration and scoring will be considered a standardized test.

Norm-Referenced Tests

Although not all standardized tests have norms, most usually do. Norms are average scores for a given group of students, which allow comparisons to be made for different students or groups of individ-

---

[10] Teacher's Guide, *California Diagnostic Reading Tests Levels A and B* (Monterey, Calif.: CTB/McGraw-Hill, 1989), p. 7.

[11] Michael Zieky, director of technical assistance and training, Educational Testing Service (ETS), Princeton, N.J., January 1990.

Norms
Average scores for a given group of students, which allow comparisons to be made for different students or groups of students.

Norm-referenced tests
Standardized tests with norms so that comparisons can be made to a sample population.

uals. The norms are derived from a random sampling of a cross section of a large population of individuals. The use of a large representative sample of students for research is obviously not possible with a teacher-made test. (See "Teacher-Made Tests" in this chapter.)

Norm-referenced tests are used to help teachers learn where their own students stand in relation to others in the class, school system, city, state, or nation. Although a child may be doing average work in a particular class, the child may be above average when compared to other norms. Similarly, it is possible for a child to be doing above-average work in a third-grade class but to be below average for all third-graders in the nation.

Teachers must be cautious in their analysis of test results. They should not be intimidated by standardized tests, and they must recognize the limitations of these tests. Teachers must determine whether a test is appropriate for their students. If the class has not covered the work in the standardized test, the test obviously would not be valid. Differences in student populations must also be taken into account in interpreting test results.

Another important factor concerns the students themselves. Students who are overly anxious or upset by a test, who are tired or hungry, or who lack motivation, will not perform as well as others not burdened in this manner. Such factors will adversely affect test performance. Read Dick Gregory's disturbing words:[12]

> The teacher thought I was stupid. Couldn't spell, couldn't read, couldn't do arithmetic. Just stupid. Teachers were never interested in finding out that you couldn't concentrate because you were so hungry, because you hadn't had any breakfast. All you could think about was noontime, would it ever come? Maybe you could sneak into the cloakroom and steal a bite of some kid's lunch out of a coat pocket. A bite of something. Paste. You can't really make a meal of paste, or put it on bread for a sandwich, but sometimes I'd scoop a few spoonfuls out of the big paste jar in the back of the room. Pregnant people get strange tastes. I was pregnant with poverty.

Classification of Standardized Tests

Standardized tests may be classified in a number of ways, one of which is according to the *way* they are administered. For example, some tests are group administered and some are individually administered, so these tests would be called group or individual tests. Some persons classify tests according to whether they have oral instructions or written instructions. Usually, tests are classified according to *what* is measured. Accordingly, standardized tests are generally divided into the following categories: aptitude (intelligence) tests; achievement tests, which include diagnostic, single subject-matter, and survey batteries; and interest, personality, and attitude inventories.

[12] Dick Gregory, *Nigger: An Autobiography* (New York: E. P. Dutton, 1964), p. 44.

Special Note

Survey batteries consist of a group of tests in different content areas. These subtests have been standardized on the same population so that the results of the various components may be directly compared.[13] Standardized achievement tests that yield a general score are usually called survey tests. They may be part of a survey battery, or they may be single-subject tests (see Chapter 7).

Selection of Standardized Tests by Teachers

Many times teachers are not involved in the selection of standardized tests. This is a mistake. The more teachers know about standardized tests, the better able they will be to use the results. The problem is that there are so many standardized tests on the market, and many of them are considered worthless. Read the following statements made by the late Oscar Buros, who was the originator of the *Mental Measurements Yearbooks*:[14]

> Unfortunately, the rank and file of test users do not appear to be particularly alarmed that so many tests are either severely criticized or described as having no validity. Although most test users would probably agree that many tests are either worthless or misused, they continue to have the utmost faith in their own particular choice and use of tests regardless of the absence of supporting research or even of the presence of negating research. When I initiated this test reviewing service in 1938, I was confident that frankly critical reviews by competent specialists representing a wide variety of viewpoints would make it unprofitable to publish tests of unknown or questionable validity. Now 27 years and five *Mental Measurements Yearbooks* later, I realize that I was too optimistic.

Buros in his *Seventh* and in his *Eighth Mental Measurements Yearbooks* reiterates the same thoughts: "At least half of the tests currently on the market should never have been published."[15]

The *Mental Measurements Yearbooks* are excellent resources for the teacher intent on choosing a standardized reading test that best suits his or her purposes. The books help acquaint teachers with most tests in the field except the very recent ones. Frank critical evaluations of tests are written by authorities in the field. Test users are also warned about the dangers of standardized tests and are told of their values. An essential contribution that the books make is to "impress test users with the desirability of suspecting all standardized tests— even though prepared by well-known authorities—unaccompanied by detailed data on their construction, validity, uses, and limitations."[16]

[13] Mehrens and Lehmann, p. 264.

[14] Oscar Buros, ed., *The Sixth Mental Measurements Yearbook* (Highland Park, N.J.: Gryphon Press, 1965), pp. xxiii–xxiv.

[15] Oscar Buros, ed., *The Eighth Mental Measurements Yearbook* (Highland Park, N.J.: Gryphon Press, 1978), p. xxxi.

[16] Oscar Buros, ed., *Reading: Tests and Reviews* (Highland Park, N.J.: Gryphon Press, 1968), p. xvi.

The Ninth Mental Measurements Yearbook, published in 1985 under a new editor, continues in the tradition of the others by giving individuals valuable information about tests. Other sources of test information that teachers would find helpful are *Tests in Print*; *Tests*, 3rd ed.; and *Test Critiques*, vols. 1–8, as well as journals such as *The Reading Teacher* and the *Journal of Reading* that periodically review various tests.

Interpretation of Some Achievement Test Score Terms

Many teachers are often confused about the terms that test makers use in discussing standardized achievement tests. What follows is a guide to some of the terms teachers will probably meet at one time or another.[17]

Raw Score

Raw Score
The number of items that a student answers correctly on a test.

The raw score is the number of items that a student answers correctly on a test. (The number of test items, as well as the difficulty of the items, may vary from one section of a test to another; therefore, the weighting of the test items should vary.) The raw score is usually not reported because it does not convey meaningful information. Test makers use the raw scores to derive their scale scores.

Scale Scores

Scale score
Used to derive other scores.

Scale scores are used most often in deriving other scores and for statistical analyses and research.

Grade Equivalent

Grade equivalents
Description of year and month of school for which a given student's level of performance is typical.

A grade equivalent is a description of the year and month of school for which a given student's level of performance is typical. A grade equivalent of 6.2 on the California Achievement Test (CAT) is interpreted as the score that is typical of a group of students in the third month of the sixth grade. (September is designated as month .0, October as .1, November as .2, December as .3, and so forth up to June, which is .9.) These scores are useful in the elementary grades because fairly regular gains are expected in basic skill development at each grade level.

Special Note

Extreme grade equivalents, those that are more than two years above or below grade level, must be interpreted with great caution because they are based on "extrapolations" rather than actual student per-

---

[17] Adapted from *Test Interpretation Guidelines, Comprehensive Tests of Basic Skills*, 4th ed. (Monterey, Calif.: CTB/McGraw-Hill, 1988).

formance. A very low or a very high score just means that the student scored quite below or quite above the national average. A grade equivalent score of 6.6 by a third-grader does not mean the third-grader is able to do sixth-grade work or should be in the sixth grade. It does mean that this third-grader is scoring well above the average for third-grade students.

Percentile

Percentile
A point on the distribution below which a certain percentage of the scores fall.

A percentile is a point on the distribution below which a certain percent of the scores fall. A test score equivalent to the 98th percentile means that the student did better, or the student's score is higher, than 98 percent of the test takers on that same test. Another way of looking at it is to say that only 2 percent of the students did better.

Special Notes

The 50th percentile score is the middle score, which is also referred to as the median; it is the point above and below which half of the students scored.

Percentile and percent correct are not the same. A percentile score of 75 on an achievement test by a fifth-grader means that the fifth-grader obtained a score higher than 75 out of every 100 students in a representative sample of fifth-graders in the nation who took the test.

Stanine

Stanine
A score in educational testing on a nine-point scale, ranging from a low of 1 to a high of 9, of normalized standard scores.

The stanine is a unit of a score scale that divides the scores of the norm population (representative sample) into nine groups, ranging from a low of 1 to a high of 9. There is a constant relationship between stanines and percentiles; that is, the range of percentiles included within each stanine is always the same (see Table 3.1).[18]

Stanines 4, 5, and 6 are generally used to describe the "average" range of achievement. Stanines 1, 2, and 3 are used to describe below average, and 7, 8, and 9 usually describe above average.

Special Note

A major problem with stanine scores is that they are not very precise. For example, a stanine score of 5 could have a percentile score as low as 41 or as high as 59.

[18] Ibid., p. 4.

TABLE 3.1 Stanines and Percentile Scale Conversion Table

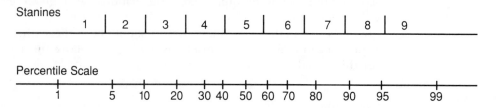

TEACHER-MADE TESTS

Informal tests
Teacher-made tests.

Teacher-made tests
Tests prepared by the classroom teacher for a particular class and given by the classroom teacher under conditions of his or her own choosing.

Classroom tests
Teacher-made tests; also called informal tests.

Teacher-made tests are also called either classroom or informal tests. These are prepared by the classroom teacher for a particular class and given under conditions of his or her own choosing.[19] Usually, teacher-made tests are the primary basis for evaluating students' school progress. Teachers can get quick feedback on learning behaviors by constructing appropriate classroom tests. The tests with which you are probably the most familiar are those used to determine students' grades; these tests are generally classified into essay and objective tests and are mostly group tests.

In the field of reading, classroom tests are generally used to help diagnose a student's reading problem or to learn more about a student's weaknesses and strengths. Many of the teacher-made tests used for diagnosis are individually administered. The informal reading inventory, which may be commercially produced or teacher-made, can be one of the teacher's most valuable aids in diagnosing reading problems (see Chapter 8).

CRITERION-REFERENCED TESTS

Criterion-referenced tests
Based on an extensive inventory of objectives in a specific curriculum area; they are used to assess an individual student's performance in respect to his or her mastery of specified objectives in a given curriculum area.

Criterion-referenced tests are based on an extensive inventory of instructional objectives in a specific curriculum. The objectives are desired educational outcomes.

Criterion-referenced tests are designed to diagnose specific behaviors of individual students. They are used to gain more information about the students' various skill levels, and the information is used to either reinforce, supplement, or remediate the skill-development area being tested. The test results help the instructor plan specific learning sequences to help the students master the objective they missed. Many criterion-referenced tests are used in individualized programs.

Criterion-referenced tests are considered standardized if they are published tests that have been prepared by experts in the field and have precise instructions for administration and scoring. They can be administered individually or to a group, and they may be teacher-

[19] Mehrens and Lehmann, p. 224.

Objective
Desired educational outcome.

made or standardized. They are not norm-based; however, some may provide a means for comparing students to a norm group (see Special Notes at the end of this section). Criterion-referenced tests are concerned primarily with mastery of predetermined objectives, which are based on classroom curriculum. On criterion-referenced tests an individual competes only with him- or herself. There is very little difference in appearance between a norm-referenced test and a criterion-referenced test; however, differences do exist, as has already been noted, in the purposes for the tests.

Content domain
Term that refers to subject matter covered.

For a criterion-referenced test to be valid, a content domain must be specified, and the test items must be representative of the content domain. Test makers identify various content-area domains and write measurable objectives within each domain; then detailed item specifications are developed. These item specifications are supposed to "ensure detailed coverage of the skills stated in the objectives."[20] Usually, there are a number of items written for each objective to ensure reliable measurement.

There does not seem to be agreement on how specifically the content domain should be defined; "A reasonable expectation is that the test constructor specify with considerable detail the subject matter topics and pupil behaviors the test is designed to sample."[21] (See Chapter 9 for more on criterion-referenced tests and Table 9.2 in Chapter 9 for the content of a published criterion-referenced test.)

Here is an example from a teacher-made criterion-referenced test. Note that the teacher has defined the content domain in general and specific terms. The test item is correlated to the objective for the specific area. The important factor is not the terminology used but whether we can infer that the test item does indeed measure what it is supposed to, in this case, the ability of the child to draw inferences. In other words, is the test item a valid representation of its content domain?

General area: Reading comprehension (interpretation)
Specific area: Drawing inferences
Objective: The student will draw inferences about the personality of the main character based on the content of reading material.

The child is asked to read a short story carefully. After finishing the reading, the child is asked to answer questions based on the story. An example of a question based on the given objective follows:

What can you infer about the personality of Dennis?

The child is then asked to choose the best answer from the given statements. (Note that in criterion-referenced testing *every* test item is related to a corresponding objective.)

---

[20] *California Diagnostic Reading Tests Technical Report,* (Monterey, Calif.: CTB/McGraw-Hill, 1989), p. 5.

[21] Mehrens and Lehmann, p. 77.

Here is an example of sample test items from a published criterion-referenced test.[22]

CDRT

■ **SAMPLE TEST ITEMS**

LEVEL B

Shown on this page are samples of the kinds of items that are used in the Vocabulary and Comprehension sections of Level B. (Illustrations are approximately two-fifths of their actual size.)

ONE This item measures the student's ability to identify the member of a category or a category common to all members.

"Find the word that tells how these three words are alike."

collies, poodles, boxers
- ○ dogs
- ○ ponies
- ○ haircuts
- ○ cats

TWO This item measures the student's ability to define words that reflect a breadth of student experience.

"Fill in the circle beside the word that answers the question."

Where are animals from all over the world kept for people to see?
- ○ theater
- ○ back yard
- ○ zoo
- ○ farm

THREE This item measures how well the student can identify the topic, main idea, or the author's purpose in a given passage.

"Find the answers to the questions."

All the Erwin children go to school a different way. Jack runs to school. The twins ride the bus. Judy walks. Will is too little for school. He stays home.

NOTE: Statements in quotation marks are read aloud by the teacher.

Sample B

What is this story mostly about?
- ○ why Judy walks to school
- ○ how fast Jack runs to school
- ○ why Will stays home from school
- ○ how the children go to school

Sample C

Why does Will stay at home?
- ○ He is sick.
- ○ He is too young.
- ○ He is a pet.
- ○ He likes his dad.

[22] Preview materials for the *California Diagnostic Reading Tests*, (Monterey, Calif.: McGraw-Hill, 1989), p. 14. Reprinted from *California Diagnostic Reading Tests* by CTB. Copyright © 1989 by McGraw-Hill, Inc. Reprinted by permission of Macmillan/McGraw-Hill School Publishing Company.

"Criterion-referenced tests and norm-referenced tests are no longer seen as a strict dichotomy."[23] Some tests are more useful for norm-referenced use than for criterion-referenced use, depending on the purpose for the test. Some tests have been prepared for use as both criterion-referenced and norm-referenced; that is, test users can compare a student's test results to a national norm or to a set of predetermined specific objectives. When a criterion-referenced test has equated norms, it means that "the scores on one test have been statistically matched to the scores on a normed test."[24]

Some test makers are including a "cutoff or passing score" with criterion-referenced tests, perhaps because the term *criterion* implies this. "Whether there should be an implied standard of proficiency or cut-off score(s) is debatable. . . . At any rate, everyone agrees that with a criterion-referenced interpretation of the scores, the focus is on 'what Johnny can do' and the comparison is to a behavioral domain."[25] It has been suggested that criterion-referenced tests should be called domain-referenced tests, a term that is more accurate for the test.

The terms *instructional objective* and *objective* are often used interchangeably.

Content domain may refer to the content of an entire book, or, for a particular test, a set of objectives would define its content domain.

Before we proceed to a general discussion of reading tests, we should differentiate between group and individual tests.

GROUP AND INDIVIDUAL TESTS

Group tests
Administered to a group of people at the same time.

Individual tests
Administered to one person at a time.

It seems evident that group tests are administered to a group of people at the same time, whereas individual tests are administered to one person at a time. It also should be obvious that it would be more time-consuming to give an individual rather than a group test. What may not be as obvious are the reasons for administering an individual test. Individual tests in reading are usually given when the teacher feels that some inconsistency exists between the student's classroom behavior or his or her reading potential and his or her test score on a group-administered standardized reading achievement

[23] Michael Zieky, director of technical assistance and training, Educational Testing Service (ETS), January, 1990.

[24] Ibid.

[25] Mehrens and Lehmann, p. 16.

test (see Chapters 8 and 9). Individual tests are administered when teachers wish to learn more about a student's specific behavior, such as oral reading, and the only way to do so would be through an individual test. An individual test may also be given if the teacher suspects that a child has difficulty following directions. On an individual test the tester can determine whether the student understands a question and whether the student is tired, hungry, or not feeling well.

Group tests are more limited in their format than individual tests because they must be administered by the reading of simple directions and answered by some kind of mark on an answer sheet. Group tests are usually given by the classroom teacher, and there are as many different types of group tests as there are individual tests. For example, there are group and individual aptitude tests, group and individual achievement tests, group and individual personality inventories, group and individual attitude inventories, and so on. There are some individual tests, such as individual IQ tests, that must be administered by a specially trained clinician or psychologist; and there are some, such as individual diagnostic tests, that can be administered by the regular classroom teacher. Whether a teacher or a specially trained person administers an individual test, it is not given as often as a group test because it is more costly and more time-consuming. However, individual tests are generally more reliable than group tests; they are more useful with students who have reading difficulties because they usually require less reading than group tests; more can be learned about a student in a clinical-test one-to-one situation than in a class; and they are usually more valid for those students who have difficulty taking tests in a group. (See Figure 3.2 on p. 48 for a diagram of the various types of tests.)

READING TESTS

There are a number of different kinds of standardized and teacher-made reading tests; some measure study skills, vocabulary, comprehension, speed in reading, oral reading, and so on. No single test or single score can tell all there is to know about a student's reading behavior. The purpose for the test should determine the type of test that is used.

Teachers in a diagnostic-reading and correction program must be knowledgeable of the many different types of reading tests that exist so that a wise selection of tests can be made. Tests used to identify a problem are different from those used to uncover specifics about the problem. For example, it is one thing to discover that a child is reading below his or her ability level, and it is another to determine *why*.

Choosing the proper standardized test for a specific purpose is difficult in reading because the name of the test may not be descriptive of it; that is, the name may be misleading. There are a number of tests measuring the same type of skills that have different names, and there are a number of tests measuring different types of skills that have the same name. Because of this, teachers must be very cautious in choosing a standardized test and make sure that they read the examiner's manual or a description of the test in publishers' catalogs.

Teachers should not depend solely on standardized tests to help them learn more about the reading behavior of their students. As stated earlier in this chapter, a teacher can get quick feedback from a classroom test. It is possible that the skill that teachers would like to learn more about may not be covered in a standardized test, or it may be easier to make up a test than to hunt one down that will reveal needed information. (See Part III for detailed information on reading tests.)

WHAT ARE DIAGNOSTIC READING TESTS?

Diagnostic reading tests
Provide subscores discrete enough so that specific information about a student's reading behavior can be obtained and used for instruction.

A diagnostic reading test is designed to break down a complex skill into its component parts to help teachers gain information about a student's specific reading weaknesses and strengths. It is generally given after a group standardized reading survey test has screened those children who seem to be reading below their ability.

Diagnostic reading tests can be standardized or teacher-made tests. Most reading diagnostic tests are individually administered and given by a special reading teacher rather than by the regular classroom teacher. However, many of these diagnostic tests can be given by the regular classroom teacher, and in a diagnostic-reading and correction program, many should be. Informal reading inventories are examples of diagnostic tools that are indispensable to the classroom teacher (see Chapter 8).

Although agreement does not exist on how to define a diagnostic reading test and what tests to include under the umbrella of diagnostic tests, it seems clear that a test on a test battery that provides subscores discrete enough so that specific information about a student's reading behavior can be attained and used for instructional purposes should be included in this category. A reading diagnostic test or test battery may consist of oral reading, silent reading, comprehension, phonic analysis, structural analysis, sight vocabulary, visual and auditory discrimination, reading and study skills, or rate of reading.

The diagnostic test that is chosen should fulfill the criteria for all tests; that is, it should be valid, reliable, easy to administer in a reasonable period of time, and easy to score. Most importantly, the test should be one that will help the teacher diagnose a student's specific problem. Teachers should check the diagnostic test carefully before administering it to make sure that it does indeed diagnose the specific skill that the teacher wishes to have diagnosed.

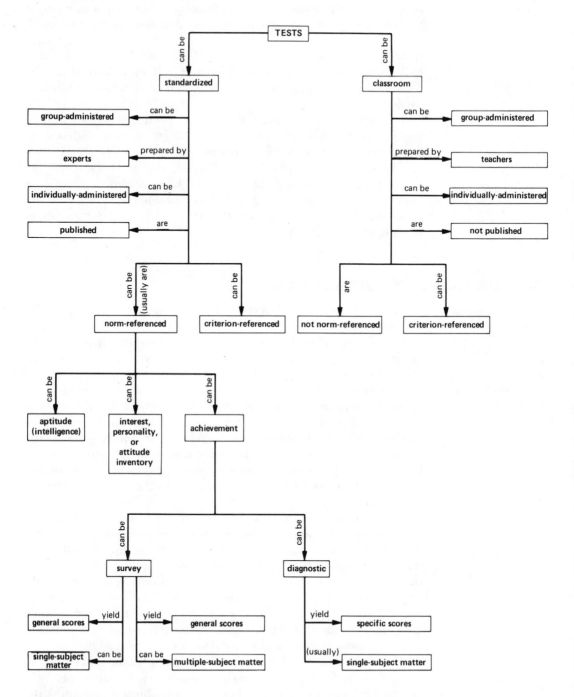

Figure 3.2   A tree diagram of the various types of tests. This diagram is a simplification, showing the relationship of the tests.

WHOLE LANGUAGE AND DIAGNOSTIC READING TESTS

Whole language
A set of beliefs in which the emphasis is on the "wholeness" of things.

Teachers should be aware that test makers are very sensitive to test criticisms and keep abreast of what is taking place in the reading field. Today many publishers of standardized reading tests claim that they are focusing on the "more holistic view of the strategic processes of comprehension, or 'whole language,'"[26] and therefore, wherever possible they present their reading skills within a context rather than in isolation. Nevertheless, for diagnostic testing, we are concerned with specific skills. It is important for teachers to recognize that they do indeed need to home in on the specific difficulties that a particular child may have. Whole language and diagnostic testing are not mutually exclusive.

Teachers must recognize that children's errors tell us about their thinking and give us insight into the children's developmental levels. Teachers can learn about their children's reading behavior whether they are involved in a reading program using only literary works or basal readers or both. The more teachers learn about the kinds of errors their children make, the better able they will be to help them. Often diagnostic tests help uncover problem areas. Good teachers should be using various diagnostic techniques throughout the day to learn more about their students' reading behavior.

SUMMARY

Chapter 3 has presented general information about what teachers should know concerning tests, measurement, and evaluation. It was stated that good evaluators use tests and other measurement techniques to avoid bias in their judgments. A discussion concerned the criteria that all good tests should have: objectivity, validity, reliability, and suitability. Because there is confusion concerning the term *standardized*, it was defined according to the way that it is currently being used in the field. A standardized test is a published test with specific instructions for administration and scoring. It may or may not be a norm-referenced test. The terms *norm-referenced* and *criterion-referenced* were also defined, and the ways that standardized tests may be classified were explored. Because there are so many standardized tests on the market, teachers need help in determining which ones to use. The *Mental Measurements Yearbooks* were given as excellent sources. Teacher-made tests, which are also called classroom or informal tests, were discussed too. In this chapter, teachers were introduced to reading tests and the fact that many different kinds exist. It was emphasized that teachers in a diagnostic-reading and correction program must be knowledgeable of the various kinds of tests so that a wise selection can be made for the proper purpose.

[26] Teacher's Guide, *California Diagnostic Reading Tests, Levels A and B*, p. 5.

SUGGESTIONS FOR THOUGHT QUESTIONS AND ACTIVITIES

1. Your school is interested in using criterion-referenced tests. You have been appointed to explain the differences between criterion-referenced and norm-referenced tests. What will you say?
2. Many teachers in your school are confused about the many different types of tests that exist. You can help them by drawing a tree diagram showing the relationships among tests.
3. Discuss some of the important criteria that good tests must have.
4. Explain some of the differences between teacher-made tests and published or commercially produced tests.

SELECTED BIBLIOGRAPHY

Conoley, Jane C., and Jack J. Kramer (Eds.). *The Tenth Mental Measurements Yearbook*. Lincoln, N.B.: Buros Institute of Mental Measurements, University of Nebraska, 1989.

Hopkins, Kenneth D., Julian C. Stanley, and B. R. Hopkins. *Educational and Psychological Measurement and Evaluation*, 7th ed. Englewood Cliffs, N.J.: Prentice-Hall, 1990.

Mehrens, William A., and Irvin J. Lehmann. *Using Standardized Tests in Education*, 4th ed. New York: Longman, 1987.

Popham, James W. *Modern Educational Measurement: A Practitioner's Perspective*. 2nd ed. Englewood Cliffs, N.J.: Prentice-Hall, 1990.

Standards for Educational and Psychological Testing. Prepared by the Committee to Develop Standards for Educational and Psychological Testing of the American Educational Research Association, the American Psychological Association, and the National Council on Measurement in Education. Washington, D.C.: American Psychological Association, 1985.

Sweetland, Richard C., and Daniel J. Keyser (Eds.). *Tests*, 3rd ed. Austin, Texas: PRO-ED, 1990.

4

Some of the Factors That Affect Reading Performance

Scenario: Angelique and Sara: A Study in Contrast

Angelique and Sara are both in Mrs. Brown's first-grade class. Angelique is a bubbly, inquisitive, alert child who is excited about learning and looks upon every day as an adventure. She loves books and reads well. She asks good questions and likes to learn about things in depth. She talks about nocturnal birds and how she saw an owl one evening. She talks about wild animals and tame animals, and she is always eager to show anyone the stories she has written about different animals.

Angelique is quite verbal. She has an extensive vocabulary and uses words correctly. She can talk about animals, books she has read, books that have been read to her, other parts of the country, and so on. She can give you opposites and words similar in meaning. She can tell if you are being "funny." In addition, she can relate present information or experiences to past ones and make predictions about various things.

Angelique is an only child, and her college-educated parents adore her. They feel she is the joy of their lives. When she was born, her mother left her position to stay home with Angelique until she started school. Her parents read to her, talk to her, and interact with her. They take trips together and have flown to various other parts of the country. She has eaten different kinds of food in various restaurants, gone to zoos, farms, museums, and so on.

Sara, on the other hand, comes from a home in which she is the oldest of six children. At seven years of age, she has had a great amount of responsibility thrust upon her. Her mother works, and often Sara has to stay home to help take care of the other children. There is no father; at times, there are various "uncles" living at home with them. Sara is a "put upon" child. She is very mature for her age and is gaining many experiences; unfortunately, these will not help her do well in school. She has never traveled, never been to a zoo, never been to a farm, never had anyone read to her; she has never had any of the kinds of things children should have. She knows about the various kinds of drugs; she knows what to do when her mother and her "uncles" drink too much. The animals she sees are stray shaggy dogs that run wild, cats that seem to live in the garbage cans sprawled on the streets, and rats that run freely in the apartment.

Here are composites of these two children. Which child would you predict will succeed in school? Why?

Angelique L.

Only child.
Upper-middle-class socioeconomic status.
College-educated parents.
Standard English is dominant language.
Both parents at home.
Both parents read to Angelique.
Many books are available for Angelique.
Newspapers, books, and magazines are available for parents.
Parents read for pleasure.
Angelique sees parents writing.
Television is supervised.
Parents discuss books and television shows with Angelique.
Family does many things together.
Angelique has pets.
Angelique helps take care of pets.
Family travels together to "fun" places.

Sara M.

Oldest of six children.
Low-class socioeconomic status.
Mother has a seventh-grade education.
There is no father present.
Various "uncles" stay at house.
Nonstandard English is spoken.
No newspapers, magazines, or books are visible.
Television is unsupervised.
No one reads to Sara.
Mother does not read for pleasure.
Sara has many home responsibilities.

You probably answered "Angelique," and if you did, you would probably be correct. You are also probably saying that the deck has been stacked in Angelique's favor. It has been; however, many children have backgrounds similar to those of Sara and Angelique. The Angeliques do well in school because they have had the preschool background and experiences that seem to correlate well with school success. The Saras are considered at-risk children. And unless these children are identified early and helped, they will remain at high risk of failing in school and eventually dropping out.

This chapter will present a number of those factors, which determine in part the reading success of children. It is important that teachers recognize how many of these individual factors affect reading success, even though there are a number—such as home environment, family makeup, and cultural differences—that educators can do nothing about. However, if educators are aware that some students come from backgrounds that are not conducive to school learning, they will try to provide those experiences that these children need to be successful readers. It is to be hoped that teachers will also recognize how important their role is in helping these children and not, as was discussed in Chapter 2, invoke the self-fulfilling prophecy, which will guarantee the children's failure.

KEY QUESTIONS

After you finish reading this chapter, you should be able to answer the following questions:

1. What are some factors that influence a child's reading performance?
2. How are some factors that influence a child's reading performance interrelated?
3. How does a child's home environment influence his or her reading ability?
4. How are language development, concept development, and reading related?
5. What is a concept?
6. What are *assimilation* and *accommodation* according to Jean Piaget?
7. What are examples of concepts that primary-grade children should have?
8. What are some informal techniques for measuring concept development?
9. What is the relationship of intelligence to reading?
10. What is the relationship of sex differences to reading?
11. What is the relationship of birth order to language development?
12. What is the relationship of language and dialect to the development of standard English?
13. What is the role of the teacher in helping nonnative speakers acquire English as a second language?
14. What is the relationship of physical health to reading?
15. Who are considered "at-risk" children?

KEY TERMS IN CHAPTER

You should pay special attention to the following new terms:

accommodation
assimilation
at-risk students
bilingual
bilingual education
black English
cognitive development
concept

dialect
educational factors
English as a second language
  (ESL)
equilibrium
home environment
immersion
noneducational factors
nonstandard English
schemata
second-language learners
standard English

DIFFERENTIATING BETWEEN NONEDUCATIONAL AND EDUCATIONAL FACTORS

Educational factors
Those factors that come under the domain or control of the educational system and influence learning.

Noneducational factors
Supposedly those factors that do not come under the domain or control of the educational system and cannot be influenced by it.

Before we proceed to some of the various noneducational and educational factors that can affect a child's reading performance, it is necessary to differentiate between *noneducational* and *educational* factors. When people talk about educational factors, they generally are referring to those factors that come under the domain or control of the educational system and influence learning. Under educational factors, we would usually include the various methods and materials that the child has been exposed to, the teacher, the instructional time, the school environment, the school district, and so on. Under noneducational factors, we generally would include physical health (general), vision, hearing, intelligence, personality, and gender. Noneducational factors are supposedly those that do not come under the domain or control of the educational system and cannot be influenced by it. However, if we were to scrutinize these factors, we would see that although gender cannot be influenced by the schools, sex roles can. Intelligence is another factor that is influenced by school and learning. Obviously, for some of the factors, overlapping exists. A case could even be made for general physical health as being influenced by educational practices. For example, children who are doing poorly in school may wish to avoid school to such an extent that they become ill every morning. The children's emotional health has influenced their physical health so that they actually get ill; that is, they may get a stomachache, headache, or throw up. Their emotional state may so affect them that they cannot eat or sleep. The physical symptoms are real, even though the cause may not be a virus or bacterium.

A child's personality can also be affected by what takes place in school. For example, the little boy Larry, who is presented in a scenario at the beginning of Chapter 8, had an undetected eye problem, and he was subjected to methods and materials in school that were not helping him learn to read. Larry soon changed from a happy, outgoing, and helpful young boy to a sullen, irritable, unhappy child who didn't like himself or anyone else.

It is imperative that teachers be aware of the interrelatedness of the various factors, regardless of whether they are educational or noneducational. A child who has difficulty learning to read usually has concomitantly many emotional and social problems, and these are compounded as the child goes through school if he or she is not helped as soon as a problem is detected or suspected.

CONCEPT DEVELOPMENT AND ITS RELATIONSHIP TO LANGUAGE AND READING

The cartoon presented in Figure 4.1 illustrates the interrelationships among language, concepts, and cognitive development. Since Punkin Head did not know what a hare or tortoise is, he could not understand the story told to him by Tiger. Punkin Head must be able to differentiate these animals from others which may have some similar characteristics. At a higher cognitive level, he must also be able to conceptualize why the tortoise beat the hare in the race, and thereby comprehend the meaning of the adage "Slow and steady wins the race."

Concept development is closely related to language development. Unless children attain the necessary concepts, they will be limited in reading as well as in all other aspects of the language arts (listening, speaking, and writing).

Knowledge of what concepts are and how children attain them is

Reprinted with special permission of King Features Syndicate, Inc.

Figure 4.1 Punkinhead needs help in concept development.

especially essential in a diagnostic-reading and correction program. Teachers in such a program must recognize early when a child is lacking certain concepts and help that child to attain them. Angelique and Sara, the two children presented at the beginning of this chapter, are in the same class at school, but they are at different concept-development levels. Unless Sara attains certain concepts, she will be limited in all aspects of the language arts.

The quality of language development depends on the interrelationships of such factors as intelligence, home environment, sex differences, cultural differences, and family makeup. The factors that influence language development also influence concept development. As a result, children who are more advanced in language development are also usually more advanced in concept development, and these children tend to be better readers than those who are not as advanced.[1]

Before discussing the factors that help shape concepts and subsequently influence success in reading, let's first look at concept development.

WHAT IS A CONCEPT?

Concept
A group of stimuli with common characteristics.

A concept is a group of stimuli with common characteristics. These stimuli may be objects, events, or persons. Concepts are usually designated by their names, such as book, war, man, woman, animal, teacher, and so forth. All these concepts refer to classes (or categories) of stimuli. Some stimuli do not refer to concepts; Miss Dawn, the hairdresser, Hemingway's "The Killers," World War II, and the Super Bowl are examples. These are particular (not classes of) stimuli, persons, or events.[2]

Concepts are needed to reduce the complexity of the world. When children learn that their shaggy pets are called dogs, they tend to label all other similar four-footed animals as "dogs." Young children overgeneralize, tending to group all animals together, and have not yet perceived the differences between and among various animals. Unless children learn to discern differences, the class of words that they deal with will become exceptionally unwieldy and unmanageable. However, if children group each object in a class by itself, this too will bring about difficulties in coping with environmental stimuli because it will also be such an unwieldy method.

The first step in acquiring concepts concerns vocabulary because concepts are based on word meanings: without vocabulary there would be no base for their development. The second step is gathering

[1] Walter D. Loban, *Language Development: Kindergarten Through Grade Twelve*, Research Report No. 18 (Urbana, Ill.: National Council of Teachers of English, 1976).

[2] John P. DeCecco, *The Psychology of Learning and Instruction: Educational Psychology*, 2nd ed. (Englewood Cliffs, N.J.: Prentice-Hall, 1974), p. 288.

data, that is, specific information about the concept to be learned. In doing this, students use their strategies for processing information—they select data that are relevant, ignore irrelevant data, and categorize items that belong together. Concepts are formed when the data are organized into categories. Based on this information, you can see how Angelique's early experiences have prepared her very well for school, and Sara's have not. Sara is deficient in vocabulary development and consequently in concept development. These deficiencies will affect how well she does in school unless teachers intervene and know how to help her.

PIAGET AND CONCEPT DEVELOPMENT

Cognitive development
Refers to development of thinking.

Concept development is closely related to cognitive (thinking) development. Jean Piaget, a renowned Swiss psychologist, has written on children's cognitive development in terms of their ability to organize (which requires conceptualization), classify, and adapt to their environments.

Figure 4.2 These children are learning the concept of opposites.

According to Piaget,[3] the mind is capable of intellectual exercise because of its ability to categorize incoming stimuli adequately. Schemata (structured designs) are the cognitive arrangements by which this categorization takes place. As children develop and take

[3] Jean Piaget, *The Origins of Intelligence in Children* (New York: International Universities Press, 1952).

Schemata
These structured designs are the cognitive arrangements by which the mind is able to categorize incoming stimuli.

Assimilation
A continuous process which helps the individual to integrate new incoming stimuli to existing concepts—Piaget's cognitive development.

Accommodation
The developing of new categories by a child rather than integrating them into existing ones—Piaget's cognitive development.

Equilibrium
According to Piaget, a balance between assimilation and accommodation in cognitive development.

in more and more information, it is necessary to have some way to categorize all the new information. As children develop, their ability to categorize, by means of schemata, grows too. That is, children should be able to differentiate, to become less dependent on sensory stimuli, and to gain more and more complex schemata. Children should be able to categorize a cat as distinct from a mouse or a rabbit. They should be able to group cat, dog, and cow together as animals. Piaget calls the processes which bring about these changes in children's thinking *assimilation* and *accommodation*.

Assimilation does not change an individual's concept but allows it to grow. It is a continuous process that helps the individual to integrate new, incoming stimuli into existing schemata or concepts. For example, when children tend to label all similar four-footed animals as dogs, the children are assimilating. They have assimilated all four-footed animals into their existing schemata.

If the child meets stimuli that cannot fit into the existing schema, then the alternative is either to construct a new category or to change the existing one. When a new schema or concept is developed, or when an existing schema is changed, it is called accommodation.

Although both assimilation and accommodation are important processes that the child must attain in order to develop adequate cognition, a balance between the two processes is necessary. If children overassimilate, they will have categories that are too large to handle and, similarly, if they overaccommodate, they will have too many categories, as we have already seen. Piaget calls the balance between the two *equilibrium*. A person having equilibrium would be able to see similarities between stimuli and thus properly assimilate them, and would also be able to determine when new schemata are needed for adequate accommodation of a surplus of categories.

As children develop cognitively they proceed from more global (generalized) schemata to more particular ones. For the child there are usually no right or wrong placements but only better or more effective ones. That is what good education is all about.

Concept Assessment

Concepts are necessary to help students acquire increasing amounts of knowledge. For example, as one proceeds through the grades in school, learning becomes more abstract and is expressed in words, using verbal stimuli as labels for concepts. Many teachers take for granted that those spoken concept labels are understood by their students, but this is not always so. Young children's literal interpretation of oral and written discourse and their limited knowledge of the world around them will, of course, affect their comprehension and ability to form correct concepts (see Figure 4.3). Many times

Figure 4.3 Linus does not understand the concept of "field trip."

concepts are learned either incompletely or incorrectly. This example illustrates incomplete concepts for *tourist* and *immigrant*.[4]

> All the tourists may be obviously American whereas all the immigrants may be obviously Mexican. The tourists may be well dressed, the immigrants poorly dressed, and so on. If the natural environment is like a grand concept-formation experiment, it may take the child a long time to attain the concepts *tourist* and *immigrant;* indeed, the environment may not be as informative as the usual experimenter since the child may not always be informed, or reliably informed, as to the correctness of his guesses. No wonder a child might form the concept that a tourist is a well-dressed person who drives a station wagon with out-of-state license plates!

When children come to school the teacher must assess their concept-development level, then help them to add the attributes necessary and relevant for the development of particular concepts, while helping them to delete all those concepts that are faulty or irrelevant.

An informal inventory test of concepts in the primary grades, such as the one given below, could be developed and easily administered to the whole class as a paper-and-pencil test, or it can be given orally to individual students, whichever is more convenient in the classroom.

Another method to determine whether children have the concept of opposites is for the teacher to ask each child to give some opposites for the following words:

no	good	fat
boy	mommy	go
happy		

In order to determine whether the children understand the

---

[4] John B. Carroll, "Words, Meanings and Concepts," in *Thought & Language: Language and Reading*, Maryanne Wolf et al., eds. (Cambridge, Mass.: Harvard Educational Review, 1980), p. 42.

concepts of left and right, the teacher could play the game "Simon Says" with the children and use directions with the words *left* and *right*. The teacher could also observe whether children understand the concept of *first* and *last* by asking children to name who is first or who is last in line. The teacher can learn much about the concept development of students by using such informal techniques.

EXAMPLE OF AN INFORMAL INVENTORY TEST OF CONCEPTS FOR PRIMARY-GRADE STUDENTS

For each concept the teacher will orally state the tested term in the context of a sentence. The children will show they understand the concept by correctly checking or putting a circle around the picture that best describes the concept. Before beginning, the teacher should make sure that all children understand the symbol for a check (✔) and that they can draw a circle around an object.

   1. Concept *over*. Concept in sentence: The check (✔) is over the ball.

Directions

Put a circle around the picture that shows a ✔ is over a ball. (Again, the teacher should put a ✔ on the board to make sure children understand this term. The teacher should make a circle on the board to make sure children understand this concept as well.)

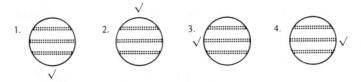

   2. Concept of *under*. Concept in sentence: The check (✔) is under the ball.

Directions

Put a circle around the picture that shows a ✔ is under a ball.

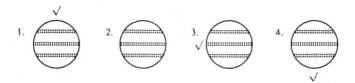

3. Concept of *square*. Sentence: Which picture shows a square?

Directions

Put a check in the square.

4. Concept of *triangle*. Sentence: Which picture shows a triangle?

Directions

Put a check in the triangle.

5. Concept of *most*. Sentence: Which box has the most balls?

Directions

Draw a circle around the box that has the most balls.

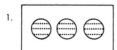  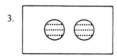

6. Concept of *least*. Sentence: Which box has the least number of balls?

Directions

Draw a circle around the box that has the least number of balls.

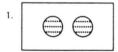 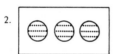 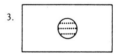

7. Concept of *smallest.* Sentence: Which ball is the smallest?

Directions

Draw a circle around the smallest ball.

1.   2.   3.   4.

8. Concept of *largest.* Sentence: Which ball is the largest?

Directions

Draw a circle around the largest ball.

1.   2.   3.   4.

9. Concept of *opposites.*

Directions

Draw a circle around the picture that is the opposite of the word that I am going to say. (For example, the teacher says, "What is the opposite of girl?")

1. girl

2. big

3. short

Published tests can also help us gain information about children's concept development. Here is a sample with directions of Test 4 from the practice test of the *Cognitive Abilities Test* (Primary Battery) that tests for the concept of verbal classification:

SAMPLE FROM A PUBLISHED TEST OF CONCEPTS FOR PRIMARY GRADE CHILDREN

Directions (Teacher reads directions aloud to the children.)

1. Put your finger on the little heart next to the first row of pictures. Look at the first three pictures in that row. There are pictures of a *daisy*, a *tulip*, and a *rose*. These three things don't *look* exactly alike, but they *are* alike in some way. (Pause.) They are alike because they are all flowers.

Now look at the rest of the pictures in the same row—the ones on the other side of the line. They have ovals under them. There are pictures of a man, a pansy, a vase, and a tree. One of those pictures is like the first three and goes with them. Which one is like the *daisy*, the *tulip*, and the *rose*?

(Pause. Give the children time to look at the answer choices. Then say:)

The picture of the *pansy* goes with the first three pictures. Pansies are also flowers. So, fill in the oval under the pansy to show that the picture goes with the first three.

(Pause. Give the children time to mark their answers. Check to make sure each child has marked the item correctly. Answer any questions. Then say:)

2.   Now put your finger on the little chair. Look at the pictures of the *apple*, the *orange*, and the *pear*. These three pictures go together because they are alike in some way. Look at them and see how they are alike. (Pause.) Now look at the rest of the pictures in that row. Choose the picture that goes with the first three. (Pause.) Fill in the oval under the picture you choose.

(As soon as the children have finished, go over the answer to the last question with them. If possible, ask them to give you the right answer. In any event, make sure they all understand what the correct answer is. Have them correct their answers if they marked them wrong. Clear up any questions before continuing with Practice Test 5.)

Instructional Implications

Studies on learning have shown that persons will retain information over an extended period of time if they are able to make generalizations about the information and if they can see relationships between what they are presently learning and material that they have already learned. Obviously, persons who have strategies for processing information will be in a better position to retain and transfer learning than those persons who do not. Good thinkers have strategies for processing information; they are able to assimilate and accommodate information; they are active consumers of information. Readers as active consumers of information must give structure or order to what they are reading. They must relate new experiences to what they already know. No one can do this for the reader; however, the teacher is the facilitator for helping the reader gain skill in higher cognitive operations. Teachers can give the students practice in many activities that help them to develop their categorizing abilities, and they can ask questions that challenge them to seek relationships and to make comparisons. Teachers can also use modeling techniques to help children gain insights into some cognitive processes. If children are exposed to these activities, they will be better prepared to do this kind of thinking when they are reading alone. (See Chapter 13 for more on concept development and categorizing.)

Let's now look at some of the factors that help shape concepts and affect reading.

HOME ENVIRONMENT

Home environment
Socioeconomic class, parents' education, and the neighborhood in which children live are some factors that shape children's home environment.

Socioeconomic class, parents' education, and the neighborhhood in which children live are some of the factors that shape children's home environments. Studies have shown that the higher the socioeconomic status, the better the verbal ability of the child.[5] Children who have good adult language models and are spoken to and encouraged to speak will have an advantage in the development of language and intelligence. Similarly children who come from homes where there are many opportunities to read, where there are diverse reading materials such as magazines, encyclopedias, books, and newspapers, and where the people with whom the children are living read frequently will be better readers than children without these advantages.[6] Parents who behave in a warm, democratic manner and provide their children with stimulating educationally oriented activities, challenge their children to think, encourage independence, and reinforce their children are preparing them very well for school.

Children who come from homes where parents have only an elementary-school education, where there are few reading materials available, where no one reads, where many people live in a few rooms, and where unemployment among the adults in the home is common will usually be at a disadvantage in learning language and in reading. These are the ones who are at risk when they come to school.

Teachers should also be aware of the adult composition of the child's home environment. Whether a child is reared by both parents, a single parent, a servant, grandparents, or foster parents will affect the child's attitudes and behavior. A child who is reared by a female single parent may behave differently from one reared by a male single parent, for instance. The death of one parent or of another family member will usually cause emotional stress in the child. Divorce can also be a traumatic experience for children. Teachers who are aware of the home environment and are sensitive to sudden changes in this important area are in a better position to understand and help such students.

How many children are born into a family and the order in which these children are born affect the achievement levels of individuals, at least to some degree. Research is still being done on these factors, but it has been hypothesized that firstborn children do better both in school and in life than other children in the family. A child without

[5] Walter D. Loban, *Language Development: Kindergarten through Grade Twelve*, Research Report No. 18 (Urbana, Ill.: National Council of Teachers of English, 1976).

[6] Ina V. S. Mullis and Lynn B. Jenkins, *The Reading Report Card, 1971–1988*, National Assessment of Educational Progress (Princeton, N.J.: Educational Testing Service, 1990), pp. 38–39.

Figure 4.4 In Melissa's home there are many books. Both her parents read, so Melissa wants to read, too; she is fascinated by books.

siblings has been shown to be more articulate for the most part than a child who is a product of a multiple birth (like twins or triplets) or a singleton (one child born at a time) who has other brothers and sisters.[7]

Studies have shown that the only child, who is more often in the company of adults, has more chances of being spoken to by the grown-ups around him or her than is the case when there are many children in the family. Then, too, twins seem to have less need to communicate with others because they have a close relationship.

Singletons with siblings also have "interpreters" near at hand, that is, older siblings who can often understand a younger child's messages so well that the younger child need not attempt to express him- or herself more effectively.

All these factors form part of the learning climate in the home and influence the degree and amount of learning the child will do in school. Angelique, our child in the scenario, is off to a good headstart. But what about Sara?

DIALECT AND LANGUAGE DIFFERENCES

Dialect and language differences are closely related to home environment because the home environment will determine whether the

[7] Mildred A. Dawson and Miriam Zollinger, *Guilding Language Learning* (New York: Harcourt, 1957), pp. 36–37. Didi Moore, "The Only-Child Phenomenon," *The New York Times Magazine*, January 18, 1981, pp. 26–27, 45–48.

child will speak standard English, a dialect of English, Spanish, French, Italian, German, Russian, Chinese, or some other language. In a diagnostic-reading and correction program, teachers must recognize that most classes will have a multicultural mix of children because we are a pluralistic society. Teachers in such classes have a tremendous challenge. They must help their students retain their cultural heritage while at the same time becoming part of the "melting pot." This is an awesome task, but with help and commitment it can be done.

Sara, the child in our introductory scenario, speaks a dialect of English. This is probably compounding her problems at school. To understand why, we need to define and discuss some terms.

According to *Webster's Third New International Dictionary*, the term *standard English* is defined as "the English that with respect to spelling, grammar, pronunciation, and vocabulary is substantially uniform, though not devoid of regional differences, that is well established by usage in the formal and informal speech and writing of the educated, and that is widely recognized as acceptable wherever English is spoken and understood."

The term *dialect* is more difficult to define, however. To some people, a dialect of English is any variation of standard English; to others, it is merely a means of expressing oneself; and to still others, it is a variety of language related to social class, educational level, geography, gender, and ethnicity. From these definitions, we can see that standard English could then be considered a dialect and that the definition of dialect is obviously intertwined with that of language. If we were to define dialect in a broad sense, we would be concerned with the language of a geographic area; if we were to define it in a specific sense, we would be looking at the language of a neighborhood, a family, or even an individual (idiolect). Generally, however, when we refer to dialect, we are talking about a structured subsystem of a language, with definite phonological and syntactic structures, that is spoken by a group of people united not only by their speech but also by factors such as geographic location and/or social status.[8]

For some people the term *dialect* seems to have negative connotations associated with it. This is unfortunate because we all speak a dialect. "Dialects inevitably arise within all languages because all languages inevitably change."[9] If the geographical separation between groups of people is very great, and the separation lasts long enough, "the dialects may diverge from each other so much that

Standard English
English in respect to spelling, grammar, vocabulary, and pronunciation that is substantially uniform, though not devoid of regional differences. It is well established by usage and the formal and informal speech and writing of the educated and is widely recognized as acceptable wherever English is spoken and understood.

Dialect
A variation of language sufficiently different to be considered separate, but not different enough to be classified as a separate language.

---

[8] Jean Malmstrom and Constance Weaver, *Transgrammar: English Structure, Style, and Dialects* (Glenview, Ill.: Scott, Foresman, 1973), p. 338.

[9] Peter Desberg, Dale E. Elliott, and George Marsh, "American Black English and Spelling," in *Cognitive Processes in Spelling*, ed. Uta Frith (New York: Academic Press, 1980), p. 70.

Nonstandard English
A variation of standard English owing to socioeconomic and cultural differences in the United States.

they become two distinct languages."[10] (Persons who speak different languages do not understand one another, whereas persons who speak different dialects do.)

In the United States, standard English is considered the "prestige" dialect and where regional dialects differ very little from each other, perhaps almost exclusively in pronunciation, we would be more likely to speak of an "accent" than a "dialect."[11] In this book, whenever the term *nonstandard English* is used, it refers to a variation of standard English owing to socioeconomic and cultural differences in the United States.

Children who speak a variation or dialect of English or another language are not inferior to children speaking standard English, nor is their language inferior. Research by linguists has shown that many variations of English are highly structured systems and not accumulations of errors in standard English. For example, William Labov states that "it is most important for the teacher to understand the relation between standard and nonstandard and to recognize that nonstandard English is a system of rules, different from the standard but not necessarily inferior as a means of communication."[12]

Children speaking in a dialect of English have no difficulty communicating with one another. However, any dialect that differs from standard English structure and usage will usually cause communication problems for children in school and in society at large. Many expressions used by children who speak a variation of English may be foreign to teachers, and many expressions used by teachers may have different connotations for the students. The similarities between the dialects of English and standard English can also cause misunderstandings between students and teachers because both groups may feel they "understand" what the others are saying when, in actuality, they may not.

Black English
A variation of standard English; in the class of nonstandard English.

These "misunderstandings" may be especially true for black English vernacular, which is in the class of nonstandard English. Black English and standard English appear similar, but they are not. Labov's research in the 1980s suggests that the differences between black English and standard English are becoming greater than narrower. He states that he would not rule out "the possibility that it is contributing to failure of black children to learn to read. How much a little child has to do to translate!"[13]

[10] Ibid., p. 71.

[11] John P. Hughes, *The Science of Language* (New York: Random House, 1962), p. 26.

[12] William Labov, *The Study of Nonstandard English* (Urbana, Ill.: National Council of Teachers of English, 1970), p. 14.

[13] William Labov, professor of linguistics, University of Pennsylvania, January 11, 1990.

Here is a sample summary of some possible phonological and grammatical interferences between standard English and black English that may affect reading:

---

1. r-lessness. Black English has a rather high degree of r-lessness. The *r* becomes a schwa or simply disappears before vowels as well as before consonants or pauses: *r* is never pronounced in four, Paris becomes Pass, carrot becomes cat.

2. l-lessness. Dropping of the liquid *l* is similar to that of dropping *r* except that the former is often replaced by a back unrounded glide (u) instead of the center glide for *r*. Or the *l* disappears completely, especially after the backrounded vowels. Examples: help = hep, tool = too, all = awe, fault = fought.

3. Simplification of consonant clusters at the end of words. There is a general tendency to reduce end consonant clusters to single consonants, particularly those ending in /t/, /d/, /s/, or /z/. In approximate order of frequency, the /t,d/ clusters affected are -st, -ft, -nt, -nd, -ld, -zd, -md, thus generating homonyms such as past = pass, meant = men, rift = riff, mend = men, wind = wine, hold = hole. The /s,z/ cluster simplification results in these homonyms: six = sick, box = bock, Max = Mack, mix = Mick. Labov found that the simplification of the /s,z/ clusters is much more characteristic of Black speakers than of White speakers.

4. Weakening of final consonants. This is another example of a general tendency to produce less information after stressed vowels, so that the endings of words (be they consonants, unstressed final vowels, or weak syllables) are devoiced or dropped entirely. Children who possess this characteristic seem to have the most serious reading problems. Most affected by this are the following: boot = boo, road = row, feed = feet, seat = seed = see, poor = poke = pope, bit = bid = big.

5. Possessive deletion. The absence of /-s/ inflection results in: John's cousin = John cousin, whoever's book = whoever book. Deletion of /-r/ makes two possessive pronouns identical to personal pronouns: their book = they book, your = you = you-all.

6. Verb suffix. Labov believes that the third person singular was not present in Black English but imported from standard English in view of the low percentage of use (only 5–15 percent in some cases) and the sharp class stratification between middle and working classes. Some illustrations of the use of the verb suffix in Black English are: Somebody get hurts. He can goes out. He always bes on the beach mosta de time. All our men ares each on side. We goes to church on Sunday. Judy go to school today.

7. Be_2 form. There are two forms of "do" and two forms of "have" in English as in "Does he do it?" and "Has he had any?" In the first question, they could be called Do_1 and Do_2. The second form in each class is a normal main verb. *Be* has a main verb Be_2 which is like other main verbs. The meaning of Be_2 is so versatile that in some instances standard English has no equivalents:

a) Habitual rather than a temporal or short occurrence. From now on, I don't be playing. He be sad. I be crying. She always be happy. Guys that bes with us.

b) Repeated occurrence. Wolfram found between 11 to 16 percent of frequency adverbs with Be_2 such as hardly, usually, sometimes, always, mostly, all the time.

c) Single nonrepeated activity in the future. This practice is used in all cases where *will* is possible or where an underlying *will* could be elicited in tag questions or in negatives: Sometime he don't be busy. He be in in a few minutes. I know he will. Sometime he be busy. I know he do.

d) Deletion of "would." She just be talking, and I wouldn't listen. If he didn't have to go away, he be home.

8. Copulation. Copula deletion is considered basically a phonological process, but it also has strong grammatical constraints which are not random. Deletion may occur with verb following, no vowel preceding, but pronoun preceding. Semantically, deletion occurs most often on short active utterances: Riff eatin. He goin. Ricky too old. Jim goin. She real tired. Carol chairman.

9. Person-number agreement.

a) In Black English, there is person-number agreement for I am, you are, and he is.

b) There is no third person singular marker, as in most languages around the world. The preferred forms are: He don't. He do. He have. *Does, has,* and *says* are used infrequently.

c) *Was* is the preferred form for past tense of *be.*

10. Past tense. Phonological conditioning weakens the regular past tense as in the reduction of /t,d/ inflection: passed = pass, missed = miss, fined = fine, picked = pick, loaned = loan, raised = raise.

11. Negative forms and negation. In Black English, *ain't* is used as past negative; for example, I told im I ain't pull it; He didn't do nothing much, and I ain't neither. Adults used *didn't* more often than *ain't.* Preteens use *ain't* less often than teenagers. *Ain't* is a stigmatized form but has special social meaning to teenagers.

In negation, Black English seems to carry negative concord principles further than nonstandard Anglo English. Examples: Nobody had no bloody nose or nosebleed. I am no strong drinker. She didn't play with none of us. Down there nobody don't know about no club.

Source: Doris C. Ching, *Reading and the Bilingual Child* (Newark, Del.: International Reading Association, 1976), pp. 15–17. Reprinted with permission of Doris C. Ching and the International Reading Association.

Bilingual
Using or capable of using two languages.

Children who come from homes where a language other than English is the dominant one may also have language difficulties when they enter school unless they are truly bilingual. The dictionary definition of *bilingual* states that one must be capable of using two languages equally effectively.[14] However, many schoolchildren who speak a language other than standard English at home are not bilingual. These children may hear only "noises" when they first enter school, because the English sounds have little or no meaning for them. They will often confuse the language spoken at home with

[14] *Webster's Third New International Dictionary of the English Language Unabridged* (Chicago: Encyclopaedia Britannica, Inc., 1981), p. 215.

Figure 4.5 Most classrooms today are multicultural.

their newly acquired English and vice versa. It is not a question of one language being better than or preferred over another, but rather one of helping children to get along in the dominant social, economic, and political culture and to become a part of it. Unless students learn to communicate in standard English as well as in a dialect or another language, they will have difficulty in finding their "places in the sun" in the economy.

Second-Language Learners

Have you heard the story of the mother mouse who was attempting to teach her baby mice how to get along in the great outside world?

> The mother mouse teaches the children how to avoid traps, how to retrieve the bait from traps without getting caught, and other similar activities, and on the final day of instruction, she says: "You know, children, a cat lives in this house—and the cat is your enemy. Today I am going to show you how to handle the cat." The mother mouse then lines up the baby mice at the entrance to their home in the baseboard of a large room, and she proceeds to run out in plain view of the baby mice and attract the attention of the cat. The unwary cat, very much surprised by the bold behavior of the mouse, is about to pounce on her when the mother mouse rears back on her hind legs and in a shrill high voice says: "Arf, arf." At this juncture every hair on the cat stands on end, he turns tail, and runs wildly in the opposite direction; whereupon the mother mouse turns and smiling broadly at her children says, "You see, children, it pays to speak a second language."[15]

When children enter school they bring with them the language of

---

[15] Virginia W. Jones. "Training Teachers of English for Alaska's Native Children," *Elementary English* (February 1971), p. 198.

their environment, of their family, home, and neighborhood. This first language learning they have acquired is the most deeply rooted, regardless of what other language learning they achieve later in their life.

Mrs. Robbins is a first-grade teacher. On the first day of school, she waits at the door and greets each incoming student. She smiles and says "Hello" to each, and each in turn usually smiles and replies "Hello" in return. This year was somewhat different. Mrs. Robbins did indeed wait at the door and did smile and say "Hello"; however, rather than greeting the teacher with "Hello" or "Hi," half her class greeted her with big wide stares. She smiled again at these children, and then they smiled back. Communication for the moment had taken place through the smile, a universal greeting.

On the first day of school, Mrs. Robbins, a monolingual teacher, learned that half her class was composed of children who had just arrived in the United States from another country. Of these, five did not understand any English, and four had limited English proficiency (LEP). Mrs. Robbins has children with multicultural backgrounds in her classroom; a microcosm of a truly pluralistic society. She has one child from Korea, one from China, two from the Ukraine, one from Brazil, two from Poland, one from Yugoslavia, and one from Pakistan. Mrs. Robbins is not alone. This heterogeneous ethnic and racial mix is happening in many classrooms in the United States, and it will become even more pronounced throughout the 1990s.

Unfortunately for Mrs. Robbins, her school system had not planned for this nor prepared its teachers. Mrs. Robbins will have to learn "on the job," and let us hope she will gain the assistance and support that she will need to help all her students.

Learning Another Language

The concept of the United States as a melting pot into which immigrant children can readily assimilate may explain why hardly any help was given for nonnative speakers to learn English. For many years, it was felt that merely being put in a classroom where English was spoken was enough to learn the language. Many did acquire English this way and did well; however, such was not the case for all immigrant children. Those who could not gain English this way soon dropped out of school.

The Supreme Court in 1974 made an important ruling on behalf of LEP students:

> There is no equality of treatment merely by providing students with the same facilities, textbooks, teachers, and curriculum; for students who do not understand English are effectively foreclosed from any meaningful education. Basic English skills are at the very core of what these public schools teach. Imposition of a requirement that, before a child can effectively participate in the educational program, he must already have acquired those basic skills is to make a mockery of public education. We know that those who do not understand English are certain to find their

classroom experiences wholly incomprehensible and in no way meaningful. (U.S. Supreme Court, 414 U.S. 563)

English as a Second Language (ESL)
Teaching that concentrates on helping children who speak a language other than English or who speak nonstandard English to learn standard English as a language.

Bilingual education
Instruction in both the student's native language and English.

Immersion
Complete exposure of a nonnative English speaker to English as soon as he or she enters school.

This milestone decision said in effect "that school districts have a duty to see that students are not discriminated against because they do not speak English."[16] The court ordered the school districts to help these children acquire English; however, it did not specify the method or form. This responsibility was left up to the school districts and lower courts.[17]

Everyone agrees that the children need to learn English; the question is how. There is no unanimity on the best way to help children acquire standard English. Also, the instructional approaches have become entangled in political and social issues. The three approaches that have generally been used are English as a second language (ESL), bilingual education, and immersion.

The ESL approach usually consists of giving nonnative English speakers instruction in English in pullout classes. The intention is to help students in their regular classes, which are taught in English. In most of these programs, audiolingual techniques are stressed. The bilingual approach gives instruction in both the students' native language and in English; that is, the students learn certain subject matter in their native language, and other subject matter in English. The immersion approach consists of being exposed completely to English.

Proponents of the bilingual approach argue that the other approaches are not viable because the emphasis is solely on the learning of English at the expense of learning subject matter. They claim that students fall farther and farther behind because of this. They feel that "instruction in the native language of LEP students allows them to participate in school, and to acquire the skills and knowledge covered in the curriculum while they are learning English. It also allows them to make use of skills, knowledge, and experiences they already have, and to build on these prior assets in school."[18] Instruction in learning English as a second language, whether formal or informal, is an important part of bilingual programs in the United States.

Proponents of the other approaches state that the sooner students learn the language of the school, the sooner they will be able to learn to read in English, and the sooner they will achieve in school. The critics of bilingual education are varied and many. Their major criticisms are that bilingual education prolongs "the 'social disadvantages' of LEP students in this society by delaying their need to learn English and to assimilate into the common culture; they are leading

[16] Lily Wong Fillmore and Concepción Valadez, "Teaching Bilingual Learners," *Hardbook of Research on Teaching*, 3rd ed. (New York: Macmillan, 1986), p. 650.

[17] Ibid.

[18] Ibid., p. 654.

to a society that is divided, not only in language and culture, but in loyalty as well; and they are not delivering the increases in academic achievement that their proponents claim for them."[19] And so it goes.

Teachers Can Help Children Learn Another Language

In a diagnostic-reading and correction program, we are interested in helping all children do the best they possibly can. Teachers like Mrs. Robbins cannot wait for the political and social issues to be resolved. They must take the lead to help their students who need to learn English as a second language. They must help not only the children who are nonnative English speakers but also those who speak variations of nonstandard English.

Good teachers need to be good observers and interacters. They need empathy. They need to be able to put themselves figuratively into the skin of nonnative speakers and feel their embarrassment and misery. They need to be patient. They need to look for subtle signs that show interest or understanding.[20] Many nonnative speakers can communicate in nonverbal ways. They can use haptics (nonverbal communication through touch) and body language. Teachers must interact with these children frequently and closely observe signs of understanding. They must encourage these students to speak, but they must do so in a nonthreatening way. They must expose children to different types of experiences to provide situations that would encourage them to speak. Good teachers recognize that "all language users demonstrate their linguistic abilities differently in different situations."[21]

The objective is to get children to want to communicate—to want to exchange ideas with others. All children in the classroom should be part of this endeavor. The attitude of the teacher is imperative. The teacher must demonstrate by his or her attitude that one language is as good as another, that it is just as useful to learn someone else's language as it is for someone else to learn English. The attitude that must prevail in the classroom is that everyone can learn from everyone else. Unless the complete classroom environment—physical, emotional, social, and intellectual—reinforces this attitude, very valuable learning opportunities will be lost, and actual damage to some children might be done.

Good teachers must be careful to avoid making judgments about nonnative speakers' cognitive ability based on their limited knowledge

---

[19] Ibid., p. 651.

[20] Celia Genishi, "Observing the Second Language Learner: An Example of Teacher's Learning," *Language Arts* 66 (September 1989): 511.

[21] Ibid., p. 514.

of English. They must be careful not to invoke the self-fulfilling prophecy concerning these children.

As stated in Chapter 2, teachers are the key. They must find out what language differences exist in their communities and check with professionals about these. Perhaps they can find tutors who can help. In a multicultural community, everyone must help everyone else.

Some Language Difference Interferences

Teachers need to recognize that children who speak another language will try to superimpose what they know intuitively about their language on the new language they are learning. Therefore, teachers would be in a better position to help their students if they knew some of the major interferences between standard English and the nonnative speaker's language. These are not easy to learn about because most teachers are not polyglots; however, they could seek help with some of the differences from bilingual or ESL teachers. Then teachers could model standard English patterns for the children, especially those that might cause the most problems for the children. (See the section "TESL Lessons.")

Here is a sample of the kinds of problems that Spanish-speaking children might have when attempting to learn standard English:

---

1. Certain vowel sounds will be difficult for the Spanish speaking child: /I/ bit; /æ/ bat; /ə/ but; and /u/ full.

2. English relies on voiced (vocal cords vibrate) and voiceless (vocal cords do not vibrate) sounds to establish meaning contrasts, but Spanish does not: bit-pit; buzz-bus.

3. The Spanish speaker does not use these sounds in his language: /v/ vote; /ð/ then; /z/ zoo; /ž/ measure; /ǰ/ jump. Often the speaker will replace these sounds with sounds he perceives to closely resemble them, or with sounds that frequently occur in similar positions in Spanish.

4. Words that end in /r/ plus the consonants /d, t, l, p/ and /s/ are pronounced without the final consonant: card-car, cart-car.

5. In Spanish the blend of /s/ and the consonant sounds /t, p, k, f, m, n, l/ does not occur, nor does any Spanish word begin with the /s/ + consonant sound. A vowel sound precedes the /s/, and the consonant that follows begins the second syllable of the word. Thus, the child has the problem not only of starting the word with the /s/, but also of pronouncing two consonants (star may thus become estar and be pronounced es-tar). The final consonant clusters /sp/ wasp, /sk/ disk, and /st/ last also present problems in consonant pronunciation.

6. Grammatical differences between the two systems may include the following: subject-predicate agreement (The cars runs.); verb tense (I need help yesterday.); use of negative forms (He no go home.); omission of noun determiner in certain contexts

(He is farmer.); omission of pronoun forms (Is farmer?); order of adjectives (The cap red is pretty.); and comparison (Is more big.).

This summary serves only as an introduction to the teacher to help him [or her] in being alert to the variations between the Spanish and English languages.

Source: Robert B. Ruddell, *Reading-Language Instruction: Innovative Practices* (Englewood Cliffs, N.J.: Prentice-Hall, 1974), p. 275. Reprinted with permission of the author.

Special Note

The director of a bilingual/ESL program in a large inner-city school district claims that often teachers feel that if the Spanish-speaking child were to learn standard English, he or she would be able to read. She feels that it is important for teachers to recognize that a Spanish-speaking child, just like any other nonnative or native English-speaking child, could have a problem learning to read even if he or she were learning in Spanish or any other native language.[22] In other words, the child may have a reading problem that is unrelated to language, but it is probably compounded by a language problem. Teachers must be aware of this possibility because often nonnative speakers are helped to learn English but not given extra help in learning to read.

In addition, she has noticed over the years that many of the Spanish-speaking children in inner-city schools, which have a large population of students who speak nonstandard English, will often pick up the phonology of black English, thereby compounding their problem.[23]

A summary of some of the phonological and grammatical variations between standard English and Chinese are also being presented because of the large population of children in the United States who come from homes where Chinese is the dominant language. The following should help teachers gain a better understanding of some of the difficulties encountered by a number of Chinese-speaking children.

There are many dialects of Chinese with Mandarin, which is spoken by approximately 70 percent of the Chinese people as the national dialect. Cantonese, another major dialect, is spoken by most of the Chinese families that come to the United States from

[22] Ellen Maldari, director of bilingual/ESL education, Trenton Public Schools, Trenton, N.J., June 1990.

[23] Ibid.

Hong Kong, Kowloon, or Macao. Thus, the Cantonese dialect is the one that is discussed below.

1. English has many more vowels than Chinese; for example, /ay/ buy; /aw/ bough; /ɔ/ bought. There is specific difficulty with production of certain vowels such as the front vowels /iy/ beat, /ey/ bait. This results in homophones for a significant number of English words: beat-bit; Luke-look; bait-bet.

2. A number of English consonant sounds are not in Chinese: /θ/ than /ð/ that; /š/ she; /n/ need; and /r/ rice.

3. Many English words end in consonants, but in Chinese many of the consonants are not used in final positions; for example, /f/ is used only initially in Chinese, and the student has difficulty producing it in a final position. Often an extra syllable will be made of the final /f/; day off becomes day offu.

4. Consonant clusters are nonexistent in Cantonese. Those which occur at the ends of words present difficulty in forming plurals and past tenses using /s, t, d, z/: cap-caps, laugh-laughed, wish-wished, dog-dogs.

5. Most grammatical relationships are indicated by word order and auxiliary words in Chinese: "He gave me two books" becomes "Yesterday he give I two book."

6. Numerical designations or auxiliary words are used to indicate plural forms in Chinese: "two books" is "two book."

7. A time word or phrase indicates the tense of a verb. An action verb followed by the auxiliary word *jaw* indicates past or completed tense: "He go jaw" means "He went."

8. Several English word classes—articles, prepositions, and some conjunctions—are reduced or absent in Chinese.

9. The question form in Chinese does not invert the noun and verb forms. Instead, the order is similar to the statement form but the "empty" words *ma* or *la* are added to the end. For example, "Are you an American?" is "You are American ma?" in Chinese.

10. A subject and a predicate are not required in Chinese when the context is sufficient for understanding. For example, "It rains" may be represented as "Drop rain" in Chinese, while "The mountain is big" may be stated as "Mountain big" in Chinese.

11. Tone or pitch in Chinese distinguishes word meanings, but in English pitch combines with intonation to convey sentence meaning.

Source: Robert B. Ruddell, *Reading-Language Instruction: Innovative Practices* (Englewood Cliffs, N.J.: Prentice-Hall, 1974), p. 278.

Special Note

> Idiomatic expressions present a great amount of difficulty for all nonnative speakers because idioms are very culturally loaded. The same is true for figurative language; many nonnative speakers will take figurative expressions literally. (A person with limited English who sees a sign that says "Chickens sold—dressed and undressed" would have great difficulty understanding this.)

TESL Lessons

Teaching English as a second language (TESL) concentrates on helping children—who speak another (foreign) language or nonstandard English speech— to learn English as another language. It does not do away with their own language but adds another one. The closer a child's language is to the print of what he or she is reading, the easier it will be for the child to learn to read. It makes sense then that children, before decoding words, should be involved in a strong aural (listening)–oral (speaking) program, which follows the developmental sequence of the language arts: listening, speaking, reading, and writing. Much inappropriate education for children who need to learn English as a second language may stem from a lack of good instruction in oral language. Although different techniques may be found feasible while working with different groups of children who do not speak standard English, the aural-oral approach is one that can be used with all children.

The lessons that follow are recommended for both nonnative speakers and those who speak nonstandard English. These directed lessons are in addition to what good teachers are doing in their classrooms throughout the day to interact with these students.

Although the TESL lessons vary according to the grouping of the children, there are a number of elements common to lessons. They usually consist of a basic dialogue presented orally by the teacher. The sentences in the dialogue, which are based on the readiness levels of the class, are usually repeated two or three times without student response.

Here is a method that the teacher can use to encourage class participation:[24]

1. The teacher models (provides the pattern) for the first sentence and gestures to the whole group.
2. The whole group repeats the sentence.
3. The teacher repeats the first sentence and gestures to each preformed small group in turn who repeat the same sentence.
4. The teacher next encourages individual responses by his or her own repetition.

The pattern is repeated for each sentence of the dialogue. (It should be remembered that each sentence must be introduced and repeated in the manner already described.) Here is an example of a simple dialogue:

Good day.
Good day.
How are you?
I am fine.

[24] Adapted from Paul Wasserman and Susan Wasserman. *"No Hablo Inglés," Elementary English* (October 1972), pp. 834–35.

The children are also given opportunities to use their new basic dialogue in role-playing situations.

Drill exercises follow the same method of instruction as the basic dialogue, except that pupils must provide the sentence pattern from one previously learned. For example: A sentence has been introduced—"This is a book." The children follow the same method as for developing basic dialogue. Then the teacher holds up a ball. A child, group of students, or the whole class then repeats the learned pattern including the new element, and states, "This is a ball." This method would be used to learn question-answer type of responses, to shorten or to expand responses, and to generate student sentences.

Based on the needs of their students, teachers should *gradually* introduce the patterns that might cause problems for their students. It is best to work on one problem area at a time and to give students enough practice in using the new pattern so that they can overlearn it.

Teachers who use such techniques as role playing, audiovisual aids, concrete materials, and other multimedia approaches to teach English as a second language will enlarge their chances for success. Students enjoy games or gamelike activities, which provide practice for students in ways that are fun.

An activity that might be used to develop speaking and listening skills involves directions. In the game, "My turn, your turn," the teacher states some directions. She points at a child and says, "Your turn." The child must then repeat and carry out the instructions.

Another activity includes "mystery" boxes. Numerous commonplace objects are put in the "mystery" box. Children must select an item from the box, state what it is, and compose a sentence in standard English naming the item.

The activities that are chosen should emphasize the aural-oral approach, stimulate interest, and encourage student participation.

Parental Involvement in TESL

An important factor in helping students learn standard English, when they have been speaking nonstandard English or another language, would involve including parents in the school programs for teaching ESL. Perhaps a program could be developed where the parents are also given ESL instruction. The more people in the family who are active in the language program, the more successful the child will be in mastering standard English.

Attitudes Toward Nonstandard English

Children who speak nonstandard English may have more problems than children who come from homes in which a foreign language is spoken because more status is generally attributed to a foreign language. It was reported in a large-scale Educational Testing Service study of Title I reading programs that teachers do hold negative attitudes toward nonstandard language.[25] Other studies with similar findings have also reported that the negative attitudes have influenced teacher practices. For example, "teachers tend to rate black English speaking students as lower class, less intelligent, and less able to do well academically then standard English speaking students."[26] In the Ann Arbor school-system case, Judge Charles W. Joiner, a United States district court judge, wrote that "a language barrier develops when teachers, in helping the child switch from the home [black English] language to standard English, refuse to admit the existence of a language that is the acceptable way of talking in his local community."[27]

The rejection of the child's language "may more deeply upset him than rejection of the color of his skin. The latter is only an insult, the former strikes at his ability to communicate and express his needs, feelings—his self."[28] The language of children who do not speak standard English has been an effective means of communication for them until they come to school. If such children are made to feel inferior because of their language by a teacher who constantly attacks their speech as incorrect, they may not attempt to learn standard English.

INTELLIGENCE AND READING

Intelligence deals with problem-solving ability and the ability to do abstract reasoning. Since reading is a thinking process, it seems reasonable to assume that highly able students who have the ability to think at high levels of abstraction and who have strategies for processing information should be good readers. To a large degree this assumption is true. However, studies have shown that not all highly able children become good readers, and these results suggest that there are factors besides intelligence that contribute to success in reading and consequently to achievement in school. (These factors are discussed in other sections.)

Most intelligence tests are highly verbal, and persons who do well on vocabulary tests also seem to do well on intelligence tests. Studies have shown also that there is a high positive correlation between reading achievement test scores and intelligence test scores.[29] Based

[25] Mary K. Monteith, "Black English, Teacher Attitudes, and Reading." *Language Arts* 57 (November-December 1980): 910.

[26] Ibid.

[27] Reginald Stuart, *The New York Times*, July 13, 1979, p. 8.

[28] E. Brooks Smith, Kenneth S. Goodman, and Robert Meredith, *Language and Thinking in the Elementary School* (New York: Holt, Rinehart and Winston, 1976). pp. 46–47.

[29] Keith Rayner and Alexander Pollatsek, *The Psychology of Reading* (Englewood Cliffs, N.J.: Prentice-Hall, 1989), p. 395.

on this, a child with a low IQ would not be expected to do as well on a standardized reading achievement test as one with a high IQ. (See Chapter 6, "Who Is Underachieving in Reading?")

The achievement tests that are generally given usually vary from one school district to another. However, since 1969, the National Assessment of Educational Progress (NAEP) has done its own national testing and issued periodic reports to Congress on the results. The good news is that all students seem to be doing well in the lower-level thinking skills and that students in lower socioeconomic levels have made special strides in this area. The bad news is that only a small percentage of students nationally do well on higher-order thinking skills. (See "A Final Word" in Chapter 7.)

The emphasis in the 1980s was on basic skills, and some of this appears to be paying off. However, the NAEP report concerning higher-order thinking skills is worrisome because schools in the 1980s after *A Nation at Risk* were supposed to be dedicated to helping students gain higher-order thinking skills. The NAEP reports suggest that the schools' efforts have not been successful.

In the 1990s educators, test makers, and basal reader series are emphasizing higher-order thinking skills. They are using literature-based programs and stressing comprehension from beginning reading onward to try to achieve their goals.

GENDER DIFFERENCES

There are vast differences between males and females besides the obvious physical ones, and teachers need to know about these. Females seem to have a biological precocity evident from birth onward.[30] The skeletal development of girls is superior to that of boys at birth, and this physical superiority continues until maturity.[31] Males, however, give off more carbon dioxide than females,[32] therefore, boys need to take in more food and consequently produce more energy. Even though the male matures later than the female, his oxygen intake is greater and continues so throughout life.[33] It has been hypothesized that sex differences in behavior may be due to these differences in metabolism.

These factors may affect the readiness levels of children in listening, speaking, reading, and writing—the language arts. Teachers must realize that some primary-grade boys may not be as mature as some girls of the same chronological age. They should not be

[30] Amram Scheinfeld, *Women and Men* (New York: Harcourt, 1944), pp. 58–71.

[31] J. M. Tanner, "Physical Growth," in *Carmichael's Manual of Child Psychology*, 3rd ed., ed. Paul H. Mussen (New York: Wiley, 1970), p. 109.

[32] Stanley M. Garn and Leland C. Clark, Jr., "The Sex Difference in the Basal Metabolic Rate," *Child Development* 24 (September-December 1953): 215–24.

[33] Ibid., p. 222.

expected to do equally well on tasks using specific hand muscles—such as handwriting. Similarly, teachers should not expect these more immature male students to be able to sit still as long as some more mature female students or to have a comparable attention span. Teachers should know that although studies reveal no significant differences between males and females in general intelligence,[34] studies continue to show differences in specific aptitudes.[35]

In the earlier studies, it was reported that males in general are superior in mathematical ability and in science, but in rote memory females are usually superior.[36] It also has been consistently shown that girls usually surpass boys in verbal ability. From infancy to adulthood, females usually express themselves in words more readily and skillfully than males. Researchers have reported that in general girls seem to learn to talk a little earlier; are usually somewhat superior during the preschool years in articulation, intelligibility, and correctness of speech sounds; and learn grammar and spelling more readily and are less likely to be stutterers.[37] It is important to note that the studies in this area are not definitive. Later studies show that for "large unselected populations the situation seems to be one of very little sex difference in verbal skills from about 3 to 11, with a new phase of differentiation occurring at adolescence."[38] Comparisons of males and females on a variety of tests have made it clear that girls and women do not have larger vocabularies than boys and men.

A recent review of research on gender differences has reported that even though the data on sex differences studies are inconclusive and contradictory, there are a few generalizations that can be made. The reviewers report that "the largest differences appear in tests of mathematical or quantitative ability, where men tend to do better than women, particularly in secondary school and beyond. In recent years, there is some evidence that this gap may be narrowing."[39] What is surprising is that the gap is narrowing between men and women in the area of verbal skills. "Women have tended to do better than men in many tests of verbal skills (particularly writing), but a

[34] Scottish Council for Research in Education, *The Intelligence of a Representative Group of Scottish Children* (London: University of London Press, 1939). Scottish Council for Research in Education, *The Trend of Scottish Intelligence* (London: University of London Press, 1949).

[35] Gita Z. Wilder and Kristin Powell, "Sex Differences in Test Performance: A Survey of the Literature," College Board Report No. 89–3 (Princeton, N.J.: Educational Testing Service, 1989)

[36] Leona E. Tyler, *The Psychology of Human Differences* (New York: Appleton-Century-Crofts, 1965), pp. 244–45.

[37] Ibid., pp. 243–44.

[38] Eleanor E. Maccoby and Carol M. Jacklin, *The Psychology of Sex Differences* (Stanford, Calif.: Stanford University Press. 1974), p. 85

[39] "The Gender Gap in Education: How Early and How Large?" *ETS Policy Notes*, vol. 2, no. 1 (Princeton, N.J.: Educational Testing Service, October 1989).

number of studies indicate that this superiority has diminished since the early 1970s."[40]

In the 1970s and 1980s females made great inroads in male bastions. As a result, the latest findings on sex differences may seem confusing because females haven't made the great strides one would have expected. What has happened is that males have gained in verbal skills, so that females seem to be losing their edge in this area, and males have continued to maintain their edge in mathematical skills.

Sex Differences and Reading

A review of the national assessments of reading between 1971 and 1988 reveals that even though, as stated earlier, the traditional female advantage in verbal skills seems to be eroding, "females at all three ages (9, 13, and 17) outperformed their male counterparts in each of the five NAEP reading assessments."[41]

It should not be surprising then that innumerable studies have found that boys usually outnumber girls in remedial reading classes,[42] and reading disabilities are "from three to ten times more common for boys, depending on how the disability is defined and what population is studied."[43] Researchers have also found "greater variability in reading scores among boys from grades 2 through 7 . . . and boys outnumbered girls among the lowest scores by about 2 to 1 in the lower grades, with the ratio decreasing thereafter."[44]

Many causes have been suggested as reasons for the sex differences. A number of researchers have hypothesized that the female superiority in reading in the United States may be caused by cultural factors, and therefore a number of cross-cultural studies have been made. A much quoted one is Preston's study comparing the reading achievement of German and American boys and girls. He found that the German boys excelled over the German girls in all reading areas tested except that of speed, and his results for the American children were similar to those of previous researchers; that is, "the incidence of 'retardation' and of 'severe retardation' was greater among the American boys than among the American girls—significantly so in almost all instances."[45] His study supported culture as a major factor influencing sex differences in reading. A review of some of the cross-

---

[40] Ibid.

[41] Ina V. S. Mullis and Lynn B. Jenkins, *The Reading Report Card*, 1971–1988, National Assessment of Educational Progress (Princeton, N.J.: Educational Testing Service, 1990), p. 17.

[42] Norma Naiden, "Ratio of Boys to Girls Among Disabled Readers," *The Reading Teacher* 29 (February 1976): 439–42.

[43] Maccoby and Jacklin, p. 119.

[44] Ibid.

[45] Ralph C. Preston, "Reading Achievement of German and American Children," *School and Society* 90 (October 1962): 352.

cultural studies found conflicting results; that is, many studies confirm the superiority of girls in reading in countries other than the United States, whereas some studies support the Preston findings.[46]

Some researchers have claimed that the differences in reading achievement in the early grades are the result of the greater educational readiness of girls for formal reading when they come to school."[47] Both cultural and biological or maturational factors have been put forth as reasons for girls' superior readiness for formal reading. A perusal of the literature seems to lend support to theories suggesting that gender differences in reading may be caused by a combination of both maturational and environmental factors. There are no definitive researches in this area.

It is interesting to note that even though in the past few decades there has been a great emphasis on trying to treat males and females the same, there is "ample evidence that boys and girls are treated differently from birth and perhaps even before, in an age of increasing knowledge about the gender of the unborn child. Parents react more positively toward their toddlers when the children are engaged in gender-appropriate behavior. Moreover, parents' behavior is not always congruent with their stated attitudes."[48]

Let's look at the environmental or cultural evidence a little more closely to see how this factor may affect children's readiness to read. Since language learning is closely related to reading success, and since girls usually surpass boys in verbal ability, it would appear that girls have an advantage over boys when they come to school. The question is why girls have this ability. It has been hypothesized that the language differences observed between the sexes in the early years may also be due to cultural factors. For example, mothers might spend more time with young females during the day than with young males because "parents tend to respond to dependency behavior in girls by encouraging them to stay close and in boys by encouraging them to move away from parents."[49] As a result, there would probably be more verbal interaction between parents and girls.

[46] Howard A. Klein, "Cross-Cultural Studies: What Do They Tell About Sex Differences in Reading?" *The Reading Teacher* 30 (May 1977): 880–85. Dale D. Johnson, "Sex Differences in Reading Across Cultures," *Reading Research Quarterly* 9 (1973–1974): 67–85. Alice Dzen Gross, "Sex-Role Standards and Reading Achievement: A Study of an Israeli Kibbutz System," *The Reading Teacher* 32 (November 1978): 149–56.

[47] Irving H. Balow, "Sex Differences in First Grade Reading," *Elementary English* 40 (March 1963): 306. Guy L. Bond and Robert Dykstra, "The Cooperative Research Program in First-Grade Reading Instruction," *Reading Research Quarterly* 2 (Summer 1967): 122.

[48] Wilder and Powell, p. 16.

[49] Ibid., p. 17.

In addition, studies have suggested that girl babies are spoken to more than boy babies.[50]

Also, studies made of sex-role standards have shown that American boys look upon reading as "feminine" and not in accord with a masculine role. It has been suggested that this factor may influence greatly how males will achieve in reading. For example, in a study made in an Israeli kibbutz, where the boys perceive reading as a desirable masculine skill appropriate for their sex, boys achieve at equally high levels, and boys and girls exhibit an equal amount of reading disability.[51] Preston suggests that the apparent reading superiority of German boys to German girls may be caused by the masculinization of the German schools. In German culture, reading and learning are considered to be more in the male than the female domain, and the teachers in Germany are predominantly males even in the elementary school.[52]

The *teacher* also has been put forth as a possible cause for boys' depressed reading achievement. Some researchers claim that American teachers *expect* their girls to read better than their boys, and that this influences sex differences.[53] Other investigators suggest that sex differences in reading achievement are the result of classroom teachers' *treatment* of boys and girls; that is, "classroom teachers treat boys and girls differently and this difference in treatment is associated with differences in early reading achievement."[54] The studies in this area are also confusing because different studies seem to find different results. For example, a review of the research comparing male and female elementary-school teachers did not find any significant differences between male and female teachers' perception or treatment of boys and girls.[55]

Interestingly, more recent studies suggest that "boys and girls receive different treatment and respond differently to such treatment.[56] However, this difference seems to be primarily in the area of mathematics.

Although it has not been shown that either sex has a preference for vision or hearing to gain information, Maccoby and Jacklin, two noted authorities in the psychology of sex differences, put forth an

---

[50] Ibid., p. 16.

[51] Gross, pp. 149–56.

[52] Preston, p. 353. Also, Ralph C. Preston, "Letters," *The Reading Teacher* 31 (December 1977): 318–19.

[53] Johnson, p. 85.

[54] John D. McNeil, "Programed Instruction Versus Usual Classroom Procedures in Teaching Boys to Read," *American Educational Research Journal* 1 (March 1964): 113.

[55] Henriette M. Lahaderne, "Feminized Schools—Unpromising Myth to Explain Boys' Reading Problems," *The Reading Teacher* 29 (May 1976): 776–86.

[56] Wilder and Powell, pp. 19–20.

intriguing possibility. It is that "modality preferences during the early school years might feed into the development of different subject-matter skills at a later time."[57] This theory is based on a study by a researcher who identified individual differences among first- and second-grade children in how they took in information. The study discussed by Maccoby and Jacklin found that the "visual" children do better in reading, and the "auditory" children do better in arithmetic. The researcher of the study, however, does not report whether there are sex differences in the perceptual orientations he has identified.[58] (See Chapter 5 for information on visual and auditory factors and their effect on reading.)

PHYSICAL HEALTH

A child who is ill is not able to do well in school. This statement is obvious; however, it may not be obvious that a child is ill. A teacher should be alert for certain symptoms that may suggest a child is not well or not getting enough sleep. For example, a child who is listless, whose eyes are glazed, who seems sleepy, and who actually does fall asleep in class may need a physical checkup. The teacher should speak to the school nurse about such a child and also discuss the child's behavior with his or her parents.

The reason a child who is ill does not usually do well in school is not necessarily the child's illness but the child's frequent absence from school. Children who have illnesses that keep recurring are generally absent from school a lot. Moreover, the illnesses may be as mundane as the simple omnipresent cold. Such children should be seen by their doctor for a complete physical checkup to determine why they are so susceptible to colds. It may be that they are run-down or not eating the proper food.

The effects of nutrition, and particularly malnutrition, on learning are not new. Many studies have shown that children who are hungry and malnourished have difficulty learning because they cannot concentrate on the task at hand; they also lack drive. Some studies have suggested that severe malnutrition in infancy may lower children's IQ scores.[59] A number of researchers have found that the lack of protein in an infant's diet may adversely affect the child's ability to learn.[60] Other studies have found that food additives may be a deterrent to learning for certain children.[61]

[57] Maccoby and Jacklin, p. 35.

[58] Ibid.

[59] Merlin C. Wittrock, "Learning and the Brain," in Merlin C. Wittrock, ed., *The Brain and Psychology* (New York: Academic Press, 1980), pp. 376–77.

[60] Nevin S. Scrimshaw, "Infant Malnutrition and Adult Learning," *Saturday Review*, March 16, 1968, pp. 64–66, 84.

[61] Eleanor Chernick, "Effects of the Feingold Diet on Reading Achievement and Classroom Behavior," *The Reading Teacher* 34 (November 1980): 171–73.

A teacher should be cautious about making any diagnosis about a child's physical health. The teacher should also not make any inferences about a student's behavior unless she or he has sufficient evidence to warrant it. For example, if a child keeps putting his head on the desk, it may mean that he is frustrated or bored rather than ill or sleepy (see Chapter 10).

EDUCATIONAL FACTORS

Educational factors in learning, as stated earlier in this chapter, come under the domain or control of the educational system. Examples are approaches to instruction, methods and materials of instruction, instructional time, teachers, school environment, and so on. If a child is having a reading problem, it's generally a good idea for the teacher to check his or her school record to see if there is any information that might shed light on the child's problem. From the records, the teacher may be able to learn about the methods and materials the child has been exposed to in previous terms. It may be that these were not effective, and something different should be tried.

Educational factors extend beyond the individual school to the entire school district and the community. The values of the community will affect the kind of education that will take place in the schools. For a diagnostic-reading and correction program to be effective, teachers need the support of their principals and other administrative and supervisory staff, as well as the support of the community and parents (see Chapter 16).

Only a short section is being devoted to this area here for a number of reasons. First, it would be prohibitive in a book such as this to present in detail all the methods and materials used to teach reading and the reading approaches; these can be found in reading method books. Also, throughout this book, there are sections that discuss educational factors. For example, in Chapter 2, the teacher as the key to a good reading program is discussed, as well as instructional time and strategies; Chapter 5 presents various listening-thinking approaches; and the chapters in the last part of the book present important educational factors, as well as a review of important reading skills and strategies.

A FINAL WORD: HELPING AT-RISK CHILDREN

The significance of children's early years in reading achievement has been amply documented; however, this should not be used as an excuse for not helping children when they come to school. Rather than putting blame on social, political, and economic factors, over which teachers and children have little control, more should be done in the schools.

The importance of learning to read in the early grades cannot be overstated. The longer children remain nonreaders, the less likely are their chances to get up to their grade levels or their ability levels, even with the best remedial help. Underachievers in reading tend to have many emotional and social problems, and these are compounded as the child goes through school. Studies have shown that severe underachievement in reading appears to follow the individual all through life.[62]

Teachers want to help children to learn—that is their intent. Those teachers who cannot help students soon lose confidence in themselves, and their own self-concept is impaired. This feeling eventually gets picked up by their students.

At-risk students
Those students who because of their backgrounds or other factors are in danger of failing in school.

Today the term "at-risk" is being used to label children who are in danger of failing in school because they lack basic literacy skills. The surfacing of a new label, however, will not make the problems these children have go away. Labels can't do that! Efforts in the right direction can. Children who come from educationally disadvantaged homes need early identification and special programs beginning in kindergarten or preschool that emphasize the language arts. They need intervention as early as possible.

It is good that the at-risk label is focusing attention on the problems of these children; however, the term "at-risk" may itself have risks. Teachers "must take special care that the term 'at risk' is not used as a prediction of failure, that it does not become a negative label that perpetuates a self-fulfilling prophecy."[63]

SUMMARY

This chapter has presented a variety of educational and noneducational factors that may affect a child's reading performance. Many of these individual differences, such as home environment, family makeup, and culture, teachers can do nothing about. However, if teachers are aware that some of their children come from environments not conducive to learning, they will try to provide experiences in school to help these children become successful readers. Since reading is a thinking act, and since intelligence measures a person's ability to reason abstractly, it seems logical that the more intelligent an individual is, the better reader he or she should be. However, studies show that not all highly able students become good readers, and these results indicate that there are other factors besides intelligence that affect a student's ability to read. This chapter explores many of these other factors, one of which is gender differences.

[62] Diane Haines, *The Long-Term Consequences of Childhood Underachievement in Reading*, doctoral dissertation (Ann Arbor, Mich.: University Microfilms International, 1979).

[63] Linda Gambrell, guest ed., "Journal of Reading: A Themed Issue on Reading Instruction for At-risk Students," *Journal of Reading* 33 (April 1990): 485.

Many studies have found that there are more boys in remedial reading classes than girls. A number of reasons have been put forth for this phenomenon, one of the most greatly researched being cultural factors; another is biological or maturational factors.

This chapter also emphasizes the interrelatedness of language development, concept development, and reading. It is shown how a child with a problem in language will also have problems in acquiring concepts, and how this will affect a child's reading performance. All of the individual factors that are discussed in the chapter affect a child's language and concept development. The area of language development is the one in which educationally disadvantaged or at-risk young children are in need of help. A special section is presented on concept development because of its importance in the reading process. Knowledge of how children attain concepts and what they are is especially essential in a diagnostic-reading and correction program because teachers in such a program must recognize *early* when a child is lacking certain concepts and help that child attain them. Some informal techniques to assess a child's concept development are presented.

In addition, educational factors were discussed. Educational factors, which are defined as those factors that come under the domain or control of the school, include instructional time, the teacher, methods of instruction, materials of instruction, and so on. It is shown how noneducational factors can be influenced by educational ones and that there are a number of factors that overlap.

SUGGESTIONS FOR THOUGHT QUESTIONS AND ACTIVITIES

1. Explain why cultural factors have been suggested as an explanation for why there are more boys in remedial reading classes or with reading disabilities than girls.
2. How have researchers tried to refute the "cultural factors theory" about why there are more boys with reading problems?
3. You have been asked to give a talk to your colleagues about why there are more reading disabilities among boys than among girls in the United States. What will you say?
4. Why is *equilibrium* necessary in concept development?
5. Reread the cartoon (Fig. 4.3) presented on page 59. Give some other humorous examples similar to the one in the cartoon.
6. What should the teacher know concerning the relationship of language development, concept development, and reading?
7. Why may children who speak nonstandard English have more problems in school than children who speak a foreign language such as French or German?
8. Why would the community be considered an educational factor that could affect children's reading?

9. What is the relationship of intelligence to reading?
10. How can the physical health of a child affect his or her work at school?
11. Who are "at-risk" children?

SELECTED BIBLIOGRAPHY

Barnitz, John G. "Toward Understanding the Effects of Cross-Cultural Schemata and Discourse Structure on Second Language Reading Comprehension." *Journal of Reading Behavior* 18, no. 2 (1986): 95–116.

Bennett, Christine I. *Comprehensive Multicultural Education: Theory and Practice*, 2nd ed. Needham, Mass.: Allyn & Bacon, 1990.

Genishi, Celia. "Observing the Second Language Learner: An Example of Teacher's Learning." *Language Arts* 66 (September 1989): 509–15.

Grohens, Joe. "Nutrition and Reading Achievement." *The Reading Teacher* 41 (May 1988): 942–45.

Maccoby, Eleanor E., and Carol M. Jacklin. *The Psychology of Sex Differences*. Stanford, Calif.: Stanford University Press, 1974.

Piaget, Jean. *The Language and Thought of the Child*, New York: Harcourt, 1926.

Rigg, Pat, and Virginia G. Allen (Eds.). *When They Don't All Speak English: Integrating the ESL Student into the Regular Classroom*. Urbana, Ill.: National Council of Teachers of English, 1989.

Smith, Nila Banton. "Early Language Development: Foundation of Reading." *Elementary English* 52 (March 1975): 399–402; 418.

Sutton, Christine. "Helping the Nonnative English Speaker with Reading." *The Reading Teacher* 42 (May 1989): 684–88.

Vacca, Richard T. and Nancy D. Padak. "Who's at Risk in Reading?" *Journal of Reading* 33 (April 1990): 486–88.

Wilder, Gita Z., and Kristin Powell. "Sex Differences in Test Performance: A Survey of the Literature." College Board Report No. 89–3. Princeton, N.J.: Educational Testing Service, 1989.

Wong Fillmore, Lily, and Concepción Valadez. "Teaching Bilingual Learners." *Handbook of Research on Teaching*, 3rd ed. New York: Macmillan, 1986.

Woolfolk, Anita E. "The Mind at Work: Cognitive Development and Language," in *Educational Psychology*, 4th ed. Englewood Cliffs, N.J.: Prentice-Hall, 1990.

5

Visual and Auditory Factors and Their Effect on Reading

Scenario: David—A Child Who Wants to Learn to Read—Will He?

David is a quiet boy with an endearing smile. He is small in stature and not well dressed; he is determined to learn to read. Although he is in the fourth grade, David cannot read. "I want to read," he told his teacher. "My father bring one big book when he came home at night. He say it for me to read. I read. You see." David has hope, so he comes to school each day. But how much longer will he do so? Will he succeed in entering and mastering the land of books filled with those magic symbols called words? Will he unlock these symbols and discover the wonders of far-off places? David is waiting. Will we, as teachers, be able to help him?

The answer depends on how well we as teachers are equipped to diagnose the reading problems of the Davids in our classrooms and on our skill in developing a corrective program that helps them to read.

David's case aptly emphasizes the interrelatedness of the language arts and how difficulty in one facet will generally carry the problem over to another. If we ask why David, in the fourth grade, is not reading, his teacher claims

that he was tested the year before and was found to have impaired hearing. Digging into the problem further, we find that David had been "tested" by another teacher in the school, who knew little about the study of hearing. When David's teacher is asked if referrals had been made for more professional opinions and testing, we are told that it doesn't really pay to bother because all special personnel from the psychologist to the remedial reading teachers are overloaded, and the teacher would only be wasting his time.

By pinning the label "hearing impairment problem" on David the teacher is psychologically relieved of his responsibility. But David has not yet lost his determination to learn to read. He does not have a hearing problem. He has a language problem, which might be mistaken for a hearing impairment difficulty in the third or fourth grade. David comes from a home where Spanish is the dominant language. His parents and peers all converse in Spanish. The school he goes to has no formal program for helping him acquire English as a second language, and, unfortunately for David, he has not had teachers who were knowledgeable enough to help him. His teachers have allowed him to while away his time, and they consider themselves a success if David does not make a "fuss" in class.

David needs lots of help. He has trouble discriminating between sounds in English; therefore he needs help in auditory discrimination.

If David does not hear English words correctly, how can he be expected to say them correctly, or for that matter, read or write them? To David, many of the words in English are mere noises because the words are not in his listening vocabulary. David needs help in learning the English language.

This chapter will help you gain a better understanding of the relationship of visual and auditory factors to reading and of the role of both in the diagnostic-reading and correction program.

KEY QUESTIONS

After you finish reading this chapter, you should be able to answer the following questions:

1. How can perceptual factors interfere with reading success?
2. What are some symptoms that indicate a possible vision problem?
3. What should a teacher know about laterality and reading?
4. What should a teacher know about eye movements?
5. What is listening?
6. How is listening related to reading?
7. What are the levels of listening?
8. What factors influence the various listening levels?
9. What is the relationship of auditory discrimination to reading?
10. What is the directed listening/thinking approach?
11. What is a listening comprehension test?
12. How is question asking a key to active listening?
13. What is the relationship of a rich oral program to reading?
14. What are some standardized listening tests?

KEY TERMS IN CHAPTER

You should pay special attention to the following new terms:

astigmatism
auding
audiometer
auditory acuity
auditory discrimination
auditory fatigue
auditory memory span
binaurality
binocular vision
crossed dominance

decoding
directed listening/thinking
  approach
egocentric speech
eye movements
fixations
grapheme-phoneme
  correspondences
hearing
hypermetropia
laterality
listening
listening comprehension test
listening vocabulary
masking
mixed dominance
morpheme
myopia
phoneme
proximodistal development
regressions
reversals
saccades
visual discrimination

PERCEPTUAL FACTORS

In Chapter 1 the importance of perception (giving meaning to sensations) as part of the process of reading was discussed. It was stated that a child who has problems in the perceptual domain will most assuredly encounter difficulty in concept development and consequently in reading. The area of perception will be pursued further in this chapter as a significant factor affecting reading achievement.

Throughout this book it is stressed that reading is a complex process and that a reading difficulty is usually due to multiple causes rather than a single one. In learning to read, children need auditory and visual perceptual skills and such sensory-motor skills as eye-movement control for scanning the pages and finger control for turning them,[1] as well as the skills in language and concept development. For example, a child would have difficulty decoding if he or she has not achieved such skills as "discrimination, retention and

[1] Marianne Frostig, "Visual Modality—Research and Practice," in *Perception and Reading*, vol. 12, ed. Helen K. Smith, (Newark, Del.: International Reading Association, 1966–1967).

recall of sounds and letters, sequential ordering of phonemes and graphemes, and the ability to interrelate one with the other.[2]

VISUAL PERCEPTION

Since reading requires the sense of sight, it seems almost absurd to say that a visual deficit will influence a child's ability to read. However, a visual problem is not always obvious and, as a result, is not always detected. Most schools have some kind of visual screening that each child must undergo. The screening is generally done by the school nurse and often makes use of the Snellen chart. This chart uses line figures for young children and letters for those who can read letters; it tests acuity (keenness of vision). The test making use of the Snellen chart requires that the child stand twenty feet away from the chart with one eye covered. The child must identify letters of various sizes with each eye. A score of 20/20 is considered normal. A score of 20/40 or 20/60 means that a child has defective vision because the child with normal vision can see the letters at a distance of forty or sixty feet, whereas the child with defective vision can only see these letters at a distance of twenty feet.

Hypermetropia
Farsightedness; difficulty with close-up vision.

Astigmatism
A defect of vision that causes blurred vision.

Myopia
Nearsightedness; difficulty with distance vision.

The accuracy of the scores obtained from the Snellen chart has been questioned because the test does not detect moderate degrees of farsightedness (hypermetropia) or astigmatism, which causes blurred vision, and fails completely to detect even severe cases of poor fusion and eye-muscle imbalance.[3] The one defect it often discloses is nearsightedness (myopia). However, there are difficulties even with detecting nearsightedness because some children may memorize the chart and appear to have "normal" distance vision even though they do not.

Another problem with the Snellen chart is that school nurses are often unable to observe children's eye movements and features because the nurses usually have to point to the figures or letters they want the children to read.

A vision screening test that school nurses seem to like is the Insta-Line produced by the Good-Lite Company. They prefer this instrument over others because it is portable and because distance measurements are already done. One of its most positive features is that nurses are free to observe a child's eye movements and features. They can observe whether a child's eyes are crossed, whether the child is straining while reading, and whether the eyes are tearing, twitching, or squinting. They can also look for eye contractions, and so on.

---

[2] Joseph M. Wepman, "The Modality Concept—Including a Statement of the Perceptual and Conceptual Levels of Learning," in *Perception and Reading*, vol. 12, ed. Helen K. Smith, (Newark, Del.: International Reading Association, 1966–1967).

[3] Albert J. Harris and Edward R. Sipay. *How to Increase Reading Ability*, 9th ed. (New York: Longman, 1990), p. 347.

Figure 5.1 This child is being tested on the Titmus Vision Tester.

The Titmus Vision Tester is another instrument that school nurses use; however, it has a major defect in that examiners cannot observe a child's eye behavior during the testing because the child is looking into a machine at slides (see Figure 5.1). There are a number of more sophisticated eye survey tests that are available, but the function of the school nurse is to do preliminary screening for a possible problem, not to diagnose, so the money spent on these more sophisticated instruments might not be warranted.

The school nurse is an important part of every school team and plays a major role in helping to detect possible vision problems that could cause reading difficulties. When a school nurse suspects a possible visual problem, she should speak to the parents and recommend that they take their child to an eye doctor for a thorough examination.

Binocular Vision

Binocular vision
The ability to focus both eyes on a similar point of reference and see one object.

A few years ago, the writer asked the students in her class to take a simple test for binocular vision, the ability to focus both eyes on a similar point of reference and see one object. She asked them to hold up their forefinger at eye level at arm's length and then to look beyond the finger at some object. When they do so, they should see two fingers; that is, they will if they have done it correctly and if they have no problems with binocular vision. (The test proves that both eyes are in use.)

The further the finger is placed away from the eyes, the less separation of the fingers they should see. If it were possible to place the finger on the object they were looking at, they would see only one finger if both eyes are working together properly.

One young man in the class who was an athlete had difficulty seeing two fingers at arm's length. He was disturbed by this result and went to an ophthalmologist (eye specialist) to find out whether he had a problem. Fortunately for him, the cause of his problem was such that it was easily treatable.

It is important that children be checked for binocular vision because there are some conditions that cannot be treated effectively after a child is a certain age.

© 1972 United Feature Syndicate, Inc.

Figure 5.2 Charlie Brown has the right attitude concerning preliminary eye screening tests.

Since the emphasis in this book is on the teacher's ability to detect a possible vision problem, here is a listing of some symptoms that teachers should look for:

1. The child complains of constant headaches.
2. The child's eyes show some of the following: red rims, swollen lids, crusted lids, red eyes, frequent sties, watering eyes.
3. The child squints while reading.
4. The child asks to sit closer to the chalkboard.
5. The child can't seem to sit still while doing close work.
6. The child holds the book very close to his or her face while reading.
7. The child skips lots of words or sentences while reading.
8. The child makes many reversals while reading.
9. The child confuses letters.
10. The child avoids reading.
11. The child mouths the words or lip reads.
12. The child confuses similar words.
13. The child makes many repetitions while reading.
14. The child skips lines while reading.
15. The child has difficulty remembering what he or she just read silently.

If a teacher notices some of these symptoms, he or she should speak to the child's parents or refer the child to the school nurse. It is important to state, however, that the presence of one or more of the listed symptoms does not mean a child has an eye problem, nor does it mean that it is the cause of the child's reading problem if one exists.

Eye Movements

Eye movements
How the eyes appear to move in the act of reading.

Fixations
Stops readers make in the act of reading continuous text.

Regressions
Eyes move backward; they move back to reread material while in the act of reading continuous text.

Saccades
Quick, jerky movements of the eyes as they jump from one fixation to another in the reading of continuous text.

When we read, both our eyes are supposed to work together, but they do not go across the page in one smooth pattern. Studies show that as we read we make stops for minutely small periods of time that are measured in milliseconds (fixations); we go back to reread text (regressions); and we make small, rapid, jerky jumps as we move from one spot in a text to another (saccades). It is during fixations that we gain visual information from text material.

Mature readers have shorter fixations, longer and fewer saccades, and fewer regressions; the converse is true for beginning readers. Beginning readers "make more and longer fixations, shorter saccades, and more regressions than skilled readers."[4] Obviously, a beginning reader would have a slower reading rate than a more mature one. Also, it makes sense to say that a more difficult text would generally require more fixations, shorter saccades, and more regressions.

Visual Discrimination

Visual discrimination
The ability to distinguish differences and similarities between written symbols.

Visual discrimination is the ability to distinguish between written symbols. If pupils have difficulty discriminating between and among letters, they will not be able to read. In learning to read, children need to be able to make fine discriminations, and therefore need activities involving letters rather than geometric figures or pictures. Also, transfer of learning is greater if the written symbols children work with are similar to those they will meet in reading.

A visual discrimination test such as the following is excellent for discovering whether a child has some reversal problem:

Directions: Put a circle around the letters that are the same as the first in the line. (Read aloud the directions for children who cannot read.)

b   d b b d p b
p   d b d p b p

[4] Keith Rayner and Alexander Pollatsek, *The Psychology of Reading* (Englewood Cliffs, N.J.: Prentice-Hall, 1989), p. 386.

Directions: Put a circle around the numbers that are the same as the first in the line. (Read aloud the directions for children who cannot read.)

```
7   6  9  4  7  9  7
9   7  8  9  7  6  9
```

Directions: Put a circle around the words that are the same as the first in the line. (Read aloud the directions to children who cannot read.)

```
saw   was   saw   saw   was   won   now
won   now   won   won   now   not   won
```

Most reading readiness tests have a subtest on visual discrimination. (See Chapters 9 and 12 for examples of more visual discrimination tests.)

Laterality and Reading

Laterality
Refers to sidedness.

Crossed dominance
The dominant hand on one side and the dominant eye on the other.

Mixed dominance
No consistent preference for an eye, hand, or foot.

Reversals
Confusion of letters and words by inverting them; for example, *b = d, was = saw,* and vice versa.

Human perceptual-motor activity is usually initiated from the one dominant side of the body, even though humans are bilateral, or two-sided. By the time children enter school they generally show a fairly consistent preference for their right or left hand, as well as preferences in the use of eyes and feet. Such preferences concern laterality or sidedness. People are said to have a dominant side if their hand, eye, and foot preferences are similar. When people have a dominant hand on one side and a dominant eye on the other, they are said to have crossed dominance. Individuals who do not have a consistent preference for an eye, hand, or foot are said to have mixed dominance. (Often the term *mixed dominance* is used also for *crossed dominance.*) It has been hypothesized that children who have crossed or mixed dominance may tend to have reversal difficulties in reading and writing, but studies made in this area have not been definitive. Children with crossed dominance can perhaps shift from a left-handed orientation to a right-handed one in writing, but this change might cause difficulties for them.

Figure 5.3 Linus proves that "a little learning is a dangerous thing."

Proximodistal development
Muscular development from the midpoint of the body to the extremities.

No substantial evidence exists concerning cognitive deficits of left-handers[5]; however, a number of left-handers have orientation problems in reading and writing. To better understand the left-handed child's problem in reading and writing we must refer to proximodistal development—development from the midpoint of the body to the extremities. Right-handed children move their right hands from left to right naturally. Left-handed children find moving their left hand from left to right against their natural inclination.

Try this simple experiment to illustrate the point: Bring both hands to the center of your body. Now, move both hands out away from your body. The right hand will follow a left to right path corresponding to the English pattern of writing; the left hand follows a right to left path. Ask some left-handed persons to write a *t*. Observe carefully how they make the horizontal line. Most of them, unless they have been well conditioned, will draw the line from right to left.

Teaching reading is a complex task, and one of the things that the child learns is that in learning to read in English, he or she must read from left to right. This follows natural development for right-handed people. However, teachers must recognize that reading from left to right is not natural for left-handed children and must be alert for possible reversal problems.

A teacher can easily test whether a child has crossed or mixed dominance. To determine hand dominance, a teacher can observe which hand the child uses to throw a ball, write, or open a door. The teacher can tell which eye is dominant by observing which eye the child uses to look through a microscope, telescope, or an open cylinder formed by a roll of paper. Foot dominance can be easily determined by observing which foot the child uses to kick a ball or stamp on the floor with.

Teachers should be cautioned that crossed or mixed dominance in a child does not mean that the child will have a problem, although the possibility exists. The teacher should give special attention to those children who are having reversal problems by emphasizing left-to-right orientation for reading and writing.

The teacher should also try to determine whether the child's reversal problem was caused by not *overlearning*[6] the word or letter being reversed. Many times if the letters *b* and *d* are presented together or taught one after the other, a child who has not sufficiently learned the first letter will confuse it with the next one. Traditionally, it is recommended that teachers should not teach letters such as *b* and *d*, or numbers such as *6* and *9*, together or one after the other. However, some research has found that confusable letters such as *b/d*

---

[5] Merlin C. Wittrock, "Education and the Cognitive Processes of the Brain," *The National Society for the Study of Education 77th Yearbook*, Part II, 1978, p. 85.

[6] *Overlearning*, unlike overcooking, is not bad. The additional practice you engage in after you think you have mastered the material is called *overlearning*.

and *m/n* should be taught together to help students notice the slight differences between them.[7] If teachers decide to teach confusable letters together, they should stress the fine detail that differentiates one letter from another rather than just having students notice that the letters are different.

THE DEVELOPMENT OF LISTENING

"Listen! Listen to me!" Children want to be heard. Whether their parents spend time listening to them, and whether they encourage them to express themselves, will affect the kind of listening the children are able to do, as well as influence their oral expression.

By the time children come to school they have emerged from an egocentric view of the world, where everything they do and say concerns *me, my*, or *I*. In this egocentric world, children speak in parallel, in a collective monologue. They are not in the role of listeners, and so there is no communication. According to Piaget, the eminent Swiss psychologist, not until children need to be social do they need to become logical in their speaking.

Egocentric speech Child speaks in a collective mono- logue or primarily in parallel, that is, speech is not di- rected to another's point of view; con- cerned with own thoughts.

Read the following noncommunicative egocentric speech of a preschooler:

Mlle. L. tells a group of children that owls cannot see by day.
LEV: "Well, I know quite well that it can't."
LEV (at a table where a group is at work): "I've already done 'moon' so I'll have to change it."
Lev picks up some barley-sugar crumbs: "I say, I've got a lovely pile of eyeglasses."
LEV: "I say, I've got a gun to kill him with. I say, I am the captain on horseback. I say, I've got a horse and a gun as well."[8]

If children are to learn effectively in school, they must first learn to listen. Since they have spent their early childhood years in egocentric thought, they have not developed this skill adequately. When children come to school they participate in dialogue, which is a giving and receiving of ideas between two persons. Though they must listen, children still need someone to listen to them.

When Lev emerged from egocentric speech, he was able to engage in a communicative conversation with other children of his age:

PIE: (6.5) "Now you shan't have it [the pencil] because you asked for it."
HEI: (6.0) "Yes I will, because it's mine . . ."
PIE: "Course it isn't yours. It belongs to everybody, to all the children."
LEV: (6.0) "Yes, it belongs to Mlle. L. and all the children, to Ai and to My too."
PIE: "It belongs to Mlle. L. because she bought it, and it belongs to all the children as well."[9]

[7] Robert L. Hillerich, *Reading Fundamentals for Preschool and Primary Children* (Columbus, Ohio: Charles Merrill, 1977), pp. 57–58.
[8] Jean Piaget, *The Language and Thought of the Child* (London: Routledge & Kegan Paul, 1959), pp. 18–19.
[9] Ibid., p. 71.

Dialogue between children and their classmates and between teachers and children is very important to children's development of listening skills and in making their thinking more objective. Teachers should listen to children; observe them at play and work; introduce new materials and ideas to them; add information; raise questions; allow opportunities for children to raise questions as well; and *talk* with children about what they see, think, and feel. It is essential that teachers show they respect their pupils' ideas and act as models of "good listeners" for them. Children must have sufficient practice or "play" in the intake and outgo of language. Unless children are given ample opportunities to engage in listening and being listened to, they may not develop their listening ability adequately.

LISTENING AS DECODING

Decoding
Listening and reading are decoding processes involving the intake of language.

Phoneme
Smallest unit of sound in a specific language system.

Listening is the intake of language. The listener is involved in decoding a message from the speaker. The listener hears sound symbols which are called *phonemes*. These are analogous to the Morse code, for the listener must be able to decode the various sounds which stand for symbols. In order to decode, listeners must be able to hear differences between and among the various sounds of their language. If you were to ask a salesperson about the price of an item and were told fifty cents a pound, how could you be sure that the salesperson didn't say ninety cents a pound or five dollars a pound? You might say, "Because with my ears I heard that person say fifty cents rather than ninety cents. Fifty cents sounds *different* from ninety cents."

However, the buyer-listener might think he or she heard fifteen rather than fifty cents because of the similarity of the sounds. The emotional bias toward wanting to hear the lower price could also influence the listener.

Morpheme
The smallest individually meaningful element in the utterances of a language.

Phonemes have no meaning in themselves except as they are combined into a specific pattern to form a *morpheme*, which is the smallest word unit. Morphemes are combined into an arrangement which gives the sentence its unique meaning. The listener must be able to assimilate the flow of sound symbols into meaningful concepts or no communication can occur. If a listener heard the sentence: "I blibed the blob," the sounds cannot be assimilated into meaningful concepts because *blibed* and *blob* are nonsense words. Similarly, if listeners heard the delightful poem "Jabberwocky" recited by Alice in *Through the Looking-Glass*, they would be as perplexed as Alice was about its meaning. Read one stanza and see if you agree.

'Twas brillig, and the slithy toves
Did gyre and gimble in the wabe:
All mimsy were the borogoves,
And the mome raths outgrabe.

AUDITORY DISCRIMINATION AND MEMORY SPAN

Auditory discrimination
Ability to distinguish differences and similarities between sound symbols.

Auditory discrimination, which is the ability to distinguish between sounds, is essential for the acquisition of language and for learning to read. The essence of what speech clinicians have learned about auditory discrimination is summarized as follows:

1. There is evidence that the more nearly alike two phonemes are in phonetic (relating to speech sounds) structure, the more likely they are to be misinterpreted.
2. Individuals differ in their ability to discriminate among sounds.
3. The ability to discriminate frequently matures as late as the end of the child's eighth year. A few individuals never develop this capacity to any great degree.
4. There is a strong positive relation between slow development of auditory discrimination and inaccurate pronunciation.
5. There is a positive relationship between poor discrimination and poor reading.
6. Although poor discrimination may be at the root of both speech and reading difficulties, it often affects only reading or speaking.
7. There is little if any relationship between the development of auditory discrimination and intelligence, as measured by most intelligence tests.[10]

For children who speak a nonstandard dialect of English or for whom English is a second language, it is well to bear in mind that the acquisition of speech sounds for any given dialect is learned very early in life and is usually established by the time the child starts school. These children especially need help in auditory discrimination if they are to learn standard English (see Chapter 4).

Auditory memory span
Amount of information able to be stored in short-term memory for immediate use or reproduction.

Auditory memory span is essential for individuals who must judge whether two or more sounds are similar or different. In order to make such comparisons, the sounds must be kept in memory and retrieved for comparison. Auditory memory span is defined as "the number of discrete elements grasped in a given moment of attention and organized into a unity for purposes of immediate reproduction or immediate use."[11] A deficiency in memory span will hinder effective listening. (See Chapter 9 for a digit-span scale for determining how well children are doing in memory span.)

The *Wepman Auditory Discrimination Test*, which was developed by Joseph M. Wepman and published by Language Research Associates, is a norm-referenced test that teachers use to discern whether students have auditory discrimination problems. (This test is similar to the

---

[10] Joseph M. Wepman, "Auditory Discrimination, Speech and Reading," *Elementary School Journal* 60 (1960): 326.
[11] Virgil A. Anderson, "Auditory Memory Span as Tested by Speech Sounds," *American Journal of Psychology* 52 (1939): 95.

first test item of the informal auditory discrimination test presented in Chapter 9.) The teacher asks the student to turn around so that he or she cannot lip-read; then the teacher very distinctly pronounces each pair of words. The student must determine if the words are the same or different. There are two forms of the test, each one consisting of forty pairs of words.

Many of the reading diagnostic tests presented in Chapter 9, as well as many of the reading readiness tests presented in Chapter 7, have subtests that test a child's auditory discrimination.

Individual intelligence tests, such as the *Stanford-Binet* and the *Wechsler*, have subtests that measure an individual's memory span. These tests are called *Digits Forward* and *Digits Backward*. The individual is told to listen carefully, and then the examiner says some numbers at the rate of one per second. After the entire series of numbers has been given, the individual must repeat them in the exact order. For the *Digits Backward*, the individual must repeat the digits in reverse order after the examiner has stopped (see Chapters 9 and 14).

DIFFERENT LEVELS OF LISTENING[12]

Hearing
The lowest level in the hierarchy of listening; the physical perception of sound.

Listening
Middle of hierarchy of listening in which the individual becomes aware of sound sequences, and is able to identify and recognize the sound sequences as words.

Auding
Highest level of listening, which involves listening with comprehension.

In order to have a better understanding of the hierarchical and cumulative nature of listening, a discussion of the various levels of listening is necessary. *Hearing*, the lowest level in the hierarchy, refers to sound waves being received and modifie ' by the ear. Someone in the process of hearing physically perceives the presence of sounds but would not be able to make out what the sounds are; they would merely be noise. Hearing, being a purely physical phenomenon, cannot be taught.

Listening is in the middle of the hierarchy of listening,[13] in which individuals become aware of sound sequences. They are able to identify and recognize the sound sequences as known words, if the words are in their listening vocabulary.

Auding is at the highest level of the hierarchy and involves not only giving meaning to the sounds but assimilating and integrating the oral message. An individual at the auding level would be able to gather the main idea of a spoken passage, discern analogies and inferences, and perform all the other high-level comprehension skills that are usually associated with reading. Creative problem solving and critical listening are also skills included in this level. Although we are looking at each level as a separate entity, the act of listening is not divided into parts but functions as a whole.

[12] Stanford E. Taylor, *Listening: What Research Says to the Teacher* (Washington, D.C.: National Education Association, 1969).
[13] The term *listening* is usually used to refer to both listening, the middle level, and auding, the highest level of the hierarchy.

Factors Influencing Hearing—The Lowest Level

Auditory Acuity

Auditory acuity
Physical response of the ear to sound vibrations.

Auditory acuity is concerned with the physical response of the ear to sound vibrations. If individuals have organic ear damage, they will not be able to hear properly, if at all, depending on the extent of the damage. Auditory acuity is the ability to respond to various frequencies (tones) at various intensities (levels of loudness).

Human speech comprises frequencies ranging from 125 to 8,000 Hertz (Hz).[14] The intensity or loudness level found in everyday speech will range typically from 55 decibels (faint speech) to 85 decibels (loud conversation). When hearing is tested, a person's ability to hear is checked across the entire speech-frequency range. If persons require more than the normal amount of volume (db level) to hear sounds at certain frequencies, they are most probably exhibiting a hearing loss. The most critical frequencies for listening to speech lie in the frequency range between 1,000 and 2,500 Hertz because the majority of word cues are within this range. Frequencies above 2,500 Hertz contribute to the fineness with which we hear such sounds as /b, d, f, g, s, t, v, sh, th, zh/ (Webster's symbols).

Audiometer
An instrument used for measuring hearing acuity.

An audiometer is used by audiologists for precise measurement of hearing loss (see Figure 5.4). But teachers can make a lot of informal measurements on their own. Teachers can observe if any of the following behavior is present:

Does the child appear to be straining to push himself or herself closer to the speaker?
Does the child speak either very softly or very loudly?
Does the child have difficulty following simple directions?
Does the child turn up the sound of the record player or tape recorder?
Does the child have difficulty pronouncing words?
Does the child seem confused?

Although these questions could be posed for a number of other problems, a teacher should have the student checked for possible hearing loss if one or more of these symptoms are manifested.

Auditory Fatigue

Auditory fatigue
Temporary hearing loss due to a continuous or repeated exposure to sounds of certain frequencies.

Auditory fatigue is a temporary hearing loss caused by continuous or repeated exposure to sounds of certain frequencies. A monotonous tone or droning voice will have the effect of causing auditory fatigue. It has been shown that exposure to continuous loud noises over an extended period of time could be permanently harmful to an

---

[14] *Hertz* is the accepted international scientific word for cycles per second, named after the great nineteenth-century German physicist who proved the existence of electromagnetic waves.

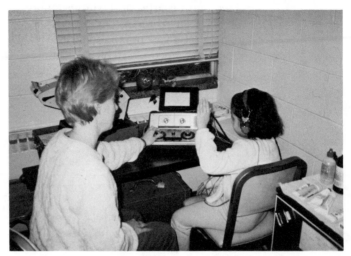

Figure 5.4 This child is being tested on the audiometer.

individual's hearing ability. Listening to music at a very high volume or being constantly exposed to cars and trucks rumbling through highway tunnels can have deleterious effects.

Binaurality
The ability of listeners to direct both ears to the same sound.

Binaural Considerations

When individuals are in the presence of two or more conversations, they must be able to direct their attention to only one of the speakers in order to be able to get the essence of what is being said. The more readily listeners are able to separate the sound sources, the more they will be able to grasp messages correctly. *Binaurality* thus refers to the ability of listeners to increase their reception sensitivity by directing both ears to the same sound.

Masking
Factor inhibiting hearing as sounds interfere with the spoken message.

Masking

Masking occurs when other sounds interfere with the message being spoken. Background noises drowning out a speaker or noisy classrooms or simultaneous group discussions will retard hearing ability.

Factors Influencing Listening—The Middle Level

Listening involves the way in which one identifies and recognizes sounds. Unless people are attentive to sounds, they will not understand their meaning, and meaning of sounds is an important part of listening. Sustained attention is concentration. If individuals are physically or mentally unwell, their chances for attending, and thus listening, are slim. Speakers play an important role in maintaining sustained attention. If they are boring, disliked, or unenthusiastic, they will not be as readily listened to as speakers who are interesting, liked, enthusiastic, and who use motivating techniques. Similarly, the physical environment of the classroom plays an important role in maintaining sustained attention. If the room is too hot or cold, if the chairs are uncomfortable, if there are provisions for writing, if the lighting is adequate and free of glare, if the acoustics are good, and if there are visual distractions—all these play a part in whether listening occurs.

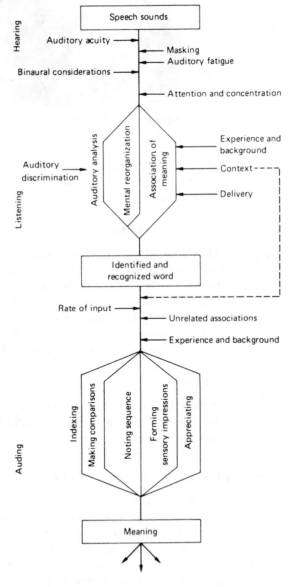

Figure 5.5 The total act of receiving auditory communication.

Factors Influencing Auding[15]—The Highest Level

Auding is the highest level of listening, as we have seen. It is not only the ability to discriminate between one word and another, or one syllable and another, but it also involves the individual's ability to assimilate the spoken message using the individual's total experience. The thinking skills used during auding are quite similar to those used during speaking, reading, and writing. Since the average speaking rate is 150 words per minute, the individual has time to formulate thoughts about what is being said, if what is being said is in the experience of the auditor. If the words are not in the listener's listening vocabulary, or if the topic is beyond the scope of his or her experiences, the listener will not understand what is being said. An individual who knows nothing about linguistics will have trouble comprehending an advanced lecture on this topic. A person with a background in linguistics may also have difficulty with the lecture if the words being used by the speaker are not familiar.

Figure 5.5[16] depicts the three stages of hearing, listening, and auding.

LISTENING AND READING

To be able to recognize expressions in print, students must have heard these phrases correctly in the past; they must be in the reader's listening vocabulary. Reading comprehension depends on comprehension of the spoken language. Students who are sensitive to the arrangement of words in oral language are more sensitive to the same idea in written language. Listening helps to enlarge a student's vocabulary. It is through listening that pupils learn many expressions they will eventually see in print. Listening takes place all the time. Teachers orally explain word meanings and what the text says. Students listen to other children read orally, talk about books, and explain their contents.

In the elementary grades, when children are learning to read, students of low and average achievement usually prefer to listen rather than to read independently. These children gain more comprehension and retention from listening because of the important added cues they receive from the speaker, such as stress given to words or phrases, facial expressions, and so on.[17] Children who are very able and who have had success in reading achievement prefer to read because these children can set their own rate of reading for

---

[15] *Auding* refers to the highest level of listening. It is defined as listening plus comprehension. The term *listening* is many times used to mean auding.

[16] Taylor, p. 5.

[17] Robert Ruddell, "Oral Language and the Development of Other Language Skills," *Elementary English* 43 (May 1966): 489–98.

maximum comprehension and retention. They do not wish to be constrained by the fixed oral rate of the teacher.

The case in which students can understand a passage when it is orally read to them, but cannot understand it when they read it themselves, indicates that the words are in the students' listening vocabulary but that they have not gained the skills necessary for decoding words from their written forms.

Listening Vocabulary
The number of different words one knows the meaning of when they are said aloud.

It may be that some words are in the children's listening vocabulary (for example, they know the meaning of the individual words when they are said aloud), but they still might not be able to assimilate the words into a meaningful concept. The instructor will have to help these children in concept development and in gaining the necessary reading comprehension and listening skills. A person who does not do well in listening comprehension skills will usually not do well in reading comprehension skills. Help in one area usually enhances the other because both listening and reading contain some important similar skills,[18] and researchers going as far back as the 1930s seem to support this view. For example, an investigation made in 1936 found that children who did poorly in comprehension through listening were also poor in reading comprehension.[19] Research in 1955 on the relationship between reading and listening found that practice in listening for detail will produce a significant gain in reading for the same purpose.[20] Other studies have also found that training in listening comprehension skills will produce significant gains in reading comprehension[21] and that reading and listening have similar thinking skills.[22]

Although there are many common factors involved in the decoding of reading and listening—which would account for the relationship between the two areas—listening and reading are, nonetheless, separated by unique factors. The most obvious is that listening calls for *hearing*, whereas reading calls for *seeing*. As has already been stated, in the area of listening, the speakers are doing much of the interpretation for the listeners by their expressions, inflections,

[18] Thomas Jolly, "Listen My Children and You Shall Read," *Language Arts* 57 (February 1980): 214–17.

[19] William E. Young, "The Relation of Reading Comprehension and Retention to Hearing Comprehension and Retention," *Journal of Experimental Education* 5 (September 1936): 30–39.

[20] Annette P. Kelty, "An Experimental Study to Determine the Effect of Listening for Certain Purposes upon Achievement in Reading for Those Purposes," *Abstracts of Field Studies for the Degree of Doctor of Education* 15 (Greeley: Colorado State College of Education, 1955): 82–95.

[21] Sybil M. Hoffman, "The Effect of a Listening Skills Program on the Reading Comprehension of Fourth Grade Students," Ph.D. dissertation, Walden University, 1978.

[22] Thomas Sticht et al., *Auding and Reading: A Developmental Model* (Alexandria, Va.: Human Resources Research Organization, 1974). Walter Kintsch and Ely Kozminsky, "Summarizing Stories After Reading and Listening," *Journal of Educational Psychology* 69 (1977): 491–99.

stresses, and pauses. Similarly, the listeners do not have to make the proper grapheme (letter)–phoneme (sound) correspondences because these have already been done for them by the speakers. It is possible for students to achieve excellent listening comprehension but not to achieve as well in reading.

Grapheme-phoneme correspondences
Letter-sound relationships.

Readers must first make the proper grapheme-phoneme correspondences and must then organize these into the proper units to gain meaning from the words. Readers must also be able to determine the shades of meaning implied by the words, to recognize any special figures of speech, and finally to synthesize the unique ideas expressed by the passage.

The relationship between listening and reading ability is succinctly summarized by these four rules:

1. When auding ability is low, reading ability more often tends to be low.
2. When auding ability is high, reading ability is not predictable.
3. When reading ability is low, auding ability is not predictable.
4. When reading ability is high, auding ability is, to a very small extent, predictable—and likely to be high.[23]

THE EFFECT OF A RICH ORAL PROGRAM IN DEVELOPING READING SKILLS

A number of studies[24] have found that children who speak nonstandard English make significant gains toward standard English when they are involved in a rich oral program, one that stresses the reading aloud of stories and the active involvement of the children in related oral activities. Teachers, beginning in kindergarten, should plan a program for linguistically different children that should include regular and continuous listening to storybooks based on their students' interest and concept development levels. Speech-stimulating activities such as choral speaking, creative drama, discussion, storytelling, and so on should follow the story so that the children can have an opportunity to express themselves.

A rich oral program is a necessary first step to prevent reading failure because it helps prepare the children for reading. The closer the children's language is to the written symbols encountered in reading, the greater their chance of success. Hearing standard English in the context of something meaningful with which they can identify helps the children to gain "facility in listening, attention span,

[23] John Caffrey, "The Establishment of Auding-Age Norms," *School and Society* 70 (November 12, 1949): 310.

[24] Dorothy Strickland, "A Program for Linguistically Different Black Children," Eric #ED 049 355, April 22, 1971. Bernice E. Cullinan, Angela M. Jagger, and Dorothy Strickland, "Language Expansion for Black Children in the Primary Grades: A Research Report," *Young Children* 29 (January 1974): 98–112.

narrative sense, recall of stretches of verbalization, and the recognition of new words as they appear in other contexts."[25] (See Chapter 15.)

Of course, a rich oral program is important for all children. Studies suggest that listening to stories read aloud helps all children increase their vocabulary, even if the story is not accompanied with teacher explanation of word meanings.[26]

Figure 5.6 This child is following along as she listens to a story read aloud.

Reading a Story Aloud to Young Children (Preschool and Kindergarten)

Answer the following statements true or false:

1. Anyone who can read knows how to properly read a story aloud to children.
2. Children should not say a word while the story is read.

If you answered both "false," you are correct.

Reading a story aloud to young children can be a wonderful interactive learning experience if it is done properly. Here are a few steps that will help ensure success.

Preparing for the Story

1. Choose a short storybook that is at the attention, interest, and concept-development levels of the children and that has large pictures that can be easily seen.

[25] Dorothy H. Cohen, "The Effect of Language on Vocabulary and Reading Achievement," *Elementary English* 45 (February 1968): 217.

[26] Warwick B. Elley, "Vocabulary Acquisition from Listening," *Reading Research Quarterly* 24 (spring 1989): 174–87.

2. Have the young children sit comfortably and in a position that allows them to see the pictures easily.
3. Make sure there are no distractions to attract their attention.
4. State the title and show the book to the children. Ask them if they can figure out what the story will be about from the title.
5. Tell them to listen carefully for certain things. (Of course, this will be based on the story being read.)

Reading the Story

Read the story aloud to the children. Stop at key points and have them predict what will happen or have them state the refrain if the story contains one. You can state more questions for them to think about while they are listening to the story. If they interject comments during the story, you should acknowledge these, say "good thinking," if it shows they are thinking, and then continue reading.

After the Story

When the story is finished, you could have the children answer some of the unanswered questions and do some of the following based on their attention and interest levels:

a. Tell what the story is about.
b. Retell the story in sequence.
c. Discuss whether the story is based on fantasy or reality.
d. Act out the story.
e. Make up another ending for the story.

Figure 5.7 This teacher reads many stories to the children in her class.

QUESTION ASKING: A KEY TO ACTIVE LISTENING

Question asking is a key way to help students become more active and better listeners. Teachers need to learn to ask questions that require interpretive, critical, and creative thinking rather than merely literal thinking. Here are examples of questions at the various listening/thinking comprehension levels.

Literal Comprehension (Based on Information Directly Stated)

What is the pet's name?
How old is John?
Where do the Joneses live?

Interpretive Comprehension (Based on Information That Is Implied Rather Than Directly Stated)

What is the speaker's central idea?
What do you think will happen next?
How do you think the talk will end?
What conclusions can you draw from the talk?
Compare this speaker's views with the one we heard previously.
What figures of speech did the speaker use?

Critical Comprehension (Based on the Passing of Personal Judgment on the Accuracy, Truthfulness, and Value of Something)

State three propaganda tactics the speaker used.
Was the speech based on fact or fiction? (Support your answer with facts.)
How objective was the speaker?
Explain whether you think what the speaker said could actually happen.
What are your feelings toward the speaker?

Creative Comprehension (Based on Going Beyond the Presented Information to Come up with Alternate Solutions)

What would you have done in that situation?
Think of another way to end this talk.
How else would you state this?
What other positions could you take?

Teachers should also invite students to ask relevant questions during and after a talk. Also, after the talk, some students can be asked to summarize the talk orally, as well as the questions asked.

Student Questioning

Students need to be helped to learn how to ask challenging questions of their own so that they can be more active listeners. Here are some

Figure 5.8 Jennifer knows that asking questions is an important part of learning.

techiques teachers can use to give students practice in formulating questions:

1. "The Question-Only Strategy"[27] can be adapted for use with intermediate-grade level students to help them learn the value of asking good questions. This strategy has four steps and one optional step. Step 1 prepares the students for the activity; the teacher states a topic and explains the rules of the interaction. The students are the question askers and the teacher is the answerer. The teacher will answer only those questions that the students ask; then a test will be given that will cover all the material that the teacher feels is important about the topic whether the students have asked the questions or not. Step 2 is the interaction; Step 3 is the test, and after the test is a discussion of the questions that were asked and those that should have been asked. Step 4 requires the students to listen to a short lecture to acquire the information they failed to attain through their questions. The last step, which is optional, is a follow-up test.

2. Suchman's inquiry method is also a good technique to make students better question askers. This technique requires students to ask questions in the form of hypotheses to solve a problem. The teacher answers only "Yes" or "No." If students formulate enough correct question hypotheses, they will subsequently arrive at the correct solution or conclusion.

[27] Anthony D. Manzo, "Three Universal Strategies in Content Area Reading and Languaging," *Journal of Reading* 24 (November 1980): 148.

THE DIRECTED LISTENING/THINKING APPROACH

Directed listening/ thinking approach
Requires teachers to ask questions before, during, and after a talk; consists of a number of steps; requires students to be active participants.

The directed listening/thinking approach requires teachers to ask questions before, during, and after a talk. The steps in this approach are as follows:

Step 1: Preparation for talk, lecture, audiotape, or film. Teacher relates to students past experiences, gives an overview of talk, presents any special vocabulary and questions at various difficulty levels that students should try to answer while listening to the talk.

Step 2: Students listen to presentation. During the presentation, the teacher stops, asks students to answer some of the previously given questions, and interjects some more thought-provoking questions to guide students.

Step 3: After the presentation. The children answer unanswered questions and are presented with some more challenging questions. In addition, the teacher asks for the central idea of the talk, as well as a short summary of it.

Step 4: The teacher asks students to devise some good questions that he or she could use as test questions.

CLASSROOM TEACHERS' ASSESSMENT OF LISTENING COMPREHENSION SKILLS

Listening comprehension test
Given to assess a child's comprehension through listening; same as a listening capacity test; it helps estimate a student's reading potential.

The informal assessment is not concerned with determining organic ear malfunctions. If a teacher feels that a student is having difficulty that might be physiological, he or she should go through the proper referral procedures and inform the principal, school nurse, and parents so that the child can be properly diagnosed by professionally trained personnel. Many times a child is diagnosed as having a "hearing impairment" problem and perceptual learning problems when the difficulty is not due to physiological factors but to experiential ones.

In order to determine the student's level of listening at the auding level, the teacher could easily develop a diagnostic instrument by choosing paragraphs based on the student's concentration and vocabulary ability according to grade levels. The selections can vary in length from grades one to six. A grade-one selection would be approximately 50 words, whereas a grade-six selection would be approximately 150 words. The teacher reads aloud the selections and then asks questions based on them. The number of comprehension questions asked would depend on the specific grade level or ability levels of students. For the first grade the teacher could ask three or four questions, whereas in sixth grade, six or seven questions could be asked. The questions asked should include interpretive and critical comprehension questions as well as literal ones. From these tests the teacher can determine whether there is a listening problem common to all students or just to a few. (See Chapter 8 for a discussion of listening capacity level and listening capacity tests.)

STANDARDIZED LISTENING TESTS

There are many different kinds of standardized tests that have listening subtests. For example, the *PRI Reading Systems*, published by CTB/McGraw-Hill, is a criterion-referenced test, which has an oral comprehension test at Level A (prekindergarten to first grade) and at Level B (first to second grade). The tests measure literal and inferred meaning.

The third edition of the *Sequential Tests of Educational Progress* (STEP III), which is published by Educational Testing Service (ETS) and distributed by McGraw-Hill, is a norm-referenced achievement test battery that includes listening subtests in its four CIRCUS levels (A to D) for the preprimary and early primary grades.

The *Stanford Achievement Test Series*, 8th ed. (1989), published by the Psychological Corporation, also includes subtests on listening vocabulary and listening comprehension skills at grades K.0–9.9.

The *California Achievement Tests/Listening Test* (1985), published by McGraw-Hill, assesses direction-following ability and interpreting oral discourse.

The Primary Battery, grades K–3 (Levels 5–8), of the *Iowa Tests of Basic Skills*, published by the Riverside Publishing Company (1990), contains a listening subtest that assesses children's comprehension of orally presented material. The specific areas measured are literal comprehension, inferential meaning, concept development, following directions, linguistic and numerical/spatial relationships, understanding sequence, predicting outcomes, and attention span. (An optional listening test is available for the Multilevel Edition, grades 3–9 [Levels 9–14].)

The *Durrell Analysis of Reading Difficulties*, 3rd ed., published by the Psychological Corporation, is a diagnostic reading test that includes both a listening comprehension subtest and a listening vocabulary subtest. "The purpose of this test is to provide an estimate of the child's reading capacity as indicated by his or her ability to understand paragraphs that are read aloud by the examiner."[28] The purpose of the listening vocabulary test is "to assess the child's listening vocabulary as a second index . . . of the child's reading capacity."[29]

There are very few tests available that measure only listening skills. One such test is the *Brown-Carlsen Listening Comprehension Test*. (Note, however, that it is a test for older students.) Here is a description of it:

> *Brown-Carlsen Listening Comprehension Test* by James I. Brown, G. Robert Carlsen; © 1953, 1955; Grades 9–13 and Adults; published by Communication Development, Inc. The test measures five important listening

---

[28] Donald D. Durrell and Jane Catterson, *Durrell Analysis of Reading Difficulty Manual of Directions* (New York: Psychological Corporation, 1980), p. 22.

[29] Ibid., p. 26.

skills: immediate recall, following directions, recognizing transitions, recognizing word meanings, and lecture comprehension.

Most informal reading inventories have listening capacity (listening comprehension) tests. (See Chapter 8 for an in-depth discussion of these. Also, Chapter 9 presents some informal digit-span tests that measure concentration ability, and Chapter 14 includes information on how to increase concentration and direction-following ability.)

Special Note

A listening comprehension test helps estimate a student's reading potential; however, if the student has some hearing problem, the test would not be an accurate estimate of that student's reading potential. Obviously, any hearing impairment would invalidate any type of listening test given to assess comprehension or concentration.

The *Detroit Tests of Learning Aptitude* have an oral direction test that measures auditory attentive ability, practical judgment, motor ability, and visual attentive ability. You can use this test as a diagnostic procedure to determine your students' concentration ability. The procedures for administering the test, the listening sheet, the scoring scale, and the norms for the test follow.

Oral Directions Test

General Directions[30]

Place the sheet before the subject. Give the directions for each set *slowly* and *very clearly* without special emphasis on any word or phrase. Be sure that the subject waits until the directions for a given set are *completed* before he or she is permitted to start. Say: "You see this page. I am going to tell you some things to do with what you see on this page. Now, listen carefully, and each time, after I get through, you do just exactly what I have said to do. Be sure to wait each time until I finish and say, 'Do it now.' Look at Number 1. It has three drawings." [Point to all three drawings on the pupil's sheet. Pause.]

Give directions for each set as indicated below. Say, "Stop" at the end of each time allowance. Any set must be entirely correct for credit.

It is best to call attention to the next set by saying, "Look at Number 2," "Look at Number 3," and so on throughout the test. Continue through three successive failures.

---

[30] *Detroit Tests of Learning Aptitude—Oral Directions* (Indianapolis, Ind.: Bobbs-Merrill, 1967).

Instructions

Time allowance is 10 seconds each for Numbers 1–6 inclusive.

1. Put a one in the circle and a cross in the square box. Do it now!

2. Draw a line from the thimble to the star that will go down under the comb and up over the hammer. Do it now!

3. Be sure to wait until I get all through. Draw a line from the rabbit to the ball that will go up over the fish, and put a cross on the fish. Do it now!

4. See the three circles. Put a number two in the first circle, a cross in the second circle, and draw a line under the third circle. Do it now!

5. Draw a line from the bottom of the first circle to the top of the second and put a cross in the second circle. Do it now!

6. Put a three in the part that is in the large box only and a cross in the part that is in both boxes. Do it now!

Time allowance is 15 seconds each for Numbers 7, 8, and 9.

7. This drawing is divided into parts. Put a number one in the biggest part, a number two in the smallest part, and a three in the last part. Do it now!

8. Draw a circle around the pig, a line under the apple, and make a cross on the cow. Do it now!

9. Draw a line under the letter *F*. Cross out the letter *K*, and draw a line above *O*. Do it now!

Time allowance is 20 seconds each for Numbers 10, 11, and 12.

10. Cross out the number that is three times five, cross out every number that is in the thirties, and cross out the largest number. Do it now!

11. Put the first letter of the first word in the first circle, the second letter of the first word in the second circle, the last letter of the first word in the fourth circle, and the last letter of the last word in the last circle. Do it now!

12. Put a cross in the big square, a letter *F* in the triangle, a number four in the little square, and a letter *H* in the first circle. Do it now!

Time allowance is 30 seconds each for Numbers 13–17 inclusive.

13. Cross out a number that is eight times eight, the number one less than one hundred, the number that is five times five, the number in the fifties, and the fourth number in the line. Do it now!

14. Put the last letter of the second word in the third circle, the first letter of the third word in the fifth circle, and the second letter of the first word in the last circle. Do it now!

15. Draw a line under the letter after *S*, cross out *J* and *V*, and draw a line over the first letter before *O*. Do it now!

16. Put the third letter of the alphabet in the third figure, a six in the diamond, the letter *L* in the first circle, a number four in the

triangle, and the first letter of the alphabet in the last figure. Do it now!

17. Cross out the even number in a square, the odd number in the second triangle, the number in the third circle, the biggest number that is in a square, and the number in a circle before twelve. Do it now!

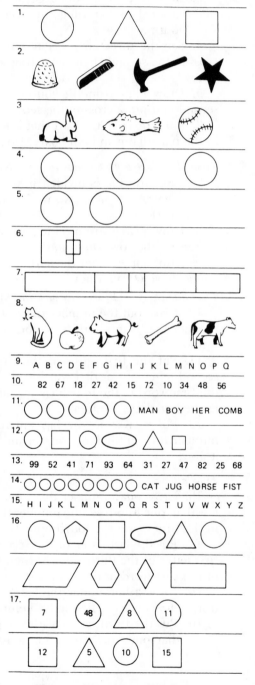

Scoring Scale*

Items 1–6, 1 point each
Items 7–9, 2 points each
Items 10–13, 3 points each
Items 14–17, 4 points each
Maximum score: 40 points

Norms

M.A. (Mental Age)	Oral Directions	M.A. (Mental Age)	Oral Directions
5-0		12-0	12
5-3		12-3	13
5-6		12-6	13
5-9		12-9	14
6-0		13-0	14
6-3		13-3	15
6-6	1	13-6	16
6-9	2	13-9	16
7-0	2	14-0	17
7-3	3	14-3	18
7-6	3	14-6	19
7-9	4	14-9	20
8-0	4	15-0	21
8-3	5	15-3	22
8-6	5	15-6	23
8-9	6	15-9	24
9-0	6	16-0	25
9-3	7	16-3	26
9-6	7	16-6	27
9-9	8	16-9	28
10-0	8	17-0	29
10-3	9	17-3	30
10-6	9	17-6	31
10-9	10	17-9	32
11-0	10	18-0	33
11-3	11	18-3	34
11-6	11	18-6	35–36
11-9	12	18-9	37–38
		19-0	39–40

* To receive credit, the student must have *everything* in the set correct.

Student's Name:_____

Grade:_____

Teacher:_____

Diagnostic Checklist for Listening

Part One: Listening (Organic)

Symptoms	Observation Dates				
The child					
1. is absent due to ear infection.					
2. speaks very softly.					
3. speaks very loudly.					
4. speaks in a monotone.					
5. complains of noises in head.					
6. turns head to one side to hear.					
7. reads lips while listening.					
8. asks to have things repeated.					
9. cups hand behind ear to listen.					

Part Two: Auditory Discrimination

	Yes	No
The child		
1. can state whether sets of words are similar or different.		
2. can state whether words begin with the same initial sound.		
3. can state whether words end with the same sound.		
4. can state whether words rhyme.		
5. can give the letter that stands for the first sound heard in presented words.		
6. can give the two letters that stand for the first two sounds heard in presented words.		
7. can give the two letters that stand for the first sound heard in presented words.		
8. can give the letter that stands for the last sound heard in presented words.		

Part Three: Listening Concentration

	Yes	No
The child		
1. is able to repeat sets of digits forward.		
2. is able to repeat sets of digits backward.		
3. is able to follow orally presented sets of directions.		

Part Four: Listening Comprehension*

	Yes	No
1. Literal listening. The child, after listening to a passage, can answer questions that relate to information explicitly stated in the passage.		

Student's Name:_____

Grade:_____

Teacher:_____

Diagnostic Checklist for Listening (Cont.)

2. Interpretive listening. The child, after listening to a
   passage, can answer questions dealing with
   a. finding the main idea.
   b. generalization.
   c. "reading between the lines."
   d. conclusions.
   e. cause–effect relationships.
   f. multiple meanings.

3. Critical listening. The child, after listening to a
   passage, can answer questions dealing with
   a. propaganda.
   b. fact or opinion.
   c. fantasy or reality.
   d. objectivity or subjectivity.

4. Creative listening. The child, after listening to a
   passage, can answer questions dealing with divergent thinking.

Part Five: Listening for Appreciation

	Yes	No
The child voluntarily chooses to listen to records, tapes, and so on.		

*The length and difficulty of the selection used are determined by the grade level and the readiness of the indi-
vidual child. Also, this is not an inclusive list of listening comprehension skills.

SUMMARY

Chapter 5 explores some of the perceptual factors that could affect
the child's reading performance. Practical information is given for
classroom teachers about how they could detect the presence of a
possible vision problem. The subject of laterality and its possible
influence on reading is also discussed, and simple tests are provided
which can help a teacher detect whether a child has crossed dominance.

Chapter 5 is also concerned with the relationship of listening to reading. Since the language arts (listening, speaking, reading, and writing) are interrelated, a problem in one area will usually carry over to another. Listening is the foundation of the language arts and closely related to reading; therefore, it deserves special attention. Auditory discrimination, which is the ability to distinguish between sounds, is essential for the acquisition of language and for learning to read. Auditory memory span is important for individuals to make comparisons of sounds. In order to make such comparisons, the sounds must be kept in memory and retrieved for comparison. Tests to assess these abilities were discussed. The hierarchical nature of listening, which includes hearing, listening, and auding, was presented as well as the factors that influence each level. In order to be able to recognize expressions in print, students must have heard these phrases correctly before; they must be in the reader's listening vocabulary. Reading comprehension depends on comprehension of the spoken language. Children need to be involved in dialogue so that they can develop their listening skills.

Techniques for developing classroom teacher assessments of listening comprehension were presented, as well as examples of standardized listening tests and a diagnostic checklist.

SUGGESTIONS FOR THOUGHT QUESTIONS AND ACTIVITIES

1. Develop a listening comprehension test suitable for primary-grade children.
2. Construct a listening comprehension test suitable for intermediate-grade students.
3. You have been asked to present a talk on the listening program in your school. Develop a talk for a hypothetical school. Present what you think a good listening program should have, and give reasons why.
4. Explain how a teacher can provide an environment conducive to listening.
5. You have been put on a committee to assess the listening program in your school. What are some of the things you would suggest to look at?
6. Explain how listening is related to reading.
7. State five symptoms suggesting that a child has a vision problem.
8. Explain crossed dominance.

SELECTED BIBLIOGRAPHY

Cohen, Alice, and Gerald G. Glass. "Lateral Dominance and Reading Ability." *The Reading Teacher* 21 (January 1968): 343–48.

Funk, Hal D., and Gary D. Funk. "Guidelines for Developing Listening Skills." *The Reading Teacher* 42 (May 1989): 660–63.

Hall, Edward T. "Listening Behavior: Some Cultural Differences." *Phi Delta Kappan* 50 (1969): 379–80.

Jolly, Thomas. "Listen My Children and You Shall Read." *Language Arts* 57 (February 1980): 214–17.

Leong, Che Kan. "Laterality and Reading Proficiency." *Reading Research Quarterly* 15 (1980): 185–202.

Rayner, Keith, and Alexander Pollatsek. *The Psychology of Reading*. Englewood Cliffs, N.J.: Prentice-Hall, 1989.

Rubin, Dorothy. "Aural Responsiveness: Listening," in *Teaching Elementary Language Arts*, 4th ed. Englewood Cliffs, N.J.: Prentice-Hall, 1990.

Strother, Deborah B. "Practical Applications of Research on Listening." *Phi Delta Kappan* 68 (April 1987): 625–28.

6

Who Is Underachieving in Reading?

INTRODUCTION

Read the following conversation between two teachers in the teachers' lounge:

Mr. Brown: I have some questions about two different students in my class. Jim scored two grade levels below his present grade level on a standardized reading achievement test. How do I determine whether he's underachieving or not, since he is a slow learner? Also, David is supposed to be gifted according to a group IQ test, but he's only reading at grade level. Isn't he underachieving? Maybe there's something wrong with the tests.

Ms. Grant: Good questions. I know that there are supposed to be formulas to help you to figure out which child is underachieving, but are they really any good? I never know which students need further testing.

Many teachers have questions and concerns similar to Mr. Brown's and Ms. Grant's. After you finish reading this chapter, you will be able to help Mr. Brown and Ms. Grant answer their questions, as well as the ones that follow.

KEY QUESTIONS

After you finish reading this chapter, you should be able to answer the following questions:

1. What does underachievement in reading mean?
2. Who is a disabled reader?
3. What is intelligence?

4. How is intelligence measured?
5. What are the major differences between individual and group intelligence tests?
6. What is a diagnostic pattern?
7. What are reading expectancy formulas?
8. What is a listening capacity test?
9. What is appraisal?

KEY TERMS IN CHAPTER

You should pay special attention to the following new terms:

appraisal
diagnostic pattern
disabled reader
dyslexia
halo effect
identification
intelligence
intelligence quotient (IQ)
mental age (MA)
motivation
reading expectancy formula
underachievement

WHAT IS A DIAGNOSTIC PATTERN?

Throughout this book it is emphasized that appropriate instruction stems from and is interwoven with accurate and pertinent diagnostic information for each child in the regular classroom. It is also stressed that diagnosis is ongoing and is necessary for prevention as well as for correction and remediation. In a diagnostic-reading and correction program the teacher is interested in determining the student's reading strengths and weaknesses, as well as the conditions causing them, as soon as possible so that any emerging reading difficulty can be nipped in the bud. To do this the teacher must first *identify* the student's present level of performance in word recognition and comprehension by using both standardized reading achievement tests and classroom tests for screening purposes (see Chapter 7). The teacher must then *appraise* the student's present level of reading performance in relation to his or her potential. The appraisal is done to determine if there is a discrepancy between the student's present reading performance and the student's reading potential, which is calculated by a reading expectancy formula (see "Who Is a Disabled Reader?" in this chapter). After appraisal, if a discrepancy exists between a student's present reading status and his or her reading expectancy, the teacher does extensive and intensive *diagnosis*. Step 3 is done to determine in detail the student's specific strengths and

Identification
Part of diagnostic pattern; the act of determining the student's present level of performance in word recognition and comprehension for screening purposes.

Appraisal
Part of diagnostic pattern; a student's present reading performance in relation to his or her potential.

Diagnostic pattern
Consists of three steps: identification, appraisal, and diagnosis.

weaknesses, as well as to discover the specific conditions and abilities that underlie the student's performance in a particular reading area. Then the teacher must help that student to set attainable goals in the area. Identification, appraisal, and diagnosis are the three steps in a diagnostic pattern.[1] This chapter is concerned with step 2—that of appraisal. Step 2 helps the teacher to determine which children are underachieving in reading.

WHO IS A DISABLED READER?

Underachievement
Achievement below one's ability level.

It is not inconceivable to have a sixth-grade class with a span of reading levels ranging from third grade to eighth grade or above. The teacher in such a class must determine who the disabled readers are. Not all students working below grade level are underachievers. A child reading at a third-grade level in a sixth-grade class may be reading at his or her ability level, whereas another child may not be. Similarly, children reading at their grade levels may be reading far below their ability levels. A teacher may be pleased that a pupil is working on grade level, but gifted children working on grade level are *not* working up to their ability levels. A gifted child working on grade level is "underachieving." However, a child with a 70 IQ in the third grade working at the second-grade level would be achieving at his or her reading expectancy level. The reading expectancy scores presented in Table 6.2 for the Bond and Tinker formula on page 138 are "idealized" ones; that is, there are many other variables that affect ability to read than just the intelligence of an individual. Usually a child with a 70 IQ on an individual IQ test would be working more than one year below grade level. Since a child with a 70 IQ would usually not be able to work in the abstract, that child would have difficulty in doing reading skills involving inferences, analogies, and so on. (See Chapter 15 for information on borderline or slow-learning children.)

Disabled reader
A reader who is reading below his or her ability level.

From this discussion, it can be seen that a disabled reader may be any student who is reading below his or her ability level; a disabled reader is one who is underachieving.

Special Note

The term *dyslexia* is a very confusing one because it is used in so many different ways by so many different people. The medical profession uses it in one way, psychologists in another, educators in another, and the public in still another way.

In the past *dyslexia* referred to any person who had word blindness; that is the person could not recognize printed words on the page; it is usually not used in this way today. Definitions range from severe

---

[1] The terms are adapted from Ruth Strang, *Diagnostic Teaching of Reading*, 2nd ed. (New York: McGraw-Hill, 1969).

reading disability of unspecified origin to any reading problem regardless of severity or cause. Often the general public uses the term in the latter sense, perhaps because dictionaries such as *Webster's Third New International Dictionary* define *dyslexia* as "a disturbance in the ability to read."

Dyslexia
Severe reading disability.

Professionals usually reserve the use of this word for those persons who have severe reading difficulties and who are at least of average intelligence. It is beyond the scope of this book to deal with an individual classified as dyslexic—that is, someone with a very severe reading difficulty.

INTELLIGENCE

Since most reading expectancy formulas are based on intelligence quotients, it is important to know what intelligence is and what intelligence tests measure.

It is difficult to pick up a newspaper, journal, or magazine without finding some reference to achievement or intelligence. Usually when intelligence—specifically an intelligence test—is brought up, the atmosphere becomes highly charged. Hardly anyone seems to regard IQ objectively.

Intelligence
Ability to reason abstractly; problem-solving ability based on a hierarchical organization of two things—symbolic representations and strategies for processing information.

Intelligence refers to the ability to reason abstractly or to solve problems. Since intelligence is a construct—that is, it is something that cannot be directly observed or directly measured—testing and research have necessitated an operational definition. Such a definition coined in the early part of the century is still much quoted: "Intelligence is what the intelligence test measures."[2] There are a variety of tests designed to measure intelligence, yet no test exists that actually does. In other words, intelligence tests cannot adequately determine an individual's absolute limits or the potential of the intelligence. Yet many persons, both lay and professional, actually behave as if the intelligence test will tell all.

This state of affairs may be due to the nature-nurture controversy. Advocates of the nature side believe that heredity is the sole determiner of intelligence, and that no amount of education or the quality of the environment can alter it. Those who believe in the nurture side claim that intelligence is determined in great part by the environment. For them, intelligence can be affected if the child is exposed to different environments and education. Most professionals take an in-between position, saying that differences in intelligence may be determined by an interaction between heredity and environment.[3] "Heredity deals the cards and environment plays them."[4] Yet the heredity theory dies hard.

[2] E. G. Boring, "Intelligence as the Tests Test It," *New Republic* 35 (1925): 35–37.
[3] M. Synderman and S. Rothman, "Survey of Expert Opinion of Intelligence and Aptitude Testing," *American Psychologist* 42 (1987): 137–44.
[4] Lee J. Cronbach, *Educational Psychology*. (New York: Harcourt, 1954), p. 204.

The majority position, which believes that intelligence is determined by some combination of heredity and environment, brings up the question as to *which* factor is more important. Conflicting studies attribute different percentages to each factor. The controversy continues to rage, as does the confusion surrounding what intelligence tests are measuring.

Most intelligence tests are highly verbal, and studies have shown that persons who do well on vocabulary tests also seem to do well on intelligence tests.[5] If a child has language problems—or if a dialect of English or a language other than English is spoken at home—the child could easily have difficulty in performing well in school. IQ tests are valid mainly for a middle-class standard English curriculum, and they predict the ability of an individual to do well in such environments. The positive correlation or agreement between individuals' IQs and their ability to work in school is neither very high nor low. There are factors other than IQ that determine an individual's success in school. One very important factor for school success is *motivation*—the desire, drive, and sustained interest to do the work.

Motivation
Internal impetus behind behavior and the direction behavior takes; drive.

The IQ test is an imperfect tool that helps teachers and parents to understand the abilities of children better. If students are doing very well in school, and if, according to their IQ scores, they are only supposed to be doing average work, one would be misusing the IQ test by thinking, "Stop, you're not supposed to be doing well."

The IQ test also helps show teachers the wide range of levels of ability in their classes. If teachers are aware of the wide span of mental age of their students, they can design programs based especially on individual needs.

However, teachers are cautioned not to see the IQ test as a perfect predictor of a child's ability to work well in school, for there are other factors, discussed in previous chapters, which influence school achievement. (See Chapter 4 for a discussion of intelligence and reading.)

DIFFERENCES BETWEEN INDIVIDUAL AND GROUP INTELLIGENCE (APTITUDE) TESTS

Teachers should recognize that differences exist between individual and group IQ tests. The most obvious difference is that an individual test is given to one person at a time, whereas a group test is given to a number of persons at one time. (See the section on individual and group tests in Chapter 3.) Although it is not difficult to administer group tests, and a person can be trained rather quickly to administer a group IQ test, there are some problems associated with these tests which teachers should be aware of. One involves administering the

[5] Leona Tyler, *The Psychology of Human Differences* (New York: Appleton-Century-Crofts, 1965), p. 80.

test to young children, who may have difficulty following directions and also paying attention long enough to finish the test. On an individual IQ test this is not a problem because the examiner can adjust the test to suit the individual needs of the child.

Individual IQ tests require people who are specially trained to give them, and scoring tends to be more subjective than on group tests. On tests such as the *Stanford-Binet*, the examiner must on many occasions use his or her discretion to determine whether a response is correct or not. The original authors of the *Stanford-Binet* were so concerned about the role of the examiner that they stated the following in their *Examiner's Manual:*[6]

> The most essential requirement for determining a valid test score on the *Stanford-Binet Scale* is an examiner who knows his instrument and who is sensitive to the needs of the subject whom he is testing.

Halo effect
A response bias that contaminates an individual's perception in rating or evaluation.

The same authors also cautioned the examiners about "halo effect." Examiners are told to judge each response on its own merits, without regard to the student's successes or failures, and to guard against allowing the scoring to be influenced by any general impression he or she has formed of the subject's ability. The authors of the *Stanford-Binet* felt that there is a natural tendency to overestimate the ability of a sprightly, self-confident, talkative child.[7]

The authors of the fourth edition of the *Stanford-Binet Intelligence Scale* in their "Guide for Administering and Scoring the Fourth Edition" continue to stress the importance of the examiner's role. They state that "the ultimate effectiveness depends upon the skills of the examiner in administering and scoring the test and observing the behavior of the examinee during testing."[8] They state further that "a qualified examiner must follow standardized procedures during test administration."[9]

In spite of the greater subjectivity of individual tests, they usually yield more valid results than group tests, especially for students who have physical, emotional, or reading problems. Actually, a group IQ test "is much less likely to yield an accurate picture of any individual's abilities."[10]

Individual tests are generally given when a teacher suspects that the group IQ test result is not valid. As stated earlier, there may be a number of reasons for this suspicion, such as easy distractability or inability to follow directions, especially with young children. Some other causes that could affect group test results could be as mundane

---

[6] Lewis M. Terman and Maud A. Merrill, *Stanford-Binet Intelligence Scale*, 1972 Norms Edition (Boston: Riverside, 1973), p. 46.

[7] Ibid., p. 55.

[8] Robert L. Thorndike, Elizabeth P. Hagen, and Jerome M. Sattler, *Stanford-Binet Intelligence Scale*, 4th ed. (Boston: Riverside, 1986), p. 2.

[9] Ibid.

[10] Anita E. Woolfolk, *Educational Psychology*, 4th ed. (Englewood Cliffs, N.J.: Prentice-Hall, 1990), p. 136.

as a student's pencil point breaking or skipping a box on the answer sheet.

The teacher should recognize also that group tests emphasize reading ability more than individual tests. If a child has a reading problem (see scenario of Larry in Chapter 8), the teacher must be careful not to interpret a low score on a group IQ test to mean a lack of intelligence, when it may actually be a lack of reading ability.

INDIVIDUAL INTELLIGENCE (APTITUDE) TESTS

Wechsler Intelligence Scale for Children, Revised (WISC-R)

The Wechsler Intelligence Scale for Children, Revised (WISC-R), which is published by the Psychological Corporation, is an individual test that is most often used with children who have reading difficulties. It was first published in 1949 and revised (WISC-R) in 1974. The original WISC was standardized for children ages 5 to 15; WISC-R was restandardized for ages 6–0 to 16–11. In the restandardization, substantial portions of the original 1949 WISC were retained, but items judged culturally biased or found unacceptable on psychometric grounds were replaced.

WISC-R, as in the 1949 WISC, has ten tests (with two alternates available if needed)[11] and these yield an IQ based on scaled scores for each age level—not on a mental age. An IQ score can be derived also from either the verbal or the performance scale alone. The verbal subtests consist of the following: Information, Similarities, Arithmetic, Vocabulary, Comprehension, and Digit Span (optional). The performance subtests consist of the following: Picture Completion, Picture Arrangements, Block Design, Object Assembly, Coding, and Mazes (optional).[12]

The Digit Span and the Mazes subtests have been retained in the WISC-R and are considered supplementary tests. They are added when time permits, or they are used as alternate tests when some other test is not appropriate or is invalidated.

The performance tests make the WISC-R suitable for students who have verbal difficulties. Poor readers usually do better on the performance scale of the WISC-R because these tests do not depend on school learning, whereas the tests in the verbal scale do.

The WISC-R, as well as the 1949 WISC, is a highly regarded testing instrument. One reviewer states the following: "The more

---

[11] Obviously, with the alternate tests, the WISC-R contains twelve tests. There are, however, only ten main tests.

[12] David Wechsler, *Wechsler Intelligence Scale for Children (WISC) Manual* (New York: Psychological Corporation, 1974), p. 8.

accurate standardization sample, the up-dated norms, and the many item changes make the WISC-R an even more valuable tool than its highly praised and well-used predecessor."[13]

Special Note

A Spanish adaptation of the WISC-R (EIWN-R) is available for use; however, this is a research edition without norms.

Stanford-Binet Intelligence Scale

The present *Stanford-Binet Intelligence Scale*, which is published by the Riverside Publishing Company, is an outgrowth of the 1916 scale, which attempted to provide standards of intellectual performance for average American-born children from age three to young adulthood—which was assumed on the basis of available information for purposes of the scale to be age 16. Tests are arranged in order of difficulty by age levels. The intellectual ability of an individual, determined by his or her performance on the scale, was judged by comparison with the standards of performance for normal children of different ages.

Intelligence ratings were expressed as mental age scores. One of Binet's basic assumptions of the original scale was that persons are thought of as normal if they can do the things a person of their age normally can do, retarded if their test performance corresponds to the performance of persons younger than themselves, and accelerated if their performance exceeds that of persons their age.[14]

In 1937 there was a second revision, in which the age level was extended downward to age two, and in 1960 there was a third revision. In 1972 a new set of norms was published to be used with the 1960 revision. In the 1960 revision the IQ tables were extended to include ages 17 and 18. This change was made because retest findings showed that mental age, as measured by the *Stanford-Binet*, extends beyond age 16.[15]

In 1986 a fourth edition was published, which maintains historical continuity with the former editions. The age level for the 1986 edition extends from age two to adult and was "developed from the assumption that general mental ability, a concept that Terman described as 'mental adaptability to new problems,' is measurable and increases with age."[16]

The fourth edition consists of a three-level hierarchical cognitive-

---

[13] Oscar K. Buros, ed., *The Eighth Mental Measurements Yearbook*, vol. 1 (Highland Park, N.J.: Gryphon Press, 1978), p. 355.

[14] Terman and Merrill, p. 5.

[15] Ibid., pp. 26–27.

[16] Thorndike, Hagen, and Sattler, p. 52.

4 Areas	Verbal Reasoning	Abstract/Visual Reasoning	Quantitative Reasoning	Short-Term Memory
15 Individual Tests	Vocabulary Comprehension Absurdities Verbal Relations	Pattern Analysis Copying Matrices Paper Folding and Cutting	Quantitative Number Series Equation Building	Bead Memory Memory for Sentences Memory for Digits Memory for Objects
Scores	Raw scores and scaled scores for each of 15 tests Scaled scores and percentile ranks for each of four area scores A composite of any combination of area scores			

Figure 6.1 Tests available for the fourth edition of the Stanford-Binet.

abilities model from which a general score and four separate cognitive scores can be obtained. There are 15 tests, and each is designed to appraise one of the major areas in the theoretical model. (See Figure 6.1 for tests included in the fourth edition.)

Slosson Intelligence Test (SIT)

The Slosson Intelligence Test (SIT) which is published by Slosson Educational Publishers for two-year-olds to adults is highlighted here because it is a useful tool that teachers can learn to use very quickly and well. This individual IQ test, which is relatively short to administer (approximately 20–40 minutes), is based on the Stanford-Binet and yields a single IQ score.

The SIT, which is useful in working with reading-disabled students because no reading is required for the test, helps teachers and clinicians gain more than just the IQ; it helps them gain insights

Figure 6.2 Yes, filling out the wrong side should count against you.

about their students' reading behavior. It can help teachers learn about their students' strengths and weaknesses from the manner in which their students respond as well as from the type of questions they can answer. Jerry Johns has developed an informal item analysis for the SIT, which helps teachers gain diagnostic insights from the test.[17]

Teachers are cautioned, however, that they must be extremely cautious in conducting an item analysis. In addition, students' strengths and weaknesses should be considered tentative and confirmed or refuted with additional evidence, and users of the item analysis for SIT are also told which items should be used in the item analysis based on the individual pupil's test results.[18]

Special Note

The Slosson Intelligence Test is also recommended for use with the Bond and Tinker formula if a Wechsler or Binet test score is not available.

Other Individual Intelligence Tests

Some other individual intelligence tests include the Kaufman Assessment Battery for Children (American Guidance Service) for 2½- to 12½-year-olds; the Woodcock-Johnson Psycho-Educational Battery, Revised (DLM) for ages three to 80; and the McCarthy Scales of Children's Abilities (Psychological Corporation) for ages 2½ to 8½.

GROUP-ADMINISTERED MEASURES OF INTELLIGENCE (APTITUDE)

Group intelligence tests are those that are generally administered by the regular classroom teacher in the regular classroom. There are a great number of group intelligence tests on the market today. The list that follows contains examples of some that are more generally used.

Cognitive Abilities Test (Riverside, 1986)

Purpose: To assess students' verbal, quantitative, and nonverbal abilities

Editions: Primary Battery: Grades K–3 (Levels 1 and 2); Multilevel and Separate Level Editions: Grades 3–12 (Levels A–H)

Administration Time: 90 minutes

---

[17] Jerry L. Johns, "Diagnostic Insights for At-risk Readers with the Slosson Intelligence Test," *Journal of Reading* 33 (December 1989): 187–92.
[18] Ibid., p. 189.

Henmon-Nelson Tests of Mental Ability (Riverside, 1973)

Purpose: To provide a quick and reliable measure of cognitive ability
Kindergarten–grade 12
Administration Time: Grades K–2, untimed (approximately 25–30 minutes)
Grades 3–12, 30 minutes

Otis-Lennon School Ability Test, Sixth Edition (OLSAT)
(Psychological Corporation, 1989)

Purpose: Designed to assess those abilities that are related to success in cognitive, school-related activities; measures verbal and nonverbal abilities
Kindergarten–grade 12
Administration Time: K–2, about 75 minutes
3–12, about 60 minutes

Here is a sample from the Practice Test of the *Cognitive Abilities Test* Levels 1 and 2 that illustrates how the Practice Test is introduced. The sample also presents Practice Test 1, which deals with relational concepts. Note that the teacher is given explicit instructions on exactly how to introduce the Practice Test, as well as on how to administer each item.

PRACTICE TEST: DIRECTIONS FOR ADMINISTRATION

(When reading the directions for each test—the words in dark type—to the children, do *not* read the item numbers aloud.)

(Pass out the booklets, face up. When you are ready to begin the test, say:)

I have given each of you a little book that has many pictures. We are going to do different things with these pictures. You should *listen* to what I say and then *do* what I tell you to do in your little book.

(Hold up your booklet to show the pictures on the front cover. Then say:)

Look at the picture of the duck at the top of the page. Do you see the shape under the duck that looks like an egg? This is called an *oval*. (Draw an oval on the chalkboard.) With your pencil, fill in the oval, like this. (Fill in the oval on the chalkboard.) Your oval under the duck should look like this. Be sure that it is all filled in. Try not to make any marks outside the oval.

(Circulate around the room, answering any questions and checking to see that all of the children are marking the oval correctly.)

Now put your finger on the little candle next to the first row of pictures. (Pause.) There are four pictures in this row. Find the picture of the baby. (Pause.) The oval under the picture of the baby has been filled in to show that this is the right picture.

(You are now ready to begin Practice Test 1.)

FORM **4**

PRACTICE TEST
BOOKLET FOR
LEVELS 1 AND 2

Cognitive
Abilities
Test

Robert L. Thorndike
Elizabeth Hagen

TEST 1: RELATIONAL CONCEPTS

(When you are ready to begin, say:)

1. Put your finger on the little flower next to the first row of pictures. (Pause.) In this row there are pictures of teddy bears. Listen carefully. Fill in the oval under the picture that shows the *biggest* teddy bear. (Pause.) Fill in the oval under the *biggest* teddy bear.

(If necessary, use the blackboard again to show the children how to fill in an oval. Point out the correct answer to the children, check to make sure they are marking the item correctly. Help children who need additional explanation.)

Now we will do the next pictures.

2. Put your finger on the little chair in front of the next row. Fill in the oval under the picture that shows that *all* of the children are standing up. (Pause.) *All* of the children are standing up.

(When the children have finished marking, go over the answer with them. Clear up any questions before proceeding to Practice Test 2.)

Now turn your booklet over to the next page.

(Demonstrate. Make sure each child is working on page 2.)

MENTAL AGE SPAN IN THE REGULAR CLASSROOM

Mental age
A child's present level of development; in intelligence testing, a score based on average abilities for that age group:

$$MA = \frac{IQ \times CA}{100}$$

The teacher in a regular classroom usually has students with a mental age span of five years. It can be more. Mental age (MA) refers to a child's present level of development; it helps to indicate the child's present readiness. As children progress through the grades the span between the borderline (slow-learning), average, and gifted child gets wider.

Children enter school based on chronological age rather than mental age; however, instruction needs to be geared to their mental ages rather than their chronological ages. For example, a child of six with an IQ (MA/CA × 100 = IQ) of 75[19] has a mental age of 4.5, and a child of six with an IQ of 130 has a mental age of 7.8 (see Table 6.1). Obviously, these children need extremely different programs, even though both are chronologically the same age. Note that

[19] Teachers may have children with IQs as low as 70 in their regular classrooms because borderline children's IQs range from approximately 70 to 85.

TABLE 6.1 Comparison of Mental Ages

Grade	CA	75 IQ MA	85 IA MA	100 IQ MA	115 IQ MA	130 IQ MA
K	5.6	4.2	4.8	5.6	6.4	7.3
1	6.0	4.5	5.1	6.0	6.9	7.8
	6.6	5.0	5.6	6.6	7.6	8.6
2	7.0	5.3	6.0	7.0	8.1	9.1
	7.6	5.7	6.5	7.6	8.7	9.9
3	8.0	6.0	6.8	8.0	9.2	10.4
	8.6	6.5	7.3	8.6	9.9	11.2
4	9.0	6.8	7.7	9.0	10.4	11.7
	9.6	7.2	8.2	9.6	11.0	12.5
5	10.0	7.5	8.5	10.0	11.5	13.0
	10.6	8.0	9.0	10.6	12.2	13.8
6	11.0	8.3	9.4	11.0	12.7	14.3
	11.6	8.7	9.9	11.6	13.3	15.1
7	12.0	9.0	10.2	12.0	13.8	15.6
	12.6	9.5	10.7	12.6	14.5	16.4
8	13.0	9.8	11.1	13.0	15.0	16.9
	13.6	10.2	11.6	13.6	15.6	17.7

Example: An eight-year-old child with an IQ of 115 has a mental age of 9.2.

$$IQ = \frac{MA}{CA} \times 100$$

$$115 = \frac{x}{8} \times 100$$

$$x = 1.15 \times 8$$

$$x = 9.2$$

Chronological age (CA) is given in years and tenths rather than in years and months so that mental age (MA) is also expressed in years and tenths.

Intelligence quotient (IQ)
Mental age divided by chronological age multiplied by 100.

students with similar mental ages and different chronological ages also do not have similar mental abilities. For example, a child with a chronological age of ten and a mental age of six has an IQ of 60. A child with an IQ of 60 will not progress in reading like a child of five with a mental age of 6 and a half, who has an IQ of 130.

Even teachers who believe in individual differences and who attempt to develop an individualized instructional program for each child in their classes will not be able to build a meaningful program for their students unless they know the cognitive styles that children at different intellectual levels possess (see Chapter 15).

Special Note

In intelligence testing, mental age is defined as a score based on "average abilities for that age group." In other words, if, on a test, the average score for eight-year-olds is 45, then the score of 45 is assigned a mental age of 8 years. For example, if a ten- or twelve-year-old child scores 45 on the test, he would have a mental age of 8. The mental age gives the child's present level of development; it is more descriptive of the child's cognitive development than chronological age.

READING EXPECTANCY FORMULAS

Reading expectancy formula
Helps teachers determine who needs special help; helps determine a student's reading potential.

Reading expectancy formulas help teachers determine who needs special help. A child's reading expectancy, calculated by a reading expectancy formula, is compared with his or her reading achievement level, measured by a reading achievement test score. If the child's expectancy level is significantly higher than his or her reading achievement score, further diagnosis should be undertaken. (See "Who Is a Candidate for Further Testing?" in this chapter for a discussion of the term *significantly*.)

Bond and Tinker Reading Expectancy Formula

This formula is used often because of its simplicity, but as stated earlier in this chapter, it is rather idealized for the child with a low IQ and underestimates the reading expectancy of a child with a high IQ. Also, many children are starting to learn to read in kindergarten, but the Bond and Tinker formula does not take this factor into account.

TABLE 6.2   Bond and Tinker Formula for Estimating Reading Expectancy for IQs 70 and 120 (Grades 1–6)*

$\left(\dfrac{IQ}{100} \times \textit{Years of Reading Instruction}\right) + 1.0$	=	*Reading Expectancy at End of School Year*
$(1 \times 0.70) + 1$	=	1.7 at end of 1st grade
$(2 \times 0.70) + 1$	=	2.4 at end of 2nd grade
$(3 \times 0.70) + 1$	=	3.1 at end of 3rd grade
$(4 \times 0.70) + 1$	=	3.8 at end of 4th grade
$(5 \times 0.70) + 1$	=	4.5 at end of 5th grade
$(6 \times 0.70) + 1$	=	5.2 at end of 6th grade
$(1 \times 1.20) + 1$	=	2.2 at end of 1st grade
$(2 \times 1.20) + 1$	=	3.4 at end of 2nd grade
$(3 \times 1.20) + 1$	=	4.6 at end of 3rd grade
$(4 \times 1.20) + 1$	=	5.8 at end of 4th grade
$(5 \times 1.20) + 1$	=	7.0 at end of 5th grade
$(6 \times 1.20) + 1$	=	8.2 at end of 6th grade

* The Bond and Tinker formula begins at grade one; that is, at the end of grade one the child is considered to have been in school one year.

In using the Bond and Tinker reading expectancy formula, teachers should keep the following considerations in mind.[20]

1. The time of reading instruction is the years and months in school from the time systematic reading instruction was started. This typically begins with first grade. (Some slower learning children may have a delay of a year or so in starting to learn to read.)
2. Readiness training in kindergarten is not counted, even though such instruction does much to diminish the chances of disabilities from occurring once reading instruction has started.
3. If an IQ obtained from a Binet or Wechsler test is not available, it is suggested that a Slosson Intelligence Test given by the teacher or that a group-performance intelligence test score be substituted temporarily.

Special Note

The authors of the Bond and Tinker formula claim that "experience and research have shown this formula to be surprisingly accurate in estimating the potential reading ability of the typical child"[21] if the three considerations they present are adhered to. The formula is very easy to calculate, and what they say is probably true for "typical" or "average" children; however, as stated before in this chapter, it appears to be "idealized" for those at the lower intelligence levels and not high enough for those at the upper limits.

Harris and Sipay Reading Expectancy Formula

This formula, like the Bond and Tinker formula, stresses intelligence—which makes sense because reading is a thinking act. The more intelligent a person is, the better thinker he or she should be; the better the person is in thinking, the better reader he or she should be.

$$\text{Reading Expectancy Age (R Exp A)} = \frac{2\ \text{MA} + \text{CA}}{3}$$

(MA and CA should be expressed in years and tenths so that R Exp A may also be expressed in years and tenths [See Table 6.3]).

Special Note

For those students who are mathematically minded, here is the formula for calculating months to decimal tenths. Take the number

[20] Guy L. Bond, Miles A. Tinker, Barbara B. Wasson, and John B. Wasson, *Reading Difficulties: Their Diagnosis and Correction*, 6th ed. (Englewood Cliffs, N.J.: Prentice-Hall, 1990), p. 42.
[21] Ibid.

TABLE 6.3 Conversion of Age Months to Decimal Tenths

	Age	
Months	Decimal-Tenths (of Year)	
0	0	
1	1	
2	2	
3	3	
4	3	
5	4	
6	5	
7	6	
8	7	
9	8	
10	8	
11	9	

To convert age months to decimal years, look in the table for months desired and read the decimal tenths next to it. For example, 5 months is approximately equal to 0.4 years. If you have 7 years 5 months to convert to tenths, it would be approximately 7.4 in tenths of a year.

of months divided by 12 and round the result to the nearest tenth. For example, 4 months converted to tenths of years = 4/12 = 0.33, and rounded to the nearest tenth equals 0.3 years. With modern hand calculators, the conversion is very easy to do.

The Harris and Sipay formula, unlike the Bond and Tinker, gives a child's reading expectancy in age rather than in grade levels. The concept of using age is a sound one and would tend to give a more realistic reading expectancy because children's entrance into school varies. Some children, because of their birthdays, may not enter school until almost a year later than some other children. Harris and Sipay's formula takes this into account. The use of age levels can, however, be confusing for teachers because they are used to working with either grade levels or with reading levels, which are easily converted to grade equivalent levels. To make the Harris and Sipay formula more useful to the teacher, it would help to convert the reading expectancy age to grade equivalent levels. This is easily done by subtracting 5 from the reading expectancy age to obtain the grade equivalent level (see Table 6.4).

When a reading test does not provide reading-age norms, Harris and Sipay suggest adding 5.2 to the reading-grade scores to attain the equivalent reading-age scores. This author, however, suggests adding 5.0 rather than 5.2 to the reading-grade score to get the reading-age scores and, conversely, subtracting 5.0 from the reading-

TABLE 6.4

Reading Grade Level	Reading Age (RA)
1.0	6.0
2.0	7.0
3.0	8.0
4.0	9.0
5.0	10.0
6.0	11.0
7.0	12.0
8.0	13.0
9.0	14.0
10.0	15.0
11.0	16.0
12.0	17.0

For reading grade level scores between the listed grade levels, add the decimal fraction to corresponding pairs of Reading Grade Level and Reading Age numbers in the conversion table. For example, if someone has a reading grade level score of 3.4, his or her reading age would be 8.4. Or, more simply, add 5.0 to the reading grade level to obtain the reading age.

age score to obtain the equivalent reading-grade score. Since we are dealing with wide variations in school starting age (there may be as much as a year's difference in age among children within the same grade), 5.0 is just as good an approximation as 5.2 in calculating reading age. Furthermore, it makes the calculation less cumbersome and easier to comprehend.

Special Note

A grade year equals only ten months, so a reading age level in *tenths* is directly convertible to a reading grade level in months.

Examples Using the Expectancy Formulas

Example 1

This example uses the Harris and Sipay formula for a student 9.0 years of age with an IQ of 100. From looking at Table 6.1, we can see that a student with an IQ of 100 who is 9.0 years of age would have a mental age of 9.0. This student, according to the Harris and Sipay formula, should be reading at a reading expectancy age of 9.0. From Table 6.4, we can see that a 9.0 year old should be reading at approximately the beginning of fourth grade.

$$R \text{ Exp } A = \frac{2(MA) + CA}{3}$$

$$= \frac{2(9) + 9}{3} = \frac{27}{3} = 9$$

Special Notes

From looking at the formula, it can be seen that any child with an IQ of 100 should be reading at his or her grade level.

For any IQ value you can compute the MA of any student if you have the student's CA and IQ score by using the following formula:

$$MA = \frac{IQ \times CA}{100}$$

Example

$$IQ = 111$$

$$CA = 9$$

$$MA = \frac{111 \times 9}{100} = \frac{999}{100} = 9.99$$

$$MA = 10.0 \text{ (rounded to the nearest tenth of a year)}$$

Examples 2 and 3

Let's look at two more examples. The first is a student who is 9.0 years of age with an IQ of 75, and the second is a student who is also 9.0 years of age but has an IQ of 130.

First we must determine the mental age for each student. From looking at Table 6.1, we can see that a student who is 9.0 years old with an IQ of 75 would have a mental age of 6.8, and a student who is 9.0 years old with an IQ of 130 would have a mental age of 11.7. Now, let's apply the Harris and Sipay formula to determine these student's reading expectancy age.

Student with 75 IQ, 9.0 years of age, 6.8 MA, fourth grade (beginning):

$$R \text{ Exp } A = \frac{2MA + CA}{3}$$

$$= \frac{2(6.8) + 9}{3} = \frac{13.6 + 9}{3}$$

$$= \frac{22.6}{3} = 7.5$$

R Exp A 7.5 is equal to a grade level equivalent of 2.5: (7.5 − 5.0 = 2.5); 2.5 is the midpoint (or fifth month) of second grade.

Student with 130 IQ, 9.0 years of age, 11.7 MA, fourth grade (beginning):

$$R \ Exp \ A = \frac{2MA + CA}{3}$$

$$= \frac{2(11.7) + 9}{3} = \frac{23.4 + 9}{3}$$

$$= \frac{32.4}{3} = 10.8$$

R Exp A 10.8 is equal to a grade level equivalent of 5.8 (10.8 − 5 = 5.8).

These children, according to the Bond and Tinker formula, should be reading at the following levels:

Student with 75 IQ, 9.0 years of age, 4th grade (beginning):

3 × .75 + 1 = 3.25 (close to the third month of third grade)

Student with 130 IQ, 9.0 years of age, 4th grade (beginning):

3 × 1.30 + 1 = 4.90 (the ninth month of fourth grade)

In comparing the Harris and Sipay and Bond and Tinker formulas, we can see that the former is more complicated than the latter; however, it is also more realistic for the slow learner and the highly able student. Teachers must remember, if they are using the Harris and Sipay formula, that R Exp A yields an age level, not a grade level. If they want or need a grade level equivalent, the age level can easily be converted to one by subtracting 5.0 (see Table 6.4).

Reading Expectancy Formulas for Early–Primary Grade Children

Harris and Sipay suggest that another formula be used for children who are younger than eight years of age because it will give a closer approximation than their own. The formula they suggest is the Horn formula, which was developed for use in the Los Angeles schools. Teachers are also aptly cautioned that any formula used to determine the reading expectancy of children under eight years of age is to be regarded with skepticism because "the weighting of MA and CA suggests an increase in the correlations between potential and reading as the pupils got older (0.50, 0.60, 0.67, and 0.75 respectively)."[22]

[22] Albert J. Harris and Edward R. Sipay, *How to Increase Reading Ability*, 7th ed. (New York: Longman, 1990), p. 170.

This observation makes sense, since reading expectancy formulas are based on intelligence quotients, and the younger a child is, the more difficult it is to obtain a reliable intelligence test score.

$$\text{Horn-L.A. formula for R Exp A} = \frac{\text{MA} + \text{CA}}{2}$$

(used with children below eight years of age)

WHO IS A CANDIDATE FOR FURTHER TESTING?

Teachers must be cautioned about using reading expectancy formulas as absolute determinants of reading potential. They are not; they are merely indicators of possible reading potential. Most reading expectancy formulas are based on intelligence quotients, which may not be valid for the child, especially if a group IQ test was used and the child has word recognition problems. (See the case of Larry, which is presented at the beginning of Chapter 8.) It may be that the child should actually be reading at a much higher level than is indicated by the reading expectancy formula. Therefore, teachers may want to administer diagnostic reading tests to children for whom there may not be any discrepancy between their present reading achievement level and their reading potential, but who exhibit behavior in class that seems to indicate that they should be reading at a higher level.

Teachers should also recognize that there really is no set rule for determining when or which child should be a candidate for further testing. Each case is different. Although some educators state that a child should be tested further or is a candidate for an informal reading inventory if a child's reading achievement score is approximately one year or more below his or her reading potential, this guideline is not very helpful or realistic. For example, a three-month underachievement in reading in first grade is probably significant and should be looked into by the teacher, whereas a three-month underachievement in sixth grade would probably not be as significant. In the former case, because we are dealing with small numbers in the first one-year period in school, small underachievements may be significant. Also, since this book is based on the premise that early diagnosis is more helpful than later remediation, it is better to err on the safe side with overzealous diagnosis in the early grades than to let the gap get too large in the later grades, which would then require extensive remediation. The adage "an ounce of prevention is worth a pound of cure" is an apt one in the field of diagnosis and reading. (See "Who Should Be Given an IRI?" in Chapter 8.)

Table 6.5 could be used as a guideline to help teachers determine whether a child is a disabled reader and a candidate for further testing. The table shows that as the child proceeds through the grades, the discrepancy between his or her reading expectancy grade

TABLE 6.5 Discrepancies Between Reading Expectancy and Achievement That Indicate Disability at Each Grade Level[23]

Grade Score Discrepancy	Grade in School						
	1	2	3	4	5	6	7 and Above
Indicating disability	0.5 or more	0.66 or more	0.75 or more	1.0 or more	1.5 or more	1.75 or more	2.0 or more
Indicating possible disability	0.3–0.5	0.4–0.66	0.5–0.75	0.7–1.0	0.9–1.5	1.1–1.75	1.3–2.0

level and actual average grade level increases. As stated earlier, a few months may be significant in grade one but would not be in the upper grades.

Harris and Sipay provide a formula not only for reading expectancy age but also for comparing a student's present level of reading with his or her reading potential.[24] This formula is actually one of appraisal because it attempts to determine which student is in need of further testing and special help.

Reading Expectancy Quotient (R Exp Q)

$$= \frac{RA}{R\ Exp\ A} \times 100$$

(RA = Reading Age)

(R Exp A = Reading Expectancy Age)

Let's see how this formula works:

Student Y has a R Exp A of 10.0 (he is in fifth grade) and an IQ of 100. He has scored at the 5.0 grade level on a standardized reading achievement test in early fall, which is equal to a RA of 10 (see Table 6.4).

$$R\ Exp\ Q = \frac{RA}{R\ Exp\ A} \times 100 = \frac{10}{10} \times 100$$

$$= 1 \times 100 = 100$$

According to Harris and Sipay, if a person scores between 90 and 100, he or she is within a normal range; this child does not need any further testing. A score below 90 would indicate that some disability exists. The greater the score falls below 90, the greater the reading disability. Obviously, you did not need any formula to determine

[23] Bond, Tinker, Wasson, and Wasson, p. 43.
[24] Harris and Sipay, p. 175.

that a child with an IQ of 100, who is 10 years of age and in fifth grade and is reading at a fifth-grade level, is reading according to his ability, assuming, of course, that the IQ score is an accurate measure of his or her ability. The formula would come in handy to uncover less obvious cases. Here is an example:

Student Z has a R Exp A of 12.0 (he is in fifth grade) and an IQ of 130. He has scored at the 5.0 grade level on a standardized reading achievement test in early fall. This is equal to a RA of 10.0 (see Table 6.4).

$$\text{R Exp Q} = \frac{\text{RA}}{\text{R Exp A}} \times 100 = \frac{10}{12} \times 100$$

$$= \frac{10}{12} = 0.833 \times 100 = 83.3$$

This student is a candidate for further testing and special help.

The standardized reading achievement test gives a score that is usually expressed in grade levels in tenths of a grade. (Some standardized norm-referenced achievement tests give the age equivalents for grade levels, but not all do.) To use the Harris and Sipay formula to determine who is a disabled reader, you must convert the reading grade level to a reading age (RA). Table 6.4 helps you to do so.

Special Note

Teachers who are in school systems that do not administer intelligence tests to their students will, obviously, not be able to use reading expectancy formulas that depend on a measure of intelligence. These teachers will have to rely on astute observations (see Chapter 10) and listening capacity tests. (See Chapter 5 for information on standardized listening tests and on the construction of informal listening comprehension tests.) Chapter 8 also discusses which children would be candidates for further testing when the teacher does not have information about a student's intelligence as measured by an intelligence test.

LISTENING CAPACITY TEST

In Chapter 5, you learned about listening comprehension tests, which are used to assess a student's reading potential, and in Chapter 8 you will learn more about these tests. Because this chapter is concerned with helping teachers determine the reading potential of students, it is necessary to mention listening comprehension or listening capacity tests here also.

The purpose of the listening capacity test is to determine the child's "potential" for reading. A child may have excellent comprehension ability, but it may be masked because of word recognition problems. Because of this, reading ability is not predictable when auding ability is high (see "Listening and Reading" in Chapter 5).

A child's word recognition difficulties could also interfere with the assessment of intelligence if a group IQ test were used rather than an individual test. Some test constructors feel that "listening comprehension may be used as the most satisfactory measure of 'potential' for reading"[25] and that listening comprehension is more directly related to reading than are most tests of intelligence. Therefore, a listening capacity test is useful also to determine reading potential if no IQ score is available for a child.

SUMMARY

Chapter 6 provides information that teachers need to determine which child is underachieving in reading. Teachers must recognize that a child can be reading on grade level yet be underachieving because the child is not reading according to his or her ability level. Conversely, a child can be reading below grade level but not be underachieving because he or she is reading according to his or her ability level. To help teachers determine the reading potential or reading expectancy of their students, reading expectancy formulas are presented and explained. Since these formulas are based on information about a student's intelligence as measured by an intelligence test, a special section is presented on intelligence and intelligence tests. Differences between individual and group IQ tests are discussed and examples of each type are given. Individual IQ tests usually require a person specially trained to administer them, whereas group IQ tests are generally given by the classroom teacher in the regular classroom.

To determine who is underachieving in reading, the teacher must compare a student's reading potential as determined by a reading expectancy formula with his or her present level of reading achievement as determined by a reading achievement test. The comparison between the present status of a child in reading with his or her reading potential is called *appraisal*, which is the second step in a diagnostic pattern. Teachers are cautioned about using reading expectancy formulas as absolute determinants of a student's reading potential. One of the reasons given for this caution is that the child's IQ score may not be a valid one for the child. It is also stressed that there is no set rule for determining which child should be a candidate for further testing. It is better to err on the safe side with overzealous diagnosis in the early grades than to let the gap get too large in the later grades. Information is also given about what a teacher can do

[25] Donald D. Durrell and Mary B. Brassard, *Manual for Listening and Reading Tests* (New York: Harcourt, 1970), p. 11.

to determine a student's reading potential if there is no IQ test score available.

SUGGESTIONS FOR THOUGHT QUESTIONS AND ACTIVITIES

1. Choose a few students for whom intelligence test scores are available, and using the Bond and Tinker formula for computing reading expectancy, determine the students' reading expectancy.
2. Compute the reading expectancy for the same students by using the Harris and Sipay formula.
3. Compare the students' reading expectancy with their present reading achievement as measured by a standardized reading achievement test. Determine which students should receive further diagnostic testing.
4. Choose three group intelligence tests and look up reviews about them in the *Mental Measurements Yearbooks.*
5. You have been asked to address this month's meeting of the Parent/Teacher Organization in your school. You have been asked to speak about intelligence and intelligence tests. There has been a lot of controversy concerning this topic in your community. What will you say? Write the address.
6. Look up reviews about the *Stanford-Binet Intelligence Scale* and the *Wechsler Intelligence Scale for Children* in the *Mental Measurements Yearbooks.* Which would you choose to use with a child who is having reading problems if you were specially trained to give these tests?
7. Explain why a listening capacity test would be useful for determining a child's reading potential if an IQ score is not available for the child or if you feel that the child's IQ score is not valid for the child.

SELECTED BIBLIOGRAPHY

Bond, Guy L., Miles Tinker, Barbara Wasson, and John Wasson. *Reading Difficulties: Their Diagnosis and Correction*, 6th ed., Chapter 3, "Description of Disabled Readers." Englewood Cliffs, N.J.: Prentice-Hall, 1990.

Boring, E. G. "Intelligence as the Tests Test It." *New Republic* 35 (1925): 35–37.

Harris, Albert, and Edward R. Sipay. *How to Increase Reading Ability*, 9th ed., Chapter 6, "What Is Reading Disability?" pp. 150–80. New York: Longman, 1990.

Hunt, McVicker, ed. *Human Intelligence.* New Brunswick, N.J.: E. P. Dutton, 1972.

Jensen, Arthur R. *Environment, Heredity, and Intelligence.* Compiled from the *Harvard Educational Review.* Cambridge, Mass.: President and Fellows of Harvard College, 1969.

Johns, Jerry L. "Diagnostic Insights for At-risk Readers with the Slosson Intelligence Test," *Journal of Reading* 33 (December 1989): 187–92.

Searls, E. F. *How to Use WISC-R Scores in Reading/Learning Disability Diagnosis.* Newark, Del.: International Reading Association, 1985.

7

Standardized Reading Achievement Tests: Survey Type

Scenario: James Brown—A Teacher Who Knows the Purpose of Tests

James Brown, a sixth-grade teacher, loves to teach. He chose this profession over others because he likes to work with children, and he feels he can make a difference. He remembers his own sixth-grade teacher who had helped him through rough times and feels good about being able to reciprocate somehow. James is never defensive about having chosen teaching as his career and resents others who are. When he is asked, "And what do you do?" he proudly replies, "I am a teacher."

However, there is one period of time during the school year that bothers James; it probably bothers many others also. In schools across the nation, you always know when it's that ominous time of the year—time for the dreaded standardized achievement tests. A hush seems to envelop the school; it's as if everyone is walking on tiptoe. Doors are closed, and anxious students and teachers are captives within. Everyone waits with bated breath for the results. Will they be an embarrassment to the school district, or will the students score substantially above the national norms? It's a tense time for all involved.

It doesn't have to be. James is frustrated because he feels that tests should be used for more than comparative purposes; they should have instructional implications. If they were administered in the fall, close to the beginning of the school year, they could be used more for instructional purposes. (Most of the standardized test batteries are normed for the beginning and end of the school year, so this procedure would not be a problem; actually, some are normed for administration even more than twice a year.)

The standardized reading tests could be used to identify students who have a potential problem. They could be used as a screening device; at the end of the year, such tests are almost counterproductive. The students know that they are used for comparison purposes and often to place children in particular classes for the fall. Also, once the tests are over, everything in the last few weeks seems to slow down; it's as if school were over, but everyone is just waiting for the official closing.

James has been pushing for a change in testing times because he feels that the fall results would be more indicative of the children's present readiness and more useful for grouping and teaching. What do you think?

This chapter will concentrate on standardized norm-referenced reading achievement tests that yield a general score, not because these are the most popular tests administered in schools, but because they play an important role in the diagnostic-reading and correction program.

KEY QUESTIONS

After you finish reading this chapter, you should be able to answer the following questions:

1. Are there major differences between a reading survey test and a reading achievement subtest of an achievement test battery? Explain.
2. What are some uses of standardized norm-referenced reading achievement or survey tests?
3. How can survey tests be used in a positive manner?
4. What are some examples of reading survey tests?
5. What are some examples of test batteries that have a reading achievement subtest?
6. When should standardized achievement tests be given?
7. What is emergent literacy?
8. What are reading readiness tests?
9. What have studies found about the predictive validity of reading readiness tests?
10. What subtests on a reading readiness test have been found to be the most effective in predicting reading success?
11. Why are reading readiness tests still used?
12. What are some examples of reading readiness tests?
13. Why should teachers be cautious about giving reading readiness tests?

KEY TERMS IN CHAPTER

You should pay special attention to the following new terms:

emergent literacy
locator test
practice test
reading readiness test
standardized reading
 achievement test
standardized reading survey
 test

STANDARDIZED ACHIEVEMENT SURVEY TEST BATTERIES (MULTI-SUBJECT-MATTER TESTS) AND STANDARDIZED READING SURVEY TESTS (SINGLE-SUBJECT-MATTER TESTS)

Some people differentiate between reading survey tests such as the *Iowa Silent Reading Tests* and the reading subtest of an achievement survey test battery such as the *California Achievement Tests*. Actually, the reading survey test and the reading subtest of an achievement survey test battery are quite similar and serve the same purposes. Both measure a student's overall reading achievement. The major difference between the two types of tests is that a standardized reading survey test, such as the *Iowa Silent Reading Tests*, only measures reading and therefore can be somewhat more comprehensive, whereas the reading achievement subtest of an achievement test, such as the *California Achievement Tests*, is part of a survey battery of achievement tests; that is, the reading achievement test is one of many tests that measure different curricula. For example, the *California Achievement Tests* are designed for measuring achievement in the basic curricular areas of reading, spelling, language, mathematics, study skills, science, and social studies. As already stated, the reading component of the survey test battery yields very similar information to a reading survey test. Both reading survey tests and reading achievement tests from survey test batteries yield a general or overall score and were not developed to be used as diagnostic instruments; however, they play an essential role in any diagnostic program. (See Special Note on page 39 in Chapter 3.) These are group tests that are usually very easy to administer in a relatively short period of time, and they are useful for screening or identification which is the first step in a diagnostic pattern (see "What Is a Diagnostic Pattern?" in Chapter 6). Standardized norm-referenced reading achievement or survey tests are used to assess the students' present achievement status. The results of these kinds of tests are used for a number of purposes. One use is usually to make comparisons among other schools in the district, state, or nation. Another use is to tell us which child is doing well and which is doing poorly; it helps to identify that child who may need help. If the teacher uses the survey test as a means for identifying those children who may need help, the instrument is being used in a positive manner.

You are probably the most familiar with standardized achievement tests such as the *Metropolitan Achievement Tests*, the *Stanford Achievement Tests*, and the *California Achievement Tests* because most schools employ these kind of tests. They are generally given either at the beginning or the end of the school year by the classroom teacher. It's usually a good idea to give the test at the same time that the test was given to the students who determined the norms for the test. For example, if you wish to give an achievement test in the fall to help you determine how to group for instruction, you should choose a test in which the norms were gathered in the fall. Standardized achievement tests that are given in the fall are usually used for instructional purposes and screening, whereas standardized achievement tests that are given at the end of the year are generally used for comparison purposes.

Before giving any tests you should study the test manual that accompanies each one. The manual usually contains information about the test, such as how norms were gathered, instructions on how to administer and score the test, and what the test measures. If teachers know that their students have not had any instruction in a specific area, the teachers would be subjecting their students to a very frustrating experience by giving them an achievement test in that area; it would be a misuse of a test instrument. The teachers do not need a test to confirm what they already know.

Special Note

As stated in the introductory section of this chapter, most standardized achievement test batteries are normed for both fall and spring administration. However, most school districts administer the tests in the spring.

Examples of Standardized Reading Survey Tests

Standardized reading survey test
Measures general reading achievement; similar to a reading achievement test; single subject-matter test.

The *Gates-MacGinitie Reading Tests*, 3rd ed., Forms K and L, are a group-administered standardized survey of achievement in reading for students from the end of kindergarten through grade 12. The 1989 edition contains nine levels, two of which are new. The first new level is Level PRE (Pre-Reading Evaluation), which is a readiness test that assesses the student's knowledge of important background concepts necessary for beginning reading (see the section on "Reading Readiness Tests"). The other new level is a separate test level for grade 4.

After the PRE Level, there is a Level R that measures beginning reading achievement in grade 1 and makes possible the assessment of growth in reading achievement between the beginning and end of first grade. After the R Level, there is another level for grade 1, grade 2, grade 3 and grade 4. Grades 5 and 6 are combined, grades 7–9 are combined, and so are grades 10–12. Each level except the PRE and R Levels yields a vocabulary, comprehension, and total score. Walter H. MacGinitie and Ruth K. MacGinitie are the authors of the third edition, published by the Riverside Publishing Company.

The *Iowa Silent Reading Tests* (ISRT) are group reading survey tests that come in two forms and consist of the following three levels: grades 6 to 9, grades 9 to 14 (high school and post-high school), and for academically accelerated high school and college students. The tests in Level 1 are vocabulary; reading comprehension; directed reading, which assesses a student's work-study skills; and reading efficiency, which uses a modified cloze technique to assess a student's speed and accuracy. Roger Farr is the coordinating editor, and these tests at present are published by the Psychological Corporation.

Examples of Standardized Achievement Survey Test Batteries

Standardized reading achievement test
Usually part of a test battery that includes other curriculum areas besides reading; measures general reading achievement.

According to Educational Testing Service (ETS) in Princeton, New Jersey, the following test batteries are those about which the most frequent inquiries are made:[1]

The *California Achievement Tests* (CAT), Forms E and F (1988), are a norm-referenced battery of overlapping tests for which criterion-referenced information is available for grades K through 12. The tests measure achievement growth of skill development in reading, spelling, language, mathematics, study-skills, science, and social studies. A locator test is available for functional level testing to determine the level at which students should begin testing (see the section "Locator Tests"). There are also practice tests that help familiarize students with taking the tests (see the section "Practice Tests"). The California Achievement Tests are published by CTB/McGraw-Hill.

The *Iowa Tests of Basic Skills*, Multilevel Edition (1990), for grades 3 through 9 (Levels 9–14), are designed for comprehensive measurement of the basic skills. The basic battery for the Multilevel Edition, Levels 9–14, contains six tests—vocabulary, reading comprehension, spelling, mathematics concepts, mathematics problem solving, and mathematics computation. The complete battery includes 11 tests; besides those already mentioned, it also has tests for capitalization, punctuation, usage and expression, visual materials, and reference materials. In addition, there is a supplemental social studies/science booklet that tests students' achievement in basic social studies and science skills. Optional listening and essay-writing tests are available also for Levels 9–14. The Iowa Tests of Basic Skills are published by Riverside Publishing Company and contain criterion-referenced reports.

The *Metropolitan Achievement Tests*, 6th ed. (MAT6), Survey Battery (1985), includes tests in the areas of reading, mathematics, language, science, and social studies for grades K.0 to 12.9. The tests also contain objective-referenced interpretations. The MAT6, which is published by the Psychological Corporation, also includes functional-level testing, and a separate score is available for higher-order thinking skills.

The *Stanford Achievement Test Series*, 8th ed. (1989), is the series that is usually used in suburban and private schools;[2] however, it may be used with any population of students. The K–13 Series has

[1] Educational Testing Service, Test Collection, 1990.
[2] Ibid.

thirteen levels, a separate level for each grade through grade 11. The eighth edition measures achievement in reading, mathematics, language, spelling, study skills, science, social studies, and listening. The series, which is published by the Psychological Corporation, also has available criterion-referenced information and practice tests. In addition, there is a special "thinking skills" score.

The *Comprehensive Test of Basic Skills* Complete Battery, 4th ed. (CTBS/4 Complete Battery) (1989), provides both norm-referenced and curriculum-referenced (or objectives-referenced) information. The K through 12 battery covers the areas of reading, spelling, language, mathematics, study skills, social studies, and science. There is also a basic skills battery available that includes only the areas of reading, spelling, language, mathematics, and study skills. The CTBS/4 offers two other testing formats as well: one for those who wish a quick survey of their students' achievement levels and do not want the curriculum-referenced information, and another for those who want only norm-referenced scores of the highest degree of accuracy. Locator and practice tests are also available. The CTBS/4 is published by CTB/McGraw-Hill.

Special Note

A number of the standardized norm-referenced achievement survey test batteries are reporting criterion-referenced *information*. John Stewart, senior product manager at CTB/McGraw-Hill, explains why standardized norm-referenced achievement tests are including criterion-referenced information. He says that "publishers have moved in this direction because it is believed that if testing does not contribute to the instructional process, then it has very limited reasons for existing. The criterion-referenced information is making testing a valid classroom exercise."[3]

The Instructional Level on Some Standardized Reading Achievement Tests

Some achievement survey test batteries such as the *California Achievement Tests* (CAT), the *Comprehensive Test of Basic Skills*, the *Metropolitan Achievement Tests*, and the *Stanford Achievement Test Series* are designed to help estimate a student's instructional level in reading. Test makers are including such information because they claim that "teachers ask for and like to have this because it helps them to identify reading materials that are appropriate for their individual students. This optional score is another way of making the test more useful for the teacher."[4]

The reporting of the instructional reading level can be very helpful

---

[3] John Stewart, senior product manager, CTB/McGraw-Hill, 1990.
[4] Ibid.

to the teacher because not all students are given an informal reading inventory (see Chapter 8); whereas all children do take the standardized reading achievement test.

Special Note

Teachers are cautioned about the use of reading achievement tests to estimate the instructional level of children with reading problems. It may not accurately reflect this children's instructional level. (See Chapter 8.)

Locator Tests

Locator test
Used to determine at what level a student should begin testing.

Many of the achievement batteries supply a locator test, which is used to determine at which level a student should begin testing, when testing out-of-level, because the U.S. Office of Education for Chapter I testing recommends functional level testing. Locator tests are becoming increasingly widespread among test makers because of the need to provide students with tests to which they can relate well. Students in sixth grade reading at a fourth-grade level will not relate well to a sixth-grade reading test. The locator test is used to determine the approximate functional level of these students, and it is recommended that those students who test out-of-level on the locator test be given the achievement test at the approximate functional level at which they tested on the locator test. Therefore, the sixth-grade students who score at the fourth-grade level on the locator test would be tested with a fourth-grade level test.

Practice Tests

Practice test
Ensures that the actual test measures what students know rather than test-taking ability; it familiarizes students with the test.

Most standardized achievement tests provide a practice test. These are designed to ensure that students know how to mark an answer *before* they take the actual test. The practice tests are supposed to ensure that the actual test measures what students know and not their previous familiarity with test-taking procedures. (See "Group-Administered Measures of Intelligence (Aptitude)" in Chapter 6 for a sample from the Practice Test of the *Cognitive Abilities Test*, Levels 1 and 2.)

EMERGENT LITERACY AND READING READINESS

Emergent literacy
That stage in literacy, which is concerned with the young child's involvement in language and his or her attempts at reading and writing before coming to school.

Today we tend to talk about levels of literacy and recognize that an individual's literacy is something that continues all through life. Emergent literacy, which is that stage in literacy prior to formal reading and writing, is concerned with the young child's involvement in language, together with his or her attempts at reading and writing before coming to school. For example, a child's scribbling or attempting to tell a story from a storybook would be considered signs of emergent literacy.

Proponents of the emergent literacy theory feel strongly that the young children engaged in such activities as listening to stories, retelling stories, and interacting with storytellers are learning to read; that is, these are legitimate reading activities that are viewed as reading rather than "precursers" to reading or reading readiness.[5]

READING READINESS TESTS

Reading readiness test
Supposed to predict those children who are ready to read. If used, it must be used with great caution.

Reading readiness tests are usually the first type of standardized achievement test a child encounters in his or her life at school. These tests, which are supposed to be designed to predict those children who are ready to read, are a direct result of the readiness movement, which believed that children are not *ready* to read until they have reached a mental age of six and a half. Even though most educators have discarded the "waiting" theory of readiness, reading readiness tests are alive and going strong. Studies show that administrators rank them as the number one criterion for determining when a child should begin formal reading instruction.[6] Because the chances are high that your school will use a reading readiness test, you should have some understanding of the kinds of tasks included and how good they are at predicting future reading success. (Note that most achievement test batteries have readiness tests.)

Reading readiness tests are not diagnostic tests.

> Although they may indicate weaknesses in certain broad areas, such as word recognition, or vocabulary, they are not designed to isolate specific reading defects. However, reading readiness and diagnostic tests do contain many item types that are similar—visual discrimination, vocabulary, motor coordination, and the like.[7]

Some of the factors that influence how well a child will learn to read are those that we discussed previously in Chapters 4 and 5: intellectual development, visual and auditory perception, concept development, desire to learn, eye-hand coordination, names of common things, and exposure to print.

Even though commercially produced reading readiness tests vary in a number of ways, which we will discuss shortly, they all seem to have some of the following types of items:

1. *Motor skills.* Examinees are required to draw lines, complete a circle, underline words, or go through a finger maze.
2. *Auditory discrimination.* The children are asked to pronounce words that have been read to them or to select which of similar-sounding words identify a picture.
3. *Visual discrimination.* The children are required to choose similarities or differences in words, letters, numbers, or pictures.

[5] Lesley Mandel Morrow and Jeffrey K. Smith, eds., *Assessment for Instruction in Early Literacy* (Englewood Cliffs, N.J.: Prentice-Hall, 1990), p. 2.
[6] Robert L. Hillerich, *Reading Fundamentals for Preschool and Primary Children* (Columbus, Ohio: Charles Merrill, 1977), p. 25.
[7] William A. Mehrens and Irvin J. Lehmann, *Using Standardized Tests in Education,* 4th ed. (New York: Longman, 1987), p. 252.

4. *Vocabulary.* Children's knowledge of the meanings of words is assessed by asking them either to define a word, name various objects of the same or different class, or select the correct word to describe a picture.

5. *Memory.* The children may be asked to reproduce a geometrical figure to which they have been exposed for a certain length of time; they may be asked to repeat a story that has been read to them; or they may be required to carry out in sequence a series of instructions that have been presented to them.

6. *Drawing/copying.* The children demonstrate their skill in copying or drawing a letter, a number, or a form.

7. *Recognition of numbers, words, and letters.* The children are required to identify numbers, words, or alphabetical letters.[8]

Examples of Reading Readiness Tests

As stated earlier, not all reading readiness tests are the same, even though they do have some similar types of items. Reading readiness tests vary as to purpose, number and kinds of subtests, and administration time. They also vary in when they are given. For example, the *Gates-MacGinitie*, Level PRE, Pre-Reading Evaluation, which is part of the *Gates-MacGinitie Reading Survey Test* (Riverside, 1989), measures understanding of literacy concepts, reading instruction, relational concepts, oral language concepts, and letters and letter-sound correspondences. It is given in grades K.6–1.2, for which norms are available, and takes about 85 to 105 minutes to administer. (See pages 158–159 for a sample with directions of this test.)

The *Metropolitan Readiness Tests*, 5th ed. (Psychological Corporation, 1986), on the other hand, has two levels. Level 1 is intended for use with four-year-olds in the preschool setting (prior to their entry into kindergarten) until the middle of the kindergarten year. Level 2 is intended for use at the middle and end of kindergarten and in the early part of grade 1. The Level 1 tests include the following: auditory memory, beginning consonants, letter recognition, visual matching, school language and listening, and quantitative language. Level 2 contains the following: beginning consonants, sound-letter correspondence, visual matching, finding patterns, school language, listening, quantitative concepts, and quantitative operations. Level 1 takes 80 to 90 minutes, whereas Level 2 takes about 100 minutes.

The *Stanford Early School Achievement Test*, 3rd ed. (SESAT) (Psychological Corporation, 1989), also has two levels. However, Level 1 (K.0–K.5) is not intended for use with preschoolers; it contains five subtests that are at a higher level than the subtests of the Level 1 subtests for the *Metropolitan Reading Readiness Tests*. They are as follows: sounds and letters, word reading, listening to words and stories, mathematics, and environment. The total administration time

[8] Ibid.

is 130 minutes, which is also longer than both Levels of the *Metropolitan Tests*, as well as the *Gates-MacGinitie Level PRE*. Level 2 of the SESAT is intended for use in grades K.5–1.5, takes 145 minutes for total administration, and has six subtests. They are the following: sounds and letters, word reading, sentence reading, listening to words and stories, mathematics, and environment.

PRACTICE ITEMS FOR *GATES-MACGINITIE READING TESTS*, LEVEL PRE (PRE-READING EVALUATION) WITH DIRECTIONS FOR P1

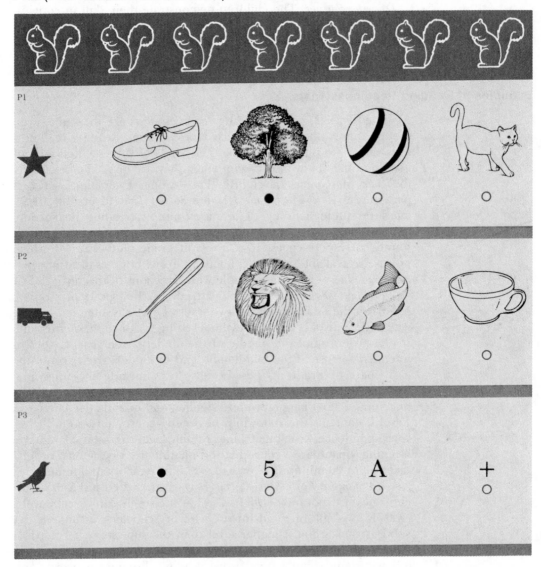

DIRECTIONS FOR P1 ON PAGE 1 OF THE TEST BOOKLET

P1 (Practice item)

Hold up the facing page of this manual, point to the star, and say: Look at my book. Wait until all the children are looking, then say: Under the squirrels, here where I am pointing, there is a star. Find the star in your book. Put your finger on the star. (or: Put your place marker under the star.)

Check to be sure that every child has found the star.

Next to the star is a row of pictures. Under each picture is a little circle. Look at the circle under the **tree**. It has been filled in with a strong, dark mark. The mark fills most of the circle. You are going to fill in some other circles so they look like the one under the **tree**.

Now look up here. Draw a small circle on the chalkboard and wait until all the children are looking, then say: When you mark a circle, fill it in like this. Fill in the circle by making a combination of vertical, horizontal, and circular strokes with the point of the chalk. (The children may use whatever kind of stroke is most natural for them.) *If the booklets will be machine scored*, add: Be sure to fill in the center of the circle. Don't let your mark go outside the circle.

The same is done for P2 and P3. The teacher must make sure that any child who has changed an answer has erased the wrong mark thoroughly.

Also, before beginning the test, every child should have marked items P2 and P3 correctly.

Uses of Reading Readiness Tests

Studies have shown that the predictive validity of reading readiness tests is not very high, that they could not predict with accuracy how well nonreaders would learn to read, and that teachers' ratings were as accurate in predicting reading success as were the tests.[9] On the other hand, there is a great amount of evidence available to support the relationship between young children's letter naming and their later reading achievement, as well as school achievement.[10] Studies

[9] Max Coltheart, "When Can Children Learn to Read—And When Should They Be Taught?" in *Reading Research: Advances in Theory and Practice*, vol. 1, ed. T. Gary Waller and G. E. MacKinnon (New York: Academic Press, 1979), p. 15.

[10] Daniel J. Walsh, Gary Glen Price, and Mark G. Gillingham, "The Critical but Transitory Importance of Letter Naming," *Reading Research Quarterly* 23 (winter 1988): 110; Marilyn Jager Adams, *Beginning to Read: Thinking and Learning about Print—A Summary* by Steven A. Stahl, Jean Osborn, and Fran Lehr (Urbana, Ill.: Center for the Study of Reading, 1990), p. 10.

have shown that the alphabet subtest of the *Metropolitan Readiness Test* "has consistently been the best predictor of scholastic achievement."[11]

It has been stated that "a great saving in testing time could well stem from using only the letters and numbers subtests or, perhaps, by not testing readiness at all. In either case, the sacrifice in information would be minimal."[12]

Such statements continue, and educators continue to decry the misuses of reading readiness tests.[13] Despite many such statements, test makers continue to produce reading readiness tests, and as has already been stated, most school systems use them. It must be that eduators feel more secure with the results of commercially produced tests than with teachers' judgments, even though evidence weighs against such security.

Why is a test needed to predict future reading success? We already know from voluminous research that high-achieving readers usually come from homes with enriched verbal environments, whereas low-achieving readers usually come from homes in which little conversation takes place with the parents. We also know that a rich verbal environment is more likely to be found among middle and upper socioeconomic classes than in lower classes.

Unfortunately, there are some dangers attached to reading readiness tests if they are misused. One danger is a self-fulfilling prophecy. If a child does poorly on a reading readiness test, the teacher may feel that the child cannot benefit from reading instruction; the child is not expected to be able to learn to read, and as a result, the teacher defers instruction in reading. Eventually, the teacher's feelings concerning the inability of the child to read become part of the child's own self-concept (see "Teachers' Expectations" in Chapter 2).

Here are some suggestions on how to choose and use reading readiness tests if they are required in your school system:

1. Use a reading readiness test that can provide you with information on a child's present level of literacy development.
2. Check the subtests to determine how directly the tasks required are related to reading. For example, some tests require children to match pictures and geometric figures rather than letters. Those children who do well in matching pictures and geometric figures may not do well in matching letters. Check to see if the subtests are similar to the activities presented in the beginning reading readiness program.

---

[11] Walsh, Price, and Gillingham, p. 110.

[12] Hillerich, p. 25.

[13] See "NAEYC Position Statement on Standardized Testing of Young Children 3–8 Years of Age," *Young Children* 43 (March 1988): 42–47; Sue Bredekamp and Lorrie Shepard, "How Best to Protect Children from Inappropriate School Expectations, Practices, and Policies," *Young Children* 44 (March 1989): 14–24; Constance Kamii (ed.), *Achievement Testing in the Early Grades* (Washington, D.C.: National Association for the Education of Young Children, 1990).

3. Check the administration time of the test. Make sure that it is suited to the attention span of your students.
4. Make sure children understand the terminology used on the test and understand the directions.
5. Do not use the results of the test to delay a child from beginning to read. Remember, our purpose is to gain information about the child's present level of development so that we can provide the best possible program for him or her rather than to determine whether a child is *ready* for reading. Unfortunately, as stated earlier, reading readiness tests often are used to test when a child is *ready* to learn to read. A child who does poorly on the test is often delayed from beginning to read, and he or she is put into programs that do not provide direct instruction in reading. This is ironic because the child who does poorly on a reading readiness test that involves the use of letters probably needs more exposure to letters and the sounds they represent than a child who does well. Delaying a child's entrance into the formal reading program is assuring failure for that child rather than success.
6. Do not use the reading readiness test as an end in itself; also use informal assessments and teacher judgment to make decisions concerning the child's readiness.

Special Note

As stated earlier in this chapter, a number of achievement test batteries have a preinstructional or readiness test as part of their battery.

Because most achievement test batteries have overlapping age levels and take into account whether a child has had instruction in kindergarten or not, these tests may be more helpful than many of the regular reading readiness tests.

A FINAL WORD

The Reading Report Card has consistently found that students through the years

> have displayed rudimentary reading skills and strategies, characterized by the ability to perform relatively uncomplicated, discrete reading tasks successfully. At the other extreme, very few students in any assessment have reached the highest level of reading proficiency defined, reflecting their difficulty in comprehending passages that are more lengthy and complex or that deal with specialized subject matter.[14]

The emphasis in the 1990s is on helping students gain higher-

---

[14] Ina V. S. Mullis and Lynn B. Jenkins, *The Reading Report Card, 1971–1988*, the National Assessment of Educational Progress (Princeton, N.J.: Educational Testing Service, 1990), p. 25.

order thinking skills, and many of the standardized reading achievement tests are beginning to include more higher-order reading test items in their batteries. For example, both the *Stanford Achievement Test Series*, 8th ed., and the *Metropolitan Achievement Tests*, 6th ed., have items throughout the battery that measure thinking skills and that provide a special thinking skills score for added information.

If standardized tests stress the interpretive and critical reading skills more, then more emphasis will probably be placed on these skills in the classroom. (See Chapter 13 for more on reading comprehension and higher-level thinking.)

SUMMARY

Chapter 7 discusses reading achievement tests that yield a general score. It is emphasized that reading survey tests such as the *Iowa Silent Reading Tests*, which measure only reading, and the *California Achievement Tests*, which have a reading test as one of their subtests, are similar and serve the same purpose. They both measure a student's overall reading achievement. Both reading survey tests and reading subtests from achievement test batteries yield a general or overall score and were not developed to be used as diagnostic instruments. They do, however, play an essential role in the diagnostic program. They are group tests that are easy to administer in a relatively short period of time, and they are useful for screening, that is, as an aid in identifying those students who may need help. Reading achievement tests that yield an overall score are generally used for comparison purposes. Various types of reading achievement tests that yield an overall or general score are discussed, and examples of some are presented.

Reading readiness tests are usually the first type of standardized achievement test that a child encounters in his or her life at school. They are designed to predict those children who are ready to read; however, teachers are cautioned about such predictions. A discussion of these tests, as well as suggestions on how to choose and use them, is given. In addition, the term *emergent literacy* is discussed and contrasted to the concept of reading readiness.

SUGGESTIONS FOR THOUGHT QUESTIONS AND ACTIVITIES

1. You have been appointed to a schoolwide committee which is interested in evaluating the testing procedures and the kinds of tests that are given during the school year. You are supposed to help committee members evaluate their use of reading readiness tests. Your suggestions will help them decide whether or not to use such tests. How will you go about helping them to make their decision? What factors should you take into consideration? What

are your views concerning reading readiness tests? What does research say about them?

2. People in your school are confused about reading survey tests and reading achievement subtests of achievement test batteries. You have been asked to give examples of each and to explain their purposes.
3. Choose three standardized achievement tests and look them up in the *Mental Measurements Yearbooks*.
4. Choose one reading survey test, such as the *Iowa Silent Reading Tests*, and look it up in the *Mental Measurements Yearbooks*.
5. Choose three reading readiness tests and look them up in the *Mental Measurements Yearbooks*.
6. Contrast the concept of emergent literacy with that of reading readiness.

SELECTED BIBLIOGRAPHY

Conoley, Jane C., and Jack J. Kramer (Eds.). *The Tenth Mental Measurements Yearbook*. Lincoln, N.B.: Buros Institute of Mental Measurements, University of Nebraska, 1989.

Cooter, Robert B., and Suzzanne Curry. "*Gates-MacGinitie Reading Tests*, Third Edition." Assessment Section in *The Reading Teacher* 43 (December 1989): 256–58.

Hopkins, Kenneth D., Julian C. Stanley, and B. R. Hopkins. "Standardized Achievement Tests." In *Educational and Psychological Measurement and Evaluation*. Englewood Cliffs, N.J.: Prentice-Hall, 1990.

Kamii, Constance (ed.). *Achievement Testing in the Early Grades*. Washington, D.C.: National Association for the Education of Young Children, 1990.

Mehrens, William A., and Irvin J. Lehmann. *Using Standardized Tests in Education*, 4th ed. New York: Longman, 1987.

Sweetland, Richard C., and Daniel J. Keyser. *Tests*, 3rd ed. Austin, Tex.: PRO-ED, 1990.

Woolfolk, Anita E. "Using Standardized Tests in Teaching." In *Educational Psychology*, 4th ed. Englewood Cliffs, N.J.: Prentice-Hall, 1990.

8

Diagnostic Reading Tests and Techniques I: An Emphasis on the Informal Reading Inventory

Scenario: The Profile of a First-Grade Failure

Larry is a blond, blue-eyed little boy, who comes from an upper-middle-class home. He has parents who care for him and who are highly educated. Larry, according to the statistics, should be doing well in school. He is not, though, and there are many others just like him. Why? If children like Larry have problems, what hope is there for those who don't have Larry's social and economic advantages?

Larry's parents had spoken to me about their little boy and told me how unhappy they were with his situation. They told me that Larry had been left back in the first grade because he couldn't read. His first-grade teacher and the principal had recommended that Larry repeat the first grade, and they, the parents, had not objected. They were told that by repeating the first grade, Larry would be happier and would do much better. Well, he was not happy, and he was not doing much better. Larry hated school. His personality was changing. He felt that he was dumb, and he didn't like himself very much. His parents spoke to the teacher, who said that Larry was having difficulty with the reading program, but it was the only pro-

gram the school was allowed to use. She was sure that Larry would soon adjust to it. The parents, not so sure, went to see the principal. The principal told them that he and his staff knew what was good for Larry. After all, they were the professionals. Also, the principal told the parents that they were justified in retaining Larry because on the group IQ test he had scored in a range that put him in the category of borderline intelligence. He told the parents not to worry, that he and his staff knew what they were doing, that Larry would have to continue in the same program, and that the same method of instruction would be used.

Larry's parents were confused and bitter. They did worry. The private schools would not accept Larry because the school term had already begun, and their son was becoming unhappier and unhappier. Larry didn't want to go to school. The parents, who had thought that their son was a bright boy, were beginning to wonder whether the IQ test score was correct and whether their son was a slow learner.

Larry's parents decided to go to outside sources for help. They asked me to test Larry, and I consented. When I met him, he said to me, "I'm the biggest one in my class because I was left back. Everyone knows that I was left back. I hate school." We talked for a little while, and I tried to learn about some of the things he liked to do. I discovered that he enjoyed looking through *National Geographic*, that he loved sports, that he went fishing and camping with his father and brother, and that he loved animals.

Even though Larry was only in the first grade, I decided to give him an informal reading inventory. When I asked him to state the words in the word recognition list, he picked up the sheet with the words and put it so close to his face that the paper was actually touching his nose. I asked Larry if he wore glasses. He said, "No." Larry had difficulty recognizing the words in isolation. I had him start at the lowest level in oral reading. Even at the preprimer level, he had trouble decoding words. His decoding problems were so pronounced that I decided to give Larry a listening capacity test because I felt his decoding problems would probably hinder his comprehension. I read aloud the passages to Larry and then asked him questions about them. Larry was able to answer the comprehension questions almost perfectly up to the seventh-grade level. He was able to tell me what a nocturnal bird was, as well as answer some very difficult and involved questions.

Larry is a highly able boy; he certainly is not "dumb." A crime has been perpetrated against him. Who is to blame? When Larry was re-tained, no one had given him any diagnostic reading tests or an individual IQ test. To give a child who is having decoding problems a group IQ test and then to use that test to assert that the child is of borderline intelligence is ludicrous. The parents should have noticed from Larry's behavior that he had some kind of eye problem. When the parents were asked about it they claimed that the school nurse had tested Larry's eyes and that no eye problem had been noticed. From Larry's behavior, the teacher also should have noticed that Larry appeared to have some kind of eye problem and should have recommended that the parents have his eyes checked by an eye doctor, since the school nurse only tests for nearsightedness and farsightedness. Based on my suggestion, Larry was taken to an ophthalmologist. The eye specialist found that Larry had very severe astigmatism, which probably would account for his decoding problems. Larry had difficulty focusing on words. This does not excuse the school for insisting that Larry adjust to the program rather than adjusting the program to suit Larry. Regardless of who is to blame, Larry sees himself as a failure. At seven years of age, he can't wait to leave school. Damage has been done to Larry, and he is still suffering from it.

This profile of Larry, which is based on fact, was not written to show the school personnel as being the devils and the author as being the angel. It has been written to raise the consciousness level of teachers to the importance of diagnosis.

In this chapter and in the next, you will encounter a number of diagnostic instruments that test a student's oral reading ability, as well as other reading abilities. You will learn how to gain detailed information about a pupil's reading behavior. This chapter will discuss oral reading and emphasize the informal reading inventory, which can be an indispensable tool for the classroom teacher if it is properly used. (See "What Are Diagnostic Reading Tests?" in Chapter 3.)

KEY QUESTIONS

After you finish reading this chapter you should be able to answer the following questions:

1. How was reading taught until the early 1900s?

2. What is the place of oral reading in diagnosis?
3. What is an informal reading inventory?
4. How does a teacher administer an informal reading inventory?
5. When does a teacher administer an informal reading inventory?
6. To whom does a teacher administer an informal reading inventory?
7. How can a teacher construct his or her own informal reading inventory?
8. How do published informal reading inventories compare with teacher-made ones?
9. How are reading levels determined on an informal reading inventory?
10. What are some controversial issues concerning informal reading inventories?
11. How are oral reading errors scored?
12. What are some of the problems concerning the scoring of oral reading errors?
13. What is miscue analysis?
14. What are the word recognition formulas for computing percent correct and allowable errors?
15. What is a listening capacity test?
16. When is a listening capacity test given?
17. What are word lists used for?
18. What is a modified informal reading inventory approach?
19. What criteria should you look for if you are interested in using a published informal reading inventory?
20. What are some points of caution concerning informal reading inventories?

KEY TERMS IN CHAPTER

You should pay special attention to the following new terms.

buffer zone
frustration reading level
independent reading level
informal reading inventory
   (IRI)
instructional reading level
listening capacity level
listening capacity test
miscue
miscue analysis
oral reading

ORAL READING

The child read aloud, of course: throughout antiquity, until the late Empire, silent reading was exceptional. People read aloud to themselves, or, if they could, got a servant to read to them.[1]

Closely associated with reading was recitation: the selected passages were not only read aloud but also learnt by heart, and it seems that beginners at least used to recite in a sing song manner, syllable by syllable: "Com-ing through, ray by ray, A-pollo, the mor-ning sun . . ."[2]

Oral reading
Reading aloud.

These excerpts help shed light on why reading was taught in a recitation manner until the beginning of the twentieth century and silent reading was ignored: It's difficult to break with tradition. As a matter of fact, in some classes today you can still find remnants of the oral tradition in reading—some teachers still have their students read in a round-robin rote fashion. Fortunately, however, this practice is not as common as in the past. Fortunately, also, the misuses and overuses of oral reading did not culminate in its complete banishment, even though there was a movement for a time to ban oral reading in the classroom.

Read the following exchange between a student and teacher. Does it sound familiar?

Teacher: You read that passage aloud very well. Now, let's see how well you do answering questions about it.
Student: Oh, I can't answer any questions on it because I wasn't listening to what I was reading.

How many times has this happened? Probably often, but why? Obviously, the child was so intent on pronouncing the words correctly that he or she was not paying any attention to the meaning of what was read. Since reading *is* meaning, we couldn't say that this child was reading. He or she was merely reciting without thinking.

Although some people may not do as well comprehending material that they read orally rather than silently, oral reading does have value. It is especially useful for diagnostic purposes and has an important place in the reading program. If properly used, it can be an essential diagnostic tool that helps teachers learn about the word recognition skills of their students.

Oral Reading as a Diagnostic Tool

Astute teachers can gain a great deal of information about a student's word recognition skill by listening to the student read aloud. A teacher can determine the reading level of the child and avoid having the child read silently at a frustration level. Oral reading helps a

[1] H. I. Marrou, *A History of Education in Antiquity* (New York: New American Library of World Literature, 1956), p. 214.
[2] Ibid., p. 215.

teacher gain insight into a student's reading difficulty, if he or she has one, as well as a student's strengths.

There are many opportunities for children to read orally during their day at school. Even though a choral reading or the reading of a book report or poem is not planned as a diagnostic testing session, knowledgeable teachers use these opportunities to study their students. Much important information is gained from informal diagnostic techniques if teachers know what to look for. The key, of course, is to know what to look for. (See Chapter 10 for a discussion on the use of observation as a diagnostic technique.)

Many standardized diagnostic reading tests test oral reading ability. Some test *only* oral reading ability, whereas others may have a subtest of this (see Chapter 9). All informal reading inventories test oral reading ability. This chapter and the next will present a number of tests that diagnose oral reading ability.

WHAT ARE THE PURPOSES OF AN INFORMAL READING INVENTORY?

An informal reading inventory (IRI) is probably one of the most valuable diagnostic aids because of the amount of information it can convey to a perceptive teacher who knows how to use it to its best advantages.

Informal Reading Inventory (IRI) A valuable aid in helping teachers determine a student's reading levels and his or her strengths and weaknesses. It usually consists of oral and silent reading passages selected from basal readers from the preprimer to the eighth-grade levels.

An essential function of an IRI is to help the teacher determine the child's levels of independence, instruction, frustration, and capacity. These are needed to make a proper match between the child and the books he or she reads.

Another important job of an IRI is to help a teacher learn about a student's reading strengths and weaknesses so that he or she can develop a proper reading program for the student. For example, if on giving a child an IRI the teacher learns that the child has difficulty answering comprehension questions that call for interpretation or inference, the teacher can develop a program for the child to help him or her gain skill in this area (see Chapters 11 and 13). From listening to the student reading orally, the teacher can learn whether the student has word recognition problems that may be interfering with comprehension when the child is reading silently.

From listening to a child's oral reading, the teacher can hypothesize possible skill deficiencies that may be limiting the student's performance. If the teacher sees that a student has a word recognition problem, he or she would probably want to administer other informal skills tests (see Chapter 9) for more specific diagnosis because there are generally not enough opportunities to observe any given skill in great depth in a relatively short passage. For example, how many initial blends are there in a selection? From listening to the child read, the teacher can determine whether the child reads with expression and observes punctuation marks or whether the student reads hurriedly without any concern for punctuation signals.

Yet another function of the IRI is to give the student feedback on his or her reading behavior. As the student reads passages at graduated levels of difficulty, he or she becomes aware of the reading level that is appropriate for him or her. It helps the student recognize his or her word recognition and comprehension strengths and weaknesses. Student awareness of a problem is a vital factor in helping the student overcome the difficulty or difficulties.

It must again be stressed that the IRI is an excellent instrument for estimating students' reading levels and for diagnosing their strengths and weaknesses, but the IRI is only as good as the person administering it and interpreting its results.

Special Note

The term *informal* implies that the inventory is teacher-made; however, many informal reading inventories are published (commercially produced) ones. In this chapter, information will be provided on how to construct an informal reading inventory, if a teacher wishes to do so, based on the basal reader series in use in the class (see "Constructing Your Own Informal Reading Inventory").

AN OVERVIEW OF THE INFORMAL READING INVENTORY

This section will give you an overview of an informal reading inventory. The sections that follow will go into detail on many of the points presented here. It is good to see the whole before discussing its parts so that you can better determine the relationship of the parts to their whole.

An IRI is individually administered and usually consists of oral and silent reading passages selected from basal readers from the preprimer to the eighth-grade levels (some exist up to the twelfth grade). Usually each selection has the following kinds of comprehension questions: factual, inferential, and word meanings. (A few may contain evaluative questions.)

Graded word lists, which usually are also taken from basal readers and generally consist of twenty or twenty-five words from each reader level, are used to determine at what grade level the student should begin reading the oral passages. The student usually begins the word list at two levels below his or her present grade level. The highest grade level at which the student has no errors on the graded word list is the grade level at which he or she begins reading the oral passage. The student reads aloud the oral passage, and the teacher records any omission, substitution, insertion, pronunciation, repetition, and hesitation errors. If the student reads the oral passage at the independent or instructional level, the student is asked the comprehension questions; he or she then proceeds to read the silent passage at the same grade level and is asked the questions to the silent passage. The student then goes to the next reading grade level, continuing until he or she reaches his or her frustration level. If the student makes so many word recognition errors in oral reading that he or she is reading at or close to his or her frustration level, the teacher begins to read the passages aloud to the student to determine his or her comprehension ability. This is called a listening capacity test.[3]

DETERMINING READING LEVELS

The IRI, which originated from the work of Emmett A. Betts and his doctoral student Patsy A. Killgallon, is used to determine three reading levels and a capacity or listening capacity level. The criteria for reading levels on the IRI were determined by Betts, and many informal reading inventories still use the same levels or modifications of them. The reason for this is that even though there is disagreement on what the quantitative reading levels should be, the research on determining reading levels is not conclusive.[4] Also, it is imperative to state again that "the valid and reliable use of IRIs must rely upon the accurate professional judgments of the person conducting the evaluation. The accurate use of IRIs requires judgment and interpretation, not the mechanical calculation or application of scores."[5]

The levels as determined by Betts and his percentages that designate the levels follow:

Betts Reading Levels

Independent Level*	Children read on their own without any difficulty.	Word Recognition—99% or above Comprehension—90% or above
Instructional Level	Teaching level.	Word Recognition—95% or above Comprehension—75% or above
Frustration Level	This level is to be avoided. It is the lowest level of readability.	Word Recognition—90% or less Comprehension—50% or less
Listening Capacity Level*	Highest level at which a pupil can comprehend when someone reads to him or her.	Comprehension—75% or above

* Betts also called the *independent level* the *basal level*, and the *listening capacity level* was called the *capacity level*.

[3] A listening capacity test may also be referred to as a listening comprehension test.
[4] Majorie Seddon Johnson, Roy A. Kress, and John Pikulski, *Informal Reading Inventories*, 2nd ed. (Newark, Del.: International Reading Association, 1987), p. 13.
[5] Ibid.

In designating these levels Betts not only gave percentage determinants but also gave other criteria that teachers should look for at each level.[6]

Independent Level

Independent reading level
Level at which child reads on his or her own without any difficulty.

This level "is the highest level at which an individual can read and satisfy all the criteria for desirable reading behavior in silent- and oral-reading situations."[7] At the independent level the child can read successfully on his or her own without any assistance. When the student is reading orally or silently at this level, he or she should be able to achieve a minimum comprehension score on literal and interpretive questions of at least 90 percent. The pupil should also be free from such observable evidence of tension as frowning, movements of feet and hands, finger pointing, and holding the book too close or too far.

For oral reading the student should have good rhythm with proper phrasing and attention to punctuation. The student's voice should be free from tension, and he or she should have an accurate pronunciation of 99 percent or more of the words. The student's silent reading should be free from lip movement or subvocalizing.

The independent level is an important one for the child, teacher, parents, and librarian. It is at this level that the child will read library or trade books in school and at home. The reference books that children choose to read for a special project or assignment should also be at their independent level because they will be reading these on their own. If they choose books to read independently that are too hard for them, that will deter them from reading. One of the ways that teachers can determine whether they have done a good job in teaching reading is to observe whether students voluntarily choose books to read during the school day.

Instructional Level

Instructional reading level
The teaching level.

The instructional level is the one at which teaching is done. This level must not be so challenging that it frustrates the student nor so easy that the student becomes bored. At this level there should be a minimum comprehension score of at least 75 percent for both oral and silent reading on literal and interpretive questions, and in the oral reading there should be accurate pronunciation of at least 95 percent of the running words. As on the independent level, there should be no observable tensions or undue movements of feet and hands. There should be freedom from finger pointing, lip movements, and head movements; and there should be acceptable posture.

[6] Adapted from Emmett A. Betts, *Foundations of Reading Instruction* (New York: American Book Company, 1946), pp. 445–54.
[7] Ibid., p. 445.

Oral reading should be rhythmical with proper phrasing; there should be proper attention paid to punctuation; and the child's voice should be free from tension.

It is possible for students to have an instructional level that spans more than one, two, or even three reader levels. (When this happens, the instructional level is reported as a range; see "Reporting Students' Reading Levels.") A student may read at more than one instructional level for a number of reasons. For example, students' interests, background information, and experience play an essential role in how well a student may do in a particular content area. It is possible that a child may be at an instructional level in one subject and not in the same instructional level in another subject. It is therefore important that the IRI that is used to determine a student's reading ability levels has a variety of materials in it.

Frustration Level

Frustration reading level
The child reads with many word recognition and comprehension errors. It is the lowest reading level and one to be avoided.

This is the level to be avoided; however, for diagnostic purposes, it is helpful for teachers to know what this level is so that they can avoid giving students reading material at this level. The fact that a child has reached his or her frustration level is evidenced by the child's attaining a comprehension score of 50 percent or less on literal and interpretive questions for oral and silent reading, and the child's inability to pronounce 10 percent of the words on the oral reading passage.

At the frustration level, the child has difficulty anticipating meanings and is not familiar with the facts presented in the selection. The child shows his or her frustration by frowning, constantly moving in a nervous fashion, finger pointing, blinking, or faulty breathing. The child may also be unwilling to read, and he or she may cry.

At this level, when the child reads silently, he or she reads at a slow rate, uses lip movements, and makes low vocal utterances. During oral reading, the child does not observe punctuation, reads in a high-pitched voice, and reads with a lack of rhythm or word by word. The child's reading is further characterized by irregular breathing, meaningless word substitution, insertion of words, repetition of words, partial and complete word reversals, omission of words, almost no eye-voice span, and an increased tendency to stutter.

Teacher judgment plays an important role in determining whether to continue testing or not. For example, it is possible to stop testing, even though a child has not reached his or her frustration level because the child is nervous or upset. (Be careful not to confuse tiredness with signs of frustration.) Also, even though minimum criteria are usually given for estimating the various reading levels of IRIs, these are actually general standards because of teacher judgment. Remember, the examiner is the final judge, not the "mechanical calculation or application of scores."

Listening Capacity Level

Listening capacity level
The highest level at which a learner can understand material when it is read aloud to him or her.

The listening capacity level, as first determined by Betts, is the "highest level of readability of material which the learner can comprehend when the material is read to him."[8] Betts also established the minimum comprehension score of at least 75 percent, based on both factual and inferential questions for listening capacity, and he designated that the term "*level* refers to the grade level at which the material was prepared for use; for example, preprimer, primer, first reader, second reader, and so on."[9] (The listening capacity level may also be referred to as the *listening comprehension level*, the *capacity level*, and even the *potential level*.)

The Buffer Zone of the IRI

Buffer zone
The area that falls between the instructional and frustration levels.

The *buffer zone* of the IRI is the area that falls between the instructional and frustration levels. For word recognition it is 94 percent to 91 percent, and for comprehension it is 74 percent to 51 percent (Betts's criteria). When a child's score falls in the buffer zone, the teacher must decide whether to continue testing or not, even though the child has not yet reached the frustration level. If the child appears interested in continuing, testing should continue. If, on the other hand, the child exhibits symptoms of frustration, testing should be stopped. Even though the decision of whether to continue testing or not is a subjective one, there are some factors that the teacher could take into consideration; for example, the types of errors the child has made, the personality of the student, the student's prior reading record, the health of the child, whether the child speaks another language at home, whether the child speaks nonstandard English, and so on.

A student who stays in the buffer zone for more than one reader level and does not exhibit signs of frustration will probably be able to gain the skills that he lacks more readily and quickly than a student who goes from the instructional level directly to the frustration level. It shows that the student has enough skills to be able to continue, as well as the interest and desire to do so.

Reporting Students' Reading Levels

The independent level is reported as one level only: the highest level at which the child can read and satisfy the criteria for the independent level. If a child reads at an independent level at reader levels 1, 2^1, 2^2 and 3^1 the child's independent level is reported as reader level 3^1.

The frustration level is also reported as one level only. The first reader level at which the child reaches frustration is reported as the

[8] Ibid., p. 452.
[9] Ibid., p. 439.

frustration level. The examiner does not continue testing after the child reaches the frustration level.

The instructional level is often not reported as one level only. It is possible that a child's instructional level is a span of a number of reading levels. When that happens, the examiner reports the range. If a child reads at the instructional level at reader levels 4, 5, and 6 before going into the buffer zone or reaching the frustration level, the child's instructional level is reported as a 4–6 range.

To determine a student's independent and instructional reading levels, the criteria for both word recognition and comprehension should be met. For the independent level, the student should meet the criteria of 99 percent accuracy in word recognition and 90 percent in comprehension. For the instructional level, the student should meet the criteria of 95–98 percent for word recognition and 75–89 percent in comprehension. For the frustration level, however, only one of the criteria has to be met, that is, 50 percent or less in comprehension or 90 percent or less in word recognition.

The examiner must use judgment in making these determinations. If a student has excellent comprehension at the independent level but makes a few minor word recognition errors while reading aloud that do not change the meaning or substance of what is being read, the comprehension level is probably more indicative of the student's reading level. Of course, the problem is in the subjectivity of determining minor errors and the ultimate consequence of possibly placing children in higher levels than they actually are. Be careful about giving students the "benefit of the doubt" when determining their reading levels. Remember, in diagnosis we want to uncover problems early and make sure we are not overlooking any possible difficulty.

Special Notes

Some examiners average the oral and silent reading comprehension scores to determine a student's reading comprehension level. This is not suggested because the oral and silent reading scores are indicative of different kinds of behavior. It is important that the examiner analyze independently both the oral and silent reading comprehension scores to gain insight into the student's reading comprehension behavior.

In addition, the averaging of the oral and silent reading comprehension scores is a violation of the spirit and intent of the IRI. A single score tends to rank students, which is not the purpose of the IRIs. "Informal reading inventories are typically not designed to rank student scores; for most, data have not been collected for this purpose nor have validation studies been conducted."[10]

---

[10] Kalle Gerritz, senior examiner, Educational Testing Service, 1990.

The silent reading comprehension score on an informal reading inventory is more indicative of what a student does in a directed reading lesson than the oral reading comprehension score of an IRI; therefore examiners may use the silent reading comprehension score combined with the oral reading word recognition score to determine at what level students should read.

Again, it must be stressed that an IRI gives a profile of a student's reading behavior, so it is important to look at the individual oral and silent reading comprehension scores, as well as the oral reading word recognition scores.

When a student does better on oral comprehension than on silent comprehension, it usually means that the student must hear the words in order to understand the message. These students are generally more immature readers, and this kind of behavior is usually more typical of younger readers. More mature readers generally do better on silent reading. If the silent reading is a level or two above the oral reading, this is usually not considered a problem.

Also, teachers should be aware that on informal reading inventories, students must rely heavily on their short-term memories, so those who have difficulties in this area will probably not do well.

CONSTRUCTING YOUR OWN INFORMAL READING INVENTORY

Although it is time-consuming to construct your own IRI, there are some teachers who would like to do so. This section will present more specific information on the parts of an IRI as well as information on how to construct and score one.

Usually an IRI, as stated earlier in this chapter, consists of word lists at varying levels which have been selected from a basal reader series; passages which are based on graduated levels of difficulty that have also been selected from a basal reader series for oral and silent reading; and comprehension questions for both the oral and silent reading passages. A separate set of passages and comprehension questions at graduated levels of difficulty are also usually included to determine the listening capacity level.

Graded Word Lists

The graded word lists usually consist of twenty or twenty-five words. There is a word list for every reader level of the basal series. The list usually starts at the preprimer level and proceeds to the highest level book available. If the IRI begins at the preprimer level and ends at the eighth-grade level, there would be a word list for each level up to the eighth. (Most basal reader series have two reader levels for certain grades, and some have three preprimer reader levels. If there are three preprimer reader levels, it's a good idea to use the second one as representative of the three.)

The words for the word lists are selected from those introduced in the basal reader for each book level. (At the back of each basal reader there is usually a list of words that have been introduced in the book.) Words for the word lists are based on a random sampling, so that each word introduced at a particular level has an equal and independent chance of being chosen.

If you are constructing your own IRI, an easy way to get a random sampling of the words for the word lists, if there are fewer than 100 words, is to put each word on a slip of paper and put the slips in a small box or hat. (Make sure the slips of paper are well mixed.) Pull 20 words from the hat. (If there are only 20 words that have been introduced at a particular reader level, you obviously would use all the words.) However, at the upper-grade levels, where there are more than 100 words presented at each level, you need a method different from the cumbersome "old hat" random sampling method. You need a formula to help you determine the number of random samples of the required sample size for a given word list. The formula for this is as follows:

$$\frac{\text{Word List}}{\text{Sample Size}} = \text{Number of Samples}$$

The number of words you want on your word list is your sample size, and the word list is the total number of words. For example, if you want to select 20 words from a 100-word list, first apply the formula

$$N = \frac{100}{20} = 5.$$

Since the number of samples is 5, number the total number of words sequentially up to 5, that is, 1, 2, 3, 4, 5. To get the 20 words from the 100-word list, select all those words that are numbered either 1, 2, 3, 4, or 5. (Choose which number you will use by any method you wish, and then choose all words that have that number.) This procedure will give you a sample of 20 words from the 100-word list covering the entire alphabetical range, if the words are presented alphabetically.

Graded Oral and Silent Reading Passages

To randomly draw sample passages for your IRI, note the number of pages in each basal reader, and then choose any one of the numbers. For example, if there are 200 pages, choose any number from 1 to 200. Open the book to the number you have chosen. Choose a selection on that page that can be easily excerpted; that is, it can stand alone and make sense. The first sentence of the selection should not have any pronouns that have antecedents in the previous paragraph. If there are no paragraphs on that page that can be easily excerpted, go to the previous page. It may be that you will have to go to the beginning of the story to get a selection that can stand alone.

The sample selections should contain approximately the following sample sizes:

Preprimer level, approximately 40 to 70 words
Primer level, approximately 50 to 85
First-grade level, approximately 70 to 100
Second-grade level, approximately 100 to 150
Third-grade level, approximately 125 to 175
Fourth-grade level, approximately 150 to 200
Fifth-grade level, approximately 175 to 225
Sixth-grade level and up, approximately 175 to 275

The paragraphs that are chosen to comprise your IRI should be representative of the readability level of the basal reader from which they were taken. There are times when this is not so; it's a good idea to double-check the chosen paragraphs with a readability formula (see Appendix B for the Fry Readability Formula). If your selection does not pass the readability formula criterion, repeat the process to choose a different passage. Each selection chosen for the IRI should have a short statement telling something about it.

Special Note

Publishers may use more complicated methods for randomizing word and passage selection than the sampling techniques just described.

Graded Oral and Silent Reading Passages: A Commentary

There is disagreement in the field as to whether the oral and silent reading passages should be from the same or different selections. The author of this text prefers to use oral and silent reading passages from the same selection to ensure a greater chance of having a similar difficulty level of concepts and vocabulary. Dissimilarity can be a problem if the basal reader series is completely literature-based because these readers seem to have a greater variation in vocabulary load between different selections in the same basal reader. It is important to have vocabulary and concepts at the same difficulty level for both oral and silent reading passages because the teacher uses the oral reading passage to determine whether the child should read the silent reading passage.

In addition, this author has found that there appears to be a much greater variation in vocabulary load and difficulty among the present literature-based basal readers than in previous series. Often there may be only a few similar words in the glossaries of different basal reader series at the same reader grade level. Teachers should be aware of these differences if they use selections from different basal reader series to construct their IRIs.

The Comprehension Questions

Both the oral and the silent reading passages must have questions based on each passage, and the questions must be text-dependent. These are usually literal comprehension questions, interpretive questions, and word meaning questions. (Some IRIs may contain critical reading questions. These may present a problem because a number of these questions are usually not text-dependent; that is, the student can answer them independently of the text.) (See Chapter 13 for an in-depth discussion of literal, interpretive, and critical reading skills.) Examples of the types of questions that can be asked to assess selected comprehension skills at each level follow.

Literal Comprehension Questions

Literal questions are the easiest to construct, and they are generally the ones most often asked. The answers for literal questions are directly stated in the selection. Here is an example of a selection and some literal comprehension questions based on it:

Sharon and Carol are sisters.
They like to play together.
They play lots of games.
Their favorite game is Monopoly.

Literal Questions:

1. Who are sisters? (story detail)
2. What do the sisters like to do? (story detail)
3. What do the sisters play? (story detail)
4. What is their favorite game? (story detail)

Interpretive Questions

Interpretive questions are more difficult to answer because the answers are not directly stated in the selection; they are implied. Interpretive questions are also usually more difficult to construct and are usually not asked as often as literal comprehension questions. Here is an example of a selection and some interpretive questions based on it:

Do you ever think of the right thing to say too late? I always do, but my friend George always has the right words and answers at the snap of your fingers. Whenever you see George, there's always a crowd around him, and they are always laughing at his jokes. He is never serious about anything. I'm always serious about everything. There's an old saying that definitely explains our friendship.

Interpretive Questions:

1. What is the main idea of the selection? (main idea)
2. What can you infer about the speaker in the selection? (inference or "reading between the lines")
3. State the old saying that explains the friendship between the two persons in the selection and then tell why it explains their relationship. (figurative language; making comparisons)
4. Choose the row with ideas from the story that belong together. (association)
   a. George, unfriendly, crowds
   b. George's friend, friendly, witty
   c. George, witty, crowds
   d. George's friend, serious, witty
5. Choose the word that best completes this analogy: George's friend is to somber as George is to _____ (analogy)
   a. people.
   b. happiness.
   c. grave.
   d. cheerful.

Critical Reading Questions

Critical reading questions are those that involve evaluation, which is the making of a personal judgment on the accuracy, value, and truthfulness of what is read. Questions that require critical thinking answers are usually more difficult to answer. Here is an example of a selection and some critical reading questions based on it:

> Fortunately, the school election will be over soon. I don't think that I can stand another week such as the last one. First, there was John, who told me that I was the only one not voting for his candidate, "True-Blue Tim." Then there was Mary, who told me that if I were a student with lots of school spirit, I'd be out campaigning for her candidate, "Clever Jane." Mary says that the majority of students are supporting her candidate. She says that even the famous local star thinks that Jane is the best person. Personally, I think that both their candidates are creeps, and I don't intend to vote for either one. I'm going to vote for Jennifer because she is so democratic and fair.

Critical Comprehension Questions

1. State at least five propaganda techniques that are used in the selection, and give examples of them. (propaganda techniques)
2. Determine whether each of the following statements are facts or opinions. (fact or opinion)
   a. The speaker in the selection doesn't think much of the candidates.
   b. The majority of students are voting for Jane.
   c. Jane is clever.

Special Note

An IRI is presented in Appendix A for your use. This IRI is adapted from the Silver Burdett & Ginn basal reader series. The directions for administration are those presented in this chapter.

Code for Marking Oral Reading Errors

Before you can administer any IRI, you must be proficient in marking oral reading errors. A number of different codes exist for this purpose. The one that you choose should be easy to use, and it should incorporate all the types of errors that are counted in the scoring scale. *Consistency* is important; that is, once you find a code that works for you, use it, rather than continuously changing. When you are listening to a child read, you must have overlearned the code so that you can quickly record the errors. Remember, the code is merely a shorthand method you are using to record information quickly; it is an aid. Table 8.1 presents a marking code that you can use to administer the IRI in Appendix A. Most of the *terms* that are used to describe the errors and the symbols that represent them are used in many published IRIs, oral reading tests, and other diagnostic tests that have an oral reading subtest.

Scoring Oral Reading Errors

The scoring scale, which is to be used with the IRI in Appendix A, is based on the philosophy that most good oral readers make some errors when they read. The counting of repetitions, hesitations of less than five seconds, and self-corrected words as errors would yield too low a score for the student. In the scoring scale of errors, multiple errors on the same word will only count as one error; mispronunciations due to dialect differences will not count as an error; mispronunciations of difficult proper nouns will not count as errors; hesitations of less than five seconds and repetitions will not count as errors, and an immediate self-correction will not count as an error. All other errors that are made will count one point (see the following Special Note). (The examiner should note all the errors, even those that do not count as errors.)

The teacher should keep a record of the errors made so that he or she can determine what kinds of strategies the student is using in figuring out words. The teacher should try to determine whether a pattern exists among the errors made and whether the student relies on graphic, semantic, or syntactic clues. The Summary Sheets on pages 191–193 and 195–197 have a checklist of possible errors, which should be helpful in recording a student's specific errors. (See "How Should Oral Reading Errors Be Scored?" in this chapter.)

TABLE 8.1   Code for Marking and Scoring Errors

Type of Error	Rule for Marking	Examples	Error Count
Omissions—leaves out a word, part of a word, or consecutive words	Put circle around omitted word or part of word.	She went in(to) the store. The (big) black dog is here	1 1
Substitutions—substitutes a whole word	Put line through substituted word, and insert word above.	home She went into the ~~house.~~ along. She went ~~alone.~~	1 1
Insertions—adds a word, part of a word, or consecutive words	Put caret to show where word or word part was inserted, and write in inserted part of word or word(s).	big The dog is black. ^ very big The dog is black. ^	1 1
Mispronunciations—mispronounces a word to produce a nonsense word (unlike substitution where an actual word is substituted)	Put line through word that was mispronounced, and insert phonetically the word if possible	herz A ~~horse~~ went into the barn. ka rōt' It weighed a ~~caret.~~	1 1
Words pronounced by examiner after a five-second pause by child	Put *P* over word or words pronounced by tester	P The anecdote was funny.	1
Hesitations—a pause of less than five seconds	Put an *H* above the word on which the hesitation occurs	H She reiterated that she wouldn't go	0
Repetitions—a word, part of a word, or a group of words repeated	Draw a wavy line under the part of word or word(s) repeated	She mumbled her acceptance. We were reluctant to go. His probation would be up soon.	0 0 0
Reversals—word order is changed	Enclose words in a horizontal *S*	The big black cat drinks milk.	1
Self-corrections—error is spontaneously corrected	Enclose incorrect word in parentheses	(brought) He bought something.	0

Special Note

If a child meets the same word a few times in a selection and makes either a substitution, omission, or mispronunciation error on it each time, it would count as *one error* the first time, and as *one-half error* each subsequent time. After the third time, the teacher should pronounce the word for the child. In addition, the examiner should not count as errors words that are pronounced or substituted with dialectical equivalents (nonstandard dialects). For example, a child may say *rat* for *right*.

Sample Marking of an Oral IRI Passage

H polet
"What is ma~~k~~(ing) the lake ~~polluted~~?" asked Jill.

s
"It could be(a)lot ∧ of things," said Mr. Brown.

"Let's go down to the lake and look at it."

big
Mr. Brown and the children went to the ∧ lake.

They looked into the water. It wasn't clean. They

about   was
walked ~~around~~ the lake. Then they ~~saw~~ why it wasn't clean.

The error on *making* is actually a mispronunciation error. The omission symbol is used because it illustrates best what the child did.

Total Error Count = 7
Polluted counts for one error only.

The error on *saw* is shown as a substitution error, even though it actually is a reversal error. To simplify the marking, only inverted word order is shown as a reversal error (see Table 8.1) because it is easier to show this than to show letter reversals. When marking errors, it is easier to assume substitution errors than reversals because a reversal error requires analysis. However, after the testing, the teacher should review all substitution errors to determine whether they have been caused by possible reversal problems. Of course, as already stated, all errors should be analyzed to determine whether a pattern exists among the errors. It is possible, also, that mispronunciation errors are caused by reversal problems.

Word Recognition Formula for Percent Correct

Here is a formula to help you to figure out the percent correct for word recognition:

$$\frac{\text{Number of words in passage} - \text{number of errors}}{\text{number of words in passage}}$$

$$\times \ 100\% = \text{percent correct}$$

Example: 150 words in passage

7 errors

$$\frac{150 - 7}{150} \times 100\% = 95\%$$

(This is at the instructional level using Betts's criteria.)

Word Recognition Formulas for Allowable Errors

It is often easier to work with the number wrong rather than with the number correct because there are fewer errors than correct readings. In working with the number wrong, you are dealing with smaller numbers. Here is the formula for allowable errors for each level:

Independent level: allowable errors

$= 0.01 \times$ number of words in a passage

Instructional level: allowable errors

$= 0.05 \times$ number of words in a passage

Frustration level: allowable errors

$= 0.10 \times$ number of words in a passage

Examples: 150 words in passage

Level	Allowable Errors
Independent	1.5 = 2.0 rounded to nearest whole word
Instructional	7.5 = 8 rounded to nearest whole word
Frustration	15

From the above, you can see that a child who makes 7 errors in a 150-word passage would be at the instructional level using Betts's criteria.

Diagnostic Checklist for Oral and Silent Reading

Coding is necessary if you are analyzing error patterns to determine a student's word recognition difficulties. If, however, you are only interested in quickly determining a student's reading level, you can simply check (✔) errors, because all you need is an error count. Diagnostic checklists are useful in recording errors, especially if you are only interested in an error count.

A checklist you can use follows. Note that this checklist is helpful in recording a student's manner of reading, as well as his or her word recognition errors.

Diagnostic Checklist for Oral and Silent Reading

Oral Reading	Yes	No	Specific Errors

1. Word recognition errors.
   The teacher listens to the child while he or she is reading orally and records whether the child makes any of the following errors:

   a. omissions
   b. insertions
   c. substitutions
   d. repetitions
   e. hesitations
   f. mispronunciations
   g. reversals.

2. Manner of reading.
   The teacher observes the child while he or she is reading aloud and records whether the child exhibits any of the following behaviors:

   a. word-by-word phrasing
   b. finger pointing
   c. head movement
   d. fidgeting
   e. voice characteristics
         high-pitched
         loud
         soft
         monotonous
   f. other.

3. Comprehension.
   (*See* Comprehension Diagnostic Checklist in Chapter 13.)

Silent Reading	Yes	No

1. Comprenhension.
   (See Comprehension Diagnostic Checklist in Chapter 13.)
2. Manner of reading.
   The teacher observes the child while he or she is reading silently and records whether the child exhibits any of the following behaviors:

   a. lip movement
   b. reads aloud
   c. head movement
   d. continually looks up
   e. finger pointing
   f. other.

ADMINISTERING THE IRI

Step 1: Establishing Rapport

Establishing rapport with the child who is to be tested is the first step. Since you are the child's teacher, you should know this child quite well and should be able to allay any fears or apprehensions that the child may have about taking the test. You should help the child recognize that the IRI is not a test that will give him or her a grade; it is a test to help you and the student to learn more about his or her reading. The IRI will give both of you more information so that the two of you can work together to help him or her overcome the reading problem.

Step 2: The Word Recognition Inventory

The Word Recognition Inventory (WRI), which is composed of the word lists selected from the basal reader series, is used to determine at what level to begin the oral reading passages of the IRI. It evaluates a student's ability to recognize (state) words in isolation and is administered to one student at a time.

Preparation

1. The WRI begins two grade levels below the student's grade level.
2. Duplicate the word lists for at least three grade levels above and below the grade level at which you will begin. (Note that the WRI in Appendix A has more than one reader level for each grade level up to grade 4.)
3. Decide how you will flash the words to the student and prepare the necessary materials. Here are two possible methods. Both require index cards.
   a. Cut out a rectangle no more than $\frac{3}{8}$ inch by $1\frac{1}{2}$ inches in the center of an index card. Expose the words being tested, one at a time, through the rectangular opening.
   b. Use one index card to cover any printed matter that appears above the word the student is being asked to state. Use a second index card to cover all matter below the card. Continue this procedure for each word on the list.

Administration

1. Because you will be working with students on an individual basis, try to use a relatively isolated part of the classroom when administering the WRI.
2. Keep the word lists covered as you explain the method of presentation to the student.
3. Begin the WRI with a flash exposure of the first word. Be sure that the word is clearly and completely shown. The student should respond immediately.

a. If the student's response is correct, place a check (✔) beside the word and proceed to the next word.

b. If an initial response is incorrect but the student makes an immediate, independent correction, place a check with a plus sign (✔+) beside the word and proceed to the next word.

4. When the student's response is incorrect and is not independently corrected, reexpose the word. Allow a reasonable length of time for the student to study the word and to apply, without assistance, any word analysis skills he or she may have.

a. If this untimed response is correct, place a check with a minus sign (✔−) beside the word and proceed to the next word.

b. If the student is unable to decode the word correctly after an untimed exposure, record a zero (0) and proceed to the next word. For later reference, you may want to record the error made, for example, *run* for *ran*. To avoid confusion or the inaccurate reporting of results, it is important to record the responses immediately.

5. After the student has responded to all the list words for a particular level, record the total number of correct responses, including flash recognitions, independently corrected recognitions, and untimed recognitions. This total is the student's WRI score for that level.

6. Continue administering the WRI until the student misses four or more words at any level. Start the oral reading at the highest level at which the child has made 0 errors.

Examples:[11]

1. Student: John X, fifth grade (the beginning)
   Begin WRI at third-grade reader level (beginning)

Results

Reader Level*	No. of Errors
3^1	4
2^2	2
2^1	1
First	0

* Refers to the grade level at which the material was prepared for use. For example, Readers 2^1 and 2^2 were prepared for use for the second grade; however, students should be reading in readers appropriate for their reading ability levels rather than those designated for their particular grade level. Also, note well that different basal reader series have different ways of keying their book levels to reader grade levels. In one series *Level 7* is equivalent to 2^2; whereas in another *Level 6* is equivalent to 2^2.

[11] Examples are based on the WRI presented in Appendix A.

Interpretation of results: Begin oral reading passages at first reader level

2. Student: Jane Y, fifth grade (middle)
   Begin WRI at third-grade reader level (middle)

Results	
Reader Level	No. of Errors
3^2	0
4	0
5	1
6	4

Interpretation of results: Begin oral reading passages at fourth-grade reader level

3. Student: George Z, fourth grade (beginning)
   Begin WRI at second-grade reader level (beginning)

Results	
Reader Level	No. of Errors
2^1	0
2^2	0
3^1	1
3^2	0
4	2
5	5

Interpretation of results: Begin oral reading passages at third-grade reader level (middle)

Note that each student is administered the WRI until he or she has made four or more errors so that you can see a pattern of the types of errors that the student has made.

Step 3: Oral and Silent Reading Passages

The student begins to read the oral passage at sight at the highest reader level at which he or she has made zero errors on the Word Recognition Inventory (see examples given in Step 2). The teacher introduces the child to the passage and tells the child that he or she will read aloud the passage and then will be asked questions on what was read. The child is asked to read aloud the passage without first looking at it.

While the child is reading aloud, the teacher records any oral reading errors the child makes (see Table 8.1). If the child's word recognition in oral reading is at the independent or instructional levels, the child is asked the comprehension questions. If the child's response is correct, the teacher puts a check (✔) next to the question. If the answer is not correct, the teacher records the student's response. The child is then asked to read the silent passage. Again, the student is not given an opportunity to look over the passage before reading it. After the student finishes reading the silent passage, he or she is asked the comprehension questions. If the child's response is correct, a check (✔) is put next to the response. If the answer is incorrect, the student's response is recorded next to the question.

The student goes to the oral passage at the next reader level. The same procedure continues until the child reaches his or her frustration level.

If the student makes many word recognition errors while reading aloud, and the errors are those that the teacher feels will interfere with the child's ability to answer the comprehension questions, the teacher usually does not have the child read the silent reading passage at the same reader level. The teacher administers a listening capacity test to the child; that is, the teacher reads aloud to the child and then asks the comprehension questions.

The Listening Capacity Test[12]

Listening capacity test
Given to determine a child's comprehension through listening. Teacher reads aloud to child and then asks questions about the selection.

A listening capacity test is given to determine a child's comprehension through listening. The teacher is interested in determining a child's ability to comprehend material that is read aloud so that he or she can gauge the child's ability to listen to instruction and oral reports. Also, a listening capacity test can help to identify those students who seem to gain information better through listening than through reading. This knowledge is important in planning proper modes of instruction for the child. (See Chapters 5 and 6 for more on listening capacity tests and for a discussion on how listening capacity tests help provide an estimate of a child's reading potential.)

The passages from the IRI are generally used to determine a child's listening capacity. The passages are evaluated in the same way that the oral and silent reading passages are evaluated except that the teacher reads aloud the selections to the child. If the passages that are to be read aloud have already been read by the child, alternate ones should be used. Some commercially produced IRIs have a separate set of selections for the listening capacity test. It is a good idea to have a separate set of selections for the listening capacity

---

[12] A listening capacity test may also be referred to as a listening comprehension test or a capacity test.

test. The IRI in Appendix A does not have this because of space limitations.

When Is a Listening Capacity Test Given?

A listening capacity test is usually given when a child has reached or is rapidly approaching the frustration level in word recognition on the oral reading part of the IRI. If a child has difficulty decoding a large number of words in oral reading, this will probably interfere with his or her ability to answer comprehension questions. Also, if a child has difficulty with a large number of words at a certain reader level, the child is usually not asked to read the silent passage at the same level because the decoding problems would probably interfere with the child's ability to answer comprehension questions. (See Example 1.) If a child does not have any extensive word recognition problems, the listening capacity test is usually given when the child is approaching or has reached his or her frustration level in silent reading on the IRI. (See Example 2 beginning on p. 193.) (Although the student in Example 1, Jim X, had reached zero errors at the 2^2 level [see chart below], the WRI was continued until he reached four errors so that a pattern of the errors could better be seen.)

Example 1[13]

Student Jim X, fifth grade (beginning). Begin Word Recognition Inventory at 3^1 level.

Reader Level	Number of Errors
3^1	2
2^2	0
3^2	4

Jim begins oral reading at the 2^2 level because he has zero errors at that level. The following chart shows his reading behavior.

Reader Level	Oral Reading				Silent Reading Comprehension		Listening Capacity	
	Word Recognition	Comprehension						
	No. Errors/ Total No. Words	% Errors	% Correct		% Errors	% Correct	% Errors	% Correct
2^2	4/131	0	100		0	100		
3^1	7/151	0	100		0	100		
3^2	10/171	20	80		25	75		

[13] Examples are based on the IRI presented in Appendix A.

Listening Capacity

Reader Level	% Errors	% Correct
4	0	100
5	0	100
6	0	100
7	20	80
8	40	60

At the 3^2 level the teacher must decide whether to let Jim read silently or whether to give him a listening capacity test. His word recognition errors may be interfering with his ability to answer the comprehension questions. The teacher decides to let him read silently, even though he is in the "buffer" zone, which is between the instructional and frustration levels, because she wants to see how well he uses context clues. Even though Jim has a word recognition problem, he seems to do quite well in comprehension. He scores 25 percent errors. The teacher has Jim read at the next level because he does not appear to be frustrated. At the next level, however, he makes 19 errors, and he has difficulty answering the comprehension questions. The teacher decides to give him a listening capacity test. She starts to read aloud the silent reading passage at the fourth-grade reader level. Then she continues to read aloud one passage from each level. The chart above shows Jim's listening capacity scores. (It doesn't make any difference whether the passage was chosen from the oral or silent reading selections.) From the listening capacity test the teacher sees that Jim has excellent comprehension but his word recognition is hindering him from working at his ability level. The teacher had decided to give Jim an IRI because his verbal behavior in class belied his reading achievement test scores.

The teacher continues administering the oral reading part of the IRI to determine Jim's independent oral reading level and to gain some more insight into the types of errors that he makes in word recognition so that she can develop a program to help him. (Jim reads the oral passage at the 2^1 level. He makes one error out of 112 words. This is his independent oral reading level.) She will probably also give Jim another word analysis diagnostic test.

On page 191 is a summary sheet, showing a complete record of Jim's reading behavior on the IRI.

Summary Sheet*

Name __Jim X__   Age __10__

Grade __5__   Teacher __Mrs. Smith__

Reader Level	Word Recognition in Isolation (No. of Errors)	Oral Reading			Silent Reading		Listening Capacity	
		W.R.	Comp.		Comp.			
		No. of Errors/ Total No. Wds.†	% Errors	% Correct	% Errors	% Correct	% Errors	% Correct
Preprimer								
Primer								
First								
2¹		1/112						
2²	0	4/131	0	100	0	100		
3¹	2	7/151	0	100	0	100		
3²	4	10/171	20	80	25	75		
4		19/187	40	60			0	100
5							0	100
6							0	100
7							20	80
8							40	60

Level at which WRI was begun   3¹

Level at which oral reading was begun   2²

*For use with the IRI in Appendix A.

†Percentages can be easily calculated using the word recognition formula on page 182, or see the IRI in Appendix A for corresponding reading levels, that is, independent, instructional, or frustration levels.

Oral reading—word recognition

Independent level   2¹

Instructional level   2²–3¹ (range)

Frustration level   4

Oral reading—comprehension

    Independent level 3^1

    Instructional level 3^2

    Frustration level   _____

Silent reading—comprehension

    Independent level 3^1

    Instructional level 3^2

    Frustration level   _____

Listening capacity level   7

Word analysis

    Consonants—single

      initial   _____

      medial   _____

      final   _____

    Consonants—double

      blends   _____

      digraphs   ch, sh, ph

    Consonants—silent   _____

    Vowels—single

      short   ă, ĕ

      long   _____

    Vowels—double

      digraphs   oa, ea

      diphthongs   ou in bough

    Effect of final *e* on vowel   _____

    Vowel controlled by *r*   _____

    Structural analysis

      prefixes   _____

      suffixes   _____

      combining forms

      inflectional endings   ignores most

    Compound words   _____

    Accent   _____

Special Notes on Strengths and Weaknesses

Jim has word recognition problems that are thwarting his comprehension ability. Jim doesn't attempt to use phonic clues. If he doesn't know the word as a sight word, and if he can't figure it out by using context clues, he skips over the word. His ability to use semantic and syntactic clues is excellent.

Comments on Behavior During the Testing

Jim seemed to like working in a one-to-one relationship. He said that he didn't like to read, but he liked to listen to persons read aloud.

Recommendations

Give Jim a complete word recognition program stressing the use of graphic clues in combination with semantic and syntactic clues. Select books of low readability and high interest content.

Example 2

Student Susan Y, fifth grade (beginning). Begin WRI at 3^1 level.

Reader Level	No. of Errors
3^1	0
3^2	0
4	0
5	0
6	4

Susan begins oral reading at the 5 level because that is her highest level of zero errors. She immediately reaches the frustration level in oral reading comprehension (see chart). Since Susan immediately reached the frustration level in oral reading comprehension, the teacher would be justified in not having her read the silent reading passage and start going down to lower grade levels to find her instructional and independent levels for comprehension. However, the teacher decides to have Susan read the silent reading passage because she wants to see if Susan was concentrating so hard on pronunciation that she didn't pay attention to what she was reading. Susan is asked to read the fifth-grade silent reading level passage. She makes 60 percent errors. The following chart shows Susan's reading behavior:

| Reader Level | Oral Reading | | | Silent Reading Comprehension | | Listening Capacity | |
| | Word Recognition | Comprehension | | | | | |
	No. Errors/Total No. Words	% Errors	% Correct	% Errors	% Correct	% Errors	% Correct
5	2/208	60	40	60	40		
4	2/187	60	40	60	40		
3^2	2/171	50	50	50	50		
3^1	2/151	40	60	50	50	50	50
2^2	1/131	25	75	25	75	40	60
2^1	1/112	10	90	10	90	25	75
6^*	9/252	—		—			

* Susan was asked to read orally only at the sixth level to find her instructional oral reading word recognition level.

From the results, we can see that Susan has excellent word recognition, but she has severe difficulties in reading comprehension. A listening capacity test is given to determine the level at which she can listen to material and comprehend it at the instructional level. From looking at the results of Susan's reading performance, the teacher decides to start reading aloud to Susan at the 3^1 level because this is the level at which she had reached frustration in silent reading. Since Susan is also at her frustration level on the listening capacity test at the 3^1 level, the teacher moves to the 2^2 level and reads aloud the passage. At this level Susan is approaching frustration. The teacher then reads the 2^1 level passage and finds Susan's listening capacity level. (The selections read aloud to Susan to determine her listening capacity level were different from those in the IRI because Susan had already read those.) It is interesting to note that Susan's listening capacity score is lower than her oral and silent reading scores. She probably has more difficulty concentrating while listening than when reading silently or orally. Her oral and silent reading scores appear to be comparable. The teacher must analyze the kinds of comprehension errors that Susan made. It seems obvious that Susan's ability to read well orally has obscured her comprehension problems. The teacher had decided to give Susan an IRI because she had noticed the discrepancy between her verbalizing in class and her inability to answer even literal questions correctly. Susan can pronounce words very well, but she doesn't have the meanings for many of them. Even when she knows the meaning of the words used in a paragraph, she can't tell you what the paragraph is about. The IRI will give Susan's teacher some insights into Susan's comprehension difficulties; however, it may be that Susan is a slow learner, and as such, is reading close to her reading ability (see Chapters 6 and 15). Since Susan's teacher does not have any IQ score for Susan, she cannot determine this possibility. However, the listening capacity test that was administered to Susan does indicate that Susan's reading potential may only be at a 2^1 grade level. Susan's teacher should probably refer Susan for an individual IQ test, but in the meantime she will have to develop a program for her based on her needs. The first step seems to be concept development.

Here is a summary sheet, showing a complete record of Susan's reading behavior on the IRI.

Summary Sheet *

Name __Susan Y__   Age __10__

Grade __5__   Teacher __Mr. Jones__

Level	Word Recognition in Isolation (No. of Errors)	Oral Reading W.R. No. of Errors/ Total No. Wds.	Oral Reading Comp. % Errors	Oral Reading Comp. % Correct	Silent Reading Comp. % Errors	Silent Reading Comp. % Correct	Listening Capacity % Errors	Listening Capacity % Correct
Preprimer								
Primer								
First								
2^1		1/112	10	90	10	90	25	75
2^2		1/132	25	75	25	75	40	60
3^1	0	2/151	40	60	50	50	50	40
3^2	0	2/171	50	50	50	50		
4	0	2/187	60	40	60	40		
5	0	2/208	60	40	60	40		
6	4	9/252						
7								
8								

*For use with the IRI in Appendix A.
†Percentages can be easily calculated using the word recognition formula on page 182, or see the IRI in Appendix A for corresponding reading levels, that is, independent, instructional, or frustration levels.

Level at which WRI was begun 3^1

Level at which oral reading was begun   5

Oral reading—word recognition
     Independent level   5
     Instructional level   6
     Frustration level

Oral reading—comprehension

Independent level 2^1

Instructional level 2^2

Frustration level 3^2

Silent reading—comprehension

Independent level 2^1

Instructional level 2^2

Frustration level 3^1

Listening capacity level 2^1

Word analysis

  Consonants—single

    initial   _____

    medial   _____

    final   _____

  Consonants—double

    blends   _____

    digraphs   _____

  Consonants—silent   _____

  Vowels—single

    short   _____

    long   _____

  Vowels—double

    digraphs   _____

    diphthongs   _____

  Effect of final *e* on vowel   _____

  Vowel controlled by *r*   _____

  Structural analysis

    prefixes   _____

    suffixes   _____

    combining forms   _____

inflectional endings   _____

Compound words   _____

Accent   _____

Special Notes on Strengths and Weaknesses

Susan has excellent word recognition skills. She is weak in word meanings. She could not give the meanings of words that she could pronounce. She could not state the main idea of the paragraphs nor could she answer inferential questions. She was able to answer literal questions, but she even missed some of these.

Comments on Behavior During the Testing

She enjoyed reading aloud. She started squirming in her chair whenever comprehension questions were asked. She also squirmed in her chair when I was reading aloud to her.

Recommendations

Help Susan expand her vocabulary. Work on literal and interpretive comprehension skills. Give her a cloze test to further check her use of syntactic and semantic clues to figure out word meanings.

PUBLISHED (COMMERCIALLY PRODUCED) IRIs VERSUS TEACHER-MADE IRIs

Teacher-made IRIs are time-consuming to construct, and many teachers do not feel secure about making one. Their prime advantage is that they are directly related to the instructional material used in class. Published IRIs, on the other hand, may not be directly related to the instructional material, but they are usually easier to administer and score because they are generally prepared by experts in the field and with specific directions. (See the Selected Bibliography at the end of this chapter for a list of some published IRIs.)

If teachers decide to use a published IRI, they must know what criteria to look for so that they can make a wise choice. A good IRI should have the following features:

1. There should be two forms, so that a pre- and posttest can be given.
2. There should be different passages for oral and silent reading.
3. The comprehension questions should consist of a variety of literal and interpretive questions. (Critical reading questions are optional.)
4. All questions should be text-driven; that is, all questions including inferential and word meaning ones should be text-dependent.
5. If a main-idea question is asked, the passage should be one for which it is possible to state its main or central idea; that is, it should be a cohesive passage.
6. The passages should be selected from the most recent basal reader series.
7. The graded word lists should be representative of the grade level from which they have been taken.
8. The passages selected for oral and silent reading should be representative of the reading material in the book; that is, the readability level should not be higher or lower than the level from which the passages have been selected.
9. Specific directions should be given for administering and scoring the test.
10. There should be a separate set of passages and comprehension questions for the listening capacity test, if possible. These should also be representative of the reading material in the book.

WHO SHOULD BE GIVEN AN IRI?

Chapter 6 is devoted to helping you determine who is underachieving in reading so that you can determine who should have further diagnostic testing. Reading expectancy formulas are presented, which help you to determine the reading potential of a child. A comparison is then made between the child's reading potential as determined by a reading expectancy formula and his or her score on a standardized reading achievement test. Another formula is then used to analyze the comparison between the child's reading expectancy and his or her score on a reading achievement test. The second formula helps you determine who is underachieving in reading to such an extent that he or she requires further diagnostic testing.

It is emphasized in Chapter 6, and it will again be stressed here, that teachers must be careful about using reading expectancy formulas as absolute determinants of a child's reading potential. A formula is based on intelligence test scores, and many times a child's IQ score is not valid because of a reading problem. As a result a child's reading expectancy would be depressed, that is, lower than it should be. Thus teachers must use their own judgment concerning whom to test further. There are times when a teacher will want to administer an IRI to a child who scored well on a reading achievement test but who seems to be having some reading problem. There are times, too, when a teacher will want to give an IRI to a student who scored at grade level on a reading achievement test and whose group IQ score was in the average range because the teacher suspects from the child's verbal ability and behavior in class that the child is a highly able child and that his or her word recognition problems may be masking this fact.

It used to be given as a rule of thumb that a child who scores about one or more years below his or her ability level on a standardized reading achievement test should be given an IRI. This is not a good rule to follow in a diagnostic-reading and correction program because the key factor in such a program is to help the child before his or her reading difficulty becomes a big problem. Also, as discussed in Chapter 6, there is a vast difference between a child in second grade with a one-year underachievement in reading and a child in sixth grade.

There are a number of teachers who will not be able to use the reading expectancy formulas that exist because in some school districts, group IQ tests have been made illegal. These teachers will have to depend on other means to determine who in their classes needs an IRI or other diagnostic tests. One good technique is to administer a group standardized listening comprehension test for an estimate of the children's reading potential (see "Standardized Listening Tests" in Chapter 5). The children's reading potential as measured by the standardized listening comprehension test could be compared to their score on a standardized reading achievement test. Along with the results of the standardized listening comprehension test, the teacher should base his or her decision on careful observation of the child's reading behavior and other behaviors that may be related. (See Chapter 10, which discusses observation as a diagnostic technique.) Another technique would be to administer the Slosson Intelligence Test, which is individually administered. (See "Slosson Intelligence Test (SIT)" in Chapter 6.)

Special Note

Some persons may say, "Why not give everyone an IRI to be on the safe side?" This would be a good idea; however, time constraints usually weigh against it.

Examples of Candidates for the IRI

The examples that follow should be especially helpful for those teachers who cannot use reading expectancy formulas to determine whether students are underachieving in reading or not because they do not have any IQ scores for their students. It may also be helpful for those teachers who can use reading expectancy formulas because it should make the teacher more sensitive to problems that may exist but are not obvious from the comparison of reading expectancy scores to reading achievement scores.

Example 1. The student answers questions that are posed orally in class very well, but he never raises his hand to read any printed material aloud. When he is called on to read, he makes many oral reading errors. He cannot decode many words that he uses with facility in his speaking vocabulary. Even though this child has scored on grade level on a standardized reading achievement test, he is a good candidate for an informal reading inventory.

Example 2. This student reads orally with excellent facility. He is always raising his hand to read orally; however, whenever he is asked to answer comprehension questions on what he has read either orally or silently, he cannot. This child has scored below grade level on a standardized reading achievement test. He would be a good candidate for an IRI. If the teacher finds that the child's reading level is a few grade levels below his present grade level, she might want to refer this child to the child study team or school psychologist for an individual IQ test.

Example 3. The student stumbles on a number of words when she reads orally. She usually has no difficulty answering questions after she has read silently. She is very verbal and seems to have quite a bit of information on a number of different topics. She has scored a few months below her grade level, which is the fourth grade, on a standardized reading achievement test. She is a candidate for an IRI because her word recognition difficulties may be interfering with her ability to answer comprehension questions.

Example 4. This student has scored below grade level on a standardized reading achievement test; however, she does not seem to have any problems answering difficult reading comprehension questions at the literal, interpretive, and critical levels. The student also reads well orally and volunteers often to read. The teacher decides to give her an informal reading inventory to check at what grade level she is reading and also to determine whether she has reading difficulties that are not obvious. If the IRI does not point out any significant reading problem, this child should take another standardized reading achievement test. It is highly probable that the standardized reading achievement test score is not valid for this child.

MODIFIED IRI APPROACHES: A CAUTION

Many teachers do not have the time to administer a complete IRI to their students, so they rely on a modified approach, whereby they use either oral reading in basal readers or graded word lists to determine a student's placement. An approach that teachers often use is the one in which a child is asked to read passages orally from various levels of a basal reader series. The level at which the child is able to read with some proficiency is the one that the teacher usually uses as the child's instructional reading level. The other technique frequently used is to expose the child to a graded list of words that has been selected from a basal reader series and have the child read aloud this list to determine his or her instructional reading level.

The on-the-spot oral reading without assessing comprehension and word lists are time-savers, and they can be helpful, but teachers must recognize the dangers of these techniques and realize that the information they are receiving may not be valid or reliable. If a teacher only uses a child's oral reading ability to determine his or her reading level, many children may be incorrectly placed. A child may have a word recognition problem but have excellent comprehension, and conversely, a child may have a comprehension problem but no word recognition problems. The latter child with no word recognition problem, who probably has a lower reading potential than the former child with the word recognition problem, would probably be placed in a higher reading group than the child with the word recognition problem.

For the on-the-spot oral reading approach to be effective, the teacher should devise some comprehension questions based on the material, or the teacher could test understanding by having the child "retell" what he or she has read in his or her own words. The teacher could also determine comprehension by asking the student to give the main idea of what he or she has read.

The problem with the use of graded word lists to determine a student's reading level is similar to the one just discussed for the on-the-spot oral reading approach. From the graded word list, you are only getting an estimate of the student's ability to pronounce words; you are not getting any information about the child's comprehension. This limitation is dangerous because reading is a thinking act. Therefore, be careful. Do not confuse the oral reading context score from an inventory with the score from a word recognition test, and do not use the results from a word recognition test to estimate students' reading levels.[14]

The on-the-spot approach is especially effective for students in the upper grades who are reading content material books and are

[14] Johnson, Kress, and Pikulski, p. 56.

not involved in reading classes. Many times these students are having difficulty because the content books are at too high a readability level for them. The on-the-spot approach would be a viable method for these students. It is a good idea to choose a passage that is representative of the book; a passage from the middle of the book would probably be best for this purpose. Have the student read aloud the passage, which should consist of a paragraph or two, and then have the student answer some comprehension questions on it, or have the student give a summary of what he or she has read.

Some people have used a group on-the-spot approach to test the readability of textbooks. There are a number of variations to this approach, but for it to be a group approach, all or a number of students must take it at the same time. In the group approach, the students usually read silently a passage close to the middle of the book, and then they write the answers to given questions on the passages, or they write a summary of the passage, or they write the main idea of the passage, and so on. Be *cautious* in using such a test to determine whether the book is at the reading ability level of the student. It may be that the student has difficulty expressing himself or herself in writing. You may be testing a student's writing ability rather than his or her reading ability. From this type of test, you are also not learning whether the student has word recognition problems or comprehension problems.

MISCUE ANALYSIS

Miscue analysis
A process that helps researchers learn how readers get meaning from language.

Miscue
Unexpected response to print.

Goodman, the prime mover in miscue analysis research, feels that miscue analysis is a viable research process that goes beyond the "superficial behavior of readers" to learn how readers get meaning from language.[15] Goodman objects to the use of the term *errors* because he feels that nothing the reader does in reading is accidental, and *error* implies randomness. If persons can understand how miscues, which are unexpected responses to print, relate to expected responses, they will better understand how the reader is using the reading process. Miscue analysis begins with observed behavior, but it tries to go beyond through analysis.

To analyze readers' miscues, an analytic taxonomy was developed that considers the relationship between the reader's expected response (ER) with his or her observed response (OR). (This taxonomy has been and is continuously modified for new inputs from miscue studies.) The strength of this taxonomy is that it attempts to analyze the causes of a reader's miscues from a number of angles. Its strengths are, however, also its weaknesses for use by the classroom teacher.

[15] Kenneth S. Goodman, "Miscues: Windows on the Reading Process," in *Miscue Analysis*, ed. Kenneth S. Goodman. (Urbana, Ill.: National Council of Teachers of English, 1973), p. 5.

The Goodman Taxonomy of Reading Miscues consists of about nineteen questions, and each miscue is analyzed in terms of these nineteen questions. The Goodman Taxonomy of Reading Miscues "is a highly complex and sophisticated research instrument calling for considerable background on the part of the user."[16] This instrument is obviously not for the classroom teacher; however, evolving from the taxonomy is the Reading Miscue Inventory (RMI), which *was* designed to be used by the classroom teacher. The inventory has condensed the nineteen questions, which involved from four to fifteen possible responses for each, to nine questions involving three choices each.

The Reading Miscue Inventory is still too involved and needs more simplification if it is to be used in the regular classroom either in place of the traditional IRI or in conjunction with it. Although the RMI is not widely used, the miscue analysis studies, with the emphasis on reading as a process in which meaning is obtained, have greatly influenced many examiners' interpretations of students' reading errors. They have heightened the consciousness level of testers using the IRI so that many are now concerned not only with the number of errors that a student makes but also with the quality or kind of error. Many recognize that getting meaning is more important than absolute accuracy of word pronunciation.

POINTS OF CAUTION CONCERNING IRIs

Teachers should recognize that an IRI can yield important information about a student's reading performance, but the results may vary from one IRI to another because of the following factors:

1. Criteria used to estimate reading levels.
2. Amount of information given before the student is asked to read aloud or silently.
3. Criteria used to record errors.
4. Type of comprehension questions asked and how scored.
5. Cut-off point for defining reading levels.
6. Readability of material.
7. Procedure for reading aloud. (Are students asked to look over material before they read aloud?)
8. Order of silent and oral reading passages. (Do students read orally first and then proceed to the silent reading passage, or do students read silently first and then proceed to the oral reading passage?)

The remainder of this chapter will discuss some of the points on this list.

[16] Carolyn Burke, "Preparing Elementary Teachers to Teach Reading," in *Miscue Analysis*, ed. Kenneth S. Goodman. (Urbana, Ill.: National Council of Teachers of English, 1973), p. 24.

Criteria for Estimating Reading Levels

The criteria as established by Betts for estimating reading levels were given in an earlier section (the section "Determining Reading Levels"). Although Betts's criteria are used by many, they are not universally accepted. One of the problems in using IRIs is that variability exists in the criteria for identifying reading levels. Two researchers summarized the criteria that various persons advocated for IRIs and illustrated the discrepancies among them.[17] They claim that differences exist in administrative procedures as well as in error classification; however, the researchers stated that the procedural differences are not enough to explain the discrepancies among the criteria put forth by authorities to estimate the instructional reading level.

Another researcher who reviewed the existing literature on informal reading inventories concludes that even though "the issues concerning IRI scoring are far from settled, several practical suggestions can be made. In general, the Betts criteria should be retained but not rigidly adhered to."[18]

Although there are a number of summaries of the literature, surprisingly, very little research exists to validate criteria for estimating reading levels. Of the studies that have been done, hardly any agree on levels of criteria.

An issue since the 1970s that has been greatly discussed concerns whether the emphasis in determining reading levels should be on error count or on the type of error that is made. It appears that both should be taken into consideration. For example, read the following sentence, and then read how three different children have read it:

The horse went into the stable.
Student 1: The horse went into the *store.*
Student 2: The *big* horse went *in* the *barn.*
Student 3: The horse went *in a* stable.

If we were to count all errors without consideration to type, Student 1 would have the fewest errors, and Student 2 would have the most. However, if we were to look at the readings of the three sentences, we would have to conclude that Student 3, with two errors, has a better understanding of the writer's message than Student 1, with one error; and Student 2, with three errors, is also a better reader than Student 1. The omission and insertion by Student 2 did not affect the meaning of the sentence, nor did the substitution of *barn* for *stable*; however, the substitution of *store* for *stable* did affect the meaning of the sentence. Student 1 made fewer errors and stuck closer to graphic cues than Student 2, but he sacrificed the meaning

---

[17] William R. Powell and Colin G. Dunkeld, "Validity of the IRI Reading Levels," *Elementary English* 48 (October 1971): 637–42.

[18] Michael C. McKenna, "Informal Reading Inventories: A Review of the Issues," *The Reading Teacher* 36 (March 1983): 674.

of the sentence. Student 1, with the fewest errors, has to be judged the poorest reader of the three.

Even though many authorities agree that both number and type of error should be taken into account, it is very difficult to devise a scoring procedure that incorporates these two concepts that would be easy and quick to use and that would eliminate subjectivity.

How Should Oral Reading Errors Be Scored?

How to score the word recognition on the graded oral passages is probably one of the biggest controversies concerning the use of IRIs. How a child is scored will determine his or her placement in a reading level; different criteria for determining reading levels will result in different reading placements, and even if similar criteria are used, different methods of scoring will affect placements. One study revealed that experienced examiners, recording the oral reading errors of an excellent-quality tape of one child slowly reading a 115-word passage, disagreed sharply on the error count. The error count of the fourteen examiners, who were reading specialists, ranged from one to fourteen.[19]

The problem seems to be twofold. It involves the classification or definition of errors and the scoring of them. There is no agreement on what should be considered an error and how the error should be scored, or even whether it should be scored. For example, some authorities note when a student has repeated a part of a word, a word, or words, but they do not count the repetitions as errors; others do. Some examiners count hesitations as errors; some do not. Some count every error made, even if it is on the same word; that is, it is possible to have multiple errors on one word, and rather than count them as one error, some testers will count each error on that word. If a student meets the same word five times in the oral reading, and each time makes an error, some examiners count this as five errors; however, some may count this only as one error. Some testers do not count errors on proper nouns; some do.

Categories of errors are also not similar among examiners. Some include reversals; some do not. Some include help from the tester; some do not. Some include provisions for dialect differences; some do not; and so it goes. Some examiners also include information about semantic, syntactic, and graphic cues and suggest that teachers should analyze their students' errors with these in mind so that they can distinguish between the trivial and the significant.

What does all this mean? It means that there is a lot of subjectivity in the scoring of errors, and you must be careful to choose a system that agrees with your philosophy and research findings.

[19] William D. Page, "Miscue Research and Diagnosis," *Findings of Research in Miscue Analysis: Classroom Implications*, ed. P. David Allen and Dorothy J. Watson. (Urbana, Ill.: National Council of Teachers of English, 1976), pp. 140–41.

Special Note

It is really only from the comprehension score that we can determine whether certain word recognition errors were indeed significant or not. Therefore, it is important that the student's word recognition behavior be accurately recorded to determine what kinds of errors may be interfering with comprehension.

A Special Look at Repetitions

An oral reading error that has caused a great amount of discussion and confusion among users of IRIs is that of repetitions. As already stated, some recommend that repetitions be counted as errors, whereas a number of others do not. One research study using the polygraph to determine the frustration level of a student found that if repetitions are not counted as errors, a child will reach the frustration level before the examiner is able to count enough errors to designate it.[20] It must be remembered that each child in this study was monitored by a polygraph. It is possible that the polygraph, itself, may have caused anxiety.

The author feels that it is not realistic to count every repetition as an error for a number of reasons. Most normal reading aloud is subject to errors even by well-known excellent readers. There are a number of reasons why a student would repeat a word or words or make some short hesitations. The student may be nervous; he or she may be unused to reading aloud or not be familiar with the type of material being read; rapport with the examiner may not be very good; the student may be shy; and, more significantly, the student may be concentrating on the meaning of what he or she is reading because the student has been told that questions will be asked after the oral reading.

Oral and Silent Reading Comprehension

Betts, in developing the IRI, suggested that silent reading be given before oral reading. However, most IRIs today present the oral reading passage before the silent one at the same level because the oral reading is used as a gauge to determine whether a student should read silently at the same level. If a student makes many oral reading errors, it is assumed that he or she will have difficulty reading silently at the same level. When the child is asked the questions after reading the silent passage, if he or she has not read orally at the same level, the teacher will not be able to determine whether the child could not answer the comprehension questions because of a comprehension problem or because of a word recognition problem.

---

[20] Eldon E. Ekwall, "Should Repetitions Be Counted as Errors?" *The Reading Teacher* 27 (January 1974): 365–67.

Most IRIs use the same criteria for scoring oral reading comprehension as for scoring silent reading comprehension, even though some persons have suggested that the former should be scored less stringently because readers concentrate more on word pronunciation during oral reading than on comprehension. Many people feel that students would score higher on comprehension after reading silently than after reading orally; however, this assumption has not been borne out by research. The comparative studies of silent and oral reading comprehension scores have been inconclusive.[21] As a result, the oral and silent comprehension criteria have remained the same.

It would appear that good readers would do better in comprehension after reading silently than after reading orally. However, there are some children who may do better in comprehension after reading orally because they need to hear the words in order to understand them. Their auditory modality may be more developed than their visual modality.

SUMMARY

Chapter 8 presents a discussion of diagnostic reading tests and techniques with an emphasis on the informal reading inventory. An IRI is a valuable diagnostic aid because it can provide information about a student's reading levels as well as help the teacher gain insight into a child's reading strengths and weaknesses. This chapter provides information on the IRI, its purposes, the criteria for estimating reading levels, how to construct one, how to administer one, how to mark oral reading errors, and how to score them. This chapter also presents information on research concerning IRIs and some information on word lists. Teachers are cautioned about the subjectivity of IRIs and are again reminded that any test, and especially the IRI, is only as good as the person administering and interpreting it. A comparison between teacher-made and published IRIs is given, with a list of criteria for choosing the latter. A section is also presented on miscue analysis and how research in this area has heightened the consciousness level of testers using the IRI so that many are now concerned not only with the number of errors a student makes but also with the quality of the errors that are made.

SUGGESTIONS FOR THOUGHT QUESTIONS AND ACTIVITIES

1. Administer an IRI to a child who has a reading problem.
2. Review three different commercial IRIs.
3. Construct an IRI using a basal reader series from the 1990s.

[21] E. H. Rowell, "Do Elementary Students Read Better Orally or Silently?" *The Reading Teacher* 29 (January 1976): 367–70.

4. Practice marking errors on an oral reading passage by listening to a tape of a child reading a passage.
5. Have a group of persons mark errors on an oral passage while listening to a tape of a child reading an oral passage. Compare the results.
6. You have been appointed to a committee to develop a coding and scoring system of oral reading that takes into account the research done on miscue analysis and the traditional coding and scoring system of most IRIs. What will you come up with?
7. What coding system would you devise for diagnosing oral reading errors?
8. Choose a few paragraphs from a basal reader series and make up comprehension questions for them, including literal, interpretive, and critical reading questions.

SELECTED BIBLIOGRAPHY

Betts, Emmett A. *Foundations of Reading Instruction*. New York: American Book Company, 1946.

Duffelmeyer, Frederick, and Barbara Blakely Duffelmeyer. "Are IRI Passages Suitable for Assessing Main Idea Comprehension?" *The Reading Teacher* 42 (February 1989): 358–63.

Duffelmeyer, Frederick, Susan R. Robinson, and Susan E. Squier. "Vocabulary Questions on Informal Reading Inventories." *The Reading Teacher* 43 (November 1989): 142–48.

Ekwall, Eldon E. *Ekwall Reading Inventory*, 2nd ed. Boston: Allyn and Bacon, 1986.

Forell, Elizabeth. "The Case for Conservative Reader Placement." *The Reading Teacher* 38 (May 1985): 857–62.

Gillis, M. K., and Mary W. Olson. "Elementary IRIs: Do They Reflect What We Know about Text Type Structure and Comprehension?" *Reading Research and Instruction* 27 (fall 1987): 36–44.

Johns, Jerry L. *Basic Reading Inventory*. Dubuque, Iowa: Kendall/Hunt, 1988.

Johnson, Marjorie S., Roy A. Kress, and John J. Pikulski. *Informal Reading Inventories*, 2nd ed. Newark, Del.: International Reading Association, 1987.

Martin, Lara, Susan G. "Reading Placement for Code Switchers." *The Reading Teacher* 42 (January 1989): 278–82.

Pikulski, John J. "Informal Reading Inventory," in Assessment Section. *The Reading Teacher* 43 (March 1990): 514–16.

Silvarali, Nicholas. *Classroom Reading Inventory*. Dubuque, Iowa: William C. Brown, 1989.

Woods, Mary Lynn, and Alden Moe. *Analytic Reading Inventory*. Columbus, Ohio: Merrill, 1989.

9

Diagnostic Reading Tests and Techniques II

© 1985 United Feature Syndicate, Inc.

Figure 9.1

INTRODUCTION

Charlie Brown may have received a D minus on his book report, but his teacher should receive an A. From an analysis of Charlie's work, she was able to discern that his report was done as an afterthought in a slipshod manner. The *Peanuts* cartoon portrays Charlie Brown's teacher as a remarkably perceptive person. Such perceptivity is important in diagnosis because the teacher is looking for the cause or causes of the student's poor performance in order to help the student improve. The teacher in a diagnostic-reading and correction program is also concerned with determining a student's independent, instructional, frustration, and capacity levels, so that the student can be given material to read that is best suited for him or her.

In Chapter 8 you learned about the importance of oral reading in diagnosing a student's reading behavior, and you were introduced to the informal reading inventory, which is an important diagnostic instrument. This chapter will continue to present diagnostic instruments and techniques that you can use.

The sections in this chapter will introduce you to a variety of diagnostic instruments. Some will be standardized, and some will be classroom-prepared.

KEY QUESTIONS

After you finish reading this chapter, you should be able to answer the following questions:

1. What are examples of some standardized norm-referenced diagnostic tests that only measure oral reading ability?
2. What are examples of some standardized norm-referenced diagnostic reading tests that measure a number of different skills?
3. What are examples of some standardized criterion-referenced reading tests?
4. What are examples of some teacher-made diagnostic tests?
5. Why are teachers interested in developing their own criterion-referenced tests?
6. What do teachers have to know in order to construct criterion-referenced tests?
7. What is the cloze procedure?
8. How is the cloze procedure used as a diagnostic technique?

KEY TERMS IN CHAPTER

You should pay special attention to the following new terms:

cloze procedure
cloze test
digit span
informal diagnostic reading
   tests
standardized oral reading tests

STANDARDIZED DIAGNOSTIC ORAL READING TESTS

Standardized oral reading tests
Individually administered tests that help teachers analyze the oral reading performance of students.

Standardized oral reading tests are individually administered and help teachers analyze the oral reading of their students. Whether the test is part of a battery of tests or is the entire test, the teacher must learn rules for recording errors and the marking symbols used in the particular test. It takes time and practice to learn a system for recording errors and to learn the marking symbols. It is important that teachers know that they cannot just pick up and administer a standardized oral reading test with which they are unfamiliar. This caution is not given to intimidate you from using a standardized oral reading test but rather to forewarn you that time is needed to become acquainted with it. It is also important that you recognize that all oral tests to not use the same recording system, symbol system, or scoring system. Obviously, if you find a test that you like and that you feel is effective for diagnosing students' oral reading strengths and weaknesses, you should stick with it. Some often-used standardized oral reading tests follow. (See the previous chapter for a discussion of oral reading errors.)

Gilmore Oral Reading Test[1]

This is an individually administered test designed to measure three aspects of oral reading ability: accuracy, comprehension, and rate. There are two forms—Form C and Form D—and each form contains paragraphs of a continuing story about a family. The paragraphs are based on graduated levels of difficulty; that is, each paragraph is a little longer and a little more difficult than the preceding one. The paragraphs begin at a first-grade level and proceed to the eighth-grade level.

Each paragraph is followed by five comprehension questions. The pupil is asked these questions as soon as he or she has finished reading each paragraph. The questions on the *Gilmore Oral Reading Test* are primarily concerned with literal comprehension. In the early 1970s, the Gilmore was highly regarded. "Despite its shortcomings, the Gilmore is among the best standardized tests of accuracy in oral reading of meaningful material now available."[2]

Gray Oral Reading Tests—Revised[3]

This is a series of standardized oral reading passages for individual administration. The two major functions of the *Gray Oral Reading Tests* are to provide an objective measure of growth in oral reading from grades 1 to 12 and to aid in the diagnosis of oral reading difficulties. Each of the two forms of this test, as in the *Gilmore*, is based on graduated levels of difficulty.

Each passage is followed by five comprehension questions. As in the *Gilmore*, the student is asked these questions as he or she has finished reading each passage; however, unlike the *Gilmore*, the questions in this revised edition are concerned with more than literal comprehension. Inferential, critical, and affective comprehension questions are asked also. The test is untimed and takes about 15–20 minutes.

The original test, which was authored by William S. Gray and later edited by Helen M. Robinson, is very highly reviewed in the *Mental Measurements Yearbooks*.

STANDARDIZED DIAGNOSTIC READING TESTS

The standardized diagnostic reading tests that are presented in this section are comprehensive tests in that they consist of a number of subtests. Many of the diagnostic test batteries contain oral reading

---

[1] John V. Gilmore and Eunice C. Gilmore, *Gilmore Oral Reading Test* (New York: Psychological Corporation © 1968).
[2] Oscar K. Buros, ed., *The Seventh Mental Measurements Yearbook* (Highland Park, N.J.: Gryphon Press, 1972), p. 1147.
[3] J. Lee Wiederholt and Brian R. Bryant, *Gray Oral Reading Tests—Revised* (San Antonio, Tex.: Psychological Corporation, 1986).

tests as well as silent reading tests and word analysis tests. Some of the tests, such as the *Botel Reading Inventory*, determine oral reading grade levels, but the tests consist of word lists rather than paragraphs. (See Chapter 8 for a discussion of the use of word lists to determine reading levels.) The first two of the tests presented in this section are also individually administered, and they, too, require some sophistication in administration and scoring. Teachers will have to study the examiner's manual carefully before administering any of the tests. It would probably be a good idea if the teacher were to practice giving the test in a simulated situation to some other person before actually giving it to children for diagnostic purposes.

Gates/McKillop/Horowitz Reading Diagnostic Tests[4]

These are individual tests, in one form only, designed to assess the oral reading, writing, and spelling skills of children in grades 1 through 6, but they can also be used to diagnose the reading difficulties of older students. The subtests consist of the following: oral reading, reading sentences, isolated word recognition, knowledge of word parts (syllabication), recognizing and blending common word parts, reading words, giving letter sounds, naming letters (capital and lowercase), identifying vowel sounds, auditory blending and discrimination, spelling, and informal writing sample. (Not all children will need to be given all the tests.)

From looking at the subtests, it can be seen that the Gates/McKillop/Horowitz Tests stress word analysis skills rather than comprehension.

The test manual contains detailed information for administering, scoring, and interpreting results. The test kit is composed of test materials (contains two tachistoscopes for words: flash test), pupil record booklet, and manual of directions.

Durrell Analysis of Reading Difficulty, 3rd ed.[5]

This test contains the following subtests: oral reading, which consists of five primary and three intermediate paragraphs with literal comprehension questions; silent reading, which consists of eight paragraphs equivalent in difficulty to the oral reading paragraphs; listening comprehension, which consists of six graded paragraphs with literal comprehension questions; word recognition/word analysis, which consists of a tachistoscope and word cards, one list for grade 1 and three lists for grades 2 through 6; listening vocabulary; pronunciation of word elements; spelling, which consists of one

---

[4] Arthur I. Gates, Anne S. McKillop, and Elizabeth C. Horowitz, *Gates/McKillop/Horowitz Reading Diagnostic Tests* (New York: Teachers College Press, 1981).

[5] Donald D. Durrell and Jane H. Catterson, *Durrell Analysis of Reading Difficulty: Manual of Directions* (New York: Psychological Corporation, 1980).

spelling list for primary and one spelling list for the intermediate grades; visual memory of words; auditory analysis of words and elements; and prereading phonics abilities inventories. The prereading phonics tests are available for nonreaders, pupils with initial reading difficulties, and kindergartners for whom more information is wanted. The prereading phonics tests consist of syntax matching, identifying letter names in spoken words, identifying phonemes in spoken words, naming lowercase letters, and writing letters from dictation.

The analysis also contains a profile chart, a checklist of instructional needs, a general history data form, supplementary paragraphs, supplementary tests, and suggestions for supplementary tests and observations.

The primary purposes of the analysis are to estimate the general level of reading achievement and to discover weaknesses and faulty reading habits so that they may be corrected.

The manual of directions provides instruction on who should be given the tests as well as directions on how to administer each. It is stated in the manual that norms are provided for most of the tests, but an analytic record of the difficulties the child displays is critical if specific help is to be given to correct weaknesses. It is also stated that the checklists for recording observations of difficulties are a very important feature. The checklist of instructional needs, an excellent guide for observing a child's reading behavior, is displayed in Table 9.1 (see Chapter 10 for information on observation).

Stanford Diagnostic Reading Test, 3rd ed.[6]

The primary purpose of the *Stanford Diagnostic Reading Test*, which is a group-administered standardized test, is to diagnose pupils' strengths and needs in reading. This test has been especially designed for remedial students and contains a significantly greater proportion of easy items than most achievement tests. As a result, the test makers claim their test is more reliable for below-average students, and students with reading problems should find the test less frustrating. In addition, the test places a strong emphasis on decoding skills because the test makers claim that any pupil's reading problems can be traced to the underdevelopment of decoding skills.

This test, which is for grades 1.5–12, has overlapping levels, contains two alternate and equivalent forms, and assesses four domains: comprehension, decoding, vocabulary, and rate. The subtests of each domain are as follows:

Comprehension—word reading, reading comprehension
Decoding—auditory discrimination, phonetic analysis, structural analysis, auditory vocabulary

[6] Bjorn Karlsen and Eric F. Gardner, *Stanford Diagnostic Reading Test*, 3rd ed. (San Antonio: Tex.: Psychological Corporation, 1984).

TABLE 9.1 Checklist of Instructional Needs*

NON-READER OR PREPRIMER LEVEL	PRIMARY GRADE READING LEVEL	INTERMEDIATE GRADE READING LEVEL
Needs help in:	*Needs help in:*	*Needs help in:*

NON-READER OR PREPRIMER LEVEL

Needs help in:

1. Listening comprehension and speech
   ___ Attention in listening
   ___ Understanding of directions
   ___ Speaking vocabulary
   ___ Speech correction
2. Prereading phonics abilities
   ___ Awareness of separate words in sentences
   ___ Syntax matching
   ___ Letter name sounds in spoken words
   ___ Phonemes in spoken words
   ___ Naming lower case letters
   ___ Writing letters from dictation
   ___ Writing letters from copy
3. Visual perception of word elements
   ___ Visual memory of words
   ___ Identifying letters named
   ___ Copying letters
4. Auditory perception of word elements
   ___ Initial or final single sounds
   ___ Initial or final blends
   ___ Phonograms
5. Reading interest and effort
   ___ Attention and persistence
   ___ Self-directed work
6. Other
   ___ _____
   ___ _____
   ___ _____
   ___ _____

PRIMARY GRADE READING LEVEL

Needs help in:

1. Listening comprehension and speech
   ___ Understanding of material heard
   ___ Speech and spoken vocabulary
2. Word analysis abilities
   ___ Visual memory of words
   ___ Auditory analysis of words
   ___ Solving words by sounding
   ___ Sounds of blends and phonograms
   ___ Use of context clues
3. Oral reading abilities
   ___ Speed of oral reading
   ___ Comprehension in oral reading
   ___ Phrasing (Eye-voice span)
   ___ Errors on easy words
   ___ Repetition of words or phrases
   ___ Ignoring punctuation
   ___ Ignoring word errors
   ___ Attack on unfamiliar words in context
   ___ Expression in reading
   ___ Speech, voice, enunciation
   ___ Security in oral reading
   ___ _____
   ___ _____
   ___ _____
4. Silent reading and recall
   ___ Speed of silent reading
   ___ Comprehension in silent reading
   ___ Attention and persistence
   ___ Recall on questions
   ___ Phrasing (Eye movements)
   ___ Lip movements and whispering
   ___ Head movements or frowning
   ___ Position of book; posture
   ___ _____
   ___ _____
   ___ _____
5. Reading interest and effort
   ___ Attention and persistence
   ___ Voluntary reading
   ___ Self-directed work; workbooks

INTERMEDIATE GRADE READING LEVEL

Needs help in:

1. Listening comprehension and speech
   ___ Understanding of material heard
   ___ Speech and oral expression
2. Word analysis abilities and spelling
   ___ Visual memory of words
   ___ Auditory analysis of words
   ___ Solving words by sounding syllables
   ___ Sounding syllables and word parts
   ___ Attack on unfamiliar words
   ___ Spelling ability
   ___ Accuracy of copy
   ___ Speed of writing
   ___ _____
   ___ _____
   ___ _____
3. Oral reading abilities
   ___ Speed of oral reading
   ___ Comprehension in oral reading
   ___ Phrasing (Eye movements)
   ___ Expression in reading; speech skills
   ___ Security in oral reading
   ___ Word and phrase meaning
   ___ _____
   ___ _____
   ___ _____
4. Silent reading and recall
   ___ Speed of silent reading
   ___ Comprehension in silent reading
   ___ Unaided oral recall
   ___ Recall on questions
   ___ Attention and persistence
   ___ Word and phrase meaning difficulties
   ___ Sentence complexity difficulties
   ___ Imagery in silent reading
5. Study abilities
   ___ Outlining
   ___ Unaided written recall
      ___ Main ideas
      ___ Details
      ___ Organization
6. Composition
   ___ Sentence sense
   ___ Spelling
   ___ Handwriting
7. Reading interest and effort
   ___ Attention and persistence
   ___ Voluntary reading
   ___ Self-directed work

Vocabulary—auditory vocabulary, vocabulary, word parts
Rate—reading rate, scanning and skimming, fast rate

The *Stanford Diagnostic Reading Test* is a norm-referenced test; that is, norms are not estimated or equated but are based on actual performance of a nationally representative sample of students. The test also supplies criterion-referenced information to help teachers diagnose students' specific strengths and weaknesses. Within each subtest there are groups of items called skills that measure specific objectives. The raw scores (the actual number correct—nonconverted or transformed scores) for each subtest can be transformed to Progress Indicators, which are the criterion-referenced scores. The Progress Indicator scores show where the student has achieved in a specific skill domain in relation to the predetermined Progress Indicator cutoff scores.

STANDARDIZED CRITERION-REFERENCED READING TESTS

Criterion-referenced tests are considered standardized if they are published, have been constructed by experts in the field, and have been developed with specific instructions for administration and scoring.

As already discussed in Chapter 3, criterion-referenced tests are based on a set of objectives, which are concerned with an individual's progress in relation to himself or herself. Before developing a criterion-referenced reading test, the test makers must decide on an inventory of desired student behaviors in reading. These must be identified, and often the standard or criterion of acceptable performance must also be identified.

The reason norms are not necessary for criterion-referenced tests is that they measure a student's mastery or nonmastery of objectives in a specific subject rather than compare the student to a national group in a subject.

Criterion-referenced reading tests are helpful diagnostic aids because they present a set of objectives that describe reading behaviors at rather specific levels. Some criterion-referenced tests are more specific than others.

Tests that supply criterion-referenced information seem to be omnipresent. Not only are a number of test publishers supplying criterion- or objective-referenced information for their norm-referenced tests to make them more useful for instructional purposes (see Chapters 3 and 7, and the earlier section "Stanford Diagnostic Reading Test, 3rd ed."), but also publishers of basal reader series are developing criterion- or objective-referenced instruments for use with their basal readers.

The tests that are presented in this section are those that have been specifically developed as criterion-referenced tests. There are not many of this kind in the field today; usually, a test is developed as a norm-referenced test, and criterion-referenced information is supplied later.

Special Note

Some criterion-referenced tests are being referred to as objective-referenced tests, curriculum-based tests, domain-referenced tests and so on.

California Diagnostic Reading Tests[7]

The *California Diagnostic Reading Tests* are a series of group-administered standardized tests that have been designed to assess the reading performance of those students who usually perform below average on tests. This series has six levels (grades 1 through 12) and assesses students' performance in four areas: word analysis (visual and auditory discrimination, whole word recognition, and structural analysis); vocabulary; comprehension; and applications. (See Table 9.2 for the test content for the whole series according to levels.)

The *California Diagnostic Reading Tests* are criterion-referenced tests; they are not norm-referenced tests; however, they can provide norm-referenced data. The tests supply criterion-referenced scores, which provide information about the student's level of proficiency in a particular content area. The criterion-referenced scores are referred to as objective performance indexes.

A Locator Test is available that makes it possible for students to take the test at their appropriate level, and the practice books for Levels D-E-F familiarize the students with the format of the test items and help them gain experience in rudimentary test-taking techniques.

The creators of these tests claim that "reading skills wherever possible, are measured . . . within a context, or limited context, rather than in isolation"[8] in order to be more in tune with the "whole language" movement. They also present detailed information on how the test results can be used as instructional planning tools. Part 4 of the Teacher's Guide, "Using a Diagnostic/Prescriptive Approach in the Classroom," contains instructional materials to guide teachers in a diagnostic/prescriptive approach.

Prescriptive Reading Inventory Reading System (PRI/RS)[9]

The *Prescriptive Reading Inventory Reading Systems* also constitute a criterion-referenced test and instruction system. This test was first

[7] Catherine Taylor (senior ed.), *California Diagnostic Reading Tests*, Teacher's Guide (Monterey, Calif.: CTB/McGraw-Hill, 1989).
[8] Ibid., p. 5.
[9] *Prescriptive Reading Inventory Reading Systems* (Monterey, Calif.: CTB/McGraw-Hill, 1984).

TABLE 9.2 Test Content of the *California Diagnostic Reading Tests*

	Test Levels	**A**	**B**	**C**	**D**	**E**	**F**
	Grade Levels	1–2	2–3	3–4	4–6	6–8	8–12
WORD ANALYSIS	Visual Discrimination	Letter Names Letter Forms Word Pairs					
	Auditory Discrimination	Single Consonants Consonant Clusters Single Vowels	Single Consonants Consonant Clusters Single Vowels Vowel Clusters	Single Consonants Consonant Clusters Single Vowels Vowel Clusters	All Consonant Sounds All Vowel Sounds	All Consonant Sounds All Vowel Sounds	
	Whole Word Recognition	Sight Words Encoding Decoding	Sight Words Encoding Decoding	Sight Words	Sight Words	Sight Words	
	Structural Analysis		Compounds	Contractions Compounds Roots and Affixes	Contractions Roots and Affixes	Roots and Affixes	
VOCABULARY	Vocabulary	Word Definition Categorization Experiential Vocabulary	Word Definition Categorization Experiential Vocabulary	Experiential Vocabulary Unfamiliar Words in Context Synonyms and Antonyms Multinyms Content Area Vocabulary	Unfamiliar Words in Context Synonyms and Antonyms Multinyms Content Area Vocabulary	Unfamiliar Words in Context Synonyms and Antonyms Multinyms Content Area Vocabulary	Unfamiliar Words in Context Synonyms and Antonyms Multinyms Content Area Vocabulary
COMPREHENSION	Oral Comprehension	Sentence/Story Listening					
	Reading Comprehension	Sentence Reading Story Reading	Sentence Reading Basic Facts / Event Sequence Inferences Central Thought	Basic Facts / Event Sequence Inferences Central Thought	Basic Facts / Event Sequence Inferences Central Thought	Basic Facts / Event Sequence Inferences Central Thought	Basic Facts / Event Sequence Inferences Central Thought Figurative Language
APPLICATIONS	Reference Skills					Graphic Displays Sources of Information	Graphic Displays Sources of Information
	Life Skills						Completing Forms Consumer Resources Life Skills Vocabulary
	Reading Speed and Accuracy				Reading Rate Skimming and Scanning	Reading Rate Skimming and Scanning	Reading Rate Skimming and Scanning

Source: *California Diagnostic Reading Tests*, Teacher's Guide (Monterey, Calif.: CTB/McGraw-Hill, 1989), p. 2. Copyright © 1989 by McGraw-Hill, Inc. Reprinted by permission of Macmillan/McGraw-Hill School Publishing Company.

published in 1980 by CTB/McGraw-Hill, and succeeds the *Prescriptive Reading Inventory*. A criterion-referenced approach to reading, the *PRI Reading Systems* include assessment and instructional materials that are supposed to supply detailed diagnostic and prescriptive information about a student's reading proficiency. The systems go beyond testing in that instructional materials, including lesson plans and activities, are provided as part of the systems.

The systems have five levels, spanning from kindergarten through grade 9. There are four skill clusters into which all *PRI Reading Systems* objectives are grouped. The objectives are presented at three different levels of specificity. Every kit includes a Systems Overview Chart, a Teacher's Guide, Teacher Resource Files, Tutor Activities, Student Worksheets, Mastery Tests, Reading Passage Books (for use with the Mastery Tests), and a Continuous Progress Monitoring Log.

TEACHER-MADE (INFORMAL) DIAGNOSTIC READING TESTS

Informal diagnostic reading tests
Teacher-made tests to help determine students' specific strengths and weaknesses.

Any test that you develop to help you learn more about a student's specific strengths and weaknesses is an informal diagnostic test. Every day teachers use informal techniques, such as word recognition tests or word lists collected from the back of a basal reader, oral reading tests, cloze tests, criterion-referenced tests, and word analysis tests, to help them learn more about their students' reading. Informal tests are excellent in giving quick feedback. They can also be structured to specifically fulfill an individual need. The classroom test that you develop will vary according to the particular situation.

Here are a number of informal reading tests you will find useful in diagnosing your students' strengths and weaknesses.

INFORMAL DIAGNOSTIC TESTS

Auditory Discrimination
(Before administering this test, make sure the child knows the difference between *same* and *different*. Also, pronounce each pair of words very distinctly, and ask the child to turn away from you when you are presenting the words to him or her so that there will not be any possibility of lip-reading.)

Listen carefully. Tell me whether I say the same word twice or if I say two different words.

1. Jim	Jim	7. rain	rain
2. Tod	Ted	8. hit	hat
3. bend	band	9. owl	our
4. top	tip	10. fond	found
5. lime	line	11. washing	watching
6. chop	shop		

1. Listen carefully. Give me another word that begins with the same sound as

   top   _____

   car   _____

   boy   _____

2. Listen carefully. Give me another word that ends with the same sound as

   bat   _____

   bed   _____

   lamb   _____

   can   _____

3. Listen carefully. Tell me a word that rhymes with the following words.

   1. walk   _____

   2. bake   _____

   3. tall   _____

   4. fell   _____

   5. let   _____

4. Listen carefully. Tell me the letter that stands for the first sound you hear in each of the following words.

1. bury	_____	2. level	_____	3. fierce	_____
4. wiry	_____	5. girl	_____	6. nephew	_____
7. dark	_____	8. tissue	_____	9. curb	_____
10. zone	_____	11. yield	_____		

5. Listen carefully. Tell me the two letters that stand for the first two sounds you hear in each word.

1. pledge	_____	2. floral	_____	3. snarl	_____
4. twirl	_____	5. dreary	_____	6. blush	_____
7. statue	_____	8. brag	_____	9. crystal	_____
10. swagger	_____	11. project	_____	12. glimpse	_____

6. Listen carefully. Tell me the two letters that stand for the first sound you hear in each word.

    1. chair _____   2. shoe _____   3. shame _____

    4. thumb _____   5. church _____

7. Listen carefully. Tell me the letter that stands for the sound you hear at the end of the word.

    1. hum _____   2. hear _____   3. mom _____

    4. buzz _____   5. thug _____   6. rain _____

    7. leak _____   8. burr _____

Visual Discrimination

Following are a number of letters. Underline the letter that is different from the first one in the line.

Example: E   E   <u>D</u>   E   E

1. U   R   U   U   U   U

2. P   P   P   P   P   D

3. d   d   d   b   d   d

4. p   p   p   p   d   p

5. m   m   n   m   m   m

6. o   o   o   o   e   o

7. K   K   H   K   K   K

Following are a number of letters. Underline the letter that is the same as the first one in the line.

Example: R   S   S   T   <u>R</u>

1. D   B   D   B   O   S

2. B   R   D   D   B   P

3. M   N   M   N   O   R

4. O   C   O   P   R   B

5. G   D   G   S   T   U

6. W   K   M   N   W   N

7. N   M   N   M   S   L

Following are a number of words. Draw a circle around the word that is the same as the first word.

Example: fun   far   fix   fat   (fun)   fall

1. was   saw   sat   won   wet   was
2. bark   dark   bark   hard   barn   bar
3. other   order   ought   other   about   ether
4. saw   set   sun   sat   saw   was
5. shame   same   shone   shame   shorn   slam
6. five   fair   find   fill   five   fix

Following are groups of letters. Draw a circle around the letter group that is the same as the first in the line.

Example: iot   tio   (iot)   oit   oti

1. tio   oit   iot   iot   tio
2. trg   rgt   tgr   trg   grt
3. sab   bsa   sab   bas   sba
4. pdb   bdp   bpd   pdb   pbd
5. oci   ico   coi   oic   oci
6. bpk   kpd   dpb   bpk   bkp
7. mbn   nbm   mbn   bmn   nmb

Memory Digit-Span Test
I am going to say some numbers, and I want you to say them just the way I do. Listen carefully, and get them just right. (Before each series repeat, "Listen carefully, and get them just right." Rate: one per second.) (See digit-span scale for digits forward and backward.)

_____ 85

_____ 62

_____ 84

_____ 374

_____ 195

_____ 837

_____ 7295

_____ 4962

_____ 6384

_____ 58274

_____ 39481

_____ 72583

_____ 362915

_____ 725816

_____ 817492

_____ 8514739

_____ 7281594

_____ 7359628

_____ 92413758

_____ 86152973

_____ 59814732

_____ 391752684

_____ 147925638

_____ 741592683

I am going to say some numbers, and I want you to say them in reverse order. For example, if I should say 5-1, you would say 1-5. Let's try another. 6-2—you say 2-6. (Before each series repeat, "Ready now, listen carefully and be sure to say the numbers in reverse order." Rate: one per second.)

_____ 92

_____ 71

_____ 38

_____ 197

_____ 638

_____ 592

_____ 7935

_____ 2976

_____ 3159

_____	72859
_____	47613
_____	94265
_____	728159
_____	597314
_____	412793
_____	8159637
_____	1742695
_____	6935148

Word Analysis Test—Auditory
Listen carefully. Each of the words I am going to pronounce has more than one syllable.
Tell me the number of syllables you hear in each word.

1. mother (2)
2. reached (1)
3. baby (2)
4. bicycle (3)
5. vocabulary (5)

Listen carefully. Tell me the vowel sound you hear in each word.

1. bake (ā)
2. coat (ō)
3. rid (ĭ)
4. not (ŏ)
5. bat (ă)

6. cute (ū)
7. leap (ē)
8. neck (ĕ)
9. nut (ŭ)
10. lip (ĭ)

Word Analysis Test—Visual
Can you pronounce the following nonsense words?

1. l o a p (lō̸ạp)
2. h a k e (hāk̸e)
3. c h i n e (chīn̸e)
4. p h a s (făs)
5. l i p o (līpō)

Special Note

When children are asked to state the letter that stands for the first sound heard in words such as *curb*, some may say *c* and others may say *k*. Neither answer is wrong. It is important to probe further to find out whether the children are saying *c* because they know the spelling of the word. It is possible but unlikely that young children will know that *c* stands for two sounds; a hard *c* and a soft *c*.

Digit-Span Scale for Digits Forward and Digits Backward

Digit span
Refers to amount of numbers an individual can retain in his or her short-term memory.

On the average, two-and-one-half-year-olds are able to repeat two digits in order, and three-year-olds are able to repeat three digits in order. Children from about the age of four and one-half to about seven years of age are able to repeat four digits in order. Seven- to ten-year-olds are usually able to repeat five digits in order. Ten- to fourteen-year-olds are usually able to repeat six digits in order. Fourteen-year-olds to more able adults usually can repeat seven, eight, and nine digits in order. (Digits refer to numbers. One-syllable words may be substituted for digits.)

On the average, seven-year-olds can repeat three digits in reverse order, and nine-year-olds to twelve-year-olds can repeat four digits in reverse order. Twelve-year-olds up to able adults can repeat five digits in reverse order. More able adults can usually repeat six and seven digits in reverse order. (See Chapter 14 for techniques to help students gain concentration ability.)

CLOZE PROCEDURE

Can you supply the _____ that fits this sentence? When you came to the missing word in this sentence, did you try to gain closure by supplying a term such as *word* to complete the incomplete sentence? If you did, you were involved in the process of *closure*, which involves the ability of the reader to use context clues to determine the needed word. To gain closure, we must finish whatever is unfinished.

Cloze procedure
A technique that helps teachers gain information about a variety of language facility and comprehension ability skills.

The cloze procedure was primarily developed by Wilson Taylor in 1953 as a measure of readability, that is, to test the difficulty of instructional materials and to evaluate their suitability for students. It has since been used for a number of other purposes, especially as a measure of a student's comprehension.

Cloze procedure is not a comprehension skill; it is a technique that helps teachers gain information about a variety of language facility and comprehension skills. A cloze test or exercise is one in which the reader must supply words that have been systematically deleted from a text at a particular grade level.

Cloze test
Reader must supply words which have been systematically deleted from a passage.

There is no set procedure for determining the length of the passage or the number of deletions that a passage should have. However, if you wish to apply the criteria for reading levels that have been used in research with the traditional cloze procedure, you must follow certain rules. First, only words must be deleted, and the replacements for each word must be the *exact* word, not a synonym. Second, the words must be deleted in a systematic manner. The researchers who have developed the criteria for scoring cloze tests state that "any departure from these rules leaves the teacher with uninterpretable results."[10]

The traditional cloze procedure consists of deleting every fifth word of a passage that is representative of the material being tested. The passage that is chosen should be able to stand alone; for example, it should not begin with a pronoun that has its antecedent in a former paragraph. The first sentence of the passage should remain intact. Then beginning with either the first, second, third, fourth, or fifth word of the second sentence, every fifth word of a 250-word passage should be deleted.

At the intermediate-grade level and higher, the passage is usually 250 words, and every fifth word is generally deleted. At the primary-grade level, the passage is usually shorter, and every eighth or tenth word is deleted. For maximum reliability, a passage should have at least fifty deletions. If we were to use this figure as our criterion, we can see that we need a passage to be at least 250 words long with every fifth word deleted. Obviously, a cloze technique would not yield as reliable a score for the primary-grade level as for the intermediate-grade level because passages for the former are shorter and have fewer deletions.

Scoring the Cloze Test

If you have deleted fifty words, the procedure for scoring the cloze test is very easy. All you have to do is multiply the number of correct insertions by two and add a percentage symbol. For example, twenty-five correct insertions would be equal to 50 percent. If you have not deleted exactly fifty words, use the following formula, in which the number of correct insertions is divided by the number of blanks and multiplied by 100 percent.

$$\text{Formula: } \frac{\text{Number of Correct Insertions}}{\text{Number of Blanks}} \times 100\%$$

$$\text{Example: } \frac{40 \text{ correct insertions}}{60 \text{ blanks}} \times 100$$

$$\frac{40}{60} \times 100\% = (40 \div 60) \times 100\%$$

$$= 67\% \text{ (rounded to nearest digit)}$$

---

[10] John R. Bormuth, "The Cloze Procedure: Literacy in the Classroom," in *Help for the Reading Teacher: New Directions in Research*, William D. Page, ed. (Urbana, Ill.: National Conference on Research in English, 1975), p. 67.

For a traditional cloze test in which only exact words are counted as correct and every fifth word has been deleted, a score below 44 percent would indicate a frustration level. A score between 44 and 57 percent would indicate the instructional level, and scores above 57 percent would indicate the independent level. It is important to note that these criteria should be used only if the exact words are used and if every fifth word has been deleted from the passage. (Do not confuse these levels with the Betts reading levels. See Chapter 8 for an in-depth discussion of reading levels.)

Reading Levels Scale for Cloze Procedure

Independent level	58% and above
Instructional level	44% through 57%
Frustration level	43% and below

Variations of the Traditional Cloze Procedure: An Emphasis on Diagnosis

Variations of the cloze technique are usually used. For example, rather than deleting every fifth or tenth word, every noun or verb is deleted, or every function or structure word (definite and indefinite articles, conjunctions, prepositions, and so on) is deleted. This technique is used when the teacher wishes to gain information about a student's sentence sense. For example:

Jane threw _____ ball _____ Mary. (the, to)

Another variation of the cloze technique is to delete key words in the passage. This technique is useful for determining whether students have retained certain information. For example:

A technique in which the reader must supply words is called the _____ procedure. (cloze)

Cloze technique can also be adapted for other uses. Students can be presented with a passage in which they must complete the incomplete words. For example:

Dick r_____ his bike every day. (rides)

Another adaptation is to present the students with a passage in which every nth word is deleted. They must then choose words from a given word list that *best* fit the blanks.

Teachers can use cloze exercises for diagnosis, review, instruction, and testing. In constructing the exercise, the key thing to remember is its *purpose*. If the purpose is to test a student's retention of some concepts in a specific area, the exact term is usually necessary; however, if the purpose is to gain information about a student's language facility, ability to use context clues, vocabulary development, or comprehension, the exact term is not as important because often many words will make sense in a passage.

Here is an example of an exercise using the cloze technique for an upper primary grade. Notice how explicitly the instructions are stated for the students, and also notice that the first and last sentences of the passage are given intact.

In addition, note that the deletion pattern is not the same throughout the passage.

Directions: Read the first and last sentences that have no missing words in them to get a clue to what the story is about. Then read very carefully each sentence that has a missing word or words in it. Using context clues, find a word that would make sense in the story and put it in the blank.

In the forest live a kind old man and woman. (1) _____ have been living in (2) _____ forest for almost ten (3) _____. They had decided to (4) _____ to the forest because they (5) _____ nature.

The kind old (6) _____ and a woman make their (7) _____ by by baking breads and cakes and (8) _____ them to the people who (9) _____ the forest. Everyone who (10) _____ the forest usually buys (11) _____ bread or cake from the old (12) _____. The kind old man and woman are happy in the forest.

Answers: 1. They, 2. the, 3. years, 4. move, 5. love, like, 6. man, 7. living, 8. selling, 9. visit, 10. visits, 11. some, 12. couple.

Here is an example of an exercise using cloze technique for an intermediate grade.

Directions: Read the first sentence of the story to get a clue to what the story is about. Then read each sentence that has a missing word or words very carefully. Using context clues, insert a word in each blank so that the story makes sense.

Everyone was looking forward to Friday night because that was the night of the big basketball game. This (1) _____ would determine the championship (2) _____ Deerville High and Yorktown (3) _____. For years Deerville High and (4) _____ High have been rivals. This (5) _____ was very (6) _____ because so far (7) _____ school had won (8) _____ equal number of games. (9) _____ game on Friday night would break the (10) _____.

Friday night finally arrived. The game (11) _____ the championship title (12) _____ being played in the Deerville High (13) _____ because the game (14) _____ year had been played (15) _____ the Yorktown High gym. (16) _____ gym was so (17) _____ that many spectators were without (18) _____. When the two teams (19) _____ the gym from the dressing areas, (20) _____ were thunderous (21) _____ and whistles from the (22) _____. Each team went through (23) _____ warm-up drills of (24) _____ baskets and passing. Then the buzzer (25) _____. The game would begin (26) _____ a moment. Just as the referee (27) _____ the ball in the (28) _____ for the starting jumpball, the lights (29) _____ the gym went (30) _____. There was complete darkness. Everyone (31) _____ taken by surprise. Almost immediately a (32) _____ on the loudspeaker (33) _____ that the game would have (34) _____ be postponed because of a (35) _____ failure. The game would take (36) _____ next Friday. All were (37) _____ to remain where they (38) _____ until someone with a flashlight came to help them.

Answers: (1) game, (2) between, (3) High, (4) Yorktown, (5) game, (6) important, (7) each, (8) an, (9) The, (10) tie, (11) for, (12) was, (13) gym, (14) last, (15) in, (16) The, (17) crowded, (18) seats, (19) entered, (20) there, (21) cheers, (22) spectators, audience, *or* crowd, (23) its, (24) shooting, (25) sounded *or* rang, (26) in, (27) threw, (28) air, (29) in, (30) out, (31) was, (32) voice, (33) announced, (34) to, (35) power, (36) place, (37) told, (38) were

Knowledge of Results and Cloze Procedure

Knowledge of results is essential if the cloze procedure is to be used for instruction or diagnosis. Students need feedback. Unless students recognize that they have made a mistake, they will continue to make the same error. Knowledge of results should be given as soon as possible, as well as an explanation for the correct response. Student involvement in the diagnostic process is important, and a student's recognition that he or she has a problem is a positive step in correcting it.

SUMMARY

Chapter 9 continues to discuss and present a number of different kinds of diagnostic tests and techniques. These tests help teachers gain detailed information about their students' reading. Oral reading, if properly used, is an essential diagnostic tool. An astute teacher can gain a great amount of information about a student's reading by listening to the child read aloud. A number of standardized oral reading and diagnostic tests were presented and described. Standardized criterion-referenced tests that are also used for diagnostic purposes were also given and described. The section on teacher-made tests gave examples of a number of diagnostic tests that teachers could use to learn more about their students' reading. The last section included a discussion on cloze procedure and examples of how this technique can be adapted for various purposes.

SUGGESTIONS FOR THOUGHT QUESTIONS AND ACTIVITIES

1. You have been appointed to a committee whose objective is to develop criterion-referenced tests for a reading program. You are responsible for the primary grades. How would you go about completing this task?
2. Generate a number of instructional objectives for word recognition, and then construct some test items to determine whether a student has achieved each specific objective.
3. Look up the reviews on three diagnostic reading tests in the *Mental Measurements Yearbooks*.
4. Develop a cloze test to learn how well a child uses syntactic clues.
5. Administer some of the teacher-made tests that are presented in this chapter to a child who is having word recognition problems.
6. Construct some of your own diagnostic tests to learn about a specific reading behavior of a student.

SELECTED BIBLIOGRAPHY

Carr, Eileen, Peter Dewitz, and Judythe Patberg. "Using Cloze for Inference Training with Expository Text." *The Reading Teacher* 42 (February 1989): 380–85.

Conoley, Jane C., and Jack J. Kramer (Eds.). *The Tenth Mental Measurements Yearbook.* Lincoln, N.B.: Buros Institute of Mental Measurements, University of Nebraska, 1989.

DeSanti, Roger J. "Concurrent and Predictive Validity of a Semantically and Syntactically Sensitive Cloze Scoring System." *Reading Research and Instruction* 28 (winter 1989): 29–40.

Gill, Doren, et al. *Defining Reading Diagnosis: Why, What, and How?* Research Series No. 46 (ED 176 211). East Lansing: Institute for Research on Teaching, Michigan State University, 1979.

Jacobson, Jeanne M. "Group vs. Individual Completion of a Cloze Passage." *Journal of Reading* 33 (January 1990): 244–50.

Sweetland, Richard C., and Daniel J. Keyser. *Tests,* 3rd ed. Austin, Tex.: PRO-ED, 1990.

10

Observation and Other Child Study Procedures as Diagnostic Techniques

INTRODUCTION

Read the following conversation overheard in the faculty lounge:

Ms. Anderson: I don't know what to do with Billy. His behavior is driving me crazy.

Mr. Johnson: Why? What does he do?

Ms. Anderson: What doesn't he do? He's forever getting up from his seat. He can't seem to sit still for a moment. He's always disturbing his neighbor. If there is any commotion or problem in the room, you can be sure that Billy is the cause of it.

Mr. Johnson: Have you spoken to Billy's parents about his behavior?

Ms. Anderson: Yes, but they say that they do not see the same kind of behavior at home, so they feel that it's something at school. I've just about had it.

Mr. Johnson: I've had Billy in my class, and I remember him as a pretty bright boy. I think that before you refer him for testing you should try to observe when Billy starts to act up. I know that I had a child who acted just as Billy does, and I thought that she was misbehaving all the time, and just to make my life miserable. Well, I had just finished a course in diagnosis, and the professor had discussed the uses of observation techniques to learn about the behavior of students. I decided to try it. My sanity was at stake. Was I surprised at the results! It also made me aware of how unfounded my statements about Susan were. Let's go to my room, and I'll show you what I did.

This chapter concerns the use of direct observation and other child study techniques such as questionnaires and inventories.

KEY QUESTIONS

After you finish reading this chapter, you should be able to answer the following questions:

1. What is the purpose of direct observation?
2. When should teachers make generalizations about students' behavior?
3. How can observations be made as objective as possible?
4. What should teachers record as worthy of observation?
5. What is an anecdotal record?
6. What are checklists?
7. What kinds of checklists are there?
8. What are some examples of checklists?
9. How can a rating scale be used with a checklist?
10. What are the advantages of informal interviews?
11. What is an interest inventory?
12. What are some examples of interest inventories?
13. What are projective techniques?
14. How can a teacher use projective techniques in the classroom?
15. What kinds of projective techniques can teachers use?
16. What are the purposes of reading autobiographies?

KEY TERMS IN CHAPTER

You should pay special attention to the following new terms:

anecdotal record
checklist
informal interviews
interest inventory
observation
projective technique
rating scale
reading autobiography

THE USES OF OBSERVATION

Direct observation is an essential part of any diagnostic program, and it is especially helpful in diagnosing reading problems. Observation is also useful for evaluation because it helps teachers become aware of students' attitudes, interests, and pleasures. It is one thing for a student to say that he or she enjoys reading, but it is another thing for the student to actually read. Through observation, teachers can observe whether students are voluntarily choosing to read in their free time and whether they voluntarily raise their hands to answer questions. The best method to determine whether students have learned something is to observe whether they are actually doing what they have learned.

Making Observations Objective

Observation
A technique that helps teachers collect data about students' behavior.

Observation is a technique; it is a means for collecting data. So that observations are of value, teachers must be as objective as possible and avoid making generalizations about a student's behavior too early. For example, by observing that Sharon on one or two occasions is reading mystery stories, the teacher states that Sharon likes mysteries. This may be so, but it may be that she is just trying them out. Sharon may actually like only a few of them, and she may read only one or two a year. Here are some helpful suggestions on how to make observations as objective and useful as possible:

1. Use checklists and anecdotal records (observed behavior without interpretations) to record observations (see next section).
2. Observe the student over an extended period of time before making any inferences about the student's behavior.
3. Avoid the projection of one's own feelings or attitudes onto the student's behavior.
4. Observations should be used in conjunction with other measurement techniques.
5. Make sure that only observed behavior is recorded.
6. Look for a pattern of behavior before making any inferences about behavior.
7. Record observed behavior immediately or as soon as possible.
8. Recognize that checklists and anecdotal records do not reveal the cause or causes of the observed behavior(s); they only help to identify patterns of behavior from which one can try to deduce the existence of possible problems.
9. Do not oversimplify a student's observed behavior.
10. Date observations.

ANECDOTAL RECORDS

Anecdotal record
A record of observed behavior over a period of time.

Teachers are often confused about what to record as worthy of observation. Because of this confusion, checklists (see next section) are very helpful; however, it is not possible for checklists to contain an inclusive list of student behavior. Therefore, teachers usually supplement checklists with anecdotal information, which is the recording of *observed behavior* as objectively as possible. In recording observed behavior, teachers should attempt to put down exactly what has taken place *as soon as possible*. The date and time of the incident should be recorded, and the teacher's interpretation of the observed behavior may be given; however, the teacher's interpretation or possible explanation for the student's behavior should be put in brackets or set off in some way to avoid confusion with the actual observed behavior. It is best for the teacher to record merely the observed behavior and to observe the student over an extended period of time before making any hypotheses about the cause or causes for the behavior. If the teacher observes the student over an extended period of time, the teacher is more likely to see a pattern of behavior.

Determining the Information to be Recorded

What information should be recorded? This is a difficult question to answer, and as already stated, is often confusing for the teacher. As a result, anecdotal information usually consists of unusual observed behavior. However, teachers may be losing important information, which could help them to gain insights into a child's problem, if they record only unusual behavior. Here is an example of a teacher who uses checklists and anecdotal records. He was losing significant information because he was only recording unusual behavior.

Mr. Jackson has a reading checklist for each student, and after each reading lesson and at other appropriate times, he checks off what he has observed. To supplement his checklist, Mr. Jackson also employs anecdotal information. Whenever he notices anything unusual, he records the observed behavior. For example, yesterday, Jerry started a fight with his best friend, and then for the rest of the day, he refused to do any work.

Mr. Jackson should have recorded Jerry's unusual behavior, but he should also be recording other kinds of observed behavior that are not on the reading checklists. For example, Mr. Jackson should be recording the following:

1/9   Jerry puts head on desk—reading period
1/13 Jerry puts head on desk—reading period
1/16 Jerry puts head on desk—reading period
1/20 Jerry puts head on desk—reading period
1/23 Jerry puts head on desk—reading period
1/27 Jerry puts head on desk—reading period

Jerry's behavior of putting his head on the desk has become such a normal occurrence that Mr. Jackson may have overlooked it. Yet, this behavior is extremely important. Jerry, over an extended period of time, puts his head on the desk *during the reading period*. Why? Mr. Jackson may not have noticed this behavior because of its frequency and because he may have thought that Jerry put his head on the desk because he was tired or sleepy. Only by recording when Jerry put his head on the desk could Mr. Jackson see that it was always during a reading period. By recording the dates, Mr. Jackson could check to see what kinds of reading lessons were involved. It may be that Jerry was tired or sleepy, but it is most unlikely. It is more probable that by checking further, Mr. Jackson will find that Jerry is bored because the work is too easy for him or that he is frustrated because the work is too hard for him. It may be that Jerry cannot do sustained silent reading because of an eye problem. It may be many things. The point is that the teacher would not be aware of these problems unless he has recorded what appeared to be "common" behavior.

From this discussion, it is obvious that exact guidelines cannot be given about what should or should not be recorded. Alert teachers, however, who are aware of the individual differences of the students in their classes will recognize those situations that warrant recording. Here are some more examples:

1. Susan always seems to want to go to the lavatory. Record when she goes and the frequency. It may be a physiological or emotional problem, or it may be that she wants to "escape" from a certain situation.
2. Michael is always causing disruptions in class. Record when Michael acts up to see whether there is a pattern. It may be that that is Michael's way of avoiding work. What is he avoiding? Is he bored or is he frustrated? Is something bothering him?
3. Maria starts walking around the room and chatting to other children who want to finish doing their work. Record when Maria does this, and try to figure out why.

It's important to note that observations do not explain the causes of behavior. As stated earlier, observation is a technique for gathering information; it helps teachers learn more about the behavior of students. If used carefully in conjunction with other techniques and test data, it can help teachers hypothesize possible causes for behavior. The possible causes must then be verified by more extensive and scientifically collected data, such as standardized and teacher-made tests.

Special Note

Teachers should be extremely careful about what anecdotal information becomes part of a child's permanent records because federal legislation now allows parents access to their children's records.

CHECKLISTS

Checklist
A means for systematically and quickly recording a student's behavior; it usually consists of a list of behaviors that the observer records as present or absent.

Checklists usually consist of lists of behaviors that the observer checks as present or absent. Checklists are a means for systematically and quickly recording a student's behavior. They are not tests, although it is possible to present or devise a test to enable the rapid filling out of a checklist of behaviors; in other words, the test is administered to get the result, which is the student's profile.

Checklist formats may vary: Some use rating scales, some are used for a whole class or group, and some are used for an individual child. The purpose for the checklist should determine the kind of checklist that is used. An example of a diagnostic checklist for a child's speech problems follows.

Child's Name: _____

Grade: _____

Date: _____

Diagnostic Checklist of Speech Problems

	Yes	No
1. Is child's voice		
a. loud?		
b. too low?		
c. nasal?		
d. hoarse?		
e. monotonous?		
f. pitched abnormally high?		
g. pitched abnormally low?		
2. Is child's rate of speech		
a. too slow?		
b. too rapid?		
3. Is child's phrasing poor?		
4. Is child's speech hesitant?		
5. Does the child show evidence of articulatory difficulties such as		
a. the distortion of sounds?		
b. the substitution of one sound for another?		
c. the omission of sounds?		
6. Does the child show evidence of vocabulary problems such as		
a. the repetition of phrases?		
b. a limited vocabulary?		
7. Does the child show evidence of negative attitudes toward oral communication such as		
a. not engaging in discussions or conversations?		
b. not volunteering to give a talk or oral report?		

Group and Individual Checklists

Checklists that are used to display the behavior of a whole class or of a group of students in a specific area are sometimes preferred by teachers because they do not have to go to individual folders to record a student's behavior; thus teachers can, at a glance, determine who needs help in a specific area and who does not. A group checklist is helpful in planning instruction for the group as well as for the individual, whereas the individual checklist is useful in assessing the strengths and weaknesses of an individual student only. Both types of formats are helpful. A teacher who, at a glance, wishes to see a complete profile of a child may prefer the individual approach, whereas the teacher who wishes to see a profile of students' strengths and weaknesses in specific skills for instructional planning will probably prefer a group checklist.

Whether a group or individual checklist is used, it should contain an itemized list of behaviors in a particular area; there should be space for dates; and there should be space for special notes.

Special Note

Group checklists usually do not have the space for notes that individual checklists have. This may be one of their disadvantages.

Diagnostic Checklist for Oral and Silent Reading

Oral Reading	Yes	No	Specific Errors
1. Word recognition errors. The teacher listens to the child while he or she is reading orally and records whether the child makes any of the following errors:			
a. omissions			
b. insertions			
c. substitutions			
d. repetitions			
e. hesitations			
f. mispronunciations			
g. reversals.			
2. Manner of reading. The teacher observes the child while he or she is reading aloud and records whether the child exhibits any of the following behaviors:			
a. word-by-word phrasing			
b. finger pointing			
c. head movement			
d. fidgeting			
e. voice characteristics high-pitched loud soft monotonous			
f. other.			

Oral Reading (Cont.)	Yes	No	Specific Errors
3. Comprehension. (*See* Comprehension Diagnostic Checklist in Chapter 13.)			

Silent Reading	Yes	No
1. Comprehension. (See Comprehension Diagnostic Checklist in Chapter 13.)		
2. Manner of reading. The teacher observes the child while he or she is reading silently and records whether the child exhibits any of the following behaviors:		
a. lip movement		
b. reads aloud		
c. head movement		
d. continually looks up		
e. finger pointing		
f. other.		

Checklists and Rating Scales

Rating scale
An evaluative instrument used to record estimates of particular aspects of a student's behavior.

A checklist that uses a rating scale is actually an assessment instrument. This type of checklist serves different purposes from one that records observed behavior. An assessment checklist can be used by the teacher at the end of a unit to help to determine a student's progress. It can be used with the student so that the student is aware of his or her progress in a specific area. When the assessment checklists are used, the checklists of observed behavior and the anecdotal records should be used as supplementary information or as aids in verifying the student's rating.

If rating scales are used, it is important that criteria be set up beforehand to help teachers determine what rating to give to a particular student. For example, if a student consistently makes errors in recognizing words that begin with certain blends, that student would receive a rating of 3 on a scale of 1 to 3 in which 1 is the highest and 3 is the lowest. If the student almost never makes an error in recognizing words that begin with certain blends, that student should receive a rating of 1 on a scale of 1 to 3. If a student sometimes makes errors in recognizing words that begin with certain blends, the student would receive a rating of 2 on a scale of 1 to 3. Here is an example of a group checklist with a rating scale.

Phonic Analysis Skills (Consonants) Rating Scale (Group)

	Maria			John			José			Susan		
	1	2	3	1	2	3	1	2	3	1	2	3
Single consonants												
Initial												
Medial												
Final												
Consonant blends (clusters)												
Consonant digraphs												
Silent consonants												

Special Note

There are diagnostic checklists in a number of other chapters in this book.

OTHER HELPFUL CHILD STUDY TECHNIQUES

There are some important student characteristics that cannot be gained through direct observation. Attitudes or feelings and interests are examples of essential characteristics that cannot be directly observed. Projective techniques, informal interviews, and inventory-type measures can help teachers learn about those aspects of students that cannot be directly observed. Achievement tests can help teachers learn about the amount of knowledge students have, and intelligence tests can help teachers learn about the students' rate of learning or their approximate potential for doing work in school; projective techniques, informal interviews, and interest inventories can help teachers understand their students better.

In a diagnostic-reading and correction program it is important for teachers to look at both the cognitive and noncognitive characteristics of their students, because students' attitudes and interests will affect what they learn and whether they learn. Reading helps reading; unfortunately, many students are not choosing to read. The reasons for this lack are varied and many (see Chapter 13). However, if teachers know about their students' attitudes and interests, they can help motivate their students and instill in them a positive attitude toward reading. For example, if a teacher has a student who is doing poorly in reading and who never chooses to read voluntarily, the teacher can learn about that child's interest and use it to motivate the child to read.

Special Note

Teachers must be cautioned against assuming the role of psychologist or therapist and should avoid any suggestion that they are searching

Figure 10.1 Rashid's teacher knows Rashid's interests, so she has books he likes in her class library.

for underlying psychological causes for a student's behavior. Teachers should avoid administering any psychiatrically oriented instrument to their students.

Informal Interviews

Informal interviews
Teachers converse with students to learn about their interests and feelings.

The easiest way to learn about students' likes or dislikes is to ask them. Teachers have many opportunities during the school day to converse with their students and learn about their feelings and interests. Teachers can also set up special times during the school day to meet with students for a consultation in the form of an informal interview. This is a good technique because it helps the teacher to build rapport with students, as well as to gain information about them. This technique is especially helpful for the lower primary grades and for those students who have reading problems. However, the informal interview is very time consuming, so other techniques are needed also.

Figure 10.2 This teacher is having an informal chat with one of her students.

Special Note

Teachers should avoid setting up special interviews to discuss students' interests after school. Students may look upon this as a punishment of some sort. Of course, if teachers, by chance, meet some of their students after school and converse with them, this is an excellent opportunity to learn about their interests.

Figure 10.3 Jennifer and her teacher are having an informal discussion about the books Jennifer enjoys reading.

Interest Inventories

Interest inventories can be standardized or teacher-made. The purpose of an interest inventory is to help teachers learn about the likes and dislikes of their students. In this book, we are particularly interested in students' likes or dislikes so that we can use this information to help stimulate them to read. For example, if we learn from an interest inventory that a student who is a reluctant reader likes mechanics and cars, we could choose books in this area at the student's ability level.

Interest inventories usually employ statements, questions, or both to obtain information. The statement or questionnaire method enables the teacher to gain a great amount of information in a relatively short period of time, but there is a major difficulty with this method. When people fill out an inventory they are not always truthful. Many times individuals give "expected responses"; that is, they answer with responses that they feel the tester expects or wants rather than with responses based on what they actually do or based on how they feel. Students who wish to create a favorable impression on their teacher may especially answer in an expected direction. Teachers cannot completely avoid the faking that is done on inventories, but they can help to control it. Teachers who have good rapport with their students and who have a good affective environment in their classrooms will be able to gain the trust of their students. Before administering the inventory, these teachers can discuss its purpose and try to impress upon the students how important it is for them to put down exactly the way they feel rather than what they think they should feel.

Interest inventories can be individually administered, administered to a small group, or administered to the whole class. The interest inventory is usually used in a group, but it is individually administered if the student's reading problem prevents him or her from filling it out. In the lower primary grades teachers can use a checklist type of questionnaire, whereby they read the question to the children and the children mark the appropriate box. Here are examples of some interest inventories that you can use with your students to ascertain their reading interests.

LOWER PRIMARY GRADES (Read aloud by teacher)

Name_____ Grade _____

1. Do you like to read?   Yes _____   No _____   Sometimes _____

2. What kinds of books do you like to read? Books about a. animals _____ b. children

_____ c. sports _____ d. adventure _____ e. fairy tales _____

3. What do you like to do after school? a. watch TV _____ b. read a book _____

c. play _____ d. do schoolwork _____ e. work around the house _____ d. work

on a hobby _____

4. What do you like to do when there is no school? a. watch TV _____ b. read a book _____ c. play _____ d. do schoolwork _____ e. work around the house _____ f. go shopping with your parents _____ g. visit the zoo _____

5. What are your favorite television shows? a. cartoons _____ b. comedy shows _____ c. movies _____ d. mysteries _____ e. musicals _____ f. game shows _____ g. adventure _____

6. What are your favorite games? a. group games played outside _____ b. indoor games _____ c. electronic (television) games _____

(For numbers 2 through 6, the child may check more than one.)

UPPER PRIMARY GRADES

Name _____ Grade _____

1. Do you like to read? _____

2. When do you like to read the best? _____

_____

3. What is your favorite subject? _____

_____

4. What is your favorite book? _____

_____

5. What do you like to do after school? _____

_____

6. What is your favorite game? _____

_____

7. What is your favorite television show? _____

_____

8. What kinds of books do you like to read? _____

_____

9. What is your hobby? _____

_____

10. Do you take out books from the library? _____

_____

Name_____ Grade _____

1. Do you like to read? _____
2. What kinds of books are your favorites? _____
   _____
3. What do you like to do after school? _____
   _____
4. What are your favorite subjects?_____
   _____
5. Name your favorite hobby. _____
6. How often during the month do you go to the public library? _____
7. How often during the week do you go to your school library? _____
8. Name your favorite book. _____
9. What do you enjoy doing the most?_____
10. What is your favorite television show? _____
11. Name your favorite movie._____
12. What is your favorite sport? _____
13. If you could go anywhere in the world, where would you like to go?_____
14. If you could visit any book character you wanted to, whom would you like to visit?
   _____
15. Name the magazines and newspapers that you read. _____
16. What part of the newspaper do you like to read the best? _____
17. What book is the most popular among you and your friends? _____
18. What would you like to be when you grow up?_____

Projective Techniques

Projective technique
A method in which the individual tends to put himself or herself into the situation and reveal how he or she feels.

Projective techniques are subtle procedures whereby individuals put themselves into a situation and reveal how they feel. Projective techniques are more revealing than inventories because the student is less likely to fake an answer. The student does not know what the *correct* or *best* answer is, for there is no correct or best answer. On a projective test students are more likely to give the answer that is natural for them, and as a result, reveal how they really feel.

There are, however, a number of problems with projective techniques. The major problem concerns the interpretation of the students' responses. Because of difficulty with interpretation, projective tests are not very trustworthy; however, they do have some definite benefits for teachers with students who have reading problems. They can help teachers gain some insights into the way students who have reading problems feel about themselves without the students realizing it. Teachers may also gain information about why the students think they have a reading problem. The teacher could then use this information to try to help the students.

The examples of projective tests that follow are simple ones that classroom teachers can administer to their students. These tests can be group- or individually administered.

Special Note

Teachers should use projective tests with caution and not try to read too much into the responses. Also, teachers should not administer tests that require clinical analysis by a psychologist.

Sentence Completion Test

The sentence completion test is easy to administer in a relatively short period of time. Students are given some unfinished sentences that they are asked to complete as rapidly as possible. This test can be given orally to those students who have trouble reading or writing, or it can be given to a whole group at once. Here are some typical incomplete sentences:

> Reading is . . .
> I believe I can . . .
> I prefer . . .
> My favorite . . .

Wish Test

The wish test is similar to the sentence completion test except that the phrase *I wish* precedes the incomplete sentence. Here are some typical examples:

> I wish I were . . .
> I wish I could . . .
> I wish reading were . . .
> I wish school were . . .
> I wish my friends were . . .
> I wish my teacher . . .

Reading Autobiography

Reading autobiography
Students write or tell about their feelings and attempt to analyze their reading problems.

The reading autobiography is not as subtle as a projective technique because the students are aware that they are writing or telling about their feelings and trying to analyze why they have a reading problem. It is a helpful technique, however, and probably not as prone to faking as an interest inventory because the students are partners in an attempt to analyze their reading difficulties. The reading autobiography is the student's own life story of his or her reading experiences. It can be presented in a number of ways, and it can be individually or group-administered.

Open-Ended Reading Autobiography

One technique that could be used is simply to have the students write their reading autobiography. They are given the following instructions:

> Since this is the life story of your reading experiences, you must go back as far as you can remember. Try to recall your earliest reading experiences, what they were, and how you felt about them. Try to recall what books you liked when you were very small, and whether you still like those kinds of books. Try to remember when you first started to read. How did you feel? Try to recall how you first learned to read, and what you think helped you the most in learning to read. If you have a reading problem, try to remember when you think it first started and why it started. Put down anything that you feel is important in helping others to understand your reading problem if you think you have one.

Students who have trouble writing could orally relate their autobiographies to the teacher, or they could tape-record them.

Questionnaire Reading Autobiography

The questionnaire autobiography is also helpful in gaining information about a student's reading history, but it is more limiting than the open-ended reading autobiography. Also, it is only as good as the questions on it because students' responses are determined by the questions. Here is an example:

READING AUTOBIOGRAPHY

	Yes	No	Sometimes
1. Do you like to read?			
2. When do you like to read?			
3. Do you like someone to read to you?			
4. Do you feel you understand what you read?			
5. Did anyone try to teach you to read before you came to school?			
6. Did anyone read to you when you were younger?			
7. Are there lots of books in your house?			
8. Do you think you have a reading problem?			

If you answered *yes* to question 8, answer the following questions:

1. What do you think your reading problem is?

2. Why do you think you have a reading problem?

3. Has anyone tried to help you with your problem?

4. When do you feel your reading problem began?

5. Who do you think has helped you the most in reading?

6. What do you think has helped you the most in reading?

7. Have you ever left the class to attend a special reading class?

If you answered *yes* to question 7, answer questions 8 and 9.

8. How do you feel about being in a special reading class?

9. Do you think the special reading class has helped you?

10. Are your parents interested in helping you in reading?

11. Do you like to read to anyone?

12. What do you do when you come across a word you do not know?

13. What do you do when you do not understand something you are reading?

14. Do you have a library card?

15. If you have a library card, how often do you go to the library?

16. What kinds of books do you like to read?

SUMMARY

Chapter 10 concerns the use of observation and other child study methods as essential diagnostic techniques that help teachers learn about their students' behavior. Direct observation is helpful in diagnosing reading problems and also for evaluation. This chapter discusses how observations can be made as objective as possible and presents techniques, such as checklists and anecdotal records, for recording students' behavior. The purposes and uses of checklists and anecdotal records are given, as well as information on the kinds of behavior that should be recorded. It is stressed throughout the chapter that observation is merely a technique for gathering information; it does not explain the causes of behavior.

Other child study techniques such as the informal interview, interest inventories, projective techniques, and the reading autobiography were also presented as viable methods to help teachers gain information about student characteristics that could not be obtained through direct observation. Interest inventories, which provide knowledge about students' likes and dislikes, help teachers plan activities and choose materials to motivate the students. Projective techniques and reading autobiographies help give teachers insight into students' feelings about themselves and reading.

SUGGESTIONS FOR THOUGHT QUESTIONS AND ACTIVITIES

1. Construct a checklist for a reading skill to use for instruction.
2. Construct a reading checklist that uses a rating scale.
3. Construct an individual checklist that lists all the reading behaviors that you feel are important.
4. Use one of the checklists given either in this chapter or in another chapter to learn more about the behavior of a particular child.
5. Observe a child at various times in class. Record his or her behavior by using a checklist.
6. Observe a child at various times in class. Record his or her behavior by using an anecdotal record.

SELECTED BIBLIOGRAPHY

Cohen, Dorothy H., and Virginia Stern. *Observing and Recording the Behavior of Young Children.* New York: Teachers College Press, 1978.

Forness, Steven R., and Karen C. Esveldt. "Classroom Observations of Children with Learning and Behavior Problems." *Journal of Learning Disabilities* 8 (1975): 382–85.

Goodman, Yetta M. "Kid Watching: An Alternative to Testing." *National Elementary Principal* 57 (1978): 41–45.

McAvoy, Rogers. "Measurable Outcome with Systematic Observations." *Journal of Research and Development in Education* 4 (1970): 10–13.

Medinnus, Gene. *Child Study and Observation Guide.* New York: Wiley, 1976.

Popham, W. James. *Modern Educational Measurement,* 2nd ed., Chapter 13: "Observations and Ratings," pp. 288–304. Englewood Cliffs, N.J.: Prentice-Hall, 1990.

Salvia, John, and James E. Ysseldyke. *Assessment,* 4th ed., Chapter 23: "Making Referral Decisions," pp. 478–97. Boston: Houghton Mifflin, 1988.

11

Helping Children Overcome Reading Difficulties

INTRODUCTION

John has trouble reading orally.
Marie needs help in learning English.
Frank needs help in concept development.
Jim has word recognition problems.
Debbie can't answer any high-level comprehension questions.
Betty's nonstandard English may be interfering with her ability to read.
Jeff has word recognition and comprehension problems.
Mike has acquired some very bad reading habits.
And so it goes . . .

The teacher Ms. Mills must decide which of these children need individual attention and which can work in a group setting. Whether she decides to work with the child individually or in a group, she must take the individual differences of each child into account and try to provide for his or her individual needs.

By now you should recognize that Ms. Mills needs to gather more data about each of the children before she can determine what to do to help them. Then she must provide each student with activities that will help him or her gain enough practice to acquire the skills they need. This chapter will present a number of scenarios showing Ms. Mills in action, and the kinds of techniques a teacher who uses diagnostic teaching utilizes.

KEY QUESTIONS

After you finish reading this chapter, you should be able to answer the following questions:

1. What is diagnostic teaching?

2. What techniques can a teacher use to help a child overcome his or her reading difficulty?
3. How does a teacher conduct an individual conference?
4. What steps are involved in helping a child in an individualized setting?
5. What is a learning center?
6. What steps are involved in the development of a learning center?
7. What is the role of record keeping?
8. What are individualized programs?
9. For whom do individualized programs work?
10. What is the place of student involvement in diagnosis?
11. How can peer tutoring be used in the classroom?
12. What is the role of computers in the reading program?
13. Is it possible to have a diagnostic-reading and correction program that stresses skill development and that still embraces the best of the whole language movement? Explain.

KEY TERMS IN CHAPTER

You should pay special attention to the following new terms:

computer-assisted instruction
diagnostic teaching
group instruction
individualized instruction
learning center
peer tutoring
sociogram

WHAT IS DIAGNOSTIC TEACHING?

Diagnostic teaching The practice of continuously trying a variety of instructional strategies and materials based on the needs of students.

In Chapter 1 we discussed the function of a diagnostic-reading and correction program; its major purpose is to "nip problems in the bud" before they become significant. To do so we must have good diagnostic teaching. Effective teachers use diagnostic teaching with all their students. "Simply put, the concept refers to the practice of systematic trial and evaluation of a variety of instructional strategies (including materials, methods of presentation, and methods of feedback) with individual students as part of their everyday educational program."[1] Teachers use a number of assessment instruments and techniques in such teaching, and they make whatever modifications they have to make on the basis of feedback from their students.

[1] John Salvia and James Ysseldyke, *Assessment in Special and Remedial Education*, 4th ed. (Boston: Houghton Mifflin, 1988), p. 525.

STUDENT INVOLVEMENT

We've stated a number of times in this book that the primary purpose for diagnosis is to determine what is causing a student's problem so that a program can be developed to help the student overcome the difficulty. For this, student involvement is crucial. Unless the student recognizes that he or she has a problem, unless the student understands what that problem is, and unless the student is interested in overcoming the problem, it is likely that nothing much will be accomplished.

The teacher can help the student to become involved in the following ways:

1. The teacher should help the student recognize his or her strengths as well as weaknesses.
2. The teacher should not overwhelm the student by listing all of his or her difficulties at once.
3. The teacher should try to elicit from the student what the student thinks his or her reading problems are, why the student feels that he or she has these problems, and what the student feels are the causes of his or her reading problems.
4. The teacher and the student together should set attainable goals to overcome a specific problem.
5. Together, the learning steps are determined.

CASE STUDIES

The scenarios that follow will illustrate how one teacher works with children who have different reading problems and how the children and she work cooperatively to try to determine the problems and overcome them.

Scenario: Word Recognition Problems

In listening to Susan S., a fifth-grader, read orally, Ms. Mills finds that the pupil consistently makes many word recognition errors. Ms. Mills decides to have a conference with Susan about this problem. Ms. Mills begins the conference by praising Susan's ideas and by telling Susan that she enjoys the endings Susan makes up for many different stories. "However," Ms. Mills says, "you have a number of word recognition problems, and these problems are preventing you from reading a lot of books that you probably want to read." Susan replies that she has always had trouble reading. "I guess I just can't read," Susan says. Ms. Mills says that Susan has a good mind and that she could be a good reader if she could overcome some of her word recognition difficulties. Ms. Mills tells Susan that she would like to give her some tests to try to determine what her word recognition problems are. Ms. Mills asks Susan if that would be all right with her. Ms. Mills also tells Susan that the tests are nothing to worry about and that Susan will not be graded on them. Susan says that she definitely does want to read better because she wants to be a writer when she grows up. "Good!" says Ms. Mills. "The first step in improving in something is knowing that you have a problem. The second step is determining what the problem is. Let's meet again tomorrow, and then I'll give you an informal reading test."

The next day Ms. Mills meets with Susan and administers an informal reading inventory (see Chapter 8). After Ms. Mills analyzes the results, she notices that there is a pattern in the word recognition errors Susan makes. The informal reading inventory also confirms Ms. Mills's other observations of Susan, namely, that she is a highly able child who has excellent comprehension skills but difficulties in word recognition.

Ms. Mills tells Susan that she will meet with her again the next day, and then they will set up a program to help her to overcome her word recognition problems.

The next day Ms. Mills meets again with Susan. Ms. Mills asks Susan if she has noticed anything special about the words she seems to have the most difficulty with. Susan says that she seems to get stuck on words that have certain vowel combinations. Ms. Mills discusses with Susan what she has discovered about her problems. One of Susan's problems does indeed deal with certain vowel combinations. Ms. Mills tells Susan that there are a number of phonic rules that she can learn to help her to be a better independent reader. "As a matter of fact," Ms. Mills says, "in the word recognition learning center there is a program just for you. Let's go to the center so that we can look at it together and see if you feel it is for you."

Ms. Mills and Susan proceed to the learning center where Ms. Mills shows Susan an instructional word recognition program. The teacher chooses the one that deals entirely with vowel combinations. Ms. Mills and Susan go over each step of the program together. The word recognition module is composed of the following steps: (1) directions for using the program, (2) pretest, (3) instructional objectives, (4) learning activities, (5) student self-assessment, (6) postassessment, and (7) recycling.

After going over each step of the program with Susan, Ms. Mills makes sure that Susan is able to operate the audio equipment and the computer that is used in the program. Ms. Mills then tells Susan that she can work at her own pace, and that if she needs any help, she should not hesitate to come to her. Susan thanks Ms. Mills and says that she is looking forward to starting as soon as possible. "It looks like fun," she says, "because there are so many different kinds of activities, and I especially enjoy doing word riddles and puzzles."

It is probable that Susan is on her way to becoming a better reader. However, Ms. Mills's job is not over. She must continue to check on Susan's progress and then, together with Susan, determine whether she is ready to go on to another area or whether she needs further help in the same area.

Outline of Steps in Individualizing a Reading Program for Susan Based on Her Needs

1. Susan has a reading problem.
2. Susan's reading problem is observed by Ms. Mills.
3. A conference is set up between Susan and Ms. Mills.
4. At the conference Susan recognizes that she has a reading problem.
5. Both Susan and Ms. Mills decide to diagnose Susan's reading problem.
6. In diagnosing Susan's reading problem, Ms. Mills and Susan analyze the types of reading errors Susan consistently makes to determine if a pattern exists.

7. Another conference is set up between Susan and Ms. Mills.
8. Susan and Ms. Mills, following an analysis of Susan's word recognition errors, determine one of Susan's problems.
9. Ms. Mills chooses a program to help Susan overcome one of her word recognition problems.
10. Ms. Mills introduces Susan to the program.
11. Susan begins work in the program.
12. Ms. Mills periodically checks on Susan's progress.
13. Ms. Mills keeps records on Susan's progress.
14. Susan keeps records on her progress.

Figure 11.1 Susan needs help in understanding something she is reading.

Scenario: Difficulty with Finding the Main Idea

Alan Y is a fifth-grader who scored at a 4.2 level on the reading comprehension subtest of the *California Achievement Tests,* which is given in the fall of the school year and is used as a screening device for instructional purposes. Ms. Mills knows that Alan has a problem in comprehension, but she does not know in exactly what skill or skills. Therefore, Ms. Mills must choose a diagnostic test that will help locate Alan's specific comprehension problem or problems. From observing Alan in his reading group and from individual sessions, Ms. Mills knows that Alan does not have problems at the literal comprehension level. His problem appears to be at the interpretive and critical reading levels. Ms. Mills administers a criterion-referenced test to Alan to determine what specific interpretive and critical reading skills are causing problems. The criterion-referenced test she uses reveals a number of specific skills that are causing problems for Alan, one of which is finding the main idea. Ms. Mills decides that she will probe further to find out what strategies Alan is using to find the main idea of paragraphs. She chooses a few paragraphs at Alan's independent word recognition level so that there is no interference from any word recognition problems. Alan reads the first paragraph silently and then attempts to state its main idea. He then reads the second paragraph silently and states its main idea. Ms. Mills notices that Alan gives the topic as the main idea. She asks Alan what he thinks the main idea of any paragraph should tell him. Alan answers, "What the paragraph is about." Ms. Mills says, "Good, but that is only part of it. What the paragraph is about is the topic of the paragraph. No wonder you keep giving the topic as the main idea."

Ms. Mills proceeds to tell Alan that there is a technique that can help him find the main idea of paragraphs. She says, "Every paragraph is written about something or someone. The something or someone is the topic of the paragraph. To find the main idea of the paragraph, you must determine what the topic of the paragraph is and what the author is saying about it that is special. Once you have found these two things, you should have the main idea. Let's try one together."

Modeling: An Instructional Technique

Ms. Mills decides to model (think out loud) for Alan to show him how she would go about finding the main idea, so she does the following:

"Here is a paragraph from one of the books you are reading. Let's go through the various steps to get the main idea of it. Remember, to find the main idea, we must first find the topic of the paragraph and then what is special or unique about it. All the details should develop the main idea."

"Let's both read the paragraph." Here is the paragraph they both read:

> Paul Smith wasn't a liar; he just exaggerated a lot. Paul exaggerated so much that people always expected him to exaggerate. Paul never disappointed them. Here are some examples of Paul's exaggerations. If Paul ate three pancakes, he'd say, "I ate fifty pancakes." Also, if he walked a mile, he'd say, "I walked a hundred miles today."

After reading the paragraph, Ms. Mills says: "First I ask myself what is the topic of the par-

agraph? Asking the question who or what can help me get the topic, so I'll try that. Alan, You try it too. I know you're good at doing this.

"Here are our choices:

a. Lying
b. Paul's lying
c. Paul's exaggeration
d. Exaggeration

"What did you choose? Good, I chose—Paul's exaggeration, also. I chose it because it best answers what the paragraph is about, but I know that this is not the main idea; it is only part of it. I have to go on and ask myself some other things. Listen carefully to what I do next. Now, I have to decide what the author is saying about Paul's exaggeration that is special and helps tie all the details together. Here are our choices:

a. It is bad.
b. It is not believed.
c. It is a problem.
d. It applies to everything he does.
e. It should not be allowed.

"I chose d. The topic is Paul's exaggeration, and what is special about it is that it applies to everything he does. Therefore, the main idea is 'Paul's exaggeration applies to everything he does.' "

"When I check to see if all the details support this, I find that they do."

Ms. Mills tells Alan that she knows finding the main idea is not easy, but with more practice, she is sure he can do it.

Ms. Mills set up a program that consisted of a number of activities to help him gain skill in finding the main idea of paragraphs. Here are some of the sample activities:

1. Find the main idea of many paragraphs such as these:

> What makes an airplane fly is not its engine nor its propeller. Nor is it, as many people think, some mysterious knack of the pilot, nor some ingenious gadget inside. What makes an airplane fly is simply its shape. This may sound absurd, but gliders do fly without engines, and model airplanes do fly without pilots. As for the insides of an airplane, they are disappointing, for they are mostly hollow. No, what keeps an airplane up is its shape—the impact of the air on its shape. Whittle that shape

out of wood, or cast it out of iron, or fashion it, for that matter, out of chocolate and throw the thing in the air. It will behave like an airplane. It will be an airplane.[2]

Main idea: What makes an airplane fly is its shape.

In many parts of Africa, the use of traps, poisons, and dogs has virtually exterminated the leopard. In my youth, we thought that the only good leopard was a hide stretched out for drying. But now we are discovering that the leopard played an important part in maintaining nature's balance. Leopards used to kill thousands of baboons every year, and now that the leopards have been largely wiped out baboons are proving to be a major control problem in many parts of the colony. The perfect way to keep them in check is by allowing their natural enemy, the leopard, to destroy them. So leopards are now widely protected and allowed to increase in numbers. Such is the strange way that

man works—first he virtually destroys a species and then does everything in his power to restore it.[3]

Main idea. Leopards are now widely protected because they play an important part in maintaining nature's balance.

2. State the topics of each of the preceding paragraphs.
3. Compare the topics of each of the paragraphs with the main idea.

Ms. Mills used the same approach to help Alan with his other comprehension problems. She also had Alan write a number of paragraphs and then state the main ideas of the paragraphs he wrote. Ms. Mills believes in integrating reading and writing wherever and whenever possible because she knows that the language arts are closely interrelated.

Scenario: Lack of Phonic Skills

George Y is another student in Ms. Mills's class who scored at a 4.2 level on the reading comprehension subtest of the *California Achievement Tests.* Ms. Mills is confused about this score because George is quite verbal; he always seems to have a lot of information on many topics, and he can answer some very difficult questions. Ms. Mills has also noticed that George never volunteers to read anything aloud. Therefore, Ms. Mills decides to give George an informal reading inventory.

Ms. Mills started George two grade levels below his grade level. George did not reach the zero level of errors for words in isolation until the first level. Therefore, George started oral reading at the first-grade level. Even at this level, he made one error. He had no problems with comprehension. George is able to answer all the comprehension questions for the oral and silent reading passages through the third level, even though he makes a number of errors in the oral reading passages. At the fourth-grade level, the number of word recognition errors are at the frustration level, and Ms. Mills suspects that even with his superior compre-

hension, George would have some difficulty answering the questions; so she decides to give him a listening capacity test. She reads aloud one passage from each level and asks George the questions. George is able to answer all the questions correctly up until the eighth level.

Ms. Mills realizes that George's word recognition problems had masked his ability to answer many questions. Although both George and Alan had made similar scores on the reading comprehension subtest of the *California Achievement Tests,* their reading abilities and needs are entirely different. George's cognitive development is quite advanced, whereas Alan's is about low average. George needs an intensive and extensive program in learning word recognition skills, and Alan needs help in comprehension.

Ms. Mills decides to look at George's school records to see what methods and materials he was exposed to in learning to read. She also decides to discuss his word recognition problems with him.

In talking to George, Ms. Mills learns that

---

[2] Wolfgang Langwiesche, *Why An Airplane Flys* (n.d.).
[3] J. A. Hunter, *African Hunter* (New York: Harper, 1952).

George's parents are both professionals and well known in their fields, that George is an only child, and that George goes everywhere with his parents and is included in their interesting conversations. George's background information certainly explains his high cognitive and language development, but it does not account for his decoding problems. Ms. Mills realizes from the types of errors he made when he was reading orally that George is probably using context clues to gain the information that he does get. Ms. Mills decides to give him an informal diagnostic word analysis test to see if she can pinpoint his word recognition problems.

Ms. Mills administers the *Informal Diagnostic Tests* presented in Chapter 9. She wants to test George's auditory discrimination because he had mentioned that he had had many ear infections when he was younger. She wants to make sure that he is able to differentiate among various sounds. George has no difficulties with auditory discrimination; however, from the results of the word analysis tests, it is obvious that he does not have any phonic or structural analysis skills. When Ms. Mills asks George about this, he says that he never had any instruction in phonics in the school that he had gone to. (George had gone to a different school in another state for the first three years of his education.) He hadn't mentioned it earlier in their talk because he didn't know that he was missing these skills.

Ms. Mills decides to set up an intensive word analysis program for George to follow. The program that George is involved in is similar to Susan's in the first scenario, except that George's program is more extensive because he has not had any instruction in phonics or structural analysis. Ms. Mills feels that George should have no difficulty gaining word analysis and synthesis skills and that he should acquire these skills in a relatively short period of time because he is a very bright individual and highly motivated. Also, when she did some blending activities to probe for his difficulties, she noticed how quickly George caught on and how he was able to apply what he learned; that is, his transfer of knowledge was excellent. George was also very excited when he saw, in his words, "how easy if was to figure out words by using graphic cues."

Here are examples of some of the probing activities Ms. Mills used to discover the strategies George uses to decode words:

1. A nonsense word—*prand*—was presented in isolation, and George was asked to pronounce the word.

When George could not pronounce the word, a familiar word using the cluster *pr* was presented to George. The word was *pretty*.

Then George was presented with the familiar word *hand,* which he had no difficulty pronouncing.

Ms. Mills asked George to blend the *pr* and the *and* to get the pronunciation of the word. George had no difficulty doing this.

Ms. Mills showed George how he could figure out many words using the phonogram *and* by just changing the initial consonant.

2. A nonsense word was presented in context. George was asked if he could figure out what he thinks the nonsense word is. "The *drend* went into the house, slammed the door, and started to cry."

Using context clues, George knew that *drend* had to be a noun because it came after *the,* and he knew from the surrounding words that *drend* must refer to a person.

3. Ms. Mills gave George a word in isolation that she thought he would have in his listening vocabulary and asked him to pronounce it. The word was *probe.*

George recognized the *pr* blend and attempted to pronounce the word, but he couldn't.

The word was then presented in context. "The police said that they would *probe* into the crime until they turned up something."

George was asked to read the sentence. He stumbled on the word *probe,* but after he had read the whole sentence, he went back and correctly pronounced *probe.* George was able to give a definition for it.

George's behavior confirmed Ms. Mills's feelings that he relied heavily on context clues, that he lacked most other word recognition strategies, and that he learned quickly. (See Chapter 12 for a review of word recognition skills and for an analysis of word recognition strategies.)

Ms. Mills introduces George to the learning center program that he will be working with and follows the same steps as with Susan.

Scenario: Integrating the Remedial Reading Program With the Regular Classroom Reading Program

This scenario involves a student in Ms. Mills's class who is attending a special reading class conducted by a reading teacher. Ms. Mills is familiar with the research findings about "pull-out" programs (see Chapter 1) and wants to make sure that Jim, the child in the pull-out program, is helped rather than hindered. She knows that for the pull-out program to be effective, Jim must be involved in the developmental reading program that is taking place in the regular classroom. The remedial reading program must be in addition to the regular classroom reading program rather than a substitute for it. Ms. Mills meets regularly with Mr. Jason, the reading teacher, to learn about Jim's progress and to correlate what he is doing in the special reading class with what he is doing in reading in his regular class. Thus Jim's remedial reading program, which takes place outside the regular classroom, is part of the developmental reading program taking place in the regular classroom. Ms. Mills meets regularly with Jim also to go over some skills and to discuss his progress. Because Jim is involved in the regular reading program in class,

he feels that he is part of the group; he is also getting the double-barreled help that he needs from his outside class.

Today's meeting with Jim is just to discuss how he thinks he is progressing. Ms. Mills also wants to talk to Jim about the books she had suggested he might enjoy reading because they are about race cars, his favorite topic. Jim appears relaxed and seems to have a good rapport with Ms. Mills. He tells her that he did enjoy reading the books on race cars and proceeds to tell her all about the books. Ms. Mills is ecstatic because this is a child who had never voluntarily chosen to read before. Buoyed by her success, Ms. Mills asks Jim if he would like her to try to get him another book about race cars. Jim says, "Yes." Ms. Mills tells Jim that she is pleased with his progress, and at the rate he is going, he will soon not need to attend the extra reading class.

Ms. Mills will use reference books such as the *Elementary School Library Collection* to help her find another book at Jim's reading ability level.

Scenario: Word by Word Reading

Vicki L is a new student in Ms. Mills's fifth-grade class. She and her family just moved into the school district. Ms. Mills is trying very hard to make Vicki feel at home because she knows how difficult it is for a young person to leave all her friends and come to a strange school where she does not know anyone. Ms. Mills tries to make a point of speaking to Vicki informally during recess and at other times so that she can get to know her. During some of their conversations Ms. Mills tries to find out what Vicki's interests are and what kinds of books she likes to read. Ms. Mills also tries to help Vicki adjust to her new environment by helping her choose books that deal with situations similar to hers. (Ms. Mills's wise use of bibliotherapy, which is the use of books to help individuals to cope better with their emotional

and adjustment problems, has helped many children in her class.)

Vicki's records from her other school haven't arrived yet, so Ms. Mills has to do some informal testing to determine at what level Vicki is reading. Actually, it really doesn't make any difference that Vicki's records haven't arrived because Ms. Mills prefers to do her own informal testing before looking at a child's past records. She feels that often records can bias a teacher.

Ms. Mills chooses a passage from the middle of the basal reader, which is equivalent to a fifth-grade level. She tells Vicki that she wants her to read the passage aloud and that she should concentrate because she will be asked some questions about what she has read. She tells Vicki something about the story before

Helping Children Overcome Reading Difficulties **257**

Vicki begins to read. Vicki's voice is loud and clear, but she reads word by word, or rather syllable by syllable. She sounds out every word she comes to. It's as if she does not recognize any word or that she does not trust herself to say it correctly unless she first sounds it out. (Now, Ms. Mills knows what people meant when they said that a child was "overphon-icked." Ms. Mills believes in using phonics to help children become self-reliant and independent readers, but she stresses that phonics is only one part of the word recognition program and that the primary goal is comprehension.) When Ms. Mills asks Vicki questions on the passage, Vicki is able to answer the literal questions, but she has difficulty answering any at the interpretive level. Ms. Mills decides to choose another passage from the same basal reader and read it aloud to Vicki. She wants to see if Vicki would do better in comprehension if she did not have to concentrate so hard on sounding out the words. Ms. Mills tells Vicki to listen carefully and see how well she can answer questions on what Ms. Mills has read aloud. After Ms. Mills finishes reading the passage to Vicki, she asks her some questions. Again, Vicki is able to answer the literal questions but not the ones requiring a higher level of thinking.

Ms. Mills asks Vicki to tell her about her reading experiences. She asks Vicki how she learned to read. Vicki tells Ms. Mills that she had learned to sound out every word and that all they did at her other school was work with words. She says very proudly that she could figure out lots of words by herself. Mrs. Mills says that she saw she could and that was very good, but she tells Vicki that she wants her to try to go beyond the words and concentrate more on the message that the words have. She also tells Vicki that she wants her to take a

chance and not sound out every word. She gives Vicki another passage to read, and asks her to look at it first and then to try to read it in thought units. Ms. Mills reads the first two sentences aloud first, and then she asks Vicki to read the complete passage aloud. Ms. Mills praises Vicki for reading it with less sounding out of words. She asks Vicki if there are any words in the passage that she does not know. Vicki says that she knows all the words. "Good," says Ms. Mills. "Let's put some in sentences." Ms. Mills asks Vicki to put a few of the words into sentences. Vicki was able to do this. Ms. Mills tells Vicki that she would like to work with her each day for a little while. She will also put her in one of the reading groups. Ms. Mills tells Vicki that her ability to sound out words is excellent, but she needs to concentrate more on understanding what she is reading and reading more smoothly. She says that she will arrange a meeting with her parents to see if they would work with her too.

Ms. Mills feels that Vicki is a bright child who should be doing much better than she is. She feels that Vicki has not had any experiences in working with higher-level thinking skills, so she will plan a program for her that will help her to develop such skills. Ms. Mills also feels that Vicki needs practice in reading for meaning rather than for pronunciation and that she needs to gain confidence in herself. It could be that she has so overrelied on the sounding out of words that she had not paid attention to the whole word. As a result, each time she met the word, it was as if she were meeting it for the first time. (Vicki appeared to lose the whole because of the parts.) Ms. Mills decides that she will have Vicki look at the *whole* word and have her say it. "Vicki is certainly a perfect example of what can happen if you use extremes."

RECORD KEEPING

Since many of the students in Ms. Mills's class are working in different areas at different levels, she cannot rely on her memory to recall exactly what each student is doing and at what level each student is working. Ms. Mills, therefore, has established a record-keeping system. She has a folder for each student in the class. In the folder she keeps a record of each student's progress in each area. For example, Ms. Mills, after meeting with Susan (the student in the first scenario), went back to her file drawer to pull Susan's folder. She wanted to record that Susan is attempting to accomplish certain objectives in the area of word recognition. She also wanted to record the specific program Susan is working in and the date that she started.

Susan's folder contains a number of items: a checklist of activities, a record of standardized achievement test scores, intelligence test scores, and criterion-referenced test information, as well as other diagnostic test information. In the folder there is also a sheet listing the particular objectives that Susan has attempted to accomplish up to that time. Next to each objective is the program chosen to achieve it, as well as the starting and completion dates.

Students as Record Keepers

The students also keep records on what they are doing. As a matter of fact, Ms. Mills initiated the program by telling the children that they were all members of a company and as such they had certain responsibilities. She explained how companies are formed and organized. She also discussed with them that companies make agreements with suppliers and others by signing contracts. She then told them that they would operate somewhat like a company and that they would be drawing up and signing contracts for work that they will then be responsible for doing. She discussed with the class the importance of keeping up-to-date and accurate records on what they as members of the company were doing. Together they also decided that they would have periodic group meetings to discuss their progress and to determine whether any changes had to be made in their operation.

Thus the Fifth Grade Dynamo Company was born, and it flourished all year long.

INDIVIDUALIZED INSTRUCTION

Individualized instruction
Student works at own pace on material based on the needs, interests, and ability of the student.

A special section on individualized instruction is being presented in this chapter because a teacher in a diagnostic-reading and correction program must know how to individualize instruction for those students who have special needs.

The many different types of individualized programs range from informal ones, developed by teachers or teachers and students together, to commercially produced ones. It is beyond the scope of this book to give a description of the organizational patterns or the individualized programs that exist; books have been written on these (see the Selected Bibliography). However, a brief description of some of the characteristics of both informal and commercially produced individualized programs would be helpful.

Teacher-Made (Informal) Programs

Informal programs can vary from teacher to teacher. However, most of the programs usually use instructional objectives, which are taken from curriculum guides, study guides, and instructors' manuals. To accomplish the objectives the teachers usually select activities and materials from a number of sources, the teacher and student confer periodically, and the teacher keeps a check on the student's progress by keeping adequate records.

Commercially Produced or Published Programs

There are a variety of different commercial programs, and they have a number of things in common. Most of them use instructional objectives for each curriculum area. Usually each area is divided into small discrete learning steps based on graduated levels of difficulty. A variety of activities and materials generally combined in a multimedia approach is used, and usually built into the commercial programs is a system of record-keeping, progress tests, and checklists.

Some Common Characteristics of Commercially Produced and Teacher-Made Individualized Programs

In almost all individualized programs, students work at their own pace. Learning outcomes in individualized programs are based on the needs, interests, and ability levels of the students. Activities are interesting and challenging, and they usually employ a multimedia approach. The activities are based on desired outcomes, students work independently, and there is some system of record keeping.

For Whom Does Individualized Instruction Work?

Students who have short attention spans, who have trouble following directions, and who have reading problems will obviously have difficulty working independently. Teachers will have to help these students set limited, short-range objectives that can be reached in a short period of time. For those students with reading problems, the teacher will have to rely very heavily on audiotapes to convey directions. Students who are slow learners (see Chapter 15) will also need special help; special programs will have to be devised for them. Students who have no discernible achievement problems but who have never worked in an individualized program before will also have difficulty unless they are properly oriented to the program. (Note: Do not confuse the need to work independently in an individualized program with the need to provide for the individual differences of each student in the class. For example, a child who is a slow learner will usually have trouble working independently, but the teacher still needs to provide an individual program for this child based on his or her special needs.)

Some Common Sense About Individual Programs

Preparing individual outcomes and a specially tailored program for each student in each specific subject can be a monumental task. Therefore, what is generally done is to use outcomes and programs already prepared, either teacher-made or commercially made, and then match these to the needs of individual students. For such an individualized program to work effectively, teachers must have a variety of individualized programs available for their students, and they must know the individual needs of each student (see the sections "Learning Centers in the Classroom" and "Group Instruction").

LEARNING CENTERS IN THE CLASSROOM

The concept of learning centers is not new. Good teachers have always recognized the importance of providing "interest centers" for their students based on their needs and ability levels. However, in the past most of the science, art, library, listening, and fun centers were just "interest attractions"; they usually were marginal to the on-going teaching-learning program rather than an integral part of it.

Learning center
An integral part of the instructional program and vital to a good individualized program. An area is usually set aside in the classroom for instruction in a specific curriculum area.

As used today, learning centers are an important and integral part of the instructional program. They are generally more formalized and are recognized as vital to a good individualized program. A place is usually set aside in the classroom for instruction in a specific curriculum area. Aims for learning centers may be developed beforehand by teachers or cooperatively by teachers and students. Some of the requirements for a good learning center are as follows:

1. Is in an easily accessible area.
2. Is attractive.
3. Provides for students on different maturational levels.
4. Has clearly stated objectives so that students know what they are supposed to accomplish (outcomes).
5. Provides for group and team activities as well as individual activities.
6. Allows for student input.
7. Asks probing questions.
8. Has some humorous materials.
9. Provides activities that call for divergent thinking.
10. Uses a multimedia approach.
11. Has carefully worked out learning sequences to accomplish objectives.
12. Has provisions for evaluation and record keeping.

Designing a Learning Center

In the following plan for developing a learning center, notice the similarity to the development of a lesson plan.

1. Motivating technique: necessary to attract attention. This could be realia (real objects), pictures, humorous sayings, and so on.
Example: Familiar commercials with pictures are listed on learning center bulletin board (propaganda learning center).
2. Objectives: necessary so that students know what they are supposed to accomplish (outcomes).
Example: Propaganda learning center.

a. Define *propaganda.*
b. Define *bias.*
c. Explain what is meant by a propaganda technique.
d. List five propaganda techniques.
e. Describe each of the five propaganda techniques you chose and give an example of each.
f. Read ten commercials and identify the propaganda technique used in each.
g. Read a political speech and state what propaganda techniques the politician uses.
h. Team up with another student, and using a propaganda technique, role-play a commercial to be presented to the class.
i. Using one or more propaganda techniques, write a commercial about an imaginary product.
j. Tape-record the commercial created by you on the imaginary product.

3. Directions to accomplish objectives: necessary so that students know what to do to accomplish objectives. Step-by-step instructions are given for the students to accomplish the objectives. For example students are told:

a. Read objectives so that you know what you are supposed to accomplish.
b. Go to file drawer one, which contains the learning activities to accomplish objective one.
c. Complete each learning activity and record your progress on each before you go on to the next objective. (This requirement depends on the learning center. In some learning centers, the students must accomplish the objectives in sequence; in others it is not necessary to do so. For the propaganda learning center, some of the learning objectives must be accomplished in order. Obviously, before students can write a commercial using propaganda and bias, they must be able to define *propaganda* and *bias,* they must be able to explain propaganda techniques, they must be able to recognize them, and they must be able to give examples of them.)

Summary of Steps in Preparing a Learning Center

1. Select a topic.
2. State objectives.
3. Identify experiences.
4. Collect materials.
5. Prepare activities.
6. Make schedules (which children use center and when).
7. Prepare record forms (each student using center must have one).

Multimedia in Learning Centers

Ms. Mills recognizes that successful individualized programs usually have learning centers that use a diversity of instructional materials to accommodate the individual differences of students. As a result, Ms. Mills has included in each of her learning centers learning sequences that use such instructional materials as textbooks, library books, programmed materials, sets of pictures, realia (real things), commercial and teacher-prepared audiotapes, filmstrips, films, television, radio, tape recorders, computer programs, maps, globes, manipulative materials, and games.

The media corner itself is not a learning center but a conveniently located storage and extra viewing place. Each learning center has its own viewing area. The media corner has two "homemade" carrels, which are helpful for viewing films and filmstrips if the learning center is occupied.

Ms. Mills realizes that she is extremely fortunate to be in a school system that not only recognizes the importance of the use of a variety of media to help students to achieve learning objectives but also provides the funds necessary to acquire the materials. (She also has a friend who helped her make the carrels for the media center.)

GROUP INSTRUCTION

The emphasis in this chapter has been on individualized instruction because children who have reading problems usually need a special program tailored to their needs. The individualized reading program discussed in this chapter is in addition to and part of, not in place of, the ongoing developmental reading program.

Group instruction
A number of students are taught at the same time; helps make instruction more manageable.

The children in Ms. Mills's class are organized into groups to make instruction more manageable. However, Ms. Mills knows that grouping does not make instruction good or bad; only teachers can do that. Most teachers have a combination of individual and group instruction in their classes. During the school day teachers usually work with individual students, with the whole class, and with small and large groups of students. As stated in Chapter 2, studies have shown that direct teacher instruction improves achievement, and time on-task also increases learning (see "Time Spent in Reading" and "Direct Instruction Time" in Chapter 2). If a number of students need help in a specific area, it makes sense to teach this skill to the children at the same time.

Toward the beginning of the term, children are usually grouped according to their reading ability levels. Teachers use informal tests, standardized tests, observation, and their own judgment in making grouping decisions. Good teachers help students understand that the grouping is flexible and that they can move from one group to another.

COMPUTER-ASSISTED INSTRUCTION AND READING IN A DIAGNOSTIC-READING AND CORRECTION PROGRAM

Ms. Mills recently read an intriguing short story, which made her stop to think about her feelings toward the influx of microcomputers in education and, in particular, in her very own classroom. Here is the story:

> John was still tired and wanted to sleep some more, but a firm voice kept saying, "Time to get up." John stretched and opened his eyes to be greeted by his faithful companion, CIPS.
> "Good morning, CIPS, couldn't you let me sleep a little longer?" asks John. "Sorry," says CIPS, "You specifically requested that you be awakened at precisely 7 A.M. It is exactly 7 A.M. Here is your schedule for today. Your outfit for today has been chosen as well as your menus."
> "Thank you, CIPS, excellent work!"
> John showered, put on the outfit that CIPS had selected and went downstairs to prepare the menu that CIPS had suggested. John always looked good, and he felt that he owed this entirely to CIPS. He didn't know what he would do without CIPS. CIPS saw to it that he was always well-groomed and that his caloric intake was perfect for the amount of activities he engaged in every day.
> After breakfast John went to CIPS to get the answer to a very complex problem that he had given to CIPS late the night before to solve. Sure enough, good old dependable CIPS had the solution. John thanked CIPS, put him in his pocket, and went to work.

CIPS is John's personal computer information processing system. CIPS is aware of John's habits, attitudes, desires, physical traits, biological makeup, abilities, and so on. Nothing about John is secret from CIPS. In John's world, anyone who is of any importance has his or her own CIPS. Incredible? Farfetched? Science fiction? Or reality?

Ms. Mills did not dismiss the short story as complete science fiction because at a conference in the late seventies she had heard the projections of some specialists in the field of artificial intelligence (the development of computer programs that display "intelligence" by solving problems or engaging in conversation).[4] These scientists talked about the "ultimate computer—the self-sufficient machine,"[5] and predicted that in the 1990s this "machine would learn natural language as people do, gain knowledge and reasoning power through experience, not just spoon-fed instructions, and be able to solve the gamut of problems that humans can solve."[6]

Computer-assisted instruction
Instruction using computers.

Ms. Mills has a number of mixed feelings about the bombardment of information about microcomputers and their educational value. She knows that computer-aided instruction is not new because when she was in college she learned about a number of programs that have been in existence for quite a long time. She has never been

---

[4] Richard E. Mayer, *Thinking and Problem Solving: An Introduction to Human Cognition and Learning* (Glenview, Ill.: Scott, Foresman, 1977), p. 136.
[5] Ibid., p. 39.
[6] Ibid.

frightened by computer-aided instruction nor does it make her feel unneeded because she realizes that it is mainly a management tool; that is, with the proper program in the computer, she could more effectively manage her class. As a matter of fact, she feels that this would be especially effective for her because she believes in early diagnosis and correction. For example, during a reading lesson, students would read a passage, and then the computer would question each student simultaneously through terminals. The pupils can answer by menu selection, whereby only one single letter or number needs to be keyed in to indicate the answer. The result to the teacher is immediate feedback of the responses of *all* the students. This type of questioning and feedback can be repeated for however much depth or breadth of coverage is required by the teacher. The teacher can not only receive immediate feedback but also see a pattern of the answers. This pattern would help the teacher immediately discern those questions that caused the most or the least difficulty for the students. The computer could also display for the teacher a pattern of an individual's responses or compare what an individual student has done over an extended period of time. The possibilities are innumerable. The teacher could also use the feedback for evaluation and grouping.

Another possibility of computer-assisted instruction is to use it in a tutorial manner, that is, in a one-to-one situation with the student. In this manner, the student knows the results in a friendly, nonthreatening way. It also diagnoses the student's problem without the teacher knowing it. (Certain programs can be developed so that only the student is aware of his or her reading difficulties.) Studies indicate that some students respond more favorably to computer diagnostics

Figure 11.2 These children are working together on a computer program.

than to teacher diagnostics. These students feel that the computer is more fair and more private, and as a result, relate better to such an impersonal diagnostic tool. Obviously, the teacher will have to know about the student's problems in order to help him or her.

There are some software programs available on the market that show "valuable potential when used sensibly and critically by trained reading clinicians."[7] Some of these programs are computer-based informal reading inventories. Jay Blanchard's *Computer-Based Reading Assessment Inventory* has two forms with eight passages, word lists based on the passages, and comprehension questions. It is an untimed test that probes a student's reading behavior using a multiple-choice format rather than the usual recall method used on traditionally administered IRIs.[8]

Another program is the *Computer-Based Reading Assessment* by Jerry Johns, which is based on his *Advanced Reading Inventory;* however, as can be gleaned from the title, this program is for more advanced students in grades 7 through college.[9]

Another program, *Computer-Assisted Reading Achievement* by Michael McKenna, interprets general information concerning a student's background, analyzes a student's oral reading errors, and provides a miscue analysis. In addition, it determines a student's reading levels, as well as some inferences concerning a student's strengths and weaknesses.

Microcomputers are certainly here to stay, and good teachers recognize that there is a place for them in the instructional program. However, teacher judgment is still the critical factor in all diagnosis.

PEER INSTRUCTION

Peer tutoring
A student helps another student gain needed skills.

Sociogram
A map or chart showing the interrelationships of children in a classroom and identifying those who are "stars" or "isolates."

Ms. Mills was pleased to learn at the professional meetings she had attended that her idea about using students to help other students was looked on as professionally sound and that it had benefits for both the tutor and the tutee. Peer tutoring usually helps the student who has been having trouble in one area gain skill in that area and also gain confidence in working with the skill. It also helps the tutee feel more at ease about participating in a large group. The tutor also gains because it helps him or her to overlearn the skill that is being taught, and it helps to enhance his or her self-concept. The tutor is looked on with respect by the teacher and his or her peers.

Ms. Mills likes using peer tutors in her class because it helps her to work with more children individually. Ms. Mills is always very careful about the pairing of the tutor and tutee. She is aware of the personalities in her class, and from administering a sociogram, she

---

[7] Renee Weisberg and Ernest Balajthy, "The Printout: Reading Diagnosis via the Microcomputer," *The Reading Teacher* 42 (April 1989): 636.
[8] Ibid.
[9] Ibid.

learned a great deal about the cliques, stars, and isolates. Ms. Mills is also very sensitive to the fact that some peer tutors, because of their popularity, can be overburdened. She does not allow this to happen. She feels strongly that the peer tutoring relationship must be one that is beneficial and satisfying to both parties.

Ms. Mills also encourages her fifth graders to work with some of the younger students in the school.

Figure 11.3 This fifth grader enjoys working with first-graders who are learning to read.

A FINAL WORD: MS. MILLS—A MASTER TEACHER

Ms. Mills is an excellent teacher who cares about the individual differences of all her students; she is a master teacher. Ms. Mills tries to keep up with what is taking place in her profession and enjoys trying new teaching strategies. She is an eclectic pragmatist; that is, she takes things from many different sources, and if something works, then it is good.

Ms. Mills knows that the language arts are interrelated; she tries to integrate reading and writing as much as possible. She knows that reading, reading, and more reading help children become better readers and writers and that they need many opportunities to do both. She also knows that she must be a good role model for her students, so she makes sure her students see her reading and writing.

Ms. Mills believes that many of the ideas the whole language movement has advocated are good. How could anyone be against using whole pieces of good literature, integrating the language arts, peer group projects, and the teacher's preparation of materials based on students' needs? These are exactly the things she does. However, at the same time, she also believes in presenting a strong skills program in her class. Also, the children in Ms. Mills's class read from both basal readers and trade books. This kind of eclectic program has worked for Ms. Mills for years. Her experiences have taught her that extremes usually do not work.

Ms. Mills recognizes also that good classroom management and organization are imperative in a diagnostic-reading and correction program. However, she realizes that whatever programs she uses to help her students are merely aids to her; she is not the aide to the program.

Ms. Mills knows that motivation is the handmaiden of discipline, so she makes sure that the students' independent work is at their ability levels. The best way to control discipline in a classroom is to prevent problems from happening.

Is it any wonder that parents fight to have their children placed in Ms. Mills's class?

SUMMARY

Chapter 11 has presented a number of scenarios in which a teacher works individually with a child to determine his or her reading difficulties and to develop a program to help the child overcome them. You are taken through the procedure step by step. A scenario is also given for a child who goes to a special reading class. A discussion of individualized programs was presented, and information was given on learning centers and how to set them up, as well as on computer-assisted instruction. Peer instruction was discussed as a sound technique that can benefit both the tutor and tutee if handled properly.

SUGGESTIONS FOR THOUGHT QUESTIONS AND ACTIVITIES

1. You are a teacher in an innovative school system. You have been appointed to a committee to suggest ways that instruction can be individualized more than it now is so that teachers can be more responsive to students' needs. What suggestions would you make?
2. A student in your class has difficulty reading orally. What would you do to help him?
3. You have thirty students in your class. What techniques would you use to learn more about their reading behaviors?
4. Suggest some reading skills you would like to have in your learning center.
5. You have no group IQ scores on any children in your class. How can you determine whether a child is reading according to his or her ability?

6. What steps would you take in your everyday reading program to assure that continuous diagnosis and correction are taking place?
7. If you have children who go to special pull-out reading classes, how do you incorporate what they do in their special reading classes with what is done in the regular reading class?

SELECTED BIBLIOGRAPHY

Allen, Vernon L. *Children as Teachers: Theory and Research on Tutoring.* New York: Academic Press, 1976.

Charles, C. M. *Individualizing Instruction.* St. Louis: C. V. Mosby, 1976.

Geisert, Paul G., and Mynga K. Futrell. *Teachers, Computers, and Curriculum: Microcomputers in the Classroom.* Boston: Allyn & Bacon, 1990.

Hiebert, Elfrieda H. "Peers as Reading Teachers." *Language Arts 57* (November/December 1980): 877–81.

Isaak, Troy, and John Joseph. "Authoring Software and Teaching Reading." *The Reading Teacher* 43 (December 1989): 254–55.

Labbo, Linda D., and William H. Teale. "Cross-Age Reading: A Strategy for Helping Poor Readers." *The Reading Teacher* 43 (February 1990): 362–69.

Pinnell, Guy Su, Mary D. Fried, and Rose Mary Estice. "Reading Recovery: Learning How to Make a Difference." *The Reading Teacher* 43 (January 1990): 282–95.

Reeves, Harriet Ramsey. "Individual Conferences—Diagnostic Tools." *The Reading Teacher* 24 (February 1971): 411–15.

Rude, R. T. *Teaching Reading Using Microcomputers.* Englewood Cliffs, N.J.: Prentice-Hall, 1986.

Singer, Harry, and Thomas W. Bean. "Three Models for Helping Teachers to Help Students Learn from Text." *Changing School Reading Programs: Principles and Case Studies,* ed. S. J. Samuels and P. D. Pearson, pp. 161–82. Newark, Del.: International Reading Association, 1988.

Spache, George D., Ken Mcilroy, and Paul C. Berg. *Case Studies in Reading Disability.* Boston: Allyn & Bacon, 1981.

Valencia, Sheila. "A Portfolio Approach to Classroom Reading Assessment," *The Reading Teacher* 43 (January 1990): 338–40.

12

Word Recognition Skills and Vocabulary Expansion: An Emphasis on Diagnosis and Correction

INTRODUCTION

In the illustration that follows you will learn a new set of phonic signals. English speech will be represented by symbols other than those of the usual Roman alphabet. Play along with the game. When you finish, you will better understand the task which children face when they are learning to read.[1]

STEP ONE

Objective: Learn sight words.

Learn to pronounce the six words below at sight. Test yourself by covering the pictures.

---

[1] Reprinted with permission of Merrill, an imprint of Macmillan Publishing Company, from *Word Attack Skills in Reading* by Carl J. Wallen, Copyright © 1969 Merrill Publishing Company, Columbus, Ohio, pp. 13–18.

Objective: Test yourself on knowledge of sight words.

Match words and pictures. Check yourself by referring back to step one.

STEP THREE

Objective: Test auditory discrimination readiness.

Answer the following questions with *yes* or *no*.

1. Do the two words represented by the pictures have the same ending sound?

2. Do the two words represented by the pictures have the same ending sound?

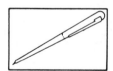 

3. Do the two words represented by the pictures have the same beginning sound?

STEP FOUR

Objective: Test visual discrimination readiness.

Circle the *words* in each column that have the same letters in the same places as those underlined in the word at the top of the column. Column 1 has been completed.

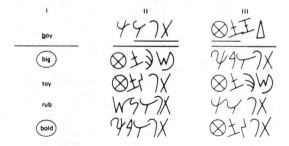

I	II	III
b̲oy		
(big)		
toy		
rub		
(bold)		

STEP FIVE

Objective: Use phonic word attack to pronounce a new word.

Follow the directions given below.

1. Pronounce the three words above.
2. How do the three words look alike?
3. How do the three words sound alike?

4. Pronounce the three words above.
5. How do the three words look alike?
6. How do the three words sound alike?

7. Above is a new word.

8. How does it look like the other two groups of words?
9. Can you pronounce the new word?

(If you cannot pronounce the new word, do steps one, two, three, and four again. Then follow the directions given in step five.)

Notice that you pronounced the new word by comparing the look of the new word with the look of familiar words. You assumed that if words have a similar spelling they will have a similar pronunciation.

Thus: 1. *oride* probably begins like *or* and rhymes with *hide*.
2. *smeek* probably begins like *smile* and rhymes with *seek*.
3. *virgule* probably begins like *virtue* and rhymes with *mule*.

In phonic word attack the child compares new words with familiar ones. When the child finds words having a similar spelling he or she assumes that the words will also have a similar pronunciation. Phonic signals are the letters and groups of letters which the reader compares. The reader learned two nonsense phonic signals in the previous exercise and used them in applying phonic word attack to the new word.

Phonic Signals Learned	New Word Attacked
⊗⊥ and Ƴ⅂Ӿ	⊗⊥Ƴ⅂Ӿ

This chapter and the two that follow will present an analytical review of some of the word recognition, comprehension, vocabulary expansion, and study skills that a good teacher must have. It seems obvious that teachers will not be able to diagnose reading problems unless they know the components of reading.

Word recognition
A twofold process that includes both the identification of printed symbols by some method so that the word can be pronounced and the association of meaning to the word after it has been properly pronounced.

Word recognition is necessary to be able to read. No one would disagree with that statement; however, people do disagree on what word recognition encompasses. In this book word recognition is seen as a twofold process that includes both the identification of printed symbols by some method so that the word can be pronounced and the attachment or association of meaning to the word after it has been properly pronounced.

This chapter will concentrate on helping you better understand word recognition strategies and will present a developmental sequence of phonic skills. It is important in a diagnostic-reading and correction program that teachers have the word analysis skills at their fingertips, as well as techniques for teaching them, so that they can interweave diagnosis with instruction and correction. In addition, this chapter will discuss techniques teachers can use to help students at both primary and intermediate grade levels to expand their vocabulary with an emphasis on using a combining forms approach.

KEY QUESTIONS

After you finish reading this chapter, you should be able to answer the following questions:

1. What is a diagnostic and correction approach to teaching word recognition skills?
2. What does word recognition encompass?
3. How is word recognition defined in this book?
4. What is the place of phonics in the reading program?
5. What is explicit phonics instruction?
6. What is implicit phonics instruction?
7. What strategies are used to help students pronounce words?
8. What strategies are used to help students get word meanings?
9. What skills are taught in phonics instruction?
10. What are consonant and vowel digraphs?
11. What are diphthongs and consonant blends (clusters)?
12. What is a phonogram?
13. How are vowel generalizations taught?
14. What is the relationship of syllabication to phonics?
15. What are the syllabication generalizations?
16. What should children know about accenting?
17. What is a vocabulary consciousness?
18. What are combining forms?
19. How can teachers help students expand their vocabulary?
20. What is the place of vocabulary in the content areas?

KEY TERMS IN CHAPTER

You should pay special attention to the following new terms:

affixes
combining forms
consonant clusters (blends)
consonant digraph
context
derivatives
diacritical marks
dictionary
diphthongs
explicit phonics instruction
implicit phonics instruction
phonic analysis
phonic synthesis
phonics
phonogram
prefix
root
schwa

silent consonants
structural analysis
structural synthesis
suffix
syllable
vocabulary consciousness
vowel digraph
whole word or "look and say"
word recognition

WORD RECOGNITION STRATEGIES

It is important that teachers be aware of the different word recognition strategies and the purpose for each so that effective teaching can take place. For example, a teacher must realize that helping a child to become proficient in phonics will not help him or her to be a good reader unless the child has developed a stock of vocabulary and has adequate concept development. A child may be able to decode all the words in a passage, but as stated in Chapter 1 when defining reading, this child would not be reading unless he or she could determine the meaning of the passage. A teacher should not only be aware of the different strategies for figuring out word pronunciation and meanings but also recognize that some strategies work better with different children. This advice should not, however, preclude teachers from helping children to become proficient in using all the strategies and from helping children to determine which strategy or strategies are best to use in a specific situation. Usually, a combination of strategies is used.

Word Recognition Strategies for Pronunciation

When we read, we are intent on getting the message and appear to do so automatically and in one step. We don't notice the individual letters, groups of letters, or even every word if we are good readers. It isn't until we stumble on an unfamiliar word that we become aware of the individual letters that are grouped together to form a word. The reason we stopped reading is because the word we stumbled on has interfered with the message. The question is: Do you remember what you did when a word interfered with your understanding of what you were reading? To understand better the concept that word recognition is a twofold process, that there are a number of strategies that can be used to figure out how to pronounce a word as well as to determine its meaning, and that these strategies are not necessarily the same, we will be involved in a number of exercises containing nonsense and actual words. Read the following sentence:

I don't like *cland* food.

You should have stumbled on the nonsense word *cland*. Imagine that you do not know that *cland* is a nonsense word. Let's look at the kinds of strategies we could and could *not* use to help us pronounce a word *independently*.

Strategy 1: Phonic analysis and synthesis
Definition: Phonics is a decoding technique that depends on students' being able to make the proper grapheme (letter)–phoneme (sound) correspondences. *Analysis* has to do with the breaking down of something into its component parts. *Synthesis* has to do with the building up of the parts of something into a whole.
Analysis: Break down *cland* into the blend *cl* and the phonogram *and.*
 We have met the blend *cl* before in such words as *climb* and *club.*
 We have met the phonogram *and* before in such words as *sand* and *band.*
 We therefore know the pronunciations of *cl* and *and.*
Synthesis: Blend together the *cl* and *and.*

Phonic analysis
The breaking down of a word into its component parts.

Using this technique, we should be able to pronounce *cland* or at least gain an approximation of its pronunciation.

Phonic synthesis
The building up of the component parts of a word into a whole.

Strategy 2: Whole word or "look and say" method
Definition: The whole word or "look and say" method, which is also referred to as the sight method, has to do with the teacher's or any other individual's directing a student's attention to a word and then saying the word. The student must make an association between the oral word and the written word, and he or she shows this by actually saying the word.

Whole word or look and say
A word recognition technique in which a child's attention is directed to a word and then the word is said.

This technique is a useful word recognition strategy that helps us to learn to pronounce words, but it will not help us to figure out the pronunciation of unfamiliar words independently.

Strategy 3: Ask someone to pronounce the word for you.

This request could be made, but doing so would be similar to using the "look and say" method, and it would not help us to figure out the word independently.

Strategy 4: Context clues
Definition: By *context* we mean the words surrounding a word that can shed light on its meaning. When we refer to context clues, we mean clues that are given in the form of definitions, examples, comparisons or contrasts, explanations, and so on, which help us figure out word meanings.

This is a word recognition technique, but it is not one that helps us to figure out the pronunciation of words. It is one that is used for helping us to gain the meaning of a word.

Structural analysis
A technique for the breaking down of a word into word parts such as prefixes, suffixes, roots, and combining forms.

Strategy 5: Structural analysis and synthesis (word parts)
Definition: Structural analysis and synthesis have to do with the breaking down (analysis) and building up (synthesis) of word parts such as prefixes, suffixes, roots (bases), and combining forms.

Structural analysis is most often used in conjunction with phonic analysis. Knowledge of word parts such as prefixes, suffixes, and roots helps us to isolate the root of a word. After the root of a word is isolated, phonic analysis is applied. If the word parts are familiar ones, then we can blend together the word parts to come up with the pronunciation of the word.

Structural analysis is a helpful word recognition technique that can aid with the pronunciation of words, but it will not help us to figure out the pronunciation of *cland* unless we apply phonic analysis because *cland* as a nonsense word is an unfamiliar root (base) word.

Structural analysis is especially helpful in figuring out the pronunciation of an unfamiliar word if the word is composed of familiar word parts such as prefixes, suffixes, and roots. The technique to use is similar to that used with phonic analysis and synthesis. For example, let's see how we would go about figuring out how to pronounce the italicized word in the following sentence using structural analysis and synthesis.

The salesperson said that the goods were not *returnable*.

Structural Analysis: Break down the word into its parts to isolate the root.

re   turn   able

If we had met *re* before and if we had met *able* before, we should know how to pronounce them. After we have isolated *turn*, we may recognize it as a familiar word and know how to pronounce it.

Structural synthesis
A technique for building up of word parts into a whole.

Structural Synthesis: Blend together *re*, *turn*, and *able*.

If *turn* is not a familiar root word for us, then we could apply phonic analysis to it and after that blend it together with the prefix *re* and the suffix *able*.

Strategy 6: Look up the pronunciation in the dictionary.

This is a viable method, but you may not have a dictionary handy, and by the time you look up the pronunciation of the word, you may have lost the trend of what you were reading.

Let's list those techniques that can help us to figure out the pronunciation of words:

1. Phonic analysis and synthesis
2. Whole word or "look and say"
3. Asking someone
4. Structural analysis and synthesis
5. Looking up the pronunciation in the dictionary

Word Recognition Strategies for Word Meaning

Being able to pronounce a word is important, but it does not guarantee that we will thereby know the meaning of the word. As previously stated, word recognition is a twofold process: The first step involves the correct pronunciation, and the second involves meaning. After we have pronounced a word, we have to associate the word with one in our listening vocabulary in order to determine the meaning of the word; that is, we need to have heard the word before and know what the word means. Obviously, the larger our stock of listening vocabulary, the better able we will be to decipher the word. However, even though we can pronounce a word such as *misanthropic*, it doesn't mean that we can associate any meaning to it. If we have never heard the word before, it would not be in our listening vocabulary; therefore, the pronunciation would not act as a stimulus and trigger an association with a word that we have stored in our memory bank. Let's see the techniques that we can use to help us unlock words that we have never encountered before.

Strategy 1: Context

Context
The words surrounding a particular word that can shed light on its meaning.

By *context* we mean the words surrounding a particular word that can help shed light on its meaning. (Context clues can be very helpful in determining the meanings of words, especially words with multiple meanings, and because of their importance, special emphasis is given to this area in Chapter 13.) Read the following sentence:

Even though my *trank* was rather long, I wouldn't take out one word.

From the context of the sentence you know that the nonsense word *trank* must somehow refer to a sentence, paragraph, paper, or report of some kind. Even though you have never met *trank* before, the context of the sentence did throw light on it. You know from the word order or position of the word (syntax) that *trank* must be a noun, and words such as *word* and *long* give you meaning (semantic) clues to the word itself. There are times, however, when context is not too helpful so that other strategies must be used.

Strategy 2: Structural analysis and synthesis for word meaning

Read the following sentence:

We asked the *misanthrope* to leave.

From the position of the word *misanthrope* in the sentence, we know that it is a noun; however, there is not enough information to help us figure out the meaning of *misanthrope*. Structural analysis could be very useful in situations where there are insufficient context clues, and the word consists of a number of word parts.

Analysis: Break down *misanthrope* into its word parts.

Mis means either "wrong" or "hate," and *anthropo* means "humankind."

Synthesis: Put together the word parts. It doesn't make sense to say, "Wrong humankind," so it must be *hate* and *humankind*. Since *misanthrope* is a noun, the meaning of *misanthrope* would have to be "hater of humankind."

Structural analysis is a powerful tool, but it is dependent on your having at your fingertips knowledge of word parts and their meanings. If you do not have these at hand, you obviously need another strategy. (More will be said about structural analysis later in this chapter.)

Strategy 3: Ask someone the meaning of the word.

This at times may be the most convenient if someone is available who knows the meaning of the word.

Strategy 4: Look up the meaning in the dictionary.

If you cannot figure out the word independently rather quickly so that your train of thought is not completely broken, the dictionary is a valuable tool for word meanings.

Let's list those techniques that can help us figure out the meaning of words:

1. Context of a sentence
2. Structural analysis and synthesis
3. Asking someone
4. Looking up the meaning in the dictionary

There are times when it is possible for context clues to help with the correction of mispronounced words that are in the listening vocabulary of the reader but not yet in his or her reading vocabulary. Here is such an example. A student is asked to read the following sentence:

The child put on her coat.

The student reads the sentence as follows:

The *chilld* put on her coat.

The reader then self-corrects and rereads the sentence correctly. What has taken place? The first pronunciation *chilld* was obtained from graphic clues. As the student continued to read, the context of the sentence indicated to the student that the mispronounced word should be *child* rather than *chilld*. Since *child* was in the person's listening vocabulary, the student was able to self-correct the mispronunciation. In this case, the context clues helped the reader to correct the mispronunciation of *child*.

It is important to state that the reader would not have been able to self-correct if the word *child* had not been in his or her listening vocabulary and if he or she had not heard it correctly pronounced.

Teachers should stress to their students that phonics usually only gives an approximation of the way a word is pronounced. Often readers must rely on sentence meaning and their familiarity with the spoken word to be able to pronounce it correctly.

Special Notes

Many foreign students who are learning English as another language or students who speak nonstandard English may pronounce a number of words incorrectly because they have heard them pronounced that way or because they have difficulty producing the sounds, but they may know the meanings of the words. The teacher must be careful in determining the cause of the child's mispronunciation; that is, is the mispronunciation due to a pronunciation problem or a comprehension problem?

THE IMPORTANCE OF DECODING IN READING

In Chapter 5, we discussed the importance of listening and the fact that children who have difficulty in listening will have a problem in oral language, as well as reading. Since reading is a process of interpreting printed symbols that are based on arbitrary speech sounds, it depends on a foundation of previously learned speech symbols. Usually, beginning readers have a substantial oral vocabulary before they begin to read, when they learn that each word they speak or listen to has a printed symbol. Students who become effective readers must be able to automatically decode written symbols which represent speech sounds. Inability to do so will prevent readers from bringing anything to or getting any message from the printed page.

PHONICS

Phonics
The study of the relationships between letter symbols of a written language and the sounds they represent.

Phonics, which is the study of relationships between the letter symbols (graphemes) of a written language and the sounds (phonemes) they represent, is a method used in teaching word recognition in reading. It is a pedagogical term. Phonics is used in the classroom as an aid to decoding words. It helps students gain independence and reliance in reading, but it is only one aspect of the reading process.

Phonics instruction in the early grades is important; however, it must be taught in conjunction with meaning and the emphasis should not be on stating the generalizations but on children's being able to internalize them so that they can become proficient readers as quickly as possible. A recent analysis of program-comparison research projects was undertaken to determine the effectiveness of beginning reading approaches.

> According to the analyses, the approaches that, one way or another, included systematic phonics instruction consistently exceeded the straight basal programs in word recognition achievement scores. The approaches that included both systematic phonics and considerable emphasis on connected reading and meaning surpassed the basal-alone approaches on virtually all outcome measures.[2]

In teaching phonics, the reading material should be interesting and related as closely as possible to the phonic skills that the children

---

[2] Marilyn Jager Adams, *Beginning to Read: Thinking and Learning about Print—A Summary* by Steven A. Stahl, Jean Osborn, and Fran Lehr (Urbana, Ill.: Center for the Study of Reading, 1990), p. 9.

are learning. This is not as simple as it sounds because the books that have attempted to do this have often been stilted and uninteresting.

Explicit Versus Implicit Phonics Instruction

Explicit phonics instruction
Each sound associated with a letter in the word is pronounced in isolation, and then the sounds are blended together.

Implicit phonics instruction
Does not present sounds associated with letters in isolation. Children listen to words that begin with a particular sound; then they state another word that begins with the same sound.

Before presenting a developmental-diagnostic and correction sequence of phonics instruction, it is important to explain the differences between explicit and implicit phonics instruction. In explicit phonics, each sound associated with a letter in the word is pronounced in isolation and then blended together. A problem with this method is that it is very difficult to produce pure speech sounds in isolation. As a result, what usually takes place in the classroom is the following. The teacher shows the children the word *cat*, points to the letter *c* and says that it stands for the sound *cuh*. The teacher then points to the letter *a* in the word *cat* and says it stands for the sound *ah* and then points to the letter *t* and says it stands for the sound *tuh*. The children are then told to blend *cuh ah tuh* together to get *cat*. Even though *cuh ah tuh* does not sound like *cat*, children are supposedly able to recognize the word *cat* from this method.

Implicit phonics instruction, on the other hand, does not present sounds associated with letters in isolation. The children are presented with a list of words that all begin with the same initial consonant such as the following:

girl   game   get

The children are helped to recognize that all the words begin with the same letter *g*. Then the children are told to listen carefully to the beginning sound of each word. The teacher pronounces each word and tells the children that the letter *g* stands for the sound at the beginning of the words *girl, game, get*. The children are then often asked to look around the room for other words that begin like *game* or with the letter *g*. (Usually, the teacher has pictures of items around the room that begin with the letter *g*.)

It appears that many teachers use a combination of both explicit and implicit phonics. The important thing to remember is that any method that helps children unlock words as quickly as possible should be used and that phonics gives children the power and independence they need to pronounce unfamiliar words. The key, of course, is for children to overlearn words after they have sounded them out a number of times so that they will become part of their sight vocabulary.

Special Note

Some writers use the terms *synthetic phonics* to refer to explicit phonics instruction and *analytic phonics* to refer to implicit phonics instruction.

A DEVELOPMENTAL-DIAGNOSTIC AND CORRECTION SEQUENCE OF PHONICS

Although the teaching of phonics will vary according to the needs and readiness levels of the students, in a developmental sequence certain skills should be achieved before others. So that teachers can properly diagnose the needs and readiness levels of their students in phonics, teachers must be proficient in this area and know the steps involved. First, the child usually learns a few sight words. Then, when the child learns that some words look alike and/or sound alike, the mastering of phonic word attack skills has begun. This task is not a simple one. (In the Introduction of this chapter an activity was presented that should have given you some insight into what children may go through when learning word attack skills.)

Following is an outline of the developmental sequence of phonics instruction. Each area will be defined, and then a sample diagnostic test or tests will be presented, as well as instructional suggestions.[3]

1. Auditory discrimination.
2. Visual discrimination.
3. Consonants.[4]
   a. Initial consonants.
   b. Final consonants.
   c. Consonant clusters (blends) (*bl, st, str*).
   d. Initial consonant blends (clusters); final consonant blends (clusters).
   e. Initial consonant digraphs (*th, ch, sh*).
   f. Final consonant digraphs (*ng, gh*).
   g. Silent consonants (*kn, pn, wr*).
4. Vowel sounds.
   a. Long vowel sounds.
   b. Short vowel sounds.
   c. Effect of final *e* on vowel.
   d. Double vowels.
      (1) Digraphs.
      (2) Diphthongs.
   e. Vowel controlled by *r*.
5. Special letters and sounds.
6. Phonograms.
7. Syllabication.
   a. Meaning of syllable.
   b. Generalizations.
      (1) Double consonant vc/cv.
      (2) Vowel-consonant-vowel v/cv.
      (3) Consonant with special *le* c/cle or v/cle.

[3] For ease of reading, the author has omitted slashes that are often used to enclose phonemic symbols.
[4] Consonants are usually taught before vowel sounds.

c. Syllable phonics.
   (1) Open syllable.
   (2) Closed syllable.
d. Accent.

Auditory and Visual Discrimination

As has already been stated, unless children are able to hear sounds correctly, they will not be able to say them correctly, read them, or write them. Not only must children be able to differentiate between auditory sounds and visual symbols in order to be ready for reading, they must also learn that the sounds they hear have written symbols.

Since they must have good auditory and visual discrimination, these samples of exercises should help in determining such discrimination.

Visual Discrimination

Visual discrimination is the ability to detect similarities and differences in written symbols.

SAMPLE DIAGNOSTIC TESTS

Directions: Draw a circle around the letter that is like the first letter.

s	c	p	c	e	s
p	d	p	b	r	q
l	t	k	h	l	d
b	p	d	b	o	u
d	s	b	p	d	q
m	n	m	s	h	w

Directions: Draw a circle around the word that is like the first word.

car	far	can	cap	car	fan
dear	bear	dark	deal	dear	bean
pail	sail	pail	bail	pain	pear

Directions: Draw a circle around the group of numbers that is like the first group of numbers.

3357	3375	3355	3357	5733
2179	2791	2179	9127	9712
5218	8125	5182	5821	5218

Figure 12.1 These kindergarten children are learning their letters.

Instructional Suggestions

If a child has difficulty with the visual discrimination tests involving letters, words, and numbers, the teacher should make sure the child understands what he or she is supposed to do. The best way to ensure understanding is to model an example for the child.

Some children need a great amount of practice to be able to make the fine discriminations necessary to read. If, however, a teacher has worked with a child and given him or her a number of activities, and the child still has problems with recognizing letters that are similar or different, the teacher might want to refer the child for an eye test (see Chapter 5).

Auditory Discrimination

Auditory discrimination is the ability to detect differences and similarities in sound symbols.

SAMPLE DIAGNOSTIC TESTS

Directions: Listen carefully. See if you can tell me which pair of words is the same.

sat	set	ball	bell
cap	cap	sing	singe
hand	hand	pan	pan
sail	sell	burn	but

Directions: Listen carefully. Give me another word that rhymes with

can _____   fat _____

sail _____   day _____

Directions: Listen carefully. Give me another word that begins like

baby	_____
door	_____
can	_____
fat	_____

Instructional Suggestions

If a child has difficulty discriminating between or among various sound symbols, the teacher should present the child with other words that have sounds similar to the ones that seem to be causing problems. This procedure will help the teacher to determine whether the child "misheard" the original words. The teacher should also model for the child what he or she is supposed to do, and then they should do some together.

Teachers should keep in mind that judging whether two or more symbols are similar or different is not easy for young children. The children must be able to keep a sound in memory and then retrieve it to make a comparison. Some five- or six-year-olds may not have developed this ability. These children need practice in auditory discrimination before they can begin a phonics program. However, if after a great amount of practice the child still has difficulty, it is possible that the inability to discern similarities and differences in speech sounds may be a symptom that the child has an auditory problem.

In addition if the child speaks nonstandard English or if standard English is not the child's dominant language, the child may not do well. For children whose dominant language is not English, certain sounds may be different or nonexistent in a student's native language (see Chapter 4).

Consonants

Initial Consonants

Initial consonants are single consonants (one speech sound represented by one letter). For example: *b* (bath), *c* (cake), *d* (damp), *f* (fat), *g* (girl).

SAMPLE INDIVIDUAL DIAGNOSTIC TEST

Directions: Listen carefully. What is the letter that stands for the first sound you hear in the following words?

dog, mother, father, girl, boy, hat, cat, family

SAMPLE GROUP DIAGNOSTIC TEST

Directions: Listen carefully. Write the first letter of each word I say. Let's do one together. The word is *baby*. Again, the word is *baby*. Did you write a *b*? Good. Here are the words:

1. girl	6. log
2. fan	7. dog
3. sit	8. bat
4. want	9. pot
5. tail	10. light

Instructional Suggestions

The instructional technique used here is generally an implicit one. Teachers state a number of words beginning with the same initial consonant. They ask the children to listen to the words *ball*, *book*, and *bee*. They also write the words on the board. Then they ask how *ball*, *book*, and *bee* are similar. They all have the same beginning letter *b*. They all start with the same sound. Teachers can then give more words that begin with *b* and ask students to state some others that start like *big*, *book*, and *balloon*.

For variety, the children can be given a series of words that begin with the same initial consonant and be told to match these words with those in a second column that start with the same letter by drawing a line from one to the other. For example:

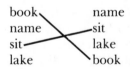

Substitution of Initial Consonants. After children have learned to recognize and are able to state single consonants, they are ready to substitute those in already learned words to generate new words. The new words must be in their listening vocabulary; that is, they must have heard the word and know the meaning of it in order to be able to *read* it. For example, children have learned the consonant letter *c* and they also know the word *man*. They should then be able to substitute *c* for *m* and come up with the word *can*.

Special Notes

The sample group tests presented in this section require the children to write the letters that stand for the sounds they hear. This test

286   *The Diagnostic-Reading and Correction Program in Action*

should not be given unless children have been exposed to the letter-sound combinations and have learned to write the letters. It would be a good idea to have a practice test first to go over the directions and tell the children what they are to do, as well as to review what will be on the test.

If children do poorly on the group-administered test, the teacher should check the results by giving an oral individual test to determine whether the problem is one of sound-letter correspondence; that is, the child cannot associate a letter with the sound. Also, the teacher should have the children read some of the words to check their letter-sound correspondence; that is, the child knows what letters stand for what sounds.

It may also be that the instructions are too confusing for the children; that is, the concept of "the letter that stands for the sound" may confuse some children. Therefore, you might change your instructions to say "the sound of the letter," even though this usage is not linguistically correct because letters do not have sounds. However, our purpose is not to teach linguistic principles to the children. It is to help them see and hear patterns in words so they can decode them as quickly as possible when they meet the words in connected text.

The oral individual diagnostic test can be given at any time during the day to determine a child's phonic analysis ability. Good teachers interweave diagnosis with instruction throughout the day.

Teachers must be especially careful to pronounce all words very distinctly; the teacher's articulation must be excellent.

Final Consonants

Final consonants are similar to the list given for the initial consonants, except that they appear at the end of the word. Examples of the most frequent single consonants are *b* (rob), *d* (road), *g* (pig), *k* (brook), *l* (tool), *m* (mom), *n* (hen), *p* (top), *r* (car), *s* (fuss), *s-z* (has), *t* (that).

SAMPLE INDIVIDUAL DIAGNOSTIC TEST

(Same as for initial consonants, except children have to give the last letter in the word that stands for the last sound they hear.)

Directions: Listen carefully. What is the letter that stands for the last sound you hear in the following words?

cab, dog, man, hat, tap, drop

SAMPLE GROUP DIAGNOSTIC TEST

Directions: Listen carefully. Write the last letter of each word I say.

1. rob	6. pig
2. pop	7. hat
3. ear	8. sled
4. hen	9. tool
5. miss	10. head

Instructional Suggestions

Some teachers teach final consonants at the same time that they teach initial consonants. This approach is preferable, for teachers are working with a particular sound that they want children to "overlearn"; that is, they want students to be able to recognize and state the sound-letter combination over an extended period of time. When the initial and final consonants in words are emphasized, the children are gaining extra practice in both the particular sound and the letter that represents the sound being studied. As the children have learned that the letter *Gg* stands for a certain sound and can recognize this sound in *girl, go, game, get,* and so on, they should also be given words such as *pig, log, leg, tag,* and so on, to see whether they can recognize the same sound at the end of the word.

Substitution of Final Consonants. In order to gain skill in the substitution of final consonants, the children are given a list of words that they can already decode and recognize—such as *bat, pet, let, tan.* Then they are asked to substitute the final letter *g* in all the words to make new words. For example, *bat* would become *bag,* *pet* would become *peg,* *let* would become *leg,* and *tan* would become *tag.* Pupils can also be asked to substitute other consonants to make new words. For example, *d* for *g* in *bag* to make *bad,* and *d* in *let* to make *led.*

Consonant Clusters (Blends)

Consonant clusters (blends)
A combination of consonant sounds blended together so that the identity of each sound is retained.

Consonant clusters are simply a way of combining the consonant sounds of a language. Clusters are a blend of sounds. (In some basal reader series, the term *consonant cluster* has replaced the term *consonant blend.*)

Initial Consonant Blends (Clusters)

Consonant blends are a combination of sounds. They are two or more consonant sounds blended together so that each sound is retained. For example: *bl* (black), *br* (brown), *cl* (clap), *cr* (cross), *fr* (frame), *gl* (glass), *gr* (grass), *pr* (prize), *pl* (please), *sk* (skip), *sn* (snow).

Directions: Listen carefully. What are the two letters that stand for the first two sounds you hear in the following words?

blame, prune, flag, glove, glass, frog, snow, clear, break, crow

SAMPLE GROUP DIAGNOSTIC TEST

Directions: Listen carefully. Write the first two letters of each word I say.

1. clear	6. plane
2. grow	7. frog
3. train	8. brake
4. slow	9. steam
5. blow	10. floor

Instructional Suggestions

Consonant blends are generally introduced in the first grade at the primer level in basal readers. The teaching of the initial consonant blends depends on the readiness levels of the children, who may be at the stage where they can benefit from added instruction in order to help them more readily decode words. The children must be able to recognize, sound, and substitute initial consonants in words before proceeding to blends. They should be given a list of sight words that have blends, such as *spin, snow, play, stop*, asked to say these words, and then tell what sounds they hear at the beginning of the words. They should also be asked to say a list of words such as *go, get, me*, and *mother* and then be asked what the difference between the two groups of words is. The children should be able to discern that in the group consisting of *play, stop*, and *spin*, they were able to hear two consonant sounds rather than one. Thus the concept of a blend is introduced. The teacher should then give the children exercises similar to those presented in the section on initial consonants. For example, the pupils could be given a list of words that they may not necessarily know as sight words:

1	2	3	4
black	big	mother	happy
ball	play	great	broom
blue	draw	farm	track
chain	down	spin	grow
train	go	run	help

Teachers would tell the children to underline only those words they pronounce—such as *black*, *play*, *spin*, and *broom*.

This exercise can also be used to see how well children listen, follow directions, and recognize blends. For example, the teacher can instruct the children to *listen carefully* and not to do anything until he or she has completed the sentence. Then, the teacher can say, "Put a circle around *black* and a cross on *blue*. Put a circle around *draw* and a line under *play*. Put a line under *great* and a circle around *spin*. Put a cross on *track* and a circle around *broom*."

Final consonant blends are usually taught after initial consonant blends, using similar techniques.

Final Consonant Blends (Clusters)

Similar to initial consonant blends except that they are at the end of the word and are different combinations of blends. For example: *nd* (kind), *rk* (park), *mp* (stamp), *rt* (start), *sk* (mask), *rp* (harp), *nt* (ant).

SAMPLE INDIVIDUAL DIAGNOSTIC TEST

Directions: Listen carefully. What are the last two letters that stand for the last two sounds you hear in the following words?

bump, cart, ask, park, sand, find

SAMPLE GROUP DIAGNOSTIC TEST

Directions: Listen carefully. Write the last two letters of each word I say.

1. bark	6. fist
2. mask	7. sand
3. camp	8. harp
4. Frank	9. slant
5. cart	10. grasp

Instructional Suggestions

As already stated, teachers should use similar techniques as those presented for initial consonant blends.

Consonant digraph
Two consonants that represent one speech sound.

Initial Consonant Digraphs

Consonant digraphs usually consist of two consonants that represent one speech sound. For example: *ch* (chair), *sh* (show), *th* (thank), *ph* (phone).

SAMPLE INDIVIDUAL DIAGNOSTIC TEST

Directions: Listen carefully. What are the two letters that stand for the first sound you hear in the following words?

chain, thumb, shall, phone

SAMPLE GROUP DIAGNOSTIC TEST

Directions: Listen carefully. Write the first two letters of each word I say.

1. phone	6. chair
2. shame	7. that
3. chain	8. photo
4. shall	9. thumb
5. child	10. shine

Instructional Suggestions

These suggestions are similar to those given for initial consonant blends; however, teachers should help children recognize that combinations such as *ch*, *th*, and *sh* represent one sound rather than two. In addition, teachers should make sure children understand that *ph* sounds like *f* in words such as *photo*, *phone*, and *phony*. Unless they have met these words and know how to spell them, they may write either the letter *f* or *fo* because you asked for the first two letters in the word. The children are writing what they hear.

Final Consonant Digraphs

Examples of final consonant digraphs are *th* (booth), *ng* (sing), *sh* (mash), *ch* (cinch), *gh* (rough). Note: It is possible to have a digraph represent one of the sounds in a cluster. In the word *cinch*, *nch* represents a cluster (blend) because *nch* represents a blend of *two* sounds. The letter *n* represents a sound, and the digraph *ch* represents another sound.

SAMPLE INDIVIDUAL DIAGNOSTIC TEST

Directions: Listen carefully. What are the two letters that stand for the last sound you hear in the following words?

flash, pinch, moth, ring, much

SAMPLE GROUP DIAGNOSTIC TEST

Directions: Listen carefully. Write the last two letters of each word I say.

1. rash	6. cash
2. touch	7. rich
3. sing	8. push
4. push	9. teeth
5. moth	10. bring

Instructional Suggestions

Similar to those given for initial consonant digraphs.

Silent consonants
Two adjacent consonants, one of which is silent, for example, *kn (know)*, *pn (pneumonia)*.

Silent Consonants

Silent consonants refer to two consonants in which one is silent. Examples are *kn* (know), *gh* (ghost), *wr* (wreck). These are analogous to consonant digraphs, for the two consonants represent one speech sound.

No special tests are being presented for these. Children learn these as they are exposed to them in print.

Vowel Sounds

Long and Short Vowel Sounds and Effect of Final e

The vowels are *a*, *e*, *i*, *o*, and *u*, and sometimes *y* and *w* act as vowels. A vowel is long when it says its name.

SAMPLE INDIVIDUAL DIAGNOSTIC TEST

Directions: Listen carefully. I will say a word. You tell me the vowel you hear in the word. Also tell me if you hear a long or short vowel sound.

cat, note, make, mice, not, pet, but, cute

SAMPLE GROUP DIAGNOSTIC TEST

Directions: Listen carefully. I will say a word a few times. Write the vowel you hear in the word. Then write the word short or long next to it.

1. cut	6. hot
2. cap	7. cape
3. mute	8. time
4. pen	9. no
5. Tim	10. nut

Special Notes

It's a good idea for the teacher to do a few examples orally together with the child before giving the group diagnostic test for long and short vowel sounds. For example, the teacher can do the following:

"Let's do one together first. Listen carefully." The teacher says, "Bat, bat," and asks, "What vowel did you hear?" If the child says *a*, the teacher asks the child to state whether the word *bat* has a long or short vowel sound. If the child has difficulty with the individual test, the group test should not be given (see "Instructional Suggestions).

Also, the words *short* and *long* should be on the chalkboard visible to all the children, and the children should know what each word stands for.

We must make sure the tests do not frustrate the children.

Instructional Suggestions

Most children have met many of the vowel generalizations in sight words and have learned to pronounce the words properly before they are able to state the generalization. Vowel generalizations are usually introduced some time in the first grade and usually taught throughout the primary grades. Again, the discussion as to when to teach vowel generalizations would depend on the readiness level of the pupils in the class. The purpose of teaching vowel generalizations is to help students become more proficient in analyzing words, so that they can be more effective independent readers.

The emphasis, however, should not be on the stating of generalizations nor on children's knowledge of specialized terminology; it should be on children's being able to recognize certain word patterns. In other words, the children's attention should be on the spelling and sound structures of the word patterns they are learning.[5]

Should long or short vowels be taught first?[6] As the long vowel sound is the name of the vowel, children might have less difficulty in hearing this sound. Therefore, it would be better to start with long vowel sounds, even though there are more words with short vowel sounds.

Whichever kind of vowel is taught first, it is important that the teacher use the children's background of experiences to help them acquire new skills.

Teachers should familiarize children with the schwa sound, represented by (ə) of the phonetic alphabet. The schwa is important in phonics instruction because it frequently appears in the unstressed

[5] Adams, p. 80.
[6] Although some linguists frown at the use of the terms *long* and *short vowels*, because they claim there are only gradations of vowel sounds, it is helpful to use these terms in the teaching of phonics.

(unaccented) syllables of words with more than one syllable. (See "Special Letters and Sounds.")

Long Vowel Sounds—a e i o u (and sometimes) y. In the teaching of this concept, attention should be drawn to the sound element. A number of sight words illustrating the long vowel sound can be placed on the board:

āpe	bē	gō
āge	hē	nō
April	ēven	ōpen
āte	mē	

The children are told to listen to the words as they are sounded. Can they hear the name of any of the vowels in the words? If they can, they can tell which ones they hear. After they correctly state the vowel they heard, "saying its name," it is explained that these vowels are called long vowels and they are marked, for example, ā.

A list of words containing long vowels should be read to the children, and the students should then say which vowel is long in each word. They can be given a list of words and asked to mark all the vowels that are long after everyone has said the words aloud. For example:

āble	gāme	hāte	mōst
boy	get	hid	nāme
cāke	girl	hīde	nō
come	gō	man	nōte
father	hat	mē	pet

After children have had practice in recognizing long vowel sounds in spoken words, the teacher presents written exercises in which the children work independently at marking the long vowel sound. The words in these exercises should all be sight vocabulary words—those the children have already met and are able to recognize.

Y represents a long vowel sound when it occurs at the end of a word or syllable and when all the other letters in the word or syllable are consonants. For example: *by, cry, baby, deny.* Note that *y* in these words represents different vowel sounds. It stands for a long *i* sound in one-syllable words containing no other vowels. (See "Special Letters and Sounds.")

Short Vowel Sounds. As the children have already had practice in long vowel sounds, a list of words with short vowel sounds can next be placed on the board and each one pronounced:

not	get	man
got	let	can
pin	put	mad
tin	cut	cap
met	hat	had

The list containing long vowels can be presented so that children can hear the differences between long and short vowel sounds. The children's attention should also be brought to the *position* of the short vowel in such words as the following:

fat	man	net	got
mat	mad	get	not
cat	can	let	
hat		pet	

Children should be helped to notice the vowel rule—*a single vowel in the middle of a word (or syllable) is usually short.* As this concept is usually introduced in the first grade, the presentation of the term *syllable* should be deferred. The concept of closed syllable is reviewed in the intermediate grades in conjunction with syllabication.

Words like *gō, nō, mē,* and *hē* should also be noticed. The vowels are all long; there is only one vowel in the word; and *a vowel at the end of a one-vowel word (or syllable) usually has the long sound.*

Special Note

In phonics, the term *generalization* is preferred to the term *rule* because the latter is a more prescriptive term and implies great consistency. However, in working with children the term *rule* is easier for them to use and understand than *generalization.* The terms are used interchangeably in this chapter.

The Effect of the Final e. Words that the children know as sight words should be listed on the board and sounded:

note	cake	cute
made	take	mile

The children are asked to listen to the vowel sound, and it is stressed that in each of the sounded words the first vowel stands for a long sound. The children are then asked to notice what all the words have in common: all of the words have two vowels; one of the vowels is an *e*, which is always at the end of the word, and this *e* always has a consonant preceding it; the first vowel is long, and the final *e* is silent. The teacher then lists the following words on the board:

hat	cap	tub
kit	Tim	rob
can	not	hug
tap	cut	hop

The students read the words and tell what the vowel is and what kind of vowel sound the word has. The teacher then asks the children to put an *e* at the end of each of the words, so that the word list becomes the following:

hate	cape	tube
kite	time	robe
cane	note	huge
tape	cute	hope

The pupils are asked to read the words aloud. If they need help, the teacher reads the word. Again they are asked to notice what all of the words have in common and what happened to the words when the final *e* was added to each of them.

The teacher, through observation and discussion, helps children develop the silent (final) *e* rule, which states that *in words (or syllables) containing two vowels, separated by a consonant, and one of the vowels is a final* e, *the first vowel is usually long and the final* e *is silent.*[7]

Some practice exercises include a list of words to which children are instructed to add a final *e* to make a new word. The children then use both words in a sentence to show that they understand the difference in meaning between them. Another exercise shows their ability to recognize differences between words:

Directions: Put in the correct word.

1. He _____ himself. (cut, cute)

2. She is _____. (cut, cute)

3. I _____ you like my pet. (hop, hope)

4. I like to _____ on my foot. (hop, hope)

5. My friend's name is _____. (Tim, time)

6. What _____ is it? (Tim, time)

Double Vowels: Digraphs

Vowel digraph
Two vowels that represent one speech sound.

Two vowels adjacent to one another in a word (or syllable) stand for a single vowel sound and are called vowel digraphs; for example, *ea, oa, ai, ei, ie* in words like *beat, boat, hail, receive, believe.*

SAMPLE INDIVIDUAL DIAGNOSTIC TEST

Directions: Listen carefully. I will say a word. You tell me the two vowels that stand for the one vowel sound.

boat, keep, pail, way, bean

[7] When we say that a letter is silent, we mean that it does not add a sound to the syllable; however, it is just as important as any other letter in the syllable. It signals information about other letters, and it helps us to determine the sound represented by other letters.

SAMPLE GROUP DIAGNOSTIC TEST

Directions: Listen carefully. I will say a word a few times. Write the two vowels that go together to make one sound. The two vowels are either *ea*, *oa*, *ee*, *ai*, or *ay*.

1. pain	6. say
2. boat	7. mail
3. load	8. may
4. keep	9. tray
5. mean	10. feet

Instructional Suggestions

In first grade the children usually learn the rule that when two vowels appear together, the first is usually long and the second is silent. This usually does hold true for a number of vowel combinations such as *ai*, *oa*, *ea*, *ay*, and *ee*; however, there are exceptions to this rule, such as *ae*, *uy*, *eo*, *ew*. These digraphs are sounded as a single sound, but not with the long sound of the first. Some examples are *sew*, *buy*, *yeoman*, *Caesar*. Note that in the word *believe*, it is the *second* vowel that is long. Some vowel digraphs combine to form one sound that is not the long sound of either vowel. For example, in the words *neighbor*, *weigh*, and *freight*, the digraph *ei* is sounded as a long *a*, and in the word *sew* the digraph *ew* is sounded as a long *o*, with the *w* acting as a vowel. Note that in the word *rough*, the digraph *ou* is not sounded as a long vowel.

Obviously, the teacher should spend time on those vowel combinations that are the most useful. These are *ea*, *oa*, *ai*, *ay*, and *ee*.

The teacher should give students a set of words with one sound pattern at a time so that children can overlearn the letter–sound relationship. For example, the word *beat* can be put on the chalkboard and pronounced. The teacher can do the same for *team*, *meal*, and *bead*. After this, the teacher puts other words on the board and asks children to pronounce them. At this time, the teacher should elicit from the children what the *ea* combination in words such as meat, meal, and tea sounds like. (They should state the long *e* sound). Then children can be asked to generate words with the *ea* sound pattern. In addition, they should be given opportunities to meet words with the same *ea* sound combination in their reading.

Special Note

A child who gives *ea* as the vowel combination for *keep* is not incorrect. *Ea* and *ee* do sound alike. The child obviously does not know the spelling of the word; however, he or she does know that the combination *ee* and *ea* have a similar sound in some words.

Diphthongs
Blends of vowel sounds beginning with the first and gliding to the second. The vowel blends are represented by two adjacent vowels, for example, *oi*.

Double Vowels: Diphthongs

Diphthongs are blends of vowel sounds beginning with the first and gliding to the second. The vowel blends are represented by two adjacent vowels. Examples include *ou, oi, oy, ow*. For syllabication purposes, diphthongs are considered to be one vowel sound.

SAMPLE INDIVIDUAL DIAGNOSTIC TEST

Directions: Listen carefully. I will say a word. You tell me the two vowels that go together in the word.

boy, boil, how, cow, out

SAMPLE GROUP DIAGNOSTIC TEST

Directions: Listen carefully. I will say a word a few times. Write the two vowels that go together in the word. The two vowels are either *oi, oy, ou,* or *ow*.

1. cow	6. toy
2. brown	7. soil
3. house	8. town
4. Roy	9. mouse
5. out	10. gown

Instructional Suggestions

Digraphs usually are presented before diphthongs because they are easier to learn than diphthongs. Some of the diphthongs can be confusing to children. For example, the *ou* in *house* is a diphthong, but the *ou* in *rough* is a digraph. Also, the *ow* in *know* is a digraph, but the *ow* in *now* is a diphthong.

A good time to teach diphthongs is when children are reading stories or material that have a number of words with diphthongs. The teacher can present these words as vocabulary words and discuss the most common diphthongs.

If children learn the representative sounds of the digraphs and diphthongs, when they meet them in words in context, their chances of being able to pronounce the words or gain an approximation of their pronunciation are good.

Teachers should emphasize to children that good readers use a combination of word recognition strategies rather than just one, and context clues help students determine which pronunciation is correct for the sentence. (More will be said about context in Chapter 13.)

Special Note

Note that in the word *how* the *w* acts as a vowel in the diphthong *ow*. (Even though a diphthong is a *blend* of two vowel sounds, for syllabication purposes you should consider it as one vowel sound.)

Vowel Controlled by r

A vowel followed by *r* in the same syllable is controlled by the *r*. As a result, the preceding vowel does not have its usual vowel sound. Examples are *car, fir, or, hurt, perch*. If a vowel is followed by *r*, but the *r* begins another syllable, the vowel is not influenced by the *r*. Examples: ī · rāte̸, tī · rāde̸.

Tests and practices similar to those for other types of vowel sounds can be developed for words that have the vowel controlled by *r*.

Review of Vowel Generalizations

1. A long vowel is one that sounds like the name of the vowel.
2. A single vowel followed by a consonant in a word (or syllable) usually has a short vowel sound.
3. A single vowel at the end of a word (or syllable) usually has a long vowel sound.
4. A vowel digraph consists of two adjacent vowels with one vowel sound, as in *beat, coat,* and *maid*.
5. In words (or syllables) containing two vowels separated by a consonant, and one vowel is a final *e*, the first vowel is usually long and the final *e* is silent, as in *bāke̸*.
6. A vowel followed by *r* is controlled by the consonant *r*.
7. When *y* is at the end of a word containing no other vowels, the *y* represents the long sound of *i* as in *my, sky*.
8. Diphthongs are blends of vowel sounds beginning with the first and gliding to the second, as in *boy, boil, house*.

Review Exercise

Clues to Vowel Sounds. Here are five clues that will help in determining which vowel sound you would expect to hear in a one-syllable word:

1. A single vowel letter at the beginning or in the middle is a clue to a short vowel sound—as in *hat, let, it, hot,* and *cup*.
2. A single vowel letter at the end of a word is a clue to a long vowel sound—as in *we, by,* and *go*.
3. Two vowel letters together are a clue to a long vowel sound—as in *rain, day, dream, feel,* and *boat*.
4. Two vowel letters separated by a consonant, and one vowel is a final *e*, are a clue to a long vowel sound—as in *age, ice, bone,* and *cube*.
5. A vowel letter followed by *r* in the same syllable is a clue to a

vowel sound that is controlled by the *r*—as in *far*, *bird*, *her*, *horn*, *care*, and *hair*.

In the blank before each word, write the number of the statement in the list that would help you determine the vowel sound in the word.

_____	cut	_____	cute
_____	bean	_____	me
_____	cane	_____	hurt
_____	fine	_____	note
_____	not	_____	coat
_____	pain	_____	my
_____	far	_____	lot
_____	man	_____	seen
_____	say	_____	go
_____	get	_____	cape

Special Note

Generalizations should not be taught unless enough cases warrant their teaching. Research on phoneme-grapheme relationships has been done with enumerated specific rule generalizations and the percentage of time that words followed the rule. Some investigators have claimed that a rule should not be taught unless it holds true at least 75 percent of the time.[8] However, the decision should depend on the words. There are some frequently used words that may conform to a rule pattern, whereas a number of less frequently used words may not conform to the same rule generalization. The percentage of these latter words that conform to a rule pattern may not be as high as 50 percent, even though the most often-used words almost always conform to the same pattern. For example, the "silent (final) *e*" rule, which is usually taught in the early primary grades, only has 63 percent applicability.[9] This 63 percent includes many frequently used words that conform to the same rule pattern. Therefore, the rule should be taught as a phonic generalization.

In addition, other evidence suggests that Clymer's research concerning utility "cannot be calculated accurately with the procedures used by Clymer and others who replicated his study."[10]

---

[8] Theodore Clymer, "The Utility of Phonic Generalizations in the Primary Grades," *The Reading Teacher* 16 (January 1963): 252–58; and Lillie Smith Davis, "The Applicability of Phonic Generalizations to Selected Spelling Programs," *Elementary English* 49 (May 1972): 706–12.

[9] Davis, p. 709.

[10] Patrick Groff, "The Maturing of Phonics Instruction," *The Reading Teacher* 39 (May 1986): 921.

Special Letters and Sounds

Y. As already mentioned, *y* is used both as a consonant and a vowel. When *y* is at the beginning of a word or syllable, it is a consonant. Examples are *yes, yet, young, your, canyon, graveyard.* In the words *canyon* and *graveyard, y* begins the second syllable; therefore it is a consonant.

When *y* acts as a vowel, it represents the short *i* sound, the long *i* sound, or the long *e* sound. *Y* usually represents the short *i* sound when *y* is in the middle of a word or syllable that has no vowel letter. Examples are *hymn, gym, synonym, cymbal. Y* usually represents the long *i* sound when it is at the end of a single-syllable word that has no vowel letter. Examples are *by, try, why, dry, fly. Y* usually represents the long *e* sound when it is at the end of a multisyllabic word. Examples are *baby, candy, daddy, family.*

C and G. Some words beginning wth *c* or *g* can cause problems because the letters *c* and *g* each stand for both a hard and a soft sound. The letter *g* in *gym, George, gentle,* and *generation* stands for a soft *g* sound. A soft *g* sounds like *j* in *Jack, jail,* and *justice.* The initial letter *c* in *cease, center, cent,* and *cite* stands for a soft *c* sound. A soft *c* sounds like *s* in *so, same,* and *sew.* The initial letter *g* in *go, get, game, gone,* and *garden* stands for a hard *g* sound. The initial letter *c* in *cat, came, cook, call,* and *carry* stands for a hard *c* sound. A hard *c* sounds like *k* in *key, king, kite, kettle.* Note that the letter *c* represents a sound that is either like the *s* in *see* or like the *k* in *kitten.*

Q. The letter *q* is always followed by the letter *u* in the English language. The *qu* combination represents either one speech sound or a blend of two sounds. At the beginning of a word, *qu* almost always represents a blend of two sounds, *kw.* Examples are *queen, quilt, quiet, queer, quack.* When *qu* appears at the end of a word in the *que* combination, it represents one sound, *k.* Examples are *unique, antique, clique.*

Schwa
The sound often found in the un-stressed (unac-cented) syllables of words with more than one syllable. The schwa sound is represented by an upside-down e (ə) in the phonetic (speech) alphabet.

The Schwa (ə). The *schwa* sound is symbolized by an upside down *e* (ə) in the phonetic (speech) alphabet. The schwa sound frequently appears in the unstressed (unaccented) syllables of words with more than one syllable. The schwa, which usually sounds like the short *u* in *but,* is represented by a number of different vowels. Examples are b*e*lieve (bə·lēvé′), p*o*lice (pə·lēs′), d*i*vide (də·vīdé′), rob*u*st (rō′·bəst), Rom*a*n (rō′·mən). In the examples the italicized vowels represent the schwa sound. Although the spelling of the unstressed syllable in each word is different, the sound remains the same for the different vowels. (Note: The pronunciations presented here come from *Webster's New Collegiate Dictionary,* but it should not be inferred that these are the only pronunciations for these words. Pronunciations may vary from dictionary to dictionary and from region to region.)

Phonograms

Phonogram
A succession of graphemes that occurs with the same phonetic value in a number of words (*ight, ake, at, et,* and so on); word family.

Phonograms, which are successions of graphemes that occur with the same phonetic value in a number of words, are very helpful in both unlocking and building words.[11] Some examples of phonograms are *an, and, old, et, at, ate, eat, ap, ash, ump, ook, ad, ock, ame, ill, ink,* and so on. All phonograms begin with a vowel, and words that contain the same phonogram rhyme. For example: *bake, cake, rake, lake, take, make, fake,* and so on. (Phonograms may also be referred to as *word families.*)

Children can build many words using phonograms in the following manner:

1. Present children with the following phonograms.
   _____ et _____ an _____ ill _____ old
2. Have the children add different single consonants, consonant digraphs, and blends to the beginning of the phonograms to see how many words they can make.

Children can use phonograms to unlock words in the following manner:

1. The child meets the unfamiliar word *tank.*
2. The child recognizes *ank* as a phonogram he has met in *bank.*
3. The child substitutes *t* for *b.*
4. The child blends *t* and *ank* to get *tank.*

Syllabication—Intermediate Grades

Syllable
A vowel or a group of letters containing one vowel sound, for example, *blo.*

A syllable is a vowel or a group of letters containing one vowel sound. Syllabication of words is the process of breaking known and unknown multisyllabic words into single syllables. This is important in word recognition because in order to be able to pronounce the multisyllabic word, a child must first be able to syllabicate it. Knowledge of syllabication is also helpful in spelling and writing. In attacking multisyllabic words, the pupil must first analyze the word, determine the syllabic units, apply phonic analysis to the syllables, and then blend them into a whole word. For multisyllabic words the result will almost always be an approximation of the pronunciation. As for one-syllable words, the correct pronunciation will depend on the student's having heard the spoken word and whether it makes sense in what is being read. Usually, students will have more success in applying phonics to monosyllabic words than to multisyllabic ones because the blending of the syllables into a whole word often changes the

---

[11] See Adams, pp. 84–85, for researches that are very supportive of this technique.

pronunciation from the syllable by syllable pronunciation. (See "Accenting Words" in this chapter.)

Syllabication Generalizations

Because a multisyllabic word must be syllabicated before applying phonic analysis, syllabication rules will be given first. (The vowel rules that the students have learned since first grade should be reviewed because these same rules will be used in the application of phonic analysis.)

Rule 1: Vowel followed by two consonants and a vowel (vc/cv). If the first vowel in a word is followed by two consonants and a vowel, the word is divided between the two consonants.

Examples: but/ter can/dy com/ment

Rule 2: Vowel followed by a single consonant and a vowel (v/cv). If the first vowel is followed by one consonant and a vowel, the consonant usually goes with the second syllable.

Examples: be/gin ti/ger fe/ver pu/pil

An exception to the v/cv syllabication rule exists. If the letter *x* is between two vowels, the *x* goes with the first vowel rather than with the second one.

Examples: ex/it ex/act ox/en

Rule 3: Vowel or consonant followed by a consonant plus *le* (v/cle) or (vc/cle). If a consonant comes just before *le* in a word of more than one syllable, the consonant goes with *le* to form the last syllable.

Examples: sam/ple can/dle an/kle bun/dle pur/ple daz/zle-bea/gle ca/ble

Rule 4: Compound words. Compound words are divided between the two words.

Examples: girl/friend base/ball

Rule 5: Prefixes and suffixes. Prefixes and suffixes usually stand as whole units.

Examples: re/turn kind/ly

Phonics Applied to Syllabicated Syllables

After the word has been divided into syllables, the student must determine how to pronounce the individual syllables. The pronunciation is determined by whether the syllable is open or closed, and whether it contains a vowel digraph or diphthong.

Open syllable—one that contains one vowel and ends in a vowel. The vowel is usually sounded as long, as in *go*.

Closed syllable—one that contains one vowel and ends in a consonant. The vowel is usually sounded as short, as in mat.

APPLICATION OF VOWEL RULE TO SYLLABICATION RULE 1—DOUBLE CONSONANT RULE (VC/CV). The closed-syllable vowel rule would apply to a syllable that contains one vowel and ends in a consonant. The vowel sound is usually short.

Examples: căn/dy ăs/sĕt

APPLICATION OF VOWEL RULE TO SYLLABICATION RULE 2—VOWEL CONSONANT VOWEL RULE (V/CV). The open-syllable rule would apply to a syllable that contains one vowel and ends in a vowel. The vowel sound is usually long.

Examples: bē/gin tī/ger ō/ver fā/tal dē/tour

APPLICATION OF VOWEL RULE TO SYLLABICATION RULE 3—SPECIAL CONSONANT *LE* RULE (V/CLE) OR (VC/CLE). If the syllable is closed as in the first syllable of *sad/dle* and in the first syllable of *can/dle*, then the vowel sound is usually short in the first syllable, for it ends in a consonant. If the syllable is open as in the first syllable of *fā/ble* and in the first syllable of *bū/gle*, then the vowel sound is usually long in the first syllable, for it ends in a vowel. The letter combinations containing *le*—such as *cle, ble, gle, tle*, and so on—usually stand as the final syllable. The final syllable is not accented; it is always an unstressed syllable containing the schwa sound.

Examples: sīm/pəl fā/bəl săd/dəl ăp/pəl bŭ/gəl

Accenting Words

Accenting is taught in conjunction with syllabication in the intermediate grades. To pronounce words of more than one syllable, pupils should syllabicate the word, apply phonic analysis, and then blend the syllables into one word. To blend the syllables into one word correctly, pupils should know something about accenting and how accents affect vowel sounds. They should know that unaccented syllables are usually softened, and if the syllable of a multisyllable word is an unstressed syllable, it will often contain the schwa sound. (Stressed syllables never contain the schwa sound.) Note: When syllables are blended together, the pronunciation is usually not the same as the syllable-by-syllable pronunciation.

Example: (kĭt) (tĕn) (kĭt′tən); (bē) (lĭēvé) (bə·lĭēvé)

There may be differences between pronunciation of homographs (words that are spelled the same but have different meanings) owing to a difference in accent.

Example: con'duct (noun)   con duct' (verb)

Procedures for Teaching Accenting. A number of two-syllable words are placed on the board and syllabicated:

pi/lot	a/ble	ap/ple	va/cant
den/tist	rea/son	help/ful	bot/tle
sub/due	wi/zard	wis/dom	tai/lor
lo/cal	col/umn	jour/nal	

The teacher explains that even though students are able to syllabicate the individual words and are able to apply the proper phonic analysis, in order to be able to pronounce the words correctly, they still must know something about accenting the words.

Students are asked to listen while the teacher pronounces each word, to determine which syllable is stressed. The teacher then asks individual students to volunteer to pronounce the words and explains that the syllable that is sounded with more stress in a two-syllable word is called the accented syllable. The teacher explains that the accent mark (') is used to show which syllable is stressed, that is, spoken with greater intensity or loudness. This mark usually comes right after and slightly above the accented syllable. (Some dictionaries such as *Webster's Third New International Dictionary* have the accent mark come before the syllable that is stressed.) The teacher further explains that the dictionary has a key to pronunciation of words and that the marks that show how to pronounce words are called *diacritical marks*. The most frequent diacritical marks are the breve (˘) and the macron (¯), which pupils have already met as the symbols for the short and long vowel sounds. The accent (') is also in the class of diacritical marks.

A list of words correctly syllabicated are put on the board:

pi'lot	a'ble	ap'ple	pro'gram
rea'son	help'ful	bot'tle	jour'nal
wis'dom	tai'lor	lo'cal	den'tist

Syllabication and vowel rules are then reviewed. The two-syllable words in the preceding list are all accented on the first syllable. Another group of words in which the second syllable is stressed are then listed:

ap point'	pro ceed'	as tound'
sub due'	pa rade'	po lite'
re ceive'	com plain'	pro vide'

Diacritical marks
Marks that show how to pronounce words.

Students are again asked to listen while each word is pronounced to determine which syllable is being stressed and to see if they notice any similarity among all the second syllables. They should notice that all stressed second syllables have two vowels. From their observations they should be able to state the following generalization: *In two-syllable words the first syllable is usually stressed, except when the second syllable contains two vowels.*

In three-syllable words it is usually the first or second syllable that is accented as in *an' ces tor, cap' i tal, ho ri' zon.*

These skills for decoding words are useful for all children, including those who speak nonstandard English. However, for those speaking nonstandard English or a foreign language, the teacher must be especially certain to utilize the aural-oral approach before attempting to teach reading. (See, for example, sections in Chapter 4.) Obviously, the child must have the words that are to be decoded in both his or her listening and speaking vocabularies in order to make the proper grapheme-phoneme associations.

VOCABULARY EXPANSION

Good vocabulary and good reading go hand in hand. Unless readers know the meanings of words, they will have difficulty understanding what they are reading. It should be stressed that just knowing the meanings of the words will not ensure that individuals will be able to state the meanings of sentences, nor does knowing the meanings of sentences assure that readers can give the meanings of whole paragraphs, and so forth. However, by not knowing the meanings of the words, the individual's chances of being able to read well are considerably lessened. Without an understanding of words, comprehension is impossible.

As children advance in concept development, their vocabulary development must also advance because the two are interrelated (see Chapter 4). Children deficient in vocabulary will usually be deficient in concept development. Studies have shown that "vocabulary is a key variable in reading comprehension and is a major feature of most tests of academic aptitude."[12]

Most teachers are aware of the importance of building sight vocabulary, and word attack skills are a large part of the beginning reading program. However, the development of a larger meaning vocabulary is often neglected.

[12] Walter M. MacGinitie, "Language Development," in *Encyclopedia of Educational Research*, 4th ed. (London: Collier-Macmillan, 1969), p. 693.

Question: When doesn't it pay to increase your vocabulary?

© 1975 by NEA, Inc.

Figure 12.2 A vocabulary riddle.

Answer: When the words you use hurt.

Defining Word Part Terms

Prefix
A letter or a sequence of letters added to the beginning of a root word.

Suffix
A letter or a sequence of letters added to the end of a root word.

Affixes
Prefixes and suffixes.

Root
Smallest unit of a word that can exist and retain its basic meaning.

Derivatives
Combinations of root words with either prefixes or suffixes or both.

In order to help students use word parts for increasing vocabulary, some terms should be defined. There are a great number of words in our language which combine with other words to form new words, for example, *grandfather* and *policeman* (compound words). You may also combine a root (base) word with a letter or a group of letters either at the beginning (prefix) or end (suffix) of the root word to form a new, related word, for example, *replay* and *played*. *Affix* is a term used to refer either to a prefix or a suffix.

In the words *replay* and *played*, *play* is a root or base, *re* is a prefix, and *ed* is a suffix. A *root* is the smallest unit of a word that can exist and retain its basic meaning. It cannot be subdivided any further. *Replay* is not a root word because it can be subdivided to *play*. *Play* is a root word because it cannot be divided further and still retain a meaning related to the root word.

Derivatives are combinations of root words with either prefixes or suffixes or both. *Combining forms* are usually defined as roots borrowed from another language that join together or that join with a prefix, a suffix, or both a prefix and a suffix to form a word. Many times the English combining forms are derived from Greek and Latin roots. In some vocabulary books, in which the major emphasis is on vocabulary expansion rather than on the naming of word parts, a *combining form* is defined in a more general sense to include any word part that can join with another word or word part to form a word or a new word.[13]

[13] Dorothy Rubin, *Vocabulary Expansion*, 2nd ed. (New York: Macmillan, 1991).

The development of vocabulary is too important to the success of a child in school to be left to chance. Teachers should, therefore, provide a planned vocabulary expansion program for children when they first enter school. "Direct vocabulary instruction is generally shown to result in an increase in both word knowledge and reading comprehension."[14]

For a vocabulary program to be successful, the teacher must recognize that individual differences exist between the amount and kinds of words that kindergarten and first-grade children have in their listening vocabulary (ability to understand a word when it is spoken). Some children come to school with a rich and varied vocabulary, whereas others have a more limited and narrow vocabulary. Some children may have a rich and varied vocabulary that can be used with their peers and at home, but it may not be useful to them in school. For example, some children may possess a large lexicon of street vocabulary and expressions, and some others may speak an English dialect that contains its own special expressions and vocabulary.

Teachers should recognize also that young children's listening vocabulary is larger than their speaking vocabulary and obviously larger than their reading and writing vocabulary. All four areas of vocabulary need to be developed. However, since children first learn language through the aural-oral approach, the teacher should begin with these areas first.

Developing Vocabulary from Literature

Reading literature aloud to children is a viable means of increasing vocabulary and reading achievement.[15] (See Chapters 5, 13 and 15.) The teacher should choose books that appeal to children. The authors of these books must be aware of what is important to a child and what is likely to be confusing so that they can build meaning out of words through the kind of imagery that makes sense to a child. For example, in *Mike Mulligan and His Steam Shovel*, the meaning of *steam shovel* is clarified by giving numerous examples in which a steam shovel is used. In Margaret Wise Brown's book *The Dead Bird*, the meaning of *dead* is given by a description of the bird's state.[16]

[14] Adams, p. 29.
[15] Dorothy H. Cohen, "The Effect of Literature on Vocabulary and Reading Achievement," *Elementary English* 45 (February 1968): 209–13, 217.
[16] See Dorothy H. Cohen, "Word Meaning and the Literary Experience in Early Childhood," *Elementary English* 46 (November 1969): 914–25, for a listing of books and examples.

Vocabulary Consciousness

In the primary grades children are beginning to meet words that are spelled the same but have different meanings, based on their context in the sentence. Pupils learn that the word *saw* in "I saw Jennifer" does not carry the same meaning as in "Andrew will help Father saw the tree." When primary-graders recognize that *saw*, *train*, *coat*, and many other words have different meanings based on surrounding words, they are beginning to build a vocabulary consciousness. This consciousness grows when they begin to ask about and look up the meanings of new words they come across in their everyday activities.

Teachers ought to challenge primary-grade children's budding vocabulary consciousness in enjoyable ways. One way to do so is to use word riddles or fun-with-word activities. Examples:

1. From a six-letter word for what you put on bread, remove two letters to get what a goat does with his horns.
2. To a four-letter word for something liquid that falls from the sky, add two letters to make a kind of damage you can do by twisting a part of the body.
3. From a five-letter word for an animal with a shell, take one letter away to make a word for something that holds things together.
4. The plural of an insect, when you add a letter to it, becomes something you wear.

Answers: (1) butter, butt; (2) rain, sprain; (3) snail, nail; (4) ants, pants.

Another way to challenge primary-grade children and to help them to expand their vocabulary is through the learning of word parts. The primary grades are not too soon to begin to help children learn about word parts such as prefixes, suffixes, and roots in order to expand their vocabulary.

The Dictionary as a Tool in Vocabulary Expansion

Although children use picture dictionaries in the primary grades more as an aid to writing than in vocabulary expansion, if young readers discover the wonders of the dictionary they can enrich their vocabulary. Primary-grade picture dictionaries consist of words that are generally in the children's listening, speaking, and reading vocabularies. They consist of alphabetized lists of words with pictures and can serve as the children's first reference tool, helping them to unlock words on their own and making them more independent and self-reliant. The children can also learn multiple meanings from a picture dictionary, when they see the word *saw*, for example, with two pictures which represent a tool and the act of seeing.

Intermediate-Grade Children

As students become more advanced in reading, more words which previously only had one meaning are being met in new and strange situations. (See Chapter 13 for sections on context clues and words with multiple meanings.) In the intermediate grades, students should be guided to a mastery of vocabulary. If they are fascinated with words, they generally want to know the longest word in the dictionary, and many enjoy pronouncing funny or nonsense-sounding words such as *supercalifragilisticexpialidocious*. These students should be helped to

1. Become aware of words they do not know.
2. Try to guess the meaning from the context and their knowledge of word parts.
3. Learn the most used combining forms.
4. Jot down words that they do not know and look them up in the dictionary later.
5. Keep a notebook and write down the words they have missed in their vocabulary exercises, giving them additional study. Learn to break words down into word parts in order to learn their meaning.
6. Maintain interest in wanting to expand vocabulary.

Vocabulary Expansion Instruction

Combining forms Roots borrowed from another language that join together or that join with a prefix, a suffix, or both to form a word.

Vocabulary expansion instruction depends on the ability levels of students, their past experiences, and their interests. If they are curious about sea life and have an aquarium in the classroom, this could stimulate interest in such combining forms as *aqua*, meaning "water," and *mare* meaning "sea." The combining form *aqua* could generate such terms as *aquaplane*, *aqueduct*, and *aquanaut*. Since *mare* means "sea," students could be given the term *aquamarine* to define. Knowing the combining forms *aqua* and *mare*, many will probably respond with "seawater." The English term actually means "bluish-green." The students can be challenged as to why the English definition of aquamarine is bluish-green.

A terrarium can stimulate discussion of words made up of the combining form *terra*.

When discussing the prefix *bi*, children should be encouraged to generate other words that also contain *bi*, such as *bicycle*, *binary*, *bilateral*, and so on.

When presenting the combining forms *cardio*, *tele*, *graph*, and *gram*, place the following vocabulary words on the board:

cardiograph   telegraph
cardiogram   telegram

After students know that *cardio* means "heart" and *tele* means "from a distance," ask them to try to determine the meaning of *graph*, as used in *cardiograph* and *telegraph*. Have them try to figure out the meaning of *gram*, as used in *telegram* and *cardiogram*. Once students are able to define *graph* as an "instrument or machine," and *gram* as "message," they will hardly ever confuse a cardiograph with a cardiogram.

When students are exposed to such activities, they become more sensitive to their language. They come to realize that words are man-made, that language is living and changing, and that as people develop new concepts they need new words to identify them. *Astronaut* and *aquanaut* are good examples of words which came into being because of space and undersea exploration.

Children come to see the power of combining forms when they realize that by knowing a few combining forms they can unlock the meanings of many words. For example, by knowing a few combining forms, students can define correctly many terms used in the metric system, as well as other words.

deca:	ten
deci:	tenth
cent, centi:	hundred, hundredth
milli:	thousand, thousandth
decameter:	ten meters
decimeter:	1/10 meter
centimeter:	1/100 meter
millimeter:	1/1000 meter
decade:	period of ten years
century:	period of one hundred years
centennial:	one-hundredth-year anniversary
millennium:	period of 1,000 years
million:	one thousand thousands

(*Centi, milli, deci* are usually used to designate "part of.")

You should caution your students that many times the literal definitions of the prefixes, suffixes, or combining forms may not be exactly the same as the dictionary meaning. For example, *automobile*.

Here is a sample lesson on combining forms:

PRESENTATION OF COMBINING FORMS: A SAMPLE LESSON

The combining form *bi* is stated and written on the board. The students are challenged to generate any words that they can think of that have this combining form, for example, *bicycle, bimonthly, biweekly*. Since the most common word is *bicycle*, the teacher asks the students if they can figure out the meaning of *bi* from *bicycle*. Someone will probably volunteer *two* because a bicycle is a *two* wheeler. Other words with *bi* are stated and put on the board. For example, *biped*: The teacher says, "We know that *bi* means *two*; let's see if we can figure out what biped means." The teacher states two sentences using biped: *All humans are bipeds. However, all animals are not bipeds.* The teacher asks, "Can anyone guess what *biped* means? Remember, you know what *bi* means." To encourage and help students more, the teacher may then say, "Let me give you another word containing the combining form *ped*. Perhaps that will help you to get the meaning of *biped*." The teacher states and puts *pedestrian* on the board and writes the following sentence on the board: *Motorists must look out for pedestrians.* If the students still need help with the analysis, the teacher may ask the students to state what they do when they ride a bicycle. It is to be hoped that someone will say "pedal." If not, the teacher should suggest "pedal" and write the following sentence on the board: *People pedal hard when they want to go fast.* Students should at this point be able to give the meaning of *ped* as *foot. Biped* should be defined as *two-footed*, and *pedestrian* as *someone who is on foot or a walker.*

The teacher should inform the students again about how helpful combining forms can be in expanding vocabulary.

Vocabulary Expansion Instruction for Students Weak in Vocabulary

Working with upper-elementary-grade students who are especially weak in vocabulary requires a relatively structured approach, one that emphasizes the systematic presentation of material at graduated levels of difficulty in ways somewhat similar to those used in the teaching of English as a second language. Each day, roots, combining forms, prefixes, and suffixes should be presented with a list of words made up from these word parts. Emphasis is placed on the meanings of the word parts and their combinations into words rather than on the naming of the word parts. For example, *auto, bio,* and *graph* are pronounced and put on the chalkboard. Their meanings are given. When *autobiography* is put on the board, the students are asked by the teacher if they can state its meaning.

The terms presented for study should be those which students will hear in school, on television, or on radio, as well as those they will meet in their reading. The word parts should be presented in an interesting manner, and those that combine to form a number of words should be given. When students realize that they are seeing these words in their reading, they will be greatly reinforced in their learning.

To provide continuous reinforcement, daily "nonthreatening" quizzes on the previous days' words may be given. Students should receive the results of such quizzes immediately, so that any faulty concepts may be quickly corrected. The number of words that are presented would depend on individual students.

The possibilities for vocabulary experiences in the classroom are unlimited. Teachers must have the prefixes, suffixes, and combining forms at their fingertips in order to take advantage of the opportunities that present themselves daily. Here is a list of some often used word parts and vocabulary words derived from them:

Prefixes	Combining Forms	Vocabulary Words
a—without	anthropo—man	anthropology, apodal
ante—before	astro—star	astronomy, astrology
arch—main, chief	audio—hearing	audiology, auditory, audition, audible
bi—two	auto—self	automatic, autocracy, binary, biped
cata—down	bene—good	benefit, catalog
circum—around	bio—life	biology, biography, autobiography
hyper—excessive	chrono—time	chronological, hypertension
hypo—under	cosmo—world	microcosm, cosmology
in—not	gamy—marriage	monogamy, bigamy, polygamy
inter—between, among	geo—earth	interdepartmental, geology
mis—wrong, bad	gram—written or drawn	telegram, mistake
mono—one, alone	graph—written or drawn,	telegraph, monarchy
post—after	instrument	
re—backward, again	logo—speak	theology, logical, catalog
trans—across	macro—large	macrocosm
	micro—small	microscope, transatlantic
	mis—hate	misanthrope, misogamist
	poly—many	polyglot
	retro—backward	retrorocket
Suffixes	ped, pod—foot, feet	pseudopod
able—able to	scope—instrument for seeing	microscope
ible—able to	phobia—fear	monophobia
ology—the study of	theo—god	theocracy
tion—the act of	pseudo—false	pseudoscience

The Dictionary as a Tool in Vocabulary Expansion

In the intermediate grades dictionaries serve more varied purposes, and there is emphasis on vocabulary expansion. Children delight in learning new words. If properly encouraged by the teacher, vocabulary expansion can become an exciting hunting expedition, where the unexplored terrain is the vast territory of words.

At any grade level teachers can show by their actions that they value the dictionary as an important tool. If a word seems to need clarification, students should be asked to look it up in the dictionary. Although at times it may seem more expedient simply to supply the meaning, students should be encouraged to look it up for themselves. If the pupil discovers the meaning of the word on his or her own, he or she will be more apt to remember it.

In order to build a larger meaning vocabulary, the teacher could use a number of motivating techniques to stimulate vocabulary expansion. Each pupil can be encouraged to keep a paper bag attached to his or her desk, in which he or she puts index cards with words on one side and the meaning of the word he or she has looked up on the other. Sometime during the day students can be encouraged to challenge one another, with one student calling out the meanings of a word and another student supplying the word. This technique should make the dictionary one of the students' most treasured possessions. (See Chapter 14 for more on the dictionary.)

Vocabulary Expansion in Content Areas

Unless students know word meanings, they will not be able to understand what they are reading. No one will dispute this statement. However, many teachers may not recognize that a student's problem in a content area may be that he or she does not have the prerequisite vocabulary to understand the concepts being presented.

Using word parts to help students expand vocabulary in the content areas is a viable approach (see previous sections). Another approach is to select words directly from students' content areas. Each week the teacher could choose a certain number of words from various books and highlight them as the words of the week. Each word would be pronounced, put into a sentence, and defined. During the week students can use these words to make up word riddles, challenging their classmates for answers. The words would become part of the week's spelling words, and students would be asked to put them into sentences that show the students understand their meaning; or the teacher could present the words in sentences to the students and ask them to define the word as used in the sentence.

Student's Name: _____

Grade: _____

Teacher: _____

Diagnostic Checklist for Word Recognition Skills

	Yes	No

1. The student uses
   a. context clues.
   b. picture clues (graphs, maps, charts).		

2. The student asks someone to state the word.		
3. The student uses the dictionary to try to unlock unknown words.		

Student's Name: _____

Grade: _____

Teacher: _____

Diagnostic Checklist for Word Recognition Skills (Cont.)

	Yes	No

4. The student uses phonic analysis by recognizing
   a. consonants.
      (1) single consonants: initial, final.
      (2) consonant blends (clusters) (*br, sl, cl, st,* and so on).
      (3) consonant digraphs (*th, sh, ph, ch,* and so on).
      (4) silent consonants (kn, gn, pn).

   b. vowels.
      (1) short vowels (*cot, can, get,* and so on).
      (2) long vowels (*go, we, no,* and so on).
      (3) final silent *e* (*bake, tale, role*).
      (4) vowel digraphs (*ea, oa, ee, ai,* and so on).
      (5) diphthongs (*oi, oy*).
   c. the effect of *r* on the preceding vowel.
   d. special letters and sounds (*y, c, g,* and *q*).
   e. known phonograms or graphemic bases (a succession
      of graphemes that occurs with the same phonetic value
      in a number of words [*ight, id, at, ad, ack*]).

5. The student is able to apply the following syllabication rules to words:
   a. vowel consonant/consonant vowel rule (*vc/cv*)
      (*but/ter, can/dy*).
   b. vowel/consonant vowel rule (v/cv) (*na/tive, ca/bin*).
   c. special consonant *le* rule (vc/cle) or (v/cle) (*ca/ble, can/dle*).

6. The student is able to apply phonic analysis to syllabicated words with
   a. an open syllable (*no/ble*).
   b. a closed syllable (*can/dy*).
   c. a vowel digraph (*re/main*).
   d. a diphthong (*foi/ble*).

Student's Name: _____

Grade: _____

Teacher: _____

Diagnostic Checklist for Word Recognition Skills (Cont.)

	Yes	No

7. The student is able to apply the following accent rule to two-syllable words:
   Accent falls on the first syllable except when the second syllable has two vowels (tailor, career).

8. The student is able to use structural analysis to recognize
   a. compound words (*grandmother, caretaker*).
   b. the root or base of a word (*turn, state*).
   c. suffixes (*tion, al, ic, y*).
   d. prefixes (*re, un, non*).
   e. combining forms (*bio, cardio, auto*).
   f. derivatives.
      (1) root plus prefix (*return*).
      (2) root plus suffix (*turned*).
      (3) root plus prefix and suffix (*returned*).

Student's Name:_____

Grade:_____

Teacher:_____

Diagnostic Checklist for Vocabulary Development (Primary Grades)*

	Yes	No

1. The child shows that he or she is developing a vocabulary consciousness by recognizing that some words have more than one meaning.
2. The child uses context clues to figure out word meanings.
3. The child can state the opposite of words such as *stop, tall, fat, long, happy, big.*

* Some of the items on this checklist such as homographs and analogies are discussed in Chapter 13.

Student's Name:_____

Grade:_____

Teacher:_____

Diagnostic Checklist for Vocabulary Development (Primary Grades) (Cont.)

	Yes	No
4. The child can state the synonym of words such as *big, heavy, thin, mean, fast, hit.*		
5. The child can state different meanings for homographs (words that are spelled the same but have different meanings based on their use in a sentence). Examples: I did not *state* what *state* I live in. Do not *roll* the *roll* on the floor. *Train* your dog not to bark when he hears a *train.*		
6. The child is developing a vocabulary of the senses by being able to state words that describe various sounds, smells, sights, tastes, and touches.		
7. The child is expanding his or her vocabulary by combining two words to form compound words such as *grandfather, bedroom, cupcake, backyard, toothpick, buttercup, mailman.*		
8. The child is expanding his or her vocabulary by combining roots of words with prefixes and suffixes. Examples: *return, friendly, unhappy, disagree, dirty, precook, unfriendly.*		
9. The child is able to give the answer to a number of word riddles.		
10. The child is able to make up a number of word riddles.		
11. The child is able to classify various objects such as fruits, animals, colors, pets, and so on.		
12. The child is able to give words that are associated with certain objects and ideas. Example: hospital—*nurse, doctor, beds, sick persons, medicine,* and so on.		
13. The child is able to complete some analogy proportions such as *Happy is to sad as fat is to* _____.		
14. The child shows that he or she is developing a vocabulary consciousness by using the dictionary to look up unknown words.		

Student's Name: _____

Grade: _____

Teacher: _____

Diagnostic Checklist for Vocabulary Development (Intermediate Grades)*

	Yes	No
1. The student recognizes that many words have more than one meaning.		
2. The student uses context clues to figure out the meanings.		
3. The student can given synonyms for words such as *similar, secluded, passive, brief, old, cryptic, anxious.*		
4. The student can give antonyms for words such as *prior, most, less, best, optimist, rash, humble, content.*		

5. The student can state different meanings for homographs (words that are spelled the same but have different meanings based on their use in a sentence), for example:
    It is against the law to *litter* the streets.
    The man was placed on the *litter* in the ambulance.
    My dog gave birth to a *litter* of puppies.		

6. The student is able to use word parts to figure out word meanings.		
7. The student is able to use word parts to build words.		
8. The student is able to complete analogy statements or proportions.		
9. The student is able to give the connotative meaning of a number of words.		
10. The student is able to work with word categories.		
11. The student is able to answer a number of word riddles.		
12. The student is able to make up a number of word riddles.		
13. The student uses the dictionary to find word meanings.		

* Some of the items on this checklist such as homographs and analogies are discussed in Chapter 13.

SUMMARY

The first part of Chapter 12 has presented an analytical look at word recognition skills. Word recognition in this book is looked on as a twofold process that includes both the identification of printed symbols by some method so that the word can be pronounced and the association of meaning to the word after it has been pronounced. The emphasis in the first part of this chapter is on helping you to gain a better understanding of the word recognition process and the skills necessary to teach word recognition skills. After the strategies for word recognition are presented, a sequential development of phonics instruction using a diagnostic and corrective approach is given, as well as information on syllabic word attack skills. The emphasis on the phonics area is warranted because knowledge of phonics helps readers become more self-reliant in decoding words. Also, unless teachers have the word analysis skills at their fingertips, they will not be able to diagnose a student's word recognition problems. You should be cautious, however, to note that phonics is but one part of the reading process and that knowledge of phonics does not mean that the student understands what he or she has read. Phonics should be taught in conjunction with considerable emphasis on connected reading and meaning.

In the vocabulary expansion section of the chapter, it was stressed that good vocabulary and good reading go hand in hand and that children who are deficient in vocabulary development will have difficulty in reading because comprehension is impossible without an understanding of words. Therefore, teachers should have a planned vocabulary program in their classes rather than leaving it to chance. Diagnostic checklists for vocabulary expansion and word recognition skills were presented as additional aids to teachers.

SUGGESTIONS FOR THOUGHT QUESTIONS AND ACTIVITIES

1. You have been appointed to a special primary-grade reading committee. Your task is to help teachers better understand the role that phonics plays in the word recognition process. How would you go about doing this?
2. You have been asked to give a workshop on creative activities that would help correct some students' word recognition problems. What are some activities you would present?
3. The administration in your school district has asked you to develop criterion-referenced tests for specific word recognition skills. What kind of tests would you construct for a primary grade? For an intermediate grade?
4. You have a child in your class who seems to have great difficulty

retaining information. He needs extensive practice in order to overlearn his letters and words. You need to develop some activities that would be fun and that would help this child in a primary grade overlearn his initial consonants. What kind of activities would you develop to help this child?

5. Present a lesson that would help a primary-grade student correct a word recognition problem.
6. Present a lesson that would help you to determine the syllabication skills of an intermediate-grade level student.
7. You are interested in developing a vocabulary expansion program using combining forms. How would you go about doing it? What kinds of activities would you develop for students weak in vocabulary?
8. How important is vocabulary development? Explain.
9. How can you diagnose vocabulary problems in content areas?
10. Construct a pretest to determine whether your intermediate-grade students have knowledge of some often used combining forms.
11. You have been asked to generate a number of diagnostic tests for intermediate-grade students in vocabulary development. What kind of diagnostic tests would you develop?
12. There are a number of children in your first-grade class who are weak in concept development. How would this affect their vocabulary development? What can you do to help them acquire the concepts they need?

SELECTED BIBLIOGRAPHY

Adams, Marilyn Jager. *Beginning to Read: Thinking and Learning About Print.* Cambridge, Mass.: MIT Press, 1990.

Chall, Jeanne S. *Learning to Read: The Great Debate*, 2d ed. New York: McGraw-Hill, 1983.

———. "Two Vocabularies for Reading: Recognition and Reading." *The Nature of Vocabulary Acquisition*, ed. M. G. McKeown and M. E. Curtis, pp. 7–17. Hillsdale, N.J.: Erlbaum, 1987.

Clay, Marie M. "Concepts About Print in English and Other Languages." *The Reading Teacher* 42 (January 1989): 268–75.

Durkin, Dolores. *The Decoding Ability of Elementary School Students.* Reading Education Report No. 49. Champaign, Ill: Center for the Study of Reading, University of Illinois, 1984.

Freebody, Peter, and Brian Byrne. "Word Reading Strategies in Elementary School Children: Relations to Comprehension, Reading Time, and Phonemic Awareness." *Reading Research Quarterly* 23 (Fall 1988): 441–53.

Groff, Patrick, and Dorothy C. Seymour. *Word Recognition: The Why and the How.* Springfield, Ill: Charles C Thomas, 1987.

Maclean, Rod. "Two Paradoxes of Phonics." *The Reading Teacher* 41 (February 1988): 514–17.

Martin Lara, Susan G. "Reading Placement for Code Switchers." *The Reading Teacher* 42 (January 1990): 278–82.

Nagy, William E. *Teaching Vocabulary to Improve Reading.* Urbana, Ill.: National Council of Teachers of English, 1988.

Purcell-Gates, Victoria. "What Oral/Written Language Differences Can Tell Us About Beginning Instruction." *The Reading Teacher* 42 (January 1989): 290–94.

Rubin, Dorothy. *Vocabulary Expansion*, 2nd ed. New York: Macmillan, 1991.

Samuels, S. Jay. "Decoding and Automaticity: Helping Poor Readers Become Automatic at Word Recognition." *The Reading Teacher* 42 (April 1988): 756–60.

Spiegel, Dixie Lee. "Reinforcement in Phonics Materials." *The Reading Teacher* 43 (January 1990): 328–29.

Stanovich, Keith E., ed. *Children's Reading and the Development of Phonological Awareness*. Detroit: Wayne State University Press, 1987.

White, Thomas G., Michael A. Power, and Sheida White. "Morphological Analysis: Implications for Teaching and Understanding Vocabulary Growth." *Reading Research Quarterly* 24 (Summer 1989): 283–304.

13

Reading Comprehension and Literature: An Emphasis on Diagnosis and Correction

INTRODUCTION

> There's no frigate like a book
>   To take us lands away,
> Nor any coursers like a page,
>   Of prancing poetry,
> This traverse may the poorest take
>   Without oppress of toll;
> How frugal is the chariot
>   That bears a human soul!
>
> *Emily Dickinson*

To take a child by the hand and help lead him or her into the exciting world of books is a wonderful thing; to ignite a spark and keep it aglow until it burns with a passion for knowledge that only books can bring is an awesome task. But there are teachers who are doing just that. James Brown is one of these teachers. His task is especially hard because many of his children who are euphemistically called "at-risk" children come to school with dull eyes that look at you and say, "I don't understand." To see these eyes light up, to see these eyes aglow with understanding is indeed what school is all about.

Mr. Brown is well read. He knows about the grim forecasts for his "at-risk" students, and he knows that the number of adults who can't read or write is increasing. He knows we are living in a highly technical society that requires students to be able to read and write at more than a literal level of proficiency. And those who can't may be unemployable.

322

The good news is that the 1990 *Reading Report Card* found that the recent "larger gains made by Black and Hispanic students served to narrow their performance gaps in relation to Whites,"[1] and "the results across the three ages (9, 13, and 17) show tremendous growth in reading comprehension as students move through school."[2] However, the bad news is that there is still a disparity between minority and white students, that the performance overall for white students did not change significantly over the seventeen-year period from 1971 to 1988, and that the gains that were made were at the literal comprehension level. "No gains were evident at the higher levels of reading ability defined by adept and advanced skills and strategies."[3] A major conclusion of the report is that "until our students are exposed through schools, individuals at home, and their own initiative—to more varied and intensive reading experiences, the reading proficiency of American students is unlikely to change dramatically for the better."[4]

James Brown has been doing and is doing a number of things in his classroom to reverse the trend. This chapter will discuss some of these things. It will discuss comprehension and its various levels and present some instructional and questioning strategies to help children reach higher levels of thinking. Also, in a diagnostic-reading and correction program, teachers must be able to diagnose their students' ability to comprehend what they are reading so that they can provide corrective measures for those students who need them. This chapter gives special emphasis to the diagnosis and correction of comprehension skills.

KEY QUESTIONS

After you finish reading this chapter, you should be able to answer the following questions:

1. How is *comprehension* defined?
2. What are the reading comprehension levels presented in this book?
3. What is direct instruction?
4. What are predictable books?
5. What is a literature-based program?
7. What is the Directed Reading-Thinking Activity (DRTA)?
8. What are some practices to help poor readers?
9. How can questioning be used as a diagnostic technique?
10. How can comprehension skills be presented using a diagnostic and corrective approach?

---

[1] Ina V.S. Mullis and Lynn B. Jenkins, *The Reading Report Card, 1971–1988*, The National Assessment of Educational Progress (Princeton, N.J.: Educational Testing Service, 1990), p. 15.
[2] Ibid., p. 35.
[3] Ibid.
[4] Ibid., p. 37.

11. How can teachers help students find the main idea of a paragraph?
12. What is the role of pictures in comprehension?
13. What are "big books"?
14. How can teachers use "big books" with their students?
15. How can literature foster better understanding in a multicultural society?

KEY TERMS IN CHAPTER

You should pay special attention to the following new terms:

analogies
antonym
attitude
big books
categorizing
central idea
comparison
comprehension
context clue
contrast
creative reading
critical reading
Directed Reading-Thinking
   Activity (DRTA)
divergent thinking
example
homographs
inference
interpretation
literal comprehension
literature webbing
main idea
Question Answer Relationships
   (QARs)
reading comprehension
reading taxonomy
repeated reading
schema theory
supporting details
synonyms

READING COMPREHENSION

Comprehension is a construct; that is, it cannot be directly observed or directly measured. We can only infer that someone "understands" from the overt behavior of the person. *Webster's Third New International*

Comprehension
Understanding; the ability to get the meaning of something.

Reading comprehension
A complex intellectual process involving a number of abilities. The two major abilities involve word meanings and reasoning with verbal concepts.

Dictionary defines *comprehension* as "the act or action of grasping (as an act or process) with the intellect," and *intellect* is defined as "the capacity for rational or intelligent thought especially when highly developed." Obviously, the more intelligent an individual is, the more able he or she is to comprehend. What may not be so obvious is that persons who have difficulty understanding may have this difficulty because they have not had certain experiences that require higher levels of thinking; they may not have learned how to do high-level thinking. Such people will have problems in all language arts areas.

Reading comprehension is a complex intellectual process involving a number of abilities. The two major abilities involve word meanings and verbal reasoning. Without word meanings and verbal reasoning, there would be no reading comprehension; and, as stated earlier, without reading comprehension, there would be no reading. Most people would agree with these statements; disagreement, however, exists when we ask, "How does an individual achieve comprehension while reading?" In 1917, Edward Thorndike put forth his statement that "reading is a very elaborate procedure, involving a weighing of each of many elements in a sentence, their organization in the proper relations to one another, and the cooperation of many forces to determine final response.[5] He stated further that even the act of answering simple questions includes all the features characteristic of typical reasoning. Today investigators are still exploring reading comprehension in attempts to understand it better, and through the years many have expounded and expanded upon Thorndike's theories.

For more than a quarter of a century, research into the process of understanding has been influenced by the fields of psycholinguistics and cognitive psychology. As a result, terms such as surface structure, deep structure, microstructure, macrostructure, semantic networks, schemata, story grammar, story structure, and so on have invaded the literature. The studies that have been done are not conclusive; that is, from the studies it is not possible to say that if a reader were to follow certain prescribed rules, he or she would most assuredly have better comprehension.

Although it is difficult to state definitively how persons achieve comprehension while reading, studies seem to suggest that good comprehenders appear to have certain characteristics.[6] Good comprehenders are able to do inferential reasoning; they can state the main or central ideas of information; they can assimilate, categorize,

[5] Edward L. Thorndike, "Reading as Reasoning: A Study of Mistakes in Paragraph Reading," *Journal of Educational Psychology* 8, No. 6 (June 1917): 323.
[6] Barbara M. Taylor, "Children's Memory for Expository Text After Reading," *Reading Research Quarterly* 15:3 (1980): 399–411; B. J. Bartlett, "Top-level Structure as an Organizational Strategy for Recall of Classroom Text," unpublished doctoral dissertation, Arizona State University, 1978; and John P. Richards and Catherine W. Hatcher, "Interspersed Meaningful Learning Questions as Semantic Cues for Poor Comprehenders," *Reading Research Quarterly* 13, No. 4 (1977–1978): 551–52.

compare, make relationships, analyze, synthesize, and evaluate information. Good comprehenders engage in meaningful learning by assimilating new material to concepts already existing in their cognitive structures;[7] that is, good comprehenders relate their new learning to what they already know. Also, good comprehenders are able to think beyond the information given; they are able to come up with new or alternate solutions. In addition, they seem to know what information to attend to and what to ignore. From what has been stated, we can see that those persons who have good strategies for processing information will be able to bring to and gain more from what they are reading or listening to than those who do not have these strategies. (See "Piaget and Concept Development" in Chapter 4 for a discussion of schemata [plural of *schema*].)

Special Note

Schema theory
Deals with relations between prior knowledge and comprehension.

Schema theory deals with the relations between prior knowledge and comprehension. "According to schema theory, the reader's background knowledge serves as scaffolding to aid in encoding information from the text."[8] From this we can see that a person with more background knowledge will comprehend better than one with less and that the preparation of readers for what they will be reading "by actively building topic knowledge prior to reading will facilitate learning from text."[9]

READING COMPREHENSION TAXONOMIES

A number of reading comprehension taxonomies exist, and many appear similar to one another. This similarity is not surprising. Usually the persons who develop a new taxonomy do so because they are unhappy with an existing one for some reason and want to improve upon it. As a result they may change category headings, but keep similar descriptions of the categories, or they may change the order of the hierarchy, and so on. Most of the existing taxonomies are adaptations in one way or another of Bloom's taxonomy of educational objectives in the cognitive domain, which is concerned with the thinking that students should achieve in any discipline. Bloom's taxonomy is based on an ordered set of objectives ranging from the more simplistic skills to the more complex ones. Bloom's objectives are cumulative in that each one includes the one preceding it. And most taxonomies that have been evolved are also cumulative.

Reading taxonomy
A hierarchy of reading comprehension skills ranging from the more simplistic to the more complex ones; a classification of these skills.

In this text an adaptation of Nila Banton Smith's model is used.

---

[7] Richards and Hatcher, p. 552.
[8] Steven Stahl, Michael G. Jacobson, Charlotte E. Davis, and Robin L. Davis, "Prior Knowledge and Difficult Vocabulary in the Comprehension of Unfamiliar Text," *Reading Research Quarterly* 24 (winter 1989): 29.
[9] Ibid., p. 30.

In her original model, she presented literal-level reading skills as requiring no thinking. In the model used in this book, literal-type questions do require thinking, even though it is just a low-level type of thinking. Also, in some other taxonomies, people differentiate between directly stated and implied main ideas and put the directly stated main idea in the category of literal thinking. This is a mistake because it somehow implies that if the main idea is directly stated it is easy to find. This assumption is not true. Finding the main idea of a paragraph is not easy, even if it is directly stated; there is no little red flag next to the main idea to signal that it is the main idea.

Finding the main idea requires more than a low-level type of thinking; it requires making some kind of interpretation. Whenever a student must interpret what he or she is reading, the student is required to do reasoning that goes beyond merely recalling what is in the text.

Categorizing Reading Comprehension

Comprehension involves thinking. As there are various levels in the hierarchy of thinking, so are there various levels of comprehension. Higher levels of comprehension would obviously include higher levels of thinking. The following model adapted from Nila Banton Smith divides the comprehension skills into four categories.[10] Each category is cumulative in building on the others. The four comprehension categories are (1) literal comprehension, (2) interpretation, (3) critical reading, and (4) creative reading.

Literal Comprehension

Literal comprehension
The ability to obtain a low-level type of understanding by using only information that is explicitly stated.

Literal comprehension represents the ability to obtain a low-level type of understanding by using only information explicitly stated. This category requires a lower level of thinking skills than the other three levels. Answers to literal questions simply demand that the pupil recall from memory what the book says.

Although literal-type questions are considered a low-level type of thinking, it should *not* be construed that reading for details to gain facts that are explicitly stated is unimportant in content-area courses. A fund of knowledge is important and necessary; it is the foundation for high-level thinking. If, however, teachers ask only literal-type questions, students will not graduate to higher levels of thinking.

Interpretation

Interpretation is the next step in the hierarchy. This category demands a higher level of thinking because the questions are concerned with answers not directly stated in the text but suggested or

---

[10] Nila Banton Smith, "The Many Faces of Reading Comprehension," *The Reading Teacher* 23 (December 1969): 249–59, 291.

Interpretation
A reading level that demands a higher level of thinking ability because the material it involves is not directly stated in the text but only suggested or implied.

implied. To answer questions at the interpretive level, readers must have problem-solving ability and be able to work at various levels of abstraction. Obviously, children who are slow learners will have difficulty working at this level as well as in the next two categories (see Chapter 15).

The interpretive level is the one at which the most confusion exists when it comes to categorizing skills. The confusion concerns the term *inference*. *Inference* may be defined as something derived by reasoning; something that is not directly stated but suggested in the statement; a logical conclusion that is drawn from statements; a deduction; an induction. From the definitions we can see that inference is a broad reasoning skill and that there are many different kinds of inferences. All the reading skills in interpretation rely on the reader's ability to "infer" the answer in one way or another. However, by grouping all the interpretive reading skills under inference, "Some of the most distinctive and desirable skills would become smothered and obscured."[11]

Some of the reading skills that are usually found in interpretation are as follows:

> determining word meanings from context
> finding main ideas
> "reading between the lines" or drawing inferences[12]
> drawing conclusions
> making generalizations
> recognizing cause and effect reasoning
> recognizing analogies

Critical reading
A high-level reading skill that involves evaluation, making a personal judgment on the accuracy, value, and truthfulness of what is read.

Critical Reading

Critical reading is at a higher level than the other two categories because it involves evaluation, the making of a personal judgment on the accuracy, value, and truthfulness of what is read. To be able to make judgments, a reader must be able to collect, interpret, apply, analyze, and synthesize the information. Critical reading includes such skills as the ability to differentiate between fact and opinion, the ability to differentiate between fantasy and reality, and the ability to discern propaganda techniques. Critical reading is related to critical listening because they both require critical thinking.

Creative reading
Uses divergent thinking skills to go beyond the literal comprehension, interpretation, and critical reading levels.

Creative Reading

Creative reading uses divergent thinking skills to go beyond the literal comprehension, interpretation, and critical reading levels. In creative reading, the reader tries to come up with new or alternate solutions to those presented by the writer.

---

[11] Ibid., pp. 255–56.

[12] Although, as already stated, all the interpretive skills depend on the ability of the reader to infer meanings, the specific skill of "reading between the lines" is the one that teachers usually refer to when they say they are teaching *inference*.

Time spent in reading seems to be an important variable for success in reading, whether it is direct instructional time or time spent reading independently. (See "Time Spent in Reading" in Chapter 2.) However, teachers cannot count on students reading outside school because of the many other enjoyable activities, as well as responsibilities, that compete for students' time and attention. Therefore, teachers must plan for students to have time to read as well as direct instruction in reading.

There are various strategies that can be used with direct instruction; some are less structured than others. Direct instruction requires teachers to present strategies to help their students comprehend the material being read; this is done in addition to asking children questions before, during, and after they read. "Direct instruction in comprehension means explaining the steps in a thought process that gives birth to comprehension."[13] Obviously, teachers must themselves be good problem solvers and thinkers in order to help their students become better comprehenders. The instructional pattern that teachers use to help students gain comprehension will vary based on the concept being learned, the uniqueness of the learners, and the ability of the teacher. The section "Modeling: An Instructional Technique" in "Scenario: Difficulty with Finding the Main Idea", which was presented in Chapter 11, is an example of a technique a teacher can use to teach main idea.

It should come as no surprise that independent reading, reading students do on their own in school or out, is directly related to reading achievement. Teachers must do all they can to encourage children to read both in and out of school.

Teachers can help students become more active consumers of information by providing instruction before, during, and after the reading activity. Before reading, teachers can prepare the students for the reading activity by doing some of the following: previewing the reading selection, going over the new vocabulary or difficult words, teaching any needed strategies that students will need to read the material, as well as actively building topic knowledge.

Teachers can give students a number of questions to think about as they read or they can encourage their students to ask questions about the text material. Teachers can challenge their students to act as investigative reporters while they are reading.

After reading, students can answer their own questions or the teacher's questions, state the main idea of the selection, summarize it, discuss their feelings toward the material, or discuss how they would rewrite or change the material.

---

[13] Richard C. Anderson, et al., *Becoming a Nation of Readers: The Report of the Commission on Reading* (Washington, D.C.: National Institute of Education, 1985), p. 72.

Figure 13.1 This teacher is having children make predictions about the book she will be reading.

The Directed Reading-Thinking Activity

The basal reader series in the 1980s began to revise the kinds of reading matter they include in their readers, as well as their approach. They began to include more literature-based material and whole pieces of literature to try to appease their critics and also started to present more questions before, during, and after silent and oral reading that require higher-level thinking. In addition, their Directed or Guided Reading Approach appears to be modeled more on the Directed Reading-Thinking Activity advocated by Russell Stauffer, whereby teachers encourage students to make predictions about what they read. This is good news.

Directed Reading-Thinking Activity (DRTA)
Requires teachers to nurture the inquiry process and students to be active participants and questioners; includes prediction and verification.

The Directed Reading-Thinking Activity (DRTA) can be an especially effective approach in the hands of good teachers, whether they use a basal reader series or have a completely literature-based program. (In literature-based programs trade books are used in the reading groups as well as for independent reading.)

DRTA requires that students be active participants. "The reading-thinking process must begin in the mind of the reader. He must raise the questions and to him belongs the challenge and the responsibility of a judgment. The teacher keeps the process active and changes the amount of data to be processed."[14] Here is an outline of the process:[15]

[14] Russell G. Stauffer, *Directing the Reading-Thinking Process* (New York: Harper & Row, 1975), p. 37.
[15] Ibid.

I. Pupil actions
   A. Predict (set purposes)
   B. Read (process ideas)
   C. Prove (test answers)
II. Teacher actions
   A. What do you think? (activate thought)
   B. Why do you think so? (agitate thought)
   C. Prove it. (require evidence)

The DRTA is not as teacher-directed as the DRA used by basal reader series, and even though there are a number of sequential steps in the DRTA, they are not as delineated as in a basal reader series. The DRTA requires teachers who know how to encourage students to ask questions that stimulate higher-level thinking; it requires teachers who are masters in nurturing the inquiry process.

Modeling (Thinking Out Loud) Strategy

Many good teachers have probably used this approach, but may not have been aware of it. Often when a teacher has students who have difficulty understanding something that is being explained, the teacher may "model" the skill for the children. That is, the teacher "thinks aloud" or verbalizes his or her thoughts to give the students insight into the process. The teacher literally states out loud exactly the steps that he or she goes through to solve the problem or gain an understanding of a concept. Many basal reader series are including modeling as part of their instructional plans. (A number of the scenarios presented in this book include modeling strategies. See "Scenario: A Sample Modeling Lesson" in Chapter 2, "Scenario: Difficulty with Finding the Main Idea" in Chapter 11, and "Scenario: Modeling the SQ3R Approach for Students in an Intermediate-Grade-Level Class" in Chapter 14.)

Repeated Reading

Repeated reading
Similar to paired reading; child reads along (assisted reading with model or tape) until he or she gains confidence to read alone.

Repeated reading is a technique that is gaining favor among a number of teachers to help students who have poor oral reading to achieve fluency in reading. A suggested procedure for repeated readings follows:[16]

Passage length: Short; about 50 to 100 words

Types of passages: Any reading materials that will be of interest to the child

Readability level of passage: Start at independent level; proceed to more difficult passages as child gains confidence in oral reading; controlled vocabulary is not imperative.

---

[16] Adapted from Sarah L. Dowhower, "Repeated Reading: Research into Practice, "*The Reading Teacher* 42 (March 1989): 504–506.

Assisted reading: Use the read-along approach (assisted reading with a model or tape) to help with phrasing and speed; use when speed is below 45 words per minute (WPM), even though child makes few errors.

Unassisted reading: Use when child reaches 60 WPM.

Literature Webbing with Predictable Books in the Early Grades

Success breeds success! If children have good experiences in reading at an early age, these experiences will help instill good attitudes about reading in the children. Predictable books appear to be one way to provide these.[17] (See the section "Attitudes and Reading" in this chapter.) Literature webbing is a story map or graphic illustration that teachers can use as one approach to guide them in using predictable trade books with their children.

Literature webbing
A story map technique to help guide children in using predictable trade books.

The literature webbing strategy lesson (LWSL), which is an adaptation by Reutzel and Fawson of Watson and Crowley's Story Schema Lessons to "provide support for early readers,"[18] includes a six-step process. The preliminary preparation includes the teacher's reading of the text and excerpting a number of samples from it that are large enough so that children can make predictions about them. (The excerpts may be accompanied by enlarged illustrations if this procedure is used early in the year.) After the excerpts are chosen, the title of the book is placed in the center of the board with various web strands projecting from the title. (There are three more strands than needed for the number of excerpts. These strands, which are used for discussion purposes, are personal responses to the book, other books we've read like this one, and langugae extension activities.) Then the children follow these six steps:[19]

1. Sample the book by reading the randomly ordered illustrations and text excerpts that are placed on the chalk tray below the literature web.
2. Predict the pattern or order of the book by placing the excerpts in clockwise order around the literature web.
3. Read the predictable book straight through. (It may be a big book or a number of copies of the normal-sized text.)
4. Confirm or correct their predictions.
5. Discuss the remaining three strands that are on the board for discussion purposes.
6. Participate in independent or supported reading activities.

[17] D. Ray Reutzel and Parker C. Fawson, "Using a Literature Webbing Strategy Lesson with Predictable Books," *The Reading Teacher* 43 (December 1989): 208.

[18] Ibid., p. 209.

[19] Ibid.

What Is the Role of Pictures in Comprehension?

Educators have debated the "picture question" for a long time; however, there is very little research in this area. According to the studies that exist, the effect seems to be that pictures neither hurt nor help comprehension of text material.[20]

Some educators have stated that the pictures detract from the text material; however, "the research provides no arguments against the presence of text-compatible illustrations."[21] On the other hand, illustrations help to make books more attractive and instill positive attitudes toward them. Certainly, pictures are of prime importance in young children's books. It seems reasonable that "parent-child discussions of pictures are key to the appreciation of language and literature that grows from picture book reading."[22] (See Chapter 16.)

Figure 13.2 This child loves to "read" picture stories to his teacher.

HELPING CHILDREN ACQUIRE COMPREHENSION SKILLS: AN EMPHASIS ON QUESTIONING STRATEGIES

All children need help in developing higher-level reading comprehension skills. If teachers persist in asking only literal comprehension

[20] Marilyn Jager Adams, *Beginning to Read: Thinking and Learning about Print—A Summary* by Steven A. Stahl, Jean Osborn, and Fran Lehr (Urbana, Ill.: Center for the Study of Reading, 1990), p. 68.

[21] Ibid.

[22] Ibid., p. 69.

questions that demand a simple convergent answer, higher-level skills will not be developed.

Unfortunately, much of what goes on in school is at the literal comprehension level. Teachers usually ask questions that require a literal response, and children who answer this type of question are generally seen as being excellent students. It is to be hoped that this perception will change now that many reading task forces across the country are emphasizing the teaching of higher-level comprehension skills.

The kinds of questions the teacher asks will determine the kinds of answers he or she will receive. Rather than asking a question that would call for a literal response, the teacher must learn to construct questions that call for higher levels of thinking. This process should begin as early as kindergarten and first grade. For example, the children are looking at a picture in which a few children are dressed in hats, snow pants, jackets, scarves, and so on. After asking the children what kind of clothes the children in the picture are wearing, the teacher should try to elicit from his or her students the answers to the following questions: "What kind of day do you think it is?" "What do you think the children are going to do?"

This type of inference question is at a very simple level because it is geared to the readiness and cognitive development level of the children. As the children progress to higher levels of thinking they should be confronted with more complex interpretation or inference problems. It is important that the teacher work with the children according to their individual readiness levels. The teacher should expect all the children to be able to perform, but he or she should avoid putting them in situations which frustrate rather than stimulate them.

Critical reading skills are essential for good readers. Teachers can use primary-graders' love of folktales to begin to develop some critical reading skills. For example, after the children have read "The Little Red Hen," the teacher can ask such questions as the following:

1. Should the Little Red Hen have shared the bread with the other animals? Explain.
2. Would you have shared the bread with the other animals? Explain.
3. Do you think animals can talk?
4. Do you feel sorry for the other animals? Explain.
5. Do you think this story is true? Explain.

Divergent thinking
The many different ways to solve problems or to look at things.

Creative reading questions are probably the most ignored by teachers. To help children in this area, teachers need to learn how to ask questions that require divergent rather than convergent answers. A teacher who focuses only on the author's meaning or intent and does not go beyond the text will not be encouraging creative reading. Some questions which should stimulate divergent thinking on the part of the reader would be the following:

1. After reading "The Little Red Hen," try to come up with another ending for the story.
2. Try to add another animal to the story of "The Little Red Hen."
3. Try to add another part to the story of "The Little Red Hen."

Divergent answers, of course, require more time than convergent answers. Also, there is no one correct answer.

Following are a short reading selection and examples of the four different types of comprehension questions. These are being presented so that the teacher can have practice in recognizing the different types of questions at the four levels.

> One day in the summer, some of my friends and I decided to go on an overnight hiking trip. We all started out fresh and full of energy. About helfway to our destination, when the sun was almost directly overhead, one-third of my friends decided to return home. The remaining four of us, however, continued on our hike. Our plan was to reach our destination by sunset. About six hours later as the four of us, exhausted and famished, were slowly edging ourselves in the direction of the setting sun, we saw a sight that astonished us. There, at the camping site, were our friends who had claimed that they were returning home. It seems that they did indeed go home, but only to pick up a car and drive out to the campsite.

The following are the four different types of comprehension questions:

> *Literal comprehension:* What season of the year was it in the story? What kind of trip were the people going on?
> *Interpretation:* What time of day was it when some of the people decided to return home? How many persons were there when they first started out on the trip? In what direction were the hikers heading when they saw a sight that astonished them? At what time did the sun set?
> *Critical reading:* How do you think the hikers felt when they reached their destination? Do you feel that the persons who went home did the right thing by driving back to the site rather than hiking? Explain.
> *Creative reading:* What do you think the exhausted hikers did and said when they saw the two who had supposedly gone home?

Metacognition and Questioning

Question Answer Relationships (QARs)
Helps students distinguish between "what they have in their heads" and information that is in the text.

The more children understand what they do when they are in the act of answering questions, the better question solvers they can be. Raphael has designed an instructional strategy, Question Answer Relationships (QARs), that teachers can use to help their students gain insights into how they go about reading text and answering questions. It helps students "realize the need to consider both information in the text and information from their own knowledge background."[23]

In the QAR technique students learn to distinguish between information that "they have in their heads" and information that is

---

[23] Taffy E. Raphael, "Teaching Question Answer Relationships, Revisited," *The Reading Teacher* 39 (February 1986): 517.

in the text. The steps that can help children gain facility in QAR are presented in the following paragraphs. Note that the amount of time children spend in the steps is determined by the individual differences of the students.

Step 1. Students gain help in understanding differences between what is in their heads and what is in the text. The children are asked to read a passage, and the teacher asks questions that guide them to gain the needed understandings. Here is a short sample:

Mike and his father went to the ball game.
They were lucky to get tickets for the game.
They saw many people they knew.
At the game Mike and his father ate hot dogs.
They also drank soda.

The students are then asked the following questions:

1. Where did Mike and his father go? (To the ball game)
2. Where did they see the people? (At the ball game)

The children are helped to see that the first answer is directly stated; whereas the second is not; it is "in their heads."

Step 2. The "In the Book" category is divided into two parts. The first deals with information that is directly stated in a single sentence in the passage, and the second deals with the piecing together of the answer from different parts of the passage. (Raphael calls this step "Think and Search" or "Putting it Together.")[24]

The children are then given practice in doing this.

Step 3. This would be similar to Step 2 except that now the "In My Head" category is divided into two parts. They are "Author and You" and "On My Own."[25] The teacher helps students recognize whether the question is text-dependent or independent. For example, the answer to the first question would require the student to read the text to be able to answer it, even though the answer would come from the student's background of experiences. However, the student can answer the second without reading the passage.

1. How else do you think the cat could have escaped?
2. How would you feel if you were lost?

The QAR approach can be very useful in introducing children to inferential reasoning; it helps children understand better what information is directly stated and what is implied. Teachers can modify the QAR approach to suit their students' needs.

[24] Ibid., p. 518.
[25] Ibid.

Questioning as a Diagnostic Technique

Asking questions is not only an important part of teaching and learning; it is also very useful in diagnosis. Teachers' questions, which can stimulate students to either low- or high-level thinking, give teachers an insight into students' ability to comprehend information. Teachers can learn from their questions whether students need help, whether they are able to see relationships and make comparisons, and whether what the students are reading or listening to is too difficult or too easy.

Students' questions are important in helping students to learn, and they are essential diagnostic aids in giving teachers feedback on students' ability to understand information. In order to ask good questions, students must know their material. As result, those students who ask the best questions usually are those who know the material best. Confusing questions are a signal that the teacher needs to slow down or reteach certain material.

Teachers can use questioning as a diagnostic technique to learn about their students' thinking ability. Here are some examples.

The teacher has the children read a short story. The story is about a little boy who wants to go to school, but he can't because he is too young. The teacher tells the children that she is going to make up some questions about the story, and the children have to tell her whether the questions that she makes up are able to be answered or not. If a question is able to be answered, the student should answer it; if a question is not able to be answered, the student must tell why. The teacher makes up the following questions:

1. What are the names of Ben's sister and brother who go to school?
2. Why does Ben want to go to school?
3. Make up an adventure for Ben.
4. Why can't Ben go to school?
5. What are the names of the bus driver's children?
6. What does Ben do in the summer?

This technique can help the teacher learn which children are able to concentrate, as well as which children are able to do different kinds of thinking. Questions 1 and 4 are literal questions; question 2 is an inferential question; question 3 is a creative question; and questions 5 and 6 are not able to be answered because no such information was given in the story either directly or indirectly.

A more difficult questioning technique that the teacher could use with highly able children is to have them make up questions for a selection that they have read.

After students have read a selection, the teacher can ask them to make up three different questions. The first question should be one for which the information is directly stated in the passage. The second question should be one for which the answer is not directly stated in the passage. The third question should be one that requires an answer that goes beyond the text.

In early primary grades the teacher can use pictures as the stimuli for questions, or the teacher can relate a short story to the children and have them devise questions for it.

Here are some questions that a group of fourth-grade children made up after reading a story about Melissa and her friend Fred, who were always getting into trouble.

1. Who is Melissa's best friend? (literal)
2. What is the main idea of the story? (inferential)
3. From the story what can we infer about the main character's personality? (inferential)
4. Relate an episode that you think Melissa could get into. (creative)

The children who made up the questions challenged their classmates with their questions and then they were responsible for determining whether their classmates had answered them correctly. (See "Asking Questions" in Chapter 14.)

SOME IMPORTANT COMPREHENSION SKILLS: A DIAGNOSTIC AND CORRECTIVE APPROACH

This section presents some comprehension skills that need special emphasis. Because this book emphasizes a diagnostic-reading and correction program, the interpretive reading skills will be presented using a diagnostic and corrective approach for both primary- and intermediate-grade children. Even though only some interpretive level skills have been chosen to demonstrate this approach, you can, of course, use it with literal, critical, and creative reading skills.

Context Clues

Unless teachers can help students learn that words have multiple meanings and help them determine the correct meanings from sentence context, students will have great difficulty in reading. Because context clues are a vital aid in comprehension and there is such ambiguity in the English language, we will begin with context clues and homographs. We will then proceed to main idea and other interpretive comprehension skills.

Context Clues (Definition, Explanation, and Description)

There are times when you can get the meaning of a word from context clues. By *context* we mean the words surrounding a word that can shed light on its meaning.

If the writer wants to make sure that you get the meaning of a word, he or she will define, explain, or describe the word in the sentence. The context clue in the form of definition, description, or explanation is the specific item of information that helps the reader to figure out the meaning of a particular word. For example, the word *context* has been defined because it is a key word in this section. The definition is the context clue. In the following examples the writer actually gives you the definition of a word. (Sentences such as these are generally found in textbooks or technical journals.)

Context clue
An item of information from the surrounding words of a particular word in the form of a synonym, antonym, example, definition, description, explanation, and so on, that helps shed light on the particular word.

Examples

1. An *axis* is a straight line, real or imaginary, that passes through the center of rotation in a revolving body at a right angle to the plane of rotation.
2. In geometry, a plane figure of six sides and six angles is called a *hexagon*.

Notice how the writer in the next example explains the meaning of the word by using a synonym. (A synonym is a word that has a similar meaning to another. Notice also how this makes his writing more expressive and clear and avoids repetition.)

Example

Although Senator Smith is *candid* about his drinking problem, he is less *frank* about his investments.

In the next examples, notice how the writers *describe* the words that they want you to know.

Examples

1. Although my *diligent* friend works from morning to night, he never complains.
2. Interior paints no longer contain *toxic* materials that might endanger the health of infants and small children.
3. The *cryptic* message—which looks as mysterious and secretive as it is—is difficult to decode.

Special Notes

The word *or* may be used by the writer when he uses another word or words with a similar meaning. Example: John said that he felt ill after having eaten *rancid* or *spoiled* butter.

The words *that is* and its abbreviation *i.e.* usually signal that an explanation will follow. Example: A human is a biped, that is, an animal having only two feet, or A human is a biped, i.e., an animal having only two feet.

Context Clues (Example and Comparison/Contrast)

Example
Something representative of a whole or a group.

Many times an author helps you get the meaning of a word by giving you examples illustrating the use of the word. In the following sentence notice how the examples that the writer gives in his sentence help you determine the meaning of the word *illuminated*.

Example

The lantern *illuminated* the cave so well that we were able to see the crystal formations and even spiders crawling on the rocks.

(From the sentence you can determine that *illuminated* means "lit up.")

Comparison
A demonstration of the similarities between persons, ideas, things, and so on.

Another technique writers employ that can help you gain the meaning of a word is *comparison*. Comparison usually shows the similarities between persons, ideas, things, and so on. For example, in the following sentence notice how you can determine the meaning of *passive* through the writer's comparison of Paul to a bear in winter.

Example

Paul is as *passive* as a bear sleeping away the winter.

(From the sentence you can determine that *passive* means "inactive.")

Contrast
A demonstration of the differences between persons, ideas, things, and so on.

Contrast is another method writers use that can help you to figure out word meanings. Contrast is usually used to show the differences between persons, ideas, things, and so on. In the following sentence you can determine the meaning of *optimist* because you know that *optimist* is somehow the opposite of "*one who is gloomy or one who expects the worst.*"

Examples

1. My sister Marie is an *optimist*, but her boyfriend is one who is always gloomy and expects the worst to happen.

(From the sentence you can determine that *optimist* means "one who expects the best" or "one who is cheerful.")

2. Frank, who is of average intelligence, appears slow in contrast to his *brilliant* cousin.

(From the sentence you can figure out that *brilliant* must mean "very smart" or "highly intelligent.")

Special Notes

The writer may use the words *for example* or the abbreviation *e.g.* to signal that examples are to follow. Example: *Condiments*, e.g., pepper, salt, and mustard, make food taste better. (From the examples of condiments you can determine that condiments are seasonings.)

An example is something that is representative of a whole or a group. It can be a particular single item, incident, fact, or situation that typifies the whole.

Many times such words as *but, yet, although, however,* and *rather than* signal that a contrast is being used. Example: My father thought he owned an authentic antique chest, but he was told recently that it was a fake. (From the sentence you can tell that authentic is the opposite of fake; therefore, authentic means "not false but genuine or real.")

Context Clues (Synonyms and Antonyms)

Often a word can be defined by another, more familiar word having basically the same meaning. For, example, *void* is defined as *empty* and *corpulent* is defined as *fat. Void* and *empty,* and *corpulent* and *fat* are synonyms. Synonyms are different words that have the same or nearly the same meaning. Writers use synonyms to make their writing clearer and more expressive. Read the three sample sets of sentences. Don't you agree that the second sentence in each set is more descriptive than the first?

Examples

    a. (1) The frightened child *looked* at the man.
       (2) The frightened child *peered* at the man.
    b. (1) We *walked* through the park.
       (2) We *strolled* through the park.
    c. (1) The *noise* brought the police to the scene.
       (2) The *uproar* brought the police to the scene.

Antonyms are words opposite in meaning to each other. Examples: tall—short; fat—thin; least—most; worst—best.

Earlier you learned that when a writer uses contrast in a sentence you can often figure out word meanings from the context. Antonyms, which are used to show contrast, help to make sentences clearer and more informative.

Examples

    a. My biology professor gives *succinct* lectures, but his assistant is *verbose.*
    b. My math professor claims that all the problems she gives us are *simple* ones, but we feel that they are *intricate* and hard to solve.

Context Clues (Words with Multiple Meanings [Homographs])

Many words that are spelled the same have different meanings. These words are called *homographs.* The meaning of a homograph is determined by the way the word is used in the sentence. For example, the term *run* has many different meanings. (One dictionary gives 134 meanings for *run.*) In the listed sentences notice how *run's* placement in the sentence and the surrounding words help you to figure out the meaning of each use.

Examples

    1. Walk, don't <u>run</u>.
    2. I have a <u>run</u> in my stocking.
    3. Senator Jones said that he would not <u>run</u> for another term.

4. The trucker finished his <u>run</u> to Detroit.
5. She is going to <u>run</u> in a ten-mile race.
6. The play had a <u>run</u> of two years.

In sentence 1 *run* means "go quickly by moving the legs more rapidly
than at a walk."
In sentence 2 *run* means "a tear or to cause stiches to unravel."
In sentence 3 *run* means "be or campaign as a candidate for election."
In sentence 4 *run* means "route."
In sentence 5 *run* means "take part in a race."
In sentence 6 *run* means "continuous course of performances."

© 1978 United Feature Syndicate, Inc.

Figure 13.3 Sally hasn't learned yet that many words have more than one
meaning.

Special Notes

Some homographs are spelled the same but do not sound the same.
For example, *refuse* means "trash"; *refuse* means "to decline to accept."
In sentence 1 in the examples below *refuse* (ref'use) meaning "trash"
is pronounced differently from the term *refuse* (re fuse') meaning
"to decline to accept" in sentence 2. In reading, you can determine
the meaning of *refuse* from the way it is used in the sentence (context
clues).

1. During the garbage strike there were tons of uncollected *refuse* on the
   streets of the city.
2. I *refuse* to go along with you in that project because it seems unethical
   to me.

Do not confuse *homonym* or *homophone* (terms to describe words
that sound alike but have different spellings and meanings) with
homograph. Here are some examples of homonyms or homophones:

pear—pare; to—two—too;
way—weigh; fare—fair;
tow—toe; plain—plane

SKILL: CONTEXT CLUES

Diagnostic Analysis

Objective: The students will use context clues to choose the word that best fits the sentence.

Test

> **Directions: Read each sentence carefully. Use context clues to help you choose the word that *best* fits the sentence. Put the word in the blank. A word may be used only once. All words are used as answers.**

Word List: rose, point, suit, box, play

1. That was a good _____ she made in the game.

2. The batter stood in the batting _____.

3. We _____ late yesterday.

4. That color does not _____ you.

5. What is the _____ of the story?

> Answers: 1. play 2. box 3. rose 4. suit 5. point
> Tell students the results.

Instructional Suggestions

Here are some techniques and instructional materials to help students recognize how context clues can help them figure out word meanings.

1. Present the following sentence to your students, which should have an unfamiliar word in it.

Mary is usually a prudent person.

Ask them if they can give you the meaning of *prudent*. If not, ask them what would help. Then present this sentence.

However, yesterday she was very foolish.

Now ask them if they can figure out the meaning of *prudent*. Elicit from the children how the second sentence gave them a clue to the word *prudent*. From the second sentence, they should have realized that prudent must mean "wise," the opposite of *foolish*.

2. Put the following sentences on the chalkboard, and have the students use the context clues to help them figure out the meanings of each underlined word. Tell them that sometimes the clue to help them figure out the word meaning is in the next sentence. Go over each sentence with the students.

1. My kitten is very tame. She will not hurt anyone. _____

2. Everyone seems to know her. She must be a famous writer. _____

3. That is such an enormous ice-cream cone. You will have to get lots of people to help you eat some of it. _____

4. That street is so broad that we can all walk side by side. _____

5. The lion is a fierce animal. _____

Here are some instructional techniques and materials you can use with your students to help them recognize that words can have more than one meaning.

1. Hold up two pictures. The first picture is that of a train, and the second picture shows a boy trying to train his dog. Ask the children what the two pictures have in common. Try to get them to make up sentences about what is taking place. Write the sentences about the two pictures on the board. Try to get them to use the word *train* for both pictures.

2. Hold up a number of pictures that depict the words *slip, root,* and *bark* in more than one way. Try to get the children to recognize that each set of pictures is different, but that the word telling what each picture in the set is about is the same. You can tell the students that words with more than one meaning are usually called *homographs.*

3. Put the following sentences on the chalkboard and have the students fill in the blanks with one word that fits all the blanks in each sentence. Go over the sentences with the children.

1. I _____ my father _____ the tree in the woods. (saw)

2. In the _____ our flowers look very pretty near our _____. (spring)

3. My mother says that I _____ help her _____ some vegetables from her garden. (can)

4. Don't you _____ when you change a flat _____? (tire)

5. After we drank water from the _____, we did not feel _____. (well)

4. Challenge the children with riddles such as the following: I can make things brighter, I do not weigh a lot; and I'm the opposite of dark. What am I? Hint: One word fits all three things.

5. Ask the children to use their dictionaries to try to make up riddles to challenge their classmates.

SKILL: CONTEXT CLUES

Diagnostic Analysis

Objective: The students will use context clues to choose a word that makes sense in each sentence.

Test

Directions: Read each sentence carefully. Use context clues to help you choose the word that *best* fits the sentence. A word may only be used once. (More words are given in the word list than you need.) Insert the word in the blank.

Word List: buy, browse, pine, economy, suit, take, play, box, bore, pinch, coat, blade, post, rose, idle, work, iron, spectacles, posture, run, flowed, clothing, happy, fast, sell, dress

1. Good looks _____ in her family.

2. At the stadium the crowd _____ through the gate.

3. The soldier remained at his _____ all day.

4. At the library, I usually _____ through lots of books.

5. They said that they would try to _____ out their difficulties.

6. The children _____ for their dog who is missing.

7. During holidays, I usually feel the money _____.

8. Unless my mother wears her _____, she has difficulty seeing.

9. The senators surveyed the _____ of foreign affairs.

10. It is not good to allow your car motor to _____.

Answers: 1. run 2. flowed 3. post 4. browse 5. iron 6. pine 7. pinch 8. spectacles
9. posture 10. idle
Tell students the results.

Instructional Suggestions

Here are some instructional materials and techniques to use with your students.

1. Present your students with the following sentence that has an unfamiliar word.

Jim behaved in a very *rash* manner.

Ask your students why this sentence does not help them figure out the meaning of *rash*. Then present them with this sentence:

He rushed in too quickly and almost lost his life.

Now ask them to try to determine the meaning of *rash*. From the second sentence, they should recognize that *rash* refers to something that is done quickly and not very carefully.

2. Give them a sentence that uses comparison and ask them to see if they can figure out the meaning of an unfamiliar word.

Fred is as *obstinate* as a mule.

Ask the students to give you the meaning of *obstinate*. Since a mule is an animal that is considered stubborn, your students should get an idea of *obstinate* as meaning "stubborn."

Here are some techniques and instructional materials you can use to help students recognize that words can have more than one meaning.

1. Present students with a number of phrases. Tell them that the same word can fit in each set of phrases. The meaning of the word changes based on the words surrounding it (context). For example: a *brush* with the law; *brush* your teeth; a *brush* for your hair.

2. State a word such as *run*. Present sentences to your students and ask them to give the meaning of *run* in each sentence. Have them note that the meaning is different for each. Have them look up *run* in the dictionary. Have them write four other sentences using *run* in different ways.

3. Put the following sentences on the chalkboard and have the students fill in the blanks with one word that fits all the blanks in each sentence. Go over the sentences with the students.

1. My mind goes ———————— every time I have to fill in any ————————. (blank)

2. In England, I paid two ———————— for a book to help me shed some ————————. (pounds)

3. The lawyer knew that he had won his ———————— when he produced the ———————— containing the murder weapon. (case)

4. A certain ———————— of dogs is easier to ———————— than others. (breed)

5. Part of the ———————— was to ———————— a course that no one could follow after we hid the jewels in the chosen cemetery————————. (plot)

Main Idea of a Paragraph

The main idea is probably the skill with which teachers and students spend the most time; this is good. It is, however, a skill that seems to cause a great amount of difficulty for students. Students especially find the construction or inventing of the main idea more difficult than selecting the main idea; that is, students have more difficulty coming up with the main idea themselves than choosing one from a given list. In fact, the main idea construction process is much more difficult.[26] Even if the main idea is directly stated, this process is a difficult one. (See "Reading Comprehension Taxonomies" earlier in this chapter.)

Because of the difficulty of the main idea construction task, sufficient time must be allotted to provide the needed "think time." In addition, research has demonstrated "that if readers' prior knowledge for the text topic is not sufficient, the difficulty of main idea construction is compounded."[27]

Confusion in finding the main idea may exist because it seems to mean different things to different people. One researcher investigating the literature found that "educators have increasingly given attention to main idea comprehension, but with no concomitant increase in the clarity of what is meant by main or important ideas. The exact nature of main ideas and the teaching practices intended to help students grasp main ideas vary considerably."[28]

Even though the concept of main idea is nebulous to some researchers and the "notion that different readers can (and should) construct identical main ideas for the same text has been questioned,"[29] the teaching of main idea is a very important skill for reading, writing, and studying that can and should be taught. It is possible that the skepticism concerning the ability to teach main idea may result from "the failure to teach students to transfer their main idea skills to texts other than those found in their readers."[30] Some studies have found that "students who have been taught to identify main ideas using only contrived texts such as those found in basal reader skills lessons will have difficulty transferring their main idea skills to naturally occurring texts."[31]

---

[26] Peter P. Afflerbach, "The Influence of Prior Knowledge on Expert Readers' Main Idea Construction Strategies," *Reading Research Quarterly* 25 (winter 1990): 44.

[27] Ibid.

[28] James W. Cunningham and David W. Moore, "The Confused World of Main Idea," *Teaching Main Idea Comprehension*, James F. Baumann (ed.). Newark, Del.: International Reading Association, 1986, p. 2.

[29] Afflerbach, p. 45.

[30] Victoria Chou Hare, Mitchell Rabinowitz, and Karen Magnus Schieble, "Text Effects on Main Idea Comprehension," *Reading Research Quarterly* 24 (winter 1989): 72.

[31] Ibid.

In reading and writing, finding the main idea is very useful. In reading, the main idea helps you to remember and understand what you have read. In writing, the main idea gives unity and order to your paragraph. (See "Summaries as a Mode of Learning" in Chapter 14.)

Main idea
The central thought of a paragraph. All the sentences in the paragraph develop the main idea.

The main idea of a paragraph is the central thought of the paragraph. It is what the paragraph is about. Without a main idea, the paragraph would just be a confusion of sentences. All the sentences in the paragraph should develop the main idea.

Finding the Main Idea of a Paragraph

To find the main idea of a paragraph, you must find what common element the sentences share. Some textbook writers place the main idea at the beginning of a paragraph and may actually put the topic of the paragraph in bold print in order to emphasize it. However, in literature this is not a common practice. In some paragraphs the main idea is not directly stated but implied. That is, the main idea is indirectly stated, and you have to find it from the clues given by the author.

Although there is no foolproof method for finding the main idea, there is a widely used procedure that has proved to be helpful. In order to use this procedure you should know that a paragraph is always written about something or someone. The something or someone is the topic of the paragraph. The writer is interested in telling his or her readers something about the topic of the paragraph. To find the main idea of a paragraph, you must determine what the topic of the paragraph is and what the author is trying to say about the topic that is special or unique. Once you have found these two things, you should have the main idea. This procedure is useful in finding the main idea of various types of paragraphs.

Reread the preceding paragraph and state its main idea. *Answer:* A procedure helpful in finding the main idea of a paragraph is described.

Now read the following paragraph. After you have read the passage, choose the statement that *best* states the main idea.

Frank Yano looked like an old man, but he was only thirty. Born to parents who were alcoholics, Frank himself started drinking when he was only eight. He actually had tasted alcohol earlier, but it wasn't until he was eight or nine that he became a habitual drinker. His whole life since then has been dedicated to seeking the bottle.

1. Frank Yano looks old, but he's not.
2. Frank Yano enjoys being an alcoholic.
3. Frank Yano was a child alcoholic.
4. Frank Yano has been an alcoholic since childhood.
5. Frank Yano would like to change his life of drinking, but he can't.
6. Frank Yano's parents helped him become an alcoholic.

Answer: #4

Numbers 1 and 3 are too specific because they each relate to only one detail in the paragraph. Numbers 2 and 5 are not found in the paragraph; that is, no clues are given about Frank Yano's wanting to change his life or about his enjoying his life as an alcoholic. Number 6 is also too specific to be the main idea because it relates to only one detail. Number 4 is the answer because what is special about Frank Yano is that he has been an alcoholic since early childhood. All the details in the paragraph support this main idea.

Special Note

The main idea of a paragraph is a general statement of the content of a paragraph. You must be careful, however, that your main idea statement is not so general that it suggests information that is not given in the paragraph.

Textbook authors usually see to it that their paragraphs have clear-cut main ideas. The main ideas of paragraphs in other books may be less obvious. The literary author is usually more concerned with writing expressively than with explicitly stating the main ideas. The main idea may be indirectly given. If the main idea is indirectly given, the steps presented earlier are especially helpful. Let's look again at the steps involved in finding the main idea.

a. Find the topic of the paragraph.
b. Find what is special about the topic. To do this, gather clues from the paragraph, find out what all the clues have in common, and make a general statement about the clues.

Special Notes

Supporting details
Additional information that supports, explains, or illustrates the main idea. Some of the ways that supporting details may be arranged are as cause and effect, examples, sequence of events, descriptions, definitions, comparisons, or contrasts.

1. The topic sentence is usually the first sentence in a paragraph, and it states what the paragraph will be about by naming the topic. From the topic sentence you can usually anticipate certain events. You can usually determine that the following sentences will supply supporting details as examples, contrasts, similarities, sequence of events, cause-and-effect situations, and so on to support the main idea.
2. The main idea can be developed in many different ways. Whatever technique is used to develop the main idea, it must support and add meaning to the main idea.
3. A topic sentence may or may not contain the main idea.
4. It is possible for any sentence in the paragraph to be the topic sentence.
5. Some paragraphs may not have a topic sentence.
6. Do not confuse the topic sentence with the main idea. The topic

sentence usually anticipates both the main idea and the development of the main idea.

7. Even though the topic sentence is stated explicitly (fully and clearly) in a paragraph, the main idea may not be stated explicitly.

UPPER PRIMARY-GRADE LEVEL

SKILL: MAIN IDEA

Diagnostic Analysis

Objective 1: The students will choose a statement that best states the main idea of a short one-paragraph story.

Objective 2: The students will state a title for a story that gives an idea of what the story is about.

Test

Directions: Read the short story. Then read the statements that follow the story. Choose the one that *best* states the main idea of the story. Also, state a title for the story. Then write the title in the blank.

Tom and Jim are not feeling very good. They have just had their first fight. Tom and Jim have never had a fight before. Tom thought about the fight. Jim thought about the fight. They both felt sad.

1. Tom and Jim are sad.
2. Tom and Jim have never fought before.
3. Tom and Jim's first fight makes them feel sad.
4. Tom and Jim fight.
5. Tom and Jim feel ill.

Answers: Number 3. *Sample Title:* Tom and Jim's First Fight
Tell students the results.

Instructional Suggestions

Here are some instructional techniques and materials to use with your students.

1. Present the following paragraph to your students:

Sharon was sad. She felt like crying. She still couldn't believe it. Her best friend, Jane, had moved away. Her best friend had left her. What would she do?

Ask your students what the topic of the paragraph is or about whom or what the paragraph is written.

Answer: Sharon

Ask your students what the writer is saying that is special about Sharon.

Answer: Sharon is sad because her best friend moved away.

Tell your students that the main idea of the story is finding who or what the story is about and what is special about the who or what of the story.

2. Present your students with exercises such as the following. Tell your students to read the short story. Tell them also to read the statements that follow the short story, and choose the one that *best* states the main idea of the story. Then tell your students to write a title for the story that gives readers an idea of what the story is about.

Tom and Jim live on the moon. They spend a lot of time in their house. They have to because it is very hot when the sun is out. It is also very cold when the sun is not out. On the moon, daylight lasts for fourteen earth days. Darkness or nighttime lasts for fourteen earth days, too.

1. It's cold on the moon.
2. Tom and Jim stay in their house a lot.
3. The moon's weather.
4. Tom and Jim's house.
5. The moon's weather forces Tom and Jim to stay in their house.
6. Tom and Jim like to stay in their house.

Answers: Number 5. *Sample title:* The Moon's Weather

3. Discuss with the children the difference between the title and the main idea. Help them to see that the title and the main idea are not necessarily the same. Help them to see that the main idea is usually more fully stated than the title.

INTERMEDIATE-GRADE LEVEL

SKILL: MAIN IDEA OF A PARAGRAPH

Diagnostic Analysis

Objective: The students will state the main idea of a paragraph.

Test

Directions: Read the paragraph carefully. Write the main idea of it in the space below.

Jim and his friends planned to go on a camping trip. For weeks, he and his friends talked about nothing else. They planned every detail of the trip. They studied maps and read books on camping. Everything was set. Everything, that is, except for asking their parents to let them go. Jim and his friends had planned everything. They had not planned on their parents not letting them go. However, that is what happened. Jim's and his friends' parents did not allow them to go.

Answer: Jim and his friends' plans to go camping are blocked by their parents.
Tell students the results.

Instructional Suggestions

Here are some instructional techniques and materials that you can use with your students.

1. Have your students read the following two paragraphs. After they read them, try to elicit from them which is a better paragraph and why. You should tell them that the first one makes sense because it is well organized. You can tell what the author is trying to say because there is only one main idea and all the sentences in the paragraph expand on the main idea. Notice how disorganized the second paragraph is and how difficult it is to discover what the main idea is because each sentence seems to be about a different topic.

Organized Paragraph

All through school, John's one goal was athletic success so that he could be in the Olympics. John's goal to be in the Olympics became such an obsession that he could not do anything that did not directly or indirectly relate to achieving his goal. He practiced for hours every day. He exercised, ate well, and slept at least eight hours every night. Throughout school, John allowed nothing and no one to deter him from his goal.

Disorganized Paragraph

All through school, John's one goal was to be the best so that he could be in the Olympics. He practiced for hours every day. John's family was unhappy about John's obsession to be in the Olympics. John's social life was more like a monk's than that of a star athlete. John's coach was a difficult man to please.

2. Have your students reread the organized paragraph. After they read the paragraph, have them choose the word or words that *best* answer the two questions that follow.

a. What is the topic of the paragraph?
(1) exercise and practice
(2) work
(3) Olympics
(4) John's goal
(5) athletic success
(6) attempts
Answer: 4
b. What is the author saying about John's goal to be in the Olympics (the topic) that is special and that helps tie the details together?
(1) That it needed time and patience.
(2) That it was a good one.

(3) That it was not a reasonable one.
(4) That it was the most important thing in John's life.
(5) That it required good health.
(6) That it was too much for John.
Answer: 4

Tell your students that if they put the two answers together, they should have the main idea of the paragraph. Main idea: The goal, being in the Olympics, was the most important thing in John's life.

3. Choose a number of paragraphs from the students' social studies or science books. First have them find the topic of each and then have them state the main idea of each. Go over the procedure for finding the main idea with them.

Finding the Central Idea of a Group of Paragraphs

We generally use the term *central idea* rather than *main idea* when we refer to a *group* of paragraphs, a story, or an article. The procedure, however, for finding the main idea and for finding the central idea is the same.

The central idea of a story is the central thought of the story. All the paragraphs of the story should develop the central idea. To find the central idea of a story, students must find what common element the paragraphs in the story share. The introductory paragraph is usually helpful because it either contains or anticipates what the central idea is and how it will be developed. The procedure for finding the central idea of a story is similar to that for finding the main idea of a paragraph.

It is important to help your students recognize that the title of a story and the central idea are not necessarily the same. The ability to state the title of a story is related to the skill of finding the central idea; however, many times the title merely gives the topic of the story. The central idea is usually more fully stated than the title.

UPPER PRIMARY-GRADE LEVEL

SKILL: CENTRAL IDEA OF A SHORT STORY

Diagnostic Analysis

Objective 1: The students will state the central idea of a short story.
Objective 2: The students will state a title for a story.

Test

Directions: Read the story. Write the central idea of the story. Then write a title for the story that gives readers an idea of what the story is about.

Once upon a time in the deep green jungle of Africa, there lived a cruel lion. This lion frightened all the animals in the jungle. No animal was safe from this lion. One day the animals met and came up with a plan. The plan was not a very good one, but it was the best they could think of. Each day one animal would go to the lion to be eaten by him. That way the other animals would know that they were safe for a little while. The lion agreed to the plan and that is how they lived for a time.

One day it was the sly fox's turn to be eaten by the lion. Mr. Fox, however, had other plans. Mr. Fox went to the lion's cave an hour late. The lion was very angry. "Why are you so late? I am hungry," he said. Mr. Fox answered, "Oh, I am so sorry to be late, but another very, very big lion tried to catch me. I ran away from him so that you could eat me." When the lion heard about the other lion, he became more angry. "Another lion?" he asked. "I want to see him." The fox told the lion that he would take him to see the other lion. The fox led the lion through the jungle. When they came to a well, the fox stopped. "Look in there," said the fox. "The other lion is in there." The lion looked in the well, and he did indeed see a lion. He got so angry that he jumped in the well to fight the lion. That was, of course, the end of the lion.

Answers: *Central idea:* A clever fox outsmarts a cruel lion.
Sample title: The Clever Fox and the Cruel Lion *or* A Fox Outsmarts a Lion.
Tell students the results.

Instructional Suggestions

Here are some instructional techniques you can use with your students:

1. Choose a short story the children know and enjoy reading. Have them state what the topic of the story is. Then have them go over the story and try to state what is the most important thing about the topic. Have them put the two together.

2. Have the children write their own short stories. Have them state the central idea of their short story. Have them go over each of their paragraphs to see if it helps develop their central idea. Have them write a title for their story.

INTERMEDIATE-GRADE LEVEL

SKILL: CENTRAL IDEA OF A SHORT STORY

Diagnostic Analysis

Objective 1: The students will state the central idea of a short story.
Objective 2: The students will be able to state a title for a story.

Test

Directions: Read carefully the following short story to determine the central idea of the story. After you have found the central idea of the story, choose a title for the story that gives readers an idea of what the story is about.

A man and his son went to the market one morning. They took along a donkey to bring back whatever they would buy.

As they walked down the road, they met a woman who looked at them with a sour face.

"Are you not ashamed," she called to the father, "to let your little boy walk in the hot sun, when he should be riding on the donkey?"

The father stopped and lifted his boy to the donkey's back. So they went on.

After a little while they met an old man. He began at once to scold the boy. "You ungrateful son!" he shouted. "You let your poor old father walk while you sit there on the donkey like a lazy good-for-nothing!"

When the old man had passed, the father took his frightened son from the donkey and got onto the animal himself.

Further on they met another man who looked at them angrily. "How can you let your child walk in the dusty road?" he asked. "And you sit up there by yourself!"

The father was troubled, but he reached down and lifted his son up where he could sit on the donkey in front of him.

A little later they met a man and his wife, each of them riding a donkey. The husband called out, "You cruel man! How can you let the poor donkey carry such a heavy load? Get off at once! You are big enough and strong enough to carry the little animal instead of making it carry two of you."

The poor man was now really perplexed. He got off the donkey and took his son off, too.

Then he cut down a young tree for a pole and trimmed it. He tied the donkey's four feet to the pole. Then he and his son lifted the pole. They trudged along, carrying the donkey between them.

As they were crossing a bridge over a stream, they met with a crowd of young men. Seeing the donkey being carried on a pole, they started to laugh and shout. Their noise startled the poor donkey who started to kick violently and broke the ropes holding his feet. As he frisked about, he tumbled off the bridge and was drowned.

The man looked sadly into the stream and shook his head.

"My son," he said to the boy, "you cannot please everybody."

Answers: *Central idea:* A man and his son learn that you cannot please everyone.
Sample title: You Can't Please Everyone
Tell students the results.

Instructional Suggestions

Here are some instructional techniques you can use with your students:

1. Choose a story they have read. Have them state the topic of the story. Then have them reread the story to state what is the most important thing about the topic. Have them put these together. Have them review the story to determine whether everything in the story is related to their central idea.

2. Have them write their own stories. Have them state the central idea of their stories. Have them write a title for their stories.

3. Choose some short stories and follow the same procedure for finding the central idea. Present the short stories without the titles. Have the students make up a title for each short story. Discuss the fact that the title and the central idea are not necessarily the same. Discuss what the differences are.

Visual Representations and Main Idea

It is difficult to read a textbook, a magazine, or a newspaper without finding a variety of visual representations in the form of graphs, diagrams, and charts. The sprinkling of these gives relief from print, and a graphic representation is often worth 1,000 words. Graphs, diagrams, and charts grab your attention, and pack a great amount of information in a short space. *USA Today* uses pictorial representations every day in each section of its newspaper for these reasons.

Writers use graphs, diagrams, and charts to convey information, and each one, like a paragraph, has a main idea. To understand the charts, diagrams, and graphs, you must be able to get the main idea of them. Not surprisingly, the technique we use to do this is similar to that for finding the main idea of a paragraph.

Here is a graph from *Health Behaviors* by Rosalind Reed and Thomas A. Lang.[32] Let's go through the various steps to get the

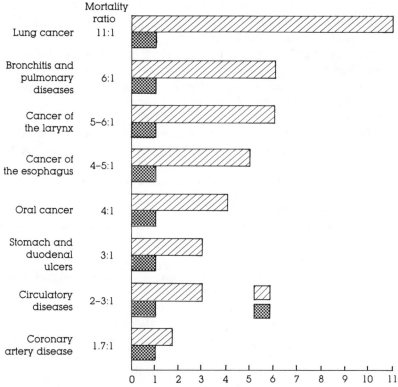

[32] Rosalind Reed and Thomas A. Lang, *Health Behaviors* (St. Paul, Minn.: West Publication, 1988), p. 328.

main idea of it. Remember, to find the main idea, we must first find the topic of the chart, diagram, or graph and then what is special or unique about it. All the details should develop the main idea. (Note that writers also usually give clues to the topic of their graphs, diagrams, and charts.)

Here are the steps I would go through:

1. I look carefully at the graph to determine its topic. I notice it deals with smokers and nonsmokers and their mortality rates for selected diseases. Therefore, the topic is

The mortality rates of smokers and nonsmokers for selected diseases.

2. Next, I need to find what is special about the topic. In looking at the graph again, I note that the writer is obviously making a comparison between smokers and nonsmokers. The comparison is about various types of diseases. In addition and what is most crucial is that the smokers have consistently higher mortality rates for all presented diseases. Therefore, the main idea must be

The mortality rates for smokers are consistently higher than for nonsmokers for all selected diseases.

Let's do one more. Here is a pictorial representation from *USA Today* (July 17, 1990). Let's go through the various steps again to find its main idea.

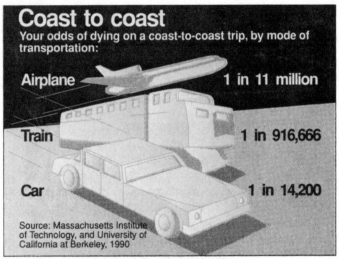

Reprinted with permission from USA TODAY.

Here are the steps I would go through:

1. I look carefully at the graph to determine its topic. I notice it deals with coast-to-coast modes of transportation and the odds of dying by each mode. Therefore, the topic is

The odds of dying on a coast-to-coast trip by different modes of transportation.

2. Next, I need to find what is special about the topic. In looking at the graph again, I note that the writer is making a comparison among the three modes of transportation—airplane, train, and car. The comparison is about the chances of dying on each one. Therefore, the main idea is

The odds of dying on a coast-to-coast trip by different modes of transportation are least by airplane and most by car.

Drawing Inferences

Inference
Understanding that is not derived from a direct statement but from an indirect suggestion in what is stated; understanding that is implied.

Many times writers do not directly state what they mean but present ideas in a more indirect, roundabout way. That is why inference is called the ability to "read between the lines." *Inference* is defined as *understanding that is not derived from a direct statement but from an indirect suggestion in what is stated.* Readers draw inferences from writings; authors make implications or imply meanings.

The ability to draw inferences is especially important in reading fiction, but it is necessary for nonfiction, also. Authors rely on inferences to make their stories more interesting and enjoyable. Mystery writers find inference essential to the maintenance of suspense. For example, Sherlock Holmes and Perry Mason mysteries are based on the ability of the characters to uncover evidence in the form of clues that are not obvious to others around them.

Inference is an important process that authors rely on. Good readers must be alert to the ways that authors encourage inference.

Implied Statements

As has been said already, writers count on inference to make their writing more interesting and enjoyable. Rather than directly stating something, they present it indirectly. To understand the writing, the reader must be alert and be able to detect the clues that the author gives. For example, in the sentence *Things are always popping and alive when the twins Herb and Jack are around,* you are given some clues to Herb's and Jack's personalities, even though the author has not directly said anything about them. From the statement you could make the inference that the twins are lively and lots of fun to be around.

You must be *careful,* however, that you *do not read more* into some statements than is intended. For example, read the following statements and put a circle around the correct answer. *Example:* Mary got out of bed and looked out of the window. She saw that the ground had something white on it. What season of the year was it? (a) winter, (b) summer, (c) spring, (d) fall, (e) can't tell.

The answer is "(e) can't tell." Many persons choose "(a) winter" for the answer. However, the answer is (e) because the "something white" could be anything; there isn't enough evidence to choose (a).

Even if the something white was snow, in some parts of the world, including the United States, it can snow in the spring or fall.

Good readers, while reading, try to gather clues to draw inferences about what they read. Although effective readers do this, they are not usually aware of it. As Sherlock Holmes says in *A Study in Scarlet,* "From long habit the train of thought ran so swiftly through my mind that I arrived at the conclusions without being conscious of intermediate steps."

UPPER PRIMARY-GRADE LEVEL

SKILL: INFERENCE OR "READING BETWEEN THE LINES"

Diagnostic Analysis

Objective: The students will read a short story and answer inference questions about it.

Test

Directions: Read the short story. Then answer the questions.

Zip and Zap are a cat and rat. They are good friends. They live on the moon. Zip and Zap love to ride in space. Their school goes on a space trip every month. Zip and Zap wear their space clothes and their air masks in the spaceship. All the other moon cats and rats wear them, too. Zip and Zap want to be spaceship pilots. This is the same spaceship that brought Zip and Zap to the moon. The spaceship has its own landing place. It is well taken care of. Special cats and rats take care of the spaceship. Zip and Zap are happy that they can ride in the spaceship.

1. Is there air in the spaceship? Explain.

2. Were Zip and Zap born on the moon? Explain.

3. Is the spaceship important to the moon cats and rats? Explain.

4. Is travel an important part of school learning? Explain.

5. Do Zip and Zap know what they want to do when they grow up? Explain.

Answers: 1. No. Zip and Zap wear their space clothes and their air masks in the spaceship.
2. No. It is stated that the spaceship is the same one that brought Zip and Zap to the moon.
3. Yes. It is their means of travel. It is stated that there are special cats and rats who take care of the spaceship and that the spaceship is well taken care of.
4. Yes. Every month the school goes on a space trip.
5. Yes. It is stated that they want to be spaceship pilots.

Tell students the results.

Instructional Suggestions

Here are some instructional procedures and materials to use with your students:

1. Present the following short selection to your students:

Sharon and Carol are going out to play. They are dressed very warmly.

Ask your students what they can say about the weather outside. They should say that it must be cold outside because the children are dressed very warmly. Even though it didn't say that it was cold outside, there was enough evidence to make this inference.

Now ask your children to tell you what season of the year it is. They should say that you can't tell because there is not enough evidence. It could be cold in the fall and spring. Some children might be able to state that you can't tell because different places of the country and world have different climates.

2. Give your students a number of opportunities to make inferences from stories they are reading if enough evidence exists.

INTERMEDIATE-GRADE LEVEL

SKILL: INFERENCE OR "READING BETWEEN THE LINES"

Diagnostic Analysis

Objective: The students will make inferences about short selections if enough evidence exists for the inferences.

Test

Directions: Read the following selection *very carefully*. Without looking back at the selection, try to answer the questions.

The two men looked at each other. They would have to make the decision that might cost many lives. They kept rubbing their hands together to keep warm. Although they were dressed in furs and every part of them was covered except for their faces, they could still feel the cold. The fire that had been made for them from pine trees was subsiding. It was getting light. They had promised their men a decision at dawn. Should they go forward or should they retreat? So many lives had already been lost.

a. Did this take place at the North Pole or South Pole? _____

   How do you know? _____

   _____

   _____

b. Circle the word that best fits the two men. The two men were: (1) trappers (2) officers (3) soldiers (4) guides. Explain why you made your choice.

Explain: _____

   _____

   _____

c. What inference can you draw from this short passage? Circle the answer.

   (1) The men were on a hunting trip.
   (2) The men were at war with Indians.
   (3) The decision that the two men had to make concerned whether to take an offensive or defensive position in some kind of battle.
   (4) The men were on a hunting trip, but they got caught in a bad storm.

Explain: _____

   _____

   _____

Answers:
(a) No. There are no pine trees at the North or South Pole. (b) Officers. Guides would not talk about *their* men. Guides usually act as advisers. They do not make decisions. Trappers trap animals for fur. Also, it is stated that the fire had been made for them. Officers do not usually prepare the camp. (c) The term *retreat* would be a commander's term. Nothing was stated about a storm nor was anything stated or suggested about Indians. Hunters would not usually hunt under such adverse conditions. It was too cold to hunt big game, and hunters would very rarely lose so many lives.
Tell students the results.

Instructional Suggestions

Here are some instructional procedures and materials that you can use:

1. Present your students with the following statements:

Jack looks out of the train window. All he sees are miles and miles of leafless trees.

Ask them whether Jack just began to look out of the window. The students would answer "no." Ask them how they know this. They should say because it says that he saw miles and miles of trees. He couldn't see "miles and miles of trees" unless he had been looking out the window for a while.

Ask them whether Jack is traveling through a densely populated or sparsely populated area. They should say that Jack is traveling through a sparsely populated area. Ask them how they know this. They should say because the area has so many trees. Ask them what kind of area it is. The students should say that it could be a forest or a park or a preserve. Enough evidence isn't given to determine this. Ask them if they can determine what season of the year it is since there are leafless trees. They should say "no." It could be any season of the year. It is not stated in what part of the country or world Jack is traveling. The trees could be leafless as a result of a forest fire, a disease, a drought, or some other cause.

2. Have students read a number of stories and see what inferences they can draw from them. Help them to recognize that enough evidence should exist to make an inference. Tell them that many times persons "jump to conclusions" before they have enough evidence. This can cause problems. Taking an educated guess is helpful in scientific activities and in searching for the truth of difficult questions. Students are encouraged to make educated guesses, but they need to recognize when they do not have enough evidence to do so.

Categorizing

Categorizing
A thinking skill involving the ability to classify items into general and specific categories.

The ability to divide items into categories is a very important thinking skill. As children advance through the grades they should be developing the skill of categorizing; that is, children should be able to differentiate and group items into more complex categories. Primary-grade children should be able to categorize a cat as distinct from a mouse or a rabbit. They should be able to group cat, dog, and cow together as animals. As these children develop their thinking skills, they should be able to proceed from more generalized classifications to more specialized classifications.

You should help your students to recognize that every time they put things into groups—such as pets, farm animals, wild animals, cities, states, countries, capitals, fruits, vegetables, colors, and so on—they are using the skill of categorizing. When they categorize things, they are classifying things. To be able to classify things, they must know what belongs together and what does not belong together. You can help your students to classify or categorize things into more general or more specific categories. For example, the category of food is more general than the categories of fruits, vegetables, or nuts. The category of animals is more general than the categories of pets, wild animals, or tame animals. The category of pets is less general than the category of animals but more general than the categories of dogs or cats.

PRIMARY-GRADE LEVEL

SKILL: CATEGORIZING

Diagnostic Analysis

Objective: The students will categorize pictures of various objects into groups.

Test

Directions: The teacher will orally give directions to students. The children are given a page which consists of pictures of things that would be found in a house. Underneath each picture will appear the name of the object. These items are presented in random order on the page. The children are asked to cut out the pictures and paste them according to their groups on another sheet of paper, which has these headings: *Furniture, Appliances, and Eating Utensils.* The teacher reads these headings aloud to the children.

The pictures on the page are as follows: sofa, bed, desk, dresser with mirror; iron, toaster, refrigerator, oven; fork, knife, plate, cup.

Tell students the results.

PRIMARY-GRADE LEVEL

SKILL: CATEGORIZING

Diagnostic Analysis

Objective: The students will group a list of words in a number of different ways.

Test

Directions: First read the list of words. Then group them in at least seven different ways.

hen	dog
drake	turkey
sow	duck
mare	elephant
colt	ape
gander	tiger
puppy	goat

kitten	mule
goose	horse
pig	

Answer:
Children will arrange the words into a number of different groups. Here are some:
    Wild animals: elephant, ape, tiger
    Tame animals: all the others
    Fowl: hen, drake, gander, goose, turkey, duck
    Female animals: hen, sow, mare
    Male animals: drake, colt, gander
    Pets: colt, mare, puppy, kitten, dog (many of the other animals can be pets)
    Baby animals: puppy, kitten
    Farm animals: hen, drake, sow, mare, colt, gander, and so on except for the elephant, ape, and tiger
    Animals: all would be included
Tell students the results.

Instructional Suggestions

Here is information that should help you plan corrective activities for your children:

Young children tend to overgeneralize and, until they are able to make discriminations, they will not be able to classify. By the time children come to school, they are able to make many discriminations and are beginning to classify.

1. Five-year-olds learn to put things together that belong together—blocks of the same size in the same place; clothes for each doll in the right suitcase; parts of a puzzle in the right box; scissors, brushes, and paints in the spaces designated for these materials.

2. First-graders may separate things that magnets can pick up from things they do not pick up by using two boxes—one marked "yes" and the other marked "no." They can think of two kinds of stories—true and make-believe stories. They can make booklets representing homes, dividing the pictures they have cut from magazines into several categories—living rooms, dining rooms, bedrooms, and so on. They can make two piles of magazines labeled "To Cut" and "To Read."[33]

3. Second-grade pupils continue to put things together that belong together—such as outdoor temperature readings and indoor temperature readings, valentines in individual mail boxes in the play post office, and flannel graph figures made to use in telling a story in the envelope with the title of the story. In addition, seven-year-olds begin to understand finer classifications under large headings;

---

[33] Although grade designations are given, teachers must take the individual differences of students into account. Some first-graders may be at a third-grade level; others may be at a first-grade or lower skill-development level.

for example, in a study of the work of a florist, plants may be classified as "plants that grow indoors" and "plants that grow outdoors." Indoor plants may be further subdivided into "plants that grow from seeds," "plants that grow from cuttings," "plants that grow from bulbs," and so on. After visiting the local bakery, second-graders, who are writing and drawing pictures of the story of their trip, can list the details in two columns—in one, "things we saw in the store" in the other, "things we saw in the kitchen."

4. Third-grade boys and girls have many opportunities to classify their ideas and arrange them in organized form. During a study of food in their community one group put up a bulletin board to answer the question "What parts of plants do we eat?" The pictures and captions followed this tabulation formulated by the third-graders:

Leaves	Seeds	Fruits	Roots
cabbage	peas	apples	carrots
lettuce	beans	oranges	radishes
spinach	corn	plums	

The file of "Games We Know" in one third grade was divided into two parts by the pupils—"indoor games" and "outdoor games." Each of these categories was further subdivided into "games and equipment" and "games without equipment." After a visit to the supermarket a third-grade class booklet was made by the children with stories and pictures of the trip. The organization of the booklet with its numbered pages was shown in the Table of Contents:

OUR VISIT TO THE FOOD MARKET

Here are examples of some exercises you can present to your children.

1. Group these words: apple, peach, potato, rice, oats, cucumber, barley, peanuts, acorn, pecans, almonds, pear.

Answer:

Nuts	Fruits	Vegetables	Grains
peanuts	apple	potato	rice
acorn	peach	cucumber	oats
pecans	pear		barley
almonds			

2. Circle the word that does not belong.

Airedale Persian Angora Siamese

Answer: You should have circled *Airedale* because all the other words refer to *cats*.

INTERMEDIATE-GRADE LEVEL

SKILL: CATEGORIZING

Diagnostic Analysis

Objective: The students will group items that belong together.

Test

Directions: First find what the items in a group have in common, and then choose a word or phrase from the list below that *best* describes the group. There are more words and phrases than are needed. Put the word or phrase on the line after each group of words.

Words and Phrases: books, fiction books, nonfiction books, fruit, vegetables, food, cooked food, desserts, dairy products, long books, writing, fowl, animals, tame animals, female animals, wood, wood products, meat, beef, pork, lamb.

1. pears, apples, bananas _____

2. meat, tomatoes, apples _____

3. milk, cheese, butter _____

4. jello, applesauce, ice cream _____

5. liver, pork chops, lamb chops _____

6. hen, mare, doe _____

7. biography, autobiography, novel _____

8. biography, autobiography, dictionary _____

9. novel, comics, fairy tales _____

10. paper, telephone pole, furniture _____

Instructional Suggestions

Here are some instructional procedures and materials to use:

1. Present students with the following list of words and have them group them in as many ways as they can think of:

chalk	book
checkers	library
pencil	auditorium
paper	science books
student	baseball
teacher	nurse
chalkboard	jump rope
desk	basketball
classroom	pen
principal	chess
history books	spelling books

2. Present the following exercise to your students. Tell them here is a group of words. Put them into five groups according to a common feature and state the common feature for each group. This activity is a more difficult one because of the vocabulary. Have students look up any words they are not sure of in the dictionary. Make sure that students remember that words may have more than one meaning so that they are not confused when they see words such as *minute*.

After students have finished the exercise, go over it carefully, discussing why they did what they did.

wood, brass, round, silk, oil, wheat, tin, wool, satin, coal, nylon, iron, barley, oats, oval, cylindrical.

1. _____
   _____ Common feature _____

2. _____
   _____ Common feature _____

3. _____
   _____ Common feature _____

4. _____
   _____ Common feature _____

5. _____

_____ Common feature _____

Answers: 1. wood, oil, coal—fuels 2. brass, tin, iron—metals 3. silk, wool, satin, nylon—fabrics 4. round, cylindrical, oval—shapes 5. wheat, barley, oats—grains

Completing Analogies (Word Relationships)

Analogies
Relationships between words or ideas.

Working with analogies requires high-level thinking skills. Students must have a good stock of vocabulary and the ability to see relationships. Students who have difficulty in classification will usually have difficulty working with analogies.

Some primary-grade children can be exposed to simple analogies based on relationships with which they are familiar.[34] Analogies are relationships between words or ideas. In order to be able to make the best use of analogies or to complete an analogy statement or proportion, the children must know the meanings of the words and the relationship of the pair of words. For example: *Sad is to happy as good is to* _____. Many primary-grade children know the meanings of *sad* and *happy* and that *sad* is the opposite of *happy*; they would, therefore, be able to complete the analogy statement or proportion with the correct word—*bad*.

Some of the relationships that words may have to one another are similar meanings, opposite meanings, classification, going from particular to general, going from general to particular, degree of intensity, specialized labels, characteristics, cause-effect, effect-cause, function, whole-part, ratio, and many more. The preceding relationships do not have to be memorized. Tell your students that they will gain clues to these from the pairs making up the analogies; that is, the words express the relationship. For example: "*pretty* is to *beautiful*"—the relationship is degree of intensity (the state of being stronger, greater, or more than); "*hot* is to *cold*"—the relationship is one of opposites; "*car* is to *vehicle*"—the relationship is classification.

It would probably be a good idea for teachers to review the word lists of the analogy exercises to determine whether their students are familiar with the vocabulary. Teachers can encourage students to use dictionaries to look up any unfamiliar words.

The analogy activities can be done in small groups or with the entire class orally as well as individually. If children work individually, it would help to go over the answers together in a group so that interaction and discussion can further enhance vocabulary development.

---

[34] See Sister Josephine, C.S.J., "An Analogy Test for Preschool Children," *Education* (December 1965): 235–37.

Special Notes

1. The term *word relationships* should be used with your primary-grade students rather than *analogies*. You might want to introduce the term *analogy* to some of your highly able upper primary-grade children. Highly able children especially enjoy working with analogies.

2. In introducing some of the relationships that pairs of words can have to one another, you should, of course, use words that are in your students' listening vocabulary. The list of some possible relationships is presented as an aid for you, the teacher.

LOWER PRIMARY-GRADE LEVEL

SKILL: PICTURE RELATIONSHIPS (ANALOGIES)

Diagnostic Analysis

Objective: The students will be able to choose a picture from the given pictures that will best complete the analogy.

Test

> **Directions: (These will be given orally by the teacher.) Present the following picture sets to your children. Tell them that the sets of pictures belong together in some way. Each set has a missing picture. Have them look at the first pair of pictures in the set. Tell them to try to figure out how they belong together. Then have them choose a picture from the large box that would *best* complete the second pair in the set. Have them draw a line from the picture in the large box to where it belongs. *All the pictures in the box are used as answers.* Do the first set with the children.**

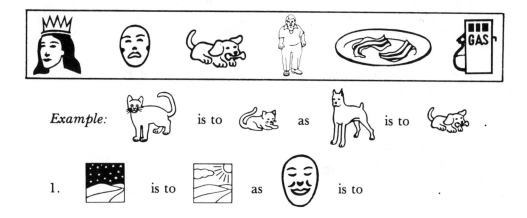

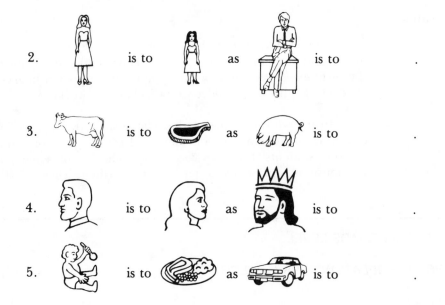

Tell students the results.

UPPER PRIMARY-GRADE LEVEL

SKILL: WORD RELATIONSHIPS (ANALOGIES)

Diagnostic Analysis

Objective: The students will complete each analogy statement with the *best* word.

Test

> **Directions: Here are sets of words that have a certain relationship to one another. Each set has a missing word that you have to supply. Look at the first pair of words. Try to figure out what the relationship is. Then choose a word from the list that *best* completes the second pair in the set. (All words do not fit in.) The first is done for you.**

Word list: hide, house, nice, proud, sire, hay, sow, stallion, ewe, gander, drake, stable, water, milk, drink, cruel, tired, great, hot.

1. *Bird* is to *nest* as *horse* is to _____stable_____.

2. *Cool* is to *cold* as *warm* is to _____.

3. *Cow* is to *bull* as *duck* is to _____.

4. *Deer* is to *doe* as *pig* is to _____.

5. *Hungry* is to *eat* as *thirsty* is to _____.

6. *In* is to *out* as *kind* is to _____.

Instructional Suggestions

Here are some instructional procedures and materials that you can use:

1. Present students with the words *hot* and *cold*. Ask them what the relationship between the two words is. Help them to recognize that *hot* and *cold* are opposites. Present students with the words *tall* and *short*. Ask them what the relationship between the words is. Again help them to recognize that they are opposites. Tell them that they are going to work with word relationships. The first relationship will be opposites. Put the following on the chalkboard:

Thin is to *fat* as *little* is to _____.

Ask them to give you a word that would fit the blank. Present a number of opposite relationships to your students.

2. Present students with the words *little* and *small*. Ask them what the relationship between the words is. Help them to recognize that these are words that have the same meaning; they are synonyms. Present students with the words *big* and *large*. Ask them what the relationship between the words is. Again help them to recognize that the words are similar in meaning. Tell them that they are going to work with word relationships. Put the following on the chalkboard:

Sad is to *gloomy* as *happy* is to _____.

Ask them to give you a word that would fit the blank. Present a number of such relationships to your students.

3. Do the same as above for different kinds of relationships.

Go over each analogy with the students. Have them explain why they chose the word that they did.

INTERMEDIATE-GRADE LEVEL

SKILL: ANALOGIES (WORD RELATIONSHIPS)

Diagnostic Analysis

Objective: The students will complete each analogy statement with the *best* word.

Test

Directions: Find the relationship between a pair of words and then complete each analogy with the *best* word. There are more words given in the list than you need.

Word list: sun, moon, light, cold, kilometer, pour, year, rate, ship, day, compass, rain, cards, blizzard, doe, time, era, kind, drove, dame, ram, century, place, ewe, love, cub, binary, meter, ecstasy, chirp, moo, friend, hate, millimeter.

1. *Happy* is to *sad* as *night* is to _____.

2. *Rain* is to *downpour* as *snow* is to _____.

3. *Horse* is to *mare* as *deer* is to _____.

4. *Chicken* is to *rooster* as *sheep* is to _____.

5. *Sad* is to *miserable* as *joy* is to _____.

6. *One* is to *thousand* as *meter* is to _____.

7. *Hint* is to *disclose* as *drip* is to _____.

8. *Distance* is to *odometer* as *direction* is to _____.

Answers: 1. day 2. blizzard 3. doe 4. ram 5. ecstasy 6. kilometer 7. pour 8. compass
Tell students the results.

Instructional Suggestions

Here are some instructional procedures and materials that you can use:

1. Discuss the various relationships that words can have to one another and have the students give examples of these. Put the examples on large newsprint so that students can refer to them. As students learn new relationships, have them add to the list.

For example:

Opposites: *hot* is to *cold*
Similarities: *thin* is to *lean*
Degree of intensity: *pretty* is to *beautiful*
Classification: *boat* is to *vehicle*
Ratio: *5* is to *10*
Part is to whole: *finger* is to *hand*
Whole is to part: *foot* is to *toe*
Parent is to child: *bear* is to *cub*

2. Have students construct their own analogies by using the dictionary. Then have them challenge their classmates by deleting the final term of the analogy statement.

Special Note

It should again be emphasized that the skill areas covered in this chapter illustrating a diagnostic and corrective approach are a sampling of some interpretive comprehension skills rather than an inclusive set. Teachers using the given examples as a guide can develop diagnostic and corrective materials for other interpretive comprehension skills, as well as for critical and creative comprehension skills.

DIAGNOSIS AND CORRECTION IN CONTENT AREAS

Diagnosis and correction in reading should not be relegated merely to the reading period. Reading is taking place all through the day at school, and teachers would be losing valuable opportunities to learn about students' reading strengths and weaknesses if they did not observe their students' reading behavior in content areas. It's in these areas that teachers can observe whether students are applying what they have learned during the reading period.

A student's problem in mathematics may not be caused by an inability to do quantitative reasoning or basic mathematical operations; it may be a reading problem. Similarly, a problem in science or social studies may be a reading problem. The teacher should have students find the main idea of various paragraphs in their content books to discern whether they understand what they are reading. Teachers should give students opportunities to read aloud from their books to determine whether the books are at the proper readability level for the students. (See "Modified IRI Approaches: A Caution" in Chapter 8.) Also, teachers should be alert to students' attitudes toward a subject. It may be that the student does not like the subject because the student cannot read the textbook. A student who is not reading at grade level would probably have difficulty reading a social studies, science, or math textbook whose readability level is at the same grade level. If teachers cannot get books for their students at their reading ability levels, they will have to make special provisions. They will have to provide a special guide that would have an outline of the material the students are supposed to read. It would also list all those vocabulary words that the teachers feel would cause difficulty. Before the students are asked to read the material, the teachers should go over the vocabulary words with the students. The words should be pronounced, presented in a sentence, and defined. After the students have read the material, the teachers should go over it with them in the same way that they would in a reading lesson. The emphasis, however, would be on gaining content concepts. (See Chapter 14 for strategies teachers can use with students to help them read content material.)

Special Note

It would be very difficult to find a subject matter book for a student who is reading below grade level at the student's reading ability that would cover the same material. If a student is in fourth grade, the subject matter book for third-grade mathematics covers different material. Also, the student may be good in mathematics but have a reading problem, and if a book from a lower grade level is used, the student would be penalized in mathematics.

Questioning Strategies in Content Areas

Children need help in developing higher-level reading comprehension skills in all their subject matter areas. James Brown understands this need and has initiated a program in his class that incorporates a special questioning technique when teaching content areas. He generally models questions at different levels of difficulty and then has his students challenge one another with their own questions. The students are responsible for knowing the answers to the questions they ask and for leading the discussion in relation to the answering of the question.

LITERATURE IN THE CLASSROOM

The emphasis in many classrooms in the United States today appears to be on literature-based programs, whether teachers use basal readers or not, and many children are being exposed to good

Figure 13.4 Jennifer chooses to read whenever she can. She learned to love books at a very early age.

literature earlier. In addition, teachers appear to be reading aloud more in their classrooms and having interactive book sessions with students. Many teachers also have attractive book displays that invite children to read, and the teachers often try to give children time in class just to read. These practices are excellent; however, many children are still not choosing to read voluntarily outside of school. And we know that reading, reading, reading, and more reading help children become better readers!

The problem is that it is difficult to compete with other enjoyable activities that vie for children's time and attention. However, some principals are trying to do just that by "going out on a limb to encourage reading."[35] They have found that the "I-dare-you approach wherein the principal offers the students a wacky reward for meeting reading goals—gets students reading in record numbers."[36] Principals have jumped into pools of Jello, sat on a roof for a day, and even worn a monkey suit and sat in a cage in the library all day.[37] (See Chapter 16 for some programs such as Reading Olympics that have been developed to encourage students to read voluntarily.)

Attitudes and Reading

The "wacky dare" program may work for the short term, but will children continue to read on their own and recognize that reading is its own reward? Long-term results need lots of nurturing, and the key is to instill a love of reading in children at very young ages before they come to school. (See Chapter 16 on parental involvement.) This is the ideal, but it does not happen for all children. Therefore, one of the greatest responsibilities that teachers of young children have besides promoting awareness of print in their pupils is to help to instill a love of books in them. What teachers do will have a profound effect on their students for the rest of their lives because it is at this stage that attitudes toward reading are developing.

Attitude
Exerts a directive and dynamic influence on an individual's behavior.

Attitudes exert a directive and dynamic influence on all our lives and once set are difficult to change. It is often the concomitant learnings such as attitudes that will remain with us more than the subject matter. Therefore, teachers must be ever vigilant that in helping children learn to read, they are not stifling their love of reading.

Instilling a Love for Reading in the Early Grades with Big Books

In preschool and kindergarten programs, the classroom should be full of print, and on display there should be many, many different

---

[35] *Reading Today* (Newark, Del.: International Reading Association, April/May 1990), p. 13.
[36] Ibid.
[37] Ibid.

Figure 13.5 These children love reading their big books. *Hairy Bear* is one of their favorites.

kinds of books that children can touch and relate to, including "big books," oversized versions of text.[38] Big books can be used in the same way as normal-sized books; however, they are much more useful when working with a large group of children. Also, children seem to love to see their favorite stories in an enlarged version.

The big books lend themselves better also for interactive sessions with a large group of young children because the pictures and print are so much easier for all the children to see. The children can relate better to the story, and they appear to be more free to ask questions and make predictions about the story.

A key feature of big books is their repetitive patterns, which give them their predictability. Big books are usually children's bedtime favorites, those with which they can associate "good feelings." They are books that children like to hear over and over again.

In reading the story, it's a good idea for the teacher to pause during the reading before coming to the repetitive passage or refrain to give the children an opportunity to state it. It is suggested that the teacher point to the words while the story is being read, so the children will gain an understanding of the relationship between the words that are being said and the print on the page, as well as that text proceeds from left to right and from top to bottom.[39] After a few repeated readings, the children will not only state the refrain,

Big books
Enlarged versions of regular children's books; known for their repetitive patterns which lend to their predictability; they are usually children's favorites.

[38] Adams, p. 69.
[39] Ibid., pp. 69–70.

but many will be able to recognize it in print. (See "Repeated Reading" in this chapter and "Parental Involvement in Regular School Reading Programs" in Chapter 16 for a discussion of paired reading.)

Special Note

The Little Red Hen is an excellent example of a book with a repetitive refrain that appears throughout the book.

Children's Literature as a Bridge to Better Understanding in a Multicultural Classroom

The importance of learning about other groups of people through literature is aptly expressed in the following:

> I never felt the world-wide importance of the children's heritage in literature more than on a day when I stood with Mrs. Ben Zvi, wife of the [then] President of Israel, in the midst of the book boxes she had filled for the centers in Jerusalem where refugee boys and girls were gathered for storytelling and reading of the world's great classics for children. "We want our boys and girls to be at home with the other children of the world," she said, "and I know of no better way than through mutual enjoyment of the world's great stories."[40]

"Young children find it easier to assimilate new information when this information is presented within the structure of a story."[41] The story acts as a bridge to help children "link their growing understanding of other cultures to their personal experience and background knowledge."[42]

The characteristics of "good" books are operative for all children regardless of background. Any book they read must help them to feel good about themselves. It must help them to view themselves in a positive light, to achieve a better self-concept, and to gain a feeling of worth.

A book that hinders a child from finding his or her identity, that portrays the child in a stereotyped role, is a book that would be considered poor reading for all children.

When selecting books for a class library, teachers should try to put themselves in the position of their students and ask, How would I feel if I read this book? Would this book make me come back for another one? Will this book interest me? Are these books on many readability levels? Does the book portray the black child or any other minority child as an individual? Are the adults portrayed in a nonchildlike manner? Are the characters supplied with traits and

---

[40] Dora V. Smith, "Children's Literature Today," *Elementary English* 47 (October 1970): 778.
[41] Jerry Y. Diakiw, "Children's Literature and Global Education: Understanding the Developing World," *The Reading Teacher* 43 (January 1990): 297.
[42] Ibid.

Student's Name:_____

Grade:_____

Teacher:_____

Diagnostic Checklist for Selected Reading Comprehension Skills

	Yes	No
1. The student is able to state the meaning of a word in context.		
2. The student is able to give the meaning of a phrase or a clause in a sentence.		
3. The student is able to give variations of meanings for homographs (words spelled the same but with more than one meaning, for example, *train, mean, saw, sole,* and so on).		
4. The student is able to give the meaning of a sentence in a paragraph.		
5. The student is able to recall information that is explicitly stated in the passage (literal questions).		
6. The student is able to state the main idea of a paragraph.		
7. The student is able to state details to support the main idea of a paragraph.		
8. The student is able to summarize a paragraph.		
9. The student is able to answer a question that requires reading between the lines.		
10. The student is able to draw a conclusion from what is read.		
11. The student can complete analogy proportions.		
12. The student can hypothesize the author's purpose for writing the selection.		
13. The student can differentiate between fact and opinion.		
14. The student can differentiate between fantasy and reality.		
15. The student can detect bias in a story.		
16. The student can detect various propaganda tactics that are used in a story.		
17. The student can go beyond the text to come up with alternate solutions or ways to end a story or solve a problem in the selection.		
18. The student shows that he or she enjoys reading by voluntarily choosing to read.		

personalities that are positive? Would all children want to read the book?

If the answers are "yes," the teacher should choose the book. But even one "no" answer should disqualify it.

The importance of providing children with books that convey hope and with which children can identify, because they mirror their lives, cannot be overemphasized. Another factor, which is as important, concerns the image that children obtain when they read a book about people with different racial or ethnic backgrounds. Since children are greatly influenced by what they read, the way that people are portrayed in books will have a profound effect on children's perceptions of them.

Good books can open doors through which can pass better understanding, mutual respect, trust, and the hope of people living together in harmony and peace. (Susan Cox and Lee Calda's "Multicultural Literature: Mirrors and Windows on a Global Community" in the Selected Bibliography is an excellent resource for some new books that "mirror" traditions of various cultures.)

SUMMARY

Chapter 13 is concerned with helping you better understand reading comprehension, as well as with helping you gain techniques for the diagnosis and correction of these skills. Reading comprehension is a complex intellectual process involving a number of abilities. The two major ones involve word meanings and reasoning with verbal concepts. It was emphasized that comprehension involves thinking, and as there are various levels of thinking, so are there various levels of comprehension. Reading comprehension was categorized into a hierarchy of four levels: literal comprehension, interpretation, critical reading, and creative reading. Then a special section on diagnosis and correction was presented for selective interpretative skills. The skills that were chosen to demonstrate the diagnostic and corrective approach were the following: context clues, finding the main idea of a paragraph and the central idea of a group of paragraphs, finding the main idea of visual representations, drawing inferences, categorizing, and recognizing analogies. An explanation and examples, as well as diagnostic tests and instructional suggestions, were given for each presented skill.

This chapter also presented a number of instructional strategies that teachers can use to help students acquire comprehension ability. In addition, some questioning strategies such as QAR were presented.

The importance of instilling a love of books in children was emphasized, and some techniques were explored, including the use of big books.

A diagnostic checklist of selected reading comprehension skills was also presented.

SUGGESTIONS FOR THOUGHT QUESTIONS
AND ACTIVITIES

1. State the four levels of comprehension presented in this chapter. State one skill for each level. Then prepare an objective and a test for the objective for each skill you have chosen (primary grades).
2. Do the same for the intermediate grades.
3. You have been appointed to a special reading curriculum committee at your school. The committee is interested in revamping their primary reading program. What suggestions would you make?
4. You are appointed to a committee that is charged with developing a diagnostic testing and correction program for reading comprehension. What suggestions would you make to the committee to proceed?
5. Generate reading comprehension questions for a selection that would elicit high level reading/thinking responses.
6. Present a reading comprehension lesson and videotape it. Note the kinds of questions you ask. Critique your lesson and state some ways in which you can improve it.
7. Compare your students' reading behavior in the content areas to their behavior when reading in reading groups. Try to determine whether interest in a subject affects the students' reading performance.
8. Choose a fairy tale. Construct questions at the literal, interpretive, critical, and creative levels for the fairy tale.
9. Use one of the strategies presented in this chapter to teach a reading lesson.
10. Choose five books that would lend themselves to being used in a predictive reading lesson.
11. Suggest three ways to encourage students to read voluntarily.
12. Prepare a lesson using a "big book."
13. You have a student in your class who has difficulty answering comprehension questions. How would you go about determining what his or her problems are? What can you do to help this student?

SELECTED BIBLIOGRAPHY

Afflerbach, Peter P. "The Influence of Prior Knowledge on Expert Reader's Main Idea Construction Strategies." *Reading Research Quarterly* 25 (Winter 1990): 31–46.

Baumann, James F. (ed.). *Teaching Main Idea Comprehension*. Newark, Del.: International Reading Association, 1986.

Beck, Isabel L. "Reading and Reasoning." *The Reading Teacher* 42 (May 1989): 676–82.

Benderson, Albert. "Critical Thinking: Critical Issues." *Focus*. Princeton, N.J.: Educational Testing Service, 1990.

Burke, Eileen. *Literature for the Young Child*, 2nd ed. Boston: Allyn and Bacon, 1990.

Cox, Susan, and Lee Galda. "Multicultural Literature: Mirrors and Windows on a Global Community." *The Reading Teacher* 43 (April 1990): 582–89.

Fitzgerald, Jill. "Enhancing Two Related Thought Processes: Revision in Writing and Critical Thinking." *The Reading Teacher* 43 (October 1989): 42–48.

Hare, Victoria Chou, Mitchell Rabinowitz, and Karen Magnus Schieble. "Text Effects on Main Idea Comprehension." *Reading Research Quarterly* 24 (Winter 1989): 72–88.

Hunkins, Francis P. *Teaching Thinking Through Effective Questioning*. Norwood, Mass.: Christopher-Gordon, 1989.

Jett-Simpson, Mary (ed.). *Adventuring with Books: A Booklist for Pre-K–Grade 6*, 9th ed. Urbana, Ill.: National Council of Teachers of English, 1989.

Mullis, Ina V. S. and Lynn B. Jenkins. *The Reading Report Card, 1971–88*. The National Assessment of Educational Progress. Princeton, N.J.: Educational Testing Service, 1990.

Reutzel, Ray D., and Parker C. Fawson. "Using a Literature Webbing Strategy Lesson with Predictable Books." *The Reading Teacher* 43 (December 1989): 208–215.

Roser, Nancy L., James V. Hoffman, and Cynthia Farest. "Language, Literature, and At-risk Children." *The Reading Teacher* 43 (April 1990): 554–59.

Rubin, Dorothy. *Teaching Elementary Language Arts*, 4th ed. Englewood Cliffs, N.J.: Prentice-Hall, 1990.

Rubin, Dorothy. *Reading and Learning Power*, 3rd ed. Needham, Mass.: Ginn Press, 1990.

Simons, Sandra M. "PSRT—A Reading Comprehension Strategy." *Journal of Reading Behavior* 32 (Februrary 1989): 419–27.

Strickland, Dorothy S., and Lesley Mandel Morrow. "Sharing Big Books." *The Reading Teacher* 43 (January 1990): 342–43.

Wade, Suzanne E. "Using Think Alouds to Assess Comprehension." *The Reading Teacher* 43 (March 1990): 442–51.

Wendler, David, S. Jay Samuels, and Vienna Moore. "The Comprehension Instruction of Award-Winning Teachers, Teachers with Master's Degrees, and Other Teachers." *Reading Research Quarterly* 24 (Fall 1989): 382–97.

14

Learning Strategies and Study Skills in a Diagnostic-Reading and Correction Program

How many times have you heard students make the following statements?

"I spent all night studying, but I did very poorly on my exams."
"I reread the chapter ten times, but I still don't understand it."
"I reread the chapter about fifteen times, and I don't even remember what I read."
"I always listen to music when I study."
"I like to be relaxed when I study."
"I don't need to study."
"I don't know how to study."
And so it goes . . .

Many students do poorly in school because they have never learned how to study. Elementary-school teachers usually do not spend time helping children acquire study skills because they themselves may lack the skills,[1] or because they feel that this is the job of high school teachers. Also, many high school teachers do not spend time in this area because they make the assumption that their students have already acquired the study skills they need. As a result, many students go through the grades without ever being helped to acquire study skills. This is a mistake. Children should be helped to acquire good study habits as soon as possible before they develop either poor study

---

[1] Eunice N. Askov et al., "Study Skill Mastery Among Elementary Teachers," *The Reading Teacher* 30 (February 1977): 485–88.

habits or erroneous concepts about studying. Children should be helped to learn that with good study habits, they could spend less time studying and learn more.

This chapter is concerned with helping you gain the information and skills that are necessary for you to help your students become better learners. This is important in a diagnostic-reading and correction program where the emphasis is on the *prevention* of reading and learning problems.

KEY QUESTIONS

After you finish reading this chapter, you should be able to answer the following questions:

1. What does studying require, and what is the key to building good study habits?
2. What is SQ3R?
3. What is the role of concentration in studying?
4. How do attitudes influence our studying?
5. What is skimming?
6. What role does skimming play in study techniques?
7. How are reading and writing used as modes of learning?
8. How can graphic organizers help in studying?
9. How do you summarize a paragraph?
10. Why should children be good question askers?
11. How can the teacher help his or her students to be better notetakers?
12. How can the teacher help his or her students to be better test takers?
13. How can teachers help students combine SQ3R and notetaking?

KEY TERMS IN CHAPTER

You should pay special attention to the following new terms:

concentration
notetaking
overlearning
questions
recite or recall
semantic mapping (graphic
   organizer)
skimming
SQ3R
study procedures
summary
survey

WHAT ARE SOME GOOD STUDY PROCEDURES?

Study procedures
(1) Build good habits, (2) devise a system that works for you, (3) keep at it, (4) maintain a certain degree of tension, and (5) concentrate.

Although there is no simple formula that will apply to all students, educational psychologists have found that some procedures will help all students. The key is in building good habits, devising a system that works for the individual student, and keeping at it.

A person cannot relax and study at the same time. Studying requires a certain amount of tension, concentration, and effort in a specific direction. Of course, the amount of tension varies with different individuals. The point is that studying is hard work, and students who are not prepared to make a proper effort are wasting their time.

Building Good Study Habits

The first step in building good study habits is to determine *when to study*. Some students study only just before an announced test. Some may even stay up until all hours and cram. All of us have probably done this once or twice. However, if this is a student's normal way of doing things, he or she will not do well in school. Cramming does not bring about sustained learning. It can be justified only as a last resort. To be a good student, the student must plan his or her study time and spread it out over a period of time. Students must realize that a regular plan will prevent confusion and help them retain what they are studying. Students, even in the elementary grades, should be helped to plan an overall time schedule in which they allow for

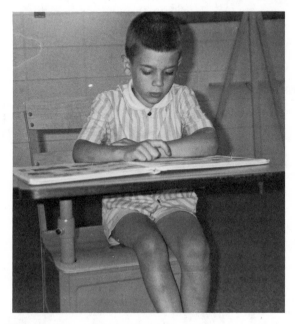

Figure 14.1 Andrew is concentrating.

social and physical activities. It is to be hoped that their time schedule also allows for some recreational reading. Students must recognize that a rhythm of activities is important. It does not matter whether they study in the evening, before or after dinner, or right after class during free periods. The important thing is for the student to follow a schedule and spread out the studying over the week.

The second step in building good study habits is to determine *where to study*. Some students are able to study well in a school or public library, but there are others who cannot. Most elementary-school students study at home. Regardless of where the student studies, he or she should choose a place that is comfortable and convenient, has enough light, and is *free from distractions*. Consistency is important.

To help children establish a comfortable, convenient, and suitable place for study at home, the teacher and the children can design such a place in the classroom. A special area can be set aside as a study area. It should be as free from distractions as possible, comfortable, and well lighted. Students should be free to go to this area whenever they wish to study. If a student is in this area, other students should recognize that it is "off bounds"; that is, other students should respect the student's desire to study and not interrupt or bother the student.

Teachers must recognize that there are some students in class who may not have a place at home to study. There may be many children in the house and not enough rooms, so that the only place to study may be the kitchen. This place, however, is not very good because it usually has too many distractions. Teachers should be aware of the home situations of their students and try to help them as much as possible without embarrassing them. One thing the teacher could do is discuss the possibility of studying at the library or at a friend's house. If these are not feasible, and if the student does not have to ride a bus to school, the teacher might make some arrangements whereby the student can study in the school. A teacher must be sensitive to the fact that students who do not have a place to do homework or study at home are actually being penalized twice— once, because they do not have a place to study, and twice, because they will probably be penalized for not doing the homework and they will also probably not do well in school.

Overlearning
Helps persons retain information over a long period of time; occurs when individuals continue to practice even after they think they have learned the material.

The third step in building good study habits is to determine the *amount of time* to spend in studying. You must help students recognize that the amount of time they spend will depend on the subject and how well they know it. It is unrealistic to set up a hard-and-fast rule about the amount of time to study in a specific subject because the amount of time will vary. In some subjects a student may need to spend a lot of time studying because he or she is weak in that area, whereas in others the student may only have to spend a short time studying. You should help students understand the concept of *overlearning* because some students feel that if they know something, they do not have to study it at all. In order to overlearn something, students must recognize that they must practice it even after they feel that they know it. *Overlearning* is not bad like *overcooking* the roast. Overlearning helps persons retain information over a long period of time. Overlearning happens when individuals continue to practice even after they think they have learned the material.

HOW TO STUDY

SQ3R
A widely used study technique that involves five steps: survey, question, read, recite or recall, and review.

Survey
To gain an overview of the text material.

After you have helped students attain positive attitudes toward their learning tasks and helped them recognize that they must exert effort to study, find a suitable place to study, and spend time in studying, you must still help them learn *how to study*. There are a number of study techniques; however, SQ3R[2] will be presented rather than some of the others because it is a widely used technique developed by a well-known psychologist that has proved helpful to many students. Here are the five steps in this technique:

1. *Survey*—Students should get an *overall* sense of their learning task before proceeding to details. They should skim the whole assignment to obtain some idea(s) about the material and how it is organized.
2. *Question*—Students should check section headings and change these to questions to set their purposes for reading.
3. *Read*—Students should read to answer the questions that they have formulated for themselves. While reading they should notice how the paragraphs are organized because this knowledge will help them remember the answer.

Recite or Recall
The process of finding the answer to a question in one's memory without rereading the text or notes.

4. *Recite or recall—This step is very important.* Without referring to their book, students should try to answer the questions that they have formulated for themselves. (Writing down key ideas will provide necessary notes for future review. See section on notetaking.)
5. *Review*—Students should take a few moments to review the major headings and subheadings of the material they have just finished studying. You should recommend to your students that it's also a good idea to try to relate what they just finished studying to the previous assignment on the same topic. (How well they are able to relate their new learning with previous learning will determine how well they will remember the new material.)

Make sure students understand that they can survey a reading assignment to determine its organization and to obtain some ideas about it, but they cannot study unfamiliar material by skimming or reading rapidly. Help your students to recognize that one of the key

[2] Adapted from Francis P. Robinson, *Effective Study,* 4th ed. (New York: Harper & Row, 1970).

Figure 14.2 Poor Linus—he'll learn.

factors in remembering information is recall or recitation and not the immediate rereading of their assignment. The time they spend answering the questions that they have formulated is crucial in learning.

Here is an example of how you can help your students adapt the SQ3R technique to suit their personal needs:

Scenario: Modeling the SQ3R Approach for Students in an Intermediate-Grade-Level Class

Ms. Mills tells her students that she is taking courses at the local college, and she has lots of reading to do. If she didn't know how to study, she would be in trouble. She tells them that she was very fortunate to have a teacher who helped her, and she wanted to do the same for her students. She will show them what she does when she has to study something.
Step 1:

Ms. Mills chooses a chapter from the students' history textbook and has her students turn to the chapter. She then says, "I always quickly skim through an assignment first to get an idea of what it's about and what it covers. So that's what I'm going to do. I also want you to do the same."

Ms. Mills then says, "As I skim through the chapter, I look at some of the section heads to see if I should break the chapter up into parts to study. I do this if it's an area I don't know anything about. Why don't you do the same?"
Step 2:

Ms. Mills says, "I try to be honest with myself. If the chapter has a great amount of new material, I should break it up into parts. Also, I know my concentration ability. I don't feel I can study the whole chapter all at once, so I will break this chapter into parts for study pur-

poses and choose a few sections to study at a time. Would you have done the same? Remember, it depends on your background of experiences."
Step 3:

Ms. Mills says, "I look over the first part of the chapter I have decided to study. I check the section heads and use these to make up questions. If there were no section heads, I would look for other clues such as words in margins, words in bold print, or words in italics. If it doesn't have any of these, then I survey or skim it more slowly and also read the first sentence to get an idea of what the selection is about.
Step 4:

"Now, I read the part I chose to study and try to answer my questions. As I do this, I try to determine how the writer has organized his paragraphs because that will help me remember the material better," says Ms. Mills. In addition, she tells her students that she makes sure she studies in an area where she will not have any distractions. When she studies, she tells them she really tries to concentrate very hard; otherwise, it's a waste of time, and she might as well be doing something else.
Step 5:

"This step is the most important for me. I

---

stop to think about the material I have read and answer my questions. If I can't answer my questions, then I go back and reread that part."

Step 6:

"Since I divided the chapter into parts, I take a few moments to go over the main points of the part I just finished studying before going on to a new part," says Ms. Mills.

Step 7:

Ms. Mills tells her students that she then goes to the next part and goes through the same steps. When she has completed the whole assignment, she reveiws everything she has studied by going back to the beginning, looking at each section heading, and trying to state the main idea of each paragraph or central idea of each section. She emphasizes to her students that they should always try to relate their new learning to their past learning because doing so will help them remember the information.

Ms. Mills also tells her students that she doesn't want to sound "preachy," but there are really no shortcuts to studying. "You have to do the work. You have to acquire the necessary skills. No one can do this for you. You have to exert effort. If you do, the rewards are great!"

Reprinted by permission of United Feature Syndicate, Inc., New York, N.Y.

Figure 14.3   In studying, the hard way out is probably the easy way out.

Activities

Here are some sample activities to give your students practice in using the SQ3R technique:

1. Choose a selection your students have not read before, and have them do the following:
   a. Survey the selection to determine what it's about.
   b. Use the given six questions to set purposes for reading. (Prepare six questions that can be used to set purposes for reading and that students can answer.)
   c. Read the selection carefully.
   d. Without looking back at the selection, try to answer the questions.
2. Choose a selection that your students have not read before, and have them formulate questions that could help them in studying.

KNOWING YOUR TEXTBOOK

Helping children to learn about the various parts of their textbooks is an important study skill that can save students valuable time and effort. Here are some things that teachers should have students do after they have acquired their textbooks:

1. *Survey the textbook.* Surveying helps students see how the author presents the material. Students should notice whether the author presents topic headings in bold print or in the margins. Students should also notice if there are diagrams, charts, cartoons, pictures, and so on.
2. *Read the preface.* The preface or foreword, which is at the beginning of the book, is the author's explanation of the book. It presents the author's purpose and plan in writing the book. Here the author usually describes the organization of the book and explains how the book either is different from others in the field or is a further contribution to the field of knowledge.
3. *Read the chapter headings.* The table of contents will give students a good idea of what to expect from the book. Then when they begin to study they will know how each section they are reading relates to the rest of the book.
4. *Skim the index.* The index indicates in detail what material students will find in the book. It is an invaluable aid because it helps students find specific information that they need by giving them the page on which it appears.
5. *Check for a glossary.* Not all books have a glossary; however, a glossary is helpful because it gives students the meanings of specialized words or phrases used in the book.

Activities

Have the students skim to answer the following:

1. Using the index of one of the students' textbooks, the students state the pages on which they would find various topics.
2. Using one of their textbooks, the students give the meaning(s) of some of the terms that are presented in the glossary.
3. Using the table of contents of one of their textbooks, the students state the pages that some chapters start on.

CONCENTRATION

Concentration
Sustained attention. It is essential for both studying and listening to lectures.

You need to help your students recognize that even though they are acquiring some good study habits, they may still have difficulty studying because they cannot *concentrate*. Concentration is necessary not only for studying but also for listening in class. Concentration is sustained attention. If you are not feeling well, if you are hungry or tired, if you are in a room that is too hot or cold, if your chair is uncomfortable, if the lighting is poor or if there is a glare, if there are visual or auditory distractions, you will not be able to concentrate.

Skill in concentration can be developed, and teachers should plan to have their students spend time in this area, which is essential for both reading and listening skills.

Concentration demands a mental set or attitude, a determination that you will block everything out except what you are reading or listening to. For example, how many times have you looked up a phone number in the telephone directory and forgotten the number almost immediately? How many times have you had to look up the *same* number that you had dialed a number of times? Probably very often. The reason for your not remembering is that you did not *concentrate*. In order to remember information, you must concentrate. Concentration demands active involvement; it is hard work. You must help your students recognize that it is a contradiction to say that you will concentrate and relax at the same time. Concentration demands wide-awake and alert individuals. It also demands persons who have a positive frame of mind toward their work. Teachers need to have a good affective environment in their classrooms and be encouraging because the students' attitude or mental set toward what they are doing will greatly influence how well they will do. Obviously if students are not interested in the lecture or reading assignment, they will not be able to concentrate. Teachers should, therefore, try to make the lectures and assignments as interesting as possible.

Of course, it is necessary to help your students understand that paying attention does not guarantee they will comprehend what they have read or heard, but it is an important first step. Without concentration, there is no hope of understanding the information. The following types of activities will help your students develop their concentration.

Activities

Activity 1: Word Concentration (Listening)

In playing this game, just two persons are needed—a speaker and a listener. It can also be played with teams. The speaker says, "Listen carefully. I am going to say some words and when I am through, I want you to repeat them. I will state the words only once and at a rate of one per second. Remember. Listen carefully and do not say them until I am finished. I'll start with two words and then I'll keep adding one word. Let's do one together."

Example: Speaker says, "Train, nail." The listener repeats, "Train, nail." And the speaker says, "Good," if the words are repeated correctly.

Set 1: can/dog . . . red/map . . .
Set 2: mail/milk/book . . . cake/pen/sad . . .
Set 3: sad/none/in/may . . . chair/help/two/six . . .
Set 4: name/sail/bike/pen/man . . . worm/boat/sick/has/more . . .
Set 5: chair/name/key/same/hop/note . . . leg/rope/teach/dance/dog/
        name . . .

Set 6:   witch/rob/sleep/some/read/check/nuts . . . ball/ape/mind/sleep/dog/king/hair . . .

Set 7:   spoon/mate/can/man/all/book/sad/show . . . love/rode/room/all/door/can/girl/pad . . .

Set 8:   boat/lamp/paint/long/dock/teach/knife/win/chair . . . draw/food/pat/car/sand/pan/size/spring/farm . . .

In this game, the words that are presented are not related to one another, so that the listener must concentrate very hard in order to be able to repeat them immediately. This game can be played each day or a few times during the week. Children enjoy playing this game and are delighted when they find that they are able to pay attention for longer periods of time and are, therefore, able to repeat more and more of the words.

See Chapter 9 for a scale that should help in determining how well your students are doing.

Activity 2: Digit-Span Concentration (Listening)

Digit-span exercises based on a graduated level of difficulty are helpful in developing concentration. The instructions for the digits are similar to those in Activity 1 for words; however, in place of words the term *numbers* is inserted. (See Chapter 9.)

Activity 3: Adding Word Concentration (Listening)

The teacher says, "I'm going to say two sets of words. The second set has all the words from Set 1 but it also has a new word. You have to write what the new word is. Example: *Set 1:* pen, dog, tall. *Set 2:* tall, dog, pen, snow. (The new word is *snow.*)"

Set 1:   stamp, week, red
Set 2:   week, stamp, red, (smoke)
Set 1:   child, help, dark, nice
Set 2:   child, (grow), help, nice, dark
Set 1:   sun, spoon, mouth, five, bet
Set 2:   spoon, mouth, five, (game), bet, sun
Set 1:   wild, rose, bread, couch, pill, cup
Set 2:   rose, bread, couch, pill, (crumb), cup, wild
Set 1:   pin, fat, net, pine, wind, swing, dog
Set 2:   fat, net, pine, wind, (damp), swing, pin, dog

FOLLOWING DIRECTIONS

Being able to follow directions is an important skill that we use all our lives. Scarcely a day goes by without the need to obey directions. Cooking, baking, taking medication, driving, traveling, repairing, building, planning, taking examinations, doing assignments, filling out applications, and a hundred other common activities require the ability to follow directions.

You can help your students to be better at following directions through practice and by having them heed the following pointers:

1. Read the directions *carefully*. Do *not* skim directions. Do not take anything for granted and, therefore, skip reading a part of the directions.

2. If you do not understand any directions, do not hesitate to ask your teacher or another student.

3. Concentrate! People who follow directions well tend also to have the ability to concentrate well.

4. Follow the directions that *are* given, not the ones you think ought to be given.

5. Reread the directions if you need to, and refer to them as you follow them.

6. Remember that some directions should be followed step by step.

7. Practice following directions. Try this activity, which will give you experience in following directions.

Directions: Read carefully the entire list of directions that follows before doing anything. You have four minutes to complete this activity.

1. Put your name in the upper right-hand corner of this paper.
2. Put your address under your name.
3. Put your telephone number in the upper left-hand corner of this paper.
4. Add 9370 and 5641.
5. Subtract 453 from 671.
6. Raise your hand and say, "I'm the first."
7. Draw two squares, one triangle, and three circles.
8. Write the opposite of *hot*.
9. Stand up and stamp your feet.
10. Give three meanings for *spring*.
11. Write the numbers from one to ten backward.
12. Write the even numbers from two to twenty.
13. Write the odd numbers from one to twenty-one.
14. Write seven words that rhyme with *fat*.
15. Call out, "I have followed directions."
16. If you have read the directions carefully, you should have done nothing until now. Do only directions 1 and 2.

Answer: The directions stated that you should read the entire list of directions carefully *before doing anything*. You should have done only directions 1 and 2. When you take timed tests, you usually do *not* read the directions as carefully as you should.

Activities

Here is a sample activity in following directions:

Directions: Read each numbered instruction once only, and then carry out the instructions on the boxed material. (This activity requires a great amount of concentration.)

1	7	3	4	play	dog	man	M	N	O
P	Q	35	32	63	15	10	stop	under	big

Instructions

1. If there are two numbers that added together equal 7 and a word that rhymes with *may,* put a line under the rhyming word.
2. If there is a word that means the same as *large,* a word opposite to *go,* and a word that rhymes with *fan,* put a circle around the three words.
3. If there are two numbers that added together equal 8, two numbers that added together equal 67, and a word the opposite of *over,* underline the two numbers that added together equal 8.
4. If there are five consecutive letters, four words that each contain a different vowel, and at least four odd numbers, put a cross on the five consecutive letters.
5. If there are six words, three even numbers, two numbers that added together equal 45, and three numbers that added together equal 16, circle the word *dog.*
6. If there are two numbers that added together equal 25, two numbers that added together equal 95, and three numbers that added together equal 79, put a circle around the three numbers that added together equal 79.

(See the oral directions test in Chapter 5.)

SKIMMING

Setting purposes for reading is a crucial factor. Students need to learn that they read for different purposes. If they are reading for pleasure, they may read either quickly or slowly based on the way they feel. If they are studying or reading information that is new to them, they will probably read very slowly. If, however, they are looking up a telephone number, a name, a date, or looking over a paragraph for its topic, they will read much more rapidly. Reading rapidly to find or locate information is called *skimming.* All skimming

Skimming
Reading rapidly to find or locate information.

involves fast reading; however, there are different kinds of skimming. Skimming for a number, a date, or a name can usually be done much more quickly than for the topic of a paragraph or to answer specific questions. (Some persons call the most rapid reading *scanning* and the less rapid reading skimming.) Teachers should help students recognize that they read rapidly to locate some specific information, but that once they have located what they want, they may read the surrounding information more slowly.

Teachers should also make sure that students do not confuse skimming with studying. Although skimming is used as part of the SQ3R technique when students survey a passage, skimming material is not the same as studying. Studying requires much slower and more concentrated reading.

Skimming is an important skill because it is used so often throughout one's life, and it is many times the only way to get a job done in a reasonable amount of time. Some skimming activities for upper-intermediate-grade students follow:

1. Skim newspaper headlines for a particular news item.
2. Skim movie ads for a particular movie.
3. Skim tape or record catalogs for a specific title.
4. Skim the Yellow Pages of the phone book for some help.
5. Skim the television guide to find a particular show.

ASKING QUESTIONS

A section on asking questions is being presented because this is an area in which students need special help. Many students become intimidated early in school about asking questions and as a result hardly ever ask any. Asking questions is an important part of learning, and this point has been made a number of times in this book. However, children must be helped to recognize this, and teachers must provide an environment that is nonthreatening so that students will feel free to ask questions. Knowing how and when to ask questions helps students to gain a better insight into a subject, gives the teacher feedback, and slows the teacher down if he or she is going too fast. Unfortunately, as has already been stated, many students are afraid to ask questions. Sometimes their fear may be caused by a teacher's attitude; however, often it's because a student doesn't know how to formulate the question or is "afraid of looking like a fool."

Questions
A good way for students to gain a better insight into a subject; questioning also gives the instructor feedback and slows the instructor down if he or she is going too fast.

Here are some pointers that teachers should try to get across to their students:

1. Students who ask the best questions are usually those who know the material best.

2. Asking questions is not a substitute for studying the material.
3. Questions help to clarify the material for students.
4. Teachers usually want and encourage questions.
5. The questions students ask will probably help a number of other students.

Here are suggestions on the kind of questions students should ask about examinations:

1. What kind of test will it be? Will it be an objective or subjective test?
2. How long will the test be? (This will help the students to know whether it's a quiz (a minor exam) or a test (one that usually counts more than a quiz).
3. Will dates, names, formulas, and other such specifics be stressed? (Whether or not these things are stressed is important for the student to know because it will influence the type of studying that he or she will do.)
4. Will it be an open-book or closed-book exam? (This option is important because it will influence the type of studying a student will do.)
5. What chapters will be covered?

Here are some suggestions on other kinds of questions students should ask:

1. In going over an examination, they should ask general questions or those that relate to everyone's papers. Tell students that if they have specific questions on their papers, they should ask the teacher their questions in private.
2. Tell students that they should not hesitate to ask questions about the marking of their papers if they do not understand it. They should especially ask the teacher about a comment on their papers that they do not understand. Help them to recognize that they learn from knowing the results and understanding their mistakes.

Here are some suggestions on how students should ask questions:

1. They should be as specific as possible.
2. They should state the question clearly.
3. They should not say, "I have a question," and then go into a long discourse before asking it. (The question may be forgotten.)
4. They should make sure that the question is related to the material.

Teachers should also help students remember that questioning is an important part of SQ3R and that questions help them set purposes for their reading. Questions help give direction and organization to their reading and help them to be actively involved while reading. Good readers usually ask questions before, during, and after the reading. The questions they ask could be triggered by a number of things. For example, they may have found some inconsistency in their reading or feel that the writer is being biased, or they may feel that what they are reading is confusing. Students who are good critical readers ask many questions of the text they are reading.

READING AND WRITING AS MODES OF LEARNING

There are a number of reading and writing strategies that teachers can help students acquire that would help the students learn better. Teachers should share with students that notetaking is an effective learning tool that they can combine with SQ3R to help them in their studying, and so are summaries, outlining, and graphic organizers. Teachers should introduce each and help the students acquire these skills.

Notetaking for Studying

Notetaking
A useful study and paper-writing tool.

Notetaking is a very important tool; it is useful not only in writing long papers but also in studying. Students are usually not concerned with notetaking until they begin writing long reports or papers. Teachers should help students learn how to take notes. Here is information on notetaking that teachers should convey to their upper-intermediate-grade students.

Notes consist of words and phrases that help persons remember important material. They do not have to be complete sentences; however, unless an individual's notes are clear and organized, he or she will have difficulty in using them for study.

Scenario: Notetaking, Studying, and SQ3R

Ms. Mills presents the following notes to her students on a transparency. (She tells the students that the notes do not belong to anyone in the class. Nevertheless, the notes are on a topic they have been studying.) She asks her students to examine the notes carefully.

Notes

1. Influenced by age
2. influenced by gender
3. skin
4. thin
5. outer layer
6. several layers
7. epidermis
8. dermis
9. tough
10. stores fat
11. thicker than epidermis

List of Main Topics

I. Age of skin
II. Layers of skin
III. Skin

She asks her students what they think about the notes. Are the notes "jogging their memories" about what they had studied? Refreshing memories is the main purpose of notes for studying. She then discusses with her students why the notes were not very helpful. Here are the things they stated:

> It is difficult to make sense of these notes because the main topics are either vaguely stated, too general, or too specific.
>
> The items in the list of notes can fit under more than one main topic; they are not precise enough; that is, they do not contain enough information to unmistakably identify or distinguish them.

Ms. Mills then tells her students that note-taking for study can be incorporated in the SQ3R study technique. Here is a suggested procedure combining SQ3R and notetaking that she presents to her students:

1. Students should read the whole selection to get an overview of what they have to study. A preliminary reading helps them see the organization of the material.
2. Students should choose a part of the selection to study, basing their choice on their concentration ability.
3. Students should survey the part chosen and note the topic of the individual paragraph or group of paragraphs. They should write the topic(s) in their notebook instead of the questions they would write in a normal SQ3R procedure.
4. Students should read the part.
5. After they finish reading each paragraph, they should state its main idea. Students should put down *only* important supporting details under the main idea.
   a. Although students do not have to use a formal outline for their notes, they should *indent* their listing so that the relation of supporting material to main ideas is clear.
   b. Students should try not to take any notes until after they have finished reading the whole paragraph. They should remember that *recall* is the essential step in the SQ3R technique. By not taking notes until they have finished reading, they are more actively involved in thinking about the material as they try to construct notes.

Semantic mapping (graphic organizer) A graphic representation used to illustrate concepts and relationships among concepts such as classes, properties, and examples.

Good notes are very helpful for review, and they can save students a great amount of time.

You should help your students recognize that for study, if the material is new to them, it's usually a good idea to write the topic for each paragraph unless the paragraph is a transitional one. You should also tell your students that textbook writers sometimes list the topics of their paragraphs in the margins and the students should be on the lookout for these helpful clues.

A number of students find that a visual representation of the material helps them to remember information they have studied. The following scenario presents the technique Ms. Mills uses to help her students.

Scenario: Semantic Mapping (Graphic Organizer) and Studying

Ms. Mills tells her students that rather than taking notes using an informal outline, they could make a graphic illustration of what they are studying. She then enumerates these steps for her students:

Step 1: Again, as in SQ3R, we choose the amount of information we will be studying. (This is usually more than a paragraph.)

Step 2: We set our purposes for reading.

Step 3: We read the material.

Step 4: We determine the central idea of what we have read and place it in the center of a blank sheet of paper.

Step 5: We reread each paragraph, state the main topic of each, and append it to the central idea.

Step 6: We go over the material once again and append the important supporting details to its main topic. (Figure 14.4 is an example of a semantic map that Ms. Mills did with her class.)

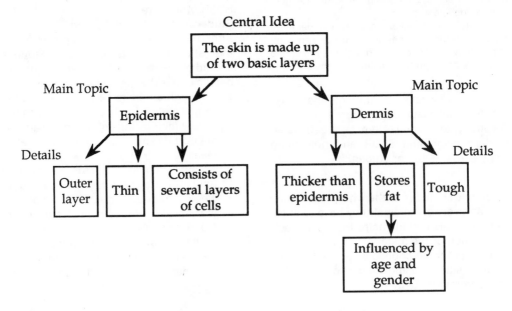

Figure 14.4   Graphic organizer as an aid to studying.

Special Note

Rather than stating the topic of every paragraph, teachers could have the students state the main idea of each one and append supporting details to each main idea. There really is no correct way to construct a graphic illustration. The test is whether it helps students recall a significant amount of information.

Summaries as a Mode of Learning

Many teachers are helping intermediate- and higher-grade level students learn how to summarize passages because they recognize summaries as a viable means of gaining the essential information. Summarizing material helps persons retain the most important facts in a long passage, and if the summary is a written summary, it helps integrate the reading and writing process.

Teachers can help elementary children learn how to summarize by beginning with paragraphs and then working up to longer

Summary
A brief statement of the essential information in a longer piece.

passages. Children should know that a good summary should be brief and should include only essential information. The main idea of the paragraph (if only a paragraph is being summarized) or the central idea of an article and the important facts should be stated but not necessarily in the sequence presented in the article. The sequence in the paragraph or article must be followed in the summary only if that sequence is essential. Teachers need to help their students include only the information stated in the paragraph or article and not what they think should have been included or their opinions.

Before teachers work with summaries, it might be a good idea for them to review with their students how to find the main idea of passages.

TEST TAKING

The term *tests* seems to make most students shudder. However, tests are necessary to help students learn about their weaknesses so that they can improve and also learn about their strengths; they help give students a steady and encouraging measure of their growth; and tests are helpful for review.

The more students know about tests, the better they can do on them. The general test-taking principles that follow are provided for you the teacher so that you can help your students to be better test takers. The principles you present to your students will depend on the grade level you are teaching as well as the students with whom you are working. Many intermediate-grade students are ready to learn about test-taking techniques and how to study for them. As a matter of fact, so are some primary-grade children. Although children today seem to be test-wise, most really are not.

Teachers should help students to be better test takers. The first thing that teachers should try to help students understand is that the best way to do well on a test is to be *well prepared*. There are no shortcuts to studying. However, research has shown that people do better on tests if they know certain test-taking techniques and if they are familiar with the various types of tests.

Here are some general test-taking principles:

1. Students should plan to do well. They should have a *positive* attitude.
2. Students should be well rested.
3. Students should be prepared. The better prepared an individual is, the less nervous and anxious he or she will be.
4. Students should look upon tests as a learning experience.
5. Students should look over the whole test before they begin. They should notice the types of questions asked and the points allotted for each question. (Students have to learn not to spend a long time on a one- to five-point question that they know a lot about. They should answer it and go on.)

6. Students should know how much time is allotted for the test. (Students need to learn to allot their time wisely and to check the time.)

7. Students should concentrate!

8. Students should read instructions very carefully. (Students need to be helped in this area because many times they read into the questions things that are not there. Students must learn that if a question asks for a description and *examples,* they must give the examples. Students also need to learn that if they do not undersand something or if something does not make sense, they should ask the teacher about it because there may be a mistake on the test.)

9. Students should begin with the questions they are sure of. This will give them a feeling of confidence and success. However, as already advised, they must learn not to dwell on these at length.

10. If students do not know an answer, they should make an intelligent guess. As long as the penalty for a wrong answer is the same as for no answer, it pays to take a calculated guess. (Of course, if the guess is wrong, students will not get any points for it.)

11. After students answer the questions they are sure of, they should work on those that count the most, that is, that are worth the greatest number of points.

12. Students should allow time to go over the test. They should check that they have answered all the questions. They should be leery about changing a response unless they have found a particular reason to while going over the test. For example, they may have misread the question, they may have misinterpreted the question, or they may not have realized that it was a "tricky" question. If the question is a straightforward one, it's probably better for students to leave their first response.

13. After the test has been graded and returned, students should go over it to learn from the results. Unless students find out why an answer is wrong and what the correct answer is, they may continue to make the same mistake on other tests.

14. Students should study the test after they get it back to determine what their teacher emphasizes on tests.

THE SCHOOL LIBRARY AND LIBRARY SKILLS

The school library should be an integrated part of the students' ongoing activities. A number of schools have designed their physical plants so that the library is actually in the center of the building, easily accessible to all classrooms. The library, properly utilized, becomes the students' storehouse of information and a reservoir of endless delight.

The atmosphere in the library should be such that children feel welcome, invited, and wanted. The librarian is the individual who is

Figure 14.5 The library is an integral part of the school program.

responsible for setting this tone. A friendly, warm person who loves children and books will usually have a library which has similar characteristics. Children should feel free to visit the library at all times, not just during their regularly scheduled periods.

An enthusiastic and inventive librarian will, by various means, act as an invitation to children to come to the library. Some librarians engage in weekly storytelling for all grade levels. Librarians should encourage teachers and children to make suggestions for storytelling, as well as to share the kinds of books they enjoy and would like. The librarian should also act as a resource person in helping the classroom teacher develop library skills in students. Once students gain the "library habit," it is hard to break, and it will remain with them throughout life.

Following are some of the library skills that children should receive in the elementary school.

Primary Grades

In the primary grades children are ready to acquire some library skills that will help them become independent library users. First, the teacher can help primary-grade children learn the kinds of books that are available in the library, for example, fiction and nonfiction books. Definitions of the terms should be given, as well as examples of each type of book. For best results, the examples used should be books with which the children are familiar.

Primary-grade children who have learned to read and can alphabetize can also learn to use the card catalog. They should learn that there are three kinds of cards for each book: an author card, a title card, and the subject card. The teacher should have samples of these for the children to see and handle. By simulating this activity in the classroom, children will be better prepared for actual library activity. Also, their chances for success in using the catalog properly to find a desired book will be increased. This useful activity can also be programmed to reinforce knowledge of alphabetizing.

Intermediate and Upper-Elementary Grades

By the fourth grade children can learn about other categories of books in the library, such as biographies and reference books.

Reference Books

Children in the elementary grades ask many questions about many topics. Teachers should use some of these questions to help children learn about reference sources. Teachers should help children understand that it is impossible for one person to know everything today because of the vast amount of knowledge that already exists, compounded each year by its exponential growth. However, a person can learn about any particular area or field if he or she knows what source books to go to for help. For example, the *Readers' Guide to Periodical Literature* will help one to find magazine articles written on almost any subject of interest. There are reference books on language and usage, such as Roget's *Thesaurus of English Words and Phrases,* which would help upper-grade students find synonyms and less trite words to use in writing.

Figure 14.6 These students are working together on a report.

The dictionary, which is a very important reference book, is probably the one with which the students are the most familiar. It is helpful in supplying the following information to a student:

1. Spelling.
2. Correct usage.
3. Derivations and inflected forms.
4. Accents and other diacritical markings.
5. Antonyms.
6. Synonyms.
7. Syllabication.
8. Definitions.
9. Parts of speech.
10. Idiomatic phrases.

The most often used reference book in elementary school, besides the dictionary, is the encyclopedia. Children should be helped to use the encyclopedia as a tool and as an aid, rather than as an end in itself. That is, children should be shown how to extract information from the encyclopedia without copying the article verbatim.

In the upper elementary grades children should learn that there are many reference books available in the library which can supply information about a famous writer, baseball player, scientist, celebrity, and so forth. The key factor is knowing that these reference sources exist and knowing which book to go to for the needed information.

Teachers can help their upper-grade children familiarize themselves with these reference books by giving them assignments in which they have to determine what source books to use in fulfilling the assignment.

Student's Name:_____

Grade:_____

Teacher:_____

Diagnostic Checklist for Reading and Study Skills

I. Dictionary	Yes	No	Sometimes

A. GRADES 1, 2

The student is able to
1. supply missing letters of the alphabet.
2. arrange words none of which begin with the same letter in alphabetical order.
3. list words several of which begin with the same letter.

Student's Name:_____

Grade:_____

Teacher:_____

Diagnostic Checklist for Reading and Study Skills (Cont.)

I. Dictionary	Yes	No	Sometimes
4. list words according to first and second letters.			
5. list words according to third letter.			
6. find the meaning of a word.			
7. find the correct spelling of a word.			

B. GRADES 3, 4, 5, 6

The student is able to

	Yes	No	Sometimes
1. locate words halfway in the dictionary.			
2. open the dictionary by quarters and state the letters with which words begin.			
3. open the dictionary by thirds and state the letters with which words begin.			
4. open the dictionary at certain initial letters.			
5. use key words at the head of each page as a guide to finding words.			
6. use the dictionary to select meanings to fit the context (homographs).			
7. use the dictionary to build up a vocabulary of synonyms.			
8. use the dictionary to build up a vocabulary of antonyms.			
9. answer questions about the derivation of a word.			
10. use the dictionary to learn to pronounce a word.			
11. use the dictionary to correctly syllabicate a word.			
12. use the dictionary to get the correct usage of a word.			
13. use the dictionary to determine the part(s) of speech of the word.			
14. use the dictionary to gain the meanings of idiomatic phrases.			

Student's Name: _____

Grade: _____

Teacher: _____

Diagnostic Checklist for Reading and Study Skills (Cont.)

2. Library Skills	Yes	No	Sometimes

A.   PRIMARY GRADES

The student is able to
1. use the card catalog to find a book.
2. state the kinds of books that are found in the library.

B.   INTERMEDIATE GRADES

The student is able to
1. state the kinds of reference materials that are found in the library.
2. use the encyclopedia as an aid to gaining needed information.
3. find books in the school library.

3. Building Good Study Habits	Yes	No	Sometimes

INTERMEDIATE GRADES

The student is able to
1. plan his or her studying time.
2. choose a place to study that is free from distractions.
3. recognize that he or she needs to study.

4. Study Procedures	Yes	No	Sometimes

INTERMEDIATE GRADES

The student is able to
1. use the SQ3R technique when studying.
2. apply the SQ3R technique when studying a chapter in a textbook.

Student's Name: _____

Grade: _____

Teacher: _____

Diagnostic Checklist for Reading and Study Skills (Cont.)

5. Concentration and Following Directions	Yes	No	Sometimes

A. PRIMARY GRADES

The student is able to
1. listen carefully and follow directions.
2. read directions and follow them carefully.
3. show that concentration is increasing by being able to pay attention for longer periods of time.

B. INTERMEDIATE GRADES

The student is able to
1. listen carefully and follow directions.
2. read directions and follow them correctly.
3. fill out some application forms.

6. Skimming	Yes	No	Sometimes

A. PRIMARY GRADES

The student is able to
1. find some information quickly by skimming.
2. skim a paragraph and state its topic.

B. INTERMEDIATE GRADES

The student is able to
1. differentiate between skimming and studying.
2. recognize the role that skimming plays in studying.
3. locate information such as the departure time of trains by skimming train schedules.

Student's Name: _____

Grade: _____

Teacher: _____

Diagnostic Checklist for Reading and Study Skills (Cont.)

7. Knowing Your Textbook	Yes	No	Sometimes

A. PRIMARY GRADES

The student is able to
1. use the table of contents to find chapter headings.
2. use the glossary to gain the meaning of a word.
3. list the parts of a textbook.

B. INTERMEDIATE GRADES

The student is able to
1. read the preface to learn about the author's purpose in writing the book.
2. skim the index to learn about the material that will be found in the book.
3. skim the index to find the page on which a specific topic is found.

8. Asking Questions	Yes	No	Sometimes

A. PRIMARY GRADES

The student is able to
1. formulate questions that will obtain the wanted information.
2. ask questions that are pertinent to the topic under discussion.

B. INTERMEDIATE GRADES

The student will be able to
1. ask questions that will help in studying for a test.
2. ask questions that will help in learning about what to study.

Student's Name:_____

Grade:_____

Teacher:_____

Diagnostic Checklist for Reading and Study Skills (Cont.)

9. Test Taking	Yes	No	Sometimes

A.   PRIMARY GRADES

The student is able to
1. read questions very carefully so that they are answered correctly.
2. follow directions in taking a test.

	Yes	No	Sometimes
1.			
2.			

B.   INTERMEDIATE GRADES

The student is able to
1. recognize that he or she studies differently for objective and essay tests.
2. take objective tests.
3. take essay tests.
4. go over the test to learn why he or she did not do well.
5. ask questions about a test to learn from the mistakes.

	Yes	No	Sometimes
1.			
2.			
3.			
4.			
5.			

10. Summaries	Yes	No	Sometimes

INTERMEDIATE GRADES

The student is able to
1. summarize a passage.
2. use a summary for study.

	Yes	No	Sometimes
1.			
2.			

11. Notetaking	Yes	No	Sometimes

INTERMEDIATE GRADES

The student is able to
1. explain why notetaking is a useful study tool.

	Yes	No	Sometimes
1.			

SUMMARY

Chapter 14 is concerned with presenting information and procedures to help teachers develop a study skills program for their students because the emphasis in a diagnostic-reading and correction program is on *prevention*. The importance of building good study habits, which includes when to study, where to study, and the amount of time to spend in studying, was discussed. In discussing how to study, the SQ3R technique was explored. Examples of how to use this technique and activities were also given. In addition, a scenario was presented in which a teacher modeled the use of the SQ3R approach in studying. Teachers were shown how to help their students gain competence in concentration and questioning. Skimming, reading rapidly to find information, was discussed, as well as how the ability to summarize passages helps students retain information. Reading and writing strategies as modes of learning were presented in scenario form, as was semantic mapping (graphic organizer), and these were suggested as ways to help students retain information they have studied. Since this chapter is a comprehensive one on study skills, topics such as "Knowing Your Textbook" and "Test Taking" were also presented, as was a diagnostic checklist for reading and study skills.

SUGGESTIONS FOR THOUGHT QUESTIONS AND ACTIVITIES

1. You have been appointed to a special committee to help develop a study skills program for your elementary school. What suggestions would you make? What kinds of skills and activities would

you recommend for the primary grades? For the intermediate grades?

2. Develop some concentration activities for primary-grade children.
3. Develop some concentration activities for intermediate-grade students.
4. You have students who seem to make careless errors on tests. What would you do to help them be better test takers?
5. What kind of program would you develop to help your students be better notetakers?
6. Some teachers in your school system feel that elementary-grade children are too immature to learn study skill techniques. What do you think? How would you convince these teachers that this is not so?
7. How can reading and writing be used as modes of learning?
8. What is the role of semantic maps in learning information?

SELECTED BIBLIOGRAPHY

Bransford, John D., Robert Sherwood, Nancy Vye, and John Rieser. "Teaching Thinking and Problem Solving." *American Psychologist* 41 (October 1986): 1078–89.

Davis, T. Zephaniah, and Michael D. McPherson. "Story Map Instruction: A Road Map for Reading Comprehension." *The Reading Teacher* 43 (December 1989): 232–40.

Hayes, David A. "Helping Students GRASP the Knack of Writing Summaries." *Journal of Reading* 33 (November 1989): 96–101.

Kuhrt, Bonnie L., and Pamela J. Farris. "Empowering Students Through Reading, Writing, and Reasoning." *Journal of Reading* 33 (March 1990): 436–41.

Rubin, Dorothy. *Reading and Learning Power,* 3rd ed. Needham, Mass.: Ginn Press, 1990.

Schmitt, Maribeth Cassidy. "A Questionnaire to Measure Children's Awareness of Strategic Reading Processes." *The Reading Teacher* 43 (March 1990): 454–61.

15

Helping Special Children

INTRODUCTION

"The success of education depends on adapting teaching to the individual differences among learners."[1] This statement, which is centuries old, has been echoed by many educators. Most educators agree that we must take the individual differences of our students into account and adjust our curriculum and instruction to their needs. The question no longer is whether these things can be done; they must be done! And they are not easy!

Scenario: Mr. Brown—A Teacher Who Cares

Let's look for a moment at the composition of Mr. Brown's self-contained sixth-grade class. He has thirty children of approximately the same chronological age, but there is a seven-year spread in mental ages. His students range from slow learners to gifted; also, he has one exceptionally creative student who is very talented in art. (Some of this child's graphic drawings are heartrending; they depict the world around him.) In addition, Mr. Brown has a num-ber of students who do not speak English; and almost all the others speak nonstandard English.

Mr. Brown is concerned because this is the year that the sixth graders are given group intelligence tests. Even though he does not put much stock in the results of these group tests for most of his students because he feels the tests are not valid for them, he knows that there are others in the system who do.

[1] Lyn Corno and Richard E. Snow, "Adapting Teaching to Individual Differences Among Learners," *Handbook of Research on Teaching*, 3rd ed. (New York: Macmillan, 1986). p. 605.

From the mix of his class, James was beginning to wonder if there were "average" children, or what it means to be average. And certainly if one were to define "at-risk" children as those who do poorly on screening measures, he was sure that he had almost a class full of those.

James Brown isn't interested in labeling children; he just wants to do the best he can to help them. One of the best ways is to learn as much as he can about them. This chapter will help James Brown do just that.

Public Law 94–142
Advocates a free appropriate education for all children in the least restrictive environment.

Public Law 94–142 advocates a free appropriate education for all children in the least restrictive environment. This law has brought to the fore the importance of the uniqueness of each child. In the regular classroom there is usually a wide range of ability, which generally includes the borderline (slow-learning) and the gifted child.[2] As a result of Public Law 94–142, exceptional children may be mainstreamed into the regular classroom. In order to be able to work with such children, all teachers, not just special education teachers, must become more knowledgeable of exceptional children. The more teachers know about the children with whom they work, the better able they will be to provide for their individual differences and needs.

This chapter provides reading and other language arts methods that are most applicable for those children whom teachers currently have in their regular classrooms, such as the borderline child and the gifted child; however, they may also be adapted for children who may be mainstreamed. Public Law 94–142 requires that exceptional children have individualized programs especially prepared for them. These individualized programs are too varied to be presented in a text with as broad a scope as this one. Teachers who have mainstreamed children in their classrooms are, therefore, encouraged to go to special education texts for more in-depth coverage.

Exceptional children
Those children who deviate so much from the "average" that they require special attention.

KEY QUESTIONS

After you finish reading this chapter, you should be able to answer the following questions:

1. Who is the "average" child?
2. Who are the "gifted" children?
3. What is mainstreaming?
4. What does the term *learning disability* mean?
5. What are the identification biases of children labeled "educable mentally retarded"?
6. What should a teacher know about the cognitive styles of students?

[2] Although gifted children are classified as exceptional children, they are generally found in the regular classroom. Borderline (slow-learning) children are not classified as exceptional children in the revised AAMD definition.

7. What are the kinds of reading and other language arts experiences that should be planned for the borderline or slow-learning child?
8. What kinds of instructional provisions should be provided for the gifted child?
9. How can children in the regular classroom be prepared for a mainstreamed child?
10. What is attention-deficit disorder (ADD)?

KEY TERMS IN CHAPTER

You should pay special attention to the following new terms:

attention-deficit disorder
  (ADD)
average children
borderline children (slow
  learners)
creativity
educable mentally retarded
  children
exceptional children
gifted children
learning disability
mainstreaming
Public Law 94–142
social promotion

THE "AVERAGE" CHILD

Average children
Often referred to children who score in the IQ range approximately from 90–110.

The first question that comes to mind whenever anyone labels someone an average child is, Is there really an "average" child? Actually, there probably is not. Every child is an individual and as such is unique. However, for research purposes we tend to look upon the average child as that individual who scores in the IQ range from 90 to 110. Studies are based on averages, and averages are necessary as criteria or points of reference. Only after we have determined the criteria for "average" can we talk about "above or below average."

THE BORDERLINE CHILD OR "SLOW LEARNER"

Borderline children (slow learners)
Children whose IQs usually range from approximately 70 to 85.

The borderline child is usually described as a dull, average child who is borderline in his or her intellectual functioning. These children's IQ scores range from approximately 70 to 85. As a result, they generally have difficulty doing schoolwork. Borderline children are not, however, equally slow in all their activities or abnormal in all their characteristics. It is difficult at times to differentiate borderline children and children with specific learning disabilities from underachievers produced by disadvantaged environments.[3]

Providing Instruction

Social promotion
Promotion of students based on chronological age rather than achievement.

Teachers in regular classrooms have many times been frustrated because they have had children who do not seem to be able to learn material that is considered "average" for the specific grade level. Not only is the teacher frustrated, but so is the child. A child with IQ test scores in the 70 to 85 range would have difficulty working at grade level. Because of social promotion (children are promoted according to chronological age rather than achievement) children are moved along each year into a higher grade. As slow learners go through the grades, their problems generally become more pronounced and compounded unless they are given special attention.

The term *slow learner* is probably a misnomer, because the term implies that a child needs more time to get a concept, but eventually will acquire it. Actually, there are some concepts that slow learners cannot acquire no matter how long they work on them because slow learners usually cannot work in the abstract. Obviously, the teacher should not use inductive or deductive teaching techniques in working with slow learners. Slow learners generally can learn material if it is presented at a concrete level. Slow learners usually must be given many opportunities to go over the same concept; slow learners must have a large amount of practice in an area beyond the point where they think that they know it, in order to *overlearn* it. The practice should be varied and interesting to stimulate them.

To motivate the slow learners, many games and gamelike activities may be used. Slow learners have a short attention span, so learning tasks should be broken down into small, discrete steps. Generally requiring close supervision, they may have difficulty working independently. Distractions must be kept at a minimum, and each task should be very exactly defined and explained. It is necessary to define short-range goals, which slow learners can accomplish, to give them a sense of achievement. Slow learners are usually set in their ways, and once they learn something in one way, they will be very rigid about changing.

The teacher should recognize that individual differences exist within groups as well as between groups. Obviously, there will be individual differences among slow learners.

Reading Instruction

In Chapter 4 you learned that children who are advanced in language development have a better chance for success in school

[3] Samuel A. Kirk, Sister Joanne Marie Kliebhan, and Janet W. Lerner, *Teaching Reading to Slow and Disabled Learners* (Boston: Houghton Mifflin, 1978), p. 3.

than those who are not. Slow development of language is a noticeable characteristic of slow-learning children. The teacher recognizes that these children need many opportunities to express themselves orally and that they learn best at a concrete level. The teacher should, therefore, plan his or her program for slow-learning children to include many *firsthand experiences* where the children can deal with real things. The teacher can take the children on trips to visit farm animals, zoo animals, the firehouse, the police station, factories, railroad stations, farms, and so on. In planning for the trip, the teacher should use the same good practices that are used for all children. The teacher should discuss the trip with the children beforehand and give them the opportunity to help plan for the trip. After the trip the teacher should encourage the children to discuss what they saw. The teacher and children could then cooperatively write an experience story about the visit.

In helping slow-learning children acquire new words, the teacher should recognize that these children will learn and retain words that they will use in their everyday conversation more readily than abstract words. It, therefore, helps for the teacher to associate the new words with their pictorial representations, real objects, or actions. Slow learners must repeatedly hear and see these words in association with objects, pictures, or actions in order to learn them. As mentioned in the previous section, the children must have a large amount of practice to *overlearn* the words.

Slow-learning children not only have problems in working with abstract words, but they also have difficulty dealing with words in isolation. Cohen's study has shown that the slower students are in academic progress, the more difficult it is for them to deal with words in isolation, unrelated to a totally meaningful experience.[4] Her study has also found that the reading aloud of stories that are at the interest, ability, and attention span level of the children is an excellent means of helping the children to develop vocabulary and sentence sense. After listening to a story, the children should be encouraged to engage in some oral expression activities. All children need many opportunities to express themselves, and slow learners are no exception. A child who feels accepted and is in a nonthreatening environment will feel more free to contribute than one who feels embarrassed.

In providing language arts instruction the teacher should provide opportunities for the slow-learning child to work with other children. Oral expression (speech stimulation) activities such as choral speaking, finger play, and creative drama are good for these purposes. The child should be given opportunities to share with the other children; all children seek approval of peers as well as of adults.

[4] Dorothy H. Cohen, "The Effect of Literature on Vocabulary and Reading Achievement," *Elementary English* 45 (February 1968): 209–213, 217.

Gifted children fall into the category of exceptional children because this group of children deviates greatly from "average" children.

When one talks about the gifted, immediately visions of small children wearing horn-rimmed glasses and carrying encyclopedias come to mind. This is a myth. There are many definitions of the gifted. In recent years the definition of the "gifted" has been broadened to include not only the verbally gifted with an IQ above 132 on the Stanford-Binet Intelligence Scale but also those individuals whose performance in any line of socially useful endeavor is consistently superior.

Marland's national definition in a congressional report alerts educators to the multifaceted aspects of giftedness:

> Gifted and talented children are those identified by professionally qualified persons who by virtue of outstanding abilities are capable of high performance. These are children who require differentiated educational programs and services beyond those normally provided by the regular school program in order to realize their contribution to self and society.
>
> Children capable of high performance include those with demonstrated achievement and/or potential ability in any of the following areas:
>
> 1. General intellectual ability
> 2. Specific academic aptitude
> 3. Creative or productive thinking
> 4. Leadership ability
> 5. Visual and performing arts
> 6. Psychomotor ability[5]

Gifted children
The academically gifted are usually those with an IQ above 132 on the Stanford Binet Intelligence Scale; however, "gifted" also usually refers to those whose performance in any line of socially useful endeavor is consistently superior.

Characteristics

Gifted children, on the average, are socially, emotionally, physically, and intellectually superior to "average" children in the population. Gifted children have, on the average, superior general intelligence, a desire to know, originality, common sense, will power and perseverance, a desire to excel, self-confidence, prudence and forethought, and a good sense of humor, among a host of other admirable traits. Their language development is usually very advanced. They generally have a large stock of vocabulary and delight in learning new words. Many have learned to read before they came to school; they usually have wide-ranging interests that they pursue in extensive depth, they tend to be voracious readers, and they delight in challenge. However, it is possible that without some guidance, a number of gifted students may not read very challenging books.

Instructional Provisions

Gifted children need special attention because of their precocious learning abilities. However, when gifted children are not given special

---

[5] S. P. Marland, *Education of the Gifted and the Talented* (Washington, D.C.: U.S. Office of Education, 1972), p. 10.

attention, they still usually manage to work on grade level. As a result, gifted children are often ignored. Regrettably, they are actually the most neglected of all exceptional children. Attention is given to those who have "more need." Margaret Mead, the renowned anthropologist, has written about this attitude toward the gifted, which is still applicable today:

> Whenever the rise to success cannot be equated with preliminary effort, abstinence and suffering, it tends to be attributed to "luck," which relieves the spectator from according the specially successful person any merit. . . . In American education, we have tended to reduce the gift to a higher I.Q.—thus making it a matter of merely a little more on the continuity scale, to insist on putting more money and effort in bringing the handicapped child "up to par" as an expression of fair play and "giving everyone a break" and to disallow special gifts. By this refusal to recognize special gifts, we have wasted and dissipated, driven into apathy or schizophrenia, uncounted numbers of gifted children. If they learn easily, they are penalized for having nothing to do; if they excel in some outstanding way, they are penalized as being conspicuously better than the peer group, and teachers warn the gifted child, "Yes, you can do that, it's much more interesting than what the others are doing. But, remember, the rest of the class will dislike you for it."[6]

Gifted children, like all other children, need guidance and instruction based on their interests, needs, and ability levels. Although gifted children gain abstract concepts quickly and are intellectually capable of working at high levels of abstraction, unless they receive appropriate instruction to gain needed skills, they may not be able to realize their potential. Gifted children should not be subjected to unnecessary drill and repetition. They usually enjoy challenge and have long attention spans, so teachers need to provide instruction that will challenge and interest them. One way that teachers can provide for their gifted students so that they can work at their own pace in many areas is through individualized programs (see Chapter 11.)

The manner in which material is presented to gifted children should be guided by a knowledge of their characteristics. The atmosphere in the classroom should be one in which gifted students are respected as persons capable of independent work and leadership, and the subject matter that is presented should allow for student involvement, choice, and interaction. Also, the instruction for gifted students should focus on those activities that involve the higher levels of the cognitive domain; that is, gifted children should spend the most time in activities that require analysis, synthesis, and evaluation. They should also be encouraged by their teachers to be intelligent risk takers, to defend their ideas, delve deeply into problems, seek alternate solutions to problems, follow through on hunches, and dream the impossible dream. In short, gifted students will know that

[6] Margaret Mead, "The Gifted Child in the American Culture of Today," *Journal of Teacher Education* 5 (September 1954): 211–12.

their teachers value their talents if they are provided with challenge commensurate with their abilities.

Reading Instruction

In an earlier section, it is stated that gifted children are usually advanced in language learning and that many have learned to read before they come to school. According to Lewis Terman, a noted psychologist who did monumental research on the gifted, nearly half of the gifted children he studied learned to read before starting school; at least 20 percent before the age of five years, 6 percent before four, and 1.6 percent before three years.[7] Most of these children learned to read with little or no formal instruction. Other studies seem to corroborate these findings. However, these findings should not be taken to mean that gifted children can fend for themselves, and that teachers should spend more time with others. It does mean that the teacher must provide alternate programs for gifted children. To not recognize that these children are reading when they first enter school and to make them go through a program geared to "average" children can be devastating.

Also frustrating for a gifted child is to be told, "Put your hand down. You're not supposed to know that yet." Such teacher statements can discourage gifted students from participating in discussions, as well as make them feel ostracized. If the teacher feels that gifted students are dominating the discussion or are answering questions too soon, the teacher should take stock of his or her program. Perhaps the teacher could have the gifted students be the discussion leaders for certain topics or ask the gifted students to provide special information about the topic that they could share with the rest of the class or group.

Gifted students usually have wide-ranging interests that they like to pursue in extensive depth, and they are generally impatient with detail. Teachers should give their gifted students the time and opportunity to pursue their interests in depth. Also, the teacher should provide a rich and varied program for his or her gifted students because they are usually able to work in a number of activities simultaneously.

While the gifted need opportunities to work with other gifted children, they also need to work with children on all ability levels. Children who work together in activities that tap the special abilities of all the children will usually learn to understand each other better. Speech-stimulating activities such as choral speaking, creative drama, and puppetry give gifted children an opportunity to work with children on all ability levels.

Although many gifted students enjoy writing and engage in it

[7] Lewis Terman and Melita Oden, *The Gifted Child Grows Up*, Genetic Studies of Genius, vol. 4 (Stanford, Calif.: Stanford University Press, 1947).

frequently for their own pleasure, some may lack basic writing skills, because it is often taken for granted that highly able students have all the basic skills that they need at their fingertips. This assumption is not so. Like other children, they must attain these skills. Also, teachers must challenge their gifted students with stimulating writing activities.

THE CREATIVE CHILD

> I see the mind of a five year old ... as a volcano with two vents, destructiveness and creativeness. And I see that to the extent that we widen the creative channel we atrophy the destructive one.[8]
>
> *Sylvia Ashton-Warner*

It is said that children come to school curious, uninhibited, and filled with enthusiasm and the desire to know, but as they proceed through school, these talents are squelched. Carl Rogers, a well-known psychologist stated, "In education we tend to turn out conformists, stereotypes, individuals whose education is 'completed,' rather than freely creative and original thinkers."[9] Another psychologist, H. H. Anderson, claimed, "Creativity was in each of us as a small child. In children creativity is a universal. Among adults, it is almost nonexistent."[10] Others have decried the stifling of the child's natural gifts by surrounding adults and blame them for destroying the child's ability to create.[11]

Defining Creativity

Confusion exists about the definition of the term *creativity* because it can mean many things to different people. Some define creativity as "something new." Yet what may be new to one may not be to another. Obviously, with such a definition, anyone can be considered creative. Other definitions of creativity are based on divergent thinking, the many different ways of looking at things.

However, since the dimension of creativity is not measured on IQ tests, E. P. Torrance, an educational psychologist at the University of Georgia, developed tests of creative thinking, which he based on his investigations of classroom situations where he felt creativity was fostered. Torrance defines creativity "as the process of becoming sensitive to problems, deficiencies, gaps in knowledge, missing elements, disharmonies, and so on; identifying the difficulty; searching for solutions, making guesses, or formulating hypotheses about the deficiencies; testing and retesting these hypotheses and possibly

---

[8] Sylvia Ashton-Warner, *Spinster* (New York: Simon & Schuster, 1959), p. 221
[9] Carl Rogers, "Toward a Theory of Creativity," *Creativity and Its Cultivation*, ed. Harold H. Anderson (New York: Harper & Row, 1959), p. 69.
[10] Ibid. p. xii.
[11] Hughes Mearns, *Creative Youth* (New York: Doubleday, Page, 1926), p. viii.

Figure 15.1 Sally has a good imagination.

modifying and retesting them; and finally communicating the results."[12] The tests are supposed to measure fluency or the number of relevant ideas; flexibility or the number of shifts in thought or changes in categories of response; originality or the number of statistically infrequent responses; and elaboration or the number of different ideas employed in working out the specifics of an overall idea.

Creativity
Difficult to define; one definition that has been given: a combination of imagination plus knowledge plus evaluation.

S. J. Parnes, a former president of Creative Education Foundation at Buffalo University, gave his definition at a symposium on creativity in the early 1960s: a combination of imagination plus knowledge plus evaluation. Although there is no universally agreed on definition of creativity, Parnes's seems to incorporate all the necessary elements. It also delimits and qualifies a broad definition, whereby anything new to the individual connotes creativity. It seems reasonable that the more knowledge individuals have, no matter in what area, the more able they will be to generate many different ideas—if they have the requisite imagination. Similarly, the more intelligent the individuals, the more able they will be to evaluate their product. Therefore, an individual who is more intelligent is bound to be capable of greater creativity than someone who is less intelligent— all other things being equal. In actuality, since "other" variables are rarely equal, it does not necessarily follow that people of great intelligence will be more creative than people of less intelligence.

Reading and Creativity

Reading teachers need to be acquainted with creativity because, as discussed in Chapter 13, good readers are good problem solvers, and the highest level in the hierarchy of reading comprehension is creative reading. Unfortunately this level of reading comprehension is probably the most often ignored.

Creativity cannot be commanded, but it is also not something that "just happens." If we want divergent thinkers and individuals who are intelligent risk takers, we must create an environment that values these traits. Teachers who are bothered by divergency will not be able to create the proper physical, emotional, and intellectual climate essential for the development of creativity.

In the reading program, teachers must allow children to give free rein to their imaginations. The teacher together with the children could brainstorm various ways that the protagonists in the stories they are reading can solve problems.

Teachers should share their ideas and "walk through" the steps that they take to arrive at their ideas. They should encourage children to present ideas, and even though criticism is avoided in the initial

[12] E. P. Torrance, "Scientific Views of Creativity and Factors Affecting Its Growth." in *Creativity and Learning,* ed. Jerome Kagan (Boston: Houghton Mifflin, 1967), pp. 73–74.

stage, they should eventually evaluate with the children those ideas that are feasible, because good creative thinkers must also be good critical thinkers.

MAINSTREAMING

As discussed earlier, the impetus of mainstreaming was triggered by Public Law 94–142, a federal law that is designed to give handicapped children a "free appropriate public education." It requires state and local governments to provide identification programs, a special education, and related services such as transportation, testing, diagnosis, and treatment for children with speech handicaps, hearing impairments, visual handicaps, physical disabilities, emotional disturbances, learning disabilities, and mental retardation handicaps. Public Law 94–142 also requires that whenever possible, handicapped students must be placed in regular classrooms. *Mainstreaming* is the placement of handicapped children in the least restrictive educational environment that will meet their needs.

Mainstreaming
The placement of handicapped children in the least restrictive educational environment that will meet their needs.

Handicapped children who are moved to a regular classroom are supposed to be very carefully screened. Only those who seem able to benefit from being in a least restrictive environment are supposed to be put into one. The amount of time that a handicapped child spends in a regular classroom and the area in which the child participates in the regular classroom depend on the individual child. Some children who are moderately mentally retarded (trainables) may spend time each week in a regular classroom during a special activity such as a story hour.

For mainstreaming to be successful, classroom teachers must be properly prepared for this role, and teachers must enlist the aid and cooperation of every student in their class. Classroom teachers must prepare their students for the mainstreamed child by giving them some background and knowledge about the child. The amount and type of information given will, of course, vary with the grade level. Regular classroom teachers should also have the students involved in some of the planning and implementation of the program for the mainstreamed child.

For example, if teachers are expecting physically handicapped children to be admitted to their class, they can help to prepare their students by reading some books to them that portray a physically handicapped child in a sensitive and perceptive manner. Teachers might read some excerpts from Helen Keller's *The Story of My Life* or Marie Killilea's book *Karen.* After reading the excerpts teachers can engage the students in a discussion of the handicapped child's struggles, fears, hopes, concerns, goals, and dreams. Teachers can then attempt to help the children in their classes recognize that they have feelings, hopes, and fears similar to many handicapped children's. Teachers should also help their students to understand that a child with a physical handicap does not necessarily have a mental handicap. As a matter of fact, many handicapped persons are very intelligent and able to make many contributions to society. The teacher can then discuss with the children how they think they can make the new child who is coming to their class feel at home. The teacher might use special films and television programs to initiate interest in the handicapped and to help gain better insights about them.

Besides preparing the children in the regular classroom for the mainstreamed child, an individualized program must be developed for each mainstreamed child in cooperation with the child's parents, the special education teacher, or consultants. The program should be one that provides a favorable learning experience for both the handicapped child and the regular classroom students. That is, the integration of a handicapped child should not take away from the program of the regular classroom children. To assure that the regular program is not diminished, the NEA in 1975 passed a resolution advocating several measures: modifications in class size, scheduling, and curriculum design to accommodate the shifting demands that mainstreaming creates; appropriate instructional materials, supportive services, and pupil personnel services provided for the teacher and the handicapped student; systematic evaluation and reporting of program developments; and adequate additional funding and resources.

Special Note

Public Law 94–142 was expanded by Congress in 1986 to include handicapped preschool children. This new set of provisions, Public Law 99–457, requires states by the school year 1990–1991 to provide a free appropriate public education to children ages 3 through 5.

LEARNING DISABILITIES

Learning disability Difficult to define; the definition given most often is: a disorder in one or more of the basic psychological processes involved in understanding or in using language spoken or written, which may manifest itself in an imperfect ability to listen, think, speak, read, write, spell, or do mathematical calculations.

The definition of learning disabilities needs special attention because there is so much confusion concerning this term. Researchers have found that the characteristics of children labeled learning disabled vary so much that it is impossible to list common characteristics.

Although there is a great amount of confusion and controversy concerning the term *learning disability* and although studies have shown that there is in existence a multitude of definitions and synonyms for this term, there is one definition that is most widely accepted and acted on. The definition that is usually given for learning disabilities is that endorsed by the federal government in 1977:

"Special learning disability" means a disorder in one or more of the basic psychological processes involved in understanding or in using language spoken or written which may manifest itself in an imperfect ability to listen, think, speak, read, write, spell, or do mathematical calculations.

The term includes such conditions as perceptual handicaps, brain injury, minimal brain dysfunction, dyslexia, and developmental aphasia. The term does not include children who have learning problems which are primarily the result of visual, hearing, or motor handicaps, of mental retardation, emotional disturbance, or environmental, cultural or economic disadvantage.[13]

From this definition, we can see that there does not appear to be any logical explanation for a child's learning disability. Also, the learning disability may go undiagnosed because the child is of average or above-average intelligence, so the teacher thinks that the child is either lazy or lacks discipline.

Teachers should be especially vigilant of those children who are of average or above-average intelligence who are having some kind of learning problems because these children may have a learning disability. Teachers should refer these children for special testing. Teachers must, however, also be leery of labeling youngsters as learning disabled without adequate and substantive documentation. For example, the Black English trial in Ann Arbor showed that the school district had labeled the Green Road children as "learning disabled" and "emotionally impaired" without due consideration to their racial and linguistic backgrounds. Unfortunately, "the staff was handicapped by their inadequate knowledge of the children's characteristics and the biased nature of the tests that they were using."[14] An example is given whereby the "speech therapists weren't aware that the Wepman test included a number of oppositions that are mergers in the Black English vernacular: *pin* vs. *pen*, *sheaf* vs. *sheath*, *clothe* vs. *clove*, and so forth."[15] (See "Dialect and Language Differences" Chapter 4.)

Attention Deficit Disorder (ADD)

Concentration, which is sustained attention, is essential for learning. Good learners must be able to attend while listening and reading; they must know what information to ignore and what to process. Unless children can attend, they will be at a great disadvantage in learning to read or for that matter any other learning.

Attention deficit disorder (ADD) Difficulty sustaining concentration at a task.

Children who have an attention deficit disorder (ADD) have difficulty concentrating at a task. They are very easily distracted by the stimuli around them; they do not have selective attention whereby they can ignore the competing stimuli in their environment and

---

[13] Federal Register, "Procedures for Evaluating Specific Learning Disabilities," Washington, D.C.: Department of Health, Education and Welfare, December 29, 1977, p. 65083.

[14] William Labov, "Objectivity and Commitment in Linguistic Science: The Case of the Black English Trial in Ann Arbor," *Language in Society* 11 (August 1982): 168.

[15] Ibid., pp. 168–69.

home in on the specific task at hand. These children's easy distractibility makes it difficult for them to learn.

The problem of hyperactivity has in the past often been treated with drugs; however, this controversial treatment has been considered by many as a "wolf in sheep's clothing for the child and the family,"[16] and this practice because of a public media outcry has subsided somewhat.[17] (The reason for the outcry is that the drugs the children receive are similar to those commonly referred to as "uppers" or "pep" pills. For some reason these drugs rather than stimulating the children have an opposite effect on them. However, many people feel that these children might become addicted to the drugs and that the drugs might have some harmful side effects.) After 1980, ADD was classified into two types, ADD and ADD with hyperactivity. Most of the children diagnosed by clinicians are put in the category of ADD with hyperactivity.[18] A child diagnosed as having an attention deficit disorder is classified as learning disabled and is entitled to special education services.

Clinicians, not teachers, do the diagnosing; however, it is the teacher who often refers the child for diagnosis because of the kinds of behavior the child is exhibiting in class. These kinds of behavior, which have been classified into three categories—coming to attention, decision making, and maintaining attention[19]—can often be disruptive. For example, a child who is constantly inattentive, has poor task-approach skills, has difficulty in getting started on an assignment, has difficulty picking out important information, and is an impulsive decision maker will obviously be more disruptive in class than one who is attentive and works on task. Children who are inattentive would get up more, talk more, fidget more, have difficulty waiting for their turn, call out more, and so on.

The problem is that many times children are diagnosed as having ADD when they are merely frustrated because they cannot read. Children who have reading problems would be prone to have many of the same characteristics as those of children diagnosed as having ADD and then classified as learning disabled.

Misclassification means that children are not given proper instructional help. Unfortunately, the children who seem to be classified as learning disabled are often those who come from educationally disadvantaged homes and who lack the kinds of experiences that are necessary to succeed in school.[20]

[16] Walter E. Sawyer, "Attention Deficit Disorder: A Wolf in Sheep's Clothing . . . Again," *The Reading Teacher* 42 (January 1989): 310.

[17] Ibid.

[18] Daniel P. Hallahan and James M. Kauffman, *Exceptional Children: Introduction to Special Education*, 4th ed. (Englewood Cliffs, N.J.: Prentice-Hall, 1988), p. 117.

[19] Barbara K. Keogh and Judith Margolis, "Learn to Labor and Wait: Attentional Problems of Children with Learning Disorders," *Journal of Learning Disabilities* 9 (May 1976): 276–86.

[20] Sawyer, pp. 311–12.

IDENTIFICATION BIASES OF CHILDREN LABELED
EDUCABLE MENTALLY RETARDED

**Educable mentally
retarded children**
Children whose IQs
usually range ap-
proximately from
55 to 70; consid-
ered mildly re-
tarded.

It appears that the incidence of educable mental retardation is not equally distributed across all segments of the population. There is a tendency to label more boys as educable mentally retarded than girls. This may be because boys are usually more likely to be mischievous than girls and as a result are more likely to be candidates for referral. There also seems to be a highly disproportionate number of children from a lower socioeconomic status. Studies show too that minority children are overrepresented in this group.

For example, in 1980, a class-action suit was "brought by Parents in Action on Special Education on behalf of 'all black children who have been or will be placed in special classes for the educable mentally handicapped in the Chicago school system.' Plaintiffs observed that while 62 percent of the enrollment of the Chicago schools was black, blacks comprised 82 percent of the enrollment of classes for the educable mentally retarded."[21]

The teacher is usually the person who first identifies the child as having a problem. Many times, as already stated, the child is referred for special testing because of nonadaptive social behavior. After the referral the child is given a number of standardized tests, of which the IQ test is the most influential in determining whether the child is retarded or not. Since studies have shown that children from minority groups and from lower socioeconomic classes usually do not do as well on IQ tests as children from the rest of the population, it is not surprising to find children from these groups disproportionately represented in the group of children labeled educable mentally retarded.

Children who are second-language learners have special problems because even the most sympathetic teachers often misinterpret children's language and learning abilities. "Perceptions regarding lack of language ability lead to mistaken assumptions about cognitive ability."[22]

There are a number of language assessment instruments available, such as the *Language Assessment Scales—Oral* (LASO), 1990, published by CTB/McGraw-Hill, that can help teachers gain a better insight into their non-English-speaking children's language and concept ability.

It cannot be emphasized enough how careful teachers must be in using such terms as *mentally retarded, emotionally disturbed,* and *learning disabled* to label a child. Once labeled, the child is hardly ever able to shed that label, even though he or she has been incorrectly labeled.

---

[21] John Salvia and James E. Ysseldyke, *Assessment in Special and Remedial Education,* 4th ed. (Boston: Houghton Mifflin, 1988), p. 45.

[22] Catherine Wallace and Yetta Goodman, "Research Currents: Language and Literacy Development of Multilingual Learners," *Language Arts* 66 (September 1989): 545.

Often children so labeled continue to function at a particular level because they, themselves, have incorporated the image that others have of them.

Special Note

"Educable" usually refers to mildly retarded children; however, the determination for this classification varies from state to state and even from school system to school system.

SUMMARY

Teachers usually have children with a wide range of abilities in their classrooms, which generally include borderline (slow-learning) and gifted children. Now, because of mainstreaming, many teachers can expect to have physically handicapped children, children with emotional problems, children with learning disabilities, and children who are mildly and moderately mentally retarded in their classes at some time. Therefore, teachers must be prepared for this role, and an individualized program must be developed for mainstreamed children in cooperation with the children's parents and the special education teacher or the consultant. In this chapter, reading and other language arts methods are provided that are most applicable for dealing with borderline and gifted children; however, they may also be adapted for some of the children who may be mainstreamed. In addition, attention-deficit disorder (ADD) and identification biases of children labeled "educable mentally retarded" were discussed. It was suggested strongly that teachers be very cautious in labeling children. A section was also presented on creativity, and it was stated that teachers must provide an environment that encourages and fosters divergent thinkers.

SUGGESTIONS FOR THOUGHT QUESTIONS AND ACTIVITIES

1. You are a teacher who will soon have a child from a special class mainstreamed into your class. How would you go about preparing for this child? To whom would you go for help? How would you involve the children in your class?
2. You have been appointed to a committee concerned with the issue of mainstreaming. What are your views about mainstreaming?
3. What recommendations would you make concerning the mainstreaming of children?
4. You have just been appointed to a committee concerned with the development of a program for gifted children. What recommendations would you make?

5. Observe a few classrooms and take note of what teachers are doing to provide for "special children" in their classrooms.
6. Discuss how you would determine the kinds of books you could make available for slow learners and for gifted children.

SELECTED BIBLIOGRAPHY

Kirk, Samuel A. *Teaching Reading to Slow and Disabled Learners.* Prospect Heights, Ill.: Waveland Press, 1988.

Labuda, Michael C. (ed.). *Creative Reading for Gifted Learners: A Design for Excellence,* 2nd ed. Newark, Del.: International Reading Association, 1985.

Larrivee, Barbara. *Effective Teaching for Successful Mainstreaming.* New York: Longman, 1985.

Pendarvis, Edwina, Aimee A. Howley, and Craig B. Howley. *The Abilities of Gifted Children.* Englewood Cliffs, N.J.: Prentice-Hall, 1990.

Supplee, Patricia. *Reaching the Gifted Underachiever: Program Strategy and Design.* New York: Teachers College Press, 1990.

Terman, Lewis M., and Melita H. Oden. *The Gifted Child Grows Up,* Genetic Studies of Genius, vol. 4. Stanford, Calif.: Stanford University Press, 1947.

Van Tassel–Baska, Joyce L., and Paula Olszewski-Kubilius (eds.). *Patterns of Influence on Gifted Learners.* New York: Teachers College Press, 1989.

16

Teachers and Parents as Partners in the Diagnostic-Reading and Correction Program

INTRODUCTION

"Mommy, what's the name of this book?" asks Jennifer.
"The name of the book is *The Cat in the Hat*," replies her mother.
"Daddy, what does this say?" asks Johnny.
"It says 'Don't touch,'" replies his father.
"Mommy, what is this word on the cereal box?" asks Paul.
"The word is 'yummy,'" replies his mother.
"Mommy, what does the sign say?" asks Sharon.
"The sign says 'Stop,'" replies Sharon's mother.
"Daddy, what's this word in the book?" asks Carol.
"The word is 'happy,'" replies Carol's father.

And so it goes. Many young children are curious about words, and they see them all around. The persons they go to for help are the obvious ones—their parents. Parents are their first teachers. This is natural, and hardly anyone would question parents' rights to help their children satisfy their thirst for learning and desire to read; that is, hardly anyone would question what these children's parents are doing today. As a matter of fact, today basal reader series, test makers, and various professional journals such as *The Reading Teacher* include special materials just for parents.

However, it was just a short time ago that educators would have questioned parents' helping their children not only formally but also informally. Educators were very jealous of their rights when it came to teaching children, especially in reading. Strong outcries emanated from professionals' lips that parents didn't know what they were doing and that they should not attempt to teach their children to

Figure 16.1 Melissa's mother knows that enjoying books together is the first step toward becoming a good reader.

read before they came to school. Reasons given included such statements as "The parents don't know the proper methods" and "The children will be bored when they come to school." Many parents believed these statements. For example, in the 1950s Dolores Durkin, a noted reading authority, in her study of early readers reported more early readers coming from homes of blue-collar families than from those of professional parents. A possible reason for this result is that the prevailing view in the 1950s was that children should learn to read in school and not before. Professional parents were usually more aware of this view and subscribed to it, whereas parents of a lower socioeconomic status were less aware of this view and did not subscribe to it.[1] As a result, if a child asked a professional parent to help him or her learn to read, the parent supposedly did not. In the early 1960s, according to Durkin, more early readers were found who came from upper-middle-class homes because it was no longer fashionable to discourage parents from teaching their children to read.[2] Many parents were beginning to take a more active role in their children's learning, and this trend has continued into the 1990s.

In this chapter we will be concerned with why this active involvement on the part of parents has continued and we will look at the role that parents are and should be playing in the reading program.

[1] Dolores Durkin, *Children Who Read Early* (New York: Teachers College Press, 1966), pp. 46–48, 136.
[2] Ibid., pp. 90, 136.

KEY QUESTIONS

After you finish reading this chapter, you should be able to answer the following questions:

1. What caused a change in educators' attitudes toward parental involvement?
2. What are educators' attitudes toward parental involvement?
3. What effect has Chapter 1 (formerly Title I) had on parental involvement?
4. What role do parents play in programs?
5. What are some examples of parental involvement programs for preschoolers?
6. What are some examples of parental involvement programs not associated with federal funding?
7. What is the role of the parent-teacher conference?
8. What factors help to make a good parent-teacher conference?
9. What is television's impact on children's reading?
10. What are parents' views toward television programming?
11. How do parents feel about input in curriculum matters?
12. What are some things parents can do to help their children?
13. What are Reading Olympics programs?
14. What is the School Entry Questionnaire for parents?
15. What is "reality time"?
16. What is the parent's role in his or her child's emergent literacy?

KEY TERMS IN CHAPTER

You should pay special attention to the following new terms:

Chapter 1
Junior Great Books Program
Newbery award books
paired reading
Reading Olympics programs

PARENTAL INVOLVEMENT IN THE SCHOOLS

Parental involvement in the schools is not a new phenomenon. Parents sit on the boards of education; they are involved in parent-teacher associations, parent councils, and parent clubs. Parents help formulate school policy, have say in curriculum, and even help to choose textbooks. Parents definitely have a voice in school matters. However, until rather recently, parents have not been encouraged to take an active role in working with their own children, particularly in reading. Teaching was considered the sole domain of the educator, and parents who wanted to teach their children were usually looked upon as meddlers, troublemakers, and outsiders. At best they were looked upon as well-meaning but unknowledgeable, and as already stated, until the late 1950s parents were admonished not to teach their children to read at home. Today in many school districts across the country parents are seen as partners and potential resources rather than as unknowing meddlers. What has caused the pendulum to swing in the other direction?

Some Possible Causes for a Change in Attitude Toward Parental Involvement

A number of things have happened not only in changing educators' attitudes toward parental involvement in reading instruction but also in changing parents' attitudes. A strong factor that cannot be overlooked is that parents began to lose confidence in the schools because of the great number of reading failures found there. With this loss of confidence came the desire for more direct involvement.

Rudolf Flesch's book *Why Johnny Can't Read—And What You Can Do About It,* which was written in 1955, probably helped to raise the consciousness level of parents concerning the role they should be playing in helping their children learn to read. Flesch's book was addressed to parents, and it was written primarily to help parents help their children learn to read by using a phonic method. Whether one agrees with the views expressed in the book or not is not as important as the impact that the book made, and indeed it did make a great impact. Parents wanted to know more about what their children were doing in reading, and many wanted to be more directly involved.

The increase of reading problems in the schools probably helped to change educators' attitudes as well as parents' attitudes. The reading problem may have caused educators to take another look at this great potential resource—parents—because many began to feel that they could use all the help they could get.

However, the greatest impetus for parental involvement probably came from the influx of federal monies to fund certain programs related to the improvement of children's reading skills. Almost all these programs in the United States mandated parental involvement. Head Start, which was initiated in the summer of 1965, is one such program. Its target audience is young children, that is, preschoolers and kindergartners. Follow Through, which is another such program, was first initiated as a pilot project in 1967 and became nationwide in 1968. Its audience is the children who participated in the Head Start program. Probably the passage of Title I in 1966 had the most effect on parental involvement because its programs cover a much larger population of children than Head Start. Under Head Start, Follow Through, and Title I programs, parental involvement is mandatory.

It wasn't until 1983 when *A Nation at Risk* knocked us out of our chairs of complacency that parents of all children again began to sit up and take note that we were on the road to mediocrity. The National Assessment of Educational Progress has continued to show that students need help with higher-level thinking and that those who achieve the best come from homes where parents read and where there are diverse reading materials available (see Chapter 4).

Today, as stated earlier, the trend is definitely to welcome parental involvement. The irony is that now, more than ever, there are more single parents and families where both parents are working; as a result, there often isn't time.

WHAT IS CHAPTER 1?

A special section is included on Chapter 1 (formerly called Title I) programs because of the great impact they have had on parental involvement in reading programs across the United States and because there is so much confusion about what Chapter 1 is itself.

Title I of the Elementary and Secondary Education Act (ESEA) was signed into law in 1965 to provide federal monies to state education agencies, which, in turn, suballocate the funds to local school districts.[3] The purpose of the law is to help educationally deprived children, ages five to seventeen, living in low-income areas. When Title I was first passed, local school districts had to have at least one hundred children or 3 percent of their local enrollment from low-income families in order to qualify. Numerous amendments have been passed through the years, and eligibility requirements have become more lenient. Although the state guidelines vary somewhat from state to state concerning the dissemination of monies and the eligibility of students in the program, the following is what generally happens: A local school district which has at least ten educationally deprived children aged five to seventeen who are receiving Aid to Families with Dependent Children (AFDC) or who come from homes that are below the poverty level can apply to the state education agency for Title I monies. Then the state disseminates the funds based on its particular formula. The school district must identify the school that these children are attending. Once the schools with the highest concentration have been identified, all educationally deprived children in that school, whether they come from low-income homes or not, are eligible for the Title I program.

Originally, Title I funds were not available for children regardless of income, but a number of problems developed with Title I programs; many did not comply with federal guidelines. In the 1970s, Congress gave more specific directions on how funds could be allocated and the kinds of programs that could be developed.

[3] *History of Title I ESEA,* U.S. Department of Health, Education and Welfare DHEW Publication No. (OE) 72–75 (Washington, D.C.: U.S. Government Printing Office, 1972).

Title I funds were now available not only for those schools with high concentrations of children from low-income families but also for those children who had major basic skills deficits, regardless of their family income. All Title I programs had to have clearly stated instructional objectives, coordination with other classes and school programs, communication with the parents and the community regarding Title I programs in their districts, and direct parental involvement.

Chapter 1
In 1981, Congress replaced Title I with Chapter 1; provides funds for children with major basic skills deficits.

In 1981, Congress replaced Title I with Chapter 1. Interestingly, one of the major differences was the decrease in parental involvement. In the 1987 reauthorization of Chapter 1, the revised legislation states that parents of children in Chapter 1 programs should be involved in decision-making processes. Also, in 1987 a study mandated by Congress found that the Chapter 1 programs did not emphasize higher-level thinking skills. In addition, another study found that the most successful Chapter 1 programs were those that emphasized instruction based on the needs of the child and used diagnostic and prescriptive instruction.[4]

The Chapter 1 programs are supposed to be in addition to the regular classroom program and in coordination with it; unfortunately, this is often not the case.

PARENTAL INVOLVEMENT IN SCHOOL PROGRAMS

Programs that involve parents vary from school to school; some have aggressive parental involvement, and some do not. When parental involvement was mandated by Title I, programs also varied from school district to school district because the specifics of the parental program were not mandated. In addition, the use of parents in the instructional aspects of the program differed since no mandate was given for their involvement in this component.

However, some Title I parental involvement programs that sprang up were excellent. One program reported in the literature consisted of a series of about five meetings on alternate weeks. The meetings were designed to make the parents feel "comfortable in school, to give them a sense of the potential importance of the role they can play with their children, and to give them specific materials and ideas for helping their children read at home."[5] In the program parents were given a taste of what it's like to learn to read; they were given books at their children's reading levels and asked to spend ten minutes a night helping their children read; and they played reading games that help reinforce skills children are learning and which can be played at home. In this program parents were encouraged to

[4] *California Diagnostic Reading Tests,* Teacher's Guide (Monterey, Calif.: CTB/McGraw-Hill, 1989), pp. 3–4.
[5] Annette Breiling, "Using Parents as Teaching Partners," *The Reading Teacher* 30 (November 1976): 188.

share their experiences with others at the meetings, which not only gave parents a feeling of security and calmed fears but also provided helpful suggestions. The topics presented at the meetings varied, but each one seemed to be concerned with helping parents learn more about the reading process and the methods and approaches teachers use. The program also included student participation, which usually consisted of a child reading for a few minutes while parents listened.

Parents' responses to the program were very good, and they reported noticeable improvement in the reading ability of their children.

PARENTAL INVOLVEMENT IN REGULAR SCHOOL READING PROGRAMS

Usually, parents become involved in school programs when their children have a specific reading problem; however, the trend appears to be for increasing parental involvement for those without reading problems.

The participation of parents in many school districts is usually dependent on how aggressive the educators and parents are in demanding such involvement. The involvement of the parents in the regular reading program seems to vary from district to district, and even in some school districts, from school to school. In one school system, you will find an organized program, and in another you will find that the program is up to the individual teacher in each individual class. The programs that do exist usually are similar in format in that they generally include workshops, instructional materials, and book suggestions. What is presented, however, will vary from district to district. The following is an example of a program that was developed in a local New Jersey school system to incorporate parental involvement in its regular reading program for all children in grades one through five. The program consists of instructional packets, book suggestions, and three workshops. At the first workshop, a reading specialist explains the reading program that is in use in the school system. The parents are acquainted with the basal reader series, and the terminology that is used is also explained. At the second workshop the parents witness a reading lesson from the basal reader series, which uses the Directed Reading Approach. The third session is entitled "A Book Talk." At this session books at different readability and interest levels are presented, and suggestions are made on how to involve children in reading them.

Another part of the program concerns instructional materials. For those children who have reading problems, parent packets are produced which consist of activities based on the skills that children are working on in class. Different parent packets are available for different grade levels. For those children who have no reading problems, materials are sent home which help parents to capitalize on their children's reading interests. A special packet which emphasizes more difficult books, especially the Newbery award winners, is sent home to the parents of children who have been identified as highly able or gifted.

A program of special interest was developed in a school system for highly able readers in grades two through six, their teachers, and parents. The program, called the "Junior Great Books Program," began in 1979 and included twelve volunteer parents and twelve teachers. A parent and a teacher were paired off, and then they worked together as a team. The parents who volunteered had to take the two-day training session, which was conducted by a special person from the Great Books Foundation, located in Chicago. The sessions consisted primarily of helping parents learn about the kinds of questions they should ask, as well as how to conduct the discussions. The children who participated in the program were considered "top readers" by their teachers. The criteria that teachers used were teacher-made and standardized test results as well as a child's ability to assume responsibility. The parent-teacher team met every week to plan for the reading discussion, which took place in the regular classroom during the regularly scheduled reading period for forty-five minutes. Both the parent and the teacher helped to lead the discussion with a particular group of children.

An exciting trend in the United States involves the Reading Olympics programs. These programs vary from school system to school system, from school to school, and even from one class to another; however, the important things are that they include the reading of books and the sharing of them in some way with parents. Here is how one such program works in the middle part of the year in a first-grade class.

There is a contest in which children are challenged to read as many books as they can. They must read these books aloud to one of their parents, and after they finish reading the book aloud, the parent asks them questions about the story, as well as asking them to retell it. The rewards are obviously manifold. Andrew, the child who won the Read-Aloud Olympics contest in his first-grade class, read 120 books aloud to his parents.

It has been reported that the "home factor that emerged as most strongly relating to reading achievement was 'whether or not the mother regularly heard the child read.' The effect was greater than that of IQ scores, maternal language behavior, or reading to the child."[6] Readers are cautioned, however, that those parents who coached were a special self-selected group, and the success may have been due to parental interest rather than to the practice of reading. Nevertheless, if it works, it's good.

Another practice that seems to be gaining favor is that of paired

[6] Kathy Johnston, "Parents and Reading: A U.K. Perspective," *The Reading Teacher* 42 (February 1989): 353.

Paired reading
The child reads aloud simultaneously with another person, usually the parent.

reading (see "Repeated Reading" in Chapter 13). This is a method whereby parents and children read aloud simultaneously. The key thing in this process is to make sure the child is actually reading rather than mimicking or echoing the parent. This technique is usually used with children who have reading difficulties. At any time during the simultaneous reading, the child may signal that he or she wishes to read alone. The parent should praise the child's desire to do so, and allow the child to read alone. "The child is encouraged to read alone by lack of criticism and by frequent praise for any independent reading."[7]

Many basal reader series, recognizing the importance of learning partnerships, have made a commitment to join in the partnership by providing parents with more than the usual letters that are sent out. Publishers have developed a package that includes the suggestions and activities that are needed to implement a "Parents as Partners" program.

On page 438 is a sample letter that children bring home for their parents. (There are English and Spanish versions of the letters that are sent home.)

Some series are also sending home a checklist for parents, which is a good diagnostic tool for parents. It lists some of the things that parents should be doing with their children. It's a good idea for parents to check the list periodically to see how well they are faring. Here is a checklist the author generated for preschoolers and early-primary-grade children that teachers might want to share with their parents.

The Parent Checklist for Preschoolers and Early-Primary-Grade Children

	Yes	Needs Improvement
I listen to my child.		
I read aloud to my child every day.		
I discuss things with my child.		
I explain things to my child.		
I spend time with my child.		
I ask my child good questions.		
I ask my child to read picture books to me.		
I watch special TV shows with my child.		
I talk about TV shows with my child.		
I encourage my child.		
I am patient with my child.		
I take my child to interesting places.		
I do not pressure my child.		
I read and write in the presence of my child.		
I am a good role model for my child.		

[7] Ibid., p. 355.

Dear Family of _____:[8]

The focus of the stories in the first part of the book is on the game of Hokey Pokey and what it's all about. To help reinforce this concept, you might wish to share these books with your child:

Mama Don't Allow, by Thacher Hurd. Harper & Row, © 1984. A traditional folk song is the basis for a humorous tale about a possum named Miles and the Swamp Band. The jazzy illustrations perfectly communicate the spirit of this story.

Louie by Ezra Jack Keats. Greenwillow, © 1983. A shy, withdrawn boy loses his heart to a puppet.

Amelia Bedelia Goes Camping by Peggy Parish. Greenwillow, © 1985. Amelia has difficulty when she follows directions literally; for example, she "pitches" a tent.

Through the stories in this unit your child has been learning about main idea/details (finding the most important idea in a story) and classification (placing words in categories). Your child has also been learning about long vowels *e, ee,* and *i*; consonant clusters with *l* and with *r* (such as *cl* in *clap* and *br* in *broom*); and consonant digraphs *ng* and *ck* (such as *ng* in *ring* and *ck* in *duck*).

Consonant clusters are two or more consonants grouped together. Consonant digraphs are two consonants grouped together to make one sound.

You might enjoy doing the following activities with your child:

1. Main Idea/Details

Have your child draw a picture of a house, a tree, and a hill. Then, on a separate piece of paper, have your child draw and color a picture of a cat. Cut out the picture of the cat. Tell your child a story about the cat: how it starts at the bottom of the tree and climbs to the top, runs to the hill, comes back to the house for a drink of milk, and so on.

Your child should move his or her picture of the cat around to show where the cat is at each point in the story. Your child might enjoy telling you a story and having you move the cat.

2. Classification

Find a fork, spoon, knife, toothbrush, tube of toothpaste, and a bar of soap. Ask your child which of the objects go together. After your child has separated the objects into two groups, ask your child how all the objects are the same. Your child might enjoy finding objects and having you separate them into groups and tell how the objects are the same.

I hope you and your child have fun sharing these books and activities.

Sincerely,

[8] From *Home Connection Letters, Level 3, Morning Bells* of the *World of Reading* series, © 1991 Silver, Burdett & Ginn Inc. Used with permission.

Test makers are also getting into the act. For example, the *California Diagnostic Reading Tests,* 1989 edition, includes a parent report that presents information on the child's strengths and weaknesses, as well as suggestions on how to help the child (see Figure 16.2).

PARENTAL INVOLVEMENT IN PRESCHOOL PROGRAMS

Many parents want help for their preschool children. Preschool help gained its greatest impetus from the federal funding of programs such as Head Start in the middle 1960s, which mandated parental involvement. Ira Gordon played a significant role in this development. All his programs used paraprofessionals who visited the home and served as parent educators to demonstrate specially designed home learning activities to the parent.[9]

The trend for preschool help and parental involvement has continued. Gallup's 1979 poll on parents' attitudes asked parents with children who have not yet started school or kindergarten, "Do you think the school could help you in any way in preparing your child for school?"

Those respondents who have no children in school represent the group most eager to have preschool help for their children (see Table 16.1). When the parents who desired help were asked "what the school could do," the suggestion offered most often was the distribution of a pamphlet or booklet telling in detail what parents should do to prepare the child for school. One parent is quoted as saying, "I would like to know exactly what they expect of the child, such as the ABCs, numbers, and other areas of learning." Another frequently made suggestion was to invite parents and their preschool children to visit the school to see what goes on in a typical day. Some parents thought that it would be a good idea to designate a day when a preschool child could actually sit in the kindergarten class with other children to see what it is like. Still other parents suggested that a regular preschool program, such as Head Start, be made part of the educational system. Many respondents said that such a preschool program already exists in their community.[10]

From the 1960s onward, we begin to see a number of programs in which parents are directly involved in teaching their young children some basic beginning reading skills. In some of the programs parents are taught certain skills that they then use to teach their children, and in some they work with preschool teachers and then provide supplementary instruction at home.

Some programs usually have preschool teachers or others model techniques for parents such as how to read aloud to children to

[9] Patricia P. Olmstead et al., *Parent Education: The Contributions of Ira J. Gordon* (Washington, D.C.: Association for Childhood Education International, 1980), p. 8.
[10] George Gallup, "The Eleventh Annual Gallup Poll of the Public's Attitudes Toward the Public Schools," *Phi Delta Kappan* 61 (September 1979): 33–44.

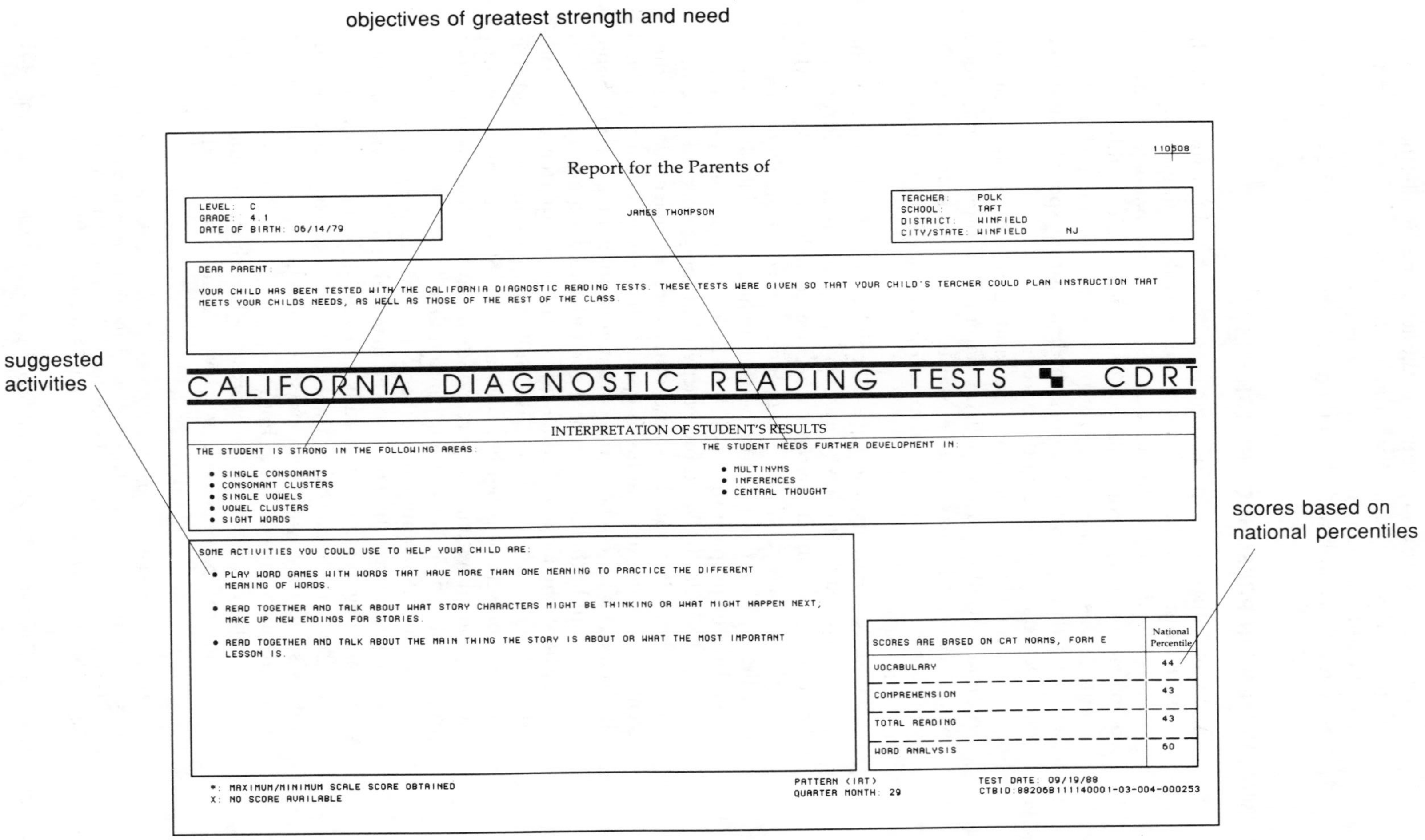

objectives of greatest strength and need

scores based on national percentiles

suggested activities

Parent Report Form from CRDT Teacher's Guide (Levels A–B) from California Diagnostic Reading Tests by CTB. Copyright © 1989 by McGraw-Hill, Inc. Reprinted by permission of Macmillan/McGraw-Hill School Publishing Company.

Figure 16.2 *California Diagnostic Reading Tests* parental report.

TABLE 16.1   (1979)

	Could School Help With Preschool Child?		
	Yes %	No %	Don't Know/ No Answer %
Parents who presently have no children in school	53	34	13
Parents with one or more children in public school	37	53	10
Parents with one or more children in parochial school	40	40	20

encourage interaction and higher-level thinking. (See "Reading a Story Aloud to Young Children [Preschool and Kindergarten]" in Chapter 5.)

Special Note

Those conducting the parent-involvement programs should help parents recognize that there is a place for "reality time" with children as well as "quality time." "Quality time" implies a value judgment and is the term most used by those who do not have much time to spend with their children.

Parents' involvement with children is good, and young children especially benefit from being with their parents. However, parents should not get into a frenzy if every moment they spend with their child is not "quality time." Teachers should help all parents recognize that "reality time" is just as important, especially for young children. Reality time is the time that parents spend with their children while making a bed, cooking, baking, going for a walk, swimming, talking, or just quiet time. When children and parents are together, every moment does not have to be filled with "pearls of wisdom."

If children perceive that the only times parents and they spend together are those related to trying to teach them something to do better in school, children may begin to react negatively to their parents and school. They may feel that if they do not do well in school, their parents will not love them.

HOW SUCCESSFUL ARE PARENTAL INVOLVEMENT PROGRAMS?

The success of any program that demands voluntary participation has to be based on turnout—not initial turnout, but continuous turnout. The programs reported in the literature and those surveyed by the author had excellent parent participation. Most of the reading coordinators claimed that parent turnout had grown and that verbal feedback had been very good. The parents in the programs claimed that since their involvement in the program their children were more interested in reading, and the parents of children who had reading difficulties claimed that their children's reading skills had improved as well as their attitude.

As stated previously, those parents who have the most interest are probably the ones who are the most involved, and we know that their children usually do the best. This success then reinforces both the parents and children to continue.

Are Parental Involvement Programs a Passing Fad?

The movement for more rather than less parental involvement in reading programs should squelch the idea that parents will lose interest in their desire to be partners in teaching. The desire for more parental involvement can be seen in the responses to some questions on the *Gallup Polls of Attitudes Toward Education*, which began in 1969. In the 1971 and 1976 opinion polls, there were questions concerning courses for parents to help their children. The responses of both parents and those persons who had no children in the schools were overwhelmingly in favor of attending such courses[11] (see Tables 16.2 and 16.3).

A number of colleges have become sensitive to parents' need and desire for more knowledge about the reading act and what the schools are doing in teaching reading. As a result, some have instituted courses for parents and some have provided special workshops designed to involve parents in their children's reading instruction. For example, in one college a summer reading clinic started a summer parent group because the instructors felt that "parents should know what their children would experience in the clinic and how they

TABLE 16.2 (1971)

A suggestion has been made that parents of school children attend one evening class a month to find out what they can do at home to improve their children's behavior and increase their interest in schoolwork. Is it a good idea or a poor idea?

	National Totals %	No Children in Schools %	Public School Parents %	Parochial School Parents %	High School Juniors and Seniors %
Good idea	81	82	80	81	75
Poor idea	13	11	16	15	21
No opinion	6	7	4	4	4
	100	100	100	100	100

[11] Stanley M. Elam, ed., *A Decade of Gallup Polls of Attitudes Toward Education, 1969–1978* (Bloomington, Ind.: Phi Delta Kappa, 1978), pp. 108, 272.

TABLE 16.3 (1976)

As a regular part of the public school educational system, it has been suggested that courses be offered at convenient times to parents in order to help them help their children in school. Do you think this is a good idea or a poor idea?

	National Totals %	No Children in Schools %	Public School Parents %	Parochial School Parents %
Good idea	77	76	78	74
Poor idea	19	18	20	25
Don't know/ no answer	4	6	2	1

could continue to help them when the clinic ended."[12] The parent coordinator of the clinic claimed that parents were responsive and that they were eager to attend.[13]

In a number of schools parents are not involved in any formal reading program, but they volunteer to be tutors in the regular reading program. Usually, the parent volunteer works with a special reading teacher or coordinator or learning disability person. These persons usually help the parent volunteers so that they will be able to tutor effectively those students who have been identified as needing help.

The 1980 Gallup poll further substantiates the fact that parents definitely want to be involved as partners in the education of their children[14] (see Table 16.4). The trend toward parental involvement,

TABLE 16.4 (1980)

Question: In your opinion, should or should not parents be asked to meet with school personnel before each new school semester to examine the grades, test scores, and career goals for each child and to work out a program to be followed both in school and at home?

	National Totals %	No Children in Schools %	Public School Parents %	Parochial School Parents %
Yes, favor this plan	84	85	83	83
No, do not favor	11	9	14	14
Don't know	5	6	3	3

[12] Helen Feaga Esworthy, "Parents Attend Reading Clinic, Too," *The Reading Teacher* 32 (April 1979): 831.
[13] Ibid.
[14] George Gallup, "The Twelfth Annual Gallup Poll of the Public's Attitudes Toward the Public Schools," *Phi Delta Kappan* 62 (September 1980): 33–46.

particularly in the area of reading, is not a fad, as further evidenced by the 1987 Gallup survey.

The 1987 survey on parental input with curriculum, instructional materials, and library books shows that parents overwhelmingly feel that parents of public school children should have more (45%) rather than less (8%) input about the courses that are offered. Also, in spite of concerns about censorship, the public's feelings are similar; that is, it wants more rather than less influence in the selection of

TABLE 16.5   (1987)

The first question: Do you feel that parents of public school students should have more say, less say, or do they have about the right amount of say regarding the curriculum, i.e., the courses offered?

	National Totals %	No Children in School %	Public School Parents %	Nonpublic School Parents %
More say	45	40	51	65
Less say	8	10	5	4
Right amount	37	37	41	26
Don't know	10	13	3	5

The second question: Do you feel that parents of public school students should have more say, less say, or do they have about the right amount of say regarding instructional materials?

	National Totals %	No Children in School %	Public School Parents %	Nonpublic School Parents %
More say	38	36	42	50
Less say	14	15	10	12
Right amount	39	36	46	34
Don't know	9	13	2	4

The third question: Do you feel that parents of public school students should have more say, less say, or do they have about the right amount of say regarding the books placed in school libraries?

	National Totals %	No Children in School %	Public School Parents %	Nonpublic School Parents %
More say	36	34	40	47
Less say	16	17	11	14
Right amount	38	36	45	33
Don't know	10	13	4	6

instructional materials (38% to 14%), and this is so also for books placed in libraries (36% to 16%; see Table 16.5).[15]

The 1987 poll also questioned the public on basics in education. It appears that at all grade levels the public feels that the schools do not give students enough instruction in the basics (see Table 16.6).[16]

TABLE 16.6   (1987)

The first question: Some school districts have been told that they must require students to take more courses in basic subjects, such as math and science, thus reducing the number of elective courses students can take. Do you think this requirement would improve or hurt the quality of the public schools in this community?

	National Totals %	No Children in School %	Public School Parents %	Nonpublic School Parents %
Improve quality	75	74	76	85
Hurt quality	11	9	16	7
Don't know	14	17	8	8

The second question: Is it your impression that the public elementary schools give enough attention, or not enough attention, to reading, writing, and arithmetic?

	National Totals %	No Children in School %	Public School Parents %	Nonpublic School Parents %
Enough	28	21	46	23
Not enough	58	62	47	67
Right amount*	6	6	5	6
Don't know	8	11	2	4

* Those who said "right amount" volunteered that answer.

The 1989 poll continues to show that parents are indeed interested in having a say in their children's education (see Table 16.7).[17] It also shows that the public feels that family influence is the most important and most positive educational influence on the young, whereas television has the least educational value and is the least positive (see Table 16.8).[18]

[15] "The Nineteenth Annual Gallup Survey of the Public's Attitudes Toward the Public Schools," conducted for *Phi Delta Kappan*, September 1987, Gallup Report No. 264, p. 6.

[16] Ibid., pp. 6–7.

[17] Stanley M. Elam and Alec M. Gallup, "The 21st Annual Gallup Poll of the Public's Attitudes Toward the Public Schools," *Phi Delta Kappan* (September 1989): 47–48.

[18] Ibid., p. 47.

TABLE 16.7   (1989)

Do you feel that parents of public school students should have more say, less say, or do they have about the right amount of say regarding the following areas in public schools?

	More Say %	Less Say %	Right Amount %	Don't Know %
Allocation of school funds	59	10	27	4
Curriculum (i.e., the courses offered)	53	9	36	2
Selection and hiring of administrators	46	14	37	3
Books and instructional materials	43	13	41	3
Selection and hiring of teachers	41	17	38	4
Teacher and administrator salaries	39	17	39	5
Books placed in the school libraries	38	15	44	3

The 1989 annual Gallup poll of the public's attitudes toward public schools also reveals some interesting findings concerning the public's feelings toward national standards and testing. The poll shows that there appears to be a consensus for more uniformity in public school programs, "as well as national standards and goals for the public schools and nationally standardized tests to measure the achievement of these standards and goals."[19] This finding confirms statements made earlier in this text that the trend seems to be going toward more rather than less testing in the schools.

The interest of parents in their children's schooling is exceedingly important and cannot be overstated, especially since a number of studies have suggested that "the potential for parents to help their children in learning to read is tremendous."[20] Therefore, it is good that the trend toward parental involvement seems to be getting stronger.

It is unfortunate, however, that parents of "at-risk" or educationally disadvantaged children are often not involved in their children's schooling. A number of Outreach programs have been established in the United States that try to encourage parents who are in low

[19] Ibid., p. 42.
[20] Timothy Rasinski and Anthony Fredericks, "Working With Parents: Can Parents Make a Difference?" *The Reading Teacher* 43 (October 1989): 84.

TABLE 16.8 (1989)

The first question: In addition to school, young people receive their education from a number of different sources. As I read off these sources, one at a time, would you indicate how important an influence you think each source is on a student by mentioning a number between zero and 10—the higher the number, the more important the influence; and the lower the number, the less important.

	Most Important Influence (Ratings of 9 and 10 Only) %
The student's family	63
School	47
The student's peers	41
Television	32

The second question: Now, as I read off each of these sources, one at a time, would you tell me how *positive* an influence you think each source is on a student by mentioning a number between zero and 10—the higher the number, the more positive the influence; and the lower the number, the less positive.

	Most Positive Influence (Ratings of 9 and 10 Only) %
The student's family	53
School	39
The student's peers	24
Television	13

socioeconomic groups to participate. Often, they begin to work with young women before they have given birth and guide them through their pregnancy.

The trend toward establishing Outreach programs in low socio-economic areas to work with parents of preschoolers seems to be increasing, and it is to be hoped that they continue.

EMERGENT LITERACY AND PARENTS

In Chapter 7, emergent literacy is defined as all those language and reading and writing activities that children engage in before coming to school. It is stated further that proponents of this theory consider these activities as learning to read rather than precursors to reading. Regardless of whether these activities are precursors to reading or actual learning-to-read activities, it makes sense that the acquiring of literacy is a continuum and that parents play an esential role in a child's emergent literacy development. The following four processes should help teachers guide parents in the kinds of activities parents should be involved in with their children to help children attain literacy abilities.

1. *Observation*—Being read to or seeing adults model reading and writing behavior.
2. *Collaboration*—Having an individual interact with the child to provide encouragement, motivation, and help.
3. *Practice*—Trying out what has been learned; for example, the child writes a story or retells it to another child, stuffed animal, or doll without any help or without being supervised by an adult.
4. *Performance*— Sharing what has been learned with an adult who shows interest and support and gives positive reinforcement.[21]

"The Parent Checklist for Preschoolers and Early–Primary–Grade Children" presented in an earlier section should also be a valuable aid.

GRANDPARENTS SHOULD BE INVOLVED TOO

Why not involve the elderly in reading programs in which they could work directly with children as tutors and helpers? Why not have children read aloud to the elderly? Why not bring the grandparents into the mainstream? Why not, indeed?

Interestingly, we are living in an era when a person's life expectancy is the greatest that it has ever been, and as a result there are many more elderly people who are visible. Even though there is an increased interest in gerontology and in more benefits for the elderly, and the elderly have become more vocal, they are usually shunned, especially by young people. Moreover, with the advent of retirement communities and nursing homes, the elderly are probably more segregated from society today than ever before.

The treatment of the elderly in children's literature has probably been the most neglected and the most poorly portrayed of all areas. Children are greatly influenced by the way elderly people are portrayed, especially in fairy tales. When children were asked how elderly people are shown in fairy tales, the children responded, "They are witches."[22] Obviously, these children have been greatly influenced by the portrayal of the old woman as a mean, cross, wicked hag or witch in such famous fairy tales as "Hansel and Gretel," "Sleeping Beauty," and "Snow White and the Seven Dwarfs."

As stated earlier, today the elderly are more visible, but not usually by children because of the burgeoning of senior communities. It is claimed that the more involved the elderly are, the happier they are, and the longer they live. It would seem to be a good idea, both for

[21] Lesley Mandel Morrow and Jeffrey K. Smith (eds.), *Assessment for Instruction in Early Literacy* (Englewood Cliffs, N.J.: Prentice-Hall, 1990), p. 3.
[22] Myra P. Sadker and David M. Sadker, *Now Upon a Time: A Contemporary View of Children's Literature* (New York: Harper & Row, 1977), p. 77.

young people and the elderly, to have them work together. If young people can see that the elderly are not like the stereotypes portrayed in print, their attitudes toward the elderly could become more positive.

The elderly take part in some community programs developed to foster parental involvement, but their involvement is usually sporadic; that is, it's based more on chance than a concerted effort to get them involved. The programs that incorporate senior citizens as aides or tutors in reading are usually based in a particular school rather than in a districtwide program. For example, in Princeton, New Jersey, some schools have a program in which fifth-graders work in a cooperative effort with the elderly. The fifth-graders eat lunch with the elderly, and at the luncheon they act as the hosts and hostesses. After the luncheon, the senior citizens work with the children as tutors.

There is one community in northern Michigan that has made a concerted effort to integrate senior citizens into its daily school life. The school system of Harbor Springs initiated a program in which senior citizens are encouraged to participate in all school activities, and the senior citizen center is housed in the school's old library, which was renovated to fit the needs of the elderly.[23] The project at Harbor Springs when it was initiated was believed to be the first of its kind.

TELEVISION, PARENTS, CHILDREN, AND READING

In a chapter on parental involvement in schools, we would be remiss if we did not discuss the impact of television on children's reading, because most television viewing is done at home.

The question of the influence of television viewing on children's reading skills has been debated since television was first introduced. The researches have not been definitive. Some studies suggest that "television viewing has a considerable negative impact on reading achievement only for children who watch for relatively many hours— more than 4 to 6 hours a day."[24] Television also seems to affect different groups of children in different ways. The reading achievement of children of high socioeconomic status decreased when they watched greater amounts of television, whereas the converse appeared to be true for low socioeconomic status children; that is, heavier viewing for these children increased their reading achievement.[25]

[23] Sara Gay Dammann, "New Older Students Join Younger Ones," *Christian Science Monitor,* September 15, 1980.
[24] Johannes W.J. Beentjes and Tom H.A. Van Der Voort, "Television's Impact on Children's Reading Skills: A Review of Research," *Reading Research Quarterly* 23 (fall 1988): 401.
[25] Ibid.

TABLE 16.9 (1989)

On the average, about how many television programs do you watch with your children each week?''

TV Viewing with Children

	Average Programs per Week
Nationwide	7.5
Men	6.9
Women	7.9
18–29 years	7.6
30 and older	7.3
Attended college	5.5
No college	9.1
$25,000 and over	6.8
Under $25,000	9.5
Children's age:	
Under 6	7.1
6–12	7.9
13–17	8.0

Parents who watch with their children (83% of parents with children under 18 living at home) were asked:

About how often would you say you feel uncomfortable about something in a television program that you are watching with your children? Would you say you frequently, occasionally, seldom or never feel uncomfortable?

Frequency of Discomfort Caused by TV

Frequently	25%
Occasionally	33
Seldom	25
Never	17
	100%

Parents watch television with their children on an average of 7.5 shows a week, and heavier viewing appears to be among parents who have less formal education. In addition, almost 60 percent of the parents who watch television with their children feel uncomfortable at least occasionally about the content of the programs they see[26] (see Table 16.9). It is not surprising, then, that the public ranks the educational value of television lower than family, school, or peers,

[26] George Gallup, Jr., "Parents Disturbed by TV Content; Most See Growth in Problem," *The Gallup Poll,* April 9, 1989.

and that television is perceived as being least positive in influence (see Table 16.8).

Interestingly, a 1990 Roper survey reports that children ages 7 to 17 are more involved in decision making than ever before because families are so busy today. Of the parents polled, 79 percent claimed that their children decide which television shows the family watches. According to the poll, which was done for *USA Today*, the higher the parents' income and the more educated they are, the more say their children have in family decisions.[27]

PARENT-TEACHER CONFERENCES

In some schools the only parent-teacher involvement may be through the parent-teacher conference. This conference is an excellent opportunity for parents and teachers to learn to feel more comfortable with one another, as well as to exchange information. Also, the parent-teacher conference may be the only way for parents to learn about the reading program and the specifics of how individual children are doing.

Some teachers look with dread on parent-teacher conferences; therefore they structure them so that very little time is allowed for parent input or questioning. Unfortunately, such attitudes are usually conveyed to parents, and a free exchange is generally inhibited. For parent-teacher conferences to work, there must be a feeling of confidence on both sides. The more confidence a teacher has, the more comfortable he or she will feel with parents.

For parent-teacher conferences to be effective, teachers must be friendly, interested, and allow for an exchange of ideas. It is also important for teachers to recognize that although they may have twenty-five or thirty students in the class, this particular child is the one who is important to the parents. Most importantly, since this conference is primarily an exchange of ideas, teachers should encourage parents to give some insights into the children that would be helpful in teaching them. Remember, it is doubtful that anyone knows these children better than their parents. If the children need any special help, teachers should point this out to parents and explain precisely what they can do.

Parent-teacher conferences need not take place only during the reporting period. Whenever a need for a conference arises is the right time to call for one. However, teachers should remember that successful parent-teacher conferences require careful planning and effort.

[27] Dan Sperling, "Parents Are Listening More to Kids," *USA Today*, January 24, 1990.

A FINAL WORD

For parents to be partners in learning with educators, "educators" will have to recognize that it's not between "them" and "us"; there is no dichotomy. For a partnership to work, there has to be equal "give and take." If parents are looked upon as parent-educators, this viewpoint "acknowledges the home-school relationship as a rich potential shared among equals, equals who bring important and divergent experiences to bear upon individual and often limited perspectives."[28]

SUMMARY

Chapter 16 is concerned with parental involvement in the schools' reading programs. In the 1950s many parents were discouraged from attempting to help their children learn to read; however, in the 1970s, 1980s, and 1990s, the trend is definitely toward more parental involvement. Parents are looked upon as partners in education, and as partners they are beginning to take a more active role. Parental involvement was triggered by a number of factors, two salient ones being loss of confidence in the schools and the input of federal funds mandating parental involvement. The reading programs that include parental involvement vary from school district to school district and even from school to school in the same school district; however, more and more school districts are developing programs that involve parents. The book publishing companies are including special materials for their reading series specifically for parents and children, and so are test publishers. Not only is there a trend for parental involvement in the reading program but there also seems to be a concerted effort in some communities to involve grandparents, too. The parent-teacher conference was discussed as an excellent means for parents and teachers to get to know more about each other and to exchange information about an individual child. In addition, suggestions were given to help teachers guide parents in activities that would help their children attain literacy abilities.

SUGGESTIONS FOR THOUGHT QUESTIONS AND ACTIVITIES

1. You have been put on a special committee in your school district to represent your school. The committee was formed to try to learn how parents can be more involved in the schools' reading programs. What suggestions would you make?

[28] Gayle Goodman, "Worlds Within Worlds: Reflections on an Encounter with Parents," *Language Arts* 66 (January 1989): 20.

2. If you were asked to conduct an opinion poll concerning parents' attitudes about school and in particular about the reading program, what kinds of questions would you ask?
3. A suggestion was made at a meeting that the elderly become more involved in working directly with children in your school. How do you feel about this? In what way do you feel the elderly can help children in the reading program?
4. Survey a school district to determine the kinds of federally funded programs that it has. Then try to find out about the ways in which parents are involved.
5. Choose a school in your area. Try to set an appointment with an administrator to learn how that school involves parents in its reading programs.

SELECTED BIBLIOGRAPHY

Fields, Marjorie V. *Literacy Begins at Birth.* Tucson, Ariz.: Fisher Books, 1989.

Fredericks, Anthony D., and Timothy V. Rasinski. "Lending a (Reading) Hand." *The Reading Teacher* 43 (March 1990): 520–21.

Henderson, Anne T. "Parents Are a School's Best Friend." *Phi Delta Kappan* 70 (October 1988): 148–53.

Hill, Mary W. *Home Where Reading and Writing Begin.* Portsmouth, N.H.: Heinemann Educational Books, 1989.

Levi, Ray. "Assessment and Educational Vision: Engaging Learners and Parents." *Language Arts* 67 (March 1990): 269–73.

Potter, Gill. "Parent Participation in the Language Arts Program." *Language Arts* 66 (January 1989): 21–28.

Rasinski, Timothy V., and Anthony D. Fredericks. "Dimensions of Parent Involvement." *The Reading Teacher* 43 (November 1989): 180–82.

Rasinski, Timothy V., and Anthony D. Fredericks. "The Best Reading Advice for Parents." *The Reading Teacher* 43 (January 1990): 344–45.

Trelease, Jim. "Jim Trelease Speaks on Reading Aloud to Children." *The Reading Teacher* 43 (December 1989): 200–206.

Wahl, Amy. "Ready . . . Set . . . Role: Parents' Role in Early Reading." *The Reading Teacher* 42 (December 1988): 228–31.

Glossary

Accommodation. The individual's developing of new categories rather than integrating them into existing ones—Piaget's cognitive development.

Affective domain. Includes the feelings and emotional learnings that individuals acquire.

Affixes. Prefixes (*which see**) that are added before the root word and suffixes (*which see*) that are added to the end of a root word.

Analogies. Relationships between words or ideas.

Analysis. Breaking down something into its component parts.

Analytic phonics. Same as implicit phonics instruction (*which see*).

Anecdotal record. A record of observed behavior over a period of time.

Antonyms. Words opposite in meaning.

Appendix. A section of a book containing extra information that does not quite fit into the book but that the author feels is important enough to be presented separately.

Appraisal. Part of diagnostic pattern—a student's present reading performance in relation to his or her potential.

Assimilation. A continuous process which helps the individual to integrate new incoming stimuli to existing concepts—Piaget's cognitive development.

Association. Pairing the real object with the sound of the word.

Astigmatism. A defect of vision that causes blurred vision.

At-risk students. Those students who because of their backgrounds or other factors are in danger of failing in school.

Attention deficit disorder (ADD). Difficulty sustaining concentration at a task.

Attitude. Exerts a directive and dynamic influence on an individual's behavior.

Auding. Highest level of listening, which involves listening with comprehension.

Audiometer. An instrument used for measuring hearing acuity.

Auditory acuity. Physical response of the ear to sound vibration.

Auditory discrimination. Ability to distinguish differences and similarities between sound symbols.

Auditory fatigue. Temporary hearing loss due to a continuous or repeated exposure to sounds of certain frequencies.

Auditory memory span. Amount of information

* Which see refers to the immediately preceding word that is defined elsewhere in the glossary.

able to be stored in short-term memory for immediate use or reproducton.

Average children. Often referred to children who score in the IQ range approximately from 90–110.

Basal reader approach. An approach involving a basal reader series. This approach is highly structured; it uses a controlled vocabulary, and skills are sequentially developed.

Bibliotherapy. The use of books to help individuals to cope better with their emotional and adjustment problems.

Big books. Enlarged versions of regular children's books; known for their repetitive patterns which lend to their predictability; they are usually children's favorites.

Bilingual. Using or capable of using two languages.

Bilingual education. Instruction in both the student's native language and English.

Binaurality. The ability of listeners to direct both ears to the same sound.

Binocular vision. The ability to focus both eyes on a similar point of reference and see one object.

Black English. A variation of standard English; in the class of nonstandard English (*which see*).

Borderline children (slow learners). Children whose IQs usually range approximately from 70 to 85.

Bottom-up reading models. Models which consider the reading process as one of grapheme-phoneme correspondences; code emphasis or subskill models.

Breve. The short vowel mark (˘).

Buffer zone. The area that falls between the instructional and frustration levels.

Capacity level. See **Listening capacity level.**

Categorizing. A thinking skill involving the ability to classify items into general and specific categories.

Central idea. The central thought of a group of paragraphs, an article, or a story. All the paragraphs develop the central idea of a group of paragraphs, an article, or a story. See **Main idea.**

Chapter 1. In 1981, Congress replaced Title I with Chapter 1; provides funds for children with major basic skills deficits.

Checklist. A means for systematically and quickly recording a student's behavior; it usually consists of a list of behaviors that the observer records as present or absent.

Classroom tests. Teacher-made tests; also called informal tests (*which see*).

Cloze procedure. A technique that helps teachers

gain information about a variety of language facility and comprehension ability skills.

Cloze test. Reader must supply words which have been systematically deleted from a passage.

Clusters. Clusters represent a blend of sounds.

Cognitive development. Refers to development of thinking (*which see*).

Cognitive domain. Hierarchy of objectives ranging from simplistic thinking skills to the more complex ones.

Combining forms. Usually defined as roots (*which see*) borrowed from another language that join together or that join with a prefix (*which see*), a suffix (*which see*) or both to form a word, for example, *aqua/naut.*

Communication. Exchange of ideas.

Comparison. A demonstration of the similarities between persons, ideas, things, and so on.

Compound word. Separate words that combine to form a new word, for example, *grandfather, stepdaughter, sunlight.*

Comprehension. Understanding; the ability to get the meaning of something.

Computer-assisted instruction. Instruction using computers.

Concentration. Sustained attention. It is essential for both studying and listening to lectures.

Concept. A group of stimuli with common characteristics.

Connotative meaning. Includes all emotional associations of the word. It's based on an individual's background of experiences.

Consonant clusters (blends). A combination of consonant sounds blended together so that the identity of each sound is retained.

Consonant digraph. Two consonants that represent one speech sound.

Construct. Something which cannot be directly observed or directly measured—such as intelligence, attitudes, and motivation.

Content domain. Term that refers to subject matter covered.

Context. The words surrounding a particular word that can shed light on its meaning.

Context clue. An item of information from the surrounding words of a particular word in the form of a synonym (*which see*), antonym (*which see*), example (*which see*), definition, description, explanation, and so on, that helps shed light on the particular word.

Contrast. A demonstration of the differences between persons, ideas, things, and so on.

Corrective reading program. Takes place within the regular classroom.

Creative reading. Uses divergent thinking skills to go beyond the literal comprehension (*which* *see*), interpretation (*which see*), and critical reading (*which see*) levels.

Creativity. Difficult to define; one definition that has been given: a combination of imagination plus knowledge plus evaluation.

Criterion-referenced tests. Based on an extensive inventory of objectives in a specific curriculum area; they are used to assess an individual student's performance in respect to his or her mastery of specified objectives in a given curriculum area.

Critical reading. A high-level reading skill that involves evaluation; making a personal judgment on the accuracy, value, and truthfulness of what is read.

Crossed dominance. The dominant hand on one side and the dominant eye on the other.

Decoding. Listening and reading are decoding processes involving the intake of language.

Deductive teaching. Students are given a generalization and must determine which examples fit the rule, going from general to specific.

Denotative meaning. The direct, specific meaning of the word.

Derivatives. Combinations of root words with either prefixes (*which see*) or suffixes (*which see*) or both; for example, prefix (*re*) plus root word (*play*) = *replay*.

Developmental reading. All those reading skills that are systematically and sequentially developed to help students become effective readers throughout their schooling.

Diacritical marks. Marks that show how to pronounce words.

Diagnosis. The act of identifying difficulties and strengths from their signs and symptoms, as well as the investigation or analysis of the cause or causes of a condition, situation, or problem.

Diagnostic pattern. Consists of three steps: identification (*which see*), appraisal (*which see*) and diagnosis (*which see*).

Diagnostic-reading and correction program. Reading instruction interwoven with diagnosis and correction.

Diagnostic reading test. Provides subscores discrete enough so that specific information about a student's reading behavior can be obtained and used for instruction.

Diagnostic teaching. The practice of continuously trying a variety of instructional strategies and materials based on the needs of students.

Dialect. A variation of language sufficiently different to be considered separate, but not different enough to be classified as a separate language.

Dictionary. A very important reference tool that supplies word meanings, pronunciations, and a great amount of other useful information.

Digit span. Refers to amount of numbers an individual can retain in his or her short-term memory.

Digraph. Usually consisting of either two consonants or two vowels which represent one speech sound, for example, *ch, ai*.

Diphthongs. Blends of vowel sounds beginning with the first and gliding to the second. The vowel blends are represented by two adjacent vowels, for example, *oi*. For syllabication purposes, diphthongs are considered to be one vowel sound.

Directed listening/thinking approach. Requires teachers to ask questions before, during, and after a talk; consists of a number of steps; requires students to be active participants.

Directed Reading-Thinking Activity (DRTA). Requires teachers to nurture the inquiry process and students to be active participants and questioners; includes prediction and verification.

Direct instruction. Instruction guided by a teacher, who uses various strategies to help students understand what they are reading.

Disabled reader. A reader who is reading below his or her ability level.

Divergent thinking. The many different ways to solve problems or to look at things.

Dyslexia. Severe reading disability.

Educable mentally retarded children. Children whose IQs usually range approximately from 55 to 70; considered mildly retarded.

Educational factors. Those factors that come under the domain or control of the educational system and influence learning.

Egocentric speech. Child speaks in a collective monologue or primarily in parallel, that is, speech is not directed to another's point of view; concerned with own thoughts.

Emergent literacy. That stage in literacy which is concerned with the young child's involvement in language and his or her attempts at reading and writing before coming to school.

Environmental psychology. Focuses on behavior in relation to physical settings.

Equilibrium. According to Piaget, a balance between assimilation (*which see*) and accommodation (*which see*) in cognitive development (*which see*).

English as a Second Language (ESL). Teaching that concentrates on helping children who speak a language other than English or who speak nonstandard English to learn standard English as a language.

Evaluation. A process of appraisal involving specific values and the use of a variety of instruments in order to form a value judgment; goes beyond test and measurement.

Example. Something representative of a whole or a group.

Exceptional children. Those children who deviate so much from the "average" that they require special attention.

Experience story. A basic teaching technique in reading founded on experiences of students.

Explicit phonics instruction. Each sound associated with a letter in the word is pronounced in isolation, and then the sounds are blended together; synthetic phonics.

Eye movements. How the eyes appear to move in the act of reading.

Fact. Something that exists and can be proved true.

Finding inconsistencies. Finding statements that do not make sense.

Fixations. Stops readers make in the act of reading continuous text.

Frustration reading level. The child reads with many word recognition and comprehension errors. It is the lowest reading level and one to be avoided.

Functional reading. Includes all reading in which the primary aim is to obtain information.

Gifted children. The academically gifted are usually those with an IQ above 132 on the Stanford Binet Intelligence Scale; however, "gifted" also usually refers to those whose performance in any line of socially useful endeavor is consistently superior.

Grade equivalents. Description of year and month of school for which a given student's level of performance is typical.

Grapheme-phoneme correspondences. Letter-sound relationships.

Graphemes. The written representation of phonemes (*which see*).

Graphemic base. Same as phonogram (*which see*).

Graphic organizer. Same as semantic mapping (*which see*).

Group instruction. A number of students are taught at the same time; helps make instruction more manageable.

Group tests. Administered to a group of people at the same time.

Halo effect. A response bias that contaminates an individual's perception in rating or evaluation.

Hearing. The lowest level in the hierarchy of listening; the physical perception of sound.

Home environment. Socioeconomic class, parents' education, and the neighborhood in which children live are some factors that shape children's home environment.

Homographs. Words that are spelled the same but have different meanings.

Homonyms. Words that sound alike, are spelled differently, and have different meanings.

Homophones. Same as homonyms (*which see*).

Hypermetropia. Farsightedness; difficulty with close-up vision.

Identification. Part of diagnostic pattern (*which see*); the act of determining the student's present level of performance in word recognition and comprehension for screening purposes.

Immersion. Complete exposure of a nonnative English speaker to English as soon as he or she enters school.

Implicit phonics instruction. Does not present sounds associated with letters in isolation. Children listen to words that begin with a particular sound; then they state another word that begins with the same sound; analytic phonics.

Independent reading level. Level at which child reads on his or her own without any difficulty.

Index. A list of topics discussed in a book and page numbers indicating where the topics are discussed.

Individualized instruction. Student works at own pace on material based on the needs, interests, and ability of the student.

Individual tests. Administered to one person at a time.

Inductive teaching. Students discover generalizations by being given numerous examples which portray patterns; going from specific to general.

Inference. Understanding that is not derived from a direct statement but from an indirect suggestion in what is stated; understanding that is implied.

Informal diagnostic reading tests. Teacher-made tests to help determine students' specific strengths and weaknesses.

Informal interviews. Teachers converse with students to learn about their interests and feelings.

Informal Reading Inventory (IRI). A valuable aid in helping teachers determine a student's reading levels and his or her strengths and weaknesses. It usually consists of oral and silent reading passages selected from basal readers from the preprimer to the eighth-grade levels.

Informal tests. Teacher-made tests (*which see*).

Instructional reading level. The teaching level.

Intake of language. Listening and reading.

Intelligence. Ability to reason abstractly; problem-solving ability based on a hierarchical organization of two things—symbolic representations and strategies for processing information.

Intelligence quotient (IQ). Mental age divided by chronological age multiplied by 100.

Interactive instruction. The teacher intervenes at optimal times to enhance the learning process.

Interactive reading models. The top-down processing of information is dependent on the bottom-up processing, and vice versa.

Interest inventory. A statement or questionnaire method that helps teachers learn about likes and dislikes of students.

Interpretation. A reading level that demands a higher level of thinking ability because the material it involves is not directly stated in the text but only suggested or implied.

IPA. International Phonetic Alphabet.

Junior Great Books Program. Program in which parent-teacher teams work together to plan reading discussions for students; sessions take place in regular classrooms during the reading period and are led by both parent and teacher.

Kinesics. Study of the gestures that may or may not accompany speech (message-related body movement).

Language. A learned, shared, and patterned arbitrary system of vocal sound symbols with which people in a given culture can communicate with one another.

Language arts. The major components are listening, speaking, reading, and writing.

Language-experience approach. A nonstructured emerging reading program based on students' experiences, which incorporates all aspects of the language arts into reading.

Laterality. Refers to sidedness.

Learning center. An integral part of the instructional program and vital to a good individualized program. An area is usually set aside in the classroom for instruction in a specific curriculum area.

Learning disability. Difficult to define; the definition given most often is: a disorder in one or more of the basic psychological processes involved in understanding or in using language spoken or written, which may manifest itself in an imperfect ability to listen, think, speak, read, write, spell, or do mathematical calculations.

Linguistics. The scientific study of language.

Listening. Middle of hierarchy of listening in which the individual becomes aware of sound sequences, and is able to identify and recognize the sound sequences as words.

Listening capacity level. The highest level at which a learner can understand material when it is read aloud to him or her.

Listening capacity test. Given to determine a child's comprehension through listening. Teacher reads aloud to child and then asks questions about the selection.

Listening comprehension test. Given to assess a child's comprehension through listening; teacher reads aloud to child and then asks questions about the selection. Same as listening capacity test (*which see*).

Listening vocabulary. The number of different words one knows the meaning of when they are said aloud.

Literal comprehension. The ability to obtain a low-level type of understanding by using only information that is explicitly stated.

Literature webbing. A story map technique to help guide children in using predictable trade books.

Locator test. Used to determine at what level a student should begin testing.

Macron. The long vowel mark (ˉ).

Main idea. The central thought of a paragraph. All the sentences in the paragraph develop the main idea. The term *central idea* (*which see*) is usually used when referring to a group of paragraphs, an article, or a story.

Mainstreaming. The placement of handicapped children in the least restrictive educational environment that will meet their needs.

Masking. Factor inhibiting hearing as sounds interfere with the spoken message.

Measurement. Part of the evaluative process; broader than test; involves quantitative descriptions.

Memory span. The number of discrete elements grasped in a given moment of attention and organized into a unity for purposes of immediate reproduction or immediate use; synonym for digit span (*which see*).

Mental age. A child's present level of development; in intelligence testing, a score based on average abilities for that age group:

$$MA = \frac{IQ \times CA}{100}$$

Metacognition. Thinking critically about thinking; refers to students' knowledge about their thinking processes and ability to control them.

Miscue. Unexpected response to print.

Miscue analysis. A process that helps researchers learn how readers get meaning from language.

Mixed dominance. No consistent preference for an eye, hand, or foot.

Modeling strategy. Thinking out loud; verbalizing one's thoughts to help students gain understanding.

Morpheme. The smallest individually meaningful element in the utterances of a language.

Morphology. Involves the construction of words and word parts.

Motivation. Internal impetus behind behavior and the direction behavior takes; drive.

Myopia. Nearsightedness; difficulty with distance vision.

Newbery Award books. The books that have received the Newbery Medal, which is given annually to the book in the United States that has been voted "the most distinguished literature" for children.

Noneducational factors. Supposedly those factors that do not come under the domain or control of the educational system and cannot be influenced by it.

Nonstandard English. A variation of standard English owing to socioeconomic and cultural differences in the United States.

Norm-referenced tests. Standardized tests with norms (*which see*) so that comparisons can be made to a sample population.

Norms. Average scores for a given group of students, which allow comparisons to be made for different students or groups of students.

Notetaking. A useful study and paper-writing tool.

Objective. Desired educational outcome.

Objectivity. The same score must result regardless of who marks the test.

Observation. A technique that helps teachers collect data about students' behavior.

Open syllable. A syllable having a single vowel and ending in a vowel. The vowel is usually long, for example, *go*.

Opinions. Based on attitudes (*which see*) or feelings; they can vary from person to person, but cannot be conclusively proved right or wrong.

Oral reading. Reading aloud.

Overlearning. Helps persons retain information over a long period of time; occurs when individuals continue to practice even after they think they have learned the material.

Paired reading. The child reads aloud simultaneously with another person.

Peer tutoring. A student helps another student gain needed skills.

Percentile. A point on the distribution below which a certain percentage of the scores fall.

Perception. A cumulative process based on an individual's background of experiences. It is defined as giving meaning to sensations or the ability to organize stimuli on a field.

Perceptual domain. Part of the reading process that depends on an individual's background of experiences and sensory receptors.

Phoneme. Smallest unit of sound in a specific language system; a class of sounds.

Phonemics. Deals with the problem of discovering which phonemes are part of the conscious repertoire of sounds made by speakers of a language or dialect.

Phonetics. The study of the nature of speech sounds.

Phonic analysis. The breaking down of a word into its component parts.

Phonics. The study of the relationships between letter symbols of a written language and the sounds they represent.

Phonic synthesis. The building up of the component parts of a word into a whole.

Phonogram (graphemic base). A succession of graphemes that occurs with the same phonetic value in a number of words (*ight, ake, at et*, and so on); word family.

Phonology. Branch of linguistics (*which see*) dealing with the analysis of sound systems of language.

Physical environment. Refers to any observable factors in the physical environment that could affect the behavior of an individual.

Practice test. Ensures that the actual test measures what students know rather than test-taking ability; it familiarizes students with the test.

Preface. A short introduction to a book.

Prefix. An affix (*which see*); a letter or a sequence of letters added to the beginning of a root word that changes its meaning, for example, *re* plus *play* = *replay*.

Principle. Refers to a rule or a guide.

Projective technique. A method in which the individual tends to put himself or herself into the situation and reveal how he or she feels.

Propaganda. Any systematic, widespread, deliberate indoctrination or plan for indoctrination.

Proximodistal development. Muscular development from the midpoint of the body to the extremities.

Public Law 94–142. Advocates a free appropriate education for all children in the least restrictive environment.

Question Answer Relationships (QARs). Helps students distinguish between "what they have in their heads" and information that is in the text.

Questions. A good way for students to gain a better insight into a subject; questioning also gives the instructor feedback and slows the instructor down if he or she is going too fast.

Rating scale. An evaluative instrument used to record estimates of particular aspects of a student's behavior.

Raw score. The number of items that a student answers correctly on a test

Readiness. An ongoing, dynamic process which teachers use to prepare students for various learning activities throughout the school day.

Reading. The getting of meaning from and the bringing of meaning to the written page.

Reading autobiography. Students write or tell about their feelings and attempt to analyze their reading problems.

Reading comprehension. A complex intellectual process involving a number of abilities. The two major abilities involve word meanings and reasoning with verbal concepts.

Reading expectancy formula. Helps teachers determine who needs special help; helps determine a student's reading potential.

Reading Olympics programs. Programs vary; however, most include a contest to challenge students to read the most books they can and the sharing of these books in some way with parents.

Reading process. Concerned with the affective (*which see*), perceptual (*which see*), and cognitive (*which see*) domains.

Reading readiness. Preparing students for the reading lesson by taking into account their maturation, past experiences, and desire to learn.

Reading readiness test. Supposed to predict those children who are ready to read. If used, it must be used with great caution.

Reading recovery program. An early individualized, one-on-one intervention program for first-graders who are experiencing difficulty in learning to read.

Reading taxonomy. A hierarchy of reading comprehension skills ranging from the more simplistic to the more complex ones; a classification of these skills.

Recite or recall. The process of finding the answer to a question in one's memory without rereading the text or notes.

Recreational reading. Reading primarily for enjoyment, entertainment, and appreciation.

Regressions. Eyes move backward; they move back to reread material while in the act of reading continuous text.

Reinforcement. Any stimulus, such as praise, which usually causes the individual to repeat a response.

Reliability. The extent to which a test instrument consistently produces similar results.

Remedial reading program. Takes place outside the regular classroom and is handled by special personnel.

Repeated reading. Similar to paired reading (*which see*); child reads along (assisted reading with model or tape) until he or she gains confidence to read alone.

Reversals. Confusion of letters and words by inverting them; for example, $b = d$, *was = saw*, and vice versa.

Role playing. A form of creative drama in which dialogue for a specific role is spontaneously developed.

Root. Smallest unit of a word that can exist and retain its basic meaning, for example, *play*.

Saccades. Quick, jerky movements of the eyes as they jump from one fixation to another in the reading of continuous text.

Scale score. Used to derive other scores.

Schemata. These structured designs are the cognitive arrangements by which the mind is able to categorize incoming stimuli.

Schema theory. Deals with relations between prior knowledge and comprehension.

Schwa. The sound often found in the unstressed (unaccented) syllables of words with more than one syllable. The schwa sound is represented by an upside-down e (ə) in the phonetic (speech) alphabet. A syllable ending in *le* preceded by a consonant is usually the final syllable in a word and contains the schwa sound.

Second-language learners. Refers to those children whose parents have usually been born in another country and who speak a language other than English; it may also refer to a child who is born in the United States, but English is not the dominant language spoken in the child's home.

Self-fulfilling prophecy. Teacher assumptions about children become true, at least in part, because of the attitude of the teachers, which in turn becomes part of the children's self-concept.

Semantic clue. Meaning clue.

Semantic mapping (graphic organizer). A graphic representation used to illustrate concepts and relationships among concepts such as classes, properties, and examples.

Silent consonants. Two adjacent consonants, one of which is silent, for example, *kn (know), pn (pneumonia).*

Silent reading. Reading to oneself; not saying aloud what is read.

Skimming. Reading rapidly to find or locate information.

Slow learners. Same as borderline children (*which see*).

Social promotion. Promotion of students based on chronological age rather than achievement.

Sociogram. A map or chart showing the interrelationships of children in a classroom and identifying those who are "stars" or "isolates."

SQ3R. A widely used study technique that involves five steps: survey, question, read, recite or recall, and review.

Standard English. English in respect to spelling, grammar, vocabulary, and pronunciation that is substantially uniform, though not devoid of regional differences. It is well established by usage and the formal and informal speech and writing of the educated and is widely recognized as acceptable wherever English is spoken and understood.

Standardized oral reading test. Individually administered test that helps teachers analyze the oral reading performance of students.

Standardized reading achievement test. Usually part of a test battery that includes other curriculum areas besides reading; measures general reading achievement.

Standardized reading survey test. Measures general reading achievement; similar to a reading achievement test; single subject-matter test.

Standardized tests. Tests that have been published by experts in the field and have precise instructions for administration and scoring.

Stanine. A score in educational testing on a nine-point scale, ranging from a low of 1 to a high of 9, of normalized standard scores.

Structural analysis. A technique for breaking a word into its pronunciation units; the breaking down of a word into word parts such as prefixes (*which see*), suffixes (*which see*), roots, (*which see*) and combining forms (*which see*).

Structural synthesis. A technique for building up of word parts into a whole.

Study procedures. (1) Build good habits, (2) devise a system that works for you, (3) keep at it, (4) maintain a certain degree of tension, and (5) concentrate.

Suffix. An affix (*which see*); a letter or a sequence of letters added to the end of a root word, which changes the grammatical form of the word and its meaning; for example, *prince* plus *ly = princely.*

Suitability. The appropriateness of a test for a specific population of students.

Summary. A brief statement of the essential information in a longer piece.

Supporting details. Additional information that supports, explains, or illustrates the main idea. Some of the ways that supporting details may be arranged are as cause and effect, examples, sequence of events, descriptions, definitions, comparisons, or contrasts.

Survey. To gain an overview of the text material.

Survey batteries. A group of tests in different content areas.

Sustained silent reading (SSR). Practice in independent silent reading.

Syllable. A vowel or a group of letters containing one vowel sound, for example, *blo.*

Synonyms. Words similar in meaning.

Syntax. Refers to word order or position of the word in a sentence.

Synthesis. Building up the parts of something, usually into a whole.

Synthetic phonics. Same as explicit phonics instruction (*which see*).

Table of contents. A listing of chapter titles, major headings, and page numbers at the beginning of a book.

Teacher-made tests. Tests prepared by the classroom teacher for a particular class and given by the classroom teacher under conditions of his or her own choosing.

Test. A standard set of questions to be answered.

Thinking. Covert manipulation of symbolic representations.

Top-down reading models. These models depend on the reader's background of experiences and language ability in constructing meaning from the text.

Topic sentence. This sentence states what the paragraph will be about by naming the topic.

Underachievement. Achievement below one's ability level.

Validity. The degree to which certain inferences can be made from test scores or other measurements; the degree to which a test instrument measures what it claims to measure (nontechnical definition).

Visual discrimination. The ability to distinguish differences and similarities between written symbols.

Vocabulary consciousness. An awareness that words may have different meanings based on their context and a desire to increase one's vocabulary.

Vowel digraph. Two vowels that represent one speech sound.

Whole language. A set of beliefs in which the emphasis is on the "wholeness" of things.

Whole word or "look and say". A word recognition technique in which a child's attention is directed to a word and then the word is said.

Word recognition. A twofold process that includes both the identification of printed symbols by some method so that the word can be pronounced and the association of meaning to the word after it has been properly pronounced.

Appendix A ─────────────

Informal Reading Inventory[*]

Summary Sheet

Name_____   Age _____

Grade_____   Teacher _____

| Reader Level | Word Recognition in Isolation (No. of Errors) | Oral Reading | | | Silent Reading | | Listening Capacity | |
| | | W.R. | Comp. | | Comp. | | | |
		No. of Errors/ Total No. Wds.	% Errors	% Correct	% Errors	% Correct	% Errors	% Correct
Preprimer								
Primer								
First								
2^1								
2^2								
3^1								
3^2								
4								
5								
6								
7								
8								

* The Informal Reading Inventory is based on the Silver Burdett & Ginn series *World of Reading*, 1989.

Level at which Word Recognition Inventory
(WRI) was begun   _____

Level at which oral reading was begun   _____

Oral reading—word recognition
    Independent level   _____

    Instructional level   _____

    Frustration level   _____

Oral reading—comprehension
    Independent level   _____

    Instructional level   _____

    Frustration level   _____

Silent reading—comprehension
    Independent level   _____

    Instructional level   _____

    Frustration level   _____

Listening capacity level   _____

Word analysis
    Consonants—single
      initial   _____

      medial   _____

      final   _____

    Consonants—double
      blends   _____

      digraphs   _____

    Consonants—silent   _____

    Vowels—single
      short   _____

      long   _____

    Vowels—double
      digraphs   _____

      diphthongs   _____

Effect of final *e* on vowel   _____

Vowel controlled by *r*   _____

Structural analysis

  prefixes   _____

  suffixes   _____

  combining forms   _____

  inflectional endings   _____

Compound words   _____

Accent   _____

Special Notes on Strengths and Weaknesses

Comments on Behavior During the Testing

Recommendations

SPECIAL NOTES

Information on the following is given in the body of Chapter 8:

1. Code for marking oral reading errors (p. 181)
2. The scoring of oral reading errors (pp. 180–182)
3. Criteria for estimating the reading levels (pp. 170–173)
4. Administering the IRI (pp. 185–197)
5. Examples (pp. 189–197)

Partial credit may be given for comprehension questions if an answer consists of more than one part. For example, if the answer to a question consists of three names, and the student has named only one, the student should get one-third credit. If the answer to a question consists of two things, and the student gives one only, the student should receive half credit.

Do not count mispronunciations of difficult proper nouns in the oral reading passages as errors. You may pronounce these for the children if necessary. Also, do not count as errors dialectical equivalents (nonstandard dialects); however, these should be noted.

In addition, the term *main idea* is used rather than *central idea*, even though the oral and silent passages are usually more than one paragraph. (See "Finding the Central Idea of a Group of Paragraphs" in Chapter 13.)

Word Recognition Inventory (WRI)

Preprimer		*Primer*		*First*	
1. water	_____	1. blow	_____	1. soup	_____
2. play	_____	2. little	_____	2. tents	_____
3. sand	_____	3. many	_____	3. afternoon	_____
4. look	_____	4. bright	_____	4. baked	_____
5. wind	_____	5. old	_____	5. family	_____
6. jump	_____	6. won	_____	6. alone	_____
7. cave	_____	7. things	_____	7. great	_____
8. make	_____	8. yellow	_____	8. white	_____
9. put	_____	9. farm	_____	9. soft	_____
10. bear	_____	10. friend	_____	10. boy	_____
11. over	_____	11. more	_____	11. dinner	_____
12. out	_____	12. thanks	_____	12. does	_____
13. cap	_____	13. snow	_____	13. wife	_____
14. could	_____	14. some	_____	14. horse	_____
15. down	_____	15. cows	_____	15. head	_____
16. sun	_____	16. game	_____	16. sorry	_____
17. have	_____	17. please	_____	17. summer	_____
18. side	_____	18. leaves	_____	18. hungry	_____
19. top	_____	19. draw	_____	19. drank	_____
20. surprise	_____	20. work	_____	20. enough	_____

Word Recognition Inventory (WRI) (*Cont.*)

2^1		2^2		3^1	
1. brave	_____	1. office	_____	1. plow	_____
2. noon	_____	2. perfect	_____	2. horn	_____
3. park	_____	3. patient	_____	3. hesitate	_____
4. strange	_____	4. enemy	_____	4. neglect	_____
5. November	_____	5. donkey	_____	5. deaf	_____
6. money	_____	6. dirt	_____	6. language	_____
7. library	_____	7. clever	_____	7. attention	_____
8. join	_____	8. company	_____	8. drawn	_____
9. angry	_____	9. candle	_____	9. complain	_____
10. apple	_____	10. beard	_____	10. fame	_____
11. carrots	_____	11. bundle	_____	11. goal	_____
12. class	_____	12. address	_____	12. familiar	_____
13. answer	_____	13. snowflake	_____	13. elevator	_____
14. loud	_____	14. sailors	_____	14. plunge	_____
15. mouth	_____	15. score	_____	15. nature	_____
16. matter	_____	16. tune	_____	16. poem	_____
17. hurry	_____	17. thirsty	_____	17. stall	_____
18. idea	_____	18. unload	_____	18. talent	_____
19. carve	_____	19. view	_____	19. worthy	_____
20. clothes	_____	20. trouble	_____	20. lung	_____
21. delicious	_____	21. south	_____	21. medal	_____
22. below	_____	22. shy	_____	22. mistake	_____
23. boil	_____	23. ambulance	_____	23. customer	_____
24. built	_____	24. tiny	_____	24. courage	_____
25. dragons	_____	25. hobby	_____	25. announce	_____

Word Recognition Inventory (WRI) (*Cont.*)

3^2	4	5
1. petal ____	1. gracious ____	1. tragedy ____
2. rein ____	2. imitate ____	2. applause ____
3. furious ____	3. defense ____	3. amazement ____
4. popular ____	4. declare ____	4. harvest ____
5. identify ____	5. electronics ____	5. thaw ____
6. forecast ____	6. punishment ____	6. original ____
7. attach ____	7. robot ____	7. balcony ____
8. bought ____	8. uniform ____	8. marvel ____
9. admire ____	9. twilight ____	9. mileage ____
10. noble ____	10. wander ____	10. cluster ____
11. migrate ____	11. stranger ____	11. architect ____
12. patient ____	12. tame ____	12. heroine ____
13. novel ____	13. technique ____	13. audition ____
14. ruin ____	14. suspect ____	14. interrupt ____
15. rescue ____	15. ordinary ____	15. landscape ____
16. unusual ____	16. native ____	16. petition ____
17. x-ray ____	17. haughty ____	17. permission ____
18. wisdom ____	18. hostile ____	18. vessel ____
19. rough ____	19. entire ____	19. promotion ____
20. protest ____	20. errand ____	20. violence ____
21. persuade ____	21. average ____	21. voyage ____
22. influence ____	22. appetite ____	22. vast ____
23. prince ____	23. uniform ____	23. nuisance ____
24. bandage ____	24. prowl ____	24. luxury ____
25. bridge ____	25. caution ____	25. lonely ____

Word Recognition Inventory (WRI) (*Cont.*)

6	7	8
1. tenement _____	1. sham _____	1. prospect _____
2. rebel _____	2. scrutiny _____	2. quest _____
3. ease _____	3. refuge _____	3. scoop _____
4. exhibit _____	4. prestigious _____	4. journalism _____
5. appoint _____	5. quarrel _____	5. invincible _____
6. shuttle _____	6. nomad _____	6. listless _____
7. unwilling _____	7. fault _____	7. mirror _____
8. recede _____	8. flattery _____	8. circuit _____
9. wizard _____	9. hindrance _____	9. defy _____
10. wrench _____	10. imperative _____	10. anguish _____
11. revenge _____	11. colleague _____	11. augment _____
12. tiresome _____	12. trifle _____	12. aristocratic _____
13. spout _____	13. souvenir _____	13. formidable _____
14. strategy _____	14. chore _____	14. faculty _____
15. pamphlet _____	15. aggressive _____	15. seizure _____
16. persist _____	16. barometer _____	16. terrace _____
17. heritage _____	17. emigrate _____	17. scrabble _____
18. conquer _____	18. verdict _____	18. undermine _____
19. humble _____	19. zodiac _____	19. sphere _____
20. arrogant _____	20. wrench _____	20. naive _____
21. astronomy _____	21. probe _____	21. plateau _____
22. distinguish _____	22. momentum _____	22. recitation _____
23. gratitude _____	23. mortal _____	23. jaunt _____
24. guarantee _____	24. exile _____	24. frugal _____
25. legacy _____	25. imitation _____	25. hysteria _____

PREPRIMER

Introduction: Read this story aloud to find out what a little boy can make. Then I will ask you questions about the story.

The sun came out.
Bob and Mom came out to play.
Bob said, "Who can play with me?"
Mom said, "Do you see what I see?"
Bob said, "All I see is sand.
I see a lot of sand.
I can make a mountain
with all the sand I see."
Mom said, "Make a sand mountain!
You will see who will come to play."

Comprehension Questions

		Points
(Literal)	1. Who came out to play? (Bob and Mom)	20
(Inference)	2. What did Mom see? (Sand)	16
(Literal)	3. How much sand was there? (A lot)	16
(Literal)	4. What did Bob say he could make with the sand? (A sand mountain)	16
(Inference)	5. What kind of day is it? (Sunny, warm, nice)	16
(Inference)	6. What did Mom think the sand mountain would do? (Bring other children to play)	16

Scoring Scale

Levels	Word Recognition Errors	Comprehension Errors
Independent	0–1	0–10 points
Instructional	2–3	11–25 points
Frustration	6 or more	50 points or more

[1] Level 2, "The Sand Mountain," *Out Came the Sun* (Needham, Mass.: Silver Burdett & Ginn, 1989), pp. 38–39.

Introduction: Read this story to find out what Bob and his friends do. Then I will ask you questions about the story. Read it carefully.

Jane said, "Can I help make it a
big mountain?"
Bob said, "I can put sand here.
You can put sand on the other side."
Fran said, "I came to play.
Can I help make the sand mountain?"
Bob said, "Come on, you can play.
You can help Jane and me."
Jane said, "Will you get water?
The wind is blowing the sand
off the mountain."

Comprehension Questions

		Points
(Inference)	1. Who came to play first? (Jane)	16
(Literal)	2. What did Jane want to do? (Help Bob make a big mountain)	16
(Literal)	3. What did Bob tell Jane she could do? (Put sand on the other side of the mountain)	16
(Literal)	4. Whom did Bob say Fran could help? (Jane and him)	20
(Literal)	5. Who said, "Will you get water?" (Jane)	16
(Inference)	6. Why did Jane want water? (To make the sand wet so that the wind would not blow it away)	16

Scoring Scale

Levels	Comprehension Errors
Independent	0–10 points
Instructional	11–20 points
Frustration	50 points or more

² Ibid., pp. 40–42.

ORAL READING (76)[3]

Introduction: Read this story aloud to find out what Sara wants. Then I will ask you questions about the story.

Sara sat and sat, looking out at the
big tree.
She looked at her mother and asked,
"Mom, do you have some string?"
    "Yes, here is some red string,"
said Sara's mother.
"Is it for your hair?"
    "No," said Sara, "It's not for my hair."
    "I know," said Mother. "You
are going to fix something with it."
    "No," said Sara. "You'll see."
Sara saw that her father had
some string, too.
She asked him for it.

Comprehension Questions

		Points
(Literal)	1. What was Sara looking at? (The big tree)	12.5
(Literal)	2. What did Sara want from her mother? (String)	12.5
(Literal)	3. What color string did her mother have? (Red)	12.5
(Literal)	4. What did Sara's mother first think the string was for? (Sara's hair)	12.5
(Inference)	5. Who thought something was broken? (Sara's mother)	12.5
(Inference)	6. How do we know Sara's mother thought something was broken? (She thought the string was to fix something.)	12.5
(Literal)	7. Who else had string? (Her father)	12.5
(Literal)	8. What did Sara do when she saw her father had some string. (She asked him for it.)	12.5

Scoring Scale

Levels	Word Recognition Errors	Comprehension Errors
Independent	0–1	0–10 points
Instructional	2–4	11–25 points
Frustration	8 or more	50 points or more

[3] Jane Mechling, "A Rainbow for Sara," Level 4, *Make a Wish* (Needham, Mass.: Silver Burdett & Ginn, 1989), pp. 32–34.

SILENT READING[4]

Introduction: Read this story to find out more about Sara and her string. Then I will ask you questions about the story. Read it carefully.

Sara ran outside to play with Peter
and Anna.
"I am keeping string in a box,"
said Sara.
"I have some green string in my
pocket. You may have it," said Peter.
"You are keeping string?"
said Anna. "What are you going
to do with all that string? Will
you and your cat play with it?"
"No," said Sara. "You'll see."
Soon Sara had all the string she needed.
She had red string, orange string,
green string, and yellow string.

Comprehension Questions

		Points
(Literal)	1. Where did Sara go? (Outside)	12.5
(Literal)	2. Why did Sara go outside? (To play with Peter and Anna)	12.5
(Literal)	3. Where was Sara keeping her string? (In a box)	12.5
(Inference)	4. Who else was saving string? (Peter)	12.5
(Literal)	5. What color string did Peter have? (Green)	12.5
(Literal)	6. Where did Peter keep his string? (In his pocket)	12.5
(Inference)	7. Does Sara have a pet? If she does, what is it?(Yes; a cat)	12.5
(Literal)	8. What were the colors of the string Sara had? (Red, orange, green, and yellow)	12.5

Scoring Scale

Levels	Comprehension Errors
Independent	0–10 points
Instructional	11–25 points
Frustration	50 points or more

---

[4] Ibid., pp. 35–36.

ORAL READING (88)[5]

> **Introduction: Read this story aloud to find out about Fritz and Anna. Then I will ask you questions about the story.**

Fritz and Anna lived on a farm. It was a small farm. It was also very dry, and things did not grow well. So Fritz and his wife, Anna, were poor.
One day there was a tap, tap, tap on the door. A woman had come to the farm. She had been walking most of the day, and she was hungry. She asked Fritz and Anna to give her something to eat. Fritz and Anna had a pot of soup. They let the woman come in to eat.

Comprehension Questions

		Points
(Literal)	1. Where did Fritz and Anna live? (On a farm)	10
(Literal)	2. What kind of farm was it? (Small, dry)	10
(Inference)	3. Why were Fritz and Anna poor? (Things didn't grow well on their farm.)	10
(Inference)	4. Why didn't things grow well? (It was too dry.)	10
(Word meaning)	5. What does poor mean? (Not having money; not having much food to eat)	10
(Inference)	6. Who knocked on Fritz and Anna's door? (A woman)	10
(Literal)	7. What had the woman been doing? (Walking all day)	10
(Literal)	8. How did the woman feel? (Hungry)	10
(Literal)	9. What did Fritz and Anna have? (A pot of soup)	10
(Inference)	10. How do we know Fritz and Anna are kind people? (Even though they are poor, they share their soup with the woman.)	10

Scoring Scale

Levels	Word Recognition Errors	Comprehension Errors
Independent	0–1	0–10 points
Instructional	2–4	11–25 points
Frustration	9 or more	50 points or more

---

[5] Verna Aardema, "The Three Wishes," Level 5, *A New Day* (Needham, Mass.: Silver Burdett & Ginn, 1989), p. 160.

Introduction: Fritz and Anna are given some wishes by the woman. Read to find out what Fritz and Anna do with one of the wishes. Then I will ask you questions about the story. Read it carefully.

For most of the day, Fritz and Anna
talked about the three wishes they
would make. They talked long after it was
time to eat again, and they forgot to cook.
They began to get hungry.

By the time Anna and Fritz made soup,
they were both very, very hungry.
As they sat down to eat, Fritz said,
"I wish we had a sausage to go with this soup."

And there on the table was a great big
brown sausage!

Comprehension Questions

		Points
(Literal)	1. How many wishes were Fritz and Anna given? (Three)	10
(Literal)	2. How long did they talk about the wishes? (For most of the day)	10
(Literal)	3. What did they forget to do? (Cook)	10
(Inference)	4. Why did they forget to cook? (They were excited about the three wishes; they were busy talking about them.)	10
(Inference)	5. How did they know they hadn't eaten? (They became hungry.)	10
(Literal)	6. What did they make to eat? (Soup)	10
(Literal)	7. How did they feel when the soup was ready? (Very, very hungry)	10
(Literal)	8. Who wished for something? (Fritz)	10
(Literal)	9. What did Fritz wish for? (A sausage to go with the soup)	10
(Literal)	10. What did the wish bring? (A great big brown sausage)	10

Scoring Scale

Levels	Comprehension Errors
Independent	0–10 points
Instructional	11–25 points
Frustration	50 points or more

[6] Ibid., p. 163.

ORAL READING (112)[7]

Introduction: Read this story aloud to find out why a farmer needs help. Then I will ask you questions about the story.

Once there was a farmer who went to the town wise man because he had a problem, and he did not know what to do. "How can
I help you?" the wise man asked.

"I have a house with one small room," sighed the farmer.

"That is not a problem," the wise man said.

"It is a problem," the farmer sighed. "I live in this one small room with my wife and my seven children.
We are always in one another's way, and we are always talking at the same time. It is so loud that I can hardly hear myself think. I cannot stand it any longer.
Can you help me?"

Comprehension Questions

		Points
(Literal)	1. To whom did the farmer go? (To the town wise man)	10
(Word meaning)	2. What is a town wise man? (A person who can help others; a man who knows lots of things; he can answer many questions.)	10
(Literal)	3. Why did the farmer go to the town wise man? (He had a problem.)	10
(Literal)	4. Where does the farmer live? (In a house with one small room)	10
(Inference)	5. How many people live in the house? (Nine: seven children, the farmer, and his wife)	10
(Inference)	6. Explain whether you think the farmer is rich or poor. (Poor, because he lives in one room with such a large family)	10
(Inference)	7. What is the farmer's problem? (It is too noisy in his house.)	10
(Literal)	8. What does everyone in the house do at the same time? (Talk)	10
(Literal)	9. What is the noise stopping the farmer from doing? (Thinking)	10
(Inference)	10. What does the farmer want the town wise man to do? (Help the farmer solve his problem)	10

Scoring Scale

Levels	Word Recognition Errors	Comprehension Errors
Independent	0–1	0–10 points
Instructional	2–6	11–25 points
Frustration	11 or more	50 points or more

[7] Michael Patrick Hearn, "Not So Wise as You Suppose," Level 6, *Garden Gates* (Needham, Mass.: Silver Burdett & Ginn, 1989), pp. 94–95.

Introduction: Read this story to find out what the farmer does to solve his problem. Then I will ask you questions about the story. Read it carefully.

The wise man stroked his chin and thought.
"Do you have a horse?" the wise man asked.
"Yes, I have a horse," the farmer said.
"Then the answer is simple," the wise man said,
"but you must do as I tell you. Tonight you must bring
the horse into your house to stay with you,
your wife, and your seven children." The farmer was
surprised to hear such a plan, but he did as he was told.
The next morning he returned to the wise man.
He was quite upset.
"You are not so wise as you suppose!" the farmer
said,
"Now my house is even louder. The horse just kicks
and neighs morning, noon, and night!
I cannot stand it any longer."

Comprehension Questions

		Points
(Literal)	1. What did the wise man stroke? (His chin)	10
(Literal)	2. What was the wise man doing when he stroked his chin? (Thinking)	10
(Literal)	3. What did the wise man ask the farmer? (If he had a horse)	10
(Word meaning)	4. What does "simple" mean? (Easy)	
(Literal)	5. What did the wise man say was simple? (The answer to the farmer's problem)	10
(Literal)	6. What did the wise man want the farmer to do? (To bring the horse into the house to stay with the farmer and his family)	10
(Literal)	7. When was the farmer supposed to bring the horse into the house? (That night)	10
(Inference)	8. Explain how you know whether the wise man's plan worked. (It didn't work because the farmer came in very upset.)	10
(Literal)	9. What did the horse do in the house? (Kicked and neighed)	10
(Literal)	10. What did the farmer think about the wise man now? (That the wise man was not as wise as he thought he was)	10

Scoring Scale

Levels	Comprehension Errors
Independent	0–10 points
Instructional	11–25 points
Frustration	50 points or more

[8] Ibid., p. 96.

ORAL READING (131)⁹

Introduction: Read this story aloud to find out what the children's surprise is. Then I will ask you questions about the story.

The children sat down in a big circle on the ground. Everyone was excited. Mr. Ortero (or-te'-rō) had promised them a surprise.

Mr. Ortero walked into the middle of the circle. He ran the after-school program in the park.

"I have a mystery today," Mr. Ortero said. "A treasure is hidden somewhere in the park. Your job is to solve the mystery and find the treasure."

Marita (mä-rē'-ta) raised her hand. "What is the treasure?" she asked.

"That's part of the mystery," Mr. Ortero answered.

Marita laughed with everyone else. Mr. Ortero liked to tease them.

"Each of you gets one clue," Mr. Ortero said.

He started around the circle, handing out the clues. Marita was sitting between Jenny and Mike.

"I'm really a good detective," Mike said. "I bet I'll find the treasure."

Comprehension Questions

		Points
(Literal)	1. How were the children sitting? (In a big circle on the ground)	10
(Literal)	2. Why were they excited? (Mr. Ortero had promised them a surprise.)	10
(Literal)	3. Who was Mr. Ortero? (The person who ran the after-school program in the park)	10

⁹ Judith Stamper, "The Treasure Hunt," Level 7, *Going Places* (Needham, Mass.: Silver Burdett & Ginn, 1989), p. 197.

(Literal)	4. What did Mr. Ortero have for the children? (A mystery)	10
(Word meaning)	5. What is a mystery? (Something that is not known; a secret; a puzzle that has to be solved or figured out)	10
(Literal)	6. What is the mystery Mr. Ortero has for the children? (He has hidden a treasure in the park and wants the children to find it.)	10
(Literal)	7. What did Marita want to know? (What the treasure is)	10
(Inference)	8. Why didn't Mr. Ortero tell the children what the treasure is? (The treasure is part of the mystery and therefore might give the mystery away; it might make it too easy to solve the mystery.)	10
(Literal)	9. What did Mr. Ortero do to help the children find the treasure? (He gave each child a clue.)	10
(Inference)	10. Why does Mike think he will find the treasure? (Because he thinks he's a good detective)	10

Scoring Scale

Levels	Word Recognition Errors	Comprehension Errors
Independent	0–1	0–10 points
Instructional	2–7	11–25 points
Frustration	13 or more	50 points or more

Introduction: Read this story to find out more about the treasure hunt. Then I will ask you questions about the story. Read it carefully.

Jenny looked at Marita and smiled. They both liked Mike, but he bragged a lot.

Mr. Ortero gave Jenny her clue. Marita was next, and then Mike. Soon, each child had a clue to open and read. Mr. Ortero stepped back into the middle of the circle.

"Listen to the rules," he said. "First, stay inside the park. The treasure is hidden here. Second, don't harm any plants or trees. Third, you must find the treasure in twenty minutes. Meet me back here in twenty minutes. Good luck!"

The children jumped to their feet and ran in different directions. Marita read her clue over and over. It said:

Thirsty, tired, and very hot?
I'm near what's cool and hits the spot.

"Near something to drink," Marita thought. She ran to find the nearest water fountain. She looked all around the fountain, but there was no treasure.

Comprehension Questions

		Points
(Literal)	1. How did Jenny and Marita feel toward Mike? (They liked him.)	10
(Word meaning)	2. What does "brag" mean? (To boast)	10
(Inference)	3. Why did Jenny smile at Marita? (Because Mike is probably always bragging; they were used to his bragging.)	10
(Literal)	4. What did Mr. Ortero do after he gave each child a clue? (He gave them rules.)	10
(Word meaning)	5. What is a rule? (Something you have to follow)	10
(Literal)	6. What were the three rules he gave the children? (Stay inside the park; don't harm any plants or trees; they must find the treasure in twenty minutes.)	10

[10] Ibid., p. 198.

(Inference)	7. How do we know Mr. Ortero is concerned about the park? (He tells children not to harm the plants or trees.)	10
(Literal)	8. What did Marita run to find? (The water fountain)	10
(Inference)	9. Why did Marita run to the water fountain? (Because of her clue)	10
(Inference)	10. What did Marita expect to find at the water fountain? (The treasure)	10

Scoring Scale

Levels	Comprehension Errors
Independent	0–10 points
Instructional	11–25 points
Frustration	50 points or more

3¹

*ORAL READING (151)*¹¹

Introduction: Read this story aloud to find out what Jason wants. Then I will ask you questions about the story.

Every time ten-year-old Jason Hardman wanted a book
from a library, he borrowed his sister's bike and pedaled six
miles to the next town, Monroe. Since Jason's favorite thing to
do was to read books, he spent hours pedaling.

Jason's town of Elsinore, Utah, had only 650 people,
too tiny for a library of its own. Elsinore was so small
that the children even went to school in Monroe.

One night, Jason said to his parents, "I want to start
a library in Elsinore." They were pleased but told him that
he would have to talk with the town council.

"What is a town council?" Jason asked.

"It's a group of about eight elected members and the mayor.
They run all the town's business," his mom said. "Elsinore,
like all towns, collects taxes from its citizens and uses the money
for public services, such as fire and police protection," she
explained.

Comprehension Questions

		Points
(Literal)	1. How old is Jason Hardman? (Ten years old)	10
(Word meaning)	2. What does "borrow" mean? (To use something that belongs to someone else after agreeing to return it)	10
(Literal)	3. What did Jason borrow? (His sister's bike)	10
(Inference)	4. Where did Jason spend a lot of time? (In the Monroe library)	10
(Literal)	5. What was Jason's favorite thing? (Reading)	10
(Literal)	6. Why didn't Jason's town have a library? (It was too small.)	10
(Literal)	7. What did Jason want to do? (Start a library)	10
(Inference)	8. Why did Jason want to start a library? (Because he loved to read and didn't want to keep pedaling to Monroe to get library books)	10
(Literal)	9. What is a town council? (A group of about eight elected members and a mayor, who run the town's business)	10
(Main idea)	10. What is the main idea of the story? (Jason Hardman wants to start a library.)	10

¹¹ Margaret Tuley Patton, "Jason Wants a Library," Level 8, *Castles of Sand* (Needham, Mass.: Silver Burdett & Ginn, 1989), pp. 184–85.

Scoring Scale

Levels	Word Recognition Errors	Comprehension Errors
Independent	0–2	0–10 points
Instructional	3–8	11–25 points
Frustration	15 or more	50 points or more

Introduction: Jason meets with the town council and tells them he wants to start a library. Read the story to find out more about Jason and his library. Then I will ask you questions about the story. Read it carefully.

Another week passed. Every day when Jason came off the school bus, he'd ask his mother: "Did the mayor phone?" Each day, the answer was, "No." Jason phoned the mayor every night for two weeks. Each night, the same answer was given: "The council is still thinking about it." Jason grew tired of waiting. Why can't I use the town hall basement for my library? he thought to himself.

During those weeks, Jason pedaled often to Monroe for library books. "I wonder if I will be biking these six miles forever for a book?" he asked himself sadly. He began to doubt that he would ever get a library for Elsinore.

At last it happened. When he phoned the mayor, Jason was invited to the council's next meeting. The mayor told him they might find space in the town hall basement. It was just too good to be true.

Comprehension Questions

		Points
(Literal)	1. What did Jason ask his mother when he came home from school? (Did the mayor phone?)	10
(Inference)	2. Explain how you know whether Jason lived close or far from his school. (He didn't live close because he rode a bus to school.)	10
(Literal)	3. What did Jason do every night? (He phoned the mayor every night.)	10
(Literal)	4. What answer was he always given? (The council is still thinking about it.)	10
(Literal)	5. Where did Jason want to have his library? (In the town hall basement)	10
(Literal)	6. What did Jason do while he was waiting? (Pedaled often to the library in Monroe)	10
(Word meaning)	7. What does forever mean? (Always)	10
(Literal)	8. What finally happened? (Jason was invited to the council's next meeting. They told him they might find space in the town hall basement for his library.)	10
(Inference)	9. How do we know Jason could hardly believe his ears. (In the story it says, "It was too good to be true.")	10

---

[12] Ibid., p. 187.

(Main idea)   10. What is the main idea of the story? (After Jason waits a few   10
weeks, the mayor finally tells Jason that he might be able to
use the town hall basement for his library.)

Scoring Scale

Levels	Comprehension Errors
Independent	0–10 points
Instructional	11–25 points
Frustration	50 points or more

ORAL READING (171)[13]

Introduction: Read this story aloud to find out what King Midas loves. Then I will ask you questions about the story.

Once upon a time there was a very rich king named Midas.
He lived in a fine castle with his daughter, Marygold.
The two things he loved best in life were gold and Marygold.
He loved to go into his treasure room and count his coins.
No one, not even Marygold, was allowed into the king's treasure room.

One day Midas was sitting in the treasure room dreaming about his gold. In his dream, he saw a shadow fall across the piles of valuable gold coins. He looked up and saw a stranger standing near him. Since no one was allowed into his treasure room, Midas was surprised. The stranger looked kind, however, so Midas wasn't afraid. He greeted the man, and they began to talk of gold.

"You certainly have a lot of gold," said the stranger.

"It's not so much," said Midas.

The stranger smiled. "Do you want even more gold than this?" he asked.

"If I had my way, everything I touched would turn into gold," Midas replied.

Comprehension Questions

		Points
(Literal)	1. What were the two things that Midas loved best in the world? (Gold and his daughter, Marygold)	10
(Word meaning)	2. What is the meaning of "valuable"? (Worth a lot such as gold, money, or jewelry.)	10
(Literal)	3. Where was no one allowed to go? (In the king's treasure room)	10
(Literal)	4. What did King Midas love to do in his treasure room? (Count his coins)	10
(Inference)	5. How do we know Midas loves gold very much? (He spends a lot of time sitting in the treasure room counting the coins. He also dreams about the gold.)	10
(Word meaning)	6. What is a stranger? (A person who is unknown to you; someone you don't know)	10

[13] "King Midas and the Golden Touch," retold by Judy Rosenbaum, Level 9, *On the Horizon* (Needham, Mass.: Silver Burdett & Ginn, 1989), pp. 130–31.

(Literal)	7. Where did Midas see a stranger? (In his dream while sitting in the treasure room)	10
(Literal)	8. Why was Midas surprised when he saw a stranger in his treasure room? (Because no one was allowed in the room)	10
(Inference)	9. How do we know Midas is not satisfied with what he has? (Even though he is very rich and has so much gold, he says that it's not so much. He also says he'd like everything he touched to turn into gold.)	10
(Main idea)	10. What is the main idea of the story? (Even though King Midas is very rich and has lots of gold, he thinks it's not so much.)	10

Scoring Scale

Levels	Word Recognition Errors	Comprehension Errors
Independent	0–2	0–10 points
Instructional	3–9	11–25 points
Frustration	17 or more	50 points or more

Introduction: The stranger tells King Midas that he will give him the Golden Touch. Everything he touches will turn to gold. Read the story to find out what happens. Then I will ask you questions about the story. Read it carefully.

Midas was so excited that he could hardly wait until morning. At last the sun rose. Still dreaming, Midas sat up and reached for the water jug by his bed. At once it became gold. Midas was so overjoyed, he got up and danced around the room, touching everything within his reach. Soon he had a room full of gleaming gold objects. When he reached for his clothes, they turned into heavy golden cloth. "Now I shall really look like a king," he said. He got dressed and admired himself in the mirror. Midas was impressed by his golden clothes, though they were so heavy he could hardly move.

His looking glass was more of a problem. He tried to use it to see his new treasures better. To his surprise, he could not see anything through it. He put it on the table and found that it was now gold, but Midas was too excited to worry. He said, "I can see well enough without it. Besides, it is much more valuable now."

Comprehension Questions

		Points
(Literal)	1. What did Midas first do after the sun rose? (He reached for the water jug.)	10
(Literal)	2. What happened to the water jug after he touched it? (It turned to gold.)	10
(Literal)	3. What did Midas do after the water jug turned to gold? (He got up and danced around the room, touching everything within his reach.)	10
(Literal)	4. What happened to everything he touched? (It turned to gold.)	10
(Inference)	5. Why were his clothes so heavy? (They too had turned to gold because he had to touch them to put them on.)	10
(Inference)	6. Why had his looking glass become gold? (He had touched it.)	10
(Inference)	7. Were all these things really happening to Midas? Explain. (No, Midas was dreaming it all.)	10
(Word meaning)	8. What does "admire" mean? (To think of someone with approval and respect)	10
(Literal)	9. What did Midas say when his looking glass turned to gold? (I can see well enough without it. Besides, it is much more valuable now.)	10
(Main idea)	10. What is the main idea of the story? (In his dream, King Midas is very excited because everything he touches turns to gold.)	10

---

[14] Ibid., p. 132.

Scoring Scale

Levels	Comprehension Errors
Independent	0–10 points
Instructional	11–25 points
Frustration	50 points or more

4

Introduction: Read this story aloud to find out how a writer begins a book for young people. Then I will ask you questions about the story.

How does a writer such as Mr. Pinkwater begin a novel for young readers? How does he work? "When I'm beginning a new book," he states, "I am almost like an actor getting into character. I listen to music. I watch television, I talk to people. I turn up at a K-Mart store and go through all the motions of being an ordinary citizen.

"When I start a novel, all I'm really doing is waiting for the characters to show up. It's like the movie *Close Encounters of the Third Kind.* The people who have been 'selected' to be in this story show up. It is a very interesting experience."

He does not sit down and write every day. "It would be terrible if I had to work that way. I show up at my office every day in the event that something may want to happen, but if nothing happens, I don't feel that I have failed to perform. If something gets started, fair enough. If it doesn't, and I feel I've given it enough time, I go to K-Mart. I showed up, the story didn't!

Comprehension Questions

		Points
(Literal)	1. To whom does Mr. Pinkwater compare himself when he first begins to write? (An actor)	10
(Literal)	2. State three things Mr. Pinkwater does when he begins to write? (Listen to music, watch television, talk to people)	10
(Inference)	3. What does listening to music, watching television, and talking to people help him do? (Get into character for his book)	10
(Literal)	4. When he first starts writing what is he waiting for? (For his characters to show up)	10
(Literal)	5. What place does Mr. Pinkwater visit? (K-Mart)	10
(Word meaning)	6. What does "ordinary" mean? (not special; usual; normal)	10
(Inference)	7. What does Mr. Pinkwater mean when he says he goes through the motions of being an ordinary person. (He is acting; he is trying to act like the people who go shopping at K-Mart, so he can learn what it feels like.)	10
(Literal)	8. What movie does Mr. Pinkwater refer to? (*Close Encounters of the Third Kind*)	10

[15] Lee Bennett Hopkins, "Daniel Manus Pinkwater," Level 10, *Silver Secrets* (Needham, Mass.: Silver Burdett & Ginn, 1989), p. 56.

(Inference)   9. What are Mr. Pinkwater's feelings about writing every day?   10
                 (He doesn't feel he has to. He doesn't feel he is a failure if he
                 doesn't perform every day.)
(Main idea) 10. What is the main idea of the story? (Mr. Pinkwater describes   10
                 what he does in beginning to write a book.)

                               Scoring Scale

Levels	Word Recognition Errors	Comprehension Errors
Independent	0–2	0–10 points
Instructional	3–9	11–25 points
Frustration	19 or more	50 points or more

Introduction: Read this story to find out how Daniel Pinkwater feels while he is writing his books. Then I will ask you questions about the story. Read it carefully.

"I love the story as it is being written. Sometimes it's as though it were happening without my doing it. I'll go to bed, excited about what's going to happen tomorrow. I know something's got to happen beause I've only got 175 pages done and I've got to do more.

"To me, the beauty in writing is making the words come out as clear as a pane of glass. That I can do, and I'm rather pleased because it took me years to learn how.

"Writing for girls and boys has helped me to remember my own childhood. And since I'm writing books for a specific reader, namely myself at different ages, I've gotten more and more expert at revisiting that person within me at different ages."

He sometimes uses a computer. "The computer allows me to think in a different way. It helps me to be a better, more daring writer. Using a computer was a breakthrough for me."

Comprehension Questions

		Points
(Literal)	1. What does Mr. Pinkwater love? (The story as it is being written)	10
(Literal)	2. How does Mr. Pinkwater feel when he goes to bed after working on a story? (Excited)	10
(Inference)	3. Why is Mr. Pinkwater excited when he goes to bed after working on his story? (He can't wait to see what will happen or how his story will turn out.)	10
(Literal)	4. How does Mr. Pinkwater know something will happen? (Because he only has 175 pages done and he has to do more.)	10
(Inference)	5. What is the beauty in writing for Mr. Pinkwater? (His being able to make words come out as clear as a pane of glass)	10
(Inference)	6. What does it mean when he says that his words are as clear as a pane of glass? (That it is easy to understand what he is saying; he gets his ideas across; his words help bring pictures to your mind.)	10
(Inference)	7. How do we know it wasn't always easy for him to make his words as clear as a pane of glass? (He said it took him years to learn how.)	10
(Literal)	8. What has writing for children helped him to do? (Remember his own childhood)	10

[16] Ibid., pp. 56–57.

| (Literal) | 9. How does the computer help Mr. Pinkwater? (It allows him to think in a different way; it helps him to be a better, more daring writer.) | 10 |
| (Main idea) | 10. What is the main idea of the story? (Mr. Pinkwater describes what he does and how he feels while writing a story.) | 10 |

Scoring Scale

Levels	Comprehension Errors
Independent	0–10 points
Instructional	11–25 points
Frustration	50 points or more

5

Introduction: Read this story aloud to find out about how the Davidsons lived years ago. Then I will ask you questions about the story.

Early in April of 1872, the Davidsons' covered wagon rolled onto their 160-acre land claim in eastern Nebraska. There was no shelter waiting for them. Like most settlers on the Great Plains, the Davidsons had to build their own shelter. At first, the family lived in the covered wagon. That was all right for a while. But by fall, they needed more protection from Nebraska's cold and windy climate.

Back east, the Davidsons had lived in a wooden farmhouse. They would have liked to build a wooden house on the Plains, too. But there wasn't a tree in sight. Lumber for building wasn't available in Nebraska, even if the family had been able to afford it.

There wasn't time for building, anyway. As farmers, the Davidsons knew they had to get on with the all-important work of plowing and planting. Only then would their new land provide enough harvest to see them through the winter.

Rabbits and foxes dig their burrows and dens in hillsides, and that's what the Davidsons did too. The settlers chose the streambank location because it was conveniently close to water. There were no building materials to buy or skilled workers to hire. After two days of digging, the Davidsons' new home was ready.

Comprehension Questions

		Points
(Literal)	1. When did the Davidsons arrive at their destination? (In April of 1872)	10
(Literal)	2. What was their destination? (A 160-acre land claim in eastern Nebraska)	10
(Literal)	3. Where did they live when they first arrived? (In their covered wagon)	10
(Literal)	4. Why did they live in a covered wagon? (There was no shelter waiting for them.)	10
(Inference)	5. How do we know that the Davidsons weren't wealthy? (The	10

[17] Duncan Searl, "A Sea of Grass," Level 11, *Dream Chasers* (Needham, Mass.: Silver Burdett & Ginn, 1989), pp. 423–24.

story said that lumber wasn't available, even if the Davidsons could afford it. Also, they needed the harvest to see them through the winter.)

(Inference)   6. During what season or seasons of the year did the Davidsons   10
live in their covered wagon? (During the spring and summer;
a student may include the beginning of fall as part of the
answer. Accept this also.)

(Inference)   7. What was the Davidsons' highest priority? (Plowing and   10
planting)

(Inference)   8. The Davidsons' home was compared to homes built by what   10
two animals? (Rabbits and foxes)

(Word meaning)   9. What is a burrow? (A hole that an animal digs in the ground)   10

(Main idea)   10. What is the main idea of the story? (The Davidsons' only   10
choice to survive the cold and windy climate was for them,
themselves, to dig a home in the hillside like the rabbits and
foxes.)

Scoring Scale

Levels	Word Recognition Errors	Comprehension Errors
Independent	0–2	0–10 points
Instructional	3–10	11–25 points
Frustration	21 or more	50 points or more

Introduction: Read this story to find out more about how the Davidsons lived years ago. Then I will ask you questions about the story. Read it carefully.

Most people believe in the old saying, "There's no place like home." The Davidsons, however, might not have felt that way about their dugout. The cramped dwelling was damp and dark, even on sunny days. Dirt from the roof sifted down into bedding and food. Insects and snakes were constant house guests.

Hoping their new shelter would be a temporary one, the Davidsons began to plow and plant. But this wasn't as easy as they had expected. In the early 1870s, more than a foot of thick sod covered almost every inch of the territory. Held together by a mass of tangled roots, this sod was almost impossible to cut through. It could take weeks to plow a single acre. Settlers like the Davidsons became known as "sodbusters."

The sod's toughness gave the settlers an idea. Why not build with it? The new fields were covered with long ribbons of sod that had been plowed up. It would be a simple matter to cut these into smaller pieces and use them as building blocks. The settlers even had a nickname for this unusual building material—"Nebraska marble."

Comprehension Questions

		Points
(Literal)	1. What is the saying that most people believe in? (There's no place like home.)	10
(Inference)	2. How would the Davidsons feel about the saying "There's no place like home"? (They would not agree because they lived in a dugout that was not very comfortable.)	10
(Literal)	3. State three problems with their dugout. (It was cramped, damp, and dark; dirt from the roof sifted down into bedding and food; and so on.)	10
(Literal)	4. Who were the Davidsons' constant guests? (Insects and snakes)	10
(Inference)	5. How long had the Davidsons planned on staying in their dugout? (Not long; they hoped their new shelter would be a temporary one.)	10
(Word meaning)	6. What is the meaning of "temporary"? (Lasting for a short time; not permanent)	10

[18] Ibid., p. 425

(Literal)	7. What covered almost every inch of the Davidsons' territory? (More than a foot of thick sod)	10
(Inference)	8. Why were the settlers known as ''sodbusters''? (Because it was very hard to cut through the sod; however, they did, even though it could take weeks to plow one acre.)	10
(Literal)	9. What idea did the sod's toughness give the settlers? (To build with it)	10
(Main idea)	10. What is the main idea of the story? (The Davidsons, unhappy with their dugout, come up with the idea to use the tough sod for building material.)	10

Scoring Scale

Levels	Comprehension Errors
Independent	0–10 points
Instructional	11–25 points
Frustration	50 points or more

6

Introduction: Read this story aloud to find out what is special about the Monterey Bay Aquarium. Then I will ask you questions about the story.

You walk through the door—and immediately freeze. Overhead, to your left, a thresher shark whips its tail. To your right are three huge killer whales. Have you wandered into a nightmare? Hardly. You've just entered the Monterey Bay Aquarium.

The shark and whales, lifesize and hanging from the ceiling, are fiberglass. The other 6,000 creatures you'll meet are not. On a visit to the aquarium, on the shores of California's Monterey Bay, you'll have a chance not only to see them swim, scurry, hunt, and court, but to pick up and handle a few as well.

One of the aquarium's most spectacular exhibits is the three-story-high kelp forest—the world's only kelp forest growing indoors. Clinging to the bottom with a rootlike "holdfast," the yellow-brown kelp reaches up through 28 feet of water, spreading out on the tank's sunlit surface. With "stipes" instead of trunks, and "blades" in place of leaves, the kelp forest resembles an underwater redwood grove. Sunbeams slant down from above, while the kelp sways gently back and forth. With a patient eye, you will begin to spot some of the many creatures that call the kelp forest home.

Long-legged brittle stars and crabs can be seen within the tangled holdfast. Watch for turban snails higher up. The fish of the kelp forest aren't as fast as those of the open ocean, but they're better at playing hide-and-seek. Special air sacs allow some of them to hover in hiding within the maze of blades. Many are completely camouflaged.

Comprehension Questions

			Points
(Literal)	1.	What do you first see when you walk through the door of the Monterey Bay Aquarium? (Overhead to your left a thresher shark and to your right three huge killer whales)	10
(Inference)	2.	Why would you immediately freeze when you first walk through the door? (Because the thresher shark and three killer whales must look very real, but they aren't.)	10
(Literal)	3.	How many real creatures are there in the aquarium? (6,000)	10
(Word meaning)	4.	What does "spectacular" mean? (Of or like a remarkable sight; showy; striking)	10
(Literal)	5.	What is one of the aquarium's most remarkable exhibits? (The three-story-high kelp forest)	10
(Inference)	6.	Why is the kelp forest so remarkable? (It's the world's only indoor kelp forest.)	10
(Literal)	7.	What does the kelp forest resemble? (An underwater redwood grove)	10
(Inference)	8.	Why are the fish in the kelp forest better at playing hide-and-	10

[19] Paul Fleischman, "The Monterey Bay Aquarium," Level 12, *Wind by the Sea* (Needham, Mass.: Silver Burdett & Ginn, 1989), pp. 395–96.

seek? (They can hover in hiding within the maze of blades so that they blend in with the blades; they are completely camouflaged.)

(Literal)   9. What allows some of the fish to hover in hiding? (Special air sacs)   10

(Main idea)   10. What is the main idea of the story? (The Monterey Sea Aquarium is a very unusual aquarium that houses the world's only kelp forest growing indoors.)   10

Scoring Scale

Levels	Word Recognition Errors	Comprehension Errors
Independent	0–3	0–10 points
Instructional	4–13	11–25 points
Frustration	25 or more	50 points or more

Introduction: Read this story to find out about one of the Monterey Bay Aquarium's residents. Then I will ask you questions about the story. Read it carefully.

Among the animals who depend on the kelp are the aquarium's most playful residents, the sea otters. Floating on their backs, doing somersaults in the water, taking part in high-speed games of tag, these smallest of the marine mammals charm every audience.

Their two-story tank lets you view them from above as well as from below the water's surface. In the wild, though, their home is the kelp beds. They live on creatures who live on the kelp. They depend on it for shelter during storms. Before sleeping, they wrap themselves in it to keep from drifting out to sea.

Why are otters so playful? No one knows, though part of the answer might lie in the fact that their constant motion helps to keep them warm. Unlike the whales and other marine mammals, otters have no layer of blubber between their warm-blooded insides and the cold water outside. So they move around a lot, which requires a lot of energy, which in turn requires a lot of eating. Could you eat 25 hamburgers a day? That's the equivalent of what an otter swallows, eating up to one-quarter of its body weight daily. If you're present at feeding time, you'll be amazed at how much fish, squid, and abalone an otter can eat. Wild otters eat so many purple sea urchins that their bones eventually turn purplish as well.

Otters have another defense against the cold—their coats. When you touch the soft sample of fur on the wall by their tank, you'll understand why they were hunted until they were nearly extinct.

Comprehension Questions

		Points
(Literal)	1. What animals are the aquarium's most playful residents? (The sea otters)	10
(Literal)	2. How do the sea otters charm audiences? (They float on their backs, do somersaults, and play high-speed games of tag.)	10
(Literal)	3. Where do they live in the aquarium? (In a two-story tank)	10
(Literal)	4. Where do they live in the wild? (In the kelp beds)	10
(Literal)	5. What is the reason given for the otter's playfulness? (Their constant motion keeps them warm.)	10
(Inference)	6. Why do the otters have to move around a lot to keep warm? (The otters have no layer of blubber between their warm-blooded insides and the cold water outside.)	10
(Inference)	7. What is the effect of the great amount of movement? (The otters have to eat a lot because they use up a lot of energy; they eat one-quarter of their body weight daily.)	10
(Word meaning)	8. What does "extinct" mean? (No longer existing; no longer living; having died out)	10
(Inference)	9. Why were otters hunted until they almost didn't exist anymore? (For their fur; it is very soft.)	10

[20] Ibid., p. 397

(Main idea)   10. What is the main idea of the story? (The sea otters are the   10
most playful aquarium residents because they need to move
around a lot to keep warm.)

Scoring Scale

Levels	Comprehension Errors
Independent	0–10 points
Instructional	11–25 points
Frustration	50 points or more

ORAL READING (263)[21]

Introduction: Read this story aloud to find out what some courageous children do. (Etienne is pronounced ā·tyen'.) Then I will ask you questions about the story.

The voice came from out of the sky, "Hey fellows, quick, grab those ropes and pull me into the wind as if I were a kite. Hurry!"

Looking up, the young people were startled to see a man waving wildly at them from a strange banana-shaped flying balloon—a balloon that was about to crash!

Sara reacted quickly and grabbed one of the ropes that dangled near her. But Sara could not even stop the flying contraption, let alone pull it in the other direction. As she attempted to dig her heels into the ground, the balloon nearly toppled her.

"Boys, don't just stand there. Help her," the man in the balloon shouted at Etienne and Louis.

Rushing to help their sister, the boys grabbed other ropes trailing from the balloon and frantically tugged at the runaway flying machine. Finally, the three of them were able to change the direction of the balloon, carrying it into the wind as the aeronaut had requested. The flying machine bobbed up like a kite.

As the young people pulled the balloon down, following the aeronaut's instructions, a crowd began to gather. The moment the flier was safe on the ground, he was surrounded by a large crowd of curious people, all talking at once.

Sara realized that the man she had rescued was the famous Monsieur Santos-Dumont, the wealthy Brazilian inventor and daredevil who predicted people would someday fly like birds.

"Where are the young people? They are the real heroes of this escape from the jaws of death," she heard him shout over the crowd.

Comprehension Questions

		Points
(Literal)	1. Describe what the children saw when they looked up in the sky. (A strange banana-shaped balloon that was about to crash)	10
(Inference)	2. How do we know the person in the balloon didn't expect the girl to help him? (He called out to the fellows.)	10
(Literal)	3. What did he want the fellows to do? (To grab the ropes and pull him into the wind as if he were a kite)	10
(Literal)	4. What happened when Sara tried to help? (She couldn't stop the balloon, let alone pull it in the other direction.)	10
(Word meaning)	5. What is an aeronaut? (Someone who navigates in the air, especially a balloon)	10
(Inference)	6. What was needed to keep the ballon afloat? (The force of the wind)	10
(Inference)	7. What did the young people have to be able to do to pull down the balloon? (Follow the aeronaut's directions)	10

[21] David Fulton, "Through Skies Never Sailed," Level 13, *Star Walk* (Needham, Mass.: Silver Burdett & Ginn, 1989), pp. 353–54.

(Inference)	8. What kind of person was Monsieur Santos-Dumont? State four characteristics. Give proof for your answer. (Creative—the story said he was an inventor; reckless, adventurous—it said he was a daredevil; well-known—it said he was famous; rich—it said he was wealthy.)	10
(Literal)	9. What did Monsieur Santos-Dumont predict people would someday be able to do? (Fly like birds)	10
(Main idea)	10. What is the main idea of the story? (A courageous girl and her brothers rescue an aeronaut by helping to bring his flying balloon safely to the ground.)	10

Scoring Scale

Levels	Word Recognition Errors	Comprehension Errors
Independent	0–3	0–10 points
Instructional	4–13	11–25 points
Frustration	26 or more	50 points or more

Introduction: Monsieur Santos-Dumont is very grateful to the children for saving his life. Read the story to see why he comes to the children's home. Then I will ask you questions about the story. Read it carefully.

"The purpose of my visit in fact is related to the events of this afternoon. I came to invite your family for an excursion in one of my balloons."

Silence filled the Cote parlor as all eyes turned to Sara's father, awaiting his reply. "I don't wish to seem overly conservative or closed minded, Monsieur Santos-Dumont, but I wouldn't consider air travel sufficiently safe to risk my whole family. This afternoon's events are evidence of that."

"I certainly wouldn't ask you to endanger your family, but flying in a balloon, which is merely a big bag filled with hydrogen, has long been demonstrated to be a safe sport.

"I wouldn't suggest taking you in a craft such as the one I was flying this afternoon. That was a 'dirigible.' Its design is the latest breakthrough in the attempt to control the direction of flight. It's a balloon that has a gasoline engine suspended beneath it to direct its movement. Unfortunately, my colleagues and I have yet to work out all the problems. But we will. In any case, the dirigible may soon be obsolete. I recently heard a report at a meeting of the Aero Club, and I understand that some Americans have actually built a glider of some sort that is heavier than the air, and it is said they use a gasoline engine to power it. Now, that is really incredible."

Comprehension Questions

		Points
(Literal)	1. What was the purpose of Monsieur Santos-Dumont's visit to the children's family? (To invite them on an excursion in one of his balloons)	10
(Word meaning)	2. What is an excursion? (A short pleasure trip)	10
(Literal)	3. How does the children's father feel about air travel? (He feels it is not safe.)	10
(Inference)	4. What evidence does the children's father give to back up his feelings? (The afternoon's events)	10
(Literal)	5. What does Monsieur Santos-Dumont claim is safe? (Flying in a balloon filled with hydrogen)	10
(Literal)	6. What kind of machine was Monsieur Santos-Dumont flying in the afternoon? (A dirigible, which has a gasoline engine suspended beneath it to direct its movement)	10
(Inference)	7. How do we know Monsieur Santos-Dumont is not working alone on developing the dirigible? (The story says that he and his colleagues have yet to work out the details.)	10
(Literal)	8. What does Monsieur Santos-Dumont feel is incredible? (The glider that the Americans have built, which is heavier than air and uses a gasoline engine to power it)	10
(Inference)	9. What does Monsieur Santos-Dumont feel the Americans' flying machine will do to the dirigible? (Make the dirigible obsolete, that is, no longer useful or in use)	10

[22] Ibid., p. 356.

(Main idea)   10. What is the main idea of the story? (Monsieur Santos-   10
                   Dumont tries to persuade the children's father to allow his
                   family to go on a short trip in a balloon Monsieur Santos-
                   Dumont insists is safe.)

                              Scoring Scale
                   Levels   *Comprehension Errors*
                   Independent   0–10 points
                   Instructional   11–25 points
                   Frustration   50 points or more

8

ORAL READING (275)[23]

Introduction: Read this story aloud to find out why Lo Tung came to America. Then I will ask you questions about the story.

Lo Tung leaned against the rattling wall of the freight car. Beneath him the floor moved as the wheels clacked over the rails. It was a long time since he'd sat or walked on anything steady. First there had been the long days and nights on the Pacific Mail Steamship that had brought him from China, then the riverboat from San Francisco to Sacramento, then the train, waiting on the levee.

He hadn't had time for more than a glimpse of the strange, iron monster belching smoke before the boss man had hustled them aboard. It was hard to believe that he was here now, in this freight car along with other Chinese workers, rolling eastward across America.

Lo Tung looked sideways at his friend, Wei. Wei was fifteen years old, too, and as small and thin as Lo Tung.

"Not more than a hundred pounds, either of you," the agent had said in disgust. "You two will not be able to do the heavy railroad work."

"Don't worry. We are strong," Lo Tung had said. He had not added "Ho Sen was strong, the strongest man in our village. And he was killed building the American railway." Now Ho Sen's bones lay somewhere in this strange country. And Chen Chi Yuen. He had gone and never been heard from again.

Sitting now in the freight car, thinking about the work, Lo Tung flexed his muscles. Strong for the work. Of course, strong and fearless.

It was growing dark. They had been closed in here together for hours, so many of them from the ship. The air was used up and the smells were bad.

Comprehension Questions

		Points
(Literal)	1. What kind of car was Lo Tung in? (A freight car)	10
(Inference)	2. How do we know Lo Tung has never seen a train before? (Lo Tung thought the locomotive was a strange, iron monster. It wouldn't have been strange if he had seen it before.)	10
(Inference)	3. How do we know it has been a long time since Lo Tung was on land? (The story states that it was a long time since he was on anything steady.)	10
(Literal)	4. What means of transportation was used to get Lo Tung to his destination? (Steamship, riverboat, and train)	10
(Inference)	5. How long did Lo Tung have between getting off the riverboat and boarding the train? (Not long; he only had time to catch a glimpse of the train before he was hustled aboard.)	10
(Literal)	6. What was the agent concerned about? (That Lo Tung and his friend were too thin to work on the railroad)	10
(Literal)	7. What had happened to Ho Sen? (He had been killed working on the American railroad.)	10

---

[23] Eve Bunting, "It's Not the Great Wall, but It Will Last Forever," Level 14, *Worlds Beyond* (Needham, Mass.: Silver Burdett & Ginn, 1989), pp. 238–39.

(Inference)	8. Why were the smells on the freight bad? (There was not much air, and there were many people crowded together.)	10
(Literal)	9. In what direction was the train rolling across America? (Eastward)	10
(Main idea)	10. What is the main idea of the story? (Lo Tung's journey from China to America to work on the American railroad has been long and hard.)	10

Scoring Scale

Levels	Word Recognition Errors	Comprehension Errors
Independent	0–3	0–10 points
Instructional	4–14	11–20 points
Frustration	28 or more	50 points or more

Introduction: Agents had advertised in Lo Tung's village for laborers to help build the railroad in California. They offered houses to live in, plenty of food, and thirty dollars a month. The passage to go was fifty-four dollars. Read the story to find out why Lo Tung signed on. Then I will ask you questions about the story. Read it carefully.

Fifty-four dollars was a fortune, and impossible for his mother! The agent had allowed them to borrow from him. That was when he'd complained of Lo Tung's size.

"Not a penny of your wages will be yours till you pay me back," he had warned.

Lo Tung had agreed. He would have agreed to almost anything. Not that he wanted to go to America. The thought of leaving his home brought tears to his eyes. But it was clearly his duty. He was, after all, the eldest son. Since his father's death the family responsibility had been his. If he went, his debt to the agent would be cleared in two months. Then he could begin sending money home for his mother and his sisters, and his little brother. He had to believe that he could save enough to go home himself some day.

Thinking of home here in the heat of the freight car made loneliness rise in him like water in a swamp. Fear was bad, but loneliness was worse. He would not allow himself to remember.

"We are slowing," Wei said. "I can see through a crack."

Someone else announced, "We are here."

Tired men and boys staggered up, swaying, hoisting their bedrolls. As the train chugged to a stop they waited quietly for what was to come.

When the doors opened Lo Tung saw that it was night outside, the sky filled with a million crystal stars.

"American stars," he whispered to Wei, pointing upward.

"Are they the same that shine over China or . . ."

"Out! Everyone out!" Men waited beside the train, big, bulky men who cast massive shadows.

"Hurry! Get a move on!"

The words were not in Lo Tung's language but he understood the tone.

Comprehension Questions

		Points
(Literal)	1. How were Lo Tung and his mother able to get enough money to go to America? (The agent had allowed them to borrow from him.)	10
(Inference)	2. Why was Lo Tung going to America? (Because his family needed the money; he couldn't earn the money they needed in his village.)	10
(Inference)	3. Why did he feel he had to support his family? (Because his father was dead and he was the eldest son)	10
(Literal)	4. How long would it take to clear his debt to the agent? (Two months)	10

[24] Ibid., p. 240.

(Inference)	5. Does Lo Tung expect to stay in America? Explain. (No, the story states that he had to believe that he could save enough to go home himself some day.)	10
(Literal)	6. What does Lo Tung feel is worse than fear? (Loneliness)	10
(Inference)	7. What simile is used to describe Lo Tung's loneliness? Explain the simile. (Loneliness rose in him like water in a swamp; when it rains, water in a swamp rises very quickly, and that's how fast his loneliness rose.)	10
(Inference)	8. How do we know it was a clear night when they arrived at their destination? (The sky was filled with a million crystal stars.)	10
(Literal)	9. What kind of men were waiting beside the train? (Big, bulky men who cast massive shadows)	10
(Main idea)	10. What is the main idea of the story? (Even though Lo Tung does not want to leave his family, he goes to America so he can earn money for his family in China.)	10

Scoring Scale

Levels	Comprehension Errors
Independent	0–10 points
Instructional	11–20 points
Frustration	50 or points or more

Appendix B ———————————————

Fry Readability Formula

———————————————

**EXPANDED DIRECTIONS FOR WORKING
READABILITY GRAPH**

1. Randomly select three (3) sample passages and count out exactly 100 words each, beginning with the beginning of a sentence. Do count proper nouns, initializations, and numerals.
2. Count the number of sentences in the hundred words, estimating length of the fraction of the last sentence to the nearest one-tenth.
3. Count the total number of syllables in the 100-word passage. If you don't have a hand counter available, an easy way is to simply put a mark above every syllable over one in each word, then when you get to the end of the passage, count the number of marks and add 100. Small calculators can also be used as counters by pushing numeral 1, then push the + sign for each word or syllable when counting.
4. Enter graph with *average* sentence length and *average* number of syllables; plot dot where the two lines intersect. Area where dot is plotted will give you the approximate grade level.
5. If a great deal of variability is found in syllable count or sentence count, putting more samples into the average is desirable.
6. A word is defined as a group of symbols with a space on either side; thus, *Joe, IRA, 1945,* and *&* are each one word.
7. A syllable is defined as a phonetic syllable. Generally, there are as many syllables as vowel sounds. For example, *stopped* is one syllable and *wanted* is two syllables. When counting syllables for

numerals and initializations, count one syllable for each symbol. For example *1945* is four syllables, *IRA* is three syllables, and *&* is one syllable.

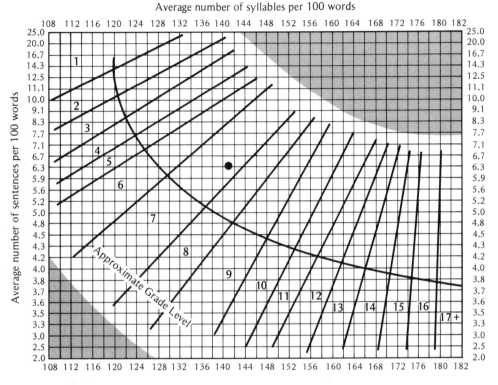

Average number of syllables per 100 words

Figure B.1 Graph for estimating readibility—Extended by Edward Fry, Rutgers University Reading Center, New Brunswick, N.J. 08904. Note: This "extended graph" does not outmode or render the earlier (1968) version inoperative or inaccurate; it is an extension. (Reproduction permitted—no copyright.)

Example:

	Syllables	Sentences
1st Hundred Words	124	6.6
2nd Hundred Words	141	6.6
3rd Hundred Words	158	6.8
	141	6.3

AVERAGE READABILITY 7th GRADE (see dot plotted on graph)

Index

Suchman's inquiry method, 113
Suffix, 303, 307
Suitability, 35–36
Summary. *See* Studying
Supporting details. *See* Main idea of a paragraph
Survey, 386
Survey battery. *See* Standardized achievement survey test batteries
Syllabication, 302–304, 403
    accenting and, 304–306
    generalizations, 303
    phonics and, 303–304
Syllable, 302
    unaccented, 304
Synonyms, 339, 341, 403
Syntactic clue, 278
Synthesis, 276
Synthetic phonics. *See* Explicit phonics

Teacher
    characteristics of, 19–21
    as classroom manager, 26–27
    evaluation, 19
    expectations, 27, 53, 75, 85, 88, 160
    instruction, 24–25
    as key person, 18–19
    in a multicultural classroom, 72, 74–75
    planning, 21
    role of, 17–18
    scenarios, 25, 26–27, 251–258, 387–388, 396–397, 397–398
    See also Diagnostic-reading and correction program; Group instruction; Instructional time; Scenarios
Teacher-made tests. *See* Tests
Teaching English as a second language. *See* English as a second language (ESL)
Television, 449–451
    reading and, 449

Tests, 33
    achievement, 38, 149, 151–152, 161, 238
    candidates for, 144–146
    criteria for, 34–37
    group, 45–46
    individual, 45–46
    reading, 46–47
    teacher-made, 42, 218–224
    tree diagram of, 48
    See also Criterion-referenced tests; Diagnostic reading tests; Informal reading inventory (IRI); Norm-referenced tests; Reading readiness tests; Standardized tests; Whole language
Test taking. *See* Studying
Textbook reading. *See* Studying
Title I. *See* Chapter 1
Top-down reading models, 11–12
Topic sentence, 349–350

Underachievement, 126, 144–146

Validity, 35, 36, 37
Vision, symptoms of problems, 96–97
Visual discrimination, 97–98, 156, 283–284
    defining, 97, 283
    tests, 97–98, 220–221, 283
Visual perception, 93, 94–98
Visual representation and main idea, 356–358
Vision screening instruments
    Insta-Line, 94
    Snellen Chart, 94
    Titmus Vision Tester, 95
Vocabulary consciousness, 309
Vocabulary expansion
    and borderline children, 415
    intermediate-grade level, 310–314
        diagnostic checklist for, 318
        dictionary skills for, 313–314
        instruction, 310–313

and listening, 107–109, 109–110
    primary-grade level, 308–309
        diagnostic checklist for, 316–317
        dictionary skills for, 309
        and literature, 308–309
        See also Content Areas
Vowels, 292
    controlled by *r*, 299
    diagnostic tests of, 292
    generalizations, 299–300
    instructional suggestions for, 293–296
Vowels, double
    digraphs, 296
        diagnostic tests of, 296–297
        instructional suggestions for, 297
    diphthongs, 298
        diagnostic tests of, 298
        instructional suggestions for, 298–299

Wechsler Intelligence Scale for Children, Revised (WISC–R), 103, 130–131, 139
Wepman Auditory Discrimination Test, 102–103, 424
Whole language, 31, 267–268
    diagnostic reading tests and, 49
Whole word or "look and say," 276
Woodcock-Johnson Psycho-Educational Battery, Revised, 133
Word analysis tests, 223
Word lists, 169, 175–176, 201, 212
Word parts, defining terms, 307
Word recognition
    defining, 273
    diagnostic checklist for, 314–316
    learning center for, 252
    meaning strategies, 277–280
    pronunciation strategies, 275–277
    scenarios of, 251–253, 255–256
    See also context clues; Decoding; Phonics
Word relationships. *See* Analogies